D1604666

REALMS OF MEMORY

European Perspectives

REALMS

COLUMBIA UNIVERSITY PRESS NEW YORK

The Construction of the French Past

REALMS OF MEMORY

VOLUME II: TRADITIONS

Under the Direction of Pierre Nora

ENGLISH-LANGUAGE EDITION EDITED BY LAWRENCE D. KRITZMAN

Translated by Arthur Goldhammer

Columbia University Press

Publishers Since 1893

 New York Chichester, West Sussex

To honor Clifford E. Rybolt, Jr. and Mary Grace Rickert Rybolt, friends of France, Edwin W. Rickert has made a gift to the Press toward costs of publishing this work.

Columbia University Press wishes to express its appreciation for assistance given by the government of France through Le Ministère de la Culture in the preparation of the translation.

Library of Congress Cataloging-in-Publication Data
Les Lieux de mémoire. English
Realms of memory: the construction of the French past / under the direction of Pierre Nora: English language edition edited and with a foreword by Lawrence D. Kritzman; translated by Arthur Goldhammer
p. cm. — (European perspectives)
Revised and abridged translation of the original work in French.
Includes bibliographical references and index.
Contents: v. 2. Traditions
ISBN 0-231-10634-3 (alk. paper)
1. France—Civilization—Philosophy. 2. Memory. 3. Symbolism. 4. National characteristics, French. 5. Nationalism—France.
1. Nora, Pierre. II. Kritzman, Lawrence D. III. Title. IV. Series.
DC33.L6513 1996
944—dc20 95493349
CIP

Casebound editions of Columbia University Press books are printed on permanent and durable acid-free paper. Printed in the United States of America

c 10 9 8 7 6 5 4 3 2 1

EUROPEAN PERSPECTIVES

A Series in Social Thought and Cultural Criticism
Lawrence D. Kritzman, Editor

European Perspectives presents English translations of books by leading European thinkers. With both classic and outstanding contemporary works, the series aims to shape the major intellectual controversies of our day and to facilitate the tasks of historical understanding.

Julia Kristeva, *Strangers to Ourselves*
Theodor W. Adorno, *Notes to Literature*, vols. 1 and 2
Richard Wolin, editor, *The Heidegger Controversy*
Antonio Gramsci, *Prison Notebooks*, vols. 1 and 2
Jacques LeGoff, *History and Memory*
Alain Finkielkraut, *Remembering in Vain: The Klaus Barbie Trial and Crimes Against Humanity*
Julia Kristeva, *Nations Without Nationalism*
Pierre Bourdieu, *The Field of Cultural Production*
Pierre Vidal-Naquet, *Assassins of Memory: Essays on the Denial of the Holocaust*
Hugo Ball, *Critique of the German Intelligentsia*
Gilles Deleuze and Félix Guattari, *What Is Philosophy?*
Karl Heinz Bohrer, *Suddenness: On the Moment of Aesthetic Appearance*
Alain Finkielkraut, *The Defeat of the Mind*
Julia Kristeva, *New Maladies of the Soul*
Elisabeth Badinter, *XY: On Masculine Identity*
Karl Löwith, *Martin Heidegger and European Nihilism*
Gilles Deleuze, *Negotiations, 1972–1990*
Pierre Vidal-Naquet, *The Jews: History, Memory, and the Present*
Norbert Elias, *The Germans*
Louis Althusser, *Writings on Psychoanalysis: Freud and Lacan*
Elisabeth Roudinesco, *Jacques Lacan*
Ross Guberman, *Julia Kristeva Interviews*
Kelly Oliver, *The Portable Kristeva*
Pierra Nora, *Realms of Memory: The Construction of the French Past*,
vol. 1: *Conflicts and Divisions*
vol. 2: *Traditions*
Claudine Fabre-Vassas, *The Singular Beast: Jews, Christians, and the Pig*

Introduction *Pierre Nora* *ix*

PART I. MODELS

I The Land, *Armand Frémont* 3
II The Cathedral, *André Vauchez* 37
III The Court, *Jacques Revel* 71

PART II. BOOKS

IV *Le Tour de la France par deux enfants:* The Little Red Book of the Republic *Jacques and Mona Ozouf* 125
V Lavisse, The Nation's Teacher, *Pierre Nora* 151
VI Vidal de La Blache's *Geography of France*, *Jean-Yves Guiomar* 187
VII Marcel Proust's *Remembrance of Things Past*, *Antoine Compagnon* 211

PART III. SINGULARITIES

VIII *La Coupole*, *Marc Fumaroli* 249
IX Monuments to the Dead, *Antoine Prost* 307
X The Good Soldier Chauvin, *Gérard de Puymège* 333
XI Street Names, *Daniel Milo* 363
XII The Pulpit, the Rostrum, and the Bar, *Jean Starobinski* 391
XIII Gastronomy, *Pascal Ory* 443
XIV The Tour de France, *Georges Vigarello* 469

Notes *501*
Index of Names *557*
Index of Subjects *569*

Introduction to *Realms of Memory* Volume II

Pierre Nora

Tradition is memory that has become historically aware of itself. In order to understand national tradition in a country the size of France, one has to combine the insider's view, the understanding of a heritage that one assumes, with the outsider's, which objectifies that heritage and establishes it as a "tradition." This entire volume is built on this conjunction: it brings the *models* that underpin social structures and shape collective representations together with the *singularities*, or distinctive characteristics associated with the image of France, in which the outsider's judgment (absent from this book as such but present in this guise) confronts spontaneous feelings that take the insider's view for granted.

In order to explore this middle ground between participant analysis and critical detachment, the historian of memory must go beyond the merely descriptive *lieux de mémoire* of Volume 1 *(Conflicts and Divisions)* to investigate "sites" that actually or allegedly constitute French identity. Of the vast array of possibilities, how is one to choose without unwarranted arbitrariness, and on what principles is one to proceed once the choice is made?

Land, Cathedral, and Court: if the choice of precisely these three models was so compelling, it was not simply because they were the most venerable, the most vivid, and the most decisive models in the shaping of peasant France, Christian France, and monarchical France. There was a more profound reason for these particular choices: they are, if I may put it this way, models of models. Quite apart from the social structures, types of organization and regimes, and historical eras that they evoke, each of these three words has accumulated, whether at a specific moment in time or as a gradually thickening patina, a certain weight of historical images and representations—images and representations which have been revised throughout the ages and which still influence us as archetypes of social memory. The symbolic and revelatory power of these models has made them basic building blocks of the national imagination, fundamental references that the collective "France" has elaborated for itself and that derive their energy precisely from the fact that they no longer exist as social and historical realities.

It bears emphasizing, moreover, that these models, whose prestige and authority derive from their venerability, did not vanish until quite recently, barely thirty years ago. Perhaps I should be more precise about dates. It can be argued that the peasant model survived until the mid-1960s, when the proportion of the working population engaged in agriculture dropped below ten percent for the first time. The Christian model came to an end when the Second Vatican Council for all practical purposes abolished the Latin mass in 1965. And one can confidently date the demise of the monarchical model from the death of General de Gaulle in 1970, for it was then that the last threat of a restoration of the monarchy was eliminated, even as the role of the president as a democratic sovereign under the constitution of the Fifth Republic was confirmed.

A similar logic guided the selection of singularities. The phenomena that seemed most pertinent—institutions, memorials, myths, and distinctive traits of culture or civilization—were not chosen in order to export some pleasant and rather traditional stereotype of France's past. The forms of tradition that I have selected—from the Académie Française to the Tour de France, from Armistice Day memorials to the conviviality of the dinner table—are here because each seemed to exemplify an important aspect of the idea of "Frenchness."

One of the central themes common to all these *lieux* is that of rite and ritual. This is not a mark of conservative or reactionary traditionalism but a reflection of the sacred character of the French national religion, the French form of civil religion: secular liturgy is an integral part of the French national phenomenon. Another central theme is the role of the French language, as embodied in an institution, the Académie Française, which for three centuries has been its official repository and guardian and whose influence has shaped French literary expression and hierarchies. Language is also present in the religious, political, and juridical forms that have made it an instrument of persuasion: the pulpit, the rostrum, and the bar. The articles on war memorials and the myth of the soldier Chauvin introduce another theme: the role of war in defining the French national spirit and the way in which a physical sense of danger encouraged the sacrificial cult of the fatherland. Finally, the article on the Tour de France embodies yet another important theme: France's relation to space, from the geographical diversity of its landscape to the political unity of its history. In the Tour that relation takes the visceral form of a popular sporting event, but the spatial theme is also present in a more intellectualized form in the chapter on the geography of Paul Vidal de la Blache.

Vidal's work is one of the key books discussed in a third section, which it seemed enlightening to place between the sections on models, rooted as they are in the *longue durée,* and singularities, with their individuating particularity. Focusing on a series of key books seemed like a good way to give a living portrait of French identity over time. Of course the books treated here are merely a selection from a much longer list of possibilities, and the principle of selection was the same as for the other two sections: all the works represented here are *lieux de mémoire,* not because they embody, like an encyclopedia, a "total memory" of France (at once historical, geographic, affective, and literary) but because the effects of time and the vicissitudes of history have enlarged our understanding of memory in such a way as to bring out new meanings in the selected works. It is this perpetual sedimentation of new meanings, this permanent metamorphosis, that turns a book already invested with a certain form of memory into a veritable *lieu de mémoire.*

Take, for example, Ernest Lavisse's celebrated history textbook, which plays a crucial role not only in this section but in this enterprise as a whole. Lavisse was essentially the author of two complementary works, both equally important: a basic history textbook from which, between 1880 and 1914, fifteen million French children learned what they were supposed to know about the history of France (the battle of Verdun is inseparable from this work), and a twenty-seven-volume *History of France,* written with collaborators who together offered the first great synthesis of scientific history and thereby established the basic frame of reference in terms of which subsequent revisions must be understood. Lavisse established one form of French memory, but at the same time he epitomized another. Without Lavisse's great history, without this great, unitary, teleological and chronological narrative, there could be no *Realms of Memory* with its method of monographic decomposition. At the same time, however, it is the method of *lieux* that has made it possible to unearth the Lavisse phenomenon, including both the objectification of that phenomenon and its ultimate embodiment as a *lieu de mémoire.*

Finally, what characterizes all these traditions is that they date from the nineteenth century. Even those whose roots can be traced back to much earlier times were revived and reformulated in the nineteenth century. The "land" would not exist as such without the ruralist and protectionist movement of the late nineteenth century. The "cathedral" would not exist without the re-Christianization of the Restoration and the Romantic movement. And so on. The British historians Eric Hobsbawm and Terence Ranger have shown that England's most ancient and venerable traditions, including "the crown" itself, are actually of quite recent confection: to this phenomenon they have applied a handsome description, "the invention of tradition." What this second volume highlights, especially in identifying continuities and deep structures, is a period of time which, in a country whose history is longer than its memory, was, broadly speaking, linked to the French Revolution and its break with the past. As in the revolutionary period, we live in age of rupture. Our aim is to pinpoint that rupture, identify the paths that have led up to it, and specify its historical roots. This is confirmation that memory thrives on great events and perceives permanence exclusively through discontinuity. It was the nineteenth century as a whole, the great century of French memory, that invented the "France" of which this book is an inventory.

REALMS OF MEMORY

PART I

MODELS

FIGURE 1.0. The land, Franche-Comté.

FIGURE 1.1. Flanders.

CHAPTER I

The Land

Armand Frémont

In France as in most of Western Europe, farmland—the peasants' land, the land that every year is sliced into furrows by plowshares and discs, the land that lies beneath the carpet of pasture and rows of vines—accounts for most of the nation's territory. Untamed land, land not subject to the farmer's dominion, occupies only a small part of the total surface: the shoreline of beaches, dunes, cliffs, and the area immediately adjacent; forests, more or less everywhere but especially in eastern France; mountainous terrain above 10,000 feet, comprising the crags and glaciers of the Alps and Pyrenees; the pine barrens and marshes of western France; and the scrub and brush of the Mediterranean Midi. What is more, all this marginal land, long feared by peasants, who were slow to trespass its boundaries, was gradually exploited, whittled away, subdued, and finally occupied, to the point where the last bear in the Alps was hunted down on the eve of World War I. Throughout France, communities and individuals developed a myriad of ways to profit from what was no longer unfettered nature. When viewed from an airplane or in aerial photographs, France thus appears to be an assiduously domesticated expanse, with virtually nothing left of the virgin forest, scrub, and wasteland that fills other countries. The cultivated land forms an intricate marquetry that extends from one end of the country to the other in a variety of forms for which the French language has no shortage of terms: *plaine, champagne, campagne, bocage, vallée, coteau, rivière, vigne, terrasse, village*. Furthermore, although the cultivated surface area has been diminishing now for a century, and especially for the past thirty years, owing to the expansion of cities and their outskirts, what agronomists call the "usable agricultural surface" still covers the majority of France: 77,803,000 acres in 1985, together with 36,094,000 of woodland, for a total of 135,163,700 acres.

FIGURE 1.2. Woods and farmland in Moselle; aerial photograph, 1958.

Even for urban Frenchmen the land is still a ubiquitous presence. It is all around them, in all of its immense diversity. It is etched into the depths of the most venerable and popular forms of their history. Ever since the Neolithic period, since the invention of agriculture and husbandry some 7,000 years ago, the land has constantly been worked and reworked down to the smallest plot. In some centuries once-cultivated land was abandoned; in others peasants made new conquests. In the nineteenth century the vast majority of the French population lived in the country and off the land: the rural population attained its peak at that time. There is scarcely a family in France without roots in the soil, roots that are not only deep but also relatively recent, attested perhaps by wedding or holiday photographs of a still familiar grandparent or great-grandparent, stored away in the bottom of a drawer. Such immediate rural ancestry is less common in England or Germany or North America, where the impact of industrialization was felt earlier and more forcefully. In France, peasant traditions remained a vital presence until after World War II, even in the cities. Thereafter, however, everything changed. Urbanization shrank the countryside. More than that, the active farm population steadily decreased to the point where by 1985 it accounted for only 8.2 percent of the total working population. Meanwhile, farm output increased in response to new demands from agribusiness and the food-processing industry. This increase was much more rapid and effi-

FIGURE 1.3. Woods and farmland in Moselle; aerial photograph, 1989. In thirty years, or one generation, the overall pattern of land use has barely changed. The distribution of woods, farmland and pasture, and inhabited area is roughly the same, and the network of roads and paths is identical: the basic pattern is all but immutable. And yet a veritable agricultural revolution occurred in this period, as evidenced by the absorption of thin strips of farmland into larger fields.

cient than when the main driving force was the needs of the ordinary peasant. With the all but inevitable disappearance of the peasant, did the land cease to be the land? Never before had it produced so much though worked by so few, to the point where France is now one of the world's leading exporters of grains and dairy products. And yet never, perhaps, has the land exerted such fascination for people who, while they no longer live on it, still wish to identify with those who did. This fascination has given rise to an abundant scholarly literature and an equally abundant popular literature and even to a few great books, particularly in the 1970s. The land of the *agriculteur,* or modern high-tech farmer, has not yet relegated the land of the *paysan,* or traditional peasant, to oblivion. The countryside has become France's playland and vacation spot, a place to spend lazy summer days and fun-filled weekends: more than ever a *lieu de mémoire.*

1. The Land Revisited

A visit to Ardèche brings with it all the charm and bounty of a trip to the land of memory. It is worth delving a little more deeply into what lies behind the sights, and

FIGURE 1.4. Ardèche, Sainte-Agrève region; aerial photograph, 1984: woods, scrub, and pasture, with terraced fields abandoned on the higher hillsides, and fields and villages on the lower slopes.

we can do this by listening to such informed guides as Pierre Bozon, Jean-François Blanc, and Michel Riou as well as by talking to schoolchildren, prominent local figures, and other tourists.

The plain truth of the matter is that the land is dying. This is even more true in Ardèche than in other parts of France, for here the changes are more palpable. The département of Ardèche, which used to be known as the Vivarais region, occupies the steep slopes that rise more than 3,000 feet from the Rhône valley in the neighborhood of Valence to the high plateau of the Massif Central. The geological substrate is extremely varied, running the gamut from volcanic to metamorphic to sedimentary. The rugged terrain is marked by the sharp contrast between valleys, interfluves, and high plateaus; and subtle or marked local climatic variations differentiate the Le Velay highlands from the Rhône valley, the almost Atlantic weather of the north from the Mediterranean climate of the south. As a result, agricultural Ardèche is extremely varied, a veritable compendium of the kinds of terrain found elsewhere in France and indeed throughout Western Europe. But here the slope of the land makes the landscape palpable. It literally reveals itself to the traveler. The land is a visible, tangible presence, along with its crops and the other works of its peasants. On the high plateaus overshadowed by volcanic peaks fairly large cattle ranches once flourished. Poor but persistent smallholders eked out a living by growing a variety of crops on carefully terraced slopes. In the valleys small industrial towns have sprung up alongside fruit orchards and vineyards that have been relatively prosperous in recent years. Except for the latter, all these activities are in visible decline. The abandonment of the countryside is quite apparent from the number of ruined farms, overgrown fields, encroaching forests, and crumbling terraces. Working farms are hemmed in by recent growths of brush and scrub. After millennia of agriculture, the fertile, much-worked soil is again covered with weeds, straggly trees, heather, and ferns. Meanwhile, the transformed terrain has been invaded by tribes of seminomadic hunters, gatherers, and fishermen, denizens of a modern Paleolithic age: city dwellers, tourists, part-time residents.

There is no dearth of studies of the demise of the French peasant. The sociologist Henri Mendras gave currency to the phrase *la fin des paysans* with a work published in 1967. The end of World War II saw the sudden acceleration of a process that had begun roughly a century earlier: the rural exodus of peasants into cities and towns, as families that had worked the land for centuries gradually abandoned it. Before World War II, however, the change was slow. According to the 1906 census, 43.8 percent of the population was at that time still living directly off the land, and in 1954 the figure was still 31 percent. These levels are much higher than the comparable figures for the leading industrial nations of Western Europe and North America. During this first stage of the peasant's demise, France, unlike Germany, Great Britain, the Scandinavian countries, and the United States, remained in large part a nation of farmers, of small to medium landowners clinging to the old farmstead and the old ways. Abandoned farms and deserted countryside were found mainly in the regions where farming was most difficult, primarily in southern France and mountainous terrain. Ardèche was such a region. Its population peaked during the Second Empire. The 1861 census counted 388,500 inhabitants in a département containing no large city. In those days every hillside was carefully terraced and every valley dotted with small factories, most of them involved in the processing of silk or the manufacture of paper. Busy towns served as social centers and marketplaces. Yet here as in many other regions where a similar system prevailed, the decline of rural industry had a negative effect on agriculture and vice versa. Within a century the population decreased by more than 140,000 owing to emigration and a declining birthrate. The 1962 census turned up only 245,600 inhabitants, a decrease of more than a third from the nineteenth century. Here, the abandonment of the land was already all but complete.

Yet still more decisive changes have come during the past thirty years. Thanks to the combined effects of the expanded European market; agronomic research and its applications in the areas of fertilizers, motorization, and mechanization; selective breeding; and agricultural rationalization, farming has achieved unprecedented levels of productivity. Agricultural output has increased. The land is yielding more than ever before with fewer and fewer farmers, while the cultivated surface has steadily diminished. Gone are the periods of scarcity whose effects were still so apparent in the eighteenth and nineteenth centuries. The shortages of World War II and the postwar years are a thing of the past. France now produces more than it needs. It exports some products and stores surpluses of others. Even unassuming, backward Ardèche has had to adjust to the new rules and cope with the new anxieties. Impressive steps toward modernization were taken at the behest of agricultural cooperatives and the food-processing industry, and the region's leading products—such as highland milk, goat cheese, fruits (primarily the cherries and peaches of the Eyrieux valley and the Aubenas area), and the wines of the Rhône valley and southern vineyards—must now meet European quality standards and compete on the European market.

Three new types of agricultural producers have emerged—psychologically and sociologically as well as statistically. The distribution of these new producers varies across France, but all three are found in Ardèche. The first is the direct heir of the traditional peasant. He lives alone or with a family whose size has been reduced by departures for the city or an absence of children. He has no diploma and no ambition other than to survive and to live independently. He is reluctant to change any of the traditional practices he learned as a child. If he has changed at all, it has been by way of adopting a more defensive posture and growing old. Although he produces little, he is king in his own castle and has every intention of remaining so. He is without peer when it comes to gathering mushrooms, collecting chestnuts, hunting rabbit and partridge, and poaching out of season. There are two aspects to his demise, individual and collective: many rooms in his house are permanently shuttered, and more and more of his fields lie unplowed and overgrown. The second type of producer resembles the first but is somewhat younger, slightly more open-minded, traces his ancestry not quite so far back into the past, may have children, is less isolated, and has even been willing to try out a few new ideas after first criticizing his neighbors for adopting them and then envying their success. The third type is ready to try anything, no matter how bold. A few brave souls led the way as long ago as the turn of the century, and a few more followed between the two world wars. After 1950 most who remained on the soil joined them. All were of peasant background, of course, but increasingly they acquired technical skills and became producers, entrepreneurs, and managers plugged into world markets rather than holed up in their farmhouses clinging to old ways and fending off unwanted changes. Before long they were achieving record yields of wheat, milk, meat, wine, fruits, and vegetables. In Ardèche they selected the finest goats from their herds to produce flawless cheeses; they filled baskets with cherries and peaches from the orchards of the Eyrieux; they improved the productivity of their vineyards and the quality of their wine; and they even coaxed top-quality vegetables from terraced and irrigated fields.

Recent developments have confirmed the demise of the peasant quantitatively as well as socially. In 1986 the National Institute for Economic and Electoral Statistics (INSEE) estimated the number of active farmers as 1,414,000 and the number of farm workers as 239,00, for a total of 7.7 percent of the working population. This was higher, to be sure, than the comparable figures for West Germany and Great Britain. Nevertheless, when these figures are compared with those for France in 1906 and 1954, the change is dramatic. The vocabulary has changed, too: France no longer has *paysans* but *agriculteurs,* a group whose social importance is far outweighed by that of workers in the tertiary sector of the economy. Indeed, there are more blue-collar workers than farmers in every region of France. Farmers are outnumbered by civil servants (2,176,000), middle managers (2,074,000), merchants and artisans (1,763,000), and the unemployed (2,500,000). Together, teachers (of whom there are 700,000 in public schools) and students (1,200,000) constitute a group roughly comparable with that of farmers. Even in Ardèche, which is known as farming country, the change is apparent. Of course it was not until 1962 that the number of blue-collar workers in the département surpassed the number of farmers and farmhands. But by 1982 the social transformation was complete: while farmers still accounted for 14 percent of the working population, they were far outnumbered by industrial workers (38 percent) and tertiary-sector employees (48 percent). The 12,000 farmers in Ardèche in 1982 barely nosed out the 11,000 unemployed (as of 1986).

Sociological and psychological changes confirm these statistics. The last peasants are without heirs. Those farmers who remain have adopted the lifestyle of the dominant middle-class consumer society, rejecting the peasant tradition. The land itself has been steadily losing value, literally as well as figuratively. It is still sought after as an economic resource or a place to build, but it has lost the patrimonial value it once possessed. The pattern of centuries past has been reversed. Over the past fifteen years, the price of farmland has dropped everywhere in France by an average

FIGURE 1.5. Ruins, upper Provence.

of 40 percent. At the same time the usable agricultural surface has diminished, as forests and uncultivated land have expanded. In order to remain competitive in the twenty-first century, the boldest farmers have dreamt up a new kind of agriculture. It is envisioned that, by turning to new techniques, three regions—Brittany for livestock, the central Parisian basin for grains, and Languedoc for grapes, trees, and vegetables—can produce as much as all of France produces today. It would take just 100,000 to 200,000 farms, a fifth to a tenth of the present number. The rest of the country could be used for building new cities, left fallow, turned into vacation land, or studied by rural archaeologists. Such ideas are by no means utopian; they are under active consideration. Are the terraced hillsides and chestnut groves of Ardèche therefore a thing of the past? And will even the peach and cherry orchards and vineyards of today prove insufficiently profitable in the future?

In view of all this, the "back to the land" movement of the Vichy years may seem nothing less than preposterous or nonsensical. Between 1940 and 1944, and thus before the acceleration of the rural exodus, the regime promoted an ideology of moral regeneration, corporatism, and a return to the soil, said to be the cornerstone of French society and the French economy. Marshal Pétain's message was to "reroot the Frenchman in French soil, from which he has always drawn not only his own subsistence and that of his fellow citizens of the cities but also the stout virtues that gave the country its strength and enabled it to endure." What happened was the opposite. Yet the "back to the earth" message did not disappear with Vichy. It reemerged in a new guise twenty years later, at a time when the depopulation of the French countryside was at its height.

Was there any sense to this? Bucking the tide, the first "new farmers" turned up in the late 1950s in the poorest, most depopulated areas of southern France: the Cévennes, the Pyrenees, the southern Alps. Isolated at first, their communities grew from shortly before 1968 until the mid 1970s, when the movement reached its peak. During this period, Ardèche received a hundred or so new arrivals each year, according to one well-placed observer. These numbers may have been small, but in the most deserted *cantons* the new arrivals could represent ten percent or more of the adult population. Wary peasants referred to the newcomers rather disdainfully as "zippies." In Ardèche the history and the legend of the *néo-ruraux* was marred by a tragic crime. In 1977, ten years after settling in the isolated hamlet of Les Boutières, Pierre Conty, a native of Grenoble, committed a holdup in Lozère and then, on a road in Ardèche, killed a policeman and two others before vanishing into thin air. Memories of the crime still linger, and while admittedly an extreme case, it suggests a region that had reverted partway to savagery, exempt not only from the law of the cities but from the law of the peasants as well. In August 1986 another rather strange crime occurred in rural Ardèche. A peasant from Lespéron killed two tourists and wounded six people after a rather murky quarrel involving payment for the sale of certain animals. *Coup de feu, coup de sang, coup de folie* read the headline in *Le Monde* on August 15, 1986. Once again the murderer vanished.

The sociologists Danièle Léger and Bertrand Hervieu have studied the "back to nature" movement. At first, they tell us, young people determined to drop out of society were attracted not so much by the land as by the idea of living on society's fringes, in a sort of desert. "Communes" thrived on utopian dreams, not on work. Nearly all failed. Those who went in search of rustic idylls or ecological paradise found themselves forced fairly quickly to throw in the towel. For a short time it may have been fashionable in certain quarters to think of opening a potter's studio or raising a small herd of goats, but such ideas soon proved vulnerable to the tide of history. Yet as Léger and Hervieu show, some of the newcomers stayed on, lived together as more or less stable couples, had children who went to school, rejoined society, entered their honey or their goat cheese in county fairs, marketed their produce, sat on town councils, and began agitating for state subsidies. So the movement was not altogether without significance.

Not all those who dreamed of getting back to the land were hippies obsessed with fantasies of the farm, however. Plenty of middle-class Frenchmen bought second homes in the countryside or even first homes at ever greater distances from the cities in which they worked. Both phenomena emerged in the 1960s and have continued to the present day, even as the last peasants were vanishing from the countryside.

Purchasing a second home was more than just fashionable. In 1982, 9.6 percent of housing units in France were second homes. Second-home ownership is far more common in France than in any other industrialized country. In Auvergne and the Mediterranean region, 15 to 20 percent of all housing units are second homes, with the record being held by Corsica, where the figure is 26.2 percent. The rate of second-home ownership was also high in rural areas on the fringes of the Paris basin, including Lower Normandy (14.9 percent), Brittany (13 percent), and Burgundy (12.1 percent), as well as in mountainous areas such as the Rhône-Alpes (12.7 percent). In many villages of the Auge region of Normandy or the hinterland of Ardèche, second homes are now far more numerous than farms or permanent residences. Many villages and hamlets come to life only on weekends or during the vacation season. The phenomenon has left its mark on French society. In 1985, 12.5 percent of French families owned a second home. Not only did 32.7 percent of top managers and 17 percent of middle managers fall into this group, but so did 10.2 percent of clerical workers and 7.8 percent of blue-collar workers. Thus even people of modest means were not altogether deprived of the joys of living amidst greenery or of the rustic pleasures of weeding beneath the apple tree or clearing a hillside field.

The figures take on a rather different aspect when one includes permanent residences built outside existing city limits. Because of such new construction, the decline of the rural population, which had been constant since France first began to take its census, ceased from 1975 to 1982. Indeed, the rural population actually increased over that period, slightly to be sure but still more than the urban population. Cities are no longer growing by the expansion of contiguous suburbs. Instead, people are building country houses over an area proportional to the size and vitality of the central town. For a large city like Grenoble, this "rurbanization" comprises a territory some twenty to twenty-five miles in radius from the center of town, including the Grésivaudan and the Cluse de Voreppe as well as the foothills of the nearby Chartreuse, Vercors, and Belledonne. These once rural areas have been forced to reopen schools, repair roads, and renovate post offices and police stations after a century of depopulation. In Ardèche, even such modest towns as Aubenas and Privas are now ringed by communities in which hillside homes are more likely to thrive than grapevines and peach orchards.

But what role does the soil play in this rediscovery of country living? To be sure, the newcomers dream of living off the land, indeed of living as much as possible in harmony with the laws of nature. Yet few have been able to translate these dreams into reality. Many plant gardens, prune hedges and trees, restore houses and barns, and tend a row or two of grapevines. But since they have only the summer season and weekends to work, they cultivate the decorative rather than the useful. Instead of grapes, apples, peaches, feed grains, and vegetables, they plant lilacs, roses, and grass. Instead of pastures they have lawns, on which one is apt to find not cows and sheep but Japanese power mowers and English lapdogs. Suburban yards will surely go the same way as converted farmsteads. The soil remains, but its use has been utterly transformed: it now serves to provide pleasure for a few hours or a few days, its utility as a productive resource having diminished to almost nil. The value of farm property is declining everywhere except where it can be converted into lots for building. "Soil" has become "land."

All of these changes are wreathed in nostalgia. It is not without sorrow and doubt that the French have uprooted themselves from the soil in which their familiar history was rooted. The demise of the peasant has been accompanied by the lament of the poets.

Ardèche's slow agony elicited little sympathy from most Frenchmen until recently. But as the end nears, and as some seek to divert or deceive themselves by returning to a simpler way of life, there has been an extraordinary literary and artistic outpouring. There have also been works of history and studies of the writings of Olivier de Serres, who developed modern agronomy in Villeneuve-de-Berg even as that city was being transformed forever. Various ethnological studies, guidebooks, dozens of village monographs, poems, expositions, museums, and rural novels should also be mentioned: among them *De la soie dans les veines* (Roger Ferlet, 1958), *Ardèche douce amère* (André Griffon, 1975), *Les Contes de La Burle* (Jean Durand, 1982), *La Burle, un médecin de campagne en Haute-Ardèche* (Paul Perrève, 1981), *Le Vent feuillaret, une enfance ardèchoise* (Thérèse Bresson, 1980). Geographers have also contributed: the most comprehensive survey of rural Ardèche,

Pierre Bozon's *Ardèche, la terre et les hommes,* was published in 1978. And Jean-François Blanc concealed his heartfelt emotion when he published a thesis on the terraced fields of Ardèche in 1984, even as those terraces, the remarkable creations of countless peasant architects, were being obliterated by scrub. From retirement in Antraigues, the popular singer Jean Ferrat intoned "Que la montagne est belle. . . ." That tiny town has become a Mecca for artists and vacationers nostalgic for rocky cliffs and games of *boules.* Fashion has penetrated to the heart of even the most remote villages. The schoolchildren of Ardèche have probably never had at their fingertips so much information about the land of their ancestors, or so many sources of inspiration, now that their fathers are no longer peasants.

Ardèche stands for all of France. One could give a similar analysis of every département, and the greater the number of *néo-ruraux,* the more solid the documentation on which to base one's arguments. Excellent historians, geographers, and writers have chronicled the change. For half a century French geography has been steeped in ruralism, as if the soil rather than towns and industry must remain forever the inspiration of disciples of Jules Sion, René Musset, André Meynier, Raoul Blanchard, Paul Marres, Pierre Brunet, Pierre Flatrès, and Jacqueline Bonnamour. As for historians, Gaston Roupnel's *Histoire de la campagne française* (1932) was a pioneering work. Scholars of the *Annales* school, greatly influenced by the geographers, cut their teeth on tracing the origins of the rural infrastructure even as it was vanishing; this was especially true of the work of Marc Bloch. The peasant's saga has also served as a subject for writers as diverse as Gustave Flaubert, Guy de Maupassant, Jean Giono, Marcel Pagnol, Henri Bosco, Henri Pourrat, Maurice Genevoix, George Sand, and hundreds of others, as well as regionalist painters everywhere, yet very few filmmakers have dealt with it.

In the 1970s some excellent books enjoyed extraordinary success because they came at the right time to provide answers to the many different kinds of questions that were then being asked. In 1967 the sociologist Henri Mendras wrote *La Fin des paysans,* the book from whose title I have borrowed the phrase "the demise of the peasant." Then, in the space of three years, three important books appeared. All three were best-sellers, to an extent that cannot be explained by fashion alone but has to point to something deeper: Pierre Jakez Hélias's *Le Cheval d'orgeuil* (1975), Emmanuel Le Roy Ladurie's *Montaillou, village occitan* (1975), and *L'Histoire de la France rurale,* a four-volume work edited by Georges Duby and Armand Wallon (1977). The soil of France, worked since the Neolithic era, tamed and appropriated over a period of five to six thousand years, became, now that the last peasants were leaving it and the first of a new breed of inhabitants were rediscovering it, a focus of all France's thoughts and emotions, as if something essential were being torn from the nation's heart.

2. The Land Made Fertile

The richest land in France lies in the center of the Paris basin, between the Oise, the Seine, and the Loire. Other soils are of course more valuable: the hillside vineyards, for example, or the Mediterranean plains with their fruit orchards, flower farms, and truck gardens. Yet nowhere else is the wealth distributed over as vast an area as in the "breadbasket" of the Île-de-France and its adjacent regions: the Plain of France itself, immediately north of Paris, and the Valois, the Soissonais, the Tardenois, Brie, Beauce, Vexin, and, a little farther out, the plateaus of Picardy and eastern Normandy together with those of Touraine, Berry, and Champagne. The heart of France, all around its capital, is also its richest farm land.

As soon as one exits one of the major highways or superhighways anywhere outside Paris's urban sprawl, the horizon expands to encompass vast fields of wheat, barley, corn, alfalfa, sugar beets, and sunflowers. In all seasons wealth springs from the flatlands and gently rolling fields at the center of the sedimentary basin. In the fall the deeply furrowed soil appears brown. In winter it turns black beneath the downpours that come from the ocean to the west or white with frost and snow. In spring shoots of wheat and barley turn it a shimmering green, while farmers pass back and forth over the fields spraying chemicals to keep down parasites. In summer the fields turn gold, as the combines come out of storage and a strong smell of ripening grain wafts over the countryside. These bucolic scenes, straight out of the pages of Roupnel, are repeated in villages throughout France. It is easy to imagine the same scenes painted not with today's mechanized tractors and combines but with yesterday's teams of horses or oxen. But here—especially here, most powerfully here, beneath the skies of Île-de-France, Picardy, and Normandy—images of the present vie with images of the past. The soil of France is rich, fertile, and highly worked. To sing its praises calls for a Péguy; to offer its fruits up to heaven requires great cathedrals; and to store its now abundant harvest takes grain elevators, modernity's cumbersome replacement for the elegant spires of old, ringing every railway station and port.

Physically, the land is the oldest of all archives. The geographers' cross-sections reveal the depths of the earth as well as the surface: one sees the geological substrate, the surface conformations, and the soil proper. The substrate is a mineral memory of the earth's history before (broadly speaking) man's arrival. France is rather neatly divided between the crystalline and metamorphic rock of the old mountain ranges, particularly the Massif Central and the Armorican Massif, and the substrates of limestone, marl, sand, and clay of the two great sedimentary basins, the Aquitanian and the Parisian, while in the east, the Alpine uplift has juxtaposed rugged terrain with elements of a more tormented geological history. The surface formations reveal the alterations to which these substrates were subjected during the Quaternary period, through the alternation of warm and cold and wet and dry periods, for example, or the distribution of alluvium over plateaus, the creation of terraces in valleys, and the accumulation of hillside moraines. Few traces of human existence are found in the depths of the earth, for prehistoric tribes were widely scattered and possessed little. Vestiges of what is believed to be the earliest European carved implements, roughly 1,800,000 years old, have been found at Chilhac in Haute-Loire. These are the oldest traces of man in Europe but not in the world, since the presence of hominids in East Africa is thought to date back some 4,000,000 years.

For historians and prehistorians alike, the soil carries a quite different meaning. Geographers and agronomists use the term "soil" to refer to the outer layer of the terrestrial epidermis, ranging in France from a few inches to a yard or so in depth. This layer is subject to the direct action of water, to erosion and accumulation, to penetration by plants and animals, to various processes that build up and alter the humus, and last but not least to the work of man. The soil is the living portion of the earth's husk. It is also what peasants mean by "the land." Georges Bertrand, an expert in such matters, argues that there is virtually no "natural" soil left in France. Nature of course plays its part through the action and interaction of climate, vegetal covering, and geological substrate, but one cannot neglect the influence of man, not only by his present actions but also by the cumulative effect of what he has done in the past. The earth offers a physical guide to understanding what is going on today at the intersection of agronomy and ecology. Sophisticated research techniques can also turn the soil itself into a veritable archive of peasant activity. Archaeologists, soil scientists, and prehistorians have been quick to seize on this evidence, using excavations as a surgeon might use a scalpel and aerial photographs as a radiologist might use an X-ray.

The history of the peasant's earth begins in the Neolithic period, when the hunter-gatherers of the Paleolithic were gradually supplanted by sedentary tribes that raised sheep or cattle or sowed wheat and barley for harvesting some months later. Certain tribes practiced both agriculture and husbandry. In France this fundamental transition took place in the fifth millennium B.C. It was primarily the work of two groups, one consisting of Mediterranean tribes, the other of migrants who traveled down the Danube from Central Europe and eventually filtered into the eastern and central portions of the Paris basin. Thereafter the land was worked, seeded, trampled by the hooves of livestock and enriched by their dung—in short, made fertile. From then until the dawn of the twentieth century, the history of the peasant was intertwined with that of climate and vegetation. Over seven millennia the land was slowly conquered, as field after field was laboriously cleared of what began as a dense covering of Atlantic or Mediterranean forest dotted with barrens, marsh, and brushland, until by the nineteenth century the domination of the soil was virtually complete. If one were to graph this progress, it would resemble a sawtooth: setbacks preceded each new advance, and the course of events was marked by an endless series of calamities, wars, famines, epidemics, and other scourges that saw fields and meadows reclaimed by scrub. The land was not only the focal point of this history but also its record book, even if that record is not always easy to decipher. Before written documents came into being, the land is the only witness we have. It fascinates the peasant because of what it contains but also because of what it conceals of what is sometimes called "the night of time." When a farmer's plow turns up an old skeleton or tool, the earth is revealed as the sepulchre of this mystery. Life and death are mingled with the soil itself.

Does the soil of France have some peculiar quality that has made it such a central part of every Frenchman's legacy? What has been said about France can in fact be said about any of the great peasant civilizations. Objectively speaking, neither history nor geography bestows any particular primacy on France. The Neolithic transformation, without which the peasant's land would not exist, occurred earlier to the east, probably as early as the tenth millennium in the plains of the Middle East (where grains were grown and sheep and goats domesticated). France, moreover, has by no means been exempt from major calamities. In addition, the differences between the soil and climate of France and those of its immediate neighbors are not sufficient to count as decisive. Yet while these qualifications are accurate, they should not be overstated. The fact is that, both within France and without, French soil has enjoyed an unshakable reputation for being rich, fertile, productive, ardently sought after, and apt to give rise to new agricultural methods and potentialities. Favorable reports have echoed down the ages, from the *villae* of Romanized Gaul to the great Carolingian estates to the pioneer clearings of the late Middle Ages and ultimately to the villages of the eighteenth and nineteenth centuries, although to be sure dark periods divided these epochs of progress. More objectively, France was of course the most populous as well as the most densely populated country in Europe even though its economy was essentially agricultural. What is more, contemporary production figures bear out this historical memory. France has always enjoyed its riches of bread and wine.

Modern historians have been careful to distinguish between the rosy legend and the harsh reality. They are as likely to write about dark times and regions in difficulty as about rich provinces and happy times. Yet the idealized image no doubt owes a great deal to the various factors discussed above. France lies on an extraordinary isthmus, and its location helped to foster a remarkable convergence of Central Europe and Iberia, the Mediterranean and the Atlantic. In speaking of "convergence" I am referring as much to the complementarity of climates and soil conditions as to the commingling of peoples and ideas of which the Neolithic settlements were a first sign. Furthermore, the French isthmus is not narrow; it is broad enough to contain vast basins and plains where favorable soil conditions could readily develop: the Paris basin, the Aquitaine basin, and the series of plains stretching from Alsace to the Saône and Rhône. Over the last millennium, moreover, first the centralizing monarchy and then the republic managed slightly better than governments elsewhere to maintain civil peace and the rule of law. Such a combination of factors is rather unusual. Everything has to be seen in perspective, however. What is unique is the combination of factors, not the situation in a single region or epoch: France is a whole that was a long time in the making. In the final analysis, however, the idealized image offers a remarkably complete résumé of the various geographical and historical factors that together gave us France: hillsides and plains under calm skies, peaceful fields kept tranquil by the authority of the king or the republic, the cycle of labors from tilling to reaping, the grapevines and forests in the distance, the rich, black earth. In their morning prayer Catholics give thanks to Mary not only for the coming harvest but also for allowing the regular cycle of labors to continue without interruption.

If there is one region in which all these various symbols come together, it has to be the center of the Paris basin, which is also the heartland of France. Here one finds the very paradigm of rich soil, spread out over vast silted plateaus and worked and reworked for ages, conceivably without interruption since Neolithic times. Its fertility no doubt owes as much to this continuity as to its nonetheless real natural qualities. The fields are vast, devouring space and light and leaving only a few domanial forests for princely pleasures, a few smaller woods for an occasional hunt, and hillsides and valleys for truck gardens, fruit orchards, meadows, and factories. Nowadays the grain and sugar-beet fields are arrayed in huge blocks suited to the needs of tractors and combines, whereas in the past they were laid out in narrow ribbons better suited to teams of horses or oxen. Compact villages where farmhands reside dot the terrain, along with medium to large farms. With deep plowing it became possible to avoid leaving fields fallow, although this agricultural revolution came somewhat earlier to Flanders and the Po valley than to France. Here in central France, early in this century, well-to-do farmers confident of their abilities and resources developed a new high-yield agriculture that soon set the pace for the entire country. Pierre Brunet studied this model system in his 1960 thesis. The great amalgamation of farms took place in the nineteenth century. But one can trace the ancestry of these developments back much farther with a fair degree of confidence, working backward in time from the eighteenth century to the progress made by various religious orders in the eleventh and twelfth centuries and back to the Carolingian *villae* and Gallo-Roman estates.

Since the publication of Brunet's work, historians have amassed much additional detail about social changes, climatic cycles, capital accumulation, and the grinding poverty in which most peasants lived. Even more exciting is what aerial photogra-

FIGURE 1.6. Coulommiers, in Brie, aerial photograph, 1987: field pattern of large-scale agriculture.

phy has revealed about periods before the first written records were kept. Roger Agache's work on Picardy, for example, has yielded astonishingly precise maps of Bronze Age burial sites, ancient plot boundaries, Gallo-Roman *villae* with their buildings arrayed around rectangular courts, Roman roads, and scattered towns and villages. Elsewhere, in Provence and Alsace, for instance, investigators have been able to penetrate beneath today's boundaries to reveal the firm contours of Roman centuriations. These surveys have been fleshed out by extensive excavations in many parts of the country. The peasant's soil has a long history, laid down layer upon layer. Archaeologists are now moving on to study medieval and early modern times. The plowman who walked behind his team was surprised when he turned up a polished stone or flint tool, and no less surprised when he unearthed a rusty plow or scythe barely a century old. In such discoveries seven millennia of half-invisible peasant life were telescoped. But does today's agricultural technician, seated high above the soil in his powerful tractor, still have eyes to see them?

"Fertile," "made fertile," "natural fertility"—today's farmers would find such terms old-fashioned. And they are, for they are terms redolent of ancient peasant traditions, religious connotations, pagan memories, and Catholic litur-

FIGURE 1.7. Cormeilles, on the fringes of the Auge region of Normandy, aerial photograph, 1988: bocage, or fields bordered by hedgerows.

gies. They also suggest yields that are mediocre by modern standards and subject to vicissitudes that were traditionally interpreted as acts of God. Now that the peasants are gone, one has to speak in terms of yields and productivity rather than fertility.

Deeply furrowed, subjected to all sorts of mechanical devices, perfected by scientifically calibrated fertilizers, purged and sterilized by insecticides, and sown with carefully selected seedstock, the soil today yields more than ever before, in some cases ten times more than a generation or two ago. Where a medieval peasant was lucky to recover five to ten times what he sowed, today's farmer regularly harvests more than 7,000 pounds per acre. France, made fertile by the work of millennia and productive by the work of a few decades, is now one of the world's major agricultural producers. The central Paris basin leads the way in the production of grains and sugar beets; western France raises livestock; and grapes, fruits, and vegetables are grown along the Mediterranean. France leads the world in the production of wine and Europe in the production of wheat (in which it ranks fifth worldwide), sugar (seventh worldwide), corn (eighth worldwide), milk (third worldwide), and beef (fifth worldwide). It is a leading exporter of all these products. Among countries in the temperate zone it ranks third in agricultural production, behind the United States and the former Soviet Union (but its yield per acre substantially exceeds that of the latter). France has never been more fertile or productive than since its peasants left the land in droves. It projects upon the past the image of a golden age while suffering in the present with the devastation and depression of abundance.

3. The Domestication of the Land

Peasants, especially in France, tamed the land completely. The farmer's job is not merely to make the land fertile, to make it produce. It involves activities both individual and collective that leave a virtually permanent imprint on the environment. The most extraordinary of France's ancestral riches—or perhaps more accurately, the most ordinary, because they are found everywhere—are its rural landscapes. Historians and geographers since Marc Bloch have been working to classify these and discover their origins. Roger Dion and Daniel Faucher made important contributions to this effort, and their work was followed by that of André Meynier, Étienne Juillard, Pierre Brunet, and Georges Bertrand.

In the early 1960s Pierre Brunet and Marie-Claude Dionnet compiled what is probably the most detailed, objective, and useful compendium of all this work in the form of an atlas of rural France, which has since been through several revisions. The atlas is based on aerial photographs, the finest tool available at the time but one that is now being supplanted by satellite imaging. These photographs offer a vertical view of peasant handiwork, a view the peasants themselves never had the privilege of enjoying. At a scale of 1:1,000,000 one immediately discerns a higher order. Until World War II the landscape could only be viewed horizontally, village by village and hamlet by hamlet, or at best in the somewhat broader vista afforded by an elevated vantage point. The new atlas was completed just as an older agrarian pattern was being transformed from top to bottom as a result of the enlargement of fields, the introduction of mechanized equipment, the expansion of uncultivated land, the growth of towns, and the encroachment of urban excrescences. Geographers mastered the agricultural landscape intellectually even as peasants were losing their grip on it. Was this a mere coincidence or an ineluctable necessity? Quickly rendered obsolete by aerial photographic technology, such traditional hilltop sites for observing the rural landscape as Sion-Vaudrémont, Solutré, and the Mont Ventoux observatory were abandoned to the hordes of tourists.

Very broadly speaking, the atlas reveals three major types of rural landscape. The central and eastern Paris basin, extending from France's northern border and the Rhine to the English Channel, is open-field country, interspersed at intervals with forests. This region extends southward into the Loire and Allier basins, along the Saône and Rhône valleys, and into Charente. The open-field country is itself divided into two subtypes. In eastern France one typically finds quartered fields stretching out along wooded areas, at times in rather long ribbon-like patterns. In the central Paris basin, Berry, and the plain of Caen, the forested area is limited, and most of the surface is covered with huge, almost square fields. Versions of these two types of open field probably cover somewhat more than half of France's total surface area. One finds similar landscapes in the plains and basins of Central and Northern Europe, especially in Germany, the Netherlands, and Belgium.

Western France, by contrast, is *bocage* country: the term refers to a field enclosed by thick hedges, shrubbery, or trees, sometimes reinforced by a low earthen berm. Such fields can be used either as pasture or for raising crops. The *bocage* is typically found in Lower Normandy, Brittany, Maine, Vendée, and the Limousin, and also on the fringes of the northern and western Massif Central, the Jura and Alpine foothills, in Bresse and Dombes and Adour. Over the past twenty years the *bocage* has been in decline nearly everywhere, but especially in Brittany, as plot boundaries have been redrawn and new mechanized techniques introduced. In some cases fields are not hedged on all sides or alternate with non-hedged fields: this is referred to as *semi-bocage* and is typical of the eastern parts of the region described above. In recent years the *semi-bocage* or modified *bocage* structure has spread even into western France and now covers roughly a quarter of the nation's surface. Unlike open-field country and in contrast to what is commonly believed, *bocage* regions are generally not thickly forested, although the hedgerows themselves are tantamount to a vast linear forest.

In France's southern fringe, along the Mediterranean coast and in the lower Rhône valley and Aquitaine basin, one again finds the contrast between open and enclosed fields, but the distinguishing characteristic of this region is different. Here, the more varied relief of the terrain, the reliance on irrigation to overcome the effects of summer droughts, and an agricultural tradition that draws more on the tradition of the Mediterranean basin than on those of Northern and Central Europe have combined to produce a countryside that bears little resemblance to either *bocage* or open-field country. In the southeast one finds the characteristic Mediterranean contrast between *saltus* and *ager,* that is, between, on the one hand, highlands (hillsides, dry plateaus, and mountains) used for grazing flocks (which leaves little trace on the landscape of wood, brush, or *garrigue*) and, on the other hand, lowland plains that are intensively cultivated wherever sources of irrigation are available. In some places, such as the Vivarais, one also finds vineyards and orchards on terraced hillsides. In the southwest one finds an Aquitanian variation on this theme, composed of similar elements but under less stringent conditions and giving rise to gentler contrasts. While the well-irrigated valleys of the Garonne and its principal tributaries are reminiscent of the Mediterranean plains with their rich vineyards, orchards, and produce farms, the surrounding hillsides have been laboriously converted into open fields of small to medium size, interspersed with vineyards and sharing space with fruit orchards; curtains of trees and small forests dot the horizon wherever one looks.

To interpret these landscapes, historians and geographers have unleashed barrage after barrage of explanations for more than half a century, ever since Marc Bloch inaugurated the history of the agricultural landscape, the science of *finages* and *parcellaires*. Some emphasize the importance of natural conditions: the thick and thin soils and the Atlantic climate of the west; the alluvial soil and semicontinental climate of the Paris basin and its offshoots; the harshness of the mountains and contrasts of the Mediterranean; and so on. Others stress the historical background, pointing to ancient traditions and the tendency to stick with tried and true methods. Accordingly, they divide the country into three zones: an oceanic (and perhaps Celtic) region in the west; an area in the center and east open to the influence of Central Europe; and a region of Mediterranean tradition in the south. Many scholars recognize the decisive importance of agricultural methods, crops, implements, and farming systems: multiple crop planting *(polyculture)* coupled with husbandry; pastoralism opposed to fixed plantations; the cultivation of grapes and fruits as opposed to crop rotation; irrigation as opposed to dry farming; cultivation with the hoe as opposed to the swing-plow or plow; different techniques for exploiting forests, barrens, and marshes; and so on. And quite a few researchers, finally, have taken an interest in forms of land ownership and exploitation as well as in the social relations on which these were or are based: the west was a region of individualists, scattered widely throughout parishes in which discipline was loose at best; in the east and center, by contrast, village communities imposed collective constraints from which the more prosperous farmers only gradually freed themselves; while in the south one had patriarchies and phratries. All of these theories are interesting to study. But reality involved a subtle blend of a great many factors of which the landscape is the visible manifestation. As the land is drained of its last peasants, that landscape itself is revealing seven millennia of history to scholars bent over aerial photographs and archival records. An open field or hedge-lined meadow; a terrace formed by a stone retaining wall; a channel dug for irrigation; scattered hamlets and compact villages; princely forests and small private woods; a Roman arch spanning a river; a star-shaped or rectilinear road intersection—all these things are the visible vestiges of an ancient human saga, the still legible signs of a disciplined domestication of the land.

The rural landscape reflects the almost total domestication of the soil. The *Dictionnaire Robert* tells us that "domestic" animals (from the Latin *domesticus*, from *domus*, house) are those "that live in close proximity to man and that aid or amuse him; these long-tamed species reproduce under conditions established by man." In the peasant's world this definition applies not only to animals but also to crops, dwellings, roads, and fields. The domestication of the earth can be seen as a historical and geographical transition between a state of nature, in which man was a predator somewhat more clever than his competitors, and a state in which peasant society learned to control nature through agricultural reproduction. There are several reasons for the extraordinary quality of the French countryside. For one thing, France is an agricultural mosaic, in which several cultures converged upon a highly variegated natural canvas. The French isthmus drew its riches from the entire continent of Europe as well as from the Atlantic and Mediterranean. The domestication of its soil proceeded, despite occasional setbacks, slowly but steadily from Neolithic times. Memories of peasant civilization are still fresh: its demise is still recent, and everyone is familiar, if only from images, with using teams of oxen to till the land, riding horseback, threshing wheat, traveling on rutted dirt roads, watching livestock at the watering hole, washing clothes in the washhouse, fishing in trout streams, and hunting in the forest. Last but not least, nature in France was domesticated with almost impeccable thoroughness and tact: on the eve of World War I, just before the peasants met their final debacle, very little of the nation's territory had eluded their grasp.

What do we know of the "natural" landscape in which tribes of hunter-gatherers lived and where the first communities of farmers and husbandmen took root? Prehistorians and geographers such as Georges Bertrand tell us that the forest in those days was by no means uniform. Indeed, it was a varied mosaic. There were thick woods dominated by species that varied with climate and soil: beech, oak, fir, and pine. There were also prairies and sand barrens, brushland and *garrigue*, marshland, bog, and muddy meadows alongside streams and rivers. To one degree or another, peasants would eventually lay claim to all these varied environments, while never totally obliterating the landscape of the hunter-gatherers whom they replaced. It is useful to distinguish four primary environmental types.

At first glance the forest might appear to be the last remnant of natural space. To charcoal burners and poachers it served as a refuge. Even today it can still inspire fear. It is a place not so much for harvest as for hunting and gathering, cutting and felling. The forests of France have been extensively studied, and we know a great deal about them from their medieval uses to their modern exploitation. Of course there is nothing "natural" about what remains of French forests, unless it is their adaptation to climate and soil conditions. To be sure, there is still something "wild" about woodlands, with a hint of the Paleolithic in such activities as hunting, gathering, and collecting dead wood as well as in the the forest's role as refuge, escape, and focal point of human fears. But the chief use of the forest today is as a productive resource. And the landscape itself, with its sections and quarters, its riding paths and crossings and rendezvous, is largely defined by the way in which the forest is exploited: whether trees are trimmed or allowed to grow to full height, grown for firewood or for lumber, clear-cut or intercut. There are vast state forests and smaller private ones and even a few majestic wooded parks laid out in solar pattern in homage to the kings of France.

A second type of space is less completely domesticated than agricultural land proper. In this category one can place land that is too steep to be farmed or where the soil is too poor or the elevation too high or the soil too waterlogged (alongside a river perhaps) or too difficult to drain (in an estuary, say, or behind a dune). This type of land was the last to be exploited in periods of agricultural expansion, such as the late Middle Ages and the nineteenth century, and the first to be abandoned when farmers fall back, as they are doing now, on the most productive areas. Such places fall, in a manner of speaking, between the Paleolithic and the Neolithic, by which I mean that they lend themselves to two kinds of uses: hunting, fishing, and gathering (along with recreation and sightseeing) on the one hand and "temporary" agriculture, forestry, and more commonly husbandry on the other. In France one has, for example, the pine barrens, swamps, and low-lying meadows of the west, along with wetlands everywhere filled with reeds, alder, willows, and poplars, mountain pastures and grasslands bordering on cliffs and glaciers, and the extensive *garrigues* and *maquis* (scrub) of the Mediterranean south.

The field is the quintessential agricultural space. In the west fields are turned into permanent pastures for livestock. Other fields may be closed or open, dry or irrigated, rotated regularly among several crops, or permanently planted with fruit trees or grapevines. The variety is astonishing. Yet in all cases—field, pasture, orchard, or vineyard—constant attention is lavished on the soil. The regular round of labors is repeated season after season, and nothing is left to chance: harvest alternates with preparation of the soil, and growers have their ways of replenishing the land and of ensuring the perpetuation of its product. In France continuity was always stressed over productivity. The peasant looked to the long run rather than to short-term profit. This was encouraged by paternalistic relations between landowners and farmers. Until the recent period of wholesale transformation, innovation was somewhat suspect, persistence was respected, and wisdom was often identified with the lessons of the past and summed up in oft-repeated proverbs. The countryside was therefore slow to change. Fields and pastures were exploited deliberately but not necessarily in the most sophisticated manner. The land was domesticated without violence to nature's rhythms, without the large-scale transformation of the landscape sometimes seen in other countries, without brute force or open warfare against the terrain or soil—in short, with understanding gentleness rather than massive attack: not for nothing is the country known as *la douce France*.

FIGURE 1.8. Ammerschwihr, near Colmar: an Alsatian village and its adjacent vineyards.

FIGURE 1.9. Saint-Georges-en-Auge in Normandy: scattered dwellings in a landscape of fields, hedgerows, trees, pasture, and a few remaining orchards.

FIGURE 1.10. Bonnieux in Provence: a compact Mediterranean village perched above its orchards.

At the heart of the system, the house together with its immediate dependencies forms the center of domestic space. Volumes have been written about the enormous variety of rural dwelling places. From the hilltop villages of the Mediterranean to the walled farms of the Beauce, veritable fortresses for the storage of grain; from Alsatian villages hemmed in by vineyards to the hedged hamlets of *bocage* country; from the large farms of Caux, surrounded by double rows of beech trees soaring upward out of earthern berms, to villages whose residents live huddled around the landlord's chateau: meaning has been imposed on the landscape in many ways. Peasants, it turns out, not only shaped the land but shaped their living space as well. At home they sought refuge from the winds of the plains and the hot sun of the semiarid south. Some were poor, others rich, with gardens, orchards, wine and storage cellars, barns and haylofts, kitchens and common rooms. Their homes were redolent of a variety of smells: apples and grapes in the kitchens, preserves in the pantry, wax on family heirlooms in the living quarters, curdled milk under the eaves. City dwellers dream of such things, while antique dealers scour the countryside for relics of a bygone era.

The house, too, is a patrimony, complementing that of the land on which it stands. The peasant never paused to measure the worth of his home, or for that matter of his land and trees, except when he stood silently after Sunday mass contemplating the ripening crop, or perhaps behind the walls of a *notaire*'s office in a festering dispute over someone's inheritance, at which time what counted was not aesthetics but money. Once the peasant disappeared, his heirs rediscovered these rural riches, but with a new eye, shaped by new interests. Memories do not vanish as abruptly as the urban migration statistics might suggest. They can take highly emotional forms: images of grandparents and the stories they told, souvenirs of country vacations, remembrances of childhood fragrances, a nostalgic yearning for moments of happiness. For many people in France, such sensations as the smell of freshly made jam or the feel of riding a bicycle down a narrow path between vineyards remain living memories. The domesticated landscape can become a sort of lost paradise. One begins to look at antique cupboards and rural villages with a loving, aesthetic eye.

In Bertrand Tavernier's film *Une semaine de vacances*, Nathalie Baye plays a young schoolteacher who goes to visit her parents in a small Beaujolais village. The young woman, who works in Lyon, is a victim of the wrenching dislocations of the late 1970s. On the edge of depression, she takes a week off from work. Tavernier only hints at her feelings during this brief return to the scene of her childhood. From the bus window he shows us the countryside in a way that mingles past and present. We witness the bus's slow ascent of one of the long, gentle ridges that are a distinctive feature of the Beaujolais landscape. We see the granular ocher soil of the granitic arenas and the vineyards that turn the ridges into waves of grapes. We see the fanciful geometry imposed by crests and hollows and the carefully thought-out pattern of paths and drainage. We see substantial villages in which vine growers live cheek-by-jowl, each family turned inward on its own courtyard. Standing somewhat apart, we also see the more ostentatious homes of the wine dealers and Lyon-based landlords, whose balconies command the better vistas. This nostalgic journey is quite evocative, even if the spectator doubts that homesickness is the whole reason for the young schoolteacher's depression or that a visit home will be enough to turn things around. The opening sequence is sufficient unto itself; silent, it tells us more than words could ever do. Childhood is lost forever. On that night as on many other nights, the hills of Beaujolais and of many other places in France were radiant with an ineffable beauty.

The French rural landscape is almost everywhere beautiful, gently cloaking the earth. It has taken somewhat more than two centuries to articulate this point. Prior to the eighteenth century the beauty of the landscape was not something one discussed: there are no literary descriptions, and it seems likely that the land was not so attractive to look at in any case. The feeling for nature and the countryside emerged with Rousseau. Nineteenth-century novelists such as Balzac, Sand, Flaubert, Maupassant, and Zola offered a fairly realistic view of rural life, though not untinged by aesthetic indulgence. Already the literary eye saw the light shimmering off the countryside of Indre or Caux. In more recent times, writers like Jean Giono and Henri Pourrat, as well as scholars like Gaston Roupnel and essayists like Pierre Jakez Hélias, have introduced a plaintive, nostalgic note. Yet few historians and geographers have bothered to analyze the representation of the landscape, as if they found it impossible to make room for the aesthetic within their notion of objective scholarship.

The beauty of the landscape now forms a part of the common understanding as well as the vocabulary of officialdom. The countryside is pretty. Mountains are pretty. Steaming, freshly-plowed fields are pretty. The land has become an object of aesthetic sublimation. Farmland and the common appurtenances of rural life have become objects of art: to be sure, they first have to be scraped clean, tidied up, and cleansed of blemishes, but anything old will do quite well: a small farmhouse in an apple orchard, a pond bordered by irises, a meadow fringed by poplars lining a stream, wisps of fog on a plowed field, a beamed ceiling darkened by smoke from the fireplace. As farmland disappears, the state has taken upon itself the duty of protecting this heritage. And so we have national and regional parks, catalogues of our national treasure, lists of protected sites, museums featuring folk arts and traditions, "ecomuseums," environmental impact studies, and what have you. The collective poem that for seven millennia was written upon the land deserved at least this definitive reprint.

4. The Land Appropriated

Since the beginning of the nineteenth century, France has maintained a cadastre of land ownership. Cadastral surveys had of course been done before, in ancient Egypt and Rome and in Savoy as early as the beginning of the eighteenth century. During the Ancien Régime land ownership was often in doubt, despite various types of land registries *(terriers, pouillés)*. In 1790 the Constituent Assembly had the idea of establishing a cadastre, but nothing was done to implement that idea. Napoleon finally gave the order in 1807, but it was not until about 1850 that all the *communes* in France had been surveyed.

The cadastre is an important modern institution. If one happens to be visiting the town hall of a rural French commune, it is worth taking the trouble, after a glance at the usual bust of Marianne and photograph of the current president of the Republic, to look at the cadastre. It consists of three items: a cadastral map, an inventory of each of the commune's sections, and a list of landowners. The map gives a detailed survey of the commune showing sectional boundaries at a scale between 1:500 and 1:5,000. The basic element of the map is the plot *(parcelle)*, which is defined as a "continuous portion of land in a specific locale *[lieu-dit]* devoted to a single type of cultivation and belonging to a single owner." Thus each "portion of land" is clearly identified. The sectional inventory is the primary land register, identifying each plot with a number corresponding to its number on the map and listing its surface area, owner's name, and tax valuation. The ownership list is a secondary land register listing all owners of property in the commune, together with the properties they own. Every commune in France thus maintains a record of all properties and their owners.

Not a single morsel of French soil is omitted from the cadastre: all property is thus recorded, be it private (the most common case) or public (whether owned by the national government, the commune, a section of the commune, or other legal entities). Most communes possess three versions of their cadastres, because the instrument has had to be revised several times since the beginning of the nineteenth century. One can thus view the history of land ownership in minute detail, at the family level, over a period of at least two centuries. To do so, however, would take a great deal of patience, given the massive amount of information available. Historians have been slow to undertake this thankless task. After World War II, however, Pierre George and his students did pioneering work in this area.

Is land ownership in France a sacred thing? It sometimes seems that way. The cadastre gives us an extraordinarily detailed picture of social relations. With each revision landowners clashed with the government over the valuation of their property. When boundary lines were disputed, the cadastre provided the legal basis for the adjudication of rival claims. Families could trace the way in which different parcels of land were assembled and disassembled by wills and sales. In France, the person responsible for sorting out the complexities of such transactions is the *notaire*, or notary. His job is to apply the law in such a way as to reconcile public and private, the rights of all and the rights of individuals and families.

Let us visit the offices of a Norman notary. The old province of the dukes enjoys a well-deserved reputation for being somewhat fussier than others and perhaps a little more tangled in red tape when it comes to questions of land ownership. To be sure, its land, from the rich pastures of Auge and Bessin to the fine fields of Vexin and Caux, the plains of the Eure, and the open country of Caen, is more valuable than land in many other places. The notary's office is apt to be located in a small town, a place such as Romain-de-Colbosc, Pont-l'Évêque, or Verneuil-sur-Avre, always near the main square where the weekly market is held but somewhat apart, on a quiet street, safe from prying eyes and at a distance from the noisy crowd and the unduly curious. A quick visit to the office is sufficient for dropping off or retrieving a document in the vestibule, but doing any serious business takes time. For such occasions the client is likely to put on his best clothes. His wife may accompany him, although she is unlikely to say anything. If she does speak up, her words will not go unnoticed. The car will have been parked some distance away, and the client will have taken care to avoid meeting anyone along the way. His welcome will proceed by degrees, a series of initiations, starting at the door, moving on to the waiting room, passing from there into the clerical offices, then to the chief clerk's cubicle, and finally into the office of the notary himself, who is referred to as *maître* (master). The room is likely to be carpeted, rather dark, and totally silent, safe from eavesdroppers, and furnished as well as if not better than the best rooms back at the farm or manor. The notary is of course a man of serious mien who has probably known the family for a long time, known it perhaps as well as the family doctor. This is a place where a man can talk, evaluate his situation, weigh serious decisions, and even take a modest risk on the future. The conversation, of course, is about land.

From the beginning of the nineteenth century, when the cadastre and the notary became national institutions, until the early 1970s, there were three dominant trends in French real estate: the price of farmland rose slowly but steadily (except for brief periods of recession); large estates were broken up, while smaller farms were gradually eliminated, with the vast majority of multicrop and livestock farms clustered in the 25- to 125-acre range (with the median gradually rising); and land was increasingly owned by the peasants—or, as they came to be called, cultivators—themselves, rather than by landlords who collected a cash rent or share of the crop. Farms became the property of those who worked them, or at any rate of their families, rather than of noble lords or landlords living in town. These trends have received a good deal of scholarly attention, so there is no need to dwell on them here. Their significance is worthy of a few comments, however.

Land ownership has traditionally embodied an important range of values. That is why it has sometimes been considered "sacred," and why in Normandy and other regions the word for property in land is the same as the word for "good": *bien. Avoir du bien* or, more colloquially, *avoir du bien au soleil,* is the expression for owning land, perhaps the supreme value in French society, the most esteemed social status.

The fertile soil, the soil that has been made fertile by the work of millennia, is valued in and for itself. For the peasant, owning land is the best guarantee against misery and death, the best assurance of survival for family and loved ones in times of famine and disease. In France, past shortages are still recent enough to survive in living memory. And one needn't go back three or four generations: many people remember grandparents from regions such as Les Ségalas or Armor who worked as sharecroppers or day laborers and survived on the poor man's daily ration of black bread. During World War II, rationing and requisitioning in a disrupted economy allowed farmers to reap substantial profits on the black market and taught the landless the meaning of the word "privation." Even today the land can still serve as a refuge for the unemployed worker fortunate enough to own a small plot.

The domesticated landscape is also valued for aesthetic and emotional reasons. Lots may be identified by numbers on cadastral maps, but they are never anonymous. Each plot possesses not only an economic value but a unique identity that everyone understands. Plots have names: the Cour Mathurin, the Grand Herbage, the Champ de la Raierie. And they have a history. They elicit memories in abundance. Sometimes land is coveted and perhaps fought over before finally being purchased. Each field is recognizable by certain unmistakable signs: a row of poplars, a certain type of fence, a handful of elms towering over grass and buttercups, a pool of runoff into which furrows disappear after every storm. There is thus an emotional resonance to ownership of the land.

It took a long time for peasants to become masters of their land. They had first to combat the traditional rights of noble landlords, still very much in evidence at the end of the Ancien Régime. From the late Middle Ages until the nineteenth century, they also had to counter the steady inroads made by urban investors who saw land as the safest place to put their money. And finally, they had to fight each other, for as the number of peasants increased as the death rate began to decline in the eighteenth century, competition among them for more land grew that much more intense.

Consider, for instance, the history of a typical Norman farm, 500 acres of excellent land and pasture between the Ouche region and the Eure valley. Farm buildings adjoin the main house, and there is an apple orchard not far from the central barnyard. Smaller fields have been combined to create larger ones, while the land along the stream has been left for pasture. A small wood has been left for hunting and woodcutting. This small bit of the Norman plain, not far from the great beech and oak forests of Conches and Breteuil, has been made fertile, domesticated like an animal and made docile, possessed as a man might possess a wife. The results of this labor of love have been mapped and recorded in the cadastre while becoming part of a long family tradition. The names of the earliest ancestors, the people who first farmed this land, appear on the oldest tombstones in the family cemetery and in the yellowest papers among the deeds of ownership. In most cases these traces date from the eighteenth century, but records going back to the sixteenth century are not uncommon. All the farms in this area began fairly modestly, with a family plot, perhaps, or with land purchased from a noble or bourgeois landlord. If the family line remained unbroken, if the heirs proved suitable to the legacy rather than the reverse, if the men did not drink and the women remained respectable generation after generation, if parents taught their children to be good farmers, and if, in addition, they enjoyed a little luck, the farm might grow inch by inch as its owners acquired more land and more knowledge, as they learned new methods and techniques, until ultimately they became today's modern agricultural entrepreneurs. In this saga, which runs from the nineteenth century to the present, a happy ending depended on a certain ruthlessness toward others, a great deal of self-discipline, and ultimately a kind of virtue. To economists and agronomists, however, the process goes by the name of "concentration of farmland."

Land as property can thus be identified with the peasant family, not only because the family lived off the land but also because the land allowed the family to reproduce and was a permanent feature of its history. The land insisted on certain moral values of a most basic and sacred kind: diligence, endurance, loyalty, and a certain measure of self-denial in the name of higher necessities. The land was *le bien*. Without the right moral climate at home, a family could hardly hope to hold on to its land. Without land, it could hardly expect to remain a "good family" for very long. Like the pagan fertility cults of old, Christianity recognized the social need for the "chosen of the earth." Except for certain backwaters of southwestern France, most of the country was Christian, and for a long time peasants were always the best Catholics, as opposed to the beggars who came to the land from other places or left it for them.

Before the recent period of concentration, ownership of French soil was widely distributed. In 1955 there were still some 1,212,000 owner-farmers in France, or 53.6 percent of the total number of cultivators. There were 580,000 others (25.4 percent of the total) who combined one form or another of tenancy with ownership, and 467,000 (20.7 percent) who rented their land or worked as sharecroppers. "Everyone a landowner" might well have been the slogan of rural France in times past, for even artisans, small merchants, factory and farm hands, and even common laborers who lived in the country often owned small plots; some still do. Tenant farming is still common in the central Paris basin, in Upper Normandy, and to a lesser extent in western France. Sharecropping persists in rather specialized forms in vine-growing regions such as Beaujolais and certain parts of the Massif Central. In recent years, however, the trend everywhere has been toward medium-sized family farms, with family members working land partly owned by themselves and partly rented from relatives and neighbors. By 1970 the proportion of farms operated by tenants or sharecroppers had declined to just 14.7 percent, whereas mixed farms now accounted for 42.6 percent.

As a result of this extreme concentration, peasants are more than ever masters of the soil, whereas aristocratic and urban investment in land has declined. Despite this, things have been headed in a negative direction. In most areas most of the land is occupied by owner-farmers. Nevertheless, land prices have been dropping for the past ten years, reversing an age-old trend. Farmers indebted to their bankers are afraid of seeing their land sold off to real-estate trusts or European competitors. Last but not least, many farmers wonder if any of their children will be willing to take over the family farm after they die. The statistical forecasts are quite pessimistic. Depending on which survey or region one looks at, anywhere from 30 to 50 percent of present-day farmers are uncertain whether there will be anyone to follow in their footsteps. The current situation stands in sharp contrast to the way things were just a short time ago, when competition for ownership of the land was acute. Increased productivity has separated the peasant family from its *bien*: increasingly one finds farmhouses occupied by an elderly couple or even a solitary bachelor, living a life completely out of step with today's fashions. If current trends continue, the land may end up simply being abandoned. Just as former farmland in southern and eastern France went out of cultivation in years past, the same thing is happening in western France today. Families that sell off their patrimony often use the money to "build" in town or restore a vacation home and thus remain in a sense property owners. Children who inherit their parents' land find themselves drawn in other directions and choose to sell what they own rather than do something with it. Spurned property becomes the graveyard of lost virtues.

Still, the best farms in the richest regions remain vital and coveted. Good land, concentrated in ever larger farms, is intensively cultivated by highly productive agribusiness operations producing grapes, fruit, lumber, grain, and livestock. But this is no longer peasant land: the capital, methods, labor, and lifestyles of the few who still cultivate have nothing in common with peasant ways. The experts who profit from the land now, many of them descendants of peasants past, have turned the land into a rare resource, highly productive economically, somewhat less remunerative financially, but aesthetically and emotionally still priceless.

The land is not only the most extensive and ubiquitous of the *lieux* of French history, it is also the most profound. It embodies the values of an age-old peasant civilization that lives on beneath the contemporary landscape. The oldest of our memories is therefore also the freshest, for the last peasants are still among us.

FIGURE 1.11. Brittany: intensive cultivation beneath plastic groundcover, 1988.

FIGURE 1.12. Livestock raised in the Sarthe.

No other major peasant civilization in Europe or elsewhere has ever valued the soil more than the French or associated it more intimately with the good. In France the soil has been cultivated longer, more widely, and more continuously than anywhere else. The natural and agricultural diversity is greater. Adapting gracefully to the exigencies of climate and terrain, man, having remained on the soil until quite recently, has created in France a landscape of unparalleled harmony. Taken together, these factors help to explain why so many French people idealize the land. There can be no doubt that it has marked their history and colored their memory.

A factor of continuity in the face of change, the land was for two centuries the cradle of French conservatism. Yet in less than a generation everything has changed. Revamped from top to bottom, French agriculture is now among the most productive in the world. The suddenly old-fashioned peasant landscape offers the French a nostalgic image of themselves, a past idealized for its now vanished stability. In reality, however, enterprise is winning out over tradition, and conservatism is becoming a conservatory.

FIGURE 2.0. *Our Ladies of Paris,* by Raoul Hausmann, 1939.

CHAPTER II

The Cathedral

André Vauchez

The fate of the great religious edifices of medieval France is a curious one: the country's principal abbeys, headquarters of orders, and pilgrimage churches, which for centuries commanded the attention of all Europe, have nearly all disappeared. Contrast this with Italy, whose principal monasteries remain intact, from Subiaco to Farfa and Monte Cassino, which was carefully rebuilt after sustaining major damage in World War II, and Spain, which jealously cares for its prized monasteries at Ripoll, Montserrat, and Las Huelgas, not to mention the more recently constructed Escorial. Of course France still possesses many splendid cloisters, abbey churches, and collegiate churches that are masterpieces of Romanesque and Gothic art. But of Cluny, Cîteaux, Prémontré, Saint-Martin of Tours, and Saint-Martial of Limoges, which in their day were numbered among the most prestigious religious monuments in all Christendom, only fragments remain, ruins that speak only to archaeologists. Clairvaux, which once owed its renown to Saint Bernard, is today known primarily as a prison, and Fontevrault, which suffered a similar fate, has yet to efface the ravages of time. By contrast, nearly all our medieval cathedrals have survived, having been restored or rebuilt each time their existence was threatened.

At first glance it might seem that if abbeys were treated differently from cathedrals, it might have had something to do with the profound crisis that affected monastic orders in France from 1730 to 1830, or with the vandalism of the so-called *bande noire*, or black gang, a group of church-wreckers active during the Revolution and Empire and responsible, among other things, for destroying Cluny in order to exploit the ruins as a source of cheap stone. Significantly, however, in all this period, during which countless monasteries and old churches were razed, only three cathedrals succumbed, all of them on France's northern borders: Arras, Boulogne, and

Cambrai. In 1797, when the cathedral of Noyon was put up for sale as a national property (that is, confiscated by the Revolution), it found no buyer. And in Strasbourg in 1793 local citizens saved their cathedral's spire, which offended the egalitarian sensibilities of local and Parisian Jacobins, by draping it with an enormous Phrygian cap made of metal and visible from German soil. Later, after church and state in France were officially separated, the secular Republic did not stint on funds for repairing war damage to the cathedral of Reims (restored from 1918 to 1938) or the cathedral of Rouen (after 1945). More recently, political leaders of both the left and the right have agreed on the need to make the restoration of France's major cathedrals a national priority, as the vote on a 1986 appropriations bill for that purpose attests. Given that only about ten percent of the population regularly attends church, such extraordinary favor can only be explained by historical and cultural factors. Indeed, such factors account for the fact that most French people view cathedrals, as distinct from other kinds of churches, not as purely religious edifices but rather as memorial embodiments of French history, both sacred and profane.

Medieval France: Monarchical and Christian

What exactly does the word "cathedral" mean? The definition is not as clearcut as one might think, for the word actually has several loosely related meanings. The first definition is administrative: ever since the Concordat of 1801, ratified on this point by the Law of Separation of 1906, the French government has officially applied the term "cathedral" to the principal church in each of the Catholic Church's dioceses in both metropolitan France and its overseas territories.[1] The definition covers some eighty-seven churches, which are officially government property even though their primary function is religious. Under a 1907 law, the cost of maintaining these buildings was transferred from the recently abolished Ministère des Cultes to the Ministère des Beaux-Arts. All were classified as historical monuments and assigned to a special department, which has been responsible ever since for all physical maintenance.

This administrative definition does not coincide, however, with that of the present-day Catholic Church, which has established a number of new dioceses with cathedrals not recognized as such by the government, or with that of Ancien Régime France, which counted 158 dioceses on the eve of the Revolution. Thus edifices as important as Notre-Dame of Laon and Senlis and Saint-Just of Narbonne and Saint-Bertrand of Comminges have not been officially counted as cathedrals since 1801, whereas a mediocre eighteenth-century neoclassical church in La Rochelle and a nineteenth-century church in Gap are entitled to be called cathedrals and enjoy the special status that goes with the title. If today's official list seems too restrictive, the list of dioceses prior to 1791 is equally unsatisfactory because it is too inclusive: in 1317, when Pope John XXII established sixteen new dioceses in southwestern France, many of them quite small, he transformed a number of abbeys, such as those of Saint-Papoul and Maillezais, into cathedrals that never really managed to live up to their newfound dignity. It is therefore best to adopt an empirical definition that may be unsatisfactory from a legal point of view but nevertheless corresponds to the general public's idea of what a cathedral is, namely, an important religious edifice that is or was the principal church of a bishopric and that dates back to medieval times. It is significant, moreover, that the only churches commonly accepted as cathedrals are those that have enjoyed the distinction since time immemorial, as if the term were only applicable to places where certain sacred functions have been performed continuously. Pushing this conceptual analysis a little further, it quickly becomes apparent that in France the term "cathedral" applies above all to the principal churches of a specific region, namely, the area bounded by Amiens to the north, Bourges to the south, Coutances to the west, and Reims to the east. In the mind of the average French person today, the cathedral is essentially a feature of the Paris basin, the birthplace of Gothic art and the heart of the Capetian royal domain, with outposts in Lorraine and Alsace (Metz and Strasbourg) and the Languedoc region of southern France (Carcassonne, Albi, Narbonne). Of course there are authentic cathedrals in Aquitaine and Provence, but these occupy only a modest place in France's memory.

Although the exclusion may seem arbitrary, this selective perception is based on certain objective realities: south of the Loire it often seems as though monasteries and other urban sanctuaries used to (and in some cases still do) command more attention than cathedrals. In Toulouse, for example, the collegiate church of Saint-Sernin is rightly more celebrated than the archbishop's church, Saint-Étienne, while in Poitiers, the cathedral, Saint-Pierre, has never enjoyed the prestige of its rivals Notre-Dame-la-Grande, Saint-Hilaire, and Sainte-Radegonde. In Provence and the southern Rhône valley the situation is somewhat different. In cities such as Vienne, Aix-en-Provence, and Fréjus, the bishop's church remains the leading religious edifice, but these monuments are modest in size and fully integrated into their urban surroundings, set apart only by their steeples, and even these hardly tower. Such restraint scarcely fits the general public's idea of what a cathedral is. The only cathedrals that count in French history are those that set themselves apart by dint of massive size, impressive height, and noteworthy works of art.

The distinction I am making here also reflects certain disparities in the ecclesiastical geography of old France: a glance at the map shows that there is a marked contrast between southern France, where dioceses were generally small, comprising no more than a few dozen rural parishes within a short distance of a relatively modest episcopal city, and northern France, where bishoprics such as those of Bourges and

Rouen might boast hundreds of parishes and support cathedrals impressive enough to dominate their surroundings.[2] This geography of course reflects the disparity that emerged in the twelfth and thirteenth centuries between the heartland of the medieval economic spurt, which was both agricultural (around Chartres, Amiens, and Laon) and commercial (in Rouen, Paris, and Strasbourg), and the area south of a line stretching from Bordeaux to Lyon, which reaped only marginal benefits from this growth. Finally, there is an obvious (if hard to pin down) connection between the flourishing of cathedrals and the growth of monarchical power, be it imperial (as at Strasbourg) or royal (as at Reims, Senlis, and Paris).[3] Because the cathedrals of northern France played a leading role in the nation's religious and political history, they are a crucial part of the national legacy, at once symbols of and models for medieval, monarchical, Christian France.

A Conservatory of the Sacred

The search for a pragmatic as opposed to an administrative or ecclesiastical definition of the cathedral has thus shown that cathedrals are not like other churches but repositories of the past, gathering up centuries of the memories of the cities and dioceses they represent. Foremost among these are of course memories associated with things sacred. Hence it is no surprise that the most prestigious cathedrals are those that can boast of being the oldest. In some cases the Christian edifice was erected on the site of a sanctuary or monument dedicated to an earlier cult. In Le Mans, for example, the cathedral's principal entrance is referred to as "*de la Pierre au lait*," no doubt a distortion of *pierre lée* (or *levée*), meaning "raised stone," a reference to a menhir of striped pink sandstone that stands in one corner of the facade, where worshippers used to seek divine favor by inserting their thumbs into a small cavity. In Chartres the cathedral was built above a cave, which until the Revolution held a statue of the Virgin. According to a local tradition, this cave had been the site of a cult honoring a virgin with child a hundred years before the birth of Christ. Crypts and wells play an important role in these religious structures, ostensibly striking roots deep into the bowels of the earth and enveloping the edifices above in the night of time.

In Christian terms the cathedral was preeminent because it was the bishop's church, the bishop being the principal religious authority in each diocese. It was therefore the *ecclesia* par excellence, the diocese's mother church, to which all other churches were subsidiary, as is attested today by the name of Marseilles's cathedral, referred to simply as *la Major*. The word "cathedral," which comes from the Latinized Greek *cathedra*, or seat, referring to the throne on which the bishop sits, did not appear in France until the eighth century and did not really take hold until the thirteenth century, when bishops consolidated their authority. Prior to the

Carolingian period one should speak rather of the "cathedral close" or "ecclesiastical quarter," for what one had in early medieval cities was not a single church but a variety of religious buildings spread over a fairly extensive area.[4] It was not uncommon to find, alongside the bishop's church, a second cathedral, which, as in Paris, served for a long time as the city's only parish church. One was also likely to find, in addition, a baptistry, an episcopal palace, housing for canons, and so on. In liturgical terms the cathedral's status was marked by the splendor of its dedicatory ritual, the ceremony marking its consecration as a religious edifice, which lasted no less than five hours. Each year the anniversary of that dedication was to be marked by a solemn commemoration in all the churches of the diocese. The subordination of the various parish churches to the mother church was reflected in certain concrete obligations, some of them financial. The cathedral was also the church where the "cathedral office" was performed: a series of prayers (canonical hours) marking the progress of the day and accompanied by the ringing of bells.

Many cathedrals were reputed to have been founded by the first person to evangelize the diocese or by one of its first bishops. Some were erected on the very site of the supposed founder's martyrdom, as in Reims, where until the eighteenth century one could see the *rouelle* of Saint Nicasius, a chapel built on the spot where the prelate was killed by Vandals in 407. But founding bishops and martyrs were not the only treasures on which episcopal churches prided themselves. From the fourth century on, the church hierarchy sought to turn cathedrals into repositories of relics and other sacred objects. The earliest cathedral dedication in France for which we possess ample documentation took place in Rouen in 396, for which the bishop, Victrice (later Saint Victricius), sent to Milan for the relics of Saints Gervase and Protase, whose bodies had only recently been discovered by Saint Ambrose. This event marked the beginning of a traffic in relics that would grow steadily until the Reformation. Whenever circumstances allowed, each cathedral added to its treasure whatever it could in the way of precious liturgical objects (gems, ivory, silk chasubles from the Orient, and what have you), reliquaries and bejeweled caskets containing the precious remains of God's servants, and, especially during the Crusades, slivers of the True Cross.[5]

Ultimately the principal function of the cathedral shifted from that of bishop's basilica to reliquary. The process took longer in some regions and dioceses than in others. The episcopal throne, originally located on the axis of the nave, was reduced to a simple faldstool, or curule chair, sometimes covered by a baldachin, and moved to one side of the choir, whereas the principal altar, containing the most prestigious relics, assumed the central position. Some cathedrals even became pilgrimage sites, which led to the construction of an ambulatory around the choir and a proliferation of lateral chapels, further reinforcing the sacral charge of the monument and its power to attract visitors. In Chartres, for example, worshippers came from the ninth century on to venerate the Virgin's veil, a gift of Charles the Bald, and, from the fifteenth century, the miraculous statue of Our Lady of the Pillar. In Laon it was the head of John the Baptist. And at Le Puy, it was the Black Virgin, a gift of Saint Louis: destroyed during the Revolution, this effigy was restored in 1817. After World War II it was sent on a tour of France, and it still draws crowds today.

Each cathedral thus became a local and regional center of the Christian religion. Many factors contributed to the cathedral's centrality: the prestige of the site, which was often associated with the advent of Christianity in a particular city or diocese; the unusual splendor of its religious ceremonies, which on some occasions, such as the Holy Thursday mass at which the baptismal oil was blessed, drew priests from all over the diocese to the bishop's side; the existence in each diocese of a distinctive local ritual (the pontifical) and local liturgical calendar; and processions during which important relics were held up to public view and solemnly carried through local streets.

A Consolidated Historical Memory

Catholicism has changed since the Middle Ages, however, and people have tended to lose sight of the cathedral's distinctive religious function. French bishops have not been princes of the Gallican Church since the nineteenth century, and the 1906 Law of Separation stripped them of the civic functions that had once earned them the sobriquet "purple prefects." Since Vatican II the Catholic Church has spurned liturgical splendor, and even the faithful no longer participate in the mysteries of incarnation once enacted in the cult of the saints and the rituals of procession and pilgrimage. Yet even if a part of the message once conveyed by cathedrals is no longer received or understood, the places themselves continue to fascinate. Alive and animated, they provide an unrivaled opportunity to travel back through time. Everything about them helps to foster and reinforce a sense of unbroken historical continuity from the beginning of time. The cathedral is thus a stratified memory, and the historian's task is perhaps to take that memory and separate reality from myth, or at any rate from retrospective reconstruction. Yet historical research will influence only specialists;, it does not affect the impression that the cathedral makes on worshippers, pilgrims, and other visitors. Since early Christian times, cathedrals have maintained lists of bishops, so-called *fasti*, or annals, at first carved on ivory diptychs, later, in the Carolingian period, inscribed or engraved in stone.[6] When the time came to record the deeds of some of these prelates, all memory of them had long since vanished, and the authors of the annals did not hesitate to fill in the blanks with their own inventions. Quite often the temptation to link the advent of Christianity in the diocese to the preaching of the Apostles was simply too strong to resist.[7] The apostolic origin of the Gallican Church was a myth that not only enjoyed early success—attested as early as the fifth century—but also proved quite durable: bitter polemics were still raging on the subject among the French clergy as late as 1900. According to tradition, most French cathedrals were supposed to have been created by one or another of the seventy-two disciples mentioned but not named in the Gospel as having been sent on missions by the twelve Apostles of Christ: Saint Martial to Limoges, for example, or Saint Clement to Metz (both associated with Saint Peter), Saints Savinian and Potentian to Sens, and Mary Magdalene herself to Marseilles—all considered to have been the founders of their respective dioceses. Over the centuries, those bishops who could not be linked to such illustrious founders nonetheless acquired prestigious ancestors in the form of local martyrs: in Nantes, for example, this role was filled by Saints Rogatian and Donatian (died 290), whose statues frame the cathedral's main entry and who figured in the annual procession held on their feast day, at which time they were represented as young Roman knights, each with an arm around the other's waist.

Even when these traditions were lost, or when scholars, following the lead of Cardinal Duchesne and positivist historiography, demolished them by demonstrating their inconsistencies, they survive in the form of art: in Strasbourg and Bourges, for example, magnificent stained glass panels portray all the bishops of each city from the founder to the last prelate to die before the cycle was completed. Such representations created an air of invincible truth and concrete proximity, especially in places where, as in Bourges, the series of twenty-six windows inaugurated by Saints Ursinus and Justus, the first to carry the Gospel to Berry, ended with a figure as familiar as Guillaume, the archbishop of the city, who died in 1201 and was canonized in 1218 by Pope Honorius III. Elsewhere, in Rouen, Amiens, and Reims, for example, the glories of the local church are preserved in a porch or cycle of sculptures dedicated to saints such as Romanus, Firminus, or Sixtus. In Chartres, the well of the Saints-Forts, which dates from Gallo-Roman times, perpetuates the memory of the local martyrs allegedly tossed into it. Though the details varied, the process was always the same, and so was its result: to give palpable presence to the major religious figures of the diocese, for which the cathedral served as a kind of pantheon.

This exaltation of history through myth and legend was aimed at abolishing distance and turning the past into an eternal present. The cathedral was in every way an illustration of the Christian conception of time: time not as mere flux but as preparation, within each individual as well as in the world, for the coming reign of God. Accordingly, cathedral facades almost always depicted the creation of Adam and Eve together with the Last Judgment, the beginning and the end, as well as the signs of the zodiac and the "labors of the months" that set the rhythm of man's brief mortal compass. To those with eyes to see, the facade also indicated the way to salvation, following in the footsteps of Christ, the Virgin, and the saints. At one time this initiatory aspect was even more apparent after the worshipper entered the church: most of the great French cathedrals contained a labyrinth, a complex, twisting pathway marked by alternating light and dark stones in the floor of the nave itself: this symbolized the pilgrimage to Jerusalem, and the faithful followed the path on their knees, reciting prayers as they went. When, after considerable physical exertion, they reached the end of the maze, often more than two hundred yards long, they felt worthy of blessed salvation. In the eighteenth century all these labyrinths (except the one in Chartres) were destroyed. I mention them here not for the pleasure of describing an archaeological curiosity but because they offer an excellent illustration of one of the specific functions of the cathedral, that symbol of the holy city and anticipation of the heavenly Jerusalem: namely, to epitomize all

FIGURE 2.1. To experience something like the rigors of a pilgrimage to Jerusalem, the faithful made their way through mazes like this one while reciting prayers. The only one still in existence in France today is in the cathedral of Chartres (depicted here).

aspects of religious experience, at once local and universal, historical and eschatological.

An Urban and Diocesan Memory

Each French cathedral was also the embodiment of a particular history, the history of the city and diocese in which it stood and of which it was the sole conservator. That history was of course first of all the history of the cathedral itself, the history of a monument that over the centuries was destroyed and rebuilt many times. For example, the Notre-Dame that we find in Paris today was built in the late twelfth century on the ruins of two churches that were razed to make room for it: an earlier Notre-Dame and the old cathedral of Saint-Étienne, which as long ago as the time of Clovis was already the largest church in Gaul. All memory of this earlier church would have been lost had one of the portals of the Gothic cathedral not been dedicated to Saint Étienne to mark the continuity of the two structures and the persistence of the cult of the early martyr celebrated on this spot. Street names in the neighborhood of the cathedral (such as the Rue Chanoinesse and the Rue du Cloître-Notre-Dame) are in some cases all that remains of whole sections of an earlier urban topography. In Paris, the demolitions ordered by Baron Haussmann in the nineteenth century cut the cathedral off from its surroundings and obscured the fact that in the Middle Ages it formed an essential element of the city. Much earlier, however, in the twelfth and thirteenth centuries, urban space and the urban fabric were already disrupted by the intrusion of new "Gothic" basilicas, especially in cities in the northern half of France, where apart from Saint-Lazare in Autun and Notre-Dame in Coutances none of the great Romanesque cathedrals has survived. For us, long accustomed to an immutable architectural setting, it is difficult to appreciate the magnitude of these vast medieval construction projects, which became, for decades and in some cases centuries on end, a focal point of the activity of hundreds of masons, stonecutters, and sculptors under the direction of a handful of architects of genius, men such as Pierre de Montreuil and Jean d'Orbais.[8] In each case a whole section of a city was reconstructed around a single edifice of enormous size, which took the place of any number of churches and chapels dating back to the early Middle Ages. There was no compunction about razing these older structures, despite their venerable nature. Old foundations and trenches had to be filled in, new streets had to be built to provide access to the work site for carts bearing stones from the quarries, and new houses and squares had to be constructed. The restructuring of the city proceeded at a frenetic pace, especially in the century between 1160 and 1260. This activity of course reflected the city's growing population and expanding economy. More than that, however, the architectural explosion was palpable evidence of the rebirth of the secular church and episcopal power after

FIGURE 2.2. Cathedrals embodied local as well as religious traditions. Here, the capitals of Chartres.

centuries of monastic dominance. The bishop's power was not over the city, where the reins of political domination slowly changed hands, but over the diocese, all of whose clergy now gathered in synod twice a year in a hall or palace adjacent to the cathedral (one such palace is still extant in Sens).[9] A reform that had been launched in the second half of the eleventh century was essentially complete throughout France by 1110 or 1120. As a result, the bishop and chapter now received a portion of the tithe and other ecclesiastical revenue from each parish in the diocese, and these funds made it possible to undertake very costly construction. Indeed, contrary to a stubborn myth born in the romantic period, the new building was financed essentially by the clergy, who in some instances diverted a considerable portion of their revenues to the purpose.[10] The princely contribution was negligible. The people, for their part, were generally content to offer donations and bequests, sometimes in return for certain favors. While Péguy was not wrong to say that the cathedrals were born "of the fertile soil," this should be interpreted to mean, not that peasants played an active role in their construction, but rather that agricultural progress and increased revenues from land were sufficient to allow landlords to make substantial long-term investments.

FIGURE 2.3. The roof of the new nave of the cathedral of Moulins, circa 1860.

The cathedral was not simply a church; it was a world. Rebuilding meant not just constructing larger, taller, and more beautiful naves and choirs in accordance with the canons of the new style but also setting up a whole array of auxiliary structures: first of all the cloister, with its *psallette* (only the one in Tours has survived), where the chapter and masters gathered to recite psalms and prepare for services; the library, for storing prayer books and classroom texts; the chapter archives; and, most important of all, the school. On several occasions during the twelfth century the papacy reminded bishops that they were required to maintain a school adjacent to the cathedral for training future clerics under the direction of a chancellor chosen from among the canons of the chapter. In the end the pope's persistence obtained the desired effect. After 1230 these chapter schools were eclipsed by the success of the universities, but they did not disappear, and one should not forget the important influence once exercised by the most prestigious of them, those of Laon, Chartres, and Paris, which boasted teachers as renowned as Bernard and Thierry of Chartres and Peter Abelard. These illustrious teachers drew large numbers of clerics and students, who in Paris soon settled on the left bank of the Seine in what came to be known as the Latin Quarter. Nearly all vestiges of this past have disappeared, and only Noyon in Picardy, Meaux, and Viviers have preserved the canonical quarters that once stood adjacent to the old cathedral. Yet if one cannot imagine the canons' houses, the cloisters protected by the right of asylum that served as a refuge for the homeless and unemployed, or the crowds of altar boys and *escoliers* (students) who, on Childermas (feast of the Holy Innocents, December 28), sat in the choir stalls reciting comic prayers, one is unlikely to understand much about a world that has long since vanished but whose social and cultural importance was significant and which left a profound mark on French urban history.

Economic difficulties in the late Middle Ages halted work for extended periods on many cathedral projects, and the delays usually resulted in decisive changes: the clergy, who saw their revenues seriously curtailed by the depopulation of the countryside and decreased agricultural production, soon found themselves unable to bear alone the financial burden of building or even maintaining vast cathedrals. From the fourteenth century on, the clergy gradually lost control. In Strasbourg, for example, when a fire destroyed the church in 1298, the municipal authorities insisted on a role in administering the Œuvre Notre-Dame and in 1395 assumed total control over the construction, restoration, and decoration of the new cathedral. Then, in the fifteenth century, using its own money and without seeking any indulgences in return, the municipality undertook to build the 466-foot spire that is the cathedral's crowning jewel.[11] Elsewhere the clergy sought the aid of princes or monarchs. In each case the result was the same: when prosperity returned in the period 1450 to 1530, construction resumed, and everywhere the focus was now on building side chapels, on adding stained glass and gables, and above all on building towers and steeples whose primary purpose was to add to the city's beauty. Urban dwellers now adopted their cathedrals, which were often portrayed in official seals as the city's emblem, and filled them with objects whose interest was more secular than religious: astronomical clocks, enormous bells whose names speak volumes (for example, the "Non pareille" of Saint-Privat in Mende, which weighed nearly twenty tons and broke in 1579, or the "Muette" in Metz, housed in a tower 289 feet high, which was used to summon the people on great occasions), and carillons of one sort or another, like the one at Rouen with fifty-five bells. As cathedrals entered into civic consciousness and became symbols of local patriotism, people invented familiar names for their parts or for details of their decoration, names that are still in use today: the Maugarni entrance of Saint-Étienne in Meaux, for example, immortalizes a long jurisdictional conflict between the cathedral chapter and the bailiff of Meaux, who in 1372 ordered a thief by the name of Maugarni hanged on this spot, which was supposed to be under ecclesiastical power. In Coutances, the two towers of Notre-Dame, flanked by slender *tourelles* and pierced by long, thin bays, are called "the Fillettes" (Little Girls), perhaps in allusion to the towers' resulting girlish lines. The late Middle Ages saw the construction of many large, handsomely decorated towers intended to finish off uncompleted facades. Among these was Rouen's celebrated Tour de Beurre (Tower of Butter), so called because it was believed that it had been built with funds from the sale of dispensations permitting the Normans to eat butter during Lent. In Rodez the cathedral tower, decorated with flamboyant lacework of incised pink sandstone, was built in fifteen years to disguise damage from a fire that occurred in 1510. By contrast, other cities prided themselves on their cathedrals' links to the remote past. In Metz, for example, visitors to the southern crypt of Saint-Étienne could see an effigy of Graouilly, the loathsome monster that Saint Clement, the city's first bishop, drowned in the Seille. In Paris relics of Saint Marcel, who had been the city's bishop in the fifth century and the vanquisher of a dragon that had terrorized the populace, were transferred to Notre-Dame between the tenth and twelfth centuries and thereafter played an important part in the city's religious rituals, along with relics of Saint Denis and Saint Geneviève.[12] Through such cults, the late medieval city, now master of its fate, commemorated its birth, invoking the civilizing hero to celebrate the triumph of urban order over the creature-infested swamp out of which man had built a city.

The same attitude was responsible for what Jean Gimpel has aptly named the "world-record mentality," that is, the propensity in each city to build a cathedral larger than that of its neighbors.[13] Early on, such rivalry took the form of seeking to build the tallest possible vaults: it is probably no accident that the nave of Notre-Dame of Chartres, whose rebuilding began in 1195, is 119.7 feet high, slightly taller than the 114.8 feet of the nave of Notre-Dame of Paris, where construction began in 1163, especially in light of the fact that the vaults of Reims reached 125 feet in 1212, those of Amiens rose to 138 feet in 1221, and the choir of Beauvais topped out at 157 feet a few decades later. But the latter's spectacular collapse in 1284 probably cooled this urban ardor for setting records, at least for a while. When work resumed in the fifteenth century, cities sought to outdo their rivals primarily by constructing unusually tall steeples, such as the 466-foot-high spire of Strasbourg, which was not surpassed until 1876, when a 495-foot cast-iron steeple was belatedly set atop the cathedral turret in Rouen.

Yet even if in the late Middle Ages cathedrals were so closely identified with cities that some became emblems or symbols of the places in which they stood, they were never mere reflections of urban power. Many were more than large enough for the needs of the population, which visited the cathedral only for great occasions, dispersing among other local churches for less exalted religious activities. By the time major reconstructions were undertaken in the late twelfth and thirteenth centuries, moreover, many cathedrals had ceased to perform ordinary parish functions: this was the case in Paris, for example, from 1183.[14] Bear in mind that under the Ancien Régime there were more peasants than townspeople in every diocese, and this gave the cathedral, as mother church of the diocese, a special status that saved

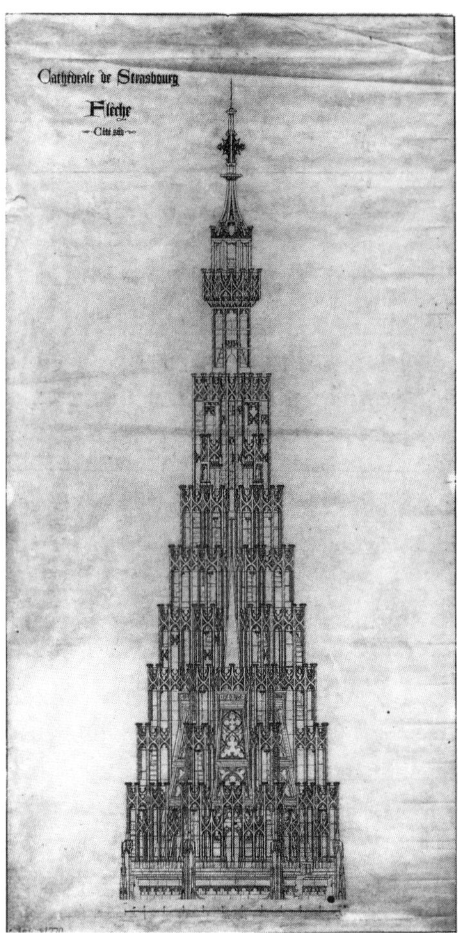

FIGURE 2.4. The tower of Rodez cathedral, with its flamboyant lacework carved in pink sandstone, was built in fifteen years to dispel the memory of damage caused by the fire of 1510; drawing by Thérond, 1859.

FIGURE 2.5. The builders of the 466-foot-high steeple of Strasbourg set out to break all records; eighteenth-century engraving.

it from falling totally under the sway of municipal authorities. The cathedral was the fruit of the harvest even more than of urban riches, and its eminence extended over an entire region. This situation was reflected in the preeminent role of the chapter, a group consisting of a few dozen canons, mostly scions of the local aristocracy, who, until the pope and the king deprived them of it, enjoyed the privilege of electing the bishop, often chosen from among their number. As a regional symbol the cathedral sometimes exerted an artistic influence as well, serving as an architectural model that more modest village churches strove to emulate. The consequences of this can still be seen in certain Alpine regions such as the diocese of Embrun, in which rural parish churches, many of them rebuilt in the fifteenth century, copied the facade and decoration of the episcopal church, as well as in Besançon, where the bell tower of the cathedral of Saint-Jean, with its four-paneled dome and four counter-curves, was a magnified version of the typical Counter Reformation church of the Franche-Comté.

A Place Where Spiritual and Temporal Could Meet

The cathedral was thus an urban church not limited by its urban setting. It was also paradoxical in another way, being at once the most sacred of religious structures and the most profane, in the sense that people frequently gathered there for ceremonies and meetings whose purposes were not purely religious. This ambiguity derived from the fact that the cathedral was always a site of power as well as a stake in power struggles.

From the earliest days of Christianity the bishop's church had been modeled on buildings used by the Roman civil authorities, particularly basilicas, and some bishops had simply occupied the old pretorian court previously used by the local representative of the Roman emperor. These buildings were suited to the needs of liturgical celebration, yet their plan reflected the fact that they had once been used for the exercise of authority, namely, in the semicircular apse where the bishop's throne now replaced that of the Roman governor or procurator. It is highly significant, moreover, that early Christians rarely chose buildings previously used by pagan cults for their churches. Temples were places in which pagan gods resided, and the faithful never entered them. Cathedrals, in contrast, were places to which clergy and faithful came to worship their God. The church was essentially a religious edifice, and above all a place for celebrating the eucharistic sacrifice, for which the community of the baptized gathered around the bishop and his *presbyterium* (council of elders). After the collapse of the Roman Empire, it was also called upon to play a political and social role as the bishop became a key figure, the acknowledged protector of a city that had been diminished but not destroyed. Cathedrals became places for electing new bishops and for holding regional or national synods, whose pronouncements were so important in the Frankish period. And it was in a cathedral—the cathedral of Senlis—that Hugh Capet, the founder of the Capetian dynasty, was elected king in 987 by *les Grands,* the principal lay and ecclesiastical lords. Even after the civil authorities built royal or municipal palaces, the cathedral's public functions did not cease. In the thirteenth century no one thought it unusual for the city council of Marseilles to meet in the cathedral. And when Philip the Fair sought to enlist the aid of social elites in his battle against Pope Boniface VIII and to mobilize public opinion in his behalf, he summoned representatives of the three estates to Notre-Dame in Paris for an April 1302 meeting that was the first public manifestation of the Gallican spirit.

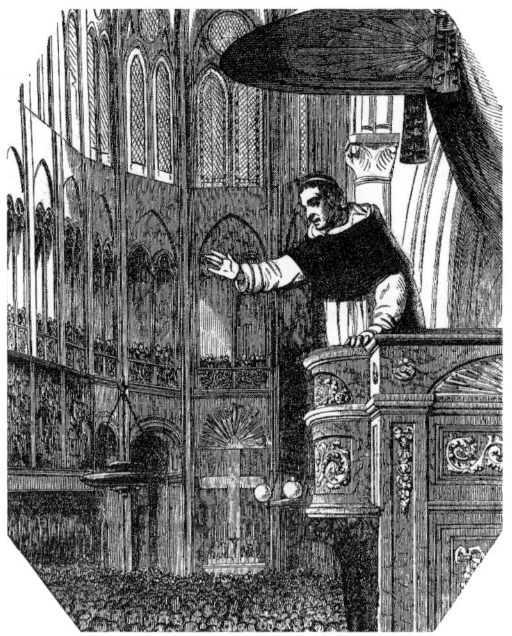

FIGURE 2.6. The clergy communicated with the faithful through the pulpit, the preeminent site of sacred eloquence: *Father Lacordaire at Notre-Dame;* engraving, 1852.

Every aspect of the cathedral, including its interior configuration, reflected its dual function as the church of God and man. The floor plan reflected changes in the relation of clergy to laity in the medieval period. In the early Middle Ages the slight elevation of the chancel was the only physical separation between the celebrant, flanked by the *schola cantorum*, and the mass of the faithful, but the exaltation of the clergy in the wake of the Gregorian reform and the growth of cathedral chapters increasingly jealous of their privileges led to the installation of a true barrier between the nave and the choir, where only clergymen were allowed to enter. This took the form of a rood screen encrusted with sculpture that prevented the laity from seeing what was going on at the altar.[15] Since most of these screens (except those at Auch and Albi) were destroyed in the eighteenth or early nineteenth century, it is hard for us to imagine how compartmentalized the now unbroken vessel of the church once was. Yet that is how we must picture the cathedrals of the last few centuries of the Middle Ages, during which clergy and laity no longer communicated through the sacrifice at the altar but only through the ministry of the word, conveyed to the people by preachers. This led to the construction in this period of splendid pulpits festooned with decorative sculpture, like the one at Strasbourg from which, on the eve of the Reformation, Geiler von Kaysersberg called upon the Church to convert, or the one in Paris, which from Maurice de Sully to Bossuet to Lacordaire has always been the place to go to hear the best in French religious oratory.

Of course any church is to one degree or another a place where clergy and laity meet. The cathedral, however, was where the confrontation between the temporal and the spiritual attained its maximum intensity and assumed its most striking forms, because symbolism there conjoined with power. In France, however, it was not until the thirteenth century that the symbiosis of the two powers, temporal and spiritual, became a permanent and significant part of the cathedral's character. During the early Middle Ages the sovereign rarely entered the cathedral, which was still primarily the bishop's church: Clovis did enter the cathedral of Reims but only to be baptized by Saint Remi. From 862 on, Carolingian and later Capetian monarchs came to Reims at the beginning of their reign to be anointed with oil from the Holy Ampulla, "invented" by Hincmar, and to receive the crown. But Reims was

FIGURE 2.7. Laity and clergy were kept apart by the construction of rood screens and enclosures covered with a profusion of sculpture, which kept worshippers from seeing what went on around the altar. Here, the rood screen of the cathedral of Albi.

and would remain a special case. There is no better proof of this than the role played by the abbeys of Fleury (Saint-Benoît-sur-Loire) and Saint-Denis in the eleventh and twelfth centuries: the Capetians preferred the prayers of monks to those of the secular clergy and chose to be buried at Saint-Denis, just as the Plantagenets in the same period elected burial in the abbeys of Fontevrault and, later, Westminster. Thus the kings of France contributed less than is generally believed to the construction of the great Gothic cathedrals.

The Temples of the "Royal Religion"

France never experienced anything like Great Britain's famous "murder in the cathedral." Unlike those in England, where the church became an oppositional force, relations between the French monarchy and the high clergy did not become embittered but grew closer and more trusting. Monarchs understood the strategic importance of the cathedrals and sought to turn them into centers of what Colette Beaune calls the "royal religion," which developed in the second half of the thirteenth century and especially after 1300.[16] There is no shortage of artistic evidence of this new royal favor: Saint Louis and his wife Marguerite of Provence commissioned images of themselves at the feet of the Virgin for one of the portals of Notre-Dame. Later, Charles V bequeathed his heart to the cathedral of Rouen, while his likeness and that of Louis of Orleans were sculpted on the buttresses of Amiens's northern tower.

As the Middle Ages waned, the cathedrals became the primary venue for celebrating the union of throne and altar: royal entries into the capital and other "good cities" of the kingdom always began with a visit to the cathedral;[17] public prayers were said for the king before battles or when his life was in danger; Te Deums were chanted after every victory. All these splendid ceremonies exalted the sacred function of the Most Christian King. Meanwhile, the monarchy tightened its control over the Church: by the fourteenth century it was taken for granted that cathedrals came under the king's protection and that among the monarch's regalian rights were certain temporal powers and, if the bishop's throne fell vacant, certain spiritual powers as well. Some Capetian monarchs took advantage of this situation to award ecclesiastical benefices to their protégés as though they had full power to hand these prizes out at will, but they were also quite generous with their largesse: the expense of restoring Notre-Dame of Reims, for example, was born by Charles VIII and Louis XII, and Henri IV, to demonstrate his gratitude to the city of Orleans, which had opened its gates to him, financed the completion of Sainte-Croix in the purest Gothic style. Henri also demonstrated his good will toward Notre-Dame of Chartres, where (contrary to custom) he had been anointed king with oil from the Holy Ampulla of Marmoutier. Relations between the two powers grew even closer later on. In the seventeenth century the Bâtiments du Roi (Royal Buildings department) had assumed responsibility for cathedral upkeep, and Louis XV would later finance the construction of the cathedral of La Rochelle out of his privy purse. By this time the balance of power had shifted toward the state, which asked the church to provide nothing more than a grandiose setting and religious pomp and circumstance for its self-glorification. Louis XIV was no longer content merely to hang captured enemy battle flags from the ceiling of Notre-Dame: indeed, the Maréchal de Luxembourg had seized so many such standards that he came to be known as the cathedral's *tapissier* (tapestry hanger). Louis used the cathedral frequently, not only for family weddings and baptisms but also to give formal welcome to foreign ambassadors. On November 16, 1663, for example, he sat in the middle of the choir on an elevated dais covered with red velvet embroidered with lilies to preside over a ceremony in which ambassadors from fifteen Swiss cantons came to renew the alliance that had tied them to France since shortly after the Battle of Marignan. Following a low mass, the bishop chanted the Te Deum and then *Domine, salvum fac regem,* which was then repeated by the choir. All the assembled then repaired to the archbishop's palace for dinner.[18] In the eighteenth century Soufflot had no compunctions about knocking down one of Notre-Dame's piers in order to make way for the royal dais. This secularization culminated with the imperial coronation of Napoleon I in Paris in 1804 and in the coronation of Charles X at Reims in 1825, though the latter in some ways harked back to the medieval ritual because the anointment ceremony was followed by the traditional touching of scrofula victims (the king was believed to possess miraculous healing powers). In both cases the sacred edifice was nothing more than a prestigious setting intended to lend nobility and sanctity to a purely political design.

During the Revolution the cathedrals paid the price for this transformation into sites celebrating the power of the monarchy. On the whole they suffered greatly in the revolutionary period. Eighteenth-century bishops and canons had already done serious damage by whitewashing walls, replacing stained glass with frosted glass, and dismantling gargoyles, grotesques, and pinnacles, whose anarchic profusion shocked classical taste. But after 1789, and even more after 1792, cathedrals were subjected to veritable profanations that threatened their very survival: the statues of the kings of Judah and Israel that decorated the facades of cathedrals in Paris, Chartres, Amiens, and Reims were partially or totally destroyed by sansculottes who, in an understandable error, believed that they depicted the Capetian monarchs, the last of whose descendants the Convention had just condemned to execution.[19] In Laon in 1793 the directorate of the Aisne département decreed that "all likenesses of former [*ci-devant*, the epithet applied to ex-nobles] angels, the former Christ, and saints male and female shall be removed within three days," and it was even proposed that the cathedral's towers should be torn down because they were "likely to awaken memories of the idea of feudalism." The roof of Chartres was stripped for its lead, while in Clermont-Ferrand, according to the report of one witness, "the statue of Notre-Dame-du-Port, after dancing the *carmagnole*, helped to illuminate the Place de la Réunion with the most delightful bonfire that philosophy ever did contemplate."[20] Many cathedrals were secularized and turned into temples of Reason and, later, of the *décadaire* religion (the Revolution abolished the seven-day week and replaced it with a ten-day week whose day of rest was known as *décadi*). Under Napoleon and of course during the Restoration the cathedrals enjoyed a respite, but in the minds of many French people they were now so closely associated with the hated Ancien Régime and the intimate union of throne and altar that some again became targets of one last wave of vandalism in the wake of the Revolution of 1830. In Paris in 1831, for example, one of Notre-Dame's portals was destroyed in a riot that ended in a sack of the archepiscopal palace.[21] The advent of the July Monarchy, which had no use for sumptuous coronation rituals and the like, and the rise of the liberal bourgeoisie appeared to mark the end of a millennial history, which the newly ascendant social and political forces resolutely rejected.

An Ideological Memory: The Nineteenth Century

Yet even as the cathedrals fell into deep disrepute and a woeful state of physical dilapidation, new cultural and national aspirations would eventually rescue them from their pitiable condition and restore them to a place of prominence. There was nothing specifically French about this astonishing reversal of public opinion: in the aftermath of the Napoleonic Wars, the Catholic Rhineland took it upon itself to complete the cathedral of Cologne, and after 1842 Prussia proved clever enough to turn this construction site into one of the workshops in which German national sentiment was forged. Initially, France was far from enjoying such enviable unanimity: the medieval past remained difficult to assimilate as conflict between proponents and adversaries of the Revolution continued to rage until the eve of World War I, especially where an obvious religious issue was involved. Barely restored, the cathedrals thus became a symbol over which various spiritual and ideological families did battle.

The shift in sensibility obviously owed a great deal to romanticism. In the *Génie du christianisme* (1802), Chateaubriand praised medieval art, especially Gothic art, which he said took its inspiration from the natural order. He stressed the continuity between the oak forests in which the Gauls had worshipped their gods and the cathedrals whose vaults were decorated with foliage and whose buttresses resembled broken tree trunks. This "constructed forest" perpetuated the murmur of the natural forest "by means of the organ and bronze, from which the sounds of wind and thunder emanate."[22] A century later Paul Claudel voiced a similar view, noting that "the Christian Church has absorbed the mystical forest" and "the cathedral finds its completion in the wind."

More than anyone else, however, it was Victor Hugo who discerned and guided the deepest aspirations of the age, turning the cathedrals into a veritable national literary myth.[23] As early as 1824, in his *Odes et ballades*, he attacked the "Black Gang," notorious for its vandalism for the previous quarter of a century. In 1825 he went to Reims for the coronation of Charles X and saw the beauty of the structure beneath "the ignoble whitewash that has spoiled it." But it was of course *Notre-Dame de Paris*, published in 1831, that established the fictional and poetic image of the cathedral that would dominate the nineteenth century. For Hugo, the cathedral was a picturesque world, teeming with life: Quasimodo and Esmeralda climb endless staircases, surrounded by gargoyles and fantastic monsters. As so often in Hugo, this image was a mixture of accurate intuitions and dubious ideas. He certainly grasped the "popular" character of the medieval cathedral, with its cloisters that served as refuges and its little world of manual laborers, clerics, and students. On the other hand, Émile Mâle has shown how little basis there is for Hugo's cherished view that cathedral art was so prolific, disorderly, profuse, and anarchic that medieval artists and stonecutters were able to convey an unofficial message, indeed a message of protest that ran counter to the dominant theological thinking.[24] Yet it scarcely matters that this interpretation was purely gratuitous. It was nevertheless extraordinarily effective, because it allowed people indifferent or hostile to Christianity and the Catholic Church to find a place for themselves in what Michelet would soon call the "house of the people."

Hugo's ideas, which earned him a place on the Commission of Arts and Monuments and a role as a volunteer inspector for the Department of Historical Monuments, were taken up and expanded by architects such as Ludovic Vitet, who in 1845 published an important *Monographie de l'église Notre-Dame de Noyon,* and above all Viollet-le-Duc, who made his mark somewhat later. Vitet made his case with singular clarity: for him, Gothic art, which flourished in the great cathedrals in the late twelfth and thirteenth centuries, was contemporaneous with the "first battles of reason against authority, of the nascent bourgeoisie against feudalism, of the popular and living languages against the ancient priestly tongue, which was all but dead."[25] Meanwhile, Augustin Thierry was publishing his *Essai sur le tiers état,* in which the birth of the commune of Laon in 1111–1112 following the murder of the city's archbishop played a central role. Vitet saw cathedral construction sites as an ideological battleground from which a new art, secular and urban, emerged victorious:

> On one side was the clerical cohort, champions of an authoritarian spirit, who sought to perpetuate the system and tradition of the semicircular arch. On the other side were free builders, *maîtres d'œuvre* as they called themselves, who seized upon the ogival arch as the basis of a new system and wielded it as a weapon to win for themselves mastery of the art of building.

In addition, Vitet stressed the role of the masonic confraternities, "a sort of lay Church within which the ogival art would be sustained and perpetuated for nearly three centuries as a mysterious and honored secret."[26]

Vitet's text is worthy of attention, if only for this last remark, which was in fact the source of many legends concerning secrets supposedly possessed by the cathedral-building masons. To the nineteenth-century mind, the only possible explanation for the architectural feats of the medieval masons was that they had been in possession of certain secret techniques and mathematical or alchemical formulas, which were passed on from generation to generation in the lodges, or barracks, in which the masons lived. The origins of the cathedrals were thus shrouded in mystery, and that mystery would deepen later when some commentators began to suggest that the secrecy that was indeed recommended in the regulations of certain construction guilds in the thirteenth and fourteenth centuries, particularly in regard to the proportions of the various elements involved in the composition of mortar, actually had something to do with an esoteric philosophical message.[27] Because the cathedrals had for centuries supported "lodges" of "freemasons," they now found themselves singled out as the birthplace of freethinking.

Viollet-le-Duc's celebrated article on the Cathedral in the *Dictionnaire raisonné de l'architecture française du XI*[e] *au XVI*[e] *siècle* must be read in this context. Written by the architect who, along with Lassus, restored Notre-Dame of Paris between 1845 and 1864, this text was to exert a profound influence on the way in which nineteenth-century French elites saw the Gothic cathedral. Expanding on Vitet's ideas, Viollet-le-Duc argued that the construction of the cathedrals from the end of the twelfth century on constituted "a striking protest against feudalism" that coincided with the rise of communal government. Inevitably, the example he chose to illustrate his thesis was Notre-Dame of Laon, whose architecture in his view made important concessions to secular thinking: "It preserves something of its democratic origins and lacks the religious aspect of Chartres, Amiens, or Reims." In a more original vein, Viollet-le-Duc stressed the way in which the Gothic cathedrals were rooted in France's deepest historical aspirations:

> The unity of monarchy and religion, the alliance of the two powers for the purpose of constituting a nation, caused the great cathedrals to be built in northern France. To be sure, those cathedrals were religious monuments, but they were also national edifices, . . . the symbol of French nationality, the first and most powerful attempt to achieve unity.[28]

It was this national aspect of the cathedrals, moreover, that according to Viollet-le-Duc had allowed them to withstand the ravages of time, particularly during the Terror, and retain their place in every Frenchman's heart:

> Today stripped bare, mutilated by time and the hand of man, neglected for several centuries by the heirs of those who had built them, our cathedrals loom like great coffins in the midst of our populous cities. Yet they still command the unflagging respect of the people. On certain public occasions they regain their voice, and with it a new youth, and the very people who a short while before repeated under their vaults the common opinion that the cathedrals were monuments of another age without significance in today's world, without a reason to exist, once again find them beautiful in old age and poverty.[29]

Freedom of thought, secular spirit, nationalism: these were the heavily charged words which would allow the liberal bourgeoisie and anticlerical liberals to acknowledge the heritage of the medieval cathedrals without betraying their most cherished values.

Yet even as this recovery of the past was going on, a no less enthusiastic and lyrical current was also on the rise, one that sought to rehabilitate the cathedrals as symbols of medieval Christendom, the ultimate embodiment of Catholicism's social and political ideals. One of the first and most eloquent champions of this view was Montalembert, who, after publishing a *Lettre sur le vandalisme en France* in 1833, waged a stubborn and ultimately successful battle in the Chambre des Pairs to secure funds from the government for the preservation and restoration of cathedrals.[30] Spurred by his overheated rhetoric, the July Monarchy, which sought to calm a nation avid for the sublime with endlessly restaged spectacles of its former glories, agreed to link Versailles with Notre-Dame in embarking on the first major effort of reconstruction, whose purpose was to save the most vulnerable sacred edifices from ruin.

As a Catholic renaissance began to develop after 1840, it became common to think of the cathedrals as the ultimate artistic expression of the Christian faith. Many writers extolled them as encyclopedias of wisdom and the faith, which by transcribing the verities of the thirteenth century's theological summas onto stone had made them accessible to the ordinary person. What was Chartres, in the words of Émile Mâle, if not "the thought of the Middle Ages made visible?"[31] The cathedrals thus became instruments of an apologetics based on sentiment and aesthetics, showing skeptics and freethinkers what heights it was possible for Catholicism to achieve when the state of society was such as to permit a harmonious synthesis of dogma and culture. If Christianity could create such beauty, how could it not be true?

Apart from such grandiose considerations, other, more down-to-earth factors also contributed to the restoration of the cathedrals' prestige. From the ecclesiastical point of view, the Revolution and Concordat deserved credit for one thing, at least: ridding the episcopate of its "rival auxiliaries" (to borrow Gabriel Le Bras's apt expression), the canons, monks, and other religious.[32] In all of French history, the bishop's power over his diocese was probably never as complete as in the nineteenth century. In the meantime, the destruction of many urban monasteries and convents or their transformation into parish churches left the cathedral the most visible religious edifice in most cities. Not content simply to restore those in need of restoration, prelates sought to complete work on still unfinished cathedrals in places such as Nantes, Limoges, and Moulins and to build new ones in Gap, Digne, and Marseilles.[33] The enthusiasm of the faithful and the cooperation of the government, particularly during the Second Empire, made it possible to embellish cathedrals in the taste of the time: painters and sculptors exalted the religious history of the diocese and the principal figures of regional hagiography in the neo-Gothic style considered to be the most sublime artistic expression of the Christian faith. In the growing number of regions where ultramontane tendencies were in the ascendant, numerous chapels were dedicated to the Virgin, while decorative art emphasized the "apostolic" origins of the diocese, all in an effort to foster the notion that in the

Church everything comes from Rome and must converge toward Rome. This climate of Catholic, monarchist restoration surrounded the first national pilgrimage to Notre-Dame of Chartres in 1873, during which Cardinal Pie proclaimed that "France is awaiting a leader, a ruler," while the faithful chanted: "Save Rome and France in the name of the Sacred Heart."

A Patrimonial Memory

The failure of this political and social program did not prejudice the cathedrals' cause. There was now a consensus about their status: no one any longer challenged their place in the realm of high art and culture. The positivist mind could only ratify the view of Viollet-le-Duc, for whom the cathedral had the rigor of a syllogism, and therefore admire these monuments "in which everything is methodical, rational, ordered, and precise, in which the place of each element is marked out in advance."[34] Yet it was poets, artists, and art critics who did more than anyone else to make the cathedrals familiar and cherished. Paul Verlaine, for example, wrote tenderly in *Sagesse* of these works of enthusiasm and faith, the quintessential expression of the "vast and delicate" Middle Ages:

> Haute théologie et solide morale,
> Guidé par la folie unique de la Croix,
> Sur tes ailes de pierre, ô folle cathédrale!
> [High theology and robust morality,
> Guided by the singular folly of the Cross,
> Upon thy wings of stone, O mad cathedral!][35]

Verlaine's contemporary the English critic John Ruskin, whose work on Amiens cathedral Proust translated as *La Bible d'Amiens* (1903) and wrote a preface for it, saw the cathedral in Picardy as one of humankind's greatest works of art, a special place affording man an opportunity to draw nearer the divine because in it were combined the True, the Beautiful, and the Good. Ruskin's message must be properly understood. For him, the cathedral was not as it was for Hugo "a Bible in stone" but *the* Bible in stone:

> The portal of any Gothic cathedral, but especially that of Amiens, the quintessential Gothic Cathedral, is the Bible. . . . Whatever your beliefs, the Bible is something real, and we have to find something in it other than its old-fashioned flavor and distraction for our curiosity.[36]

Yet the Cathedral that exerted the greatest fascination on French writers of the late nineteenth and early twentieth centuries was surely Notre-Dame of Chartres. In 1898, Chartres made its literary debut in Joris-Karl Huysmans' *La Cathédrale*, whose plot is merely a pretext to celebrate, in a lyrical vein, the "formidable and charming" aspect of the edifice that is the book's main character. The author seeks to bring the monument back to life:

> How grandiose and yet weightless, this cathedral, sprung from the exertions of the soul that created it in its own image, recounting its ascension along mystical ways, mounting little by little into the light, crossing over into the contemplative life of the transept, and then, in the choir, hovering in the brilliance of the unitive way, far from the dark purgative way of the nave! In its assumption this soul was accompanied and sustained by the host of angels, apostles, prophets, and the just, all erect in their glorious bodies of flame, that form an honor guard to the cross that lies upon the stony floor and the images of the Mother that sit upon the heights of this vast shrine, opening its walls to reveal, in an eternal holiday, bouquets of jewels budding in fiery nurseries of stained glass.[37]

Along with the many views of the Rouen cathedral that Monet painted in the same period, as well as Claude Debussy's composition *La Cathédrale engloutie*, Huysmans' book transformed these uncommon churches into masterpieces of mysticism in which anyone, regardless of faith, could feel lifted above himself and placed in contact with the realm of transcendence. This spiritualization of aesthetic emotion would attain its peak a few years later when Charles Péguy, after a three-day pilgrimage to Chartres in June 1912 to beg the Virgin to heal his ailing son, composed his famous poem *Présentation de la Beauce à Notre-Dame de Chartres*, the first part of his *Tapisserie de Notre-Dame*, in which he immortalized *la flèche unique au monde* (the spire unlike any other in the world):

> Tour de David, voici votre tour beauceronne!
> C'est l'épi le plus dur qui soit jamais monté
> Vers un ciel de clémence et de sérénité,
> Et le plus beau fleuron dedans votre couronne.
> [Tower of David, see this, your tower in the Beauce!
> This is the hardest head of grain that ever did grow
> Toward a clement and serene heaven,
> And the brightest jewel in your crown.][38]

This poetic celebration gives voice to a prayer that harks back to medieval ways of thinking. With Péguy and Paul Claudel, who some years later regained his faith while leaning against a pilaster of Notre-Dame in Paris, the cathedral became the best of all places to encounter the supernatural, the transformative experience of the divine. "Go to Chartres," Péguy told a friend, "you'll return a better man." From 1935 until the late 1960s, students from Paris, following in Péguy's footsteps, embarked on an annual pilgrimage to Chartres led by Jean Aubonnet. This redis-

FIGURE 2.8. The cathedral of Chartres looming above the plain of the Beauce.

covery of the religious, indeed mystical, aspect of the cathedrals after a lapse of several centuries may seem surprising. But surely Marcel Proust offered a convincing explanation as long ago as 1907: "The cathedrals are not only the finest ornaments of our art but the only ones that are still connected with the purpose for which they were constructed."[39]

A Memory to Identify with: The Genius of France

This rediscovery of the cathedrals' religious origins and functions, coming as it did at a time when the state was shedding the last of the bonds that linked it to the Church and militant anticlericalism was widespread in France, affected only a handful of artists and intellectuals. But the general favor that the cathedrals enjoyed was in no way diminished by the vicissitudes of political and ideological struggle, because for several generations people had been accustomed to looking at these monuments as one of the purest, most authentic expressions of the French national genius. Already Michelet, in the fourth book of his *Histoire de France,* had exalted the humble laborers whose cumulative efforts had produced artistic masterpieces: "How carefully they worked, obscure though they were and submerged in numbers, yet how fully they denied themselves! To appreciate this one must explore the cathedrals' remotest, most inaccessible parts."[40]

A half-century later Péguy produced an equally emotional description of these same workmen, the common men of old France, who prided themselves on a job well done: "Throughout my childhood I watched chairs being stuffed with the same spirit and the same heart and the same hand that these same people had brought to the crafting of the cathedrals."[41]

After the middle of the nineteenth century, moreover, historians of art and architecture no longer felt qualms about calling Gothic art the quintessential French style. The last of classicism's champions, who claimed with Beulé and Quatremère de Quincy that Gothic architecture was not French but "Teutonic, that is, German and Frankish," ultimately succumbed.[42] After Viollet-le-Duc, who saw the cathedral of Amiens as the pinnacle of "ogival" art and "the Parthenon of French architecture,"[43] no one came forward to challenge the idea that the century of Philip Augustus and Saint Louis was for France what the Age of Pericles had been for Athens. At the beginning of the twentieth century, Émile Mâle brought much learning to his thesis that the Gothic cathedrals were the quintessence of French genius, and in 1914 Rodin passionately urged the view that they were the expression of France's very soil and climate:

> The cathedral epitomizes the country. . . . The north's cliffs, forests, gardens, and sun are all summed up in that gigantic carcass. All our France is in the

> cathedrals, as all Greece is summed up in the Parthenon. . . . Our gentle, mild air has given our artists grace and refined their taste.[44]

And then, since France's genius is by definition universal, art historians had no trouble proving that most of Europe's other great cathedrals were little more than an emanation of the French spirit: thus for Henri Focillon, Cologne's cathedral, a colossal copy of Amiens, was merely "a French import in a Germanic setting," while Toledo's was "a wider, lower replica of the nave of Bourges."[45] No matter how one looked at it, Gothic architecture was associated with France and proof of its civilizing influence.

A Mythological Memory

Thus France's cathedrals became national treasures, expressions of the cultural and artistic genius of the French people. Their metamorphosis into national myths would be completed in the period 1870–1918 by the addition of an aureole of suffering. The first to acquire it were the cathedrals of Metz and Strasbourg, which became living, repeatedly invoked symbols of the lost provinces of Alsace and Lorraine following their annexation by Germany. All France quivered with rage when Kaiser Wilhelm II, who had ordered major restoration work on the cathedral of Metz, chose to adorn its main portal with a likeness of himself as the prophet Daniel (which was promptly smashed to smithereens in November 1918). But the nation's greatest indignation was reserved for the shelling of the cathedral of Reims on September 19, 1914. Every schoolchild in France had to learn by heart Edmond Rostand's ode to the martyred church, the tragic victim of German barbarity. Through a remarkable twist of fate, the very cathedral in which the union of throne and altar had been forged and celebrated for centuries now became the darling of the secular Republic. When the war was over, large sums were appropriated for its reconstruction, with additional aid coming from the United States. Shortly after the restoration was complete came the outbreak of World War II, which caused grave damage to several French cathedrals, beginning with Rouen.[46] The cathedral of Strasbourg now became a symbol of the suffering nation and its desire for resurrection. Free France invoked that symbol in many ways, including the famous oath of Koufra (1941), in which General Leclerc and his men swore not to lay down their arms until the French flag once again flew from Strasbourg's spire. Since then, the cathedrals have remained one of the few symbolic sites about which all Frenchmen can agree, more perhaps even than the Pantheon: on August 26, 1944, one of General de Gaulle's first acts in a Paris only just liberated was to call for a Magnificat (and not a Te Deum) to be sung at Notre-Dame (the cardinal-archbishop, accused of Pétainist leanings, was absent). Thus was an authority made

FIGURE 2.9. The aureole of suffering: Reims after shelling in 1916.

FIGURE 2.10. The cathedral remains, immutable, as French symbols are swept away: the Gallic cock, Marianne, Hansi, *Les Oberlé*, the képi; Strasbourg, German poster, 1940.

FIGURE 2.11. In this poster, Nazi symbols are banished: the eagle, the swastika, *Das Reich, Mein Kampf*, etc.; Strasbourg, French poster, 1944.

legitimate by the ovations of Parisians lined up along the Champs-Élysées blessed in the eyes of God as well.

Twenty-six years later, heads of state from all over the world assembled at the same spot, Notre-Dame of Paris, to join in France's tribute to the man who had twice saved the country from humiliation and disgrace. And finally, in 1987, in an equally symbolic moment, the Count of Paris (the pretender to the French throne) and President François Mitterrand came together beneath the Gothic arches of Amiens to celebrate the millennium of the Capetian dynasty and the birth of France.

Although the history recounted above is still quite recent, it has already faded into the past. Today, with building the European Community the priority of the moment, even Notre-Dame of Strasbourg, "the cathedral about which neither the Germans nor the French can speak in calm terms" (Émile Mâle) and which the Nazis tried to turn into a museum of Germanic art, has become, most appropriately, a symbol of efforts by both countries to bury their troubled past. It seems clear that the cathedrals are no longer monuments that speak to the younger generation, to whom the history they symbolize is all but unknown and the religious message they embody is largely inaccessible. Nowadays, who knows who the Queen of Sheba was or what the tree of Jesse signifies? Since the cathedrals became an unchallenged national myth, they command admiration and

FIGURE 2.12. Model of a cathedral to be built in Évry, designed by architect Mario Botta.

respect, but as a result they have been severed from their roots. In the nineteenth century Haussmann and his epigones demolished the neighborhoods that surrounded them and constituted their natural environment. Today's cathedrals are liked beached vessels, stranded in the midst of vast plazas or parks, cut off from the city and delivered up to the curiosity of the tourists who scour their naves with the *Guinness Book of Records* in hand.[47] Even the Church no longer seems to know quite what to do with these edifices, many of them too big for their dwindling ranks of worshippers yet not big enough to receive the crowds that, say, a visiting pope can draw, for which a stadium rather than a cathedral seems to be the preferred venue.

Thus, paradoxically, at a time when the national and local governments are doing so much to promote the cathedrals as a fundamental part of France's national patrimony, they are in danger of losing the religious, political, and cultural function that once guaranteed their survival and of becoming *lieux de mémoire*—conservatories of memory about which the last word, perhaps, has yet to be said. In recent years the need to build buildings transcending everyday human needs has again been felt. In Évry, for example, a suburb on Paris's southern fringe, the diocesan authorities, with support from local officials and city planners, have proposed plans for a new cathedral in the heart of the city and issued an appeal for contributions from people throughout the Paris region. It is too early to tell whether their efforts will meet with success. Yet the mere fact that the plans were formulated and that the call for contributions has met with initial approval suggests that people living in the late twentieth century have concluded that they are no longer satisfied solely by temples of consumption and entertainment. No human community worthy of the name can do without symbolic monuments unrelated to its immediate needs, monuments whose primary function is precisely their otherness: a presence, in other words, that reminds man of Him who is at once the absolute Other and the transcendence of all our differences.

FIGURE 3.0. Versailles: cliché.

CHAPTER III

The Court

Jacques Revel

Royal residences have their own peculiar melancholy, which no doubt stems from their being too large for the small number of their inhabitants, from the silence that one is surprised to find there after so many fanfares, and from their changeless luxury, whose old age gives proof of the fugitive nature of eternal dynasties, the eternal wretchedness of all things. And this exhalation of time, as numbing and depressing as the scent of a mummy, affects even the most naïve. Rosanette yawned inordinately. They went back to the hotel.

Gustave Flaubert, L'Éducation sentimentale (1869), in Œuvres complètes, ed. Conard (Paris, 1923), p. 462.

1. In the spring of 1833, Chateaubriand, dispatched by the Duchesse de Berry on delicate negotiations, called upon Charles X in Prague, where the deposed monarch had found asylum in the Hradčany. In this dark, deserted, all but unfurnished palace he lived on in the company of his family and a few loyal subjects who had followed him into exile. Yet this small company maintained the appearance of a court. Courtly forms were rigidly maintained. Shortly after the emissary's arrival, his not unexpected presence was announced to a monarch with few opportunities to escape his solitude. Yet the reception still conformed to the old rules: "M. de Blacas left me in the third hall while he went to inform the king, observing the same etiquette as in the Tuileries." Nothing had changed, though everything was different. In introducing the members of the court into his narrative, Chateaubriand instinctively adheres to the immutable order consecrated by so many previous memoirists: the dauphin, the "children of France," the principal lords, the ministers. The ritual, though diminished, remains the same. Dinner is "meager and rather poor." The conversation is wretched: interrupted by long silences, suffocating with boredom, it remains confined within "a circle of commonplaces." Inevitably, the evening is for games: "Illuminated by two candles in the corner of a dark room, a game of whist began among the king, the dauphin, the Duke de Blacas, and Cardinal Latil. Along with O'Hegerty, the page, I was the only

witness. Through the windows, whose shutters were not drawn, the twilight mingled its pallor with that of the candles. Between those two expiring lights the monarchy was dying. Profound silence, apart from the rubbing of the cards and a few shouts from the king, who grew angry." Yet this moribund court had by no means given up on passion or intrigue. A triumvirate (consisting of de Blacas, the Baron de Damas, and Cardinal Latil) sought to supervise the dauphin's upbringing. "The rest of the castle's inhabitants caballed against the triumvirate. The children themselves headed the opposition. There were, however, various shades within this opposition," which one still had to identify and classify. Flattery, slander, and ambition fueled this "masquerade of valets and ministers changing costumes."

As so often in Chateaubriand's *Mémoires d'outre-tombe,* the very lengthy description of the visit to Prague combines two distinct levels of style: a tone of sadness, which grips the visitor at the thought of the fallen king "shut up in the black walls" of his borrowed palace, and a tone of political intelligence that sparkles with inimitably perceptive cruelty. By combining these two styles, Chateaubriand makes us see that behind the parody there exists something other and greater than parody. The sad fate of the last of the Bourbons is played out within forms that are an intimate part of the reality of monarchy, ridiculous though they have become. Failure, banishment, and isolation have left the court of Charles X little more than a "tissue of realities and fictions." But the formula might equally well be applied to any court.

Here I am not referring to that anticurial tradition which, in the West, at any rate, is probably as old as the reality it denounces. It runs from the *Roman de Renart* to the *Caractères* of La Bruyère, and its tone is at once moral and political. Instead, I have in mind another commentary that has come down through the centuries, according to which every court is the fulfillment, generally unstable and imperfect, of an ideal and a memory. This was of course true of nineteenth-century courts, which were often tempted by an unsatisfiable desire to reconstitute the past. But already in the last decades of the Ancien Régime, Louis-Sébastien Mercier liked to describe the still quite vital court at Versailles as a tourist attraction, a sumptuous park full of sights that Parisians liked to visit on Sundays in springtime. Everything one saw there was magnificent and pointless. Indeed, "the word *court* no longer impresses us as it did in the time of Louis XIV." Was this disillusioned comment nothing more than an instance of the Enlightenment's corrosive irony? Perhaps, but Mme Campan, Marie-Antoinette's first lady-in-waiting, who lived at Versailles in this same period and who was by no means spoiled by philosophy, was no less disabused, despite her position and her continued devotion to the old values. A century earlier, at the height of the Sun King's brilliance, such critical distance was impossible. All the effort of the court went to proclaiming the personal majesty and glory of the monarch, who was transformed into a hero. Yet no other reign produced an analysis of the court as acute or precise as this one. None so mercilessly exposed the mechanism and workings of the courtly machine. However inhospitable to doubt, this was also the age that produced Mme de La Fayette's *La Princesse de Clèves* (1678), which opened with this celebrated affirmation, tantamount to the throwing down of a gauntlet: "Splendor and gallantry in France were never more spectacular than in the final years of Henri II." Nor was she alone in looking backward, seeking models of courtly honor and virtue in the "old court" of Anne of Austria or that of Louis XIII or, even more frequently, in the now forgotten refinement of the last Valois. It is as if the court (the actual court, that is) was never anything other than a pale imitation of an irretrievably vanished past. In this sense it was already a *lieu de mémoire*. It was always obsessed with remembered models whose perfection it could not match.

This more or less explicit understanding was the source of the ambivalence evident in so many surviving reports of the court. This abundant, often repetitious literature wavers between two extremes that it often manages to combine. On the one hand, the court is presented as something natural. This was true not only of its champions, whose arguments Voltaire collected in his canonical interpretation of the *Siècle de Louis XIV* (1751), but also of writers whom one might assume to be less likely to rehearse the vulgate. Take, for example, the *Encyclopédie,* to which Diderot contributed the following:

> *Court, modern and ancient History,* is always a place in which a sovereign lives. It is composed of princes, princesses, ministers, lords, and leading officeholders. Hence it is not surprising that it should be the center of manners *[politesse]* of a nation. Manners flourish there owing to the equality to which the extreme grandeur of a single individual relegates those around him, and taste is refined by continual use of the superfluities of wealth. Among those superfluities, one inevitably encounters artificial productions of the most exquisite perfection. Knowledge of that perfection extends to many other far more important objects. It passes into language, judgment, feeling, bearing, manners, tone, humor, works of the mind, gallantry, attire, and customs themselves.

The court was thus the center of absolutist society. Yet there is also a second version of the court, very different from the first, in which it appears as opaque, impenetrable, mysterious, and dangerous. Mme de Sévigné, though not a member of court, visited often and was always well received. Yet, keeping her distance, she often spoke of it as "that place." She kept herself informed about the goings-on there but still felt "ill-educated." Her lapidary judgment, pronounced in 1680, was that the court "is no place for me." One finds a hundred variations on this theme on the part of numerous authors, some of whom were quite firmly established at court and not all of whom had the marquise's Paris connections: for the Abbé de Bellegarde, the

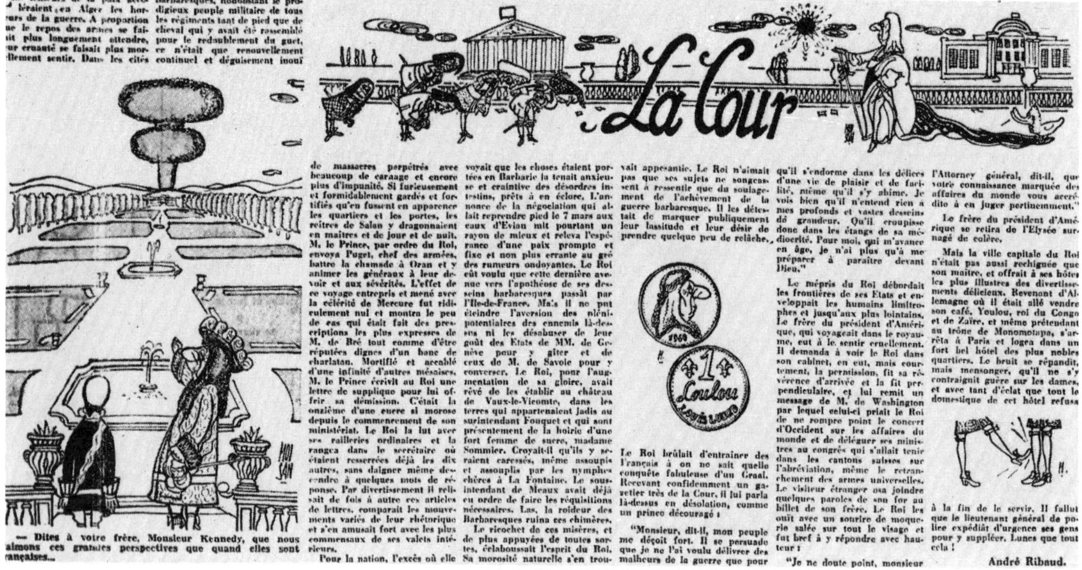

...teurs de la paix acco... laient en Alger les hor-... eurs de la guerre. A proportion que le repos des armes se faisait plus longuement attendre, sur cruauté se faisait plus mortellement sentir. Dans les cités barbaresques, nonobstant le prodigieux peuple militaire de tous les régiments tant de pied que de cheval qui y avait été rassemblé, ce n'était que renouvellement continuel et déguisement inouï

La Cour

de massacres perpétrés avec beaucoup de caraage et encore plus d'impunité. Si furieusement et formidablement gardés et fortifiés qu'en fussent en apparence les quartiers et les portes, les reitres de Salan y dragonnaient en maitres et de jour et de nuit. M. le Prince, par ordre du Roi, envoya Puget, chef des armées, battre la chamade à Oran et y animer les généraux à leur devoir et aux sévérités. L'effet de ce voyage entrepris et mené avec la célérité de Mercure fut ridiculement nul et montra le peu de cas qui était fait des prescriptions les plus expresses de M. de Bré tout comme d'être réputées dignes d'un banc de charlatan. Mortifié et accablé d'une infinité d'autres mésaises, M. le Prince écrivit au Roi une lettre de supplique pour lui offrir sa démission. C'était la onzième d'une encre si morose depuis le commencement de son ministériat. Le Roi la lut avec ses railleries ordinaires et la rangea dans le secrétaire où étaient resserrées déjà les dix autres, sans daigner même descendre à quelques mots de réponse. Par divertissement il relisait de fois à autre ces articles de lettres, comparait les mouvements variés de leur rhétorique et s'en amusait fort avec les plus commensaux de ses valets intérieurs.

Pour la nation, l'excès où elle voyait que les choses étaient portées en Barbarie la tenait anxieuse et craintive des désordres intestins, prêts à en éclore. L'annonce de la négociation qui allait reprendre pied le 7 mars aux eaux d'Evian mit pourtant un rayon de mieux et releva l'espérance d'une paix prompte et fixe et non plus errante au gré des rumeurs ondoyantes. Le Roi eût voulu que cette dernière avenue vers l'apothéose de ses desseins barbaresques passât par l'Ile-de-France. Mais il ne put éteindre l'aversion des plénipotentiaires des ennemis là-dessus ni les désabuser de leur goût des Etats de MM. de Genève pour y gîter et de ceux de M. de Savoie pour y converser. Le Roi, pour l'augmentation de sa gloire, avait rêvé de les établir au château de Vaux-le-Vicomte, dans les terres qui appartenaient jadis au surintendant Fouquet et qui sont présentement de la hoirie d'une fort femme de sucre, madame Sommier. Croyait-il qu'ils y seraient caressés, même assoupis et assouplis par les nymphes chères à La Fontaine. Le sous-intendant de Meaux avait déjà eu ordre de faire les réquisitions nécessaires. Las, la roideur des Barbaresques ruina ces chimères.

Le ricochet de ces misères, et de plus appuyées de toutes sortes, éclaboussait l'esprit du Roi. Sa morosité naturelle s'en trouvait appesantie. Le Roi n'aimait pas que ses sujets ne songeassent à ressentir que du soulagement de l'achèvement de la guerre barbaresque. Il les détestait de marquer publiquement leur lassitude et leur désir de prendre quelque peu de relâche.

Le Roi brûlait d'entraîner des Français à on ne sait quelle conquête fabuleuse d'un Graal. Recevant confidemment un gazetier très de la Cour, il lui parla là-dessus en désolation, comme un prince découragé :

"Monsieur, dit-il, mon peuple me déçoit fort. Il se persuade que je ne l'ai voulu délivrer des malheurs de la guerre que pour qu'il s'endorme dans les délices d'une vie de plaisir et de facilité, même qu'il s'y abîme. Je vois bien qu'il n'entend rien à mes profonds et vastes desseins de grandeur. Qu'il croupisse donc dans les étangs de sa médiocrité. Pour moi, qui m'avance en âge, je n'ai plus qu'à me préparer à paraître devant Dieu."

Le mépris du Roi débordait les frontières de ses Etats et enveloppait les humains limitrophes et jusqu'aux plus lointains. Le frère du président d'Amérique, qui voyageait dans le royaume, eut à le sentir cruellement. Il demanda à voir le Roi dans son cabinet, en eut, mais courtement, la permission, fit sa révérence d'arrivée et la fit perpendiculaire, et lui remit un message de M. de Washington par lequel celui-ci priait le Roi de ne rompre point le concert d'Occident sur les affaires du monde et de déléguer ses ministres au congrès qui s'allait tenir dans les cantons suisses sur l'abréviation, même le retranchement des armes universelles. Le visiteur étranger osa joindre quelques paroles de son for au billet de son frère. Le Roi les ouït avec un sourire de moquerie salée sur tout le visage et fut bref à y répondre avec hauteur :

"Je ne doute point, monsieur l'Attorney général, dit-il, que votre connaissance marquée des affaires du monde vous accrédite à en juger pertinemment."

Le frère du président d'Amérique se retira de l'Elysée surnagé de colère.

Mais la ville capitale du Roi n'était pas aussi rechignée que son maître, et offrait à ses hôtes les plus illustres des divertissements délicieux. Revenant d'Allemagne où il était allé vendre son café, Youlou, roi du Congo et de Zaïre, et même prétendant au trône de Monomotapa, s'arrêta à Paris et logea dans un fort bel hôtel des plus nobles quartiers. Le bruit se répandit, mais mensonger, qu'il ne s'y contraignit guère sur les dames, et avec tant d'éclat que tout le domestique de cet hôtel refusa à la fin de le servir. Il fallut que le lieutenant général de police expédiât d'urgence ses gens pour y suppléer. Lunes que tout cela !

André Ribaud.

— Dites à votre frère, Monsieur Kennedy, que nous aimons ces gratuites perspectives que quand elles sont françaises...

FIGURE 3.1. Versailles: caricature; "The Court," a column from the satirical weekly *Le Canard enchaîné,* March 7, 1962, with illustrations by Moisan.

court was a "strange country," "an unknown country," and "incomprehensible," while for Saint-Réal it was a "foreign nation." There was probably a certain amount of affectation in thus pretending to be alienated from a court whose accelerated institutionalization and very success were tending toward a certain normalization of its role. Yet one senses something else as well: a society whose customs and rules differed in every respect from the conventions governing people elsewhere.

The court: commonplace or curiosity? There was of course no need to choose between the two, and the most valuable testimony about the court comes from those who played it both ways, who wrote as both insiders and outsiders, describing and interpreting from inside with an anthropologist's objective eye. Saint-Simon (whose accounts of court life so fascinated Proust) is still the best example, even in his excesses and biases.

2. But the court was also the center of a state. It combined a particular form of social organization with a particular modality of power. In this respect, too, it lives on in French memory. In France one tends to assume as a matter of course that, even in the midst of a modern democratic society, no powerful executive or centralized authority can exist without in some way surrounding itself with a court. The best example of this is the political culture of the Fifth Republic. From the beginning the regime had a monarchical tinge that no doubt owed a great deal to the ideas and practices of its founder yet remained after he was gone. The institutional role of the

FIGURE 3.2. The grandeur and servility of the republican monarchy: the *Refurbishing of the Grand Trianon;* a cartoon by Moisan for *Le Canard enchaîné,* April 3, 1963.

president is reinforced by a symbolic apparatus whose scope and pervasiveness are probably without equivalent in comparable political systems. Very quickly, however, it also turned out to be inextricably intertwined with a welter of personal loyalties, rivalries, and exclusions that immediately called to mind the relation of a king to his court. It was no accident that the satirical newspaper *Le Canard enchaîné* instinctively turned to Saint-Simon as a literary source for its running political and moral commentary on the Gaullian Republic: an imperious, Louis XIV–style court under the general, degraded into a bourgeois regency or Louis-Philippe–style monarchy under Pompidou and then a frivolous spectacle under Giscard d'Estaing. As everyone knows, moreover, the election of a Socialist president changed none of the court's settled ways, quite the contrary. Someone may object that the kinds of comparisons I'm making here are at best rough analogies and at times caricatures; that they are generally based on anecdote or rumor; and that nothing in republican institutions supports the contention that the regime has been monarchized or curialized. And the objection is correct as far as it goes, but the point is that the effectiveness of monarchy and court have at least as much to do with representations, beliefs, expectations, and rumors as with "objective" arrangements. No one ever knew whether or not the king really could cure scrofula, but for centuries it was crucial that people believed he could. No one in 1661 could guarantee that young Louis was the handsomest and most accomplished man in the kingdom, but it was crucial that people convinced themselves that he was. As for the prodigious amount of detailed information available about the courts of Charles de Gaulle and François Mitterrand, most of it is unverifiable. But whether it is true or false surely matters less than whether it is plausible, that is, whether or not it resonates with an everyday understanding of the political consistent with the regime's projected self-image.

In this second sense, too, the court is quite obviously a *lieu de mémoire*. It points up a recurrent modality of power in France along with certain social arrangements incidental to it. The court phenomenon exists in many cultures and in Europe alone has exhibited many aspects over a very extended period. Yet there is no counterpart in the experience of other nations to the court's dual role in French history, as both reference and model. It almost seems as if the courtly monarchy is an essential element of France's exceptionality, even an invariant of French history that can always be pressed into service when needed. In description after description and commentary after commentary, an endless series of texts from both before and after the Revolution offer us countless variations on familiar themes: the loneliness of power, the ostentation and capriciousness of the monarch, the arbitrariness of favor, the eminence, uncertainty, and abjection of the courtier. When François Mitterrand lampooned the peculiarities of de Gaulle's presidency (in terms that twenty years later would be used against Mitterrand himself), one has the sense that he was drawing on the finest authors: "The members of the government know that their fate hangs on a mood and so submit to a discipline that softens their spines. Most will succeed without much violence to their nature. Some will suffer from it, yet claim an additional merit from their difficulty in demonstrating servility. A strong character that lowers itself will always be more zealous than a weak one that can get all it needs without going against its nature." But Mitterrand's 1964 book *Le Coup d'État permanent* is not a pastiche or a moral treatise. It is a political polemic that homes in on a weak spot: in the political culture of republican France, one can injure an adversary by charging him with monarchical and courtly tendencies (as under other circumstances one could injure an enemy by invoking the Jacobin hydra or the government of the Terror).

To be sure, such charges are utterly without institutional foundation. France in the final third of the twentieth century is a democratic country, and simple common sense tells us that a regime in which human rights and freedom of political expression are guaranteed by law is different from other kinds of regimes. Hence the persistence of the Ancien Régime is to be looked for not here but in certain social, political, and cultural forms that shape the exercise of authority. This brings us to the realm of representations, where what people think and believe is just as important as what is. This is true not only of power but also of the beholders of power. It is also true for political actors, whose behavior, style, and efforts to create a public image show that they are not unaware of the enduring memory of the court. The lesson of that memory is ambiguous, moreover, because it contains the best as well as the worst, much that is grand along with much that is vile.

3. A memory rather than a history. In France experience of the court is ancient and highly diverse. Outside a small circle of specialists, however, what draws our attention is not this prolonged evolution of five or six centuries, much less its hesitations and contradictions. The model of the court in France (and elsewhere for that matter) is the court of the Sun King, together perhaps with the courts of his eighteenth-century successors. It defines a type and at times is taken for an absolute. This can lead to serious misunderstandings: Louis XIV's very long personal reign (1661–1715) was not an undifferentiated expanse of time, and during it the court was redefined, at times in important ways. But the court is almost always treated as a global model whose contingent variations are supposedly of relatively minor importance. Saint-Simon is a good example of this. No one ever scrutinized more closely than he the changes in court life, the innovations (to which he was generally hostile), the shifts in the political balance, the ascents to favor and the falls from grace. But neither has anyone ever been more convinced that, beyond the everyday vicissitudes of court life, there was a general mechanism that explained how things worked. Though he had reservations about the great king and expressed them frequently, Saint-Simon nevertheless credited the monarch with the talent of a skilled horologist, a man who could keep this complex machine ticking perfectly. In the eyes of the memoirist, Louis invented this social form, then magnified it to such proportions that it became difficult to distinguish between greatness and monstrosity, calculation and absurdity:

> In everything he loved splendor, magnificence, and profusion. He made this taste his political maxim and in every way instilled it in his court. To bring him tables, costumes, coaches, ships, and games was to please him. These were occasions for him to talk to people. In the end he tried in this way to exhaust everyone by attaching honor to luxury, and, for some, necessity, and he succeeded; and thus he gradually reduced everyone to depending entirely on his boons in order to exist. He found further satisfaction for his pride in a court superb in every way, and in an increased confusion, which more and more reduced natural distinctions to nothing.

Saint-Simon is without a doubt the writer who did most to create the court of Louis XIV as an ideal type, though not without certain notable distortions. But he was by no means alone. Anyone at all diligent in reading other contemporary memoirists, letter writers, moralists, novelists, and champions and critics of the court soon becomes convinced that this was an exceptional and in some ways exemplary historical experience. In one way or another, all these writers participated in the mythification of the regime of Louis le Grand, and their view of that regime is often highly one-sided. Together, however, they created an image of the court that in most respects we still share. Their bias and privilege have been further reinforced by the vast (and generally mediocre) literature that has been devoted to the court for the past three centuries, a literature for the most part content to paraphrase the prolific testimony of the court's earliest students.

The consequences of this are ambiguous. There is a tendency to forget that the actual history of the court is long, extending far beyond the age of Louis XIV. By foreshortening our perspective, we risk turning portraiture into caricature. Last but not least, we can all too easily miss allusions to the before and the after, the original perfection and the imperfect realization, which are ubiquitous in memories of the court, because Versailles saw itself as, among other things, a unique creation, standing outside time. Still, despite the distortion and selectiveness, the oversights and excesses, of the Sun King stereotype, we will begin with it because it was the court of Louis XIV that made "courtliness" a symbolic value in the French mind and that still symbolizes courtliness even today. Here I shall attempt not so much to write a history of that symbol as to explore the ways in which it has been used to generate certain models and representations whose meaning we are still capable of deciphering.

To Raise and to Lower

4. When it came to the court, only superlatives would do. To get an idea of the tone, consider this commentary from a medallion depicting Versailles in 1680:

> Of all the Royal Houses, Versailles is the one that the King loves most and did the most to embellish. Here he has brought together all that is most extraordinary and surprising in art and splendor. And here one finds buildings so sumptuous, gardens so pleasant and varied, fountains so abundant, aqueducts so prodigious in their construction, and a multitude of ornaments so rich and beauties so varied that it would take more than a volume to describe them. Not only is the King superbly housed, but the princes, lords, and all the officers of the court have equally ample and splendid apartments. Finally, His Majesty's residence has attracted so many people and led to the building of so many houses that the city has become quite populous and considerable.

Beyond the excellence of the place one notes the accumulation of works and people: the first sign of the court's preeminence is its extraordinary amassing of signs of exception.

The court is therefore worthy of endless commentary. The question needs to be made explicit: Why did people talk and write so much about the court? Not because remarkable things happened there, surely, but because whatever did happen was ipso facto remarkable. On this point both Saint-Simon and the Marquis de Dangeau, upon whom Saint-Simon heaped criticism and scorn, agreed, as did Sourches and

FIGURE 3.3. Versailles in 1680, in *Médailles sur les principaux événements du règne de Louis XIV*, 1702, showing the king and his work on the face and reverse of the medallion.

Mme de La Fayette and all the other memoir writers. They wrote about the court because the court was an important place. In one way or another each of them says so. Dangeau, who doubtless deserves better than a slanderous tradition affords, makes much of this. He was trusted, and certain contemporaries, such as the Abbé de Choisy and Mme de Maintenon, relied on his journal as an indispensable source. Sourches, who kept his text secret, wrote for posterity. More of his memoirs are taken up with commentary, and he writes at a greater remove from events, although he, too, gives a day-by-day chronology. Saint-Simon, of course, is something else entirely: he seeks to explain, to press home his point of view. In his eyes Dangeau is little more than a quasi-official diarist and spokesman: "He adored the King and Mme de Maintenon; he adored the ministers and the government. He made such a show of his reverence that it insinuated itself into the very marrow of his bones. He inwardly adopted their tastes, their likes and dislikes." Saint-Simon, for his part, claimed to be without illusions, and to reveal to unlikely readers the court's hidden underside and its denizens' intimate secrets. Yet in their different ways and despite their different motivations, both men shared the conviction of having penetrated to the essence of the thing itself.

This may seem astonishing. Without the amplitude afforded by a Saint-Simon's style and inventiveness, court chronicles can often seem boring and repetitive, as Mercier unequivocally stated in the late eighteenth century: "One knows the spirit of the château after a day's exploration. What was done yesterday will be done exactly the same way tomorrow. See one day and you've seen the whole year." Mercier was right. When the king was present, one day was a great deal like the next, and it was rare indeed for some noteworthy event to disrupt the monotony. Here,

FIGURE 3.4. Renown, an allegory of Louis XIV, 1662. The court is held up as an unrivalled model of perfection to those who are not of it. But renown is also the rarest and most precious of goods in the eyes of courtiers, as well as the most bitterly disputed.

reduced to the essential, are several days at Versailles in December 1684, based on Dangeau's account:

> Monday 11: The king went to shoot in his park. Monseigneur went to hunt deer at Saint-Germain. At night there was the Comédie Française.—One learned of the death of Mlle de Jarnac, Mademoiselle's *fille d'honneur.*—Madame de Jarnac, her mother, was *dame d'honneur* and died early this year. It was learned that Mlle de la Valette, the youngest daughter of Mme de Navailles, stated that she wished to marry her cousin, M. de Laurière, and that her mother was most unhappy with her and with the boy, who is her nephew *à la mode de Bretagne.*
>
> Tuesday 12: Monseigneur went wolf-hunting; the king went shooting. At night there was a reception.—M. le Maréchal d'Estrées obtained the survivorship of his post as vice-admiral *du Ponant* [that is, in the west, of the Atlantic fleet] for the Comte d'Estrées, his son, on condition that he remain another year as ship's captain and three years as squadron commander.
>
> Wednesday 13: The king drove in his carriage through the small park. Monseigneur did not go out. At night, the Comédie Italienne.—The Comte d'Estrées was sworn in as vice admiral although he is not to assume his post

FIGURE 3.5. *The Gardens of Versailles Viewed from the North Terrace,* Allegrain (detail).

immediately. Mme de Béthune obtained a continuation of her pension of 9,000 francs, such as she had always enjoyed during the queen's lifetime.

Thursday 14: The king drove through his small park in his calash. Monseigneur took medicine. At night there was a reception.—Mme la Marquise de Richelieu appeared at court for the first time.—M. le Comte de Soissons returned from Savoy, where he had been unable to prevent the marriage of the Prince de Carignan.

And so it went, one thing after another, an endless round of repetition. The work, recreation, and health of the king and his family; favors and honors; news of war and diplomacy; ceremonies and holidays; deaths, births, and marriages: the main elements of surprise in this high-society datebook are the names, which change, while the situations are almost always predictable. The restitution of discipline in the court during the reign of Louis XIV, especially after 1680, further accentuated this sense of regularity, which affected the occupations not only of the sovereign but of the whole world that revolved around him. Mercier was right: court life was immutable, even stagnant. The vast literature devoted to it only reinforces this impression, for by emphasizing what seemed emblematic the writers involuntarily stressed the repetitious aspects. Yet the observation makes sense only from a point of view deliberately alien to the workings of the court. Mercier is right,

FIGURE 3.6. *The Château of Versailles,* Patel (detail), 1668.

but he fails to hit his target because his statement expresses the thinking, and the values, of another world.

What did people do at court? Strictly speaking, nothing: they were simply there. The intrigues, amours, ceremonies, and celebrations were not the whole story. To be at court was first of all to exist in a certain state. Living day after day in proximity to the sovereign gave the courtier a special place in the social hierarchy, an exceptional status. Saint-Simon cruelly mocks the Duc de La Rochefoucauld, in his day the model of the perfect courtier, who is forced by old age and blindness and infirmity into a kind of semi-retirement. The commentator is ironic about the duke's belated "decision, so difficult for a courtier who has nothing but the court." Yet despite Saint-Simon's air of superiority, did he behave so very differently? When he quit the king's service in April 1702, nothing required him to remain with a monarch who had dealt with him all in all rather harshly. He had little taste for the ordinary occupations of Versailles, and he detested the idea of "what people at court call doing business." He had no illusions with regard to royal distinctions and favors. He neither hunted nor gambled, and he had no taste for dalliances or amorous adventures. Yet he chose to stay. To be at court, whose hazards and deceptions he repeatedly denounced, was for him tantamount to an official duty, an occupation compatible with his rank.

5. To be admitted at court was a kind of recognition, and it is not surprising that most of the memorialists were careful to list all newcomers. Here, everything was

couched in the language of vision: one had to see and, if possible, be seen. Listen to this account of the first introduction of Mme de Sévigné's grandson, Louis-Provence de Grignan, newly arrived from his province:

> I come from Versailles, Madame, where I went Sunday to make an appearance. I went first to the apartments of M. le Maréchal de Lorges to beg him to introduce me to the king. He gave me his promise and told me to meet him at the door of Mme de Maintenon's apartment so as to greet the king when he came out. So I greeted him; he stopped and nodded to me with a smile. The next day I greeted Monseigneur, Madame la Duchesse, Monsieur, Madame, and the princes of the blood, and everywhere I was well received.

After an initial exchange of greetings, an expanded social circulation becomes possible. The spectacle of majesty and the king's regard result in a change of identity.

This preliminary rite of passage, generally informal, was necessary but not sufficient. The courtier needed to be in constant contact with the sovereign in order to replenish whatever it was that set him apart from others. Of course it was always in one's self-interest not to be forgotten. More profoundly, however, court society was based on a tacit pact between the monarch and his entourage. Of course their positions were not comparable, yet each needed the other to exist fully. The courtier's proximity to the king gave him status and allowed him to live in a microsociety held up as a peerless model. The court's size and brilliance provided the social background against which the sovereign could affirm his glory. Whence the king's constant preoccupation with enhancing the court's importance and reputation: "The king was much concerned to see his court full, even of people for whom he cared not and who in themselves merely swelled the crowd, and it was a certain demerit to appear there but little and infrequently, as the king made the offender feel whenever the opportunity arose."

With this remark we come to the most powerful and persuasive sociological analysis of the court, that of Norbert Elias. Here I can recall only its main outlines. For Elias, who treats the French case as paradigmatic, court society is a distinctive social pattern whose significance can only be interpreted in the context of a long-term social and political evolution. The court of Louis XIV was thus the culmination of a centuries-old process, a brief moment of equilibrium. From the thirteenth century to the end of the seventeenth century, the monarchy had consolidated its power, ending in absolutism. To do so it had regained control of the instruments of power, most notably by establishing a monopoly of violence and the power of taxation. The king's army and administration established him as the sole legitimate authority. The powers that he gathered into his hands were taken from the old feudal aristocracy, which was gradually stripped of its ancient prerogatives. In this complex social game there was therefore a winner, and there were also losers. But the game was complicated by the involvement of a third player: the new nobility of state (or office), which opened the ranks of privilege to the ambitions of the bourgeoisie. Placed in the position of a referee, the king, according to Elias, derived most of his power from manipulating the tensions that opposed the various protagonists. This is probably the most original part of Elias's interpretation. It suggests that we should look upon the long rise of the absolute monarchy not as the expression over the centuries of a continuous will to power but rather as the logical culmination of a particular system of social relations. The configuration of the field of social tensions called for constant regulation, and this was the function of the monarch. Elias's interpretation of court society is rooted in this analysis. In order to maintain the balance among groups whose rivalry was the source of his strength, the king could not simply take; he also had to give. The court offered the old nobility material as well as symbolic compensation for what it was forced to give up. Material: the king's generosity compensated for lost resources by granting courtiers posts, pensions, and, best of all, gifts that demonstrated his largesse. Symbolic: the court gradually became the preeminent place to be in society. Indeed, with Louis XIV it became a place outside society and absolutely above it (this was the meaning of its removal to Versailles in 1682). What had to be given up in the way of real power was regained in prestige.

This double compensation was ambiguous, however, and perverse in its effects. Henceforth the court nobility depended for its status and the means to support its rank on the king's good will. This dependence was crucial, all the more so in that living at court and maintaining the luster of the family name required steady increases of expenditure, sometimes resulting in spectacular indebtedness. Maintaining one's rank could ultimately mean relying on the sovereign's generosity in all things. Finally, the risks taken did not guarantee even the court nobles that their privileges would remain untouchable, and Louis XIV did not hesitate, through his grants of favor and choice of collaborators, to make them aware of the insistent pressure of the new state elites.

Although Elias's model was slow to be recognized, its scope, elegance, and persuasiveness are such that it is now accepted almost without demur. Yet there remains a great deal to be said about it. A sociologist, Elias worked with dated information, mainly from literary sources—Saint-Simon primarily, and the moralists—and at times these introduce strong ideological biases. The social evolution that he sketches in broad outline has been contradicted on many points by recent research. The case for a domestication of the nobility in the first years of Louis XIV's reign is difficult to argue in a France where the distribution of wealth, privilege, and authority failed to change in any notable way after the Fronde, assuming that one looks outside the very visible center of power and takes local realities into account. In the provinces the monarchy had to rely on the very real power of noble families to which it was in fact allied by a "congruence of interests." The spectacular consolidation of the monarch's power should not be allowed to mask the inertia and continuity of the monarchical state. Given these facts, Elias's impressive sociological fresco is not to be taken literally. Yet neither is it to be rejected in toto. Instead, we must distinguish more carefully between what was taking place so visibly at court and what was slow to change in Ancien Régime society.

6. While it is highly unlikely that a radical mutation occurred in the absolute monarchy after Louis XIV's assumption of personal power, and hard to believe that a general program of reining in the nobility was successfully undertaken, major changes were evident in at least one place: the court. Those who were admitted to court and placed above the common run of the king's subjects were thereby abased as much as they were elevated. The court magnified and made visible the effects of power on those who got too close to it without participating in its exercise (and in this sense the solar symbolism of Louis XIV's court was fully justified).

"The court," Saint-Simon wrote, "was another stratagem in the politics of despotism." This formula has often been cited to suggest that the organization of the court was one element in an authoritarian subjugation of the kingdom. Here I want to argue that the court should be seen not as evidence for such a strategy but rather as a representation of it. It was a social form that made a highly symbolic operation practicable. There is little doubt that Louis was aware of this and fully appreciated the political resources at his disposal. An episode from the very beginning of his reign clearly demonstrates this: the celebrated *carrousel* in June 1662, at the Tuileries.

The event was a military display for which the king was joined by the leading lords of France, some of whom had played prominent roles in the recent Fronde. Louis; his brother, Monsieur; the Prince de Condé; the Duc d'Enghien; and the Duc de Guise each commanded a squadron of ten horsemen, respectively the Romans, the Persians, the Turks, the Indians, and the American Savages. To make the message perfectly clear, the king and his men occupied the center of a circle (the *carrousel*), with the other protagonists distributed around the circumference. Emblems and mottoes further underscored the significance of this *mise en scène:* while Louis held up a sun to dissipate the clouds and announced *Ut vidi, vici,* the other principals represented figures of lesser importance (a moon, a crescent, a star) that merely reflected the light of the sun, as the mottoes made clear: *Uno sole minor* (for Monsieur), *Crescit ut aspicitur* (for Condé), *Magno de lumine lumen* (for Enghien). The scene emphasized the centrality, majesty, and authority of the monarch, and Perrault provided a lengthy commentary in which the solar theme was freighted with political insinuations. The significance of the spectacle was further reinforced by the fact that the *carrousel* was a form of quasi-military exercise that had replaced

FIGURE 3.7. The greatest names in the kingdom gather at the site of the Fronde to witness a spectacle underscoring the king's greatness and the subjugation of all the kingdom's energy to his exclusive glory: the Grand Carrousel of 1662, with Louis XIV as a Roman emperor; engraving by Chauveau, 1662.

the tourney, banned since the accidental death of Henri II in 1559: it offered not the reality of military power but a mock spectacle. In the end it was only a parody, which returned the leading figures of the kingdom to the role they should never have given up. This lesson was understood at once, as a contemporary commentary attests: "The *carrousels* were invented only to exercise the French nobility, which can be idle only when it savors the fruits of a profound peace, having long garnered laurels on the glorious fields of war."

This was indeed the court's political purpose in the king's mind. Its function was to represent the pacification of social space: not to establish peace but to demonstrate it and accredit the notion that it was possible. Louis in any case wanted to believe it. In the same year, 1662, he congratulated himself on having created a "society of pleasure, which gives the persons of the court an honest familiarity with us, touches them and charms more than one can say. The peoples, meanwhile, are pleased by the spectacle, whose goal is basically always to please them. And all our subjects, in general, are delighted to see that we love what they love and what they are most successful at. In this way we hold their minds and hearts, in some cases more firmly perhaps than through rewards and benefits." Here was an admirable lesson in political calculation from a young king anxious from the beginning of his reign to leave maxims for the instruction of the dauphin. Such was the doctrine of the court: it was designed to exalt the king's glory by associating it with the carefully differentiated beholders who were required to contribute to that which they beheld. The higher one rose in the hierarchy of honor, the more one was subjected to the one honor that could not be equaled, the majesty of the sovereign. The distances

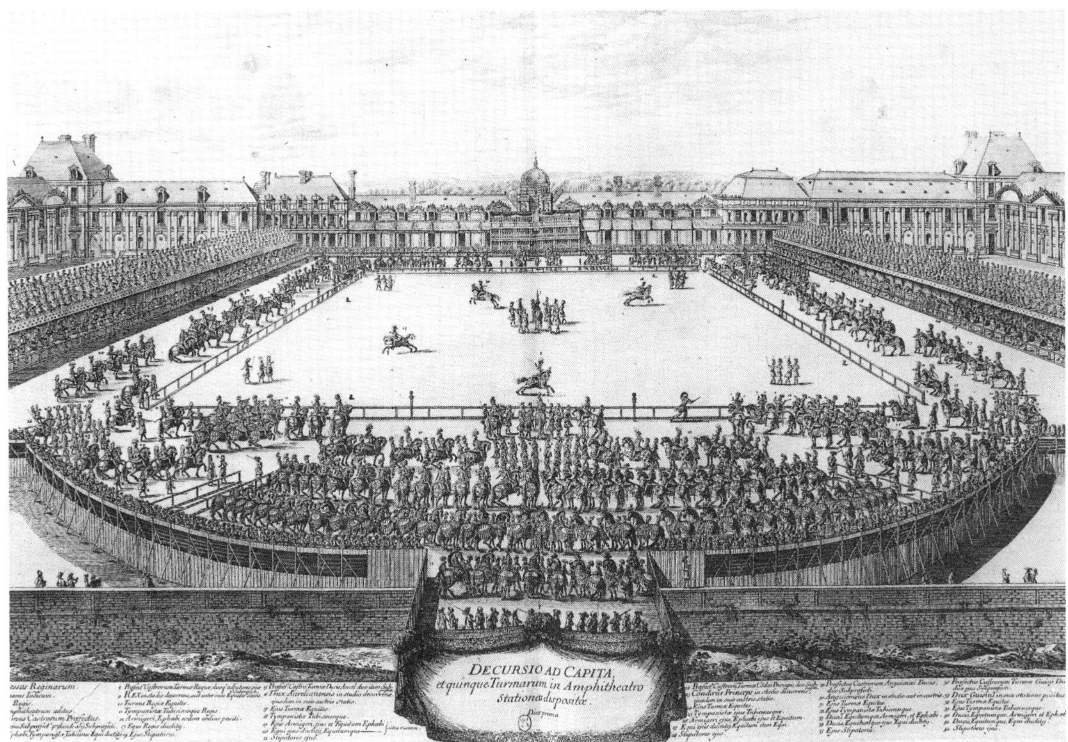

FIGURE 3.8. *Le Grand Carrousel, June 5, 6, 7, 1662;* engraving by Israël Silvestre.

that were created within the court matched those that separated it from the larger society.

On the subject of the court's brilliance, Louis XIV very lucidly observed that "what one sees prejudices judgment in favor of what one does not see." The court was precisely what one could not help seeing. The order and mechanisms that governed it were those that one hoped to see regulate society as a whole. *Faute de mieux*, the court provided a way of staging a representation of absolute power.

The Logic of Rank

7. In essence the court was a society ordered hierarchically around the man who provided its raison d'être and dominated it from an incommensurable height. Accordingly, descriptions of it always had to begin with the monarch and his family and proceed in order of decreasing proximity to the king. This orderly perception from top to bottom is present in most of the surviving reports, whether quasi-official documents such as the diplomat Spanheim's report to the Elector of Brandenburg in 1690 or private documents such as Sourches's memoirs, composed in the same period. It impressed itself even more forcefully on the actors of the

court, who constantly had to know where to situate themselves and others in the hierarchy—even those who were naturally reluctant to participate, such as the Princess Palatine in a celebrated letter of December 27, 1713:

> My son is a *grandson of France*. The grandsons of France are above the princes of the blood. It is true that they haven't as many privileges as the children of France, but they have many more than the princes of the blood. For example, my son eats at the king's table, while the princes of the blood do not. He has never taken the title of first prince of the blood, because he is not a prince of the blood but a grandson of France, and that is why he is called Royal Highness. But his son, who is the first prince of the blood, is called Most Serene Highness and not Royal Highness. He is not with the king morning and night but only in great ceremonies, when the whole family eats with the king. He therefore has none of the privileges that his father has, such as the cloué carriage, the first equerry, the first chaplain, and so on. His officers cannot and must not serve him in the presence of the king. He has no castle guards and a hundred other things of the sort, unlike my son. I must have made a mistake in writing, for my son has never been a prince of the blood. The king has indeed granted the Duc du Maine, his sons, and his brother the rank of princes of the blood, but after all the other princes and princesses of the blood: so true is this that, in his own house, the wife of the Duc du Maine is also above him; she has precedence in all things over her husband, and when a contract is signed she signs according to the rank accorded her by birth, while he puts his name only after the names of all the princes and princesses of the blood. He is therefore very far below my son: between them are all the princes of the blood.

Appellations, privileges, and customs thus reflected each person's rank in court society. Emmanuel Le Roy Ladurie has identified three main criteria of rank, each distinct and independent of the other two. The first, based on blood, was supposed to be objective, which is why it was so important for the good courtier to know his genealogies in order to know which way to turn in society: Saint-Simon was an expert in this area, as were Dangeau and a few other well-known connoisseurs at Versailles. Yet the "ranked" segment of the court was strictly speaking a fairly small elite, consisting of the children and grandchildren of France, the princes of the blood, the royal bastards, the dukes-and-peers, the dukes, the foreign princes, and, after 1700, the Grands d'Espagne. Outside this circle, in which a person's title alone had a recognized value, things were much more confused, and other criteria had to be called into play. The members of this tiny elite were distinguished by certain specific privileges: the right to be seated in the presence of sovereigns and the type of seating on which one sat (for example, the "divine stool" that Mme de Sévigné described and about which so much ink has been spilled, or, in church, the *carreau*, or pillow); access to the sovereigns' presence, table, games, or carriages at various times of day; and place in various rituals. All of these were visible signs of the ranked nobility. Of course these signs were not equally distributed among the members of the elite: *la main* (that is, the place of honor to the king's right), *le haut du pavé* (the center of the road), ceremonial precedence, and the "Pour" (the right to have the words "For Monsieur or Madame" marked on the door of reserved apartments when the court traveled) were in theory strictly regulated. There were endless quarrels over such matters, and the privileged fought hard to defend their individual status and the status of their rank.

The second set of rank criteria stemmed not from supposedly imprescriptible rights but from various presumptuous claims and usurpations. Rules were sometimes imposed from above by the most privileged, anxious to enforce wider recognition of their exceptional status: the princes of the blood, for example, tried to insist that when untitled gentry and marshals of France made condolence visits they should wear cloaks, as they did for the children and grandchildren of France. Conversely, signs of distinction could be seized upon by people of lower rank, as when velvet clothing, once reserved for the highest nobility, was (to Saint-Simon's indignation) adopted by others in the last years of Louis XIV's reign. Here the battle for prestige was waged not by the few hundred people of the "ranked court" but by the few thousand who constituted the larger court.

The final criterion of rank was not a criterion as such but a matter of the royal will. Although the system was supposed to be immutable, the king constantly shuffled people about and redistributed prizes. This manipulation of ranks could take a variety of forms, but in each case the effects were similar. The first technique was to increase the number of signs of privilege. As the court ritual became increasingly complex and minutely detailed, each sequence could become the basis of new signs of favor. People mocked these, especially Saint-Simon. When, for example, the memoirist was granted the right to hold the king's candlestick while the sovereign prepared for bed, he wrote: "This was a distinction, a favor, for the king had a way of conferring existence upon trifles." Though no fool, Saint-Simon was nonetheless honored by a gesture that indicated the honor to others. A foreign observer like Spanheim echoed him on the matter of the "Pour": "This distinction, which in itself seems of little importance, nevertheless creates a very large difference between those who have it and those who do not." Saint-Simon, the unrepentant conservative, was therefore wrong to believe that such inflation of the signs of privilege would result in their devaluation: issued by an unquestioned authority, these tokens of favor were immediately made legal tender by people whose social exchanges and arrangements depended on them.

Favor was a more obvious as well as a more arbitrary way of demonstrating whom the king's grace had touched and whom it had rejected, independent of any

FIGURE 3.9. *Olympus, or Louis XIV and His Family;* a painting by Nocret for the antechamber of Monsieur, 1665. The mythological garb ignores the strict logic of rank with its rigorous constraints and incessant disputes.

position they might have acquired. The king's favor could be expressed in various ways: through help in arranging a marriage, through a grant of office or a pension or a gift, through the assignment of an apartment in the palace, or through more liberal access to the sovereign's intimate company. Such decisive proofs of personal favor redounded to the credit of an entire household. Yet they probably counted less than the way in which the king received a particular courtier before the court. One can see many examples of this in Saint-Simon's tortured relations with Louis XIV. In 1708, when enemies used a slip of the tongue against him, the duke was forced to avoid a probable public disgrace by taking refuge on his estate at La Ferté. He timidly returned to Versailles toward the end of the following year. But he was not fully rehabilitated until the entire court was put on notice of his return to favor by a private conversation with the king "of more than half an hour," news of which promptly spread throughout the palace. Four years later, Louis XIV settled the interminable quarrel over rank among the dukes-and-peers in Saint-Simon's favor, rejecting the pretensions of M. de la Rochefoucauld. Having scored a triumph, Saint-Simon had to make sure that it was recognized: "I went . . . to wait for the king as he left his study on his way to Mme de Maintenon's. When people saw me there, they understood that I had won." The sovereign confirmed his decision in public and rejoiced in the happy outcome: "All ears had been most attentive to the king's response, which quickly passed from mouth to mouth; and more compliments." Once again it was the king's will that created social value on the stage of the court.

8. The more minutely regulated the court, the more it became a machine, a mechanism, for producing social distinctions. Emmanuel Le Roy Ladurie has recently suggested thinking of the court as a holistic microsociety organized around an indivisible power and hierarchized along two dimensions, one running from the sacred to the profane, the other from the pure to the impure. Though stimulating, this interpretation is not completely convincing. To my mind, it assumes a social continuity of values that did not necessarily exist at the court of Louis XIV. As the court became more strictly hierarchical, it also opened itself up to a more heterogeneous public. Saint-Simon, who opposed the change, insisted in his *Mémoires* on the rights of blood and seniority (the rights of purity, if you will), but his was a rear-guard action. In fact, the Sun King devoted his efforts to "separating [and] dividing." If he generalized the hierarchical principle, he did so by creating new hierarchies of rank and opposing one to another, separating the sphere of power from the order of grandeur while combining both forms of competence in himself alone. Here was a court in which the king wanted his nobles to serve, in which "subjects vied to ruin themselves so as to be in his service," yet where no employment, not even the highest, bestowed rank on the person who filled it; a court in which military careers were, at Louvois's behest, theoretically governed by an official promotion roster but where in fact promotions in the army and the Ordre du Saint-Esprit were always

uncertain and unexpected; a court in which values constantly reaffirmed in order to justify the ranking of individuals and families were regularly undermined at the whim of the monarch. What is more, the policy of privilege took less and less account of a person's family. Individuals were elevated and lowered at will, with priority to individual merit rather than to accumulated family prerogatives. It was as if the assertion of an authoritarian order in the court sowed disorder among the ostensibly honored hierarchies.

The paradox, however, was more apparent than real. The court of Louis XIV actually functioned on two levels. It established and gave visibility to a pyramid of honors and social esteem culminating in the matchless majesty of the sovereign. Each courtier contributed in his or her own way to this magnificent construct, which can legitimately be called holistic. This was one of the languages in which the court spoke of itself. But there was also another, quite different language, used to make the point that all ranks emanated from the king's grace and were his to do with as he pleased. More than that, the king demonstrated his absolute authority by disrupting orders that he had created and that seemed to culminate in him. Once again, proximity to power lowered those whom it seemed to elevate.

The court itself was divided between these two forms of recognition. On the one hand there was an etiquette to dictate even the most ordinary forms of behavior and social gestures. Everyone was subject to a code coordinated with the hierarchy of prestige—everyone, including the king, who conducted himself like the foremost and most punctilious of courtiers. This code objectified each person's position in the court order and thereby made that order more acceptable. Norbert Elias aptly characterized this as the court's "self-representation." By the late eighteenth century, however, people no longer understood the purpose of this self-representation and, finding it impossible to bear, sought to escape from its consequences. Mme Campan not so naïvely pointed out the ultimate significance of etiquette: "These rules were established as a kind of code. To a Richelieu, a La Rochefoucauld, or a Duras they brought, in the exercise of their domestic functions, opportunities for contacts that served them well. And as a sop to their vanity, they loved the customs that made honorific prerogatives of the right to offer a glass of water, carry a nightgown, or remove a basin." Make no mistake: the court of France did not invent etiquette, nor did it invent the courtly servility that the anticurial tradition has always reviled. What changed with the reign of Louis XIV, however, was the relation between the two. The humility required of the man at court was converted into prestige, and prestige was turned into risible services—as if to underscore the fiduciary nature of these tokens of social esteem.

Alongside the official rank that was made visible through the ritualization of behavior, however, there was also a de facto rank that was anything but immutable yet was ultimately decisive. It began of course with the sovereign's declaration of favor. Like disgrace, favor could manifest itself in spectacular ways. The history of Louis XIV's reign was punctuated by endless demonstrations of favor and disfavor. The currency of favor was often impossible to grasp. It could take the form of a word, a mark of attention, or even a simple glance, as one ironic observer noted: "When the king opens his mouth, the courtier's passion to be noticed defies belief. When the king deigns to cast his eyes on someone, the object of his attention thinks that his fortune is made and boasts of it, saying, 'The king looked at me.' You may count on the king's being a clever man! How many people has he paid off with a glance!" Naturally the value of this currency depended on the unlimited credit of the monarch, the creator and distributor of all courtly wealth. This currency had value because the court honored it.

Anything could serve as a token of royal favor and thus become an object of collective evaluation. Informal marks of attention vied with all too formal expressions of grace. But there were also more reliable indicators of the ever-changing map of the court, and these received perhaps the greatest attention of all. One such sign was the assignment of apartments, a scarce resource at Versailles and one subject to continual redistribution. To experts such as Dangeau, this was therefore an excellent indicator of who was up and who was down on the stock exchange of courtly values: in each instance Dangeau reported not only the name and relations of the new beneficiary but also, to round out our knowledge of the subject, the name and fate of the previous occupant and the identity of the favored individual's immediate neighbors, all details that helped to gauge more precisely the nature and importance of the favor granted. Any occasion could serve to establish a provisional ranking. A good example of this was the performance of Racine's *Esther* by the female pupils of Saint-Cyr early in 1689. The play was staged under the explicit patronage of Mme de Maintenon and the king, which transformed it into an all but obligatory social occasion. It was important to attend and to be seen. Mme de Coulanges described the event to Mme de Grignan, banished to the depths of her province: "Mark this well: if you wish to pay court, you must ask to see *Esther*. You know what *Esther* is. All worthy people find it charming; you would find it more charming than anyone. It is no great trouble to come from Grignan and spend the night at Versailles." The countess did not go, however, but her mother, Mme de Sévigné, who often professed her estrangement from the affairs of court, awaited her turn while keeping track of those invited to see the play ahead of her. Her turn came at last on February 19, the last performance. Every detail was carefully weighed: her place (in the second row, behind the duchesses), her manner ("we listened . . . with an attentiveness that was noticed"), and of course the few words that the king was kind enough to exchange with her after the performance. "His Majesty departed, leaving me the object of envy."

Much of the attention and energy of those who lived at court were thus taken up with the permanent task of taking the measure of the market of favor. Since what was given to one was necessarily taken from another, the only way to know where one stood was to know where everyone else stood: there was no necessary relation between apparent rank and actual standing. The best available information was therefore essential, information, along with royal favor, being the most precious of courtly commodities. With information one could deduce standing and prospects and thus plan strategies and alliances, as Saint-Simon did after a series of deaths of people close to him forced him to evaluate what he calls his "situation at court": these losses, he perceptively noted, "left a void (and I am not speaking here of my heart, for which this is not the place) that nothing could fill or even diminish." The "news"—and the evaluation of one's forces that it made possible—dictated the conditions under which one must act.

Although favor was by definition unpredictable, the courtier was by no means reduced to impotence. To figure out what was about to change, if possible before anyone else figured it out, was a central element of courtly rationality: "Here people are always looking out to see which way the wind from the court is blowing," observed Primi Visconti, cynical as usual but speaking from experience: had not his own rating soared after Louis XIV complimented him in public? "The Marquis de Louvois, Dangeau, the Marquis de La Vallière, the Duc de Grigny, and all the courtiers were prodigal in their compliments and repeated the king's flattering words about me. For the king has only to open his mouth to speak of someone and that person is immediately sought out as a saint or banished as a reprobate." To gather information was both to maximize one's chances and, just as important, to minimize one's risks.

This court rationality was powerful enough to dictate alliances. Some were based on old allegiances of family, friendship, or politics. Others were ephemeral and intended simply to exploit some opportunity of the moment. The most complex were organized as "cabals," or as people sometimes said, "parties." These vague and shifting alliances, whose organization and action, to believe Saint-Simon, required both close attention to detail and considerable breadth of vision, were in fact, as Le Roy Ladurie has shown, vast syndicates of basically similar interests in which all elements of the court were represented. According to Le Roy Ladurie, these alliances of overlapping ambitions were at first a way of diversifying investments so as to reduce risk. For while all courtiers were obliged to distinguish themselves from the rest and obtain whatever advantage they could, they were still all basically helpless in the face of the uncertainty of royal grace, on which ultimately everything depended.

This was where the sovereign's manipulation of the system of ranks came into play. The king did not have to intervene permanently. As Elias has shown, the court system was set up in such a way that the courtiers essentially assumed responsibility for keeping it going in accordance with a logic that unbeknownst to them determined their actions. All the king had to do was establish a hierarchical order and sow doubt about each person's place in it, thus initiating a generalized competition that he took care to perpetuate. The game could go on indefinitely. This is where the mechanical metaphors that Saint-Simon liked so much are most appropriate, yet we can also see their limits. To be sure, the clever courtier was much preoccupied with perfecting "machines and combinations" and then "setting them in precise and measured motion with exquisite harmony and a leveraged force." But this human clockwork, however perfectly conceived, was always at the mercy of an unpredictable clockmaker.

9. At court the logic of rank always came down to the exaltation of pure power. Although it embodied a formalization of social relations, it was implemented in such a way as to remind everyone that he who upheld the overall order could modify its rules whenever he pleased. Indeed, he could do more than that: he could demonstrate his absolute power by pretending to suppress all order. At Louis XIV's behest Marly became the laboratory for this ultimate experiment.

No sooner had the king settled in Versailles than he felt the need to create a refuge for himself away from the inconveniences of a large and cumbersome court. It was in 1679 in Marly, a few leagues from the chateau on the road to Saint-Germain, that Mansart began work on a residence where the king might "relax and pass his time in a domestic setting." Louis first went to Marly in 1686 and thereafter continued to visit at irregular intervals until the end of his reign. At first the residence was quite small: it contained only forty apartments, twenty-four of which the king could make available to those he wished to take with him. This was a very small number of apartments compared with the several thousand courtiers who frequented the palace. The necessity of choosing created the conditions for a bitter competition among all who felt any chance of being chosen. The king's choice immediately became a visible sign of favor. Because this distinction was rare, it was also incomparable. Over time more subtle distinctions developed within this general election: while all who had been "named for Marly" in the past and especially those who were so named in the present were set apart from everyone else, there were different ways of being chosen. One could be invited to "ordinary Marlys" or one could be invited with a more select company to "special Marlys." There were "Marlys for the ladies" and "Marlys for the gentlemen." And since the logic of distinction is always to generate further distinctions, it was even possible to come up with an alternative to Marly that temporarily shook things up and sowed trouble in the ranks.

Lists of the chosen were naturally drawn up. The memoirists scrupulously recorded the favorites, indicating who was being invited for the first time and who was back in favor after an absence of how long. The gazettes published the names, sometimes coupled with complimentary comments. The importance of being chosen was even greater because the king personally drew up the list of those who would accompany him. This was unusual and thus added to the luster of an invitation. Anyone who wished to be invited had to do everything possible to please the king and, even more important, avoid doing anything likely to incur royal displeasure. According to the Princess Palatine, the ladies "were so afraid of saying something that might displease and prevent them from going to Marly that they spoke of nothing but clothes and games, which seemed quite boring." Saint-Simon, who for a time thought he was a fixture of the scene (but who would be cruelly disappointed later on), knew what the distinction was worth: "I went often to Marly. He [the king] spoke to me sometimes, which was something much remarked on and counted. In a word, he treated me well, and better than others of my age and sort." This open competition among courtiers, who were constantly evaluating themselves in this way, became, in the hands of Louis XIV, an instrument of pressure and manipulation. The instrument was all the more effective in that the king, who decided without giving reasons for his decisions, forced the candidates to beg. When he passed, the supplicant was reduced to humbly beseeching, "Sire, Marly?" There were no guarantees that one's wishes would be granted. But beware those who, like Saint-Simon, eventually grew tired of not being heard and thought they could stop giving the king the "satisfaction of refusing." The disfavor incurred through such behavior had considerable consequences. Like the Jansenists' God, the sovereign distributed his favors to whomever he wished however he wished, but he expected his flock to perform acts of faith without hope of reward. What was given was then given freely.

At Marly the sojourn was as informal as possible. Visitors went there without pomp or servants. Dress was simplified, etiquette forgotten, and one could stroll about the grounds without removing one's hat in the king's presence. The myth of an enclave of freedom in which all hierarchy was forgotten cannot stand up to scrutiny, however. The small chateau was under constant surveillance, and no one could leave without permission. Amusements were compulsory. And the gravest danger awaited those who took seriously the illusion that at Marly there existed a society in which the distances of rank had been abolished. In 1707, Mme de Torcy fell into this trap. The wife of Colbert de Torcy, then secretary of state for foreign affairs, and the daughter of Arnauld de Pomponne, she inadvertently sat down one day "near Madame, above the Duchesse de Duras, who arrived a moment later. Mme de Torcy in fact offered the duchess her place. But the lady had already sat down. It was taken as a compliment." The king, who happened by, found such impudence intolerable, grew angry, and forcefully pointed out the difference in prestige between such bourgeois dynasties as the Arnaulds or the Colberts and the noble lineage of the Duras. He deplored the fact that "both women were so ignorant, the one of what was due her, the other of the respect—his term—she owed to rank and birth." The affair ended in near disgrace for Mme de Torcy, who had involuntarily committed such an impertinent act. This episode should be seen as more than a whim or momentary displeasure, and no psychological explanation can fully account for it. Rather, it points up one of the underlying mechanisms of court society: the king alone set the rules of the game, and those who came closest to his glory were also the most vulnerable to his arbitrariness.

The Control of Appearances

10. Here is another paradox. In the judgment of most of the writers who observed and commented on the court, it was a place of falsehood and lies. The duplicity of the courtier and the vanity of court life are in fact themes as old as courts themselves. The court of Louis XIV was no exception. Did not the indulgent Mme de Sévigné discover, to her horror, while receiving her friend Pomponne, "the hidden underside of all the things we think we see but really do not?" And did not the very official Bishop Bossuet resort to similar imagery when he denounced "the eternal underside of courts" and "this disguise of faded fabric?"

Nevertheless, people still came to this cesspool of falsehood in search of truths about man. Indeed, the court was supposed to be an ideal place for psychological observation and for painting true portraits of the human soul. *La Princesse de Clèves* is a famous example, but the novel describes a society of the past in nostalgic colors. Yet when Henriette of England asked Mme de La Fayette to sketch a portrait of her in words, she defended the excellence of the court as a subject, this time in the present: " 'Don't you think,' she tells me, 'that if everything that has happened to me and the things related to those events were written down, it would make a fine story? You write well,' she added. 'Write, I will supply you with good memories.'" No doubt the first Madame was blessed with all the qualities of a character from fiction: she had beauty and adventures and would even meet a tragic end. In general, however, the court elicited narratives and portraits, even (perhaps especially) from those who did not care for it, such as La Bruyère, or who were without illusions about it, like Saint-Simon. Whatever came out of the court was good to know about, good to relate and comment on, and ultimately good to think about. Mme de Sévigné was surrounded by a circle of informants whose news she received and passed on, thus making her correspondence a sort of "handy gazette." Not that there was much surprising in what one learned: intrigues of power, family, and love occupied an obligatory place. But in all the authors we have looked at, one feels that something more fundamental was at stake: the court, owing to its very density, to the concentration of greatness, ambition, and wealth that it attracted, was like a hugely magnified image of the whole of society. Anecdotes about the court had exemplary value, portraits from the court immediately became universal, and individual characters were sharpened to the point of caricature. Last but not least, the court was an endless source of intrigue.

It should come as no surprise, then, that the court so readily lent itself to literature or that literature so readily turned to the court for its inspiration. Of course the theater was often a forum for denouncing the conventions and artificialities of the court, which existed only as pure representation. For Primi Visconti "the court is the finest comedy in the world" and in public Louis exhibited "the gravity of a theatrical king." Derision aside, the passage from court to stage and vice versa was always easy. But the passage to the pages of fiction was in a way even more significant because it permitted many plots to be intertwined. When Mme de La Fayette recounted Henriette of England's amours with the Comte de Guiche (under Henriette's watchful gaze), nothing was omitted: the emotional doubts ("M. de Guiche did not know Madame's feelings toward him"), the misunderstandings, the need to take blind action, the hand of fate, and the effects of surprise. Take, for instance, the masked ball at Mme de La Vieuville's, which Madame and Monsieur attend: "They met a masked troupe at the door. Without knowing who they were, Monsieur proposed joining them and took one of them by the hand. Madame did the same. Imagine her surprise when she discovered the Comte de Guiche's withered hand, while he recognized the scents with which she perfumed her bonnets. Both were so surprised that they came close to uttering a cry." Court life was a novel, or, rather, the court re-created in life conditions ordinarily found only in fiction.

Thus there was no opposition between the falseness and the truth of court life, because both reflected the same order of realities. The falseness of the court was denounced in the name of morality; the truth of the court stemmed from the possibilities it afforded for understanding social life and the springs of action. Unlike the discourse of denunciation, this second discourse did not invoke transcendent values that were supposedly flouted or neglected. Rather, it took for granted that court life involved an interplay of representations that had to be taken seriously because they formed an essential part of the bond among human beings.

11. Everything can be seen at court, and everything must be visible. The court is a public space in the strongest sense, and nothing can be hidden. This rule, which affected the king and his family first of all, was probably one of the distinctive features of French court culture. In the collective spectacle that Versailles was from the outset, it was important for every individual to have access to the sovereign or at any rate to see him. Because the life of the court, centered on the king, gradually supplanted the great rituals of monarchy, the king's body became the tangible incarnation of majesty and the principle of sovereignty. More than anyone else, Louis was

LES APPARTEMENTS.

LE ROY, afin d'augmenter les plaiſirs de ſa Cour, voulut que ſes Appartements fuſſent ouverts certains jours de la ſemaine. Il y a de grandes Salles pour la danſe, pour le jeu, pour la Muſique. Il y en a d'autres où l'on trouve toutes ſortes de rafraichiſſements avec profuſion, & ce qui fait le comble de la joye, on y joüit de la préſence d'un ſi grand Roy & d'un ſi bon Maiſtre.

C'eſt le ſujet de cette Médaille. On voit dans une eſpece de Salon magnifique trois Divinitez. Une Muſe, qui tient ſa Lyre deſigne la Muſique; Pomone, qui tient une corbeille de fruits, marque les rafraiſchiſſemens que l'on y ſert; & Mercure préſide aux jeux. Les mots de la Légende, COMITAS ET MAGNIFICENTIA PRINCIPIS, ſignifient, l'*affabilité, & la magnificence du Prince.* Ceux de l'Exergue, HILARITATI PUBLICÆ APERTA REGIA. M. DC. LXXXIII. veulent dire, *le Palais du Roy ouvert aux plaiſirs de ſes Sujets. 1683.*

FIGURE 3.10. *Hilaritati publicae aperta regia.* The court must be open to the pleasure of all; from *Médailles sur les principaux événements du règne de Louis XIV,* 1702.

convinced of this, and that is why he was so punctilious in his daily comportment. Saint-Simon, who heaped criticism on Louis's head, nevertheless conceded that he always maintained taste and decorum:

> It was a very useful thing, this consistent dignity and continual outward discipline. His dignity meant that, whenever he could be seen, he projected a majestic decency that commanded respect, and his discipline meant that for hours and days on end, wherever the king might be, one had only to know the day and the hour to know what he was doing, with never the slightest alteration except to use the time he spent outdoors either to do things or simply to walk. It is unbelievable how much this exactitude contributed to his service, to the luster of his court, and to the convenience of paying him court and speaking to him.

Death and disease were not supposed to disrupt this visible order, which was the law of the court. Because Louis XV and Marie-Antoinette, the Sun King's eighteenth-century successors, forgot this and boldly attempted to carve out a private life for themselves, out of the public eye, they paid dearly. In the palace everything was to be seen, and therefore one saw everything, from the king's waking in the morning to his going to bed at night, from his work and play to his love affairs and even his final agony. So powerful was Louis's symbolic presence that at times it could do without his real presence, which was taken for granted. Long after he ceased to be present in the "apartments" where he received several evenings each week, courtiers still felt obliged to come listen to the concerts and gamble as if the king were still actually with them.

The courtiers were of course bound by the same rules. The king detested secrecy and intrigue, which nevertheless flourished at court. He was wary of the passions and dreamed of imposing a generalized transparency on his world. Another function of etiquette was to assign each person a place and a clearly identifiable behavior, to regulate relationships and situations in a predictable way. To enforce obedience, moreover, the king had few scruples when it came to ferreting out the court's secrets. A system of surveillance, or rather espionage, therefore developed at Versailles to keep tabs on individuals, conversations, and correspondence. Once again the sovereign merely had to set the machinery in motion. The court then took it upon itself to maintain and extend the system. In the chateau, observed Primo Visconti (and many others), "the walls have ears and a tongue." Indeed, "in this court, words are considered crimes." So fierce was the competition among courtiers that any means of undermining a rival's advantages and thwarting his ambitions were legitimate. Everyone observed everyone else and was in turn an object of scrutiny. One need look no farther to explain the court's evident taste for psychological and action portraits. The eye learned to discern weaknesses, to penetrate secrets, to divine what was left unsaid. Analyzing people's actions and emotions ultimately became a courtly convention, a shared taste, but before that it was dictated by the need to maintain one's position and, if possible, to get ahead.

The paradoxical consequence of this was that the insistence on visibility produced the greatest imaginable dissimulation. Expressing one's feelings and passions meant exposing oneself to others, so one had to learn to master them. Once again the king set the example. Open and accessible to everyone at almost all times, he completely controlled what he allowed to be seen. He governed by glance and silence, "for [he] never spoke too much." Blessed with an incomparable memory, he knew everything but revealed little of what he knew. Limiting his activity further increased his power: "I wish you could see the king. He has the look of a great deceiver and the eyes of a fox. He never speaks of affairs of state except with the ministers in council. Otherwise, if he says a few words to his courtiers, they invariably have to do with the respective attributions or professions of each. But no matter what he says, no matter how frivolous, it is an oracle who speaks." The courtiers also dissembled, though in their case it was impossible to hide behind official maxims. Because everything was visible, nothing important could be shown. As Norbert Elias has so persuasively demonstrated, the extraordinary density and aggressiveness of social relations at court called for a protective discipline and system of self-restraint that made the court the ideal place for the modern civilizing process to occur.

12. It seems reasonable to assume that the problem of appearances was functionally at the heart of court culture. It was repeatedly invoked in similar terms by moralists, memorialists, and ordinary chroniclers. It had its own vocabulary and imagery (masks, theater, artifice). In short, it was a *topos.* The persistence of this theme over a long period can, however, mislead us by obliterating the temporal perspective. In fact, the values and functions of appearance changed considerably over time, and these changes can help us to understand what was distinctive about the French case.

Comparison will help to bring this out. In the massive literature of court treatises, one text occupies a unique place as reference, source, and grammar of court life: Baldassar Castiglione's *Il Cortegiano (The Courtier).* Published in Venice in 1528, the book was reprinted, translated, adapted, and plagiarized throughout Europe. There were three French translations which went through a far greater number of editions in the sixteenth and seventeenth centuries. Everywhere the book served as a model. It was a best-seller in its day, and its success and almost universal acceptance can all too easily make us forget that it was a text written at a certain date and in a very particular social and political context. A contemporary of Machiavelli, Castiglione described the courts of the Italian Renaissance, a society on the eve of being overwhelmed by a more warlike age.

The book was cast in the form of a Platonic, or rather Ciceronian, dialogue, which portrayed a fictional situation: the duke of Urbino has fallen ill and taken to his bed, and during the four days of his absence his courtiers gather to discuss the question of what it is that a courtier does. We are thus confronted with a representation of characters discussing their own representative function and the justifications for the reign of appearances. This mirror composition actually proposes a threefold model (and legitimation) of court society. The first function of the court is rhetorical: as Cicero proposed to train the perfect orator, Castiglione's characters propose to "form in words a perfect courtier." This is possible, however, only because the court is by its very nature a *locus amoenus*, a place conducive to thinking. The courtier is also a creature of language, whose action is ideally constructed in words (and whose language, conversely, is a discourse of action).

The second model of the court refers to an implicit phenomenology. The courtier's whole being consists in what he shows in society. But this absolute primacy of appearances is possible only because the courtier is fundamentally different from other men. The vocabulary here is that of grace, of a gift that is exhibited only in its effects, but fully exhibited there (here we hark back to the rhetorical model). A man is a courtier to the extent that his peers recognize him as such, and his peers recognize only those who already possess the requisite qualities. Appearances are therefore a serious matter, because they are the basis of the social bond that unites the few who constitute the entourage of the prince. A serious matter but an evanescent and ineffable judgment because the determination is actually made in advance and all that remains is to confirm the grace by which the courtier already is a creature apart. The courtier must therefore cover his tracks so that no one can discover how he shapes his appearance. Effort, which would cast doubt on the courtier's status, is forbidden. What is required is *sprezzatura,* the elegant nonchalance that makes the courtier's every gesture and attitude seem at once spontaneous and inevitable. His social function exonerates him of any imputation of deception. For Castiglione, dissimulation is "honest" because it indicates a willingness to use artifice to create a truer, more sociable nature, better than nature itself. Like rhetoric and painting, the arts of the court enrich reality. Honest dissimulation permits the collective invention of a social fiction, the court, where life is incomparable because it is based on a set of freely chosen, freely accepted conventions.

The third and final model is political. In *The Courtier* the prince is symbolically absent. The courtiers assume responsibility for defining themselves. The suggestion is that the relation of courtiers to prince is one not of dependence but of reciprocity. Of course the court exists only because some kind of power exists. But the court civilizes that power and mediates between the source of sovereignty and the invention of social forms. The heir to political authority recognizes the recipients of the gift of grace. They in turn recognize one another and demand to be recognized outside their circle. One can therefore speak of a curial contract in the same sense in which one speaks of a social contract. This construct is of course a fiction that serves the courtiers' interests by legitimating their status and function as well as the rules that bind them. It is not, however, mere ideological window dressing intended to mask something real. Renaissance Italy, whose waning Castiglione witnessed with intense nostalgia, was an archipelago of courts among which men could choose (as Castiglione himself had done). Anyone dissatisfied with what he received from his prince in the way of esteem, position, or rewards could always try his luck elsewhere. The relation of courtier to prince was certainly not egalitarian (the word would have made little sense in Renaissance culture) but was at least reciprocal.

A hundred and fifty years later Castiglione's treatise was still read, and still consulted as an encyclopedia of court culture, even in France, although at the price of adaptations that were in some cases outright distortions. But the book's themes and values were now interpreted in a radically different social and political context. The court of Louis XIV was unique, and the centrality of the monarchical apparatus meant that courtiers had nowhere else to turn. One had to be accepted and recognized at court; there was no other place to succeed. Anyone too gauche or without sufficient resources (in every sense of the word) or unable to win the king's favor sufficiently to make his mark at court had no alternative but to withdraw from the scene, and such withdrawal was often seen as a form of exile. Anyone whom the king could no longer bear to see, or chose not to see, ceased to exist for himself as well as for everyone else. Saint-Simon bluntly recognized this when, disappointed at not being named brigadier, he decided to quit the service, thereby incurring the king's wrath: "He no longer spoke to me; his glance no longer fell on me except by accident." The best one could do was to try to survive while awaiting a turn in one's fortunes; failing that, there was no choice but to accept that one had become a cipher.

The function of appearance thus changed. It was no longer an ingredient in the joint creation of a social scene but rather a way of demonstrating conformity with the requirements of one's place. Etiquette defined the rules of sociability and, at a deeper level, a kind of behavior modification. Conformity was inescapable, all the more so since the king, as we have seen, was the first to conform and the most exacting in his compliance with the rules. Even as the court was undergoing rapid institutionalization, the ideal to which it aspired was that of a mechanism so perfectly adjusted that it could run on its own.

But that was not all. Because the court became the theater of all ambitions, and success was impossible outside it, controlling appearances had important strategic implications. The role that one played in public—the only role that mattered—was conceived with an eye to the social benefits it might bring. The courtier was always calculating and plotting. It is no accident that gaming metaphors are so common in the writings of court observers. Mme de Sévigné, who described Dangeau as "a naturally algebraic mind, full of the art of combinations," instinctively used a chess metaphor in writing of her friend Pomponne's sudden disgrace in 1679: "It was a sudden checkmate, which came when it seemed one's position could not have been better, with all one's pieces in place." Other writers preferred images from fencing or warfare. But chess, the royal game, with all its rigorous complexity, was best for capturing the implacable will to slay and win that was an essential part of the courtier's equipment. The marquise, who set herself the goal of learning chess, drew an important lesson from the game: "I see no better way of humbling one's pride. It [chess] makes one aware of the mind's wretchedness and limitations." Competing for prestige in the presence of power was a harsh discipline. La Bruyère, more moralist than sociologist, put it this way: "Court life is a sad, serious game."

FIGURE 3.11. Recreation was disciplined and repetitive, and attitudes were standardized. In both of these depictions of courtly pleasures, the king sets an example of perfect deportment. Here, in the Third Apartment, Louis XIV plays billiards with gentlemen of the court; engraving by Trouvain, 1694–1698.

To play this game, therefore, one had to prepare. The first rule was secrecy: "A man who knows the court is master of his every gesture and glance; he is deep, impenetrable." The second was dissimulation: not the honest self-fashioning recommended by Castiglione but the art of deception. The mask was the great weapon of intrigue because it allowed one to choose where and when to strike. It could also be used to fend off an attack or to buy time for the next engagement. Even Saint-Simon, that paragon of virtue and defender of the most venerable courtly values, had to accept this when he learned what he least wanted to hear, the news of Louis's imperious legitimation of his bastard son the Duc du Maine, in 1714. Saint-Simon encountered the duke at Marly and was forced, against everything he believed in, to offer his congratulations. "This indispensable falsehood cost me so prodigiously that I was in constant fear that my face, my voice, and my entire bearing would betray me. It is impossible to express the battle that rages in the depths of an upright, natural, honest soul, which has never been able to go masked even amid the perils of the world's most dangerous court, even about trifles, and which has paid dearly for

FIGURE 3.12. *A Ball at the Petit Parc of Versailles, July 18, 1668;* engraving by Le Pautre, 1678.

it many times without ever having drawn the lesson from its exigencies." But war has its reasons, which virtue knows not of.

The third rule was action. As the influence of *The Courtier* waned, a new reference began to take its place. The Jesuit Baltasar Gracián's anthology of maxims, *El oráculo manual y arte de prudencia,* originally published in Huesca in 1647, was translated from the Spanish by Amelot de La Houssaie in 1684 and given a French title, *L'Homme de cour.* A work of the darkest pessimism, Gracián's book was a treatise on social warfare that bluntly taught its readers how to win by dissimulating, deceiving, and striking hard. Its central value was "the art of self-containment," self-control and the suppression of passion.

The shrewd man knew how to protect himself against others, for he lived in a world of potential enemies. "The adroit man employs the stratagems of intention. He never does what he exhibits a desire to do. He aims at a goal but only to deceive those who may be watching. He tosses out a proposition and then does something no one thought of. . . . And then, when his artifice is known, he refines his dissimulation by using the truth itself to deceive. He changes his game and his weapons in order to change his ruse." The entire text is an apology for winning by any means necessary. Originally, the *Oráculo* was written for a broad, ill-defined public of ambitious men anxious to succeed in society, and in that form it appears not to have made much of a mark. It was only after the French translation appeared with its new title that the work found its true audience, not only in France but throughout Europe in the late seventeenth and eighteenth centuries. This history reveals the book's true nature. It was at court that naked violence hidden beneath a composed exterior found its most obvious use. Gracián's pugnacious language caught on only because relations among courtiers were so tense, and given the unknowability of royal favor, the stakes were so high.

The Exception and the Rule

13. Voltaire was of course the inventor of *The Century of Louis XIV*, of which he bequeathed to French memory a canonical version in the book that bears that title, a book that is harmoniously composed, reasonable, and carefully argued. Published in the middle of the eighteenth century, Voltaire's history is a dual portrait of the Great Century alongside the Great King, but its argument is in fact that without the latter the former never would have come to pass. Louis is portrayed as a civilizing hero, whose stature, initiative, and political genius engendered a unique moment in the history of nations and cultures: he is the "master" who conceived "all these broad views with the firm intention of fulfilling them." In that process the court played an important role. It was the place where the grandeur of the age fully revealed itself as well as the instrument that made such grandeur possible, "drawing all the handsomest, shapeliest men and women." Under Louis and alongside him, the court embodied the perfection of classical balance: "Between him and his court there was a constant commerce of all that majesty possessed of grace, without a hint of degradation, and of all that the eagerness to serve and to please could yield of refinement, but without a hint of baseness."

Voltaire polished this view of the court and left it to posterity, yet he was not the first to conceive it. Panegyrics to the king and court were common during the reign of Louis XIV, and their method was more assertive or imperious than argumentative. Countless variations on the theme found their way into the Apollonian mythology of the period 1660–1690. The god to whose status the king was elevated was the one whose light gave "objects their shape and color" (Benserade) and revealed the created world to itself. Although the solar theme did not originate with Louis XIV, under him it became an insistent refrain of royal propaganda, which the king's military exploits, amorous adventures, and good works ultimately served only to substantiate. Everything could be traced back to him, to his decisions and actions. He was responsible for everything. And he concerned himself with every detail, if Félibien's account of the great celebrations of 1668 is to be believed: "When he wanted to give a collation, supper, ball, or fireworks display, he cast about for the people most capable of arranging things properly. He himself pointed out to them the spots whose natural beauty was most apt to enhance the effects of their decoration." And not only was Louis an architect and scenarist, he was also an actor, at least in the early years of the reign, and always played himself, no matter what the role. In 1670 he acted for the last time, in *Les Amants magnifiques,* a sprawling, complex spectacle of which Molière claimed to be only the scribe, obedient to the king's will: "The king, who wants all his undertakings to be extraordinary, proposed to distract his court with an entertainment encompassing everything the theater had to offer. To encompass this vast idea, His Majesty chose as subject two rival princes who, while awaiting the celebration of the Pythian Games in the rural Valley of Tempe, vie with each other in regaling a young princess and her mother with all the gallantries they can think of."

But it was the creation of Versailles (even before the court finally established itself there on a permanent basis in 1682) that best illustrated the king's civilizing genius. To contemporaries there was nothing attractive about the site. It was judged to be unpromising, inconvenient, and insalubrious, and if a new chateau were built there, the work would never end. Mme de Sévigné repeated the jest that the palace was an "unworthy favorite," and Saint-Simon found it "sad," "barren," and "in such bad taste." Yet even these doubts contributed in their own way to making a hero of the builder-king. He took a shapeless, abominable natural setting and turned it into a perfect work of art, gathering there everything that could possibly attest to the triumph of culture: "There you will see all that the world has ever had to offer in the way of beauty and surprise. Admire the skill, the knowledge, the art, and the delicacy of the workers. Admire the grandeur, sumptuousness, magnificence, and generosity of the prince. And admit that Versailles outshines all the enchanted palaces of history and myth." Yet this collective creation was the work of one man, who conceived it and willed it into being.

More than that, he caused it to exist. The king became a demiurge, whose word, like the word of God in Genesis, caused things to exist and subjected nature to a will that dominated and completed it. Charles Perrault was explicit: "No sooner had the prince who gave it being said 'Let there be a palace' than an admirable palace rose from the earth. . . . The same prince willed that there should be a long road lined with trees with tops taller than the trees in the nearby forests. At once that road was built, and the work of one day equalled two or three centuries of the work of nature." Here, the striking rhetorical concision paints an image of a king capable of overcoming every constraint, including that of time itself. The more boundless his creation seems, the more effectively it demonstrates his limitless power. For Louis it was no longer enough to be a friend of the arts, a patron and protector like so many others before him: he had to fashion the world to his own liking. Witness the insistent cosmological symbolism surrounding the palace and, even more perhaps, other undertakings valuable primarily for their gigantic proportions. Take, for instance, the Eure Canal, designed in 1680, whose construction, after immense difficulties, was finally halted by financial difficulties stemming from the War of the League of Augsburg: its only purpose, after all, was to supply water for the fountains of Versailles and Marly, but it symbolized a great deal more, and those who saw the failure as a punishment of the king's hubris showed that they understood what was really at stake.

The *grands travaux* thus became proof of power, inaugurating a political tradition that continues to this day. Great public works are important signs, symbols of an era. The more arbitrary and gratuitous they are, the better they express the potential power of the sovereign. From Versailles to the Grande Arche de la Défense (constructed under President Mitterrand), they partake of the same will to change the world (metonymically at any rate). France is peculiar among nations in that major cultural projects are more often than not imputed to the prince rather than to their actual author: the architects of the Centre Culturel at Beaubourg are forgotten in favor of Georges Pompidou, the former president for whom the center is named, just as Pei and Spreckelsen are forgotten in favor of François Mitterrand. None of the Sun King's successors went as far as he, however, for Louis even tried to dictate how his creations should be received and admired: witness the text he wrote, "How to Show the Gardens of Versailles" in March 1705. And in the celebrations he so carefully staged early in his reign, he suggested that the court was just as much his handiwork as the palace that housed it.

14. The "court atmosphere" was therefore beyond comparison. It emanated directly from the king's glory, which it magnified, because it was the product of a socialization ordered by the sovereign. Memoirists frequently noted Louis's interest in the number and quality of his courtiers as well as their rank and occupations, and we have already discussed at length the strategic considerations that accounted for this interest. Yet the court had a value in itself, beyond its usefulness in the manipulation of others. Saint-Simon, always quick to denounce the "politics of despotism," was lucid enough to see this. Among his recommendations to the future regent, the Duc d'Orléans, when they spoke in anticipation of the king's death in the summer of 1715, was his advice to maintain the court: "I told him that, having so often passed the bounds of discretion in our detailed conversations about the king, we must nevertheless remember that we also agreed about one of the most useful aspects of his greatness, which his successor surely ought to be induced to imitate; and I expressed my passionate hope that his successor would wish, in this respect, to make himself in the king's image, emulating his unwavering dignity and steadfast public discipline." Saint-Simon, the outspoken critic of Versailles, became its ardent champion, opposing the plan to move the court back to Paris and invoking the very arguments

FIGUFE 3.13. The creation of the world: the king and his works. *Les Ouvrages magnifiques du roy Louis le Grand;* allegorical engraving, 1689.

that had probably weighed in favor of the definitive move to Versailles in 1682: the visibility that the court achieved by concentrating a large number of people in one place, the social and political distance that geographical remoteness symbolized, and the affirmation of the court as a society whose rules and customs were totally different from those of ordinary society.

The court atmosphere was easier to recognize than to define. It reflected the quality of individual courtiers as well as the superiority of a certain form of sociability. Selection and emulation were thus essential ingredients. The two went hand in hand. Learning how to behave at court was by its very nature a noble activity. And the courtier confirmed his distinctive place in society by agreeing to conform, as befitted his station, to the ideal defined by the king. A whole series of practices—conversation, dance, horsemanship, gaming, bodily techniques, customs of speech—revealed how well a given individual had adapted his behavior to the rules of the courtly art. Those rules could be explicitly stated and even taught, as a whole literature of treatises of various kinds demonstrated in the seventeenth century. But was learning them enough to make a courtier? Perhaps not, because the texts, which prescribed gestures, attitudes, and ways of presenting oneself in society, always ended by promising the diligent reader that by observing the forms of courtly civility he might hope to be rewarded by a change of nature. Only after the lesson was transformed into a gift of nature could the would-be courtier's true career begin.

Paradoxically, the values at issue here were to a large extent inherited from social experiences and institutions that developed on the fringes of the court or even in opposition to it. It was outside the king's entourage, deemed too large, too indiscriminate, and too vulgar, that the courtly ideal of the Italian Renaissance was preserved and cultivated, in aristocratic salons of which the Hôtel de Rambouillet is the most famous example. Seventeenth-century salons were private microsocieties governed and controlled by women. Esteem determined who was invited to join; status had little to do with it. Members, once accepted, recognized no hierarchy other than that of admiration. Like the characters in *Il Cortegiano,* they were preoccupied mainly with endless discussions of what defined the group and made it such excellent company. Conversation, correspondence, literary writing, and reading thus became parlor games whose assiduous practice helped to define and refine the requirements of a higher sociability. Love was the great thing, so great that it was a social duty. As at the court of Paphos, described by Mlle de Scudéry in *Le Grand Cyrus,* love here "is not a simple passion as it is everywhere else but a necessary and mannerly one: the men must all be in love, and the women must all be loved." The salons thus revived one of the oldest courtly traditions, dating back to the Middle Ages, according to which women play a fundamental civilizing role. As in an improvised play, each member of the company constructed a character for himself or herself, while the group as a whole devised situations to test the mettle of these characters in confrontations to be judged by all. Could a person stop loving? Could a person decide that he or she would stop loving in the future? What sort of love was best? Were all lies equally reprehensible? Which of love's sorrows was the greatest? To these questions and a hundred others like them there were no fixed answers, and in any case fixed answers would have been less interesting than the collective debate that the questions provoked and encouraged. Indeed, one of the group's core values was not to justify its answers or explain its rules. What made things right could not be articulated, much less prescribed. What was esteem or gallantry or politeness or naturalness? Around such themes one could embroider an endless casuistry, but in the end the conclusion was always that conclusions were impossible. Ultimately, what justified the complicity of the chosen and their place outside the common run of humankind was a *je ne sais quoi*.

At court, which supplanted the salons in the final third of the seventeenth century, the rules of the game could hardly be the same. Here, space was arranged according to a strict hierarchy, and social values were dictated from above. Situations were not left to collective improvisation but carefully regulated by etiquette and the sovereign's favor. Courtiers had no need to demonstrate the possibility of a form of sociability that was in any case imposed on them and could justify itself without them. They had no choice but to submit. Some—few in number—did so only against their will and adopted a tone of nostalgia: for the more open court of the Valois, which Mme de La Fayette evoked in *La Princesse de Clèves*, or the honorable court of Louis XIII, to which Saint-Simon looked back with dreams of a time before things had become all mixed up. Even fewer enjoyed the signal privilege of personal distinction: there were major historical figures such as Condé and Turenne, and there were families, like the Mortemarts, who for generation after generation were said to possess an elusive, hard-to-define legacy, a "spirit" or style or grace that set them apart from the rest. For most, however, there was no choice but to conform to the rules of the court. What they gave up as individuals was compensated for by their participation in the excellence of the group. They maintained their prestige, but at the price of being entirely subordinated to the one value that really mattered, the majesty of the king. Indeed, their prestige was even enhanced, because the court, as it was now redefined, stood as a model for everyone it excluded, a model more impossible than ever to match. Toward the end of the seventeenth century the Abbé de Bellegarde pointed this out to anyone who might have forgotten it: "People born into an obscure station spoil themselves by wishing to have commerce with the people of the court: instead of distinguishing themselves, they further reveal the baseness of their birth by lending themselves to invidious comparison."

Henceforth, as Saint-Simon succinctly observed, "in great things as in small, form implies substance." By form he meant the compulsory acceptance of an order

FIGURE 3.14. The atmosphere of the court was not only incomparable but also impenetrable: the king's court in 1665; engraving.

imposed rather than freely chosen. From now on the prestige of court society would be contained in that form. It was now enough to belong to the court to be, by law, different from everyone else. And yet the courtier's prestige was reduced to nothing more than the reflection of the firmament's single star.

15. The relation between court and culture was similarly recentered, although for a limited time. Was there really a court culture? The question is worth asking, because both before and after Louis XIV's reign the real vitality of cultural production and circulation was to be found in the city rather than the court and in private institutions rather than public ones. By contrast, between 1661 and 1715, everything could apparently be traced back to king and court, because the arts existed only to serve the great monarchical creation. Think, for instance, of the enlistment of artists and the development of institutional arrangements for tightly controlling their work (although to be sure this policy began to take shape before the beginning of Louis's

personal reign, under Mazarin and even Richelieu). Royal bonuses increasingly supplanted private patronage. The most deserving artists were appointed to official positions. Public academies took precedence over private ones to the point of replacing them altogether. Think, too, of the novel forms of recognition that the court afforded to those called there, whose status was profoundly altered by the experience. Carefully orchestrated royal patronage substantially transformed the conditions of artistic labor, bestowing through the major projects it sponsored a new legitimacy and important new resources.

Equally important was the new conviction that the court was the alpha and omega of all true cultural values. What earned the sovereign this privilege was once again his civilizing role. He was not only the inspirer and benefactor of the arts but the foremost and greatest of artists, as the always zealous Charles Perrault proclaimed in the dedicatory epistle he drafted for the Academy's dictionary when it was presented to the king in 1694: "You are, Sire, naturally and without artifice what we strive to become through labor and study: in all your discourses there prevails a sovereign reason, bolstered always by vigorous and precise expressions, which make you fully the master of every soul that listens to you and leaves them with no will but your own. And eloquence, to which we aspire through our late nights and which to you is a gift of Heaven, owes everything, does it not? to your heroic actions." A constant barrage of propaganda in image and text sustained the court in its belief that the reign of Louis le Grand—*le Grand Siècle*, as people began to call it in the 1670s—marked the beginning of a moment in history unlike any other. The court was the designated audience for the king's exploits and marvels, and it participated in the spectacle of royal glory. It spent its days among the creations of the prince's will and could of course be thought of as one of them. It was at court that the agenda was set and at court that the results were admired, so that the judgment of the court took on a new importance.

That judgment was based not on any competence but rather on shared experience. What formed the taste of the court was not knowledge but a way of being and living in society.

"Though their taste is very good, most of them know very little, and they set themselves up as perfect connoisseurs in all things only because they always know the right words and in their presence everyone else is silent out of respect." Saint-Réal's words of course suggest a strategy based on the privileges of rank, but he also points to two other factors that were just as important as social prestige. First, a conception of culture that defined itself in opposition to scholars and men of letters, and second, a mastery of the means of expression. In both cases taste was defined as a quintessentially social art. Against the jargon of the learned, the court insisted on the appreciation of the connoisseur, a generalist by nature. Until Louis's favor forced the court to accept her, Mme de Maintenon was for a long time suspected of belonging to "societies of idle people whose sole occupation is to savor their emotions and judge works of the spirit." Racine and Boileau, professional writers who were named royal historiographers in 1676, worked hard to gain acceptance, yet they were branded "poets," "philosophers," and "pedants" whose dubious talents failed to make up for their foolishness and naïveté. They were "foreigners," and made to feel it. The culture of the court had no value in itself but only as a means of social circulation. Hence it was to be displayed without ostentation, with grace and nonchalance that betrayed no effort. The mentors of the latter part of the century, especially Bellegarde and Callières, repeatedly contrasted the mediocrity of professional scholars, "who do not study society . . . and consult only their books," with the taste of "polished gentlemen" who refuse "to bury themselves among words to learn to converse with the living." The cultural model established at the time was based on detachment and the absolute priority of form. Since the goal was to create a distinctive form of sociability, the manner in which this was done outweighed every other consideration. Hence the importance of courtly language, which was defined not by rules but by shared usage: it was a language purged of old, impolite, technical, and vulgar words (for Bouhours, "fine language is like pure, clear water that has no taste") and regulated by exchange (particularly among women) and above all by conversation. It was a civil language, whose "sweetness" expressed a privileged relational mode.

Nevertheless, the court's privilege was not as obvious as it seemed. In any case it was provisional: although in La Bruyère's day it was still possible to persuade oneself that "the city apes the court," by the time of the Regency and for the remainder of the eighteenth century the city once again became the center of cultural activity. The court's primacy was often proclaimed and affirmed, yet it was less assured than it might seem. Erich Auerbach was among the first to show that the two terms "court" and "city," which were and still are automatically opposed, were used conjointly from the mid-seventeenth century on to refer to the cultivated public in general *(la cour et la ville)*. Vaugelas foresaw this unification of the cultivated as early as 1647, when he defined linguistic correctness *(le bon usage)* in the preface to his *Remarques sur la langue française*: "This term refers to the manner in which the better part of the court speaks, in conformity with the way in which the better authors of the age write. When I say the court, I include women as well as men, and various people in the city in which the Prince resides, who, through communication with the gentlemen of the court, partake of its politeness." The conditions surrounding cultural activity were transformed in the following decades, and the court did distance itself from the capital, initially in a geographic sense. Yet the compromise between the two poles was not seriously challenged. It exhibited itself in the role of a new agency: the public. This was not a sign of any effacement of social hierarchies. Rather, it reflected the common acceptance of a new definition of culture as a form of commerce between *honnêtes gens,* respectable people. The reception of the classical theater, of its values and conventions, exemplifies the triumph of this formula, as Molière himself pointed out as early as 1663 in the *Critique de l'École des femmes.*

But if the distinction between the court and the city tended to blur in this way, wherein did the exceptional status of the court scene lie and how was it to be justified? In its most routine operation, the court could of course claim to embody a formal model applicable elsewhere. More to the point, the court had no reason to exist other than the presence at its center of the one person from whom all values emanated and around whom cultural circulation was both possible and necessary. In this as in every other realm, everything depended on the king's unquestioned credit. Charles Perrault made just this point in a comparison that leaves little room for doubt: "In France the only language that can be used in a serious work is pure French, or, to put it more clearly, the language of the court, because in a kingdom language is like currency: neither is valid unless stamped with the mark of the Prince." Once again, the privileges of the court were all guaranteed by the worth of the king.

A Republican Court?

16. We have dwelt at length on a relatively brief moment in the long history of the French court. The reason for devoting so much space to the court of Louis XIV is not that his reign was exceptional (and, I might add, exceptionally well-documented), but rather that in the memory of the court there is no comparable reference. The inexhaustible fund of anecdotes, situations, and *exempla* that it has left us is evidence of this. Nothing in this welter of stories is truly important, but almost everything makes sense as an instance of or at any rate an allusion to some peculiarity of France. Political and moral satires on the court and portraits of courtly attitudes predate the second half of the seventeenth century. Yet one turns as if by instinct to La Bruyère and Saint-Simon for examples that are then treated as definitive, timeless illustrations of a reality permanently etched into the history of France. This habit first took hold, moreover, in the court of Louis XIV itself. Saint-Simon, that indefatigable collector of information about "all things, great and small," knew that "this is all the food one has to live on at court, and without it one merely languishes." He was nevertheless convinced that these trivialities matter, that they were worth reporting and commenting on for the instruction of future generations.

Memories of the court have thus been passed down to us through seemingly endless repetition. The history of the court did not end in 1715 or even with the fall of the absolute monarchy. Between the First and Second Empires there was no shortage of attempts to revive the court or make it over in a new image, imposing under

Napoleon and during the Restoration, more pragmatic under Louis-Philippe and Napoleon III. These efforts, though sporadic, cannot be ignored, yet we tend to look upon them as inopportune or illegitimate experiments. When people think of the court, they generally pass over these episodes in silence or dismiss them as parodies. For the genuine article we generally look to the heart of the Ancien Régime, not to crude nineteenth-century bourgeois revivals. The old courtly values were incompatible with the social arrangements and representations of the postrevolutionary world and survived only as vestiges of a bygone era. The *hôtel* of the Guermantes, that creation of Marcel Proust's imagination, is one of the few places in which one can still glimpse, as social epiphenomena destined for oblivion, choices and attitudes suggestive of a society with no reason to exist except as a reminder of things past. Fossil forms become paradoxical when their only purpose is to indicate a difference: "Owing to a vestige left over from the time of the courts, something called social polish, which was anything but superficial because, owing to a strange inversion of outside and inside, what was on the surface became essential and profound, the Duke and Duchess of Guermantes considered it a duty more essential than those, fairly often neglected by at least one of them, of charity, chastity, pity, and justice, rarely to speak of the Princess of Parma in other than the third person." No one knew or cared exactly how or when such forms originated. They mattered only because they attested to the residual presence of a model of social relations whose significance and justification were unknown to those who stood in belated witness to them. The "spirit" of the court had been held up as an example in its time of splendor. Now it was no more than a puzzling curiosity that survived only with difficulty.

Hence there was a profound hiatus between courtly experience and the democratic societies it continued to fascinate. It is therefore quite surprising to discover how emphatically that experience is still invoked in France in the second half of the twentieth century. What we find, however, is not the tyranny of a majority worshipful of its own virtues and legitimacy, which Tocqueville prophesied in a celebrated passage of *Democracy in America* and thought would lead to a generalization of the courtly spirit "brought within reach of the multitude." Rather, we see a resurgence of attitudes and forms of behavior that seem reminiscent of the classical court. As I said at the beginning of this essay, under the Fifth Republic the French have been remarkably suspicious of what they take to be monarchical tendencies of one sort or another accompanied by a revival of courtly habits.

Readers of these pages may have felt oddly at home in the alien world of the court. The manners of those we have elected to govern us in some cases remind us of the last of the absolute monarchs, even though the world around them has changed utterly. Out of facts and rumors we compose a portrait reminiscent of the work of Saint-Simon (and at times inspired by it). To be sure, the Republic needs

FIGURE 3.15. The legacy of the court includes not only the Guermantes salon in Proust but also the sumptuous kitsch of *Si Versailles m'était conté,* a film conceived, written, and produced by Sacha Guitry, who also played the starring role (1955).

public rituals and even an official protocol (which was recently revised). Yet it is in the invention of new forms, the presentation of the prince, and the manipulation of favor and disfavor—in everything that has to do, in other words, with the socialization of power—that we are most immediately and powerfully reminded, at times to the point of caricature, of the ways of the ancient court.

Among the similarities, those connected with presidential authority are, not surprisingly, the most obvious. The president (not only the present incumbent [François Mitterrand] but his predecessors as well) shrewdly apportions his activity between obligatory political display and confidential or secretive intervention. He is seen often and everywhere, but everyone knows that except for official routine and in brief, dramatized periods of political life he is to be sought not in his apparitions or appearances but elsewhere. A strict, self-imposed economy regulates the manipulation of the presidential image. The chief executive's words are measured, and on important matters they are rare. Most of what he allegedly says is unverifiable, for it is transmitted only through a series of intermediaries and therefore almost impossible to authenticate. These screens give his words power even more awesome than they would otherwise command because their source is normally inaccessible. Hence the president's utterances require commentary, which enhances their effectiveness yet if necessary can always be contradicted. Glosses abound, but the last word is always the president's.

The management of interpersonal relations in the prince's entourage is a second area in which the courtly model is applicable to the Republic. The president chooses his collaborators and confidential advisors as he sees fit, and there is of course nothing unusual about that. But he uses that freedom in a demonstrative way, not least in the discretion with which most of his choices are made. Confounding the commentators, those choices are not governed by any sociological laws or even by politics in any ordinary sense. They are based on competence, to be sure (although this is generally a secondary consideration), loyalty (at times surprising), and even whims. Sometimes they are inexplicable. All in all, they obey no laws because they are primarily the reflection of a personal choice. The members of the court are the president's men, and they know it because it is the president who makes or breaks them. Hence it is no surprise that the palace chronicle is full of both boasts of favor and complaints of ingratitude. The president's men derive their power from their master alone. The exaggerated role of the president in the institutions of the Fifth Republic no doubt justifies the constant intervention from the top in all areas of political life. Again, however, what matters is not the institutional logic so much as the style that seems to be an inextricable part of its operation. A sometime observer of the presidency, remote (as we all are) from the center of power, reportedly collected a hundred anecdotes all conveying one version or another of the same story: the humblest of the prince's advisors, the last person one would expect to invoke his authority, obtains the desired decision by opportunely pointing out that "the president thinks such-and-such," without issuing an official presidential order of any kind. Are most of these anecdotes made up? I have no way of knowing, but in the end what difference does it make? If people believe them, they become true in the sense that they establish a plausible image of how politics works. If people think things work this way, in a certain sense they actually do. *Exempla* of this kind create a picture of a certain mode of authority, of its sources and exercise.

Of course not all courtiers are created equal. The president, like the king before him, spends his time manipulating and arbitrating among rival ambitions. Everyone wants something: support, advantage, position. But they are primarily interested in what matters most, namely, proximity to the prince, even at the expense of a more visible success that would take them away from the center of power. There may be a significant disparity between the visible hierarchy of governmental posts and the ranking determined by favor, esteem, and confidence. The former is objective and public, whereas the later is quasi-private and dependent on discreet signs, whose value comes entirely from their being all but imperceptible and, by definition, pre-

FIGURE 3.16. The Republic in majesty: Charles de Gaulle, 1968.

carious. As a result they demand the most scrupulous attention: the audiences the president grants, the memos he deems worthy of personal comment, the informal conversations he has, and the readiness he displays to accord this or that individual a degree of personal intimacy are signs that are constantly being totted up, probably to no avail. Just like Louis XIV's visits to Marly, François Mitterrand's annual trip to Burgundy to climb the mountain at Solutré provides an opportunity for the president to exercise a subtle blend of personal favoritism and high politics. The excursion has no official significance whatsoever, but that does not mean the stakes are not high.

What accounts for these continuities, which make the memory of the court such a vital presence today? Surely this way of interpreting things has something to do with the fact that the Fifth Republic is a highly presidential regime. But that cannot be the whole explanation, because then one would expect to find equivalents in even more highly presidential regimes such as the government of the United States, and that is not the case. Institutional practice has of course heightened some of the original features of the French system, so that the formal prerogatives reserved to the president under the constitution tell only part of the story. Power in France is extremely concentrated and individualized, and the road to achieving that power is narrow. In addition, the role of the parliament has been marginalized. Taken together, these two factors have transformed the mechanics of ambition. The political parties are nowadays little more than proving grounds for those who aspire to high office. People believe that power effectively exists in one place only, and therefore everything tends to converge toward the person who has that power. His regard, his choices, his declared or, more commonly, presumed favor rule the political world. Under constant surveillance from this lofty vantage, ambitious politicians, for reasons of logic as well as self-interest, devote their energies to cutting the proper figure. Of course this is only the barest sketch of how the system works. There is no need to interpret the hypertrophy of the role of the president and the frequency of his intervention as signs of a thirst for limitless power or of the supreme arrogance of the prince. It suggests, rather, a widely felt need for arbitration, a need that the head of state must fill because the strictly hierarchical and centralized configuration of political space means that everything leads back to him. The issue is not so much his will as the system of reciprocal relations under which the leading political players operate, a system that also dictates the role of the president and the conditions under which he works. It would of course be absurd to compare the absolute monarchy directly to the presidential republic. Yet if my hypothesis makes sense, there is clearly a sort of functional homology between the two. There may exist, episodically at any rate, a distinctive form of power that does not depend exclusively or even primarily on a monopoly of legal prerogatives but rather on the possibility of a single individual's manipulating the tensions that exist among other participants in the system. This of course brings us back to Elias's most powerful thesis, according to which the existence of court society is linked to a distinctive pattern of competing forces. One major difference must be noted, however: if the social system underlying the court of Louis XIV encompassed all the elites of the society of that time and perhaps even the whole of society, it seems clear that whatever courtly tendencies may exist in the Fifth Republic are limited to *la société politique*, that is, to officialdom, the press, and others in the presidential orbit

FIGURE 3.17. President François Mitterrand, January 1988.

I shall venture one further suggestion. The long persistence of the court as a point of reference may well have to do with another distinctive feature of French culture and politics: the emphasis on executive power and, more particularly, on representations of that power. France is a country in which the head of state is appreciated as such, independent of (and often more than) what he does. The test of his mettle is his demonstrated capacity in the realm of pure power. He is expected to undertake, and to succeed in, maneuvers that connoisseurs will appreciate. Even when the head of state is democratically elected on a specific political platform, his talent is judged in terms of his ability to invent strategies, to shroud himself in secrecy, and to create the conditions for surprise attack. This language seems strangely Machiavellian, yet it lingers on in a society that for two hundred years has wanted to think only in terms of transparency while valuing nothing so much as mystery in what politicians do; a society that is obessed with legitimacy in government yet is pleased to imagine governing as the exercise of absolute power independent of any reference other than itself. This may explain a fact that many commentators have noted: that the reinforcement of presidential power has resulted in a devaluation of the political, since the very logic of that power causes it to push the maxims of politics to the point of absurdity.

Court society does not and did not develop from such an extreme conception of sovereign power. But in its French version, at least, the two are inseparable. The court offers a visible manifestation of power, a stage on which it can impose its image and work its effects by assigning roles to each individual. It is therefore a pointless but also a deadly serious game: the representation of a representation of power.

PART II

BOOKS

A pedagogical beehive: the Fouillée family.
FIGURE 4.0. (Top left) Augustine Fouillée, alias G. Bruno.
FIGURE 4.1. (Top right) Alfred Fouillée, her second husband.
FIGURE 4.2. (Bottom) Jean-Marie Guyau, Mme Fouillée's son by her first husband.

CHAPTER IV

Le Tour de la France par deux enfants: The Little Red Book of the Republic

Jacques and Mona Ozouf

A friend of ours, a farmer from the Perche, was amazed when he saw the book on our desk. Was it really still available? he asked. So we bought him a copy, and now there is at least one book in his house, a reminder of a childhood that, despite compulsory schooling, was not particularly studious. He will use our gift not to read but to contemplate: for him, it is a book with memories pressed between its pages, a crystal ball filled with dark pine forests, busy ports, aqueducts, and sewing machines, the Orléanais and the Camargue, dusty highways, cool meadows, the sounds of Paris, and above all two children on a lengthy hike. In fact, just about all that our neighbor, M. Mortier, remembers of his irregular and not particularly happy school days, is what he refers to as "André and Julien's trip."

French readers would hardly need reminding that André and Julien are two orphans from Lorraine who, in the fall of 1871, secretly crossed the German border into France and set out, through fire, sickness, and storm, in search of an uncle and a mother. The uncle's last name is the same as their father's; and the mother, whose name their father whispered as he lay dying, his final word, was France. The story of the two boys was recounted in 1877 in *Le Tour de la France par deux enfants,* "a reader for the *cours moyen* [elementary school], with more than two hundred instructive illustrations on various topics, by G. Bruno," a book that in many rural homes (such as Pierre-Jakez Hélias's in Pouldreuzic) came to rival that other guidebook—also the sole companion of many a child—the *Lives of the Saints.* Bruno's secular saints were extraordinarily fortunate, and we can now, thanks to the work of Aimé Dupuy, measure their success.[1] The first wave, which lasted from 1877 to 1887, flooded France with three million copies. Then came a period of relative calm, which saw an average 200,000 copies published each year and lasted through the turn of the century. By 1901 some 6 million copies had been printed, and by 1976 the total had reached 8.5 million. It is hard to estimate the total number of readers, which is surely many times greater. For this was the book most frequently borrowed from school libraries, the book that allowed the teacher to give her sewing lesson in relative quiet—of all French literature, the only book whose title many people who never owned it could readily cite.

Much has already been written about the reasons for this success.[2] *Le Tour de la France*, which portrays two "grownup" children burdened with real tasks and exposed to real dangers, accomplished the feat of pleasing adults as much as children.[3] It was studied in parochial as well as public schools and was attacked from the left[4] as readily as from the right.[5] It was a mix of disparate styles and genres, at once a *Bildungsroman*, a treatise on the good life, and a manual filled with information about filling out bureaucratic forms, tending cattle, and coping with the post office. It was a textbook for all subjects, and the accompanying teacher's handbook, which furnished a barrage of questions to go with each chapter, contributed to the work's encyclopedic ambitions: by asking the proper questions, teachers could use the *Tour de la France* as a geography text, an ethics handbook, a primer in the natural sciences, or a basic introduction to French law, with which every citizen was supposed to be familiar.

What is more, *Le Tour de la France* seemed only to reveal what was self-evident, to be a shining example of the authorless work, for its author was so self-effacing that he simply vanished into his work. Or, rather, *she* vanished into *her* work: the success of *Le Tour* would not have been possible without the skill of Mme Fouillée, the woman who for so long concealed her identity behind the pen name and colors of "G. Bruno." One has only to compare her work with the book—also a reader—that her son Jean-Marie Guyau wrote two years earlier to gauge both the similarity of inspiration (about which we shall have more to say later on) and the difference that true talent makes.[6] Mme Fouillée's stroke of genius was to take her son's moral homilies and combine them into a seamless work of fiction, collecting their scattered lessons and drawing in the reader anxious to know how things turn out. She also had the knack of making readers identify with her characters: as "perfect"[7] as her heroes are, they are no strangers to fear, bluster, or foolhardiness. Children's feelings are rendered with something of the psychological realism of William James. In *Le Tour de la France* characters blush and feel shame; their hearts hang heavy in their breasts; they "puff up" with pride; they sigh heavily when sad, they clap their hands and jump for joy. As reasonable as André and Julien are, they are still creatures of emotion. They seem to be children out for a stroll, following a roundabout path, so that their journey, whose purpose is nothing less than to save their lives, nevertheless has something of the festive air of two children playing hooky. Mme Fouillée excels at alternating between necessity and chance, the emo tional and the intellectual. Why is little Julien so interested in fortresses? Because for him the siege of Phalsbourg was the primal scene. Why is André so interested in precision instruments? Because he is an apprentice locksmith by trade. These basic interests afford Mme Fouillée ample opportunity to indulge in didactic exercises, but that duty out of the way, she eagerly returns to the emotional key: even the most austere lessons are frequently interrupted by Julien's yelps of joy. Pedagogy out of the way, the story enthusiastically resumes. And Mme Fouillée was a felicitous writer as well as a professional: her demanding ear was loath to accept the changes demanded by the new public school curriculum.[8] She tried as far as possible to keep her paragraphs intact, replacing deleted passages with others having the same number of syllables or similar phrasing.

The teacher's handbook suggests the following question for the end of the book: "Will you forget the story you have just read?"[9] The question has become rhetorical: we now know that the answer was no. The book carved out a place for itself in France's collective memory, and there it remains, for the publication by Belin of a sumptuous centennial edition has reawakened dormant images and tied the book to a new kind of memory, a memory tinged with the emotional colors of a past that has become a subject for ethnography rather than history. But the question also revealed the scope of the author's ambition: to write a book that would spark memories. Not simply to draw up an inventory of the way things were in France in the early days of the Third Republic. Not simply to remind readers of the glorious past of a country that, though shorn of part of its territory, remained a great nation. Not simply to tie up in a compact bundle the kinds of things about which French schoolchildren knew or dreamed. But to teach the importance of "never forgetting" itself: the education of André and Julien is complete only because they have not forgotten their tour of France, nor will they ever forget it (this is the epilogue's leitmotif). The book, even as it was being written, was thus explicitly intended to be a lesson in the "art of memory." But what memory, exactly? A memory of places or of times? The memory of a present already pregnant with the future or of a transcended present, already anachronistic and nostalgic? A partisan memory or a national memory? A memory of France in its entirety or only of the Republic? Such questions are an inevitable consequence of the work's ambiguity.

A French child today is likely to have seen something of France and of the world but unlikely to have much of an idea of geography. Could any of today's students locate the Confolentais, the gateway to the Naurouze, on a map? Having spent our childhoods staring at the maps of Vidal-Lablache, which, when attention flagged, could be depended on to stimulate dreamy fantasies of journeys along the blue lines marking the routes of canals or the black ones indicating railroads, we tend to think that yesterday's pupils knew everything about geography. Let us not underestimate their ignorance. Above all, let us not underestimate the degree to which André and Julien's extraordinary journey served as an escape for young readers, many of whom only rarely visited the nearest town and never went anywhere else except when summoned to military service.

André and Julien's journey began in early autumn ("in a thick September fog"), with the school year. It ended as the trees were once again turning green and summer vacation lay just in the offing. It took the boys from Phalsbourg to the hills of the Perche, in a circular, enveloping movement from periphery to center and east to west, following the classic route of *compagnons,* or journeymen, making their "tour of France."[10] As the children make use of every imaginable means of transportation (foot, buggy, barge, boat, railroad), over all kinds of roads and through all sorts of weather, *Le Tour de la France* is a physical exploration of space. The reader knows if the road is ascending or descending, if Pierrot's pace is slowing or accelerating, if a storm is threatening, or if the boys are shivering "at the very break of dawn."

There can be no doubt that the book represents an appropriation of French territory. At every step of the way André and Julien ask themselves "Where exactly are we?" And their companions, the schoolchildren of France, chime in along with them. To answer that question one had the map of France, ignorance of which had ostensibly led France into humiliation and misfortune.[11] Teachers were just now beginning to hang such maps on the walls of their classrooms. Mme Fouillée was not content simply to link her text to the map. Her genius was to turn an intellectual aid into a vital necessity. Studied, memorized, and ultimately related to the terrain itself (where the Sarre was no longer a line but a flash of liquid between "two rows of beech and willow"), the map allows the two boys to cross the border, taking advantage of the lapses of the forest patrol. To Tolstoy's complaint about geography lessons (why learn about different places when the coachman will always take you where you need to go?), Bruno's book responded that learning is living—indeed, that learning is survival.[12]

Mingling the lessons of life with the lessons learned from books is a good thing, because it means that those lessons will never be forgotten. Lived experience rectifies intellectual experience (Julien had learned that the Rhône was one of the most beautiful rivers in France but "hadn't imagined it that way") and gives it roots: "Tomorrow we will pass through Moulins, and after that you'll never forget it," Julien hears from M. Gertal, who will himself never forget the Cantal because he has "gone up" there. Julien is sure that when his adventure is over he will be first in his class, because he will have absorbed knowledge of "his" France through the soles of his shoes.

Since André and Julien cannot go everywhere, the author contrives to complete their appropriation of the territory and link their imagination to places they will not visit by arranging chance encounters with people and things: an image of Descartes occasions a visit to Touraine, while an earthenware dish serves as an excuse for an excursion to Limousin. This didactic device was amplified by the teacher's handbook, which at every mention of a new city mechanically recited the Guide-Joanne: "Vesoul, chief town of the Haute-Saône, 380 kilometers from Paris, fine promenade on the Cours, cavalry headquarters." But this secondary appropriation was less important than what the boys took from their own experience. What readers remembered was the territory that André and Julien actually passed through on foot or horseback. For even the journey by ship, which offered an opportunity to visit ports and describe coastlines seen in the distance, was far less effectively detailed than the trips on foot or under the rain-battered hood of their buggy. Despite the ordeals of the ocean voyage, *Le Tour de la France* is less compelling when the heroes travel by water rather than by land. It is the physical contact with the land that gives the journey its dynamic intensity. In this sense the book is something other than a tranquil survey of the territory in which each place is treated on a par with all the others.[13]

Indeed, the trip's charm depends on the diversity of the places visited, on their quiet exoticism. André and Julien encounter "thrifty, conscientious folks" in Auvergne, energetic inhabitants of the Dauphiné, and Corsicans quicker to seize their rifles than their plows. The boys themselves are as stalwart and solid as the trees of their native Vosges. They pass through northern France, to which nature has not been excessively kind, and southern France, which groans happily beneath an abundance of lemons. They eat lard omelettes in Lorraine and fish soup in Marseilles. And among the peasants of Provence, who speak an unintelligible language, they feel as disconcerted as if visiting a "farm in a foreign land."

For children who have fled a foreign country in search of the security of identity, however, the experience is a traumatic one. This accounts for the treatment of regional differences in *Le Tour de la France*. To begin with, the book strives to show that there is nothing really threatening in these differences and to accredit the idea that all of France is basically similar, an idea that Fouillée calls essential to the French temperament.[14] At a deeper level, it presents regional differences as gifts to the nation: local chauvinism prides itself on the boons that each regional temperament contributes to France in general, on the original contribution of each locality.[15] Thus in the end the project of drawing up an honor roll of the provinces has to be given up: little Julien, diligent pupil that he is, would have liked to complete it. Each province contributes its own distinctive color to the bouquet—such is the explicit metaphor used. Hence the temptation of separatism has waned: so says the teacher's handbook, always blunter than the text itself. Separatism was an option only "in the past." Nowadays there is but one France. Within that one France, opposing, hostile parties still maneuver (the teacher's handbook, quite "Ferryist" in its conception, always treats French divisions in political rather than ethnographic terms). One day, however, the parties will fade away, and all Frenchmen "will be united on the fundamental issues."

One reason why national unity can largely be taken for granted is that two of the principal activities featured in the book, learning and traveling, themselves helped to create it. Further progress in education promised to complete France's unification. When André and Julien find themselves isolated and confused by the Provençal dialect that surrounds them at the inn, they discover that they can speak with the children who return in the evening, for these children, at least, have been to school. The teacher's handbook dwells at length on this brief episode. It defines patois as "corrupt, popular dialect," catalogues the various French patois with gloomy severity, and bluntly asks how they can survive. Why should the bilingual "burden their memories" rather than learn "useful" things? And how "shameful" to speak only one language, if that language is not French! In other words, regional dialects are either frivolous or sinful. Not for much longer, however. Compulsory schooling will do away with them, as it will do away with Corsican combativeness and Savoyard poverty. Hence the ostensible differences between French regions were deceptive. In reality, the "backward" regions were like the involuntarily backward pupils one could find even in the best of classrooms, who with proper teaching could be brought "up to the mark."

Travel, moreover, was clearly another way of fostering unity. Traveling by highway, canal, and railroad, the two boys discover that beyond the boundaries of their native canton lay other regions that were neither mysterious nor savage—a discovery that according to Émile Guillaumin was still a novelty.[16] All the regions of France could be linked together: they traded not only their products but also their qualities.[17] Brittany might be far away, but the Breton cow was everywhere, and Besançon told all Frenchmen the time. As they walked, André and Julien proved to themselves that all France was cut from the same cloth, that all its people and places belonged together.

The geographical unification of France is completed by the joyful homecoming with which the book ends. In the text, departures are never lyrical, always wrenching. When Julien inadvertently lets slip a remark about how pleasant it would be to be able to travel "as if one had a private income," M. Gertal quickly corrects him, and the teacher's handbook echoes his reproach: "Is a life of perpetual travel as desirable as it may seem at first sight?" The response is unambiguous: the teacher is told to emphasize the pleasures of permanence in both family and professional life. Moreover, the epilogue to the 1906 edition associates the delights of home with the various people with whom the boys are sadly obliged to part company along the way: the Alsatians, the Normans, the Jurassians, and the Auvergne orphan. It also sums up what they have learned about hygiene, agriculture, diet, and home economics. "André and I haven't forgotten. We remember," Julien repeats. Memories of their year on the road have been transformed into rules for a settled existence.

Memories of places are paramount, memories of times secondary. To begin with, Mme Fouillée was always less precise about chronology than about topography. Date and season mattered less to her than place. She was also quite careless about the sequence of events and the chronology of French history. She preferred to recount history through the lives of famous men. Her biographies are like ornaments hung upon the national Christmas tree: they can be taken down as well as hung up, and their brightness is the only thing they have in common. Other memories are made to seem genuine by being associated with memories of place. It is well and good to know something about Vauban, but one really learns about him only by studying the vestiges he left behind: "What!" little Julien exclaims. "You mean it was Vauban who fortified both Phalsbourg, where I was born, and Besançon, whose walls I studied so carefully?" History not only illustrates the provinces but explains what makes them illustrious. The epic is pieced together from the physical evidence.

If the memory of *Le Tour de la France* is more topographic than historical, surely it is because Mme Fouillée, good teacher that she was, understood that collective memory depends more on places than on dates. More than that, however, the book, which, as Dominique Maingueneau has put it so well, is for the two boys a "journey of reintegration with the mother," is obsessed with security.[18] The children from the border region come to nestle in the lap of *la Patrie*, not far from the spires of Chartres, in *le Perche beauceron*, the most French of all regions according to Péguy. The security that geography affords them is not something for which they can turn to history, that black cauldron of conflict in which they have only recently seen their native Phalsbourg swallowed up. We understand why the book chooses to treat history only through exemplary lives, and why among the great it selects only those who delivered messages of reconciliation. The only conflicts that appear in the lives of great men (between worldliness and abnegation, for example) are regularly and triumphantly forgotten by a grateful posterity. The text extended the sweep of national memory back to Vercingetorix and forward to Pasteur, the hero of the epilogue.[19] It ignored kings and conquerors. It bestowed its affection primarily on two groups of great men: creative scientists and patriotic military leaders. The latter brought not war but boons to mankind: German peasants referred to Desaix as "the good general." When the author is forced to choose, her instincts are to make peace: among the great men of the eighteenth century she includes Montesquieu but eliminates Voltaire and Rousseau. The richest sections of the book were devoted to the same glories with which Christian primers were filled. This reflected not cautiousness but conviction. If *Le Tour de la France*, a book reputed to be secular in its leanings, could be used in both public and parochial schools, it was not because Mme Fouillée had her eye on her sales figures. Her aim, rather, was not to recount history but to explore French heroism. Her great personages form not a sequence in time but a circle around France, paying homage not to the country's history but to its eternity.

This conciliatory work, which had the gift of including rather than excluding, was nevertheless treated by some as a partisan text, a composition in which light and darkness were shrewdly apportioned. Daniel Halévy, who deserves credit for drawing attention to this republican best-seller, had some brilliant things to say about the text's silences, which are more eloquent than its narratives.[20] In Halévy's view, the France through which the two boys travel has been adroitly edited. Gone are all cassocks, masses, pilgrimages, factories, and uniforms. We encounter not a single priest, soldier, or proletarian. Also absent is any hope of taking back Alsace and Lorraine, or even any resentment of Germany. André and Julien leave Phalsbourg with no intention of going back. Last but not least, one would search in vain for any mention of the Ancien Régime.

Halévy drew two conclusions from this catalogue of omissions: that the France of the *Tour* was a France of the past, an entirely rural France, a lost world already portrayed in nostalgic terms, and that it was a France without historical or religious roots. It was a book of memory because it preserved for the readers of 1877 a portrait in sepia tones of a France already receding into the past. Yet it was book without memory, since it cut France off from its traditions. This ambiguity, Halévy alleges, Mme Fouillée carefully preserved out of conformism, opportunism, or both.

The proof? The appearance in 1906 of a "revised" edition. In order to bring her work into line with the new regulations, Mme Fouillée revised the original text. Her cuts only made what was omitted from the 1877 text that much more visible, evidence, Halévy argues, of a bias in the original conception. Like the two successive editions of *Francinet*,[21] the two editions of *Le Tour de la France* ostensibly demonstrated the "steady decline of the idea of God" in Mme Fouillée's mind.[22]

These assertions, which are still cited by excellent authors in spite of Aimé Dupuy's careful critique, deserve close scrutiny.[23] But before turning to a discussion of them, it is worth glancing at the revised edition, whose rigorous recomposition and mysterious "author" the parliamentary right wing lampooned in 1910.[24] The contested edition tacked an epilogue, situated in 1904, onto the classic text. Old Guillaume was given an extra daughter so that there could be a happy ending with three marriages instead of two. But it was not these innocuous additions that fueled the parliamentary debate. It was the cuts, all made at the expense of a God who was no longer included in the curriculum and who was here ruthlessly ostracized, down to the very last "My God!" of amazement or pity.[25] In place of such ejaculations, the new text preferred "What joy!" or "Alas!" The boys now avoid visiting churches, and in Marseilles they go to the Château d'If without so much as a glance at Notre-

Dame-de-la-Garde. Among the great men they are permitted to admire, Bossuet and Fénelon have been eliminated, along with Saint Vincent de Paul, whose disgrace extends to the whole département of Landes, with which he had been closely associated. The right eagerly exposed the omissions from the text and ridiculed the mechanical elimination of all clergymen, including even a quotation from Du Guesclin: "In the 328th edition, they've absconded with the towers of Notre-Dame! The Hôtel-Dieu no longer exists!"[26] Even Jaurès could not believe his eyes: he was unwilling to accept "that a man of M. Alfred Fouillée's quality could have lent himself to an operation of this kind."[27]

In fact, however, the substitutions are more interesting than the omissions that the author's high-minded conception of neutrality required. Mme Fouillée, reflecting the views of an intellectual milieu in which it was common to say that the Republic was right to proclaim its neutrality but wrong not to worry about replacing what it had eliminated, was reluctant simply to make cuts. When she took God out of her text, she replaced him either with euphoric, fraternal effusion (as when the boys, who in the 1877 edition had lifted their spirits up to the Lord, now joyously embraced) or with patriotic emotion (where once the glory of nature celebrated God, now it elicited memories of the first contact with French soil, when the boys had sworn to be "worthy" of France). Fraternal as opposed to religious emotion, oath as opposed to prayer, and in both cases a reaching out from the self to one's human brothers or motherland. One has a clear sense of the text's disapproval of what Fouillée called "limiting one's thoughts and words and acts to finite things" *(l'en deça)*.[28]

These observations cast some doubt on the notion that the text was dramatically altered. The name of God was indeed eliminated and the patriotic vibrato was heightened, but was the spirit of the text really changed, as Halévy suggests? In order for Halévy to be correct, God would have to have had a greater presence in the original version and patriotism would have to have been virtually absent. A close reading shows that that was not the case. Let us return, then, to the original text. The choice is less arbitrary than it may seem, since the original edition continued to sell even after the publication of the revised edition. Statistically speaking, it was the first edition that left its mark on French memory.[29]

In the 1877 edition André and Julien did indeed visit churches, but churches devoid of priests, in which masses seemed never to be celebrated and confessions seemed never to be heard. Even more significant, the pace of the boys' journey was not set by Sundays and religious holidays.[30] Christmas is mentioned only once, and then because the New Year celebration calls it to mind. Churches without priests, life without holidays, France without rituals. Yet in this apparently deserted world, prayers were spoken: people recited "Our Father, who art in Heaven." Once again the teacher's handbook offers a crib to help unravel the meaning of this prayer. Why

"Our Father?" The teacher is instructed to point out that if God is referred to as "our Father," it is because "all men belong to the same family," and to follow this with a lesson in fraternity. In other words, the emphasis is to be not on the ties that bind man to God but on those that bind man to man. As for heaven, the teacher is urged to encourage the students to interpret the term not literally but in the sense of immensity, of "the supreme power that is the cause of everything and everywhere present in its action." It would be easy to cite numerous examples from the teacher's handbook in which God is defined as "the human term by which we designate that which makes possible the world's movement toward a state of reason, concord, and harmony." What is Providence? The governance of the world by beneficent laws. What is the soul? A synonym for *esprit* (meaning mind as well as spirit). What is prayer? A wish to be granted "the enlightenment and strength necessary to do what is right." The deist catechism had an answer for everything.

Thus the original version of *Le Tour de la France* was perfectly consistent: beliefs concerning the cause of the world and human destiny were far from being treated as superstitions (in the etymological sense, meaning secondary, superfluous structures). They were associated, rather, with the deep, the primary, structure of the human mind. Morality stood in an immediate relation to these beliefs, which were common to all men. The words "God," "soul," and "destiny" could and even should be uttered in school, but without bringing in words such as "mass," "paradise," or "hell." To believe in God, universal justice, or an ideal state was all one: the important thing was to believe. Now we can see how easy it must have been for Mme Fouillée to substitute the civic spirit or fraternity for God, and how easy it was to make the cuts required by the new regulations.[31] Not because of "the steady decline of the idea of God" in her work, but because all forms of human devotion converged in the common religion. And that religion France had aplenty, even if the country was devoid of priests and pilgrims and its bells pealed no more. As in Michelet, France was her own faith and religion.

And we must for the same reason exonerate Mme Fouillée of a second alleged omission: that of Alsace-Lorraine, which Halévy charges she wrote off as early as 1877. In the first place, it is simply wrong to say that André and Julien turn their backs on Phalsbourg never to return. In fact, they do return (to obtain the papers necessary for acquiring French nationality and, symbolically, to make two pilgrimages, one to their father's grave, the other to the home of their teacher). More than that, Phalsbourg, that archetypal city plucked straight from the pages of Erckmann-Chatrian, is the cause of an acute case of homesickness in brave little Julien, and throughout the book remains the child's standard of reference: "Phalsbourg is much better situated than Lyon, because it sits on a hill" (and is therefore protected from flooding). The siege of Alésia "is like at Phalsbourg where I was born, and where I was when the Germans surrounded it." And the sight of La Grand-Lande

LE

TOUR DE LA FRANCE

PAR DEUX ENFANTS

I. — Le départ d'André et de Julien.

Rien ne soutient mieux notre courage que la pensée d'un devoir à remplir.

Par un épais brouillard du mois de septembre deux enfants, deux frères, sortaient de la ville de Phalsbourg en Lorraine. Ils venaient de franchir la grande porte fortifiée qu'on appelle *porte de France*.

PORTE FORTIFIÉE. — Les portes des villes fortifiées sont munies de *ponts-levis* jetés sur les fossés qui entourent les remparts, le soir on lève ces ponts, on ferme les portes, et nul ennemi ne peut entrer dans la ville. — La petite ville de Phalsbourg a été fortifiée par Vauban. Traversée par la route de Paris à Strasbourg, elle n'a que deux portes : la *porte de France* à l'ouest et la *porte d'Allemagne* au sud-est, qui sont des modèles d'architecture militaire.

Chacun d'eux était chargé d'un petit paquet de voyageur, soigneusement attaché et retenu sur l'épaule par un bâton. Tous les deux marchaient rapidement, sans bruit ; ils avaient l'air inquiet. Malgré l'obscurité déjà grande, ils cherchèrent plus d'obscurité encore et s'en allèrent cheminant à l'écart le long des fossés.

L'aîné des deux frères, André, âgé de quatorze ans, était un robuste garçon, si grand et si fort pour son âge qu'il paraissait avoir au moins deux années de plus. Il tenait par la main son frère Julien, un joli enfant de sept ans, frêle et délicat comme une fille, malgré cela courageux et intelligent plus que ne le sont d'ordinaire les jeunes garçons de cet âge. A leurs vêtements de deuil, à l'air de tristesse répandu sur

FIGURE 4.3. The first page of the original 1877 edition.

ruined by the war elicits this laconic but eloquent cry: "I feel as though I'm back in Phalsbourg!"[32]

The charge that Mme Fouillée never mentions the military service that her heroes will one day be called on to perform is also incorrect; on the final page of the book we are told that André is preparing to enlist. Indeed, André and Julien begin their military careers the minute they cross the border and their feet begin to pound the French roadway "like young conscripts." There are discreet allusions to Alsace and Lorraine throughout the text: the goodhearted gendarme turns out to be Alsatian, for example, and the nice lady from Mâcon takes pity on the boys the moment she finds out where they are from. In 1877, moreover, there was no need to say much more than where the boys where born: the phrase "two orphans from Alsace-Lorraine" economically conjoined innocence with misfortune.

In fact, *Le Tour de la France* neither forgot about Alsace-Lorraine nor taught readers to "turn their backs on it" and get on with their lives. It was rather a text that kept memory of the amputation alive, as any number of examples from the teacher's handbook demonstrate. In the handbook one finds a brief, discreet account of the Franco-Prussian War together with detailed, lengthy questions: How much did the war cost? How did France pay its debt? What cunning man was responsible? The book is full of observations designed to make its readers feel secure. Before plunging into the heart of the country, the boys of course make a "tour" of France, which offers them an opportunity to inspect borders, visit fortifications, and test the patriotism of frontier provinces. When the subject of Briançon comes up, it serves as an occasion to remark that "if the Italians ever tried to invade us, they would encounter the energetic, patriotic people of the Dauphiné, ready to defend themselves against any foreign invasion." And when André and Julien return to Phalsbourg, they have a chance to see "what keeps a people from perishing."

Someone might object that all this was only a decent way of cloaking resignation to the status quo and that the text consistently eschews revanchist language or thinking. But that would be to forget that in 1877 Gambetta's rule of silence was rarely violated and to ignore the fact that military service was the second of a citizen's duties to the nation, ranking just after the obligation to attend school and ahead of paying taxes and voting. Teachers put the question bluntly to their students: "When will you be soldiers and conscripts?" What *Le Tour de la France* tried to do, in fact, was to shift the focus of militancy: the text teaches that a country's greatness depends not on the extent of its territory but on the strength of its national soul, on the generosity of its people's undertakings, on the totality of its history. The book did not prepare students for a frontal assault but sought to compensate for the pain of defeat by reminding them of successes and triumphs in other areas. Clearly there were two conceptions of "revenge": through force of arms, which was the course Germany chose after Jena, and through work and moral progress, counting on immanent justice for the future. The latter was the French way.

In this respect, the epilogue added to the 1906 edition is exemplary. It gives us a snapshot of André, Julien, and their family in 1904, thirty-three years after their departure from Phalsbourg. Alsace-Lorraine is still German, but everyone has been working hard. Their modest efforts to keep their homes and their accounts in order are their way of "withstanding" their ordeal and "repairing" the nation's disasters, a sort of tacit general mobilization. France's colonial conquests have demonstrated its greatness to the world (and reestablished the lost provinces on new ground, as the colonists in *Les Enfants de Marcel* do when they dub their farm in Algeria "Petite-Alsace").[33] And her scientific conquests have shown the world that France's *raison d'être* is to bestow upon mankind the idea of a universal society. Clearly, the loss of French territory has not been accepted with resignation. It is constantly in mind. The text, far from being guilty of the "regrettable omission" that Halévy deplored, meticulously maintained memory of the lost provinces.

Must one also quibble with Halévy over the third of the insidious exclusions of which he accuses the author, namely, that of large-scale industry and the proletariat (despite the visit to Le Creusot, a *topos* that would have been difficult to avoid)? Wondrous modern machinery gets only twenty pages, according to the critic, while workers are entitled to only a few lines. As a literary genre, textbooks are afflicted with a remarkable inertia. *Le Tour de la France* takes its place in a long line of textbooks that portray France as an artisanal, agricultural nation. Big cities, which the boys visit only briefly, are vividly portrayed as unreal, fantastic places. A walk in Paris elicits from Julien a rather stiff cry of admiration: "I love Paris with all my heart." He is tired, though, and in a hurry to get back to the countryside. As a result, the book has something of the faded charm of an old photo album. We see logs being floated downstream from the Morvan, and the text celebrates Jean Rouvet of Nièvre, who had the idea of floating logs some four hundred years earlier (the practice would in fact die out in the 1880s). The boys travel on France's network of canals and sing their praises (the canals were already losing out in competition with the railroads).

In this case Halévy's intuition is more accurate than in his previous two criticisms. His accusation is a bit too sweeping: in fact, industrial labor, from the cutlery shop to the paper factory, is by no means missing from the text, and a broad range of technologies are discussed, including some that are quite up-to-date. It is true that Mme Fouillée's descriptions of workers are a trifle nonchalant: miners vanish into their mine and out of the boys' sight, and the workers of Lyon bring forth "shiny fabrics from their somber dwellings" as if by magic. What Halévy rightly senses is the degree to which the book was addressed to a rural France, to the peasants who "populate or depopulate a region."[34] How could it be otherwise, in a country where the number of agricultural jobs was still on the rise?[35] The unchanging nature of field work and the changelessness that it imposed on people's calculations and expectations constricted the horizons of both Mme Fouillée and her heroes.

Primary education was of course designed for those who would remain in the country, those who would not be "pushed" on to other things. Oddly enough, Julien, though first in his class, feels no call to any walk of life other than the peasant's. For some reason he failed to receive that first commandment of the good student, "Thou shalt be a teacher," the incantation that opened all doors. And in an earlier book, Francinet received private lessons from his employer's daughter but derived no benefit from them other than to become a better worker. If Mme Fouillée's thinking evolved in any respect, surely it was here: when she wrote *Le Tour de la France* in 1877 (and *Francinet* eight years earlier), rural democracy was a world unto itself in which social stability seemed to be the rule. By contrast, when she wrote *Les Enfants de Marcel* in 1887, or when she added the epilogue to the revised edition of *Le Tour* in 1906, she devoted a considerable amount of space to the social advancement of good pupils. M. Gertal's son takes a position at the Institut Pasteur, Louis goes to the military academy at Saint-Cyr, and Lucie becomes a postmistress. In 1877, Mme Fouillée believed that the destiny of hardworking students was to become better peasants and better soldiers. A few years later she had them attending the École Polytechnique. In this we see a gradual shift in perception and get a sense of the extent to which education as "the road to success" has triumphed over the "school of the road."

All this makes us want to know more about how *Le Tour de la France* was written, what the author's intentions were, and exactly what sort of memory she sought to evoke. We write "she" because we know the author was a woman. But for a long time that author passed for a man, and the work was regularly attributed to Alfred Fouillée, whose public image at the time was that of a prolific writer, the author of amiable works of philosophy as well as textbooks. Indeed, it was Alfred who dealt with the publisher and resolved problems of foreign rights and translations[36] on behalf of a mysterious author to whom he always referred in the masculine and whom he characterized exclusively in negative terms: he *was not* an academic. Apparently, Fouillée decided to reveal the truth of the author's identity only when his wife's ecumenical work was directly attacked. In January 1899 a man named Fournière[37] published in the *Revue socialiste* an article criticizing Fouillée for striking a cautious compromise between religion and irreligion and filling his "ethics textbooks for children" with exotic philosophical pap. Fouillée immediately responded that he was not the author, noting that it was "Mme Fouillée who, under the pen name G. Bruno, published the books that are found in schools everywhere."[38] It nevertheless took a long time for this truth to become widely known, since Jaurès, in a parliamentary debate in 1910, again attributed the work to Fouillée, obliging him once more to deny authorship.[39]

This publishing secret was so well kept for so long because it concealed another, more private secret. When it comes to the woman whom the *Grande Encyclopédie* described only as a "distinguished lady," one is forced to rely on guesswork. Mme Fouillée was present in her work as the housewives who appear frequently in her books are in their homes: efficient, watchful, but silent. Her few biographers have been discouraged by her thoroughgoing clandestinity. For G. Bruno, at the time *Le Tour de la France* was first published, was called Mme Guyau, née Tuillerie, and although she was living with Alfred Fouillée, she could not marry him until divorce was legalized. Twenty-eight years of a secret kept—we can imagine at what price—in and out of university towns, from colleagues and even intimate friends,[40] so fiercely that no one guessed,[41] not even the conservative press, who missed the opportunity in 1910 to attack the book as the work of a "divorcée." In fact, some thirty years before her marriage to Fouillée, G. Bruno had separated from a husband who beat her and apparently once tried to murder her. The enormous scandal that this caused, in 1855, in upper-crust Laval society had an impassioned witness, a distant cousin who was a student of rhetoric at the time and madly in love with the unfortunate victim, five years older than he: his name was Alfred Fouillée, and he would devote his life to helping his companion overcome her misfortune.

The abominable M. Guyau had, however, given his wife a son, the very same Jean-Marie who would later write *L'Irreligion de l'avenir* and who was the passion of her life. That passion was shared: it was his mother's hand that Jean-Marie Guyau wished to hold as he lay dying,[42] and he himself recounted the nightmare of a little boy who hears his mother speaking in a voice oddly devoid of its normally affectionate tone. It was also as an ideal mother that Alfred Fouillée most liked to paint the portrait of the woman it took him thirty years to marry. He wrote of her in a tone of devoted affection, echoes of which one can detect even now in his "differential psychology,"[43] according to which the second sex enjoys a monopoly "of the great talents of subtlety and delicacy, of genius for psychology and child rearing." Others, however, saw her as a wife: her son wrote verse about the aging couple.[44] And in 1907, when Fr. García Calderón visited the Fouillée home in Menton (capping the experience with a visit to Guyau's grave), he divined in the pair a "poem of beautiful intimacy, of working together for the good and the ideal."[45]

The scene of the couple's life together soon shifted to the French Riviera, far from all professional obligations. Fouillée had been the gifted son of the manager of a slate quarry. The memory that stood out from his childhood was of a riot of workers, who drew back out of respect for his father's cool courage but who frightened and horrified the boy, already an enemy of conflict in both situations and people. The death of his father (a constant theme in his wife's texts) deprived the brilliant student of a chance to attend the École Normale Supérieure. Instead he was obliged to support his mother. He studied alone for the *agrégation* in philosophy, obsessed with the goal of capturing a first place in order to erase the original sin of

Femme de la Lorraine brodant. — On appelle broderie un dessin tracé en relief sur un tissu avec du fil de soie, de coton, de laine, d'or ou d'argent. — Le métier de brodeuse est très fatigant pour la vue ; l'immobilité qu'il exige et la position assise sont également fâcheuses pour la santé. Il serait bon que les brodeuses eussent toutes un second état qui leur permit de temps à autre de se délasser du premier.

not being a *normalien*. He succeeded and ultimately, after completing several theses, became a teacher at a prestigious school. After three short years of teaching, however, his precarious health forced him to retire to the south. With him he took his companion and her son, "that child of my thought, whom I cherished more perhaps than if he had been my own son."[46] Later, the three were joined by the young wife they had so arduously sought for Jean-Marie. Eventually a little boy was born, and the four adults raised the child together until Guyau's premature death,[47] after which the three survivors carried on, deceiving the boy with the painful though touching story that his father was away on an ever-extended journey.

One imagines their home in the hills of Menton as something of a pedagogical beehive.[48] Year in and year out, Alfred Fouillée turned out his volume of philosophy and

FIGURE 4.4. An allusion to the lost provinces of Alsace and Lorraine.

FIGURE 4.5. The family phalanstery.

Le travail du soir dans une ferme du Jura. — C'est dans les fermes du Jura que se fabriquent en grande quantité les ressorts de montre les plus délicats. En passant près des fermes, il est rare qu'on n'y entende pas le bruit du marteau ou de la lime. — Le *métier à bas*, auquel travaille la fermière de droite, a été inventé par un Français, un ouvrier serrurier des environs de Caen. Avec ce métier on fabrique, bien plus vite qu'avec la main, des bas presque aussi solides.

FIGURE 4.6 AND 4.7. The fir trees in the Vosges and an immense steam hammer made an indelible impression on readers' minds.

truckload of articles and toyed with the idea of writing elementary textbooks,[49] which in the end his wife wrote for him. Jean-Marie Guyau also published philosophical works along with poetry and textbooks.[50] In 1875 he published a reading primer and in 1884 a text for pre-readers. His wife wrote short, melancholy novels for adolescents under the male pen name Pierre Ulric.[51] All four admired and liked one another. Fouillée credited his wife with suggesting to him the idea of "reparative justice" and with it the essence of "contemporary social science."[52] Guyau dedicated to Fouillée his poem on solidarity. Fouillée published and wrote introductions to Guyau's posthumous works. And he wrote a preface for one of his daughter-in-law's books, a text that conceals the truth (he resorts, as was his wont, to the fiction of a mysterious male author, a "noble and generous spirit") while offering a knowing wink to the happy few by including in the preface Guyau's last words: "What has lived will live again." Guyau himself had habitually larded his texts with quotations from Fouillée.

What emerged from beneath the climbing roses of this utopian setting was a collective work of pedagogy. Although Guyau's textbooks lack the talent that distinguished his mother's works, he shared her concerns: to make children constantly aware of the things that constituted their daily environment, much in the spirit of a book that served as a model at the time, the *Histoire d'une bouchée de pain*.[53] (It was Guyau who invented the somewhat sadistic tale of the teacher who invited his pupils to a year-end feast, where the children could eat as much as they wanted provided they could say where each item—tea, sugar, chocolate, and so on—came from. Thus the dunces came away hungry, while the good students stuffed themselves.) Children were also taught about the people who worked around them and for them, as well as about great personages (such as Benjamin Franklin, who, when he returns to his native land, visits first his father's home and then his school, just like André and Julien). Last but not least, they learned about God, *that is,* about supreme justice. While Guyau and his mother wove webs of reciprocal allegiances around each individual pupil, Fouillée theorized their devices in weighty, soporific tomes.[54]

This pedagogical gardening, in which each of the four cut, layered, and grafted bits of the others' work onto his or her own, had its practical side: the education of little Augustin, the "young child" from whom Guyau took his "philosophical examples"[55] and whose progress all four adults attentively monitored. No effort was spared: in addition to daily lessons from his parents and grandparents, the child had teachers from the lycée of Nice, tutoring from Janet,[56] the company of a young cousin to relieve the solitude of an only child, and of course his grandmother's books. The only great blow in his life was the death of his grandfather; his father's had come too soon. Augustin Guyau was to die in the war, but not before confiding to notebooks (piously published after his death with prefaces by Mme Fouillée[57]) all that this "radiant" phalansterian childhood had meant to him. He thanked his educators and confirmed that he, at least, had accurately and scrupulously received their message, for as he tells it, his love of country was awakened one day in the garden bower in the very instant his grandmother gave him a copy of *Enfants de Marcel.*

Did nothing disturb the contemplative order of this secularist hothouse? Neither Guyau nor Fouillée was antireligious. In what was supposed to be Guyau's most provocative book, *L'Irreligion de l'avenir,* he recommended patience with an "absurd old prejudice, given that it has been mankind's traveling companion for perhaps ten thousand years." Still, Fouillée asked for a civil burial, and he himself recounted the funeral of Guyau: "At Easter, while believers around the world celebrated the hope of total deliverance, we, removed from this religious pomp, followed the one who was being taken to his grave, accompanied only by his friends."[58] From various confidences that he lets drop, as well as from the preface he wrote for one of his daughter-in-law's books, we sense that, more than the men, the two women remained attached to what Fouillée delicately terms "the legitimacy of certain hopes."[59] In 1886, responding to Professor Hovelacque's attack on the religious nature of *Le Tour de la France,* he remarked that "his wife did not hide her belief in God today, when it might engender a certain disregard, any more than she hid her liberal beliefs at times when they might have been viewed with suspicion."[60] As for Mme Guyau's indolent narratives, the thread that runs through all of them is an almost obsessive concern with the metaphysical conflict between men and women: now between a geologist father, a man "devoted to an exclusive science," and a daughter steeped in the ideal; now between a Christian mother and a socialist son; now between a positivist history professor and his young wife, who holds that the sense of eternity is more important than "immediate certainties."[61] Mme Guyau's great theme is the damage done to the delicate souls of women by the materialist brutality of their men: fathers, sons, and husbands.

Would it be distorting reality to imagine that this dissonance of male and female sensibilities (which Fouillée systematized in his psychology of the sexes, where he described the "feminine spirit" as "naturally inclined to seek, above this world, a living justice and a living love"[62]), while it may not have divided the tight-knit pedagogical clan, must at the very least have influenced the distribution of roles within it? If so, the religious inspiration of the first version of *La Tour de la France* would be corroborated; we would understand how a woman's savoir-faire had contributed to the sacralization of the feminine figure of France; and we would see, here somewhat diluted in the generalizations of differential psychology as well as tempered by mutual affection, a source of genuine and growing cleavage in republican families.

Republican? Just how republican were they? Was the memory they sought to foster in their readers the memory of France or of the Republic? Daniel Halévy found eloquence in the silence of *Le Tour de la France* on the Ancien Régime, and once again his partiality is clear: while it is true that the boys visit few monuments of old France, it is also true that in this intellectual milieu, monuments, unlike men, were not counted among the nation's crowning creations. It is also true that kings are not portrayed as exemplary figures but rather as rulers always in need of enlightenment by great men or women: Louis XIV by Colbert, Charles VII by Joan of Arc. The book's true target, however, is not monarchy but Caesarism. Although *Le Tour de la France* was discreet on the subject of Napoleon, the teacher's handbook was openly hostile: "Napoleon's reign was a great lesson to all nations." No nation should ever abandon itself to a leader, however inspired, for in the Napoleonic adventure "France lost the conquests of the Revolution and the conquests of the Empire." Not to mention Alsace-Lorraine, yet another loss by yet another Caesar.

Clearly, if the people in this group were republicans, it was chiefly because they repudiated the Empire. Only the memory of that detested regime can rouse Fouillée's usually conciliatory prose to a vigorous tone. In an effusion of admiring gratitude toward the universities, he wrote: "Under the Empire, when the army was busy shooting, the magistrates deporting, and the clergy blessing, who else refused to take oaths?"[63] After the fall of the Empire, he was reputed to be a pillar of the republican party, especially after his thesis defense, which Challemel-Lacour and Gambetta attended.[64] Yet there was nothing terribly revolutionary in the accommodation he worked out between liberty and determinism. Nevertheless, when a member of the jury criticized the author for writing that "one has to love in order to understand," the right-wing press went to town lambasting such audacious laxity. Msgr. Dupanloup threatened to challenge the government over the matter in the Chamber of Deputies, and a squadron of cavalry was dispatched to protect Fouillée. Jules Simon urgently requested a copy of the thesis, occasioning a flutter of excitement in the courtyard of the École Normale. A faintly heretical odor continued to hover about Fouillée, however, and it was enough to keep him out of the Institut.[65] He was rumored to be a socialist. The suspicions were unwarranted: he was a moderate enough Dreyfusard to appreciate that, however blindly, the other side too might be concerned with justice and the national honor. And as for socialism, with which he was thought to be carrying on a flirtation, nothing was more alien to his way of thinking: Fouillée regarded class struggle as a "German invention."

Fouillée and his companions saw no farther than a temperate humanism in a temperate Republic. What is surprising about *Le Tour de la France*, then, is not the silence about the Old Regime but the silence about the new one: one could easily come away from reading the work with the impression that only ants live in republics. What needs to be explained is why the Republic, though indisputably present, is never mentioned.

Let us not forget the date: 1877. When André and Julien visit the Chamber of Deputies and the Senate, both legislative bodies were still in Versailles, not yet back in Paris. The Republic was barely two years old, and hostility and possible sedition still lingered around its cradle. Hence certain words could not be spoken too loudly. Remember, too, that this innocent newborn was the daughter of the French Revolution, a fact that *Le Tour*, for all its concern with continuity, is not keen to recall. Mirabeau, Portalis, and a few generals: that is all the book has to say about the history of the Revolution, which might so easily poison unifying communal memories. What the text conceals, the teacher's handbook flatly states: André and Julien visit the Place de la Concorde, and the pupils are to be urged to ponder the significance of this name. Was this site always dedicated to concord? Unfortunately not, for after "Louis XVI's flight from the Tuileries" (a euphemism for the Tenth of August), the "unfortunate Louis paid for his father's crimes with his head, and three thousand people perished on the scaffold." The name "Concord" was thus chosen to "efface" (the very word the handbook uses) the memory of past discord. The place itself was designed to make visible the common love of country: the circle of

French cities (including Strasbourg, in those days often wreathed with immortelles) was a *tour de France* in stone.

But if the Republic was missing from the book as a regime and as a product of history, it was nevertheless present as an idea. Mme Fouillée was skillful enough to link the unnamed regime to the clear superiority of the present over the past. An obscure past, a luminous present—which could be illustrated equally well by the installation of urban streetlights or the proliferation of lighthouses. The chronological dividing line between the two was vague enough for today's superiority not to be ascribed directly to the Revolution. On this point, however, the teacher's handbook was careful to dot its *i*'s, this time without rhetorical precautions, because the issue was no longer the stormy history of the Revolution itself but rather what one might call its timeless "work." In speaking of Portalis the teacher was instructed to praise the "legal codes" as one of the Revolution's benefits. In speaking of Monge, he was to point out that before 1789 the burden of taxation fell unequally on the various classes of the king's subjects. In speaking of Desaix, he was to give credit to the National Assembly and the Convention for abolishing slavery (and then slyly add that it was reestablished by Napoleon). If the subject of inheritance came up, it was an opportunity to point out that before the French Revolution "the eldest child received more than younger ones." In all this history the last word was this: that the law, which "once" expressed the will of a single individual, "now" expressed the will of the nation.

The obviousness of today's superiority, together with the acceptance of today's law as an eternal verdict—tacitly linked to the permanence of the Republic—had the implicit consequence of discrediting rebellion, not only political but also social protest of any kind. What most irritates anyone who reads *Le Tour de la France* today is Mme Fouillée's paternalism, her ingenuous remarks on the gentle ways of the poor, her extraordinary equanimity in describing child labor in factories, her refusal to envision exploitation (the definition of which falls to a scoundrel), and the way she strives to make each individual accept his or her fate. This is not to say that she lacked compassion for the unfortunate.[66] Rather, like a fairy godmother, she simply slipped into André and Julien's bundles what they needed to compensate for social disadvantages: a measure of understanding and will.

What they understood was what they saw en route: how much better things were today, how wonderfully the human condition had improved! "But this is no fairy tale," Mme Fouillée frequently feels compelled to point out. The effect is to suggest that it might well have been one, so numerous are the marvels the boys glimpse, as in a magic lantern. The paper factory in Épinal, the spinning machine, the great public works built so quickly and so well with the aid of steam—all these make one think of Mme Gertrude's fairies in a world where Julien nevertheless "knows full well that there are no fairies." Indeed, what the boys see all around them every day would have been marvels only a short while ago. Guyau has a teacher tell his schoolboy character Michel that if the king of France could have visited his father's home (the father is a farmer), "he would have been quite envious of any number of things you own."[67] Since Michel's mother has more blouses in her closet than Isabeau of Bavaria, it must indeed be true that the republican cottage has surpassed the royal palaces of old.

Along with this understanding went a will, which for Mme Fouillée was the key to the resolution of what was then called the social question. *Le Tour de la France* is a *mise en scène* of human solidarity. In the modest but powerful image of the workers' association in the Jura cheese works, one finds an idea of cooperation not based on either organic solidarity (although an extended organic metaphor is explicitly used) or formal solidarity (for there is no need to spell it out in the form of a contract). Part organic, part contractual, part biological, part juridical, this solidarity in fact stemmed from a moral will, a community that shaped each of its members and was in turn shaped by them. In 1879, Fouillée defined France as forty million wills with mutual commitments to one another. Two years earlier, his wife had written a book whose heroes repeatedly promise to help each other from motives of fraternal solidarity. Her confidence in this sort of "quasi-contract"[68] explains her neglect of social class relations.

It is not absurd to credit Mme Fouillée with inventing "the contractual organism," since she was also the person who inspired her husband's idea of reparative justice,[69] that is, the collective debt that present generations contract with past generations, so that they owe benevolence, assistance, and instruction "to children who may yet find themselves abandoned."[70] The two orphans from Alsace-Lorraine are not charity cases, for to help them in their misfortune is not charity but simple justice. Again the teacher's handbook is more enlightening than the text itself: charity, it says, is just another word for fraternity.[71] Given the date, 1877, it was this subsumption of charity by justice that signaled the work's progressive, republican character. Reactionary critics,[72] scandalized to be told that "if, from the moral point of view, everything must be love, even justice, then from the social point of view everything must be justice, even love," were not mistaken.[73] The quasi-contract, which they interpreted as critical of private charity, was to them the new republican religion in its most detested form: heedless of time, outside history, and incorporating the idea of a universal society.

In a book heedless of republican chronology, which sought doggedly—and effectively—to construct a seemingly eternal memory, there was nevertheless a moment of inception, a Year One of Liberty: the establishment of compulsory education. There is an obvious paradox here. How can we say this about a book written in 1877, when the law establishing compulsory education was not passed until 1882? But that is just the point: there is, in this text dismissed as out of date from the

FIGURE 4.8. Guyau, the young philosopher, ardently unveils Truth, while the sage Fouillée gently moderates his gesture; Fouillée-Guyau monument by Denis Puech, inaugurated in Lyons in the presence of the two widows and Édouard Herriot in 1920 and demolished in 1959.

moment of its publication, something like a presentiment of impending changes. *Le Tour de la France* noted how rapidly new schools were being opened, extolled départements where literacy had made early inroads, and looked forward to a day when the rest of France would catch up with them. From Phalsbourg the only relic of his early life that Julien takes with him is a school notebook.[74] The 1877 edition looked forward to the future, so much so that the 1885 teacher's handbook could easily make its points by posing questions: Are new schools being opened in France every day? When did the country start building schools? There was no need to tinker with the original text: five years before the official curriculum was published, it was somehow miraculously in step with the future law on compulsory education, the key event in a history without kings, a history in which only schoolteachers were anointed. Yet it is precisely the anticipatory nature of the text that makes it seem so dated today. *Le Tour de la France* stands as witness to that moment in French history when everything was invested in the schools. We have completely lost our faith in the realm of pedagogy, which is why Mme Fouillée's sharply etched portrait seems to us so blurred; that is what makes *Le Tour de la France* a *lieu de mémoire,* investing what we can no longer see with the tremor and succulence of life.

FIGURE 5.0. Ernest Lavisse, Pope and Marshal of the university.

CHAPTER V

Lavisse, The Nation's Teacher

Pierre Nora

Ernest Lavisse (1842–1922) was the author of the basic history textbook popularly known as the *Petit Lavisse*, millions of copies of which spread the republican gospel to the humblest cottages in France. With Alfred Rambaud he edited the twelve-volume *Histoire générale du IV*e *siècle à nos jours*, and he was also the guiding spirit behind the twenty-seven volume *Histoire de France*. To posterity he is the spokesman for the generation of Léon Gambetta and Jules Ferry, which worked to reshape the national spirit after France's defeat at the hands of the Prussians in 1870 and to establish republican institutions on a firm footing. "His whole life was guided by a single concern," one of his students remembered: "To revitalize historical studies and thus transform them into a powerful instrument of national education."[1] His disciple C.-V. Langlois went even further: "How fortunate that the teaching of French history was for so long guided by a man who was such a perfect embodiment of the French national type in its most distinctive and finest form."[2]

When it comes to the formation of national feeling in France between 1870 and 1914, there is no point trying to separate Lavisse's personal contribution from the more general republican determination of which he was himself the product. Lavisse lacks the dimension of a man like Hippolyte Taine, who preceded him at the École Normale Supérieure by fifteen years, and no republican Roemerspacher paid him a solemn call like the one Maurice Barrès described in his novel *Les Déracinés*.

Lavisse was a teacher only in the academic sense of the word. Charléty remarked that "he may never have personally *educated* a single youngster." His only contact with the young people of France was in the aggregate, and none took their conception of France from Lavisse as they did from Taine or Charles Maurras. These great names seem to overshadow his. Yet while his influence may have been less prestigious, was it any less profound?

No French man of letters occupied a role equivalent to that of a Ranke, Sybel, Treitschke, Mommsen, Delbrück, or Strauss, the great historians who helped shape the German national conscience. That role was filled, in the early decades of republican France, by history teaching itself.

At the time, the prestige of public education was high: along with the army until the Boulangist crisis and alone afterwards, education was respected to an almost unprecedented degree (matched only by the enthusiasm it once elicited within certain committees of the Convention during the French Revolution). The educational system enjoyed an esteem that it has since forfeited. And within the system of public education, from the end of the nineteenth century until World War I, Lavisse occupied an unrivaled place, as Jules Isaac recounts: "Close to sixty, he reigned and presided over everything: on the Rue des Écoles, in the Sorbonne, in historical studies; . . . on the Boulevards Saint-Germain and Saint-Michel, in major publishing houses such as Hachette and Armand Colin, in historical publications and even textbooks; on the Rue de Grenelle, where the Ministry of Public Education was located, in its Conseil Supérieur; not to mention heaven knows how many commissions and ceremonies."[3]

The superteacher achieved his greatest influence in the generation after that of the Republic's founders, although his work would be associated with theirs. Far from the scene of political battle, protected from the ravages of power, he worked within one of the most typical of republican institutions, perpetuating and disseminating ideas marked by the humiliation of defeat and an obsession with revenge. The relative belatedness of Lavisse's contribution to the Republic is in itself reason to treat his case as special. Some contemporaries were quick to recognize this: as early as 1894, for instance, René Doumic wrote that "M. Lavisse represents something distinctive, original, and interesting."[4]

1. A Republican Lavisse?

The Young Lavisse and the Republican Regime

Lay preacher of a republican regeneration to be accomplished by the combined efforts of those twin pillars of *la Patrie,* the schoolteacher and the military officer: such was the mythical image that Lavisse painted of himself in his *Souvenirs,* in which he recounted his youth through November of 1862, when he entered the École Normale Supérieure: "That date marked the end of a chapter of my life." Although Lavisse's account is invaluable to the historian, his testimony is unreliable. Written in 1912, his memoirs are a reconstruction of the past by a seventy-year-old man who, having devoted his life to national education and received every academic award the Republic had to offer, could not, try though he might, refrain from editing his memories in such a way as to make his past compatible with his self-proclaimed vocation: that of a republican pedagogue.

That vocation, he tells us, was born of the bitterness of a failed education. The son of a merchant who sold notions in a shop called Au Petit Bénéfice in Nouvion-en-Thiérarche, he found his entire educational career, from primary school through the École Normale by way of the *collège* of Laon and the Massin Institute ("the most reputable boarding school in the Marais"), to be one of moral squalor and intellectual grimness. "Everything was jumbled together, and no perspective guided my eyes. My youth was nothing but a thick, shifting fog." As the story continues, Lavisse charges the entire educational system with being "narrow, formal, disciplinary, and coercive," bringing his indictment on behalf "of all men of my generation": "I blame the humanities, as they were taught to us, for having constricted France. . . . We were not prepared to understand things that men of our time must understand. We were not prepared to use our freedom." Autobiography, transformed into history, became the justification of a life. The elderly pedagogue portrayed himself as the product of a failed pedagogy. On his own account, Lavisse's wish was to take the education he had been obliged to acquire on his own and turn it into the basis of a modern system of public education inspired by a great national ideal.

"Personal Education" is the title of the longest chapter of the *Souvenirs*, in which Lavisse tells how his provincial ties to his family and his Picardian roots, together with an admiration for Victor Hugo that he shared with a small cenacle of fellow disciples, became intimately intertwined with a republican faith steeped in the spirit of 1848. What he knew about life, he says, he learned from visits to Nouvion, where he spent vacations long before returning, burdened with academic honors, to deliver sermons at annual school prize ceremonies.[5] Members of his family were the first to foster his taste for history: "I learned about the death of Louis XVI, the Emperor's triumphs and disasters, the conquests and invasions, not from books but from an old man who had seen the king die on the scaffold, from soldiers of the Emperor, from people who had fled into the woods as the enemy approached."

His first pocket money was used to purchase information about the entrance requirements for Saint-Cyr, the military academy. Eventually he renounced his military ambitions, but only for equally noble literary ones: he hoped to write in a garret. But there is something quite academic about the way he describes the "literary shivers" that reading Lamartine and Musset sent up his spine. He devoured the work of Michelet. "His *Introduction à l'histoire universelle* excited me. I lingered a good while over this sentence: 'What is least fatal, most human, and freest in the world is Europe; and what is most European is my homeland, France!'" Thus Michelet, we are given to believe, was his great teacher. "We were therefore republicans, but we did not ask ourselves how the Republic might be established in France. The word, being miraculous, seemed to us sufficient unto itself. We believed that the Republic would liberate not only France but all humanity, which awaited our signal."

The details in the *Souvenirs* appear to be accurate, but the sentiments adduced to account for them seem to belong to a later time. The outward signs of Lavisse's republicanism are mostly jejune: wearing a red tie and long hair, writing eulogies to Brutus in *Jeune France*, keeping vigil over a plaster statue of Marianne while singing "La Marseillaise," naming his dog Badinguet (the derogatory nickname given to Napoleon III by his enemies), and pretending to live in clandestinity. Sometimes his actions were more direct, however. When a collection was taken up to pay the fine imposed on Eugène Pelletan by the imperial courts, Lavisse sought out Clemenceau to offer his personal contribution, and he assisted Jules Simon, Ernest Picard, and Garnier-Pagès in their campaigns for office. The anecdote about Saint-Cyr was probably genuine, but since it must have occurred in 1856, it was probably inspired more by the victory at Malakoff and the imperial epic than by republican ardor.[6] And isn't there something a little suspect about the exclusive predilection for Hugo and Michelet? At that date Hugo was proscribed and Michelet's course was still suspended.

A brief and unexpected admission in an 1895 article, "Jeunesse d'autrefois et jeunesse d'aujourd'hui," probably comes closer to the truth.[7] Here, too, Lavisse was lavish in his praise of the Republic, which stood "high in the heavens, a vague, beautiful figure wreathed by a glowing halo," and he wrote at length about his meetings at the Procope (a Paris café) with Charles Floquet and Léon Gambetta, with whom he recited the farewell speech that Oedipus delivered before going into exile. But then, surprisingly, he adds: "In truth, I was never deeply involved in these youth movements. Contradictory tastes and feelings battled within me." What tastes and feelings? "My upbringing in a family most respectful of authority; my admiration for the Emperor's greatness and strength; my ambition to get started as soon as possible on an active, vigorous life that would lead somewhere." Yes, Lavisse was above all a good provincial student on scholarship in Paris, a boy in whom his family had invested so many hopes, a student who hoped to make his mark and who would soon see those hopes fulfilled beyond his wildest dreams.

No sooner had he graduated from the École Normale than Lavisse was noticed by Victor Duruy, the minister of public education since 1863, who asked the young teacher at the Lycée Henri-IV to join his staff, indeed to become in effect his chief of staff without the formal title, and ultimately adopted him as a spiritual son.[8] And, on the recommendation of the minister, with whom the emperor was reluctant to part company, Lavisse in 1868 became the preceptor of the prince imperial and served in that position until the fall of the Empire.

Accordingly, the defeat of 1870 came as a most serious shock. To be sure, Lavisse reacted to the news first and foremost as a Frenchman of his generation, who "loved his country, loved liberty, and loved men, whether individuals or a nation, especially those who suffered." The humiliation of the dictated peace went straight to his heart. "Reasons, principles, feelings all conspired after our misfortune. Our cause had the honor of being mankind's cause." But the national crisis was compounded in Lavisse by an individual crisis. He was nearly thirty. The collapse of the Empire may have altered his diagnosis of the political situation. It certainly destroyed his very legitimate expectations. Preceptor to the prince imperial at the age of twenty-six: what future might not have lain in store for this new Fénelon to a latter-day Duc de Bourgogne?

A mark of this inner turmoil was Lavisse's abrupt decision to depart for Germany, where he would remain for three years on a meager annual stipend of 500 francs. In an 1871 letter to the minister requesting leave, he wrote: "No one has felt these misfortunes more bitterly than I, and I shall never get over them, and no one is more determined than I to devote all my strength to the work of reparation."

The subtitle of the thesis he brought back from Germany in 1875 gives a clear idea of the historian's ambition: *The Mark of Brandenburg Under the Ascanian Dynasty: Essay on the Origins of the Prussian Monarchy*. In his first book Lavisse revealed the nature of his interest in history: his ambitions were not purely scientific. The history of Prussia did not absorb him fully. What aroused the passions of the French historian was the enigma of the German victory, and he wanted to reveal to his vanquished compatriots the secret of their defeat. He had not fought in the war, but, as a historian, he would contribute in his way to the "work of reparation." Beyond the history of Prussia, therefore, he was already preoccupied with the national history of France. The proof of this is that immediately after finishing his thesis and already regarded as a specialist, he abandoned the history of Prussia and, after some hesitation, recruited the team that under his direction would write first *L'Histoire générale* and later the great *Histoire de France*. Of course he never stopped being interested in Germany. But his works remained quite general and sporadic and were more attuned to the curiosities of the French audience than to those of the German. They include the *Études sur l'histoire de Prusse* (1879), the *Études sur l'Allemagne impériale* (1881), and the comparative portrait *Trois Empereurs d'Allemagne* (1888). His only really scholarly work, on Frederick of Prussia, remained unfinished: the *Jeunesse du grand Frédéric* appeared in 1891 and the *Grand Frédéric avant l'avènement* in 1893. German history remained but one aspect of a work whose bulk was devoted to the history of France.

Until a very late date, however, Lavisse continued to hope for a Bonapartist restoration. His correspondence with the prince in exile reveals an attachment far more political than it was personal. On November 14, 1874, he wrote to the prince in England: "Haven't the latest election results once again cast light on the future, showing the Empire at grips with the radical rabble *[radicaille]?* A fair portion of the nation has yet to make up its mind. The day it decides for the Empire, as it surely will, the Empire will be a reality."

The whole correspondence is worth consulting.[9] In describing the state of mind of his département, the Aisne, for example, Lavisse has nothing but sarcasm for the republicans: "The peasant is definitely not republican, nor is the bourgeois. The worker, outside of a few small areas, is barely republican. And yet in the last elections all these people voted for republican candidates. What accounts for this contradiction? Human cowardice. All of these folks, who to my knowledge were five years ago such faithful servants of the Empire, have yet to get it into their heads that it might be wise to keep faith with the fallen Empire."

Later, he recommends that the prince buy up republican newspapers, "filthy but ephemeral rags that hector loudly, so that anyone who chanced to read them or listen to our deputies—assuming they can speak—would think we were a bunch of Thierists with some Gambettists thrown into the mix. What will it take to rend this veil of lies?"

A few weeks before the crisis of May 16, his judgment was still severe: "The Republic is ripe with menace. Its men are paltry and its ideas nonexistent. There is nothing in prospect. We are stricken with sterility. Opportunism is an excuse for impotence. Radicalism is an old mask that hides only base passions. The center left has no balls *[n'a pas de sexe]*. What to do with all this? . . . You are the only one who can possibly pull it all together [February 18, 1877]."

It was not until 1878, one year before the prince's death, that Lavisse began to change: "I definitely do not believe that the Republic can endure for long. I am more convinced of this than ever. But I used to think that only the Empire could succeed it. I no longer think so [April 30, 1878]."

The conclusion is inescapable: a proud patriot, Lavisse was slow to accept the Republic, and his patriotic fervor wrapped itself in republican colors only after the Republic had firmly taken hold and defense of the regime became one with defense of the nation.

Lavisse's Place in the Republic's Institutions

Even when major crises posed a direct threat to the Republic's existence, Lavisse, with a caution for which many would later criticize him, never took up cudgels in its behalf. During the Boulangist crisis, he did not take sides. In the Dreyfus Affair he also abstained. In October 1899 he published in the *Revue de Paris* his only article on the case, just before the trial to overturn the verdict opened in Rennes: it was a call for "national reconciliation." For Lavisse, the Affair was a clash between two different national experiences, but the one to which he devoted all his attention was the experience invoked by the anti-Dreyfusards. He devoted considerable space to a portrait of the secular trinity on which the national order rested, a trinity destroyed by the Revolution: Church, King, Army. The Church and the Army, "corporations" with long memories, were founded on obedience and devoted to a past that was their time of power and glory: they could feel no fondness for "the disorder of liberty." They could not but grieve for the king. "This state of mind is absolutely legitimate." He therefore dismisses the arguments of both sides: "Since a terrible *misunderstanding* has pitted the Army against the Courts, begin, warring brothers, by doing your country the justice of acknowledging that it is perhaps the only country in the world where so many people are capable of torturing one another for noble sentiments. Offer up your hatreds in sacrifice to the Fatherland. And then console yourselves with this idea, that together you are France."

Thus Lavisse never engaged in politics, despite a temperament that seemed to destine him for a political life. Lecturer at the École Normale Supérieure in 1876, professor at the Sorbonne in 1888, director of the École Normale in 1904, he enjoyed a distinguished academic career. But his social influence extended well beyond the bounds of the university. Elected to the Académie Française in 1893, editor in chief of the *Revue de Paris* from 1894 until his death, *éminence grise* at the Quai d'Orsay, and a familiar oracle in the most prominent Parisian salons, especially the Napoleonic salon of Princess Mathilde, "he was a personage," René Doumic remarked as early as 1894, "whom people have become accustomed to reckoning with." Indeed, he was a great personage rather than a great personality. "Everywhere," Jules Isaac wrote,

> he impressed by dint of a certain natural Olympian majesty, which associated him with a Mounet-Sully or a Victor Hugo and inspired in him a marked preference for the most majestic of historical personages such as Charlemagne or Louis XIV. In his broad, calm face, his very pure blue eyes had a meditative look of remarkable and appealing humanity. It was for that that I liked him: he was human, very human, and kind to young people.

And here is another description, as he appeared to Pierre Benoît, his successor in the Académie, when the two men first met at the ministry of education after a meeting of the Conseil Supérieur de l'Université chaired by Lavisse:

> Stocky, large, clad simply in a sturdy navy blue suit. His squarish, solid head sat close to his shoulders, and his eyes below the bushy arcades of his eyebrows. He gazed at the rain with the indifference of country folk and seafarers, who are not afraid of getting wet. People spoke to him with respect. He answered in monosyllables. The man produced a curious impression of poise and melancholy combined. He looked for all the world like an anxious peasant.

Along with this presence, this willful, determined look of a prefect who means business, he possessed a mastery of both the spoken and the written word: "As a lecturer," Jules Isaac tells us,

> he subjugated his audience with his marvelous diction, which gave life and relief to his slightest remark. . . . How many times did I say to myself, on leaving the lecture hall to which I had come to hear him, What a great orator this man would have made! What a great actor! More than history, what he taught me was the art of speaking, of which he was an incomparable master.

As a writer, Lavisse had the gift of synthesis, an ability to turn a phrase, a vigorous, colorful, yet unaffected style, and considerable natural elegance in his presentation. Last but not least, he had the no less rare gift of attracting all kinds of talent and using (not always with the greatest of scruples, to be sure[10]) whatever competence was available and then masterfully orchestrating the results.

But Lavisse's influence stemmed not so much from his undeniable individual qualities as from the organic union he was able to create between his work as a historian of France and his profession as an educator of youth. Though apparently distinct, these two activities were intimately related in an almost functional way. Therein lies the profound originality, the vital source of his influence on the formation of French national feeling.

As a historian Lavisse was in no sense a scholar. Although he wrote at a time when Langlois and Seignobos were developing their positivist methodology of historical criticism, one would search Lavisse's work in vain for any sign of similar concerns. After finishing his thesis, he set his students to work on research projects. His spirit was not that of the École des Chartes, nor that of a philosophical historian like Taine or a master of profound synthesis like Fustel de Coulanges. He rejected specialization: "History's great duty is to follow the highway of humanity stage by stage down to our own time."

But at the end of the nineteenth century, all humanity's highways passed through Europe and indeed through France. Lavisse had not forgotten the lesson of Michelet. Witness the preface he wrote in 1890 to the *Vue générale de l'histoire de l'Europe*, which met with considerable success:[11] "I have done my best to avoid the prejudices of patriotism, and I do not think that I have exaggerated France's place in the world. But the reader will soon discover that, in the struggle among opposing factors that is history, France is the most redoubtable adversary of the *fatality of outcomes*.[12] . . . If the conflicts that are arming Europe and threatening to destroy it can be quelled, it will be thanks to the spirit of France."

Even more for Lavisse than for Michelet, France epitomized Europe. In 1885—the coincidence with his own political evolution is striking—he concluded that it was both necessary and possible to write a "history of France." It had not previously been possible to erect such a monument owing to the succession of regimes, the polemical use of science, and the lack of historical competence.[13]

The intention behind the enterprise thus signaled a historical judgment about France's past that is revealed in the conclusion: "Reasons for Confidence in the Future" (vol. 9). Along with the volume on Louis XIV, this chapter was the only part of the vast joint work that Lavisse personally wrote and signed. Of the reasons given for confidence in the future, the principal one was the quasi-eternity of *both* France *and* the regime. France's recovery from every crisis from the Hundred Years' War to the defeat of 1870 made him think that in "French solidity" there was a providential and "indestructible" element. The age of revolutions and coups d'état was over, and "the country is finally equipped with a government in whose permanence it is possible to believe." Patriotic and republican sentiment had come together and now dictated the task before the nation: "To cultivate every Frenchman for maximum yield." No one had a better sense of how intimately teaching was linked to the working of democracy. Thus even the great encyclopedic tomes responded to this unique preoccupation. Until these volumes appeared, fascicle after fascicle, students in search of an overview of historical development had nowhere to turn other than to a multitude of specialized works. What a service the "Lavisse and Rambaud" did for them!

Thus the same principle inspired both the historian's scientific work and all his efforts of reform (in both elementary and higher education).[14] From Dupuy he acquired a taste for academic reforms carefully matured and bureaucratically implemented. He was one of the drafters of the Poincaré Law of 1896 dealing with higher-educational reform and the creation of provincial universities. This marked the culmination of a long propaganda campaign in which Lavisse played a considerable part.[15] The benefit he anticipated from the founding of a university was primarily moral: young people would learn to associate reverence for the nation with reverence for learning. The universities were not to be conservators of the past like the academic corporations of the Ancien Régime but rather seminaries for the future. "The high university must be intimately involved in the life of the nation." Lavisse wished to make the university topical and present.

Even more than in these vast projects of national regeneration, the signs of Lavisse's tireless labor are evident in the reform of teaching itself. Courses were no longer intended for an audience of amateurs but rather for students preparing for examinations that would open up careers in teaching. A new advanced studies degree *(diplôme d'études supérieures)* was created. The history *agrégation* (qualifying examination for secondary teachers) was reformed. In the eyes of nonspecialists, these measures cast Lavisse in the role of an intellectual leveler. When he took the reins of the École Normale in 1904, his new program earned him an unenviable reputation: his goal was to require *normaliens* to adhere to the curriculum of the

Sorbonne, thereby reducing the Rue d'Ulm to a mere residential annex of the Rue des Écoles.[16] The most bitter sarcasms were reserved for the new student associations, the first of which had the misfortune to be established in Nancy, where Maurice Barrès, the future author of the *Culte du moi,* was then studying. "Regimentation of youth!" Barrès proclaimed, "Clampdown on all initiative, criminal education, peculiar rage for uniformity of type, modern mania for crushing the individual. The truth is, I can't see twenty-year-old Taines, Renans, and Michelets feasting their minds on the meager fodder afforded by 2,000 petty-bourgeois youngsters with nothing in common but their wretched experience as *lycéens,* their hereditary timidity, and the ruckus they raise in carrying on like young law clerks *[tapage de basochiens].* But since this," he mocked, "is the place where the nation's soul is being forged, if our future notaries, physicians, lawyers, and assistant prosecutors must have cut-rate billiards in order for M. Lavisse to promote his most noble patriotic idealism, I resign myself to it without hesitation."[17]

Even in such silly trifles Lavisse's guiding ideal stands out. To fortify republican democracy was now, in his mind, to arm France. Thus Germany was, in a manner of speaking, the connective tissue that held the new system of national education together. Germany's ever-present image served a purpose. It was an obsessive reference, which Lavisse used sometimes as an example, sometimes as an object lesson, a goad to do better.

Lavisse was not the only person in France to study Germany for what it had to teach about education.[18] From his observation of France's neighbor across the Rhine, Lavisse came away with an admiration for the way in which German universities took responsibility for shaping the public spirit. But German institutions were not to be servilely imitated.[19] Rather, they were to be transplanted into French soil in such a way as to preserve what was essential, namely, the link between knowledge and patriotism. Lavisse explicitly stated that in creating his monumental history of France and in drafting new programs of primary education, his goal was the same: to transmit that *pietas erga patriam* that gave Germany its strength.[20]

Furthermore, the portrait of Germany that emerges from the works of Lavisse offers an image of that country antithetical to that of France. The two countries differ not just on account of their different national histories and political institutions but, in a deeper sense, by their very nature: the Germans received civilization from the outside. The Germanic nature, left to its own devices, was incapable, in Lavisse's view, of creating anything; it took Latinity to bring it light. Despite his efforts to understand, despite his admiration for the stability of the German regime and even, toward the end of the century, for its economic expansion, Lavisse's judgments of Germany always tended toward caricature. That tendency took its most extreme form during the two Franco-German wars that occurred in Lavisse's lifetime: the "barbarian" Germany depicted in the *Invasion dans le département de l'Aisne* (1872) was scarcely different from that contained in the two World War I pamphlets, *Discours aux soldats: Pourquoi nous nous battons* and *Procédés de guerre allemands* (intended for an American audience). The historian here became a propagandist.

The image of the Republic was opposed to that of Prussia. To describe one was to describe the other:

> At the beginning of the new era inaugurated by the Prussian victory, we must abandon all hope of peaceful progress for mankind. Hatred today, war tomorrow: that is Europe's present and future.

As for France, in contrast:

> Ever since the European coalition forced us back within our borders, our policy has never been violent or provocative. Ultimately we took the view that any conquest that forces human beings to choose against their will is unjust.[21]

Hence the question of Alsace-Lorraine was nothing less than a matter of international morality:

> Against an Empire founded on force and sustained by it, an Empire that has sacrificed the rights of thousands of men to the rules of strategy, the French Republic stands for those violated rights. If, some day, in a great European melee, it reclaims the territory stripped from the indivisible Fatherland, it will be able to do so in the name of humanity.

This was not a national question. For Lavisse, revanchism was one thing, the issue of Alsace something else entirely. In his own eyes, his hawkish attitude was based on justice and justified by feeling:

> Since that dreadful year I have not for one minute given up hope. I have tirelessly preached that hope, and the confidence I feel, to millions of children. I have said that we have a permanent duty to the lost provinces, and repeated it often. Strasbourg's spire has never vanished from my horizon. To me it has always stood apart, soaring heavenward: "I am Strasbourg, I am Alsace, I salute you, I am waiting."[22]

Péguy's Critique of Lavisse and Its Meaning

Ultimately, then, Lavisse's role in the Republic was that of official sage and mentor to the nation, a role not unlike that of Henry Martin, whom Lavisse blasted as a "flatterer" *(bénisseur)* in 1874 but whom he had in many respects replaced by the eve of World War I. Under the circumstances, it is easy to see why the aging Lavisse struck the militants of the Dreyfus Affair as the very type of the prudent moderate, heaped with the favors of the Republic, "the Pope and Marshal of the University."[23]

The most vehement attack came from Charles Péguy. It stemmed from a personal incident: in 1911 the Académie Française decided for the first time to award a *grand prix de littérature* for which there were two candidates, Romain Rolland and Péguy. Lavisse debated the issue with the writers Paul Bourget and Maurice Barrès. Lavisse, urged on by Lucien Herr, opposed Péguy, and the phrase he used to condemn the candidate made its way back to Péguy: "Péguy is a Catholic anarchist who has diluted his petrol with holy water." Péguy flew into a rage: "All it took was an order delivered by M. Lavisse. All it took was an order from the Intellectual Party, the party of the Rue d'Ulm, and the Academy gave in." Out of this dispute came two successive pamphlets, whose ostensible targets were Fernand Laudet, the director of the *Revue hebdomadaire,* or "Langlois tel qu'on le parle" [the pun is rich but untranslatable], and Salomon Reinach (along with Gustave Lanson), but whose real target was Lavisse:

> Let me say it loud and clear: personally, I will not allow a man like Lavisse, all puffed up with subventions and pensions and stipends and honors (in the plural, in the plural), a man with a bellyful of prebends given him for having sown disasters in the Republic and the University—I will not allow a man like Lavisse, though he belong to twenty academies, to come with impunity and tell his crude and silly jokes, however *normaliennes* they may be, about the career of toil and woe, the multifarious labor and suffering, that have been our lot for the past twenty years.[24]

What drove Péguy to ask Lavisse for "the only reckoning, alas, that anyone has ever asked of him?" Was he simply settling a personal score? Yes, but in this instance Péguy's case is of general interest. Amid the pointless repetitions and vengeful hammerblows, it is easy to make out three distinct arguments.

First of all, Lavisse symbolized a generation of parvenus. Péguy felt that an intolerable injustice had been done and therefore wrote some angry words that he later regretted.[25] Had his generation fought so long and hard only to keep the previous generation in its high positions and honors?

> There is, I think, no people among whom one can find, in any age, a generation, a graduating class, that was ever so sure of itself, that ever presented a metaphysics as impudently, or with such impunity, as a physics rather than a metaphysics.

Was the spiritual heroism of *Notre jeunesse* to be confiscated "by a few turn-tails who, at the least sign of danger, slinked off fifteen years ago all the way to Nouvion-en-Thiérache and quaked in their boots while digging themselves a hole to hide in?" For Péguy, Lavisse was a usurper. His argument ran like this: We saved your Republic for you, and you took it from us. He apostrophized an "avaricious generation, temporally as well as spiritually greedy, which sat on its winnings and kept them all for itself." The Sorbonne ceremony honoring Lavisse's jubilee, over which Poincaré presided in 1912, was a masquerade: "For the policy that has won M. Poincaré's election is diametrically opposed to the policy that kept M. Lavisse in power for those fifty years."

Lavisse was also, along with Lanson, Langlois, and Seignobos, the symbol of the "intellectual party." For Péguy, Seignobos was the man who had humiliated culture, despiritualized France, and bureaucratized intelligence:

> For thirty years they set themselves up to destroy everything left standing in France along with France herself. . . . For thirty years, thirty years, they worked to bring down God, the Church, France, the Army, manners, and laws, and today they say we don't even have the right to bring down M. Lavisse.

This destructive brand of medicine was practiced above all at the École Normale. In place of the organization that Reinach proposed to aid the school's graduates, Péguy suggested an organization to aid the school itself: "Maybe by working hard, we can save a few relics from the hands of the politicians, from the senile hands of M. Lavisse."

Last but not least, Lavisse was the center of a conspiracy:

> He is none other than the back door through which so much disorder has intruded upon order and so much anarchy upon government, especially the government of the university and the distribution of honors. He is the linchpin, the chink in the armor!

Lavisse might reign, but it was Lucien Herr who governed, and Lucien Herr was the link to Jaurès and the socialists. "This small group of *normaliens* has become a source of political infection, of contamination, a spreader of virus." It had corrupted one thing after another, to wit:

- Dreyfusism, which began as a system of absolute liberty and became a system of fraud and turpitude.
- Socialism, which in the form of Jaurèsism had become an effort to sabotage any just organization of social labor.
- Secularism, which began as freedom of conscience and became the most redoubtable of systems for the oppression of conscience.

- Internationalism, which began as a system of social and political equality and became "a sort of vicious bourgeois cosmopolitanism."
- And finally, the Republic, which began as a mystique and ended in politics.

Lavisse was blamed, indiscriminately, as the author of all confusion. He was the front in the bourgeois world for the diabolical trio of which Jaurès was the champion in the socialist world. All these charges converged, moreover. In Péguy's eyes, Lavisse was guilty of high treason. As the supreme high lord of "republican defense," he had corrupted, demolished, and destroyed the France for which he was responsible. He was an enemy within. Péguy even accused him of playing into Germany's hands:

> M. Lavisse obviously spills no blood. But he spreads ruin, he spews spinelessness and shame and weakness and just plain laxity and vulgar, garden-variety misery. And anyway there's blood in back of it all. For if M. Lavisse and his generation had succeeded in turning France into what they wanted, namely, people like themselves, as spineless as they are, and if, taking advantage of the universal cowardice and spinelessness and vileness, 800,000 Germans had set upon us, blood would have flowed, my young comrade.[26]

An attack like this cannot be understood except in the intellectual climate of the prewar years. It is still ambiguous, however, and all the more interesting for mixing arguments of both left and right. Now, it so happens that Lavisse was protected against official attacks from the right after his election to the Académie Française, and he was protected against official attacks from the republican left by his ties to intellectual circles and his *laïque* loyalties. The attack could only come from an irregular, someone not beholden to any political clan.

At the time Lavisse was seen as the symbol of a school of positivist historians who had drastically overhauled historical study in the Sorbonne and promoted a concern with scientific truth and scrupulous rationalism. By caricaturing their ridiculous side, Péguy discredited what was best in the Sorbonne's contributions to historical research: respect for the facts, precision of terminology, and rigorous method. Rather than separate the wheat from the chaff, Péguy tried to submerge the historical science that Lavisse exemplified in the false ideology, moral turpitude, and sorry politics he discerned behind it. What is more, Péguy issued his condemnation of this shadowy menace in the name of a nostalgic mystique of old France, which the whole generation whose principles Lavisse finally accepted had fought against. Thus Péguy's attack, though leftist in inspiration, turned reactionary in its arguments.

It is revealing nevertheless. Péguy directs his fire not so much at Lavisse the individual as at his work, which he castigates as a cultural, political, and national crime. Yet he says nothing about the content of Lavisse's teaching. Wasn't this because the whole episode was in the end a misguided controversy? When the moment of truth came and France was put to the test, Maurras himself was the first to salute "Lavisse retrouvé": "I hardly know if I can find words strong enough to express our joy," he exclaimed in the *Action française* for August 24, 1914, in response to an article by Lavisse in *Le Temps* entitled "Découverte de la France par les Français." "We missed M. Lavisse, we who were to one degree or another his former pupils. . . . Having been, from 1885 to 1890, a sort of academic Boulanger, professor and doctor of a most militant kind of intellectual patriotism, he was of assistance to nationalism though not a partisan of it!"

But when Maurras saw Lavisse paying homage to Malvy for suspending the laws against the teaching congregations and to Augagneur for assigning chaplains to French warships, he felt that the historian had finally

> rediscovered his natural abode, the birthplace of his spirit. . . . And if I am aware that M. Lavisse's ideas spur my thoughts about various subjects, and if I cannot help but notice that every now and then my thinking has the same effect on him, I can only be reminded of an odd remark of Jules Lemaitre's in the early days of the daily *Action française*: "And Lavisse?" he liked to say. "Do you think there's any hope for Lavisse?" Sadly we shook our heads. . . . How wrong we were!

So leave aside Péguy's outrage and Barrès's ironic gibes. If Maurras could feel that what separated him from Lavisse was a misunderstanding, wasn't it because once the Republic was accepted as the regime that left France least divided, there was not really very much in Lavisse's *sentiment national* to shock the most ardent of nationalists?

2. National Feeling

An Introduction to the Textbooks

Perhaps Lavisse gave so much of himself to primary education because the only thing studied in the elementary schools was the history of France. The scholar's predilections and his genius for talking to children blended nicely with democracy's principal imperatives. The slim textbooks whose phrases millions of schoolchildren learned by heart are in themselves the history of a certain France as much as a narrative of that history. It is here that we must look for Lavisse's ideology in a stylized form. The textbooks epitomized and crystallized his energetic national philosophy. The *Petit Lavisse* was a continuous creation, perpetually reworked. Yet we can map out the main phases of its development without undue violence to reality.

The actual basic textbook, the one in which Lavisse invested his heart and his art, was written in 1884. Conceived according to the curriculum of 1882, the book covered the first year of French history.[27] At the top of its blue cover, it was identified as a "new work." The leading authorities afforded it a warm reception: "This is it: the short, truly national, and truly liberal history that we have been looking for as an educational and even a moral tool!" These words, from a letter to Lavisse, were written by Ferdinand Buisson, director of primary education, close collaborator of Jules Ferry, member of the Ligue des Droits de l'Homme, and future Sorbonne professor of the science of education. "There are pages and even illustrations with captions that bring tears to my eyes, for the book is so true, so impartial, and so courageous in taking on all comers."[28] The new book was an abridged synthesis of two longer textbooks that appeared at the same time: the first and second years of French history (355 and 439 pages, respectively), which themselves were a new, augmented version of an earlier attempt, published in 1876. Instead of the patriotic preface on the role of teachers, "who know that in Germany teachers repeat every day that it was German schoolteachers who won the battles of Sadowa and Sedan," there was now a notice "To Pupils": "A hundred years ago, France was governed by a *king*. Today, France is a *republic*, and the French *govern themselves*." The text itself, up to but not including the Revolution, was virtually identical. But major changes in form and substance had altered the appearance of the book and its interpretation of the past. For one thing, a number of difficult words and "useless" facts had disappeared, and the text of each page, broken up into short, numbered sentences, was set like a figure in a medallion. Above all, the contemporary portion of the book was substantially developed, and three long dissertations, on the French *patrie*, the monarchy up to François I, and then to the Revolution, gave a whole new look to the Ancien Régime. These two characteristics were further accentuated in the editions of 1895, the fruit of a decision made in 1894: the contemporary portion tripled in size, and a fourth dissertation, "The French Revolution and Its Consequences to the Present," completed a conception that allowed the entire history of France to be presented not as a juxtaposition of regimes and sequence of reigns ending in the tragic accident of 1789 but as an orderly development infused with purpose by the revolutionary event, a history that the caesura of 1789 transformed into an intelligible diptych, of course greatly favoring the second panel.

Already in 1882 the intention, according to the book's foreword, was to be "simpler, more moral, [and] more civic-minded."[29] The inception of the 1884 text, which was rewritten several times, appears to have been arduous. Significantly, the early versions, subjected to the criticism of sharp-eyed schoolteachers, failed to satisfy their republican standards. One of them, Eugène Boutemy, who headed the people's library in the Fifth Arrondissement of Paris, wrote to Armand Colin:

> I cannot refrain from sharing my judgment of this work with you. From beginning to end it is written from the clerical standpoint, and very skillfully, I might add. One example will suffice: read the final paragraph on page 71.

> Not a word of criticism of the Inquisition (even though it never took hold in France). Its excesses, if one can call them that, are attributed to the "barbarity of the times." More than that, the text appears to be saying that it was thanks to the Inquisition that the Midi became a "French province." The import of the following sentence is similar. The entire history of the Revolution seems just as deficient to me. Rather than glorify that great episode in the history of humanity, that triumph of reason over the odious abuses of the Ancien Régime, the book disparages or diminishes it.

The final judgment brooks no appeal: "In order to correct this book, in my opinion, you would need to ask the author to rewrite it in an *entirely* different spirit, to infuse it with a different soul."[30]

Great care was taken with the book's physical appearance. This was the personal contribution of Armand Colin, an inspired publisher who was able to involve the author in a close and continuous collaboration and was rewarded with an unparalleled technical success.[31] The typography made judicious use of bold and italic fonts, and the book's 240 pages were embellished with nearly a hundred carefully selected plates. Pedagogically speaking, this early Lavisse marked a clear advance over both the best public-school textbooks, those of Edgard Zévort, and the many private-school ones.[32] Its popularity probably owed as much to its form as to its content. The Mame texts by the Christian Brothers adopted a similar presentation.[33] The three-volume Lavisse course *(Nouvelle Année préparatoire, Première Année,* and *Seconde Année d'histoire de France)* met with unprecedented success: by 1895 it was already in its seventy-fifth edition.

The textbooks proper were complemented by two readers, compilations of civics pamphlets and primers written by Lavisse under the pseudonym Pierre Laloi. Later he received help from Thalamas. These consisted mainly of tales of military exploits and instruction in military matters. In 1888, Lavisse's brother, at the time a major in the army, wrote a pamphlet entitled *Tu seras soldat* (1888). The whole series had virtually no rivals in the public schools,[34] and its near monopoly was not seriously jeopardized, apparently, when another series was introduced between 1894 and 1908. The presentation of this new series was less original, and its republicanism more militant. It included textbooks by Aulard and Debidour (published by L. Chailley in 1894), Guiot and Mane (published by Delaplane in 1906), Gauthier and Deschamps (published by Hachette in 1904), and Rogie and Despiques (published by Rieder in 1908). Except for the first, which enjoyed some success, and the last, which appeared too late, the new series apparently suffered as a result of an episcopal condemnation issued in late 1907.

After the separation of church and state, textbook choices became a political issue.[35] The Lavisse remained above the fray, however, and pursued its triumphal course.

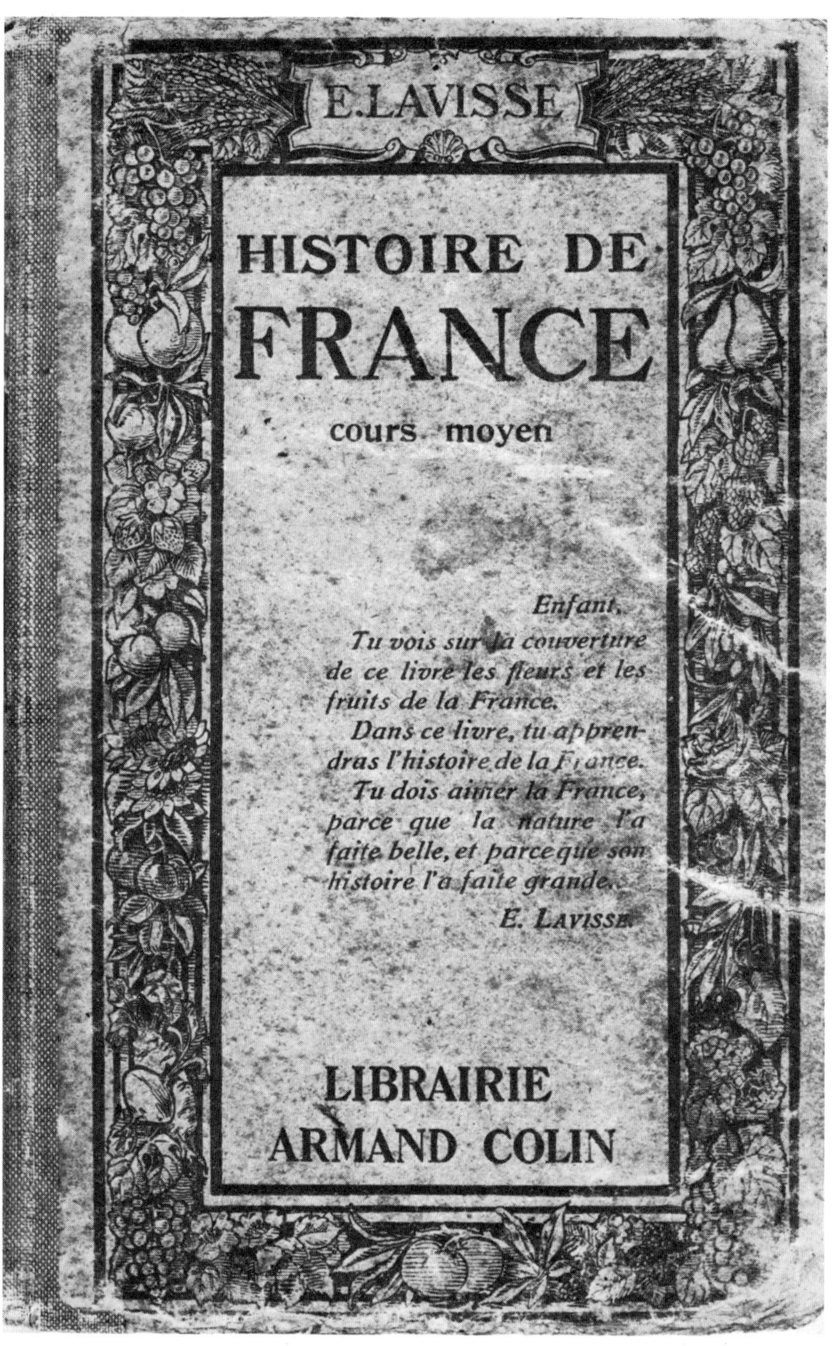

FIGURE 5.1. Here is the short, truly national and truly liberal history we have been waiting for.

A new version supplanted the original in 1912. "I have entirely redone my history course," the note on the cover page shrewdly stated. "I have simplified it considerably." According to Esmonin, "Max Leclerc persuaded Lavisse to publish this revised version for commercial reasons. Lavisse set to work without enthusiasm, as if doing a punishment assignment." Yet this was the version that was to become definitive: 272 pages, 142 plates, and 17 maps sandwiched between white covers with a garland in blue framing this notice: "Child, you see on the cover of this book the flowers and fruits of France. In this book you will learn the history of France. You should love France because nature made her beautiful and history made her great." In this form the two-year course is still in print today (the fiftieth edition appeared in 1950). Changes in the curriculum in 1925 and 1934 required two further updates of the 1912 text. This task was undertaken by Pierre Conard, but it resulted in few noteworthy modifications of either the work's style or its content.

Though quite innovative in its day, the *Petit Lavisse* now seems dated. Even the illustrations have a turn-of-the-century feel. The plate showing a "modern chemistry lab" features white-coated scientists sporting eyeglasses and beards that make them all look like Pasteur. The picture of the "most modern locomotive" continued to show a 1933 model until the 1960 edition: children who wished to see one like it in real life had to go to a museum.

Yet like old brand names that continue to inspire confidence, the venerable *Petit Lavisse* derives its authority from its antiquity. It is a political and military history. In that respect it was little different from any other history textbook until recently. Its ideology is more readily decipherable from the absence of any philosophical, social, or religious reference. Other textbooks included historical judgments and dispensed with moral ones. Lavisse did the opposite. In a remarkably clear style, he juxtaposed and related facts set forth in the form of brief propositions composing a linear narrative. In the 1912 edition, explanatory passages offering psychological and moral judgments were set apart by being printed in italics. Take, for example, the Albigensian crusade. Consider the following three opposing views, first from Aulard and Debidour, then from the Christian Brothers, and finally from Lavisse.[36]

Aulard and Debidour (*cours moyen*, 1895, p. 22) condemned the crusades across the board:

> These wars were not just. . . . They ultimately failed, moreover, and their result was to exacerbate the hatred of *Muslims* toward *Christians* that is so much to be regretted today.

> The authors continue:

> Furthermore, the popes, after preaching crusades against the Muslims, also ordered them against Christians. Thus the Albigensians, living in the south of

> France, who did not see the Christian religion in the same way as the Catholics and who had every right to their opinion, were exterminated at the beginning of the thirteenth century at the behest of Innocent III in the course of an abominable war in which the crusaders behaved like savages and wild animals. . . . The Albigensian War further enlarged the royal domain by adding half of Languedoc (1229).

For the Christian Brothers (*cours moyen*, 1901, p. 74), by contrast:

> The Albigensians were heretics who spread doctrines as harmful to civil society as they were to religion in Languedoc and the Cévennes. Protected by the comte de Toulouse, Raymond VI, by Roger, vicomte de Béziers, and by Pedro II, king of Aragon, they mistreated priests and destroyed churches. Pope Innocent III hoped to win them over through the preaching of virtuous missionaries, most notably Saint Dominic. But they mistreated the apostles who were sent to them and murdered the papal legate, Pierre de Castelnau. A crusade was then preached against them in the north of France. The valiant Simon de Montfort . . .

Finally, Lavisse, who in the 1876 edition was reluctant to discuss the "Albigensian War" and who in editions published between 1884 and 1895 still hesitated to treat the question under the head of "Progress of the Royal Domain in the Midi," had this to say on the subject of "The Albigensian Crusade" in 1912:

> In the time of Philip Augustus terrible things came to pass in the south of France. Many people in the Midi were *heretics*, that is, they did not wish to believe what the Church was teaching. They were called *Albigensians*, after the city of Albi, where heretics were very numerous.
>
> The pope preached a crusade against them. The lords of northern France took part in this crusade, in which atrocities were committed. The pope established a tribunal known as the *Inquisition*. The judges of this tribunal sought out heretics and sentenced them to very harsh punishments, including death. *Acquisition of provinces in southern France.* Philip Augustus did not take part in this crusade, but he sent his son. The son, who became King Louis VIII, added the areas around *Beaucaire* and *Carcassonne* to the royal domain.

And here is the conclusion, in italics:

> *And so it was that the king's domain was first extended into the Midi, a region that seemed quite remote, since it took six times longer to go from Paris to Carcassonne in those days than it does to go from Paris to Constantinople today.*

Such examples, which could easily be multiplied, show how indifferent Lavisse's textbook was to both religious and social issues. To be sure, the method was in part a matter of prudence. Concerning the coup d'état of December 2, 1851, which made Louis Napoleon emperor, the Christian Brothers offered a realistic assessment: "Still frightened by memories of the June Days, France sacrificed its political liberties on the altar of order." Aulard and Debidour commented ironically on "this act of piracy, following which he [Napoleon III] prided himself on having saved religion, the family, and liberty and, after reestablishing universal suffrage, granted it the opportunity to bestow upon him full powers to make a new constitution." Lavisse, in all editions published before 1912, pointed to the approbation of the masses, the seven million "yes" votes, and concluded: "Once again, France, frightened by the dangers of liberty, gave herself a master." But that very prudence *reflects* the years in which the 1884 text was drafted. The audience for which Lavisse was writing consisted mainly of peasants and artisans, and the image of France that he was presenting aged more rapidly than the presentation itself. Conceived before the Boulangist crisis, the text was obliged to be too brief about the rapidly evolving contemporary world. A national history, it isolated France from other nations. With each new edition, the history of the past sixty years was tacked on as a kind of artificial "extension" of a history whose center of gravity was the Revolution. The absurd culmination of this procedure is that in the editions prepared by Pierre Conard, World War II is presented as a continuation of World War I, when to a child the war of 1914 clearly seemed like ancient history. Historical perspective was defined in terms of the Revolution. Pupils thus arrayed events in relation to a "vanishing point" that lay beyond their historical horizon.

The internal rhythm of Lavisse's text, its vital pulse, was that of a period in which the Republic had to prove itself to a France with a peasant majority, a country still torn by the great debate initiated in 1789. Since in those days antirepublicanism drew almost entirely on the rhetoric of monarchism, the textbook reproduced the dialogue between Republic and Monarchy.

The Critique of the Ancien Régime and the Republican Apology

A systematic study, edition by edition, of the way in which the text dealt with the Revolution would show how Lavisse's judgment of that event gradually evolved toward an identification of the *patrie*, or fatherland, with the Republic. The 1876 edition vehemently condemned the course that the Revolution took after "that mournful event," the execution of the king. It had nothing to say on the subject of "the Fatherland in danger" and was reserved in its judgment of the Constituent Assembly: "It found the monarchy too powerful and rendered it too weak, unable to resist the steadily rising passions." By the 1884 edition these reservations were gone: the king's death was justified by a "conspiracy of émigrés plotting an invasion of France" and by the civil war starting up in the Vendée, "where the monarchy still had many supporters" (as opposed to a place "where faith in religion and the monarchy had remained intact"). The Festival of the Federation, the Brunswick Manifesto, and the burst of joy following the French victory at Valmy all appear in the text, and the introduction to the section on the Revolution admonishes students "never to forget, in reading the history of the Revolution, that everyone in France was alarmed by the dangers to the Fatherland. The revolutionaries who committed crimes were guilty of a great deal, but so were the émigrés and the Vendée insurgents, *for they betrayed France.*"

A major change was initiated in 1895 (especially with the inclusion of new illustrations, particularly those portraying republican soldiers) and culminated in 1912, when the point of view of the work itself changed. Henceforth the king's death was not simply excused but approved: "He paid for the mistakes" of the monarchy and for Louis XV's "après moi le déluge." As for Louis XVI, he "failed to live up to the oaths he had taken to obey the Constitution. He called upon foreigners to invade France in order to deliver it." The revolutionary psychology of betrayal and anxiety is fully portrayed. The term "suspect" is printed in italics and defined as a person "suspected of not loving the Revolution." The bill of charges against the Revolution, which at one time included the Constituent Assembly's passage of the Civil Constitution of the Clergy, was now limited to the brief period of the Terror proper, for which Robespierre now bore full responsibility. The September Massacres were presented as the work of a band of madmen and introduced by the following sentences: "Enemies had entered France. They had taken cities and were on the march." Shortly after this came an account of Valmy, energetic and galvanizing in its concision:

> The enemy was still on the march. It had entered Champagne. It believed that it had but to show itself to make our soldiers flee. But on *20 September 1792* it found itself facing the French army near *Valmy*. Generals *Dumouriez* and *Kellermann* were in command.
>
> The enemy attacked. Our soldiers held firm. Kellermann stuck his hat on the end of his sword and shouted "Vive la Nation!" Our soldiers repeated "Vive la Nation!" A salvo of cannon halted the Prussians, who withdrew. France was saved.

Anything that exalted popular patriotic enthusiasm was thrust into the limelight: the revolutionary *journées,* the Night of August Fourth, the enlistment of volunteers. The summary of the Declaration of the Rights of Man occupies an entire page, topped by a Phrygian cap, while the Festival of the Federation takes up a full two-thirds of a page:

> *The crowd was full of enthusiasm. The Fédérés had come from all over France. But they forgot that they were Bretons, Normans, or Gascons. They felt French above*

all, and proud to be so because they were free men. They fraternized and exchanged kisses.

The armies of Year II occupy a central place. They take up three pages at the conclusion of the section on the Convention, featuring illustrations of "soldiers in rags," Rude's *La Marseillaise*, and "Little Bara" volunteering for duty at the *mairie* of Palaiseau. Revolutionary Jacobinism is summed up in a few virile phrases: "Carnot, the logistician of victory. . . . They aimed to deliver nations, all mankind, from their kings." We meet Rouget de l'Isle as well as Hoche and Marceau, the sons, respectively, of a stable boy and a clerk, who began as a corporal and a private in 1789 and were both "generals commanding divisions by 1793, when Hoche was twenty-five and Marceau twenty-four. . . . Heroic children, they hastened from victory to victory." The chapter ends with a section on "the grandeur of France": "*In three years the Republic had done more for the country than François I, Henri IV, Louis XIII, and Louis XIV.*"

This reconsideration of the past, by attributing an increasingly decisive role to the Revolution, created a *before* and an *after*. Anything that was credited to the account of one was subtracted from the account of the other. It is worth pausing a moment to total things up.

The Ancien Régime was still given credit for work the Republic took over and developed for its own benefit. The kings were accepted to the extent that they contributed to the country's *unity:* territorial unity in the case of the early Capetian acquirers of land, moral unity in the case of Saint Louis, and administrative unity in the case of François I and Louis XIV. Thus the kings were associated with the deepest aspects of the republican sensibility. The most topical themes were also the most ancient: Alsace-Lorraine triggered reflexes whose source can be traced back to the Battle of Bouvines, about which Lavisse wrote an entire pamphlet already filled with hatred of "the foreigner," shame at the thought of "invasion," and references to the "security of France's borders." Other republican symbols gravitated toward Louis IX: the idea that the true France rests on a strength it never uses, that it is an arbiter for the world and an example for mankind, and above all that the true French hero is one who places his individual qualities in the service of popular aspirations for justice and peace. Finally, the monarchy's great effort to achieve administrative centralization embodied the highest virtue: a respect for order based on the authority of the state.

In contrast, everything the Republic rejected was deducted from the monarchy's account: the pride of all-powerful kings, the misery of a nation racked by taxes, the wars of prestige, the abandonment of territorial sovereignty, and the cosmopolitanism of the great princely families. Two kings epitomized these complaints and served as Lavisse's main target: Louis XIV and Louis XV. The only illustration depicting the court of Versailles was one showing the "serving of the royal meat course," a caricature of luxury made all the more revolting by the fact that it appeared opposite a terrifying scene of the "women of Paris repulsed by cavalry on the Sèvres bridge" during the famine of 1709. The section on the War of the Spanish Succession, in which it is strongly condemned, fully warrants the recommendations of the dying king: "I loved war too much. Do not imitate me in that, or in the excessive expenditures I made for the purpose." Yet the final judgment of Louis XIV is tempered with praise that is utterly absent in the case of Louis XV. The former "repented too late of great errors that did so much harm to France and to the monarchy," whereas the latter could not invoke mitigating circumstances. The War of the Austrian Succession was "pointless." The Seven Years' War was "inexcusable and punished by great disasters," including loss of colonies, bankruptcy, and debauch: "Under his reign and through his fault, France ceased to be the great and glorious nation it was. . . . Louis XV was the worst king France had ever had."

As for the final quarrel with the nation, Lavisse placed the blame squarely on the monarchy. The "General Reflections" on the Ancien Régime (1912 edition) conclude with this remark:

> It is said that we are a people with no consistency in our thoughts, a fickle people, but this is not true. For centuries our fathers loved the kings, and it was the kings' fault if the monarchy did not endure.
>
> The flaw could be traced all the way back to 1356:
>
> Étienne Marcel, who was the mayor of Paris, was one of the deputies. He wanted the Estates General to meet often and believed that the king should not be able to do anything without consulting it. *If he had succeeded, France would have been a free country from that time on.* This would have been a great boon for us. But Étienne Marcel did not succeed. He was assassinated. Afterward, the kings almost never convoked the Estates General. They preferred to do as they pleased without consulting anyone. (p. 47 of the 1912 edition)

The dividing line between the positive and negative actions of the kings was marked by the inevitable moment when they ceased to be instruments of nation building and became obstacles instead. In the end, Lavisse wove his narrative around this central thread. He summed up his philosophy in passages portraying France's growth in terms of human development. The defeated Gaul of Vercingetorix was not yet a *patrie*, "that is, a country whose children would sooner die than submit to foreign rule." The *patrie* was born with Joan of Arc:

> One day, in order to bolster Charles VII's courage, she spoke to him of Saint Louis and Charlemagne. This daughter of common people knew, in other

> words, that France had existed for a long time and that its past was filled with great memories. . . . Thus it was in the midst of great national misfortunes that our forefathers' love of France was awakened. The kings unified France; the people defended it.[37]

The monarchy inevitably took a turn for the worse once this national collaboration was complete and authority turned to despotism, with its train of wickedness, financial disaster, and political blunder. Then came the Estates General of 1789: "The Estates General, which aimed to reform the whole state from top to bottom, plunged into the immense task of creating a France in which *despotism would be replaced by liberty*, privileges by equality, and abuses of every kind by justice."

Royal despotism, republican liberty: once the major antithesis was established, Lavisse never missed an opportunity to drive it home. The final chapter of his textbook, "What the Republic Did," began with this passage: "*Liberty*: The Republic gave France freedom of the press, freedom of assembly, and freedom of association. And since then France has been one of the freest countries in the world." Lavisse thus saw liberty as the cornerstone of the Republic and its reason for being, but he never defined it as anything other than the *opposite* of the despotic regime.

Now, the defense of a regime founded on liberty raised, for Lavisse and the rest of the first republican generation, the fundamental political problem of liberalism. For centuries the unity of France had hinged on the marriage of Throne and Altar. If the liberty that supplanted despotism knew no limits and affirmed nothing in the way of positive content, was it not then, as its detractors maintained, a potential source of disunity, a permanent threat of anarchy? Throughout the nineteenth century, liberal thought had had to contend with this problem, and Lavisse, the pedagogue of a Republic at last in power, needed an unambiguous answer. Here we touch on a key aspect of republican feeling. Lavisse apparently feared a reproach that was often leveled at republicans. The Republic had killed the king and "rent the Church's robe." Republicans could therefore be charged with sowing *division*. Lavisse accordingly never passed up an opportunity to turn the charge of divisiveness back on the monarchy. The clearest example was the Revocation of the Edict of Nantes. Not only does this fill a whole section entitled "The Absolute Power of Louis XIV," which tends to identify absolutism with abuse of power; but two-thirds of the passage is devoted to the Protestant exodus to Germany, where the economic activity of banished Frenchmen is presented as the principal reason for Germany's greatness. From there it was but a short step to portraying Louis XIV as a cause of war between France and Germany. That step was taken in the final sentence: "Thus, as a result of Louis XIV's mistake, the city of Berlin grew, and today it is the capital of Germany." By contrast, Lavisse invariably sought to show how the Republic, though accused of sowing division, could succeed precisely where the monarchy had failed. Thus, where Louis XV had squandered France's colonial empire, the Republic had expanded it:

> Our explorers and colonizers pressed deep into Africa. We first made our way up the Senegal River. . . . We laid hold of the Sudan. . . . Later we linked the Sudan to North Africa. We settled first in Guinea, then in the Ivory Coast and Dahomey. . . . Our explorers, our soldiers, and our administrators, many of them unknown, were the artisans who created this admirable work.

Such repetition of the first-person plural pronoun is unusual. It is as though Lavisse deliberately echoed the royal "we" in order to show that the Republic could beat the monarchy on its own terrain, that of unity.

Yet it was not enough to show that the monarchy could claim no monopoly on national unity. In the name of liberty the Revolution had provoked a divorce between moral and political values. These now had to be reconciled. Liberty required a positive content. A new legitimacy had to be established.

A New Legitimacy

"Since this old unity is dead, another must be found at all costs."[38] Patriotic duty, in other words, is the corollary of republican liberty. In many respects the history of France was merely a source of examples for Lavisse to use in his textbook on civics. The originality of that textbook, the *Manuel d'instruction civique,* which Lavisse published under the pseudonym Pierre Laloi, struck commentators even at the time. Émile Boutroux, writing in the *Revue pédagogique* for April 1883, drew a sharp distinction between it and the forty-five other textbooks of the same genre that had appeared over the previous two years. "There is no question of principle," he noted. "There is no delving into morality from a philosophical or religious or even a political point of view, only from a patriotic one." And unlike all the other texts, added the astonished Boutroux, this one presented an idea of the fatherland not based on either reason or the students' feelings: "It is conceived as a categorical imperative." The text closest to Laloi's, that of Charles Bigot, began with these words: "French youngster, my young friend, my little brother, listen to me. I have come to speak to you about the greatest and most sacred thing in the world: *la patrie.*" Laloi did not write in a voice like this, as if choked with emotion. He did not enchant or argue but hammered home revealed truth: "*La Patrie* is France in the Past, France in the Present, France in the Future. *La Patrie:* I love it with all my heart, with an exclusive and jealous affection." Boutroux seems to have been quite struck by the purely legal aspect of Laloi's textbook (was Lavisse playing on words with his choice of pen-name, Laloi: the law?). "Reason complements the necessarily limited prescriptions of civil and political law," he wrote, "but it, too, is a law. It does not advise; it does not propose this or that decision for free choice. It commands, as God did in

[*Cartes p.* 188 *et* 206.] LE CONSULAT 179

761. Pourtant nous avions vaincu les Anglais en Hollande, et les Russes et les Autrichiens en Suisse, quand Bonaparte arriva d'Égypte.

762. Bonaparte voulait devenir le **maître de la France.** Ses victoires d'**Italie** et d'**Égypte** l'avaient rendu célèbre, et l'armée l'aimait et l'admirait.

763. Le Directoire au contraire n'avait pas d'autorité. Il était attaqué tour à tour par les révolutionnaires et les monarchistes, et il se défendait très mal.

Fig. 77. — **Le coup d'État du 18 brumaire. — Bonaparte se rend au conseil des Cinq-cents et fait envahir la salle par ses grenadiers.**

764. Bonaparte profita de cette situation. Le 9 novembre 1799, il se rendit au Conseil des Cinq-cents pour y dicter ses volontés. Comme on ne voulut pas l'entendre, il fit entrer des grenadiers dans la salle et chassa les députés (fig. 77).

765. Cet, acte par lequel le général Bonaparte viola* les lois de son pays, est connu sous le nom de coup d'État du **18 brumaire** (37e récit).

766. Le Consulat (1799-1804). — Bonaparte fit alors une Constitution qui donnait le pouvoir législatif* à quatre

---

37e Récit. — **Le calendrier révolutionnaire.** — La Convention avait décrété qu'une ère * nouvelle commençait le 22 septembre 1792, date de la proclamation de la République. Les noms des mois et des jours furent changés. Les mois d'automne s'appelèrent *vendémiaire*, ou mois des vendanges; *brumaire*, ou mois des brouillards; *frimaire*, ou mois des frimas;

761. Quelle était la situation en Hollande et en Suisse lorsque Bonaparte arriva d'Égypte? — **762**. Quelle était l'ambition de Bonaparte? — **763**. Quelle était, à cette époque, la situation du Directoire? — **764**. Que fit Bonaparte le 9 novembre 1799? — **765**. Comment cet acte est-il appelé? — **766**. Comment les pouvoirs furent-ils partagés? — **767**. Quel était, en réalité, le pouvoir de Bonaparte?

FIGURE 5.2. The design of the book, by Armand Colin, was an unparalleled success.

the Ten Commandments." The book offered students a series of maxims in which *la patrie* figured as a transcendent ideal justifying their daily obligations: "You must love your parents, who love you, feed you, and raise you. You must obey them. Do not argue with them."

In practice, this patriotic dogmatism culminated in an apologia for the social and moral values of the bourgeoisie, on which political legitimacy hinged. Good government as portrayed by Lavisse meant a government which, through hard work, thrift, and monetary stability, managed the house of France as if it were a business. For instance, the text overlooked the conservative side of Colbert's activities to offer this idealized portrait of the man:

> Colbert was the son of a Reims merchant. He wanted France to make lots of money so that it could pay its debts and so that the king would be the richest man in the world. For that reason he wanted everyone to work. He did not like people who lived without working. He felt that there were too many monks in France. He also felt that there were too many judges, lawyers, and bailiffs. He liked farmers, merchants, and soldiers.

This is followed by an account of the expansion of agriculture, manufacturing, roads, trade, the navy, and the colonies, culminating in a comment on the minister's relations with the king:

> Colbert was greatly troubled because the King spent too much and went into debt. He criticized him for loving his pleasures more than his duties. But Louis XIV was unwilling to listen, and Colbert grew sad. He no longer took as much pleasure from his work.

Thus the religious tolerance that was a key bourgeois value never extended to tolerance in the political sphere. In contrast to the way civics was taught in, say, Britain, Lavisse never granted that two parties in a dispute could both be right. He had no respect for the opposition. In his account of the Revolution he first took the side of the Girondins, then of the Dantonists, and condemned Robespierre in no uncertain terms:

> Danton was a revolutionary. . . . He was a patriot. When France was invaded, he bolstered people's courage. To frightened people he repeated the words, "Audacity, always audacity!" But in the end the terror came to seem abominable to him, and he wanted to end it.

A half page is given over to his oratorical duel with Robespierre, his heroic death, and his last words: "Show my head to the people. It's worth seeing!" By contrast, Robespierre gets only one line: "In the end the Convention rebelled against Robespierre. He was guillotined on 9 Thermidor, Year II, and the Terror ended shortly thereafter." The only opposition that Lavisse deemed justifiable was that which existed under the Restoration, for the simple reason that it drew its inspiration from the thinking of the liberal bourgeoisie.

To establish the new republican legitimacy and put an end to revolution: the two ambitions were identical. Has he words harsh enough for the Commune? To be sure, all textbooks condemned the Commune, but compare Lavisse with Aulard and Debidour:

> These disasters were followed by *civil war*. The *National Assembly* had a royalist majority that loudly proclaimed its hatred of the Republic. A portion of the population of Paris, fearing a restoration of the monarchy and unfortunately led astray, rose on March 18 against the Assembly, which had moved to Versailles, where the government had been forced to take refuge. Paris was governed by an insurrectional authority known as the *Commune*.
>
> A civil war then broke out, and the presence of the Prussians made it even more painful and regrettable. The second siege of Paris lasted two months, and when government troops reentered the capital, it was drenched in blood by eight days (May 21–28) of terrible battles. The acts of arson and execution ordered by the Commune, the horrifying severity of the victorious army, and the shedding of French blood make the memory of this period odious to good citizens. A large number of insurgents were shot. More than 10,000, tried later by *courts martial*, were deported, and many did not return to France until 1880. (Aulard and Debidour, *Histoire de France [cours moyen*, 1895])

And here is Lavisse (*Nouvelle Deuxième Année*, 1895):

> The disasters of war were compounded by a most shameful event and still further disasters. The Assembly had moved from Bordeaux to Versailles and the government had established itself in Paris when the population of the city rebelled and appointed a municipal government, known as the *Commune*, which took charge of the capital (March 1871). Exercising control over the city's forts and ramparts, small arms and artillery, the insurrection held out until May. With the Germans looking on, a French army under the command of Marshal *Mac-Mahon* was forced to place the French rebels under siege and take the capital of France by force. Before going down to defeat, the Commune burned several of the capital's monuments: the Tuileries, the Cour des Comptes, and the Hôtel de Ville. It shot the archbishop of Paris, Monsignor Darboy, and the prisoners it held hostage. . . . [definition omitted] During the battle, many soldiers were killed. A larger number of insurgents died in the fighting or were shot by firing squad after being judged by courts martial. . . . [definition omitted] True, the suffering endured during the siege,

> the rage against the government, which many people blamed for its failure to defend Paris, and the fear that the Assembly in Versailles would restore the Monarchy, anguished many Parisians and thus contributed to this terrible insurrection.[39] But of all the insurrections that history records, *the most criminal was certainly that of March 1871, carried out under the nose of France's triumphant enemy.*

In Aulard and Debidour, then, we have a statement of the Commune's motives, a parallel between the atrocities committed by the rebels and those committed by Versailles's troops, and a concluding emphasis on the harshness of the repression. In Lavisse, by contrast, we have a shameful, criminal rebellion and a one-sided emphasis on the acts of arson and the murder of the prelate committed by the rebels. Furthermore, the accusation that the Commune was unpatriotic is all the more remarkable in that it was eliminated from the 1912 edition:

> People in Paris were upset by the end of the siege. Some patriots were exasperated by our defeats. Many republicans were suspicious of the National Assembly, which had moved from Bordeaux to Versailles and seemed ready to restore monarchy. Some revolutionaries wanted to change all of society. Finally, in Paris as in all large cities, there were men who liked disorder and violence.

Nevertheless, even in this modified judgment, the disapproval of class tensions is as strong as ever. In listing republican social legislation, Lavisse says nothing about the right to strike or the workers' movement in general. His indifference to social issues is clear. Père Grégoire, the hero of the little vignettes in the Laloi text, is made to praise the competition of free labor as "the right way to rise in society" and to condemn collectivism. He is not an industrial worker or a wage earner but an artisan, an old cobbler. Furthermore, the conclusion of the chapter on social organization is unambiguous: "French society is governed by just laws, because it is a democratic society. All French people have equal rights, but there are inequalities among us that stem from nature and wealth. These inequalities cannot disappear."

Universal suffrage had put an end to social conflict. "The revolutions that were necessary in the past are no longer necessary today."[40]

This new political legitimacy would have remained fragile, however, if the only goals ascribed to it were conservative ones. By itself, liberty, defined as the opposite of despotism, was a source of division. In order to survive, it had to conquer, or else the nation would dissolve. Accordingly, Lavisse's text ultimately assimilated all the expansionist dynamism of Jacobin thinking. Patriotism ended in mysticism—mystical in the sense that its goal was to meld three distinct notions into a single indissoluble whole: a historical notion, *la patrie;* a political notion, the Republic; and a philosophical notion, liberty. In order to do this, the teacher was obliged to appeal not so much to reason as to the reflexes of passion. "Love of the fatherland is not something one learns by heart, but rather through the heart." "Let us not study history with the calm appropriate to learning the rules of participles. What is at stake here is the flesh of our flesh and the blood of our blood."[41] Here was a response adequate to the curriculum that Jules Simon, Waddington, and Paul Bert developed in the wake of the defeat. The mission assigned to history was crucial: to train good citizens for the ballot box and battlefield.[42] Of teachers this national mission demanded a special fervor akin to that of the cathedral builders:

> To sum up, if the pupil does not come away with a vital memory of our national glories; if he does not know that his ancestors went into battle for noble causes; if he has not learned that it took blood and hard work to bring Unity to our country and then to distill from the chaos of our old institutions the laws that have made us free; if he does not become a citizen imbued with a sense of duty and a soldier who loves his rifle; the teacher will have wasted his time.

Whence the bellicose enthusiasm of the text and the martial ideal it held up to young Frenchmen. The history of France culminated in heroism. To the idea that France had toiled steadily and collectively in an effort to which countless generations and individuals had contributed was added the conviction that the Revolution had made France a nation apart, exemplary, unlike any other—in a word, universal. In describing the physical embodiment of this chosen nation, elected to symbolize the progress of all humanity, to serve as the spearhead of history, the historian was overcome by intense feelings: "I never once spoke of the geography of France without emotion," Lavisse said. Here, battle history found its justification. The regular cadence of the sentences conveyed the duty of the teacher who, "by discreetly appealing to the natural generosity and ancient temperament of the race, leads tomorrow's soldiers to the flag with a quick and joyful step."[43] "You, children of the people! Know that you are learning history in order to etch the love of your country into your hearts. The *Gauls, your ancestors,* were valiant people. The *Franks, your ancestors,* were valiant people. The *French, your ancestors,* were valiant people." Thus the theme of revenge was the keystone of the entire pedagogical edifice. It first made its appearance in the little book on the invasion of the Aisne, which Lavisse dedicated in September 1871 "to the schoolchildren" of France: "If you keep the vivid image of our past glories firmly in mind, something will be missing in your lives: you will feel nostalgia for our lost grandeur. One does not die of such pain: it ennobles life, raises it above vulgar material interests. It gives it an aim, one that you know so well."

This was the goal that would define, a half-century later, the final paragraph of the *Manuel.* Once again let us compare texts. Here is the last paragraph of the *Manuel Mame* (*cours moyen,* 1904), on "Contemporary Society":

> The condition of the workers, thrifty and hardworking, has improved. Still, much misery remains to be relieved. . . . Socialism promises to cure all these ills by abolishing individual property. False promise. Its social doctrines would only lead to greater misery, disruption of society, and an end to freedom.
>
> Society will regain the security it needs only through the practice of religion, respect for justice, and sound freedom. Leo XIII has given the true solution to the social question in his encyclical on *The Condition of Workers.* There the great pope confidently explains how to bring about a harmonious accord between employers and workers.
>
> May all decent people, and especially Catholics, who, thank God, still constitute the vast majority of the nation, understand these teachings of the vicar of Jesus Christ and establish concord among all the citizens of France, children of one God and one nation!

Here, next, is the final paragraph of Aulard and Debidour's *Manuel* (*cours moyen*, 1905), on the "Present Condition and Needs of the Working Class":

> The condition of workers has markedly improved, owing to increased wages and to the right that they have enjoyed since 1864 to form *coalitions,* that is, to unite, and to *strike* in order to obtain better wages, and, further, thanks to the spread of *cooperative societies, mutual aid societies,* and *savings associations [Caisses d'Épargne],* as well as the ability of the various trades to form associations or unions to protect their interests.
>
> The working class also owes a great deal to *public welfare* institutions (such as hospitals, mental asylums, orphanages, crèches, shelters, and so on) for which national and local governments have lately sacrificed so much.
>
> Yet it is still clamoring, through the voice of the *socialist party,* for additional improvements in its lot. The chambers, which represent the people, will see what can be done. Just improvements will come to pass, but peacefully. In a Republic, in which everyone takes part in the election of deputies, the people have no need to rebel in order to claim justice for themselves, and they have no right to do so. They should have confidence in the deputies whom they themselves have chosen. If they are not happy, they can choose others. But if they were to resort to force, they would actually be rebelling against themselves, and this would be unworthy of their freedom.

And here, finally, is the last paragraph of the *Manuel Lavisse* (*cours moyen*, 1912), on "Patriotic Duty":

> War is unlikely, but it is possible. That is why France must remain armed and always ready to defend herself. *Although she has an ally and friends, she must above all always count on herself.*

> In defending France, we defend the land of our birth, the fairest, most generous land in the world.
>
> In defending France, we behave as good sons should. We fulfill a duty toward our fathers, who over the centuries worked so hard to create our homeland.
>
> In defending France, we are working for the people of all countries, for France, since the Revolution, has spread the ideas of justice and humanity throughout the world.
>
> France is the most just, most free, most humane of countries.

What distinguishes Lavisse's teaching is not its nationalist character but the nature of its nationalism. Surely it represents the most coherent effort to establish one form of political legitimacy while at the same time declaring that the age of revolution was at an end. With his militant conception of education, Lavisse made the cult of the nation dependent on the cult of liberty, and thus a simple notion dependent on a notion fraught with ambiguity.

But Lavisse's late adherence to republican ideals gave his teaching certain distinctive traits. Ideologically, he remained a contemporary of the generation of the defeat rather than that of the Dreyfus Affair. He therefore saw the connection between the conclusions of his conservative doctrine and the attendant risks of psychological demobilization: "We are telling young people that the great political work is finished," he declared in 1895. "That the battles have died down and the Republic is in tranquil possession of the future. We tell them that the peace of the world is assured and that there will never be another war." Immediately, however, he begins worrying about this disarmament of energies: "At times I fear that, in spite of all our efforts and of the definite progress we have made in the education of the young, we may, out of lack of foresight and in the absence of a general conception of present duties, be fashioning rudderless derelicts."[44]

He suggested that the Conseil Général des Facultés should sponsor a course in social economy to thwart the efforts of an independent school that Brousse, Allemane, Jaurès, Guesde, Bernard Lazare, and Vaillant had set up on the Rue Mouffetard. But the only response he received was from the Comte de Chambrun, and Lavisse once again felt alarm: "I am not unaware that I am going to be accused of calling the bourgeois state and bourgeois capital to the rescue." But then he added: "I have never known exactly where the bourgeoisie begins and where it ends, or whether I am a bourgeois or something else." Lavisse took only the patriotic content of republican thinking, not the social content, and therefore found it all the more exalting.

The conservative right of the late nineteenth century and the out-and-out nationalists of the early twentieth century were not wrong. Both groups heaped Lavisse with abuse as well as marks of consideration, sometimes simultaneously, in the hope of winning over a man whom both felt to be very close to them and yet very distant.

His teaching took the form of a simple but crucial inversion of the meaning and values of neo-monarchism: he shared the obsession with the weakness of national feeling in France, the rootedness in the French tradition, the cult of the soil, the sky, and the dead, all invoked as ultimate articles of faith, as well as a religious sense of unity and duty: Lavisse transposed the arguments in favor of monarchy into a secular republican key. The Republic became France's Providence. It *called* citizens to national *unity* for the *salvation* of the country, just as for Bossuet the king rallied his subjects for their salvation. Deep down, and despite the temporary, albeit quite important, differences, Lavisse's *Histoire de France* has, by virtue of its very syncretism, more intimate affinities with Jacques Bainville's *Histoire de France* than with Charles Seignobos's *Histoire sincère de la nation française*.

Politically, however, Lavisse, like it or not, was plunged into the rapid currents flowing out of the Republic's many crises, particularly that of the Dreyfus Affair. He was forced to take the side of the "intellectual party" and become the figurehead of the new Sorbonne. And that accounted for both the rage he provoked and the respect he commanded. V. Jeanroy-Félix deplored the fact that the gathering of youth that Lavisse envisioned appeared to exclude the youth of the private schools.[45] For Pierre Lasserre, a few phrases such as "unfinished kingdom" and "gloomy *fin de règne*" were enough for "his Louis XIV to reveal the naked systematizer, pinched schoolmaster, and bitter man within."[46] But the critic hastened to add that "M. Lavisse does not represent the new Sorbonne. He opened the gates to new methods and encouraged them, but those methods were not his." Barrès and Péguy buried him in sarcasm and scorn. Yet both *recognized him*, Barrès before Péguy: for twenty years before the latter criticized Lavisse's "system" and thirty years before both were to die in the same year, Barrès denounced Lavisse as "one of the most active philosophers of the age."[47]

FIGURE 6.0. Paul Vidal de La Blache.

CHAPTER VI

Vidal de La Blache's *Geography of France*

Jean-Yves Guiomar

Paul Vidal de La Blache's *Tableau de la géographie de France*, published in 1903, is one of those fundamental texts that since the Revolution of 1789 have pondered the question, "What is France?" and the further question, "What is a nation?"[1] A masterpiece, the work has become a national institution. It is impossible to understand the spirit that animates a work like the *Memoirs* of General de Gaulle without having read the *Tableau*, whose primary purpose is to answer the following question: "How did a fragment of the earth's surface which is neither a peninsula nor an island and which from the standpoint of physical geography is not, strictly speaking, a unit *[un tout]*, come to achieve the political status of a country *[contrée]* and ultimately become a nation *[patrie]?*" (p. 8; all references are to the Tallandier edition of the *Tableau*, published in Paris in 1979).

Vidalian geography, like all French geography, grew out of German geography, which Humboldt and Ritter had developed into a mature discipline in the first half of the nineteenth century.[2] But German geography lacked a solid foundation for its determinism until Darwin, by recognizing time as a key factor in any theory of living organisms, provided geography with the unity it required.[3]

Ratzel, who was influenced by Haeckel and in 1869 published the Darwinian treatise *Sein und Werden der organischen Welt*, was the creator of ecology, which gave geography its central notion: that of a stable environment evolving slowly in response to persistent, powerful forces. The German influence was not the only one that affected Vidal, and he took what he learned and added to and refined it while rejecting some aspects; still, it was of the utmost importance in his work.[4] The environment determines the way of life *(genre de vie)*, that is, the enduring features of existence in any particular locality: this is the central idea of the *Tableau*, the source of its organic unity.

The environment is shaped by internal and external factors and the relations between them. This gives rise to a fundamental principle of Vidalian geography: a country can be understood only in and through its environment. That is why the first part of the work ("France's Geographic Personality") is devoted to an analysis of the relation of France to its European environment. Vidal situates France as a space "in which the lines delineating the larger continental mass come together and almost converge in such a way as to trace a sort of bridge between the Mediterranean and the Atlantic" (p. 9). This position is what determines the "geographical being" (p. 22) that is France and at the same time defines France as a "country situated at the junction of two oceans" (p. 10). Vidal thus reformulated an idea that had appealed to many nineteenth-century writers, and to Michelet in particular, of France as a crossroads of the civilized peoples.[5]

A problem soon emerges, however: in fact, the external influences that Vidal actually deals with are not the two oceans but the Mediterranean on one side and the continent on the other. Clearly, Vidal, who spoke fluent German and traveled extensively beyond the Rhine, visiting many of his colleagues, considered France's attachment to the continental mass along its northern and eastern borders to be a structural factor of far greater importance than the linking of the two seas. This view is fully reflected in the regional analysis that occupies the second part of the work: book one is devoted to northern and eastern France, starting in Flanders and Ardenne; book two considers the France that lies between the Alps and the Atlantic, with the Atlantic facade receiving only the barest sketch; book three deals with western France; and book four is devoted to southern France, the Midi.

The gap between the principle—France as the link between two seas—and the actual object of study—France linked to the continent—has important consequences, in particular the fact that the west of France and the whole Atlantic coast are neglected. It almost seems that Vidal was not sure what to do with the west, which is dealt with in thirty most unsatisfactory pages, because he could not find a place for it in his organic conception. In a debate with Émile Durkheim in 1905, he said: "I can readily accept that the west is what is most distinctive in our country."[6]

In view of the age-old relations between the west of France and the British Isles, dating back millennia, it is tempting to ask whether Vidal's relative neglect of this part of France might not be related to his negative feelings about the Anglo-Saxon archipelago. Indeed, the virtual absence of the British Isles from Vidal's discussion of France's environment is astonishing. The solution to this little puzzle becomes clear when we read (p. 59) the rather aggressive remarks (quite out of keeping with the otherwise serene tone of the work) about "a new form of Germanism, the most invasive of all, namely, maritime and insular Germanism," followed soon after by these lines on the formation of England: "From seeds planted along the coasts grew a state, England. And so it was that, instead of Celtism, which it had warded off, France saw Germanism established on the opposite shore." This judgment is persistent in Vidal's thinking. We encounter it again in the chapter on England in *États et nations de l'Europe* (1886), where, while acknowledging the vigorous and distinctive personality of the English people, he nevertheless notes their "Germanic physiognomy" and is sharply critical of their egoism. These views apparently made it difficult for Vidal to take account of France's connection with the Atlantic Ocean and the North Sea, without which it is impossible to understand the west.

There is another aspect of the work that stands in contradiction with its overall plan. One would expect the Midi to occupy an important place. But in fact the region is glossed over fairly rapidly, and the Atlantic and Mediterranean portions of the south are lumped together. Marseilles, which deserved to shine as France's gateway to *Mare nostrum*, is almost nonexistent in the book. Indeed, for Vidal, there was no symmetry between the Mediterranean south and the north of France: "The Mediterranean illuminates our origins, but it was in the north that the French state was formed" (p. 57). Was this a reflection of his training as a historian or a consequence of the time he spent at the École Française in Athens? In any case, the *Tableau* begins with a definition of France at the crossroads of Europe that clearly owed something to nongeographical considerations.

Vidal's analysis of France's relation to its European environment led him to the most important conclusion of the first part of the book: his rejection of the idea that the whole of France was somehow inscribed *a priori* in nature. Nothing marked France out as a distinctive natural unit: not climate, not flora or fauna, and not geology. Vidal thus rejected not only the theory of climates but also the attractive theory of natural borders, which had been so influential throughout the nineteenth century. This was a major and lasting accomplishment of the *Tableau*. Nor did Vidal see any greater unity from the standpoint of human geography: "There is no evidence of any consistent pattern of internal distribution in France" (p. 7). Hence there was no need for a central coordinator, an orchestra conductor, as it were, which Michelet obviously situated in Paris.

Immediately thereafter, however, Vidal agreed with Michelet in defining France as "a person," stressing that "personality" was a term that had a place in the vocabulary of geography. How, then, did he propose to show that there was something on the earth's surface that could be singled out and defined as France?

The answer to this question is to be found in the way in which Vidal applied the principles of his general geography to the analysis of France. It was France's very diversity, he explained, that created its unity. Here he applied a Ratzelian principle, which he explained in a fundamental article, "Le Principe de la géographie générale," published in the *Annales de géographie* (1896): the various parts of a whole form a "reciprocal system *[foyer]* of active forces,"[7] and contrast always produces movement. An *Ausgleichung* (equilibrium or, better still, equalization) is established between physically different zones through exchanges of products and populations determined by physical contrasts. "No civilized country," he emphatically states, "is the exclusive artisan of its own civilization" (p. 17).

France, he says, has a "physiognomy unique in Europe" (p. 41), owing to a "wealth of variety found nowhere else" (p. 49). Within a relatively small expanse, geomorphological evolution had created an extreme diversity of living conditions, whose interaction gave rise to the nation France. This insight is responsible for the very style of the *Tableau* and the enchantment it exerts on the reader: everything is brought into contact with everything else. Contrasts are minutely described—contrasts between one region and the next, or between one valley and its adjacent plateau. A nation is formed out of a myriad of daily interactions, complicated over the centuries by the possibility of new kinds of relations. The French people are thus the product of "services of mutual neighborliness" (p. 15). Implicit in this is nothing less than a social ethic: the nation is a locus for the exercise of solidarity, a working out of complementarities.[8]

Ratzelian environmentalism was transformed in Vidal's work into what since Lucien Febvre has sometimes been referred to as "possibilism." Vidal himself never used the word, and it is a distortion of his thought to reduce it to a doctrine.[9] Nothing could be more alien to the spirit of a writer whose motto, as Paul Claval reminds us, was "First describe, then define and explain."[10] Yet the word captures something in Vidal, for whom "a country is a repository in which nature has placed a seed whose use depends on man. It is man who, by bending nature to his own use, displays his individuality. He establishes a link between disparate features. He takes the incoherent effects of local circumstances and replaces them with a systematic constellation of forces" (p. 8). The terminology here is worth pausing over: link, constellation of forces, and, earlier, reciprocal system of active forces. The idea of contingency is essential to understanding Vidal, but so is the physics of his time, which one finds in more systematic form in the work of his students Camille Vallaux and Jean Brunhes.

The passage quoted in the previous paragraph is crucial for understanding Vidal's regional analysis. Consider, for example, this statement from the beginning of the chapter on Paris: "It was then easy for the populations that settled here to take advantage, little by little, of the varied benefits of the region in which they had chosen to live. In twists of the rivers, notches in the hillsides, and clearings in the forest a host of new possibilities revealed themselves to their ingenuity" (p. 139). This series of possibilities naturally led to permanent settlements firmly rooted in the soil. An even clearer application of the principle can be seen in the analysis of factors affecting the creation of cities: these developed not in sheltered places but in zones of passage, where varying influences mingled and long-standing relationships intensified. In the same vein, the most vital regions were those most fully in communication with the rest: the north, the Lyons region, and above all the Touraine and the southern part of the Paris basin, to which Vidal devoted the longest and most dazzling chapter of the book.

France greeted the "diversities that assailed and penetrated it" with "its powers of assimilation," for its very variety allowed it to "transform what it received" (p. 40). Thus, in one of those striking formulas that are strewn throughout the *Tableau,* Vidal described France as "a land seemingly made to absorb the greater part of its own emigration" (p. 15).

Vidal's arguments are integrated into a tightly knit account of France as a system of organically related parts, a system that is supposed to explain the country's nature and personality. Vidal's book certainly marked a break with the historical and geographical tradition of the nineteenth century.[11] Hence it is interesting to compare Vidal's *Tableau* with Michelet's, since Vidal, by his very choice of title, acknowledged his debt to Michelet while adding the word "geography," which made all the difference.

Michelet's *Tableau de la France* was published in December 1833 as the first part of volume two of his *Histoire de France.*[12] It was intended to link volume one, which dealt with France from the beginning to the tenth century and in which the races making up the French people were the central focus, to the rest of the work. Now, on the question of race, Michelet differed with Augustin Thierry, and as Paul Vaillaneix notes, "When Michelet became a geographer, he completed his proof of the inadequacy of racial theory."[13] And here indeed, at the beginning of a history that would show how France transcended its ethnic components to create a French people, Michelet ascribed a synthetic function to the nation's physical foundation.

But was Michelet's *Tableau* really a geographical study? Michelet embarks on a tour of France. He starts in Brittany, descends the Atlantic coast, proceeds from the Pyrenees through Languedoc to Provence, heads back north through the Rhône and Meuse valleys, crosses northern and central France, and ends in Paris. Nothing in this itinerary is the result of geographic considerations (even if one refers to works of the period such as Malte-Brun's). On the contrary, Michelet begins with Brittany, Celtic since prehistoric times and still the virginal "eldest daughter of the monarchy," and moves from there to the "mixed" regions conquered by the Roman and Germanic invaders. He can therefore write: "We have now studied geography in chronological order, traveling in both space and time" (p. 85). In terms of organization, this is a far cry from Vidal's method, with only one point of contact between the two, namely, when Michelet insists that "the sap of life was in the north" (p. 82).

When Michelet distinguishes between provinces, moreover, he does not do so in geographic terms. The transition from the Armorican west to the regions south of the Loire is marked by three chronological points: the slate quarries of Angers, at the geological limit of Brittany; the great "Druidic" monument at Saumur; and Tours, the ecclesiastical metropolis of Brittany in the Middle Ages. Later he calmly observes: "I could enter the Rouergue through the great valley of the Midi . . . but I prefer to go by way of Cahors" (p. 104). This is the remark of a traveler as opposed to an analyst. Yet here, too, we note a point of contact with Vidal, when Michelet notes that "France has no region more winning, more capable of reconciling the north and the south, than Burgundy" (p. 138). But observations of this kind are rare in Vidal.

For Michelet, provincial units are compact, juxtaposed rather than linked. Each province is described as if Michelet intended to pile up as much historical significance as possible. The three pages on Lyons are a good example of this. This profusion (which Hugo also employed in *Le Rhin,* written in 1842) was meant to convey the genius of each province over time, to draw out the substance and portray the characteristic vitality of the French personality. But for Michelet the totality of that personality was the result not of interaction among its constituent parts but rather of a transcending of those parts at their center, the Île-de-France, "the seed around which everything was to crystallize" (p. 151). Once again, history is paramount: "There is only one way to acquaint you with the center of the center, with Paris and the Île-de-France, and that is to recount the history of the monarchy" (p. 155). This was poles apart from Vidal's view, as we shall see.

The rest of Michelet's text is summed up in maxims as celebrated as they are sublime: "The center knows itself and knows all the rest." "The provinces gaze upon themselves in it [the center]; in it they love themselves and admire themselves in a higher form" (pp. 156–157). With this hymn to France Michelet resolved in his own peculiar fashion the question of the relation between the local and the national. "Diminish, without destroying, local, particular, life for the benefit of the general and common life" (p. 159). Fine, but what is this sentence worth in the light of what he wrote on the next page: "The local spirit disappeared every day. The influence of soil, climate, and race gave way to social and political action. The fatality of places was vanquished, man escaped the tyranny of material circumstances" (p. 160). These observations are far-reaching. They express Michelet's national passion, a passion that one also finds in Vidal and that makes the work of both an excellent introduction to France. But Vidal could never have referred to the tyranny of local circumstances, for he showed that, however tyrannical, those circumstances were also profuse and diverse and by no means fatal in their consequences. Above all, he proposed not a hierarchical vision of France in which the center transcended its constituents, but a firmly egalitarian vision. It was no accident that he, along with his friend Pierre Foncin, ardently defended regional ideas and helped to inspire laws intended to promote regional interests.[14]

Michelet's humanism was passed on to Vidal, who studied with students of the great historian. The *Tableaux* of both were parts of histories of France that came to stand on their own as masterpieces. It would be easy to establish a dialogue between them on many points. But Michelet was bent on synthesis, Vidal on analysis, and the synthesis in his analysis must be read between the lines.

At the beginning of the twentieth century, the question of the always problematic relation between history and geography received, from the new French school, an answer that marked a major epistemological advance. The *Tableau de la géographie de la France* is the most impressive formulation of that answer. Camille Jullian acknowledged this in a reference to Vidal in volume one of his *Histoire de la Gaule* (1908): "A nation's ultimate contours are compromises between the recommendations of nature and the results of human effort."[15] In this connection the most significant passage of the *Tableau* was the third part of book one, "The Rhine Region," in which Vidal, including without comment regions that had passed to Germany in 1871, demonstrated that there was no natural or necessary reason why France should end in the middle of the Rhine valley.

Let us examine in detail how Vidal proceeded in his regional analyses in view of the structure of the work explored above. Despite Vidal's supple style, one can discern a constant pattern, evident in the very first region he looks at, Flanders. First he gives a general description in which visual details figure prominently, with frequent notations such as "one sees" (p. 61), "we have before our eyes" (p. 62), "the eye instinctively seeks" (p. 128). Then comes a transition: "But the geographer must not concern himself only with the present" (p. 72). He moves next to a study of structure, emphasizing geology rather than tectonics. And then he goes on to analyze the diversity of soils and landscapes, the distribution and types of habitation, and the location of cities, ending in some cases with psychological observations on the regional character.

Surface relief occupies a central place throughout. For Vidal, of course, relief was as much an effect of water as of great tectonic forces. I say water and not hydrography (or climatology) even though the new and soon to become standard terminology of W. M. Morris was being introduced in France at the time by Emmanuel de Margerie and others.[16] Vidal was not unaware of such concepts as the cycle of erosion, the base level and equilibrium profile, the location of rivers relative to land structure, and so on. Yet he was writing for a nonspecialist audience, and in any case what enchanted him was above all the endless variety of ways in which water flowed on the surface of the earth and below it. For him the Somme was "one of the rivers whose existence can be traced farthest back in the history of the earth" (p. 96). Of Paris he wrote that "the river was the soul of the growing city," it "threw a great shaft of air and light" through the urban landscape (p. 141). The rivers of Berry are "rare but pure and luxuriant" (p. 155). "The limestone plateaus of Berry, like all the regions the Gauls preferred, had few but copious springs" (p. 156). And in calcareous Poitou, "caverns gave rise to fine springs, fountains of clear water" (p. 315).

One passage that I cannot resist quoting is the marvelous one in which Vidal wonders about the primacy of the Seine among the streams of the southeastern Paris basin:

> In such attributions people are not guided by the same considerations as hydraulic engineers. The waters whose memory they honor most are either those that have guided them in their migrations or, even more, those that, owing to the mystery or beauty of their sources, have impressed themselves on the imagination. This, surely, is the reason for the primacy of the Seine. It is the first permanent river that springs, amid nearby mountain passes, from a beautiful source, fed by subterranean reservoirs. The Seine's original *douix* [a Burgundian word for spring], located in a narrow recess in the surrounding plateaus, is a surprising sight. It is the only source of life in these desolate expanses. Mills, villages, abbeys, and forges press in around it, and fine meadows stretch out alongside. True, it lacks tributaries. Some dry up along the way. But at the foot of the Roc de Châtillon a splendid *douix* suddenly surges forth. Slowly at first, as if welling up from the earth, it emerges, pure and deep, from the surrounding basin. Through fields and trees the Seine gathers speed, as if in recognition of the divine place ascribed to it in our ancestors' naturalistic religions. (pp. 116–117)

If Vidal was fond of sources, the network of rivers was far more than a subject of emotion: it was the true embodiment of Vidalian geography. For the rivers stood at the precise intersection of physical geography (revealing the effects of land structure and differential erosion of soft and hard layers) and human geography (being key factors in determining the distribution of habitation and trade). Vidal makes this point in his description of the Ardenne: "This form of fluvial energy was worth dwelling on, for it determines where crops are grown and where humans settle in the pinched valleys" (p. 66). Sometimes he uses the river network to structure his description of a region. The third chapter on the Paris basin is entitled "The Paris Basin Upstream from Paris." And the next chapter begins with this sentence: "Following the courses of the rivers has brought us now to the region in which Paris grew" (p. 124). Although Vidal had rejected the theory of basins that Philippe Buache had developed in the eighteenth century, he remained captivated by them.

While Vidal "commemorated" all of France's rivers, none is treated with greater respect or love than the Loire. It is obvious that he had spent many hours walking along its banks. How cleverly he sees and makes us see every twist in its tortuous course, as deformations of the earth's structure in the Tertiary era forced the river to deviate from its northward path and head west, then north again though never east, until finally, in a more recent geological epoch, it took the majestic turn that caused it to renounce its former union with the Seine basin. Vidal tells a story, the story of the "late divorce of the Seine and its tributaries from the system of the Loire," from which he deduces that "the influences of the west and south vied with those of the north" (p. 152). This he clearly saw as a major problem, a complication in the interaction of geological history with the history of the French people and nation, a difficulty that had to be overcome if the nation was to be unified. It was a problem to which he would return often, because it was connected with the famous link between northern and southern France. Perhaps the clumsiness of the treatment of western France in the *Tableau* has something to do with this problem of the course of the Loire. One could argue that the clumsiness was a consequence of Vidal's failure to carry his analytic "interpretation" of France all the way through to the end.

France—the surface features of French territory—is thus a product of water's effects. Given the variety of the country's terrain and the complexity of its geological history, erosion created contrasts (in elevation as well as at a given elevation) in the nature of the soil, which encouraged various types of farming, gave rise to complementary forms of economic activity, and thus gave substance to trade and to life itself. Vidal emphasized the importance of the presence or absence of lines of villages along the edges of valleys, close to sources of water that emerged from the earth at the height of an impermeable layer. Writing of Normandy, he remarked that "it was through its valleys that Normandy became industrial" (p. 175). "On the slopes there is neither a source level nor a change of relief capable of facilitating the establishment of mid-slope villages. Hence valleys and plateaus are virtually isolated from each other" (p. 176). Whence the division between the innovators who arrived via the valleys (that is, the Normans) and the more conservative populations that had settled at an earlier date on the plateaus. "Nowhere was the antagonism of internal and external influences as marked as it was in Normandy. . . . The prospect changes as soon as one leaves the coast." (p. 179). The Caux region is distinct from the rest of Normandy, "and the peasant knows it" (p. 174). The Cauchois "is a stranger in the valleys" (p. 174). Here, then, is a fine example of close geographic analysis, combining location, structure, influences of the network of streams, and way of life.

An important consequence of the Vidalian approach described above is that the *Tableau* is essentially a portrait of rural France, the France of *pays*. More precisely, it is a portrait of the distinct landscapes within rural France, of the places in which rural life unfolds.[17] Although streams are preeminent in Vidal's account, he also dealt in lavish passages with forests and their fauna. By contrast, agricultural production is treated relatively superficially—quite the opposite of the usual textbook with its figures on bushels of wheat and gallons of wine. (Statistics are rare throughout the *Tableau.*) If Vidal mentions wine at all, as in his discussion of Touraine, it is to comment on "the joyous life of the vintners, compared with whom the people of Les Gâtines and the plateaus seem poor wretches indeed" (p. 168)—yet another contrast.

Little attention is paid, as I said earlier, to cities. Although there are rudimentary analyses of Paris and Lyons, other cities, such as Lille, Marseilles, Nantes, Toulouse, Clermont-Ferrand, and Rouen merit only a few lines about their site and the conditions under which they were created. And even though he mentions Lyons's importance as an international financial and commercial center, his conclusion is that in the life of this city "the most important role belongs to the Alps" (p. 253). Even Paris "was an interior capital in the past as it is today" (p. 143). Vidal's sole concern is with each city's relation to its region.

Another well-known feature of the book, not unrelated to the foregoing, is the lack of attention to industrial activity. In his preface to the recent edition of the *Tableau,* Paul Claval attributes this to Vidal's strict adherence to the task that Lavisse set him in 1894: to provide an introduction to the *Histoire de France* (which in the original plan was to end with the Revolution). Presumably Vidal did not wish to encroach upon the turf of his historian colleagues. True enough.

It is also true that economic, urban, and political geography did not really come into their own until after World War I, thanks to the work of Vidal's students, especially Albert Demangeon.[18] And it was not until quite recently that scholars began to acknowledge the importance of social divisions and the laws of the market, which play a far more important role in regional and national life than do so-called facts of nature.[19] Nevertheless, even without getting into the Industrial Revolution, Vidal could have said more about fairs and trade routes, mines, and the great public works projects of the monarchy (such as roads, canals, and ports), all of which helped to shape the French countryside. Indeed, he frequently mentions Roman roads. In the end, one cannot avoid the conclusion that the weakness of the work in urban and economic geography reflects the author's personal predilections as much as the place of the volume in Lavisse's series.

For one thing, Vidal sometimes lets his feelings about modern industry show. Speaking of the scattered descendants of the original settlers of the Vosges valleys, he says: "The awesome power of modern industry, along with the habits it all too often brings in its wake, may well deal a death blow to these survivors" (p. 193). Again speaking of the Vosges, he writes: "The erstwhile importance of mines led to an artificial colonization of the region, bringing together a patchwork of settlers from outside" (p. 196). When it came to industry, in other words, population movements in response to the exploitation of natural economic potential no longer obeyed the "laws" that he himself had identified: they became "artificial." This hostility was not limited to industry but extended to all forms of productive activity, including agriculture. Speaking of the chestnut forests of the Massif Central, he castigates man as "the great destroyer of the forests," responsible for "ravages" stemming from "excessive planting and pasturing" (p. 281). These remarks shed revealing light on Vidal's remark in the preface that he intends to portray France as a "country profoundly humanized but not bastardized by the works of civilization" (p. 4).

If, then, Vidal was not interested in even agriculture or mining, ancient and enduring sources of exchange, what was the real substance of the *Tableau*? It can be summed up by a concept that Vidal did not invent and that he had already used in his book *Marco Polo* (1880), a concept for which Lucien Febvre would later attempt to provide a theory: the way of life *(genre de vie)*.[20]

Economics played a large part in Febvre's version but not in Vidal's. For Vidal, the characteristics of a way of life include the manner in which people situated themselves in a particular location, the type of dwelling they chose, and the design of their homes, all interpreted as a direct reflection of the nature of the soil. Vidal's black and white maps essentially showed the distribution of different types of dwelling. In this respect Vidal's work came close to sociology, and in elaborating the way-of-life concept he delved into anthropology in the very years during which he was working on the *Tableau*.[21] He liked to draw contrasts between, say, villagers and peasants, that is, farmers who lived in closely packed houses and farmers who lived in relatively isolated dwellings: "In Lorraine, Burgundy, Champagne, and Picardy, the inhabitants of the countryside are mostly villagers. In the west they are peasants" (p. 311). In every region he focused on the sequence running from soil to crop to occupation of the land to dwellings to psychological traits, yet he also acknowledged that there was nothing absolutely necessary in this sequence and that its specific details could vary (though even if they did, the sequence remained). The geographer, he explained in a 1904 lecture to the Société d'Économie Sociale (founded by Frédéric Le Play, who is cited in the *Tableau*), is there to help distinguish between what is permanent and what is subject to change, and to comfort "minds fundamentally attached to the soil of France with ideas, memories, and impressions to which that soil gives rise."[22]

In 1911, Vidal published an article, "Genres de vie dans la géographie humaine," which reflects the spirit of the *Tableau*. The key passage is the following: "Agriculture thus shows us one of the ways in which men have rooted themselves in the soil and left their mark on it: this is the *Einwürzelung*, the incorporation of themselves into a portion of the earth, that Peschel and Ratzel have so admirably described. The persistence of rural domains is a fact that can be observed in France

TYPES D'ÉTABLISSEMENTS ANCIENS

LE ROCHER DES EYZIES (VALLÉE DE LA VÉZÈRE).

Falaise de calcaire creusée de cavernes — entre autres celle de Cro-Magnon — qu'habitèrent les hommes primitifs. Le village moderne est installé au pied. (Cf. p. 369). Cl. Boulanger.

MONACO.

La péninsule rocheuse, abritant un port et facile à défendre vers la terre, est un type d'établissement phénicien. Là était un sanctuaire de Melkhart, que les Grecs remplacèrent par un sanctuaire d'Héraclès « Monœcos » (qui habite seul), d'où le nom de la ville.

Cl. Neurdein.

FIGURE 6.1. Typical ancient settlement sites: Les Eyzies and Monaco; from Vidal de La Blache's *Tableau de la géographie de la France* (1903).

through the study of old maps."[23] To balance this assertion, however, he immediately adds: "But the laws of evolution dominate and can call even the most firmly established judgments and maxims into question." Clearly, the caveat, here as elsewhere in Vidal, is far more hypothetical than the principle itself, which is crucial to Vidal's practice. He was constantly forced to correct overly deterministic assertions because he had not really found a satisfactory solution to the problem of determinism in geography and still relied on nineteenth-century concepts, though he was well aware of their inadequacies and dangers. His writings from 1910 to his death (*La France de l'Est* [1917] and the *Principes de géographie humaine*, which his son-in-law Martonne published in 1922) reveal a greater distance from Ratzel's determinism than the writings contemporary with the *Tableau*.

In composing his detailed portraits of local life, Vidal came to be interested in the way people think about the places they live. He attached great importance to local names for regions and types of landscape and never passed up an opportunity to point them out, underscoring his point through the use of italics.[24] For example: "In the region that geographers call *Faucilles* and peasants the *Vôge*" (p. 237); "features that the language of the people sums up in the word *Bocage*" (p. 307). He also commented on names that did not arise from any intimate connection between the land and its inhabitants, such as "Massif Central, which like most such generic terms is a scholarly invention" (p. 276).

This quite modern attentiveness to the ways in which people think about the places they live in is by no means the least attractive part of Vidal's work. If he was interested in popular names, he was even more interested in the popular imagination, the stuff of dreams and myths, and dabbled in what one might nowadays call the formation of ideologies (without of course using the term). Here is a good example:

> The popular geographic vocabulary was limited. It consisted of names repeated by merchants and pilgrims. . . . These were points of light in the obscurity that enveloped the outside world. Legend drew upon this popular geography. It materialized its memories in an object, an edifice, and everywhere that roads penetrated the renown of the holy place also traveled. . . . Given this state of mind, it is hardly surprising that many pilgrims came from far away to partake of the sanctity of these holy places. This was long the source of the fame of Tours and the basilica of Saint Martin, the holiest of holy places, whose sanctity was transmitted to pacts sworn upon its altar. Hence to possess the venerated sanctuary was an enviable thing. Whoever gained control of Tours and of the famous places that fired the popular imagination thereby stood out above all others. Tours, like Reims and Mont-Saint-Michel, upon which Philip Augustus strove skillfully to place the seal of the French monarchy, was the source of a power of opinion that was easily trans-

BEAUCE ET BRIE

UNE COUR DE FERME.

Tableau de N. Lépicie, vers 1784. Type d'une ferme de Brie. Cour grouillante d'animaux et de gens, où se concentre la vie de la ferme. En arrière, un bouquet d'arbres. Cf. p. **126** *et t.* VIII, **2**, *pl.* **22**.

Cl. Lévy.

LA MOISSON EN BEAUCE.

Plaine uniforme dont le sol est fait de calcaire lacustre, recouvert de limon. Au fond, une ferme avec un bouquet d'arbres. Les nombreuses meules de blé témoignent de la richesse des moissons.

Cl. Neurdein.

FIGURE 6.2. A farmyard in Brie. Harvest in Beauce. Ibid.

LE JURA

PATURAGE DU HAUT JURA.

Vers 1.200 mètres d'altitude, on trouve généralement des surfaces herbeuses, bossuées de roches calcaires, et parsemées de sapins; elles portent le nom de prés-bois, et alimentent de nombreux troupeaux.

Cl. Hitier.

UN PLI DE CALCAIRE JURASSIQUE.

Le « Chapeau de gendarme » sur la route de Saint-Claude à Septmoncel. L'érosion a mis à nu la tranche des assises plissées en forme d'anticlinal, lors de la surrection du Jura.

Cl. Boulanger.

FIGURE 6.3. The Jura: pasture in Haut-Jura and a fold in Jurassic limestone. Ibid.

formed into an instrument of political power. The idea associated at the time with the words 'king of France' drew on memories associated with what was most sacred in the old land of the Gauls. (pp. 169–170)

It is no accident that this passage, which touches on Christianity, ends with a reference to Gaul. The book is full of allusions to pre-Christian cults. Of the Puy de Dôme, for example, Vidal wrote: "This peak was a sacred place in old Gaul, one of those well-known and celebrated sites which symbolize a whole region in the imagination" (p. 299). The interest in ancient cults is clearest in regard to Brittany: "When the people assembled, as they did periodically as if to steep themselves once more in the local spirit, they sought not the most attractive places but high mountain springs, cliffs, isolated outcroppings, and moors. In these places where clocks ran slow, they could unconsciously revert to the old cults and return to their ancient gods" (p. 333). In this astonishing passage Vidal resolutely ignored the Christian nature of the Breton *pardons.* In a thesis on lower Brittany defended in 1906, Camille Vallaux, a student of Vidal's, also paid close attention to Armorican paganism but without minimizing the role of the Catholic religion.[25] Vidal was to some degree hostile to Catholicism (although not to abbeys, which he saw as rooted in local life). He speaks, for instance, of the spread of "Christian propaganda" from the Paris basin northward to Flanders (p. 58).

The frequent references to ancient cults in the *Tableau* are crucial to Vidal's deep-seated naturalism. This is one of the things that connects his masterpiece to Michelet's: both were interested in the roots of the national genius. But whereas Michelet, a rushed (and at times nocturnal) traveler, delivered from on high interpretations intended to exalt the divinity of France, Vidal always remained the minute analyst, receptive to the many messages emanating from the soil and its inhabitants and delighted to be their vessel. Julien Gracq might have had him in mind when he wrote: "Every great landscape is an invitation to take possession of it on foot. The type of enthusiasm it conveys is the intoxication of passage."[26]

While writers like George Sand have contributed to geography, the *Tableau* is the unique example of a geographer, a full-fledged scholar, venturing into realms of sensitivity to nature that are usually the province of writers and artists. Who is to say that the *Tableau* did not somehow inspire writers such as Maurice Genevoix, Jean Giono, or the Marcel Aymé of *La Vouivre*?

In any case, the true significance of Vidal's hymn to beautiful springs and pure rivers lies in the realm of naturalism. That is why the *Tableau* has so little to say about economic matters even of times past. For the economy lives by the clock, whereas Vidal dissolves into eternity.

I have tried to convey a sense of the inner richness of the *Tableau,* of its subtle description of the relation between the soil and the people who live on it, between places and the populations that dwell in them and give them names. Now it is time to take a broader view of the conception of France that emerges from the work.

What, to begin with, is France? We come back to a question raised earlier: How does a geographic entity become a country, a nation, and a state? Vidal offers no comprehensive answer to this question, but his regional studies offer numerous opportunities to discuss the formation of political entities in relatively limited areas. Burgundy, he says, is "a political country to the utmost degree" (p. 245), but it always lacked "a territorial base commensurate with the scope of the relations it maintained. Its position was such as to inspire boundless ambitions of increase and grandeur. . . . Yet in its geographic structure lay an intrinsic source of weakness for those powers that sought to use it as their base" (p. 246). A geopolitical conception emerges from many similar analyses: Vidal tried to show how a political entity could form in a region whose geographic circumstances facilitated both relations with the outside world and the consolidation of power at home.

Why, then, did France as a whole fulfill these conditions when no smaller region or locality did? This brings us back to the problem of the Loire, which is a key to the entire work. For Vidal, the crucial point is that once the Loire had taken its ultimate westward turn, the lure of Normandy did not prevail over the transitional region south of the river, the famous "threshold of Poitou." "The linkage of the two rivers, which draw close together between Paris and Orléans, though not achieved without effort, steered the routes from central and southern France toward Paris. Nothing did more to 'southernize' the city" (p. 149). Later he adds: "An important crossroads, Orléans was historically one of the linchpins of French territory" (p. 162), so that when the monarchy gained control of it, "Paris was from then on irrevocably associated with the south of France" (p. 163). The course of the Loire thus crystallized the various geographical bonds that over time "cemented the two principal parts of France" (p. 236): the north, where the state was born, and the south, the cradle of civilization. At the heart of this crucial region lay Touraine, whose analysis could thus be expected to reveal the essence of France.

Yet one cannot help thinking that Vidal de La Blache did not answer the question of how the physical characteristics of a certain expanse of territory made France France. Was he unable to give an answer, or was it not his intention to give one? I favor the latter hypothesis (though of course he never stated the problem in such stark terms). The question is a complicated one. Many nineteenth-century scholars tried to give a scientific answer, and some believed they had succeeded. Yet at bottom the question is metaphysical, and Vidal was not a metaphysician.

More than that, in order to give an answer he would have had to rely on social and political evidence in order to show the ways in which geographical factors were not decisive. Yet it is not until page 98 that he mentions the French monarchy in passing, and indeed the monarchy is not much in evidence throughout the volume.

It is unlikely that Vidal was silent simply because he did not wish to usurp the place of the historians. In discussing the vast forests around Paris, "preserved for hunting and the seigneurial life" (p. 128—as if he could have been unaware of the splendid *Carte des chasses du roi*, compiled and engraved between 1767 and 1807), or "the seigneurial and princely life [that] gave rise to the châteaux" in the Loire valley (pp. 150–151), he never uses the words "kingdom" or "monarchy," and one is obliged to note this as a singular reluctance. And that is not all. In countless passages he depicts unlovely feudal castles and cathedrals erected on high ground as edifices dominating local life, to be sure, but above all cutting themselves off from it. "Five rivers converge at the foot of the slight prominence atop which sits the cathedral of Bourges, all but ensnaring it in their marshes and stagnant branches" (p. 156; bodies of stagnant water disgusted Vidal). An even more striking example is this comment on political developments in the Alps: "Only the Briançonnais, master, like Uri, of one of the main passes, came close," but "what ultimately determined the outcome was the feudal fortress, the château that can still be seen, part intact, part in ruins, looming on its cliff and blocking the way" (p. 265). In other words, there was a mountain pass, hence a region that might have become, according to Vidal's theory, a "node" (as he defined it in the *Principes de géographie humaine*), but the feudal castle barred the way: the image speaks volumes.

Thus the monarchy was all but nonexistent for Vidal: feudal castles and cathedrals dominated the landscape but did not make it fertile. Political and military matters, whether ancient or more recent, stood above "real life" and indeed outside it. What, then, was real life? The life of country people, who embodied the "*genius loci* that laid the groundwork for our national existence," that "*je ne sais quoi* that transcends regional differences" (p. 51).

Yet this *genius loci*, which might seem to be compatible with the teleological theories of the nineteenth century and to depend somehow on a *deus ex machina*, in fact had quite the opposite meaning: Vidal (and his contemporaries) rejected any attempt to find a "scientific explanation" for France, that is, a necessary principle, implicit in the nature of things, in virtue of which France could not have been other than what it was.

In fact, Vidal expressed what is at first sight a surprising vision of the place of certain regions in the French constellation. Of Normandy he wrote that "a new shoot was grafted onto northern France. This vigorous new growth superimposed itself on preexisting divisions without destroying their foundations" (p. 181). Of the Alpine valleys he wrote that "scant as they may seem, they added a feature to France's physiognomy" (p. 266). And of the Midi: "These regions remain to be examined; they add many varied elements to France's overall physiognomy" (p. 339). *Superimposed, added:* nothing necessary, merely an enrichment to France's central core, the north and the regions watered by the Loire, as if in recognition of their *bounty.*

This notion of enrichment, of a gift freely given, was dear to Vidal. It recurs frequently, as in this magnificent passage on Burgundy: "One can understand how the Côte d'Or became the radiant place in which the Burgundian genius manifested itself. The region was more than just prosperous: it had something of that superfluity that is necessary if the local genius is to flourish" (p. 242). *Necessary superfluity:* here more than anywhere else in the text Vidal disclosed his ultimate view of determinism. He paid his respects to life in its most generous manifestations, to the liberality that gives rise to liberty. In these remarks on the connection between liberty and local circumstances, Vidal echoes Michelet, indeed goes beyond Michelet.

If Vidal minimized or downplayed the monarchy, feudalism, urban life, and even economic activity, it was because these spheres were guided, directed, or ruled by external principles. Vidal rejected anything that might constrain or alter the intimate, local connection between the land and its inhabitants, anything that might impose an order or hierarchy on the free aggregations that made France (in this he neglected certain things that history had to teach about the construction of France). Ultimately Vidal disliked generalization. He also disliked full stops: that is why none of his analyses of border regions really attempts to explain how their frontiers came to be defined.

Now we can understand the eulogy to France with which he begins his book: "It is the abundance of 'goods of the earth,' as old folks say, that for them is identical with the name [of France]. For the German, Germany is above all an ethnic idea. What the Frenchman sees in France, as his homesickness shows when he is away, is the bounty of the earth and the pleasure of living on it. For him France is the country *par excellence,* something intimately associated with his instinctive ideal of life" (p. 50). Is there any more eloquent expression of the naturalist credo?

But what does this credo really mean, if not the idea, born in 1789, that a nation is the product of its inhabitants' wish to live together, as opposed to the determinist conception prevalent in Germany? The geographer is asserting that the French nation as a whole transcends the geography that informs each of its localities. This is a fine and subtle lesson in the *esprit de finesse.* In local analyses Vidal remained quite faithful to Ratzel's determinism, which he nevertheless completely rejected when it came to the national territory as a whole.

Vidal wished to transmit this vision to subsequent generations. In the conclusion he is under no illusions: "Neither the soil nor the climate has changed. Why, then, does this portrait seem so superannuated? Why does it no longer correspond to the present reality?" (p. 385). This, he adds, is a question he should not try to answer, because of his volume's place in Lavisse's collection, nor does he wish to answer it, because while he is perfectly aware of the effects of the "great economic revolutions" (p. 385) of the nineteenth century, he nevertheless believes that "the great changes that we have witnessed will not fundamentally alter the essence of our national temperament. The robust rural constitution that climate and soil have given our country is a fact solidified by nature and time. It is reflected in the number of landowners in France, which no other country can match" (pp. 385–386). Whence the final sentence of the book: "More than ever before, careful study of what is fixed and permanent in France's geographical conditions should be, or become, our guide" (p. 386).

"Fixed and permanent," "should be or become": these phrases describe a future for France as if inscribed in the heavens—an eternal France. Has Vidal been proved right? As far as geography as a scientific discipline is concerned, the debate remains open, for despite the prestige and achievements of the French geographical school, which Vidal inspired, other approaches—economic, social, and urban—have since his day profoundly altered our understanding of man's relation to the earth. His determinism, despite the many reservations he expressed, seems in some ways too close to the nineteenth century and too total in scope. His *Tableau* has more in common with Michelet's than with a present-day geographical work.

The *Tableau* sums up the nineteenth-century French geographical tradition and brings it to a magnificent end. It takes up and breathes new life into the revolutionary idea of France as enjoying a unity freely chosen rather than imposed. It reformulates the great vision of France as a crossroads of civilization (without ever succumbing to the jingoism of France as the synthesis of all other civilizations). And, through the importance he attached to hydrography, Vidal looked back beyond the nineteenth century to refurbish the old idea of river basins, which he presented in a new, less schematic way.

The *Tableau* cannot be judged, however, exclusively in relation to geography. The fact that it was reprinted six times between 1905 and 1979 as well as published in a sumptuous illustrated edition in 1908 shows that the work stood on its own, apart from the *Histoire de France* to which it served as an introduction. One would like to gauge its influence, which it is safe to say extended far beyond the discipline of geography.

The *Tableau* and indeed all of Vidal's work was of great importance to the historian Lucien Febvre, who developed his own ideas and his conception of the relation between the synchronic and the diachronic through his reading of Vidal. Beyond Febvre, the *Tableau* influenced the entire *Annales* school of historians. To take just two examples: Fernand Braudel wrote that "the *Tableau de la géographie de la France*, which came out in 1903 as the first volume of Ernest Lavisse's *Histoire de*

France, is, I would say, one of the great works not only of the French geographical school but also of the French historical school."[27] And Georges Duby told Guy Lardreau that "it was not my history teachers who made me aware" of the *Annales* school "when I was studying at the University of Lyons but my geography teachers . . . because in those days, now long gone, the French geographical school was in the forefront of the human sciences."[28]

Duby went on to say that the geographical school lost this dominant position because of the growing divorce between physical geography and human geography. The "miracle" of the *Tableau* lay precisely in the intimate association of the two branches, which was a distinctive feature in the triumph of French geography at the beginning of the twentieth century. One reason for this was that Vidal fully recognized the importance of anthropology and that his intention was to write an anthropological geography, even though the price for doing so was a naturalism that today seems rather old-fashioned. If history and other disciplines have in recent times placed greater emphasis on material and intellectual forces operating over the long term and played down the role of heroic individuals, autonomous political forces, and the sovereign human spirit, it is men like Vidal de La Blache that we have to thank.

It is Vidal's view of the long run that is most exciting in his work, for it is the long run that reveals the true meaning of that interaction between geographical conditions and the human response to those conditions which was his constant preoccupation. Listen to him once again as he describes the Beauce:

> Here there is only the life of the plain, with none of the variety that always goes with life in the valley. This life of the plain was concentrated in large villages clustered around wells that had to be dug deep before water was reached, villages without the trees and gardens that surrounded the villages of Picardy. The limestone layer, everywhere close to the surface, provided good material for the construction of homes and the paving of roads. The farmer of the Beauce, comfortably housed, traveled by cart along endless roads that stretched all the way to the horizon. The idea of abundant and luxuriant life became associated with the country in which he lived and colored his habits and needs. (p. 147)

This passage is composed in an admirably sober style yet manages to touch on a great many things: the nature of the soil, the structure of the subsoil (evoked through its effect on water), the surface relief of this type of landscape, its humanization through the construction of housing and roads, the prevailing peasant prosperity, and the creation of a rhythm of existence and a mode of thought. Such a tight-knit fabric left no room, however, for other factors to account for such things as superhighways, industrial parks, and housing projects. The France of which Vidal left an irreplaceable portrait is France prior to 1914—and only that France, despite the intention stated in the book's final sentence.

The intellectual and political climate in which Vidal worked is well known. At the École Normale and the Sorbonne, those bastions of the Republic, he worked closely with his colleagues Lavisse, Rambaud, Langlois, and Seignobos. He was certainly pro-Dreyfus, though not deeply engaged in the Affair. And it was no accident that Armand Colin was the publisher of his principal works: Colin was a republican, while Delagrave published the more conservative liberals and Mame the Catholic writers. Hachette, the other great publisher of geography, had no strong political leanings. Vidal's thinking also influenced that other great institution of the Third Republic, the École Libre des Sciences Politiques, where he taught after 1909 and where his disciple André Siegfried would succeed him in the chair of geography.[29]

And yet Vidal's relations with the disciples of Frédéric Le Play, his interest in colonial questions[30] and above all in the *solidariste* potential in regionalism and various kinds of association (such as the cooperative cheese dairies in the Jura) suggest a man hopeful of transcending narrow political differences to achieve a truly national position. Was not the same thing also true of Lavisse, whom the Maurrassians hated yet also recognized?[31]

Vidal's geography played a part in what was then the most urgent task that republican thought and practice had to face in the realm of the human sciences: to lay the foundations of patriotism.[32] There was a deep affinity between the *Tableau* and the ardent national thinking that inspired all the work of Ernest Lavisse, although Vidal was a suppler, subtler writer than his historian colleague. In any case, the *Tableau de la géographie de la France* is a more politically engaged work than it may at first appear.

It was the expression of a fundamentally spiritualist way of thinking, part of the great movement of thought that had been attempting, since the middle of the nineteenth century, to establish, in opposition to Catholicism, a new morality and even a natural religion. This informed Vidal's thinking about contingency and its neo-Kantian roots, as Vincent Berdoulay has shown in his thesis.[33]

Using the principle of contingency, Vidal and his school, influenced by Cournot and Henri Poincaré, tried to answer the question raised by François Simiand: How to relate a unique and singular event such as a region or a nation to a causal series?[34] The Vidalians' answer was to look at both the specific features of the place and at general, universal truths, combining regional geography with general geography. They identified a series of phenomena linked by chains of circumstances: "The influences of the environment," Vidal wrote, "reveal themselves to us only through a mass of historical contingencies, which mask them."[35] The *Tableau* is certainly the text in which this epistemology is put to the most rigorous empirical test.

Vincent Berdoulay has commented on the affinities between this philosophy of contingency and the opportunist politics of Gambetta and Ferry. Is this the source of a certain weakness in the *Tableau* and in Vidalian thought generally, a certain artistic vagueness for which his dissident disciple Camille Vallaux criticized him and which he attributed to the disproportionate influence of German thinkers? For my part, I think Vidal was acutely aware of the fragile conceptual basis of geography, which is constantly torn between the physical and the social sciences.

Still, no philosophical or political position can account for the inspiration that was Vidal's alone and that is evident in every sentence of the *Tableau*: his sense of the concrete plenitude and density of things, his Vergilian eloquence, his search for a profound understanding of rural France, of the France of *pays* that so many politicians, from the radical Édouard Herriot to the most conservative men of the right, strove so hard to protect from the upheavals of the twentieth century.

FIGURE 7.0. Proust between Mozart and Rembrandt in the bookstore of the Bibliothèque Nationale; window designed by Bénédicte Taveling, with book-sculptures by Marie-Christine de La Rochefoucauld.

CHAPTER VII

Marcel Proust's *Remembrance of Things Past*

Antoine Compagnon

One day, a certain M. Proust arrived with a shopping cart full of groceries at the checkout counter of a supermarket. Upon examining his check, the cashier said, "Too bad, Monsieur Proust. Take away one letter and your name would be famous." The renown of the writer, who died some seventy years ago, simply cannot hold a candle to that of Formula 1 race-car driver Alain Prost, who has won several world championships. But who will remember Alain Prost in fifty or a hundred years? As for Proust's madeleine, even if not everyone has tasted it and few have read *A la recherche du temps perdu* (entitled, in C. K. Scott-Moncrieff's English translation, *Remembrance of Things Past*) all the way to the end, where that morsel's true meaning finally becomes clear, the madeleine is apparently the most famous object in all French literature. It will endure: "The little madeleine dipped in the tea recalls a forgotten flavor and thus causes [the hero] to relive his entire childhood," according to the *Petit Larousse illustré*. And to think that in early drafts of the novel the madeleine was just a piece of toast! Who nowadays can bite into a *petite madeleine de Commercy* without thinking of Proust? The madeleine attests to the almost magical notoriety of the writer and to his preeminent place in French collective memory.

In the village of Illiers, the model for Combray in *Du côté de chez Swann (Swann's Way)*, "Aunt Léonie's house" welcomes 4,000 visitors annually, and the pastry shop sells five hundred madeleines each week. In Cabourg, the model for Balbec, a hotel room, number 414, has been fitted out as "Proust's room," complete with the bookshelves whose glass doors reflect the changing sky, as described in *A l'ombre des jeunes filles en fleurs (Within a Budding Grove)*. This is for "nostalgic readers captivated by Marcel Proust," explains the manager of the Grand Hotel, who recommends making advance reservations. "Marcel Proust" has the name recognition of a trademark, as evidenced by the T-shirts bearing the writer's image, the quartz watches on whose dials the famous first sentence of the novel is inscribed in a spiral, and the countless other knickknacks that one eminent American Proustian nicely described as "para-Proustology" but that an advertising executive would very likely see as the triumph of the "personal product" or "human trademark." The Conseil Supérieur de la Langue Française sought to demonstrate the moderate character of the 1990 spelling reform by calculating that it would require changing no more than one word per page of the Pléiade edition of *A la recherche*. Proust, who wrote *grand'mère, en tous cas,* and *bonhommie* (instead of *grand-mère, en tout cas,* and *bonhomie*) has become the standard of reference for modern French, like the official meter, marked on a bar of iridized platinum carefully preserved in Sèvres. Just as it is enough for most people to know that a standard meter exists without actually having to go see it, most French people, who will henceforth write *bonhommie* as Proust did, are no longer capable, if they ever were, of reading one of the typically long sentences that were the writer's speciality as the specialty of Argenteuil is asparagus. Yet what reader of Proust does not think of him the morning after dining on such asparagus, which can change "a chamber pot into a vial of perfume" (I, 119).[1] One of the functions of a great writer is to legitimate such sentiments.

Proust is the great French writer of the twentieth century: "He towers over the history of the French novel in the twentieth century," is the judgment of the *Petit Larousse*. Some even see him as dominating all modern literature. Jean-Yves Tadié, a Proustian if ever there was one, did not hesitate to begin a widely read monograph with the statement that "Marcel Proust is the greatest writer of the twentieth century."[2] Although the German translator of the work saw fit to tone down the assertion by adding "perhaps," textbooks intended to teach French literature to foreign students can no longer begin as they used to, namely, by making the point that while every other European literature can boast of a universal genius, a Dante, a Shakespeare, a Cervantes, or a Goethe, the history of French literature is instead a history of schools, movements, and groups. French classicism, for example, is great not because of one commanding figure but because it includes Corneille, Molière, and Racine, to say nothing of La Fontaine, La Bruyère, and La Rochefoucauld. No single writer embodies the essence of French literature, but together France's writers have produced a literature without peer. In this way historians of French literature consoled themselves, perhaps, for the lack of a Dante or a Shakespeare. Later they attempted to give Hugo the universality that neither Rabelais nor Rousseau achieved, but about Hugo, it turned out, there was no consensus. If today's textbooks have had to abandon the cliché that French literature must, like the Revolution, be taken *en bloc*, it is because Proust has for some time now, in some mysterious way, achieved a place alongside Dante, Shakespeare, Cervantes, and Goethe as the giant of French literature, which he has somehow subsumed.

FIGURE 7.1. Marcel Proust's bedroom in Illiers.

FIGURE 7.2. Restoration of Proust's bedroom at the Grand Hôtel of Cabourg.

Since the *Recherche* entered the public domain in 1987, editions have proliferated, and apparently the market has yet to become saturated, as if supply created its own demand. The phenomenon has not been limited to France: there are now three Italian translations, a new English version is under way as well as a revision of the German translation, a complete new Russian translation, and even a Chinese translation, the first volume of which recently appeared: "This," according to Luo Dagan, who wrote the preface, "is a work that transcends time and space," while Han Fulin, who heads the team of translators, protests that "it is shameful for the Chinese to know absolutely nothing about Marcel Proust."[3]

Proust has not always enjoyed such preeminent status among great French writers—far from it. Hugo achieved extraordinary stature during his lifetime: the street where he lived was already called Rue Victor-Hugo, and his state funeral in 1885 was one of the great celebrations of the Third Republic.[4] By contrast, for Proust, who died in 1922 at the age of only fifty-one, unanimous glory was not immediately forthcoming, though it did not tarry long. The question thus becomes all the more insistent: how and why did a writer at first marginal on account of his Jewish origins, his sexuality, his poor health, and his snobbery, a writer who was for a long time an object of veneration by a sect of initiates, conquer such a central place, to the point where he alone epitomizes all of French literature, indeed all of Western civilization? The sociology of the reception of Proust's work has yet to be written. But to explain this disconcerting evolution one needs to look at both external, or "para-Proustological," reasons and internal ones, for if Proust's book is today the quintessential *lieu de mémoire* of French literature, it cannot be altogether unrelated to the fact that memory is a central theme of the work, which was itself conceived as a *lieu de mémoire.*

Proust himself conceived of his work in monumental terms. In a sense he established the work's canonical status in *Le Temps retrouvé (Time Regained),* not trusting the task to anyone else. But when the narrator in that volume sets to work on what is to become the *Recherche,* he asks himself if his book is not destined to remain "like a Druidic monument on an island peak, forever unvisited" (IV, 618). He also compares his work to a cathedral, to the very architecture of memory.[5] That was his plan. "And in those great books," he wrote, "there were parts that had time only to be sketched out and that will never be finished owing to the very magnitude of the architect's plan. How many great cathedrals remain uncompleted!" (IV, 610). The extraordinary thing is that we have ratified this inconceivable ambition: we recognize the *Recherche* as having the immensity of a cathedral. We grant it the eternity that Proust envisioned for art and literature, which are based on involuntary memory reuniting past and present through metaphor.

The death of Bergotte, the fictional writer who is a character in the *Recherche,* gives rise in *La Prisonnière (The Captive)* to a rare meditation on immortality:

> He was dead. Dead forever? Who can say? . . . The idea that Bergotte was not dead forever was not implausible. They buried him, but throughout the funeral night, in lit windows, his books, arranged three by three, watched like angels with wings outstretched, seeming to symbolize resurrection for him who was no more (III, 693).

We know the autobiographical source of this passage, which was written in the months that preceded Proust's death, after a visit to the Jeu de Paume, where he suffered a spell while looking at Vermeer's *View of Delft* and had a premonition that his own end was near. Catholic writers such as Claudel, Bernanos, and Mauriac criticized the absence of God in Proust's work, the lack of transcendence, of open-endedness in his introspections. But art was Proust's religion, and because of this he was able to foresee the posthumous glorification of his work. As for Bergotte, art bestowed life after death upon Vinteuil, Proust's fictional musician. His music is played in public after his daughter and her female lover, who had precipitated his death of a broken heart, rescue it from oblivion and incompletion: "Vinteuil had been dead for some years. But among these instruments, which he had loved, he was allowed, for an unlimited time, to continue at least a part of his life" (III, 759). This idea is a constant with Proust, whose memory we cultivate as he wished: "People sometimes say that something of a person can live on after his death if that person was an artist and put a little of himself into his work" (IV, 105). Proust has survived. To us, his work now seems to provide a compendium of all French literature. Yet he bears no resemblance whatsoever to the image of the great French writer invented by the Third Republic.

The Great Writer and the Society of Leisure

A great writer is not necessarily a writer whom people have read. Proust's "magnitude" is incomparably greater than the number of his books in print. *Du côté de chez Swann,* initially published by Grasset in 1913 in a press run of 1,750 copies, sold 1,500,000 copies between 1913 and 1987 (roughly 200,000 in the NRF edition, 250,000 in the Pléiade, and more than a million in various paperback, illustrated, and book club versions). This is at once a large number and a not-so-large number.[6] The subsequent volumes of the *Recherche* are far less widely read: fewer than a million copies for *A l'ombre des jeunes filles en fleurs*, 500,000 of them in paperback, and roughly 600,000 copies, 200,000 in paperback, for each of the remaining volumes. Compared to bestsellers that achieve such sales figures in less than a year, these numbers are obviously small. And for regular sales by a literary publisher over a long period, Proust's figures are substantially smaller than Camus's (as many as 6 million copies) or Gide's (3 million) or even Céline's, whose *Voyage au bout de la nuit (Journey to the End of the Night)* sold 112,000 copies between 1932 and 1944, whereas *Swann* sold 87,000 between 1919 and 1940. But Proust's numbers are large for a work of considerable difficulty long saddled with the reputation of being unreadable, which had nevertheless reached sales of 100,000, a large figure in literary publishing, when it was chosen for the Pléiade in 1954, and sales have grown steadily since the first paperback edition in 1965.

If sales figures alone do not give an adequate idea of Proust's stature, can we turn to the colossal bibliography concerning him, larger than the bibliography for any other French writer? In Klapp's annual bibliography of French literature, Proust beats all records with roughly 200 annual publications in recent years, almost twice the number for his closest rivals: Montaigne, Stendhal, Balzac, Hugo, Flaubert, Baudelaire, Rimbaud, Gide, and Sartre. The catalogue of the Bibliothèque Nationale lists more works on Proust (191) published between 1980 and 1989 than on Napoleon (139) or de Gaulle (130), and there are by now more than 2,000 books on the author. The Société des Amis de Marcel Proust et de Combray envisions a database of more than 17,000 references to published works on Proust. But even here things were not always easy: between 1934 and 1938, when the annual sales of *Du côté de chez Swann* dipped below 2,000, bottoming out at 1,400 in 1936, barely one or two books were published on the writer each year.

In 1894, Gustave Lanson had this to say in an article on literary immortality:

> There is abundant material for philosophical reflection in the fate of writers and books: Why does anyone write if not to become immortal? But of those who try, how many succeed? And what is the reason for the success of those who do? Why them and not others? Why these rather than those? Here, then, are three themes that lend themselves to all sorts of amusing speculations, after dinner, among literate people, when the day's work is done and no one cares to argue about politics.[7]

Lanson characterized this sort of discussion as "ideological," by which he meant "idle." Yet it was in his day, just before Proust's, that the canon of French literature was fixed in a form that has not greatly changed since. Indeed, Lanson was one of those chiefly responsible for casting literature in the role of a national treasure and great writers as patrons of the Republic. Nevertheless, it is a good bet that he had no inkling that Proust would become their pope.

A celebrated collection, Les Grands Écrivains Français, was launched by the Librairie Hachette in 1870. It was a series of monographs on famous writers. The first was devoted to Victor Cousin, and subsequent volumes treated all the great

French writers, starting with those of the seventeenth and eighteenth centuries. For some time Hachette had already been publishing a superb collection of critical editions, Les Grands Écrivains de la France, the equivalent of today's Pléiade and one of the earliest ventures in critical publishing. The first titles, published in 1862, were by Sévigné and Malherbe, and subsequent volumes in the series were also devoted to seventeenth-century writers until 1915, when Lanson himself inaugurated a second series, on the eighteenth and nineteenth centuries, with Lamartine's *Méditations*. Certain of these volumes still stand as monuments, outdated as to their content but still remarkable for their scholarship and documentation: among them are Marty-Laveaux's Corneille, Mesnard's Racine, Boislisle's Saint-Simon, and Régnier's Sévigné, all works that Proust knew.

The rising fortunes of the notion of "great French writer" coincided with the expansion of literary history in the second half of the nineteenth century, in rivalry with German scholarship. Boileau spoke of an "illustrious" writer, Lamartine praised a "heavenly" writer, and others, according to Furetière, praised a "famous" or "good" writer. The adjective "great" was sometimes ascribed to a writer, as in this example cited by Littré: "Racine is a great writer." But the "great writers," in the plural, in the sense of a community, an areopagus, a pantheon, a congregation of secular saints on the model of "great men," did not exist prior to romanticism and the celebration of national literatures. Larousse found the expression in the works of Joseph de Maistre and Louis de Bonald ("The works of great writers are always new") as well as Joseph Joubert ("From the reading of great writers one draws an invisible, hidden essence"). None of this is remarkable, and it is not what I have in mind. That we find in Lamartine: "What we like best in great writers is not their works but themselves." Or in Jules Janin: "Molière has been dead for a hundred and sixty years. Yet he has remained the youngest, the most vital, and the truest of France's great writers." Or in Eugène Pelletan: "The writer represents the genius of a people." Great writers are patriotic. They are sacred by virtue of their difference from the *minores,* the cohort of second-rate writers not worthy of a monument in the Hachette collection. The "Great Writers of France" are our heroes—Carlyle said that writers had replaced warriors as modern heroes. They are the Fathers of the Third Republic, the summits of French literature, forming a continuous ridge along which one moves from genius to genius.[8]

What was the great writer, however, after this early period, the time of the founding of the Third Republic? With the (real or imagined—it matters not) acceleration of history that this century has witnessed, great writers have been crowned, and consumed, more quickly than ever before. After Victor Hugo many were tapped during their own lifetime: Anatole France, André Gide, Paul Valéry, André Malraux, Jean-Paul Sartre, Albert Camus. While they were still alive excerpts from their works were being read as dictations to elementary school students. Candidates

FIGURE 7.3. Commemorative Proust stamp; 1966.

for the *baccalauréat* were required to explicate their texts. And the old custom that no thesis could be written on a living author was finally discarded. These men lived as great writers: Roland Barthes has reported his emotion at the sight of Gide eating a pear in 1939. In *Les Mots,* Sartre recounts how the myth of the great writer alienated him from his childhood and even his adulthood until the war.

Paradoxically, however, Proust, the greatest writer of all, does not fit this mold. He was not an author of *dictées;* his style was far too complex for that. He did not deal with great social issues, other than those of Sodom and Gomorrah. It would be hard to characterize him as a Founding Father of the Third Republic. Not that one can say he wasn't a republican, even if he did owe his Prix Goncourt to Léon Daudet, the founder, along with Charles Maurras, of the (antirepublican) *Action Française.* But too many things set him apart, as Lanson clearly perceived. In notes[9] written late in his life, in 1925, he observed that the Proustian idea of reading, so subjective and liberal, emphasizing the reader's individual reactions, ran counter to the egalitarian intentions of the *explication de texte* and literary history, which strove to uncover the universal significance of literature or at any rate the author's intention. What Lanson clearly grasped was that Proust represented something quite different from the ideal of the great writer with which the Third Republic had identified itself. While he does incorporate much of French literature, what is missing, by no means insignificant, is the entire eighteenth century, which seems miraculously to have escaped Proust's notice. Voltaire and Rousseau were not among his favorite writers, nor was there Diderot to preach republican civic virtues: Proust's novel was not a book for educating citizens.

Proust is not, even now, a great writer for the schools, where he has never been part of the curriculum. His notoriety is more diffuse, more complex. At first there was a small circle of fanatics, known as *proustolâtres* as early as the 1920s, who awaited each new volume of the *Recherche* with wild enthusiasm. And now there are the multitudes who recognize Jacques-Émile Blanche's portrait as Proust's "logo," as the very icon of literature. Between these two extremes, things are less clear. There are people who can quote the first sentence of *Du côté de chez Swann*; people who know that Albertine was a boy named Alfred; and people who know the legend of the cork-lined room on Boulevard Haussmann or the story of the rats that Proust pierced with hatpins in the bordello. Proust in fact became the greatest French writer only after the era of the great republican schools had come to an end, indeed not until the Fifth Republic. Since it is difficult to believe that today's young people identify with the work's themes more than their elders—their loves are far simpler, their society is less select, their world is a world in which young people go to school, for example, and serve in the military, and their psychology is surely less neurotic—this success remains bizarre. In any case it is striking that while the sagas of Georges Duhamel, Romain Rolland, Roger Martin du Gard, and Jules Romains have all more or less sunk into oblivion, most people learn what little they know of the turn of the century from the Proustian cycle, in which the Dreyfus Affair, still present in its own right in *Jean Santeuil*, and World War I are seen only through the wrong end of the telescope: one learns about them through their repercussions on the salons of the Verdurins and of Odette Swann, one hears echoes of the war in houses of ill fame, and one discovers the beauty of the Paris sky under bombardment.

The apotheosis of Proust dates from the time when the intellectual underpinnings of the Third Republic were relegated to oblivion by the advent of a society of leisure. Proust speaks of painting and music, neither of which had much if any place in republican schools. Proust's culture is that of the late-nineteenth-century bourgeoisie, the last cultivated bourgeoisie before the schools corrupted it and the last classical culture before the avant-gardes got rid of it. But it was this culture, now somewhat kitsch, that became everyman's culture in the 1960s. There is no better tourist guide than Proust: one can tour Venice with *Albertine disparue (The Sweet Cheat Gone)* in hand, as Proust toured Venice with Ruskin in 1900. One can attend a concert with "Un Amour de Swann," listening for Vinteuil's *petite phrase* in César Franck, Saint-Saëns, and Gabriel Fauré. One can visit the Jeu de Paume, or nowadays the Musée d'Orsay, with Elstir's impressions in mind. When the bookstore chain FNAC opened a provincial branch in 1985, it chose to advertise the occasion with a photograph of Proust displayed with with this caption: "Hi, Marcel. Welcome to the FNAC and its new bookstore."

"Three hundred pages to tell us that Tutur buggers Tatave is too much"

Céline did not hold Proust close to his heart. He had some rather nasty words for his rival writer in *Voyage au bout de la nuit*:

> Proust, half-ghostly himself, lost himself with extraordinary tenacity in the infinite, the deliquescent futility of the rituals and situations that society people get tangled up in, people with empty lives, ghosts of their desires, irresolute revelers always waiting for their Watteau, languid seekers after unlikely Cytheras.[10]

These complaints are typical and epitomize the charges long leveled against Proust: that he described the rich and idle, the decadent aristocracy, a dead or dying era, in an invariably amphigoric style.

One is reminded of the polemics stirred by the award of the Prix Goncourt to Proust in 1919 for *A l'ombre des jeunes filles en fleurs,* by six votes to four for Roland Dorgelès's war novel, *Les Croix de bois.* The left, veterans' groups, and spokesmen for French youth all hammered away at Proust, who a year later produced this pastiche of their attacks:

> This verdict is quite a change from last year, when that filthy pig Proust, a guy practically a hundred years old to boot, won by skullduggery and intrigue . . . over any number of sound and brilliant young veterans from the war, among whom all they had to do was choose whose masterpiece to honor instead of the soporific, etc.[11]

The articles that followed the Prix Goncourt foreshadowed the negative reception that the *Recherche* would long face: the author, it was said, was interested only in the social aspect of love and of course his language was precious and his style impossible. Yet Proust's Goncourt was the most noteworthy prize the jurors ever awarded. In 1919 the Prix Goncourt was not as well known as it has since become, and if the jurors had passed over Proust as they did Céline in 1932, it is likely that the prize would not be what it is today. In hindsight, if you will, Proust did more to legitimate the Goncourt than the Goncourt did to honor Proust.

In *Bagatelles pour un massacre,* Céline's tirade against the novelistic legacy of Paul Bourget and Marcel Proust quickly took an anti-Semitic turn: "Now we're truly into shit, we've taken a tumble, fallen into the cellar of sub-*Prousteries,*" which Céline immediately associated with "the Jewish tide, the communistic, levitic flood, the Jew's ark, the Jew prison, all the flotsam on the ocean of Jew murders."[12] In 1943, Céline was annoyed that the collaborationist writer Robert Brasillach was still backing Proust, whose style he now found "Talmudic": "The Talmud is constructed and designed almost like Proust's novels, tortuous, arabescoid, a chaotic mosaic."[13] One wonders if Proust, who was quite tolerant, indeed altogether too tolerant, of anti-Semitism, would have reacted as he advised Gallimard to react in 1921, when the *Action française* agreed to run a paid advertisement with an excerpt from an article by Fernand Vandérem on *Sodome et Gomorrhe (Cities of the Plain)* only if the journalist's name was cut, because he was Jewish, and the title of the book was omitted, because it was indecent:

FIGURE 7.4. Poster advertising the opening of a new bookstore, 1985.

> Since above all I have no desire to anger Léon Daudet, I would be prepared to accept the *écho* they are proposing (I don't think anti-Semitism had anything to do with it, but "filthy Jew" is a "Homeric epithet *dans la maison*") if it were sufficiently laudatory to compensate for the imprecisions.[14]

Let us not speak of commercial strategies, but Proust was obviously prepared to make any sacrifice for the success of his book. For Céline, Proust's Judaism, homosexuality, snobbery, and style were all one: "the hairsplitting analysis of buggery in Prout-Proust, the 'subtle-straddle' half-sting of a quarter-fly," was the way he characterized Proust's manner in *Bagatelles*.[15]

But the moment when Céline stopped assailing Proust in public is also quite significant, though in private he never abandoned his negative opinion of Proust's constricted classicism, long sentences, and absence of affect, which raised his hackles to the very end: "HORROR of *explanation* . . . Proust explains a lot for my taste—three hundred pages to tell us that Tutur buggers Tatave is too much," he wrote in 1947.[16] Yet after the mid-1950s, when Céline himself was competing for a place in the literary pantheon, trying to refurbish his image and promote his new book, *D'un château l'autre*, he went so far as to encourage comparisons with Proust in his interviews. Surely this was because by 1957 it was no longer fitting to attack a writer now held to be authoritative. True, Céline was now also published by

Gallimard, but he was not always capable of self-restraint: "Proust obviously found himself in society, so he wrote about society, no? because that was what he saw, along with the petty dramas of pederasty."[17] Except for the raving anti-Semitism, the champions of a popular, populist, proletarian, communist, committed literature (the adjectives changed frequently) might have said much the same thing from the 1930s to the 1960s.

When *Du côté de chez Swann* first appeared in 1913, after which Gide and Gallimard asked Proust to sign with the Éditions de la Nouvelle Revue Française, which had rejected his manuscript in 1912, and again, from the time of the Prix Goncourt to his death, Proust was immediately acknowledged as a great writer, already a classic: "You are truly 'our master,'" Gallimard wrote him in November 1920.[18] A special issue of *La Nouvelle Revue française*, published in homage to Proust in January 1923 and reprinted in 1927 as the first volume of the *Cahiers Marcel Proust*, brought such Gallimard authors as Paul Valéry, André Gide, Albert Thibaudet, and Pierre Drieu La Rochelle together with friends of Proust (at the express command of Gaston Gallimard and Jacques Rivière). A clan of *proustolâtres* quickly formed. In 1928, Gallimard published an index to the characters of the *Recherche* along with a volume of selected passages, which went through many editions. In 1935 a thematic index appeared. Nevertheless, Proust soon went into relative eclipse. Sales of *Du côté de chez Swann* dropped from nearly 8,000 in 1927, the year in which *Le Temps retrouvé* appeared, to fewer than 1,400 in 1936, the year of the Popular Front. By the early 1950s, before the publication of the Pléiade edition, the sales figure had climbed back to just above 2,000. Although excerpts from Proust appeared in a few textbooks as early as the 1920s, they subsequently vanished for an extended period.[19] Léon Pierre-Quint, in the 1928 edition of his very laudatory *Marcel Proust, sa vie, son œuvre* (1925), observed, because it was now in fashion to do so, that Proust never pronounced the word "God" and was indifferent to all morality: "Such fecklessness," he concluded, "somewhat diminishes the humanity of his novel."[20] In the 1936 edition of the same work, Pierre-Quint noted the "indifference of some young people toward a writer who took no interest in the social question" and a work that features not a single manual laborer, peasant, or worker, while the few characters who do have professions, such as doctors, military officers, and ambassadors, are seen only at leisure.[21] He tried to save the work from the now universally acknowledged defects of the writer: his snobbery and his disturbed sexuality. In 1926, the literary magazine *Les Marges* published the results of a survey blaming Proust for the wave of homosexuality that had engulfed French literature. How fortunate that in 1919 no one yet knew the passages of *Le Temps retrouvé* concerning the war or Proust's terrible irony on the subject of patriotism!

Yet in order for Céline to have deemed it necessary to attack Proust in 1932, ten years after his death and five years after the publication of *Le Temps retrouvé,* his renown, though at its lowest ebb, could not have been negligible, for it was still of the utmost importance for a writer to define himself in relation to Proust. The same can be said of Sartre's expression of pleasure in 1939 that Husserl's phenomenology had rendered the analytic spirit of the French novel obsolete once and for all: Husserl "has made room for a new treatise on the passions, one that would take as its inspiration this simple truth, so profoundly ignored by our sophisticates: that if one loves a woman, it is because she is lovable. Thus we are delivered from Proust."[22] In the "Présentation des *Temps modernes*" in 1947, Proust was still the only writer discussed at any length in Sartre's systematic attack on what he saw as the height of bourgeois irresponsibility:

> A pederast, Proust thought he could call upon his homosexual experience to describe Swann's love for Odette. A bourgeois, he presents the feeling of a rich, idle bourgeois for a kept woman as the prototype of all love. What this means is that he believes in the existence of universal passions. . . . Proust *chose* to be a bourgeois, he made himself the accomplice of bourgeois propaganda, because his work helped spread the myth of human nature.[23]

For Sartre, Proust was at this time public enemy number one, the leading exponent of a literature of interiority in the service of class privilege. Sartre had come a long way. The end of *La Nausée,* in which Roquentin, listening to a jazz tune, thinks he sees a possible redemption in literary creation, seemed to ratify the religion of art of *Le Temps retrouvé,* a form of aesthetic alienation that Sartre would repeatedly attack after the war, in particular in *Les Mots.*

The publication of the final two volumes of the *Recherche, Albertine disparue (The Sweet Cheat Gone)* in 1925 and *Le Temps retrouvé (Time Regained)* in 1927, initiated a fairly widespread reaction against Proust. The two volumes were not well received, being dismissed as unfinished drafts that attested to the author's decline. In his acceptance speech to the Académie Française in 1947, Paul Claudel gave voice to a widely shared feeling about Proust's portrait of the turn of the century: "Still, there were things going on in those respectable years . . . other than Mme Verdurin's gossip and the amours of M. de Charlus."[24] But if Proust remained the property of a sect until the end of the 1940s, of those who "were in," as Mme Verdurin's habitués used to say, it was above all because the dominant currents in literature, not only at the *Nouvelle Revue Française* but elsewhere, particularly at Grasset in the heyday of the "four M's"—Mauriac, Montherlant, Maurois, and Morand—were persistently hostile to him, with surrealism in the forefront. Some writers, such as Gide and Mauriac, were at best ambivalent. Aragon, rather than join the *N.R.F.*

homage to Proust in 1923, published in *Littérature* an article with an eloquent title: "Down on a Dead Man." André Breton, "the charming *dada* who read the proofs [of *Guermantes I*]," as Proust called him,[25] cited him along with Barrès in the *Surrealist Manifesto*'s condemnation of the analytic novel. Few writers seemed as remote from Proust as those that were in the limelight in the 1930s, not only Céline but also Malraux, of whom Proust said, when his work appeared in the *N.R.F.* in 1922: "I don't know who all these new *N.R.F.* writers are . . . but I find their notes as devoid of thought as they are written in a jargon that is vulgar as well as incomprehensible."[26]

The late 1920s and early 1930s saw the publication of Proust's correspondence along with a number of memoirs such as Princess Bibesco's *Au bal avec Marcel Proust* (1928), all of which tended to associate Proust with the Guermantes or Verdurin side of his work. The publication of Proust's letters to Montesquiou in 1930 and to Anna de Noailles in 1931 (in the first two volumes of the *Correspondance générale*) "did a disservice to his memory," as Pierre-Quint noted in 1936, accentuating the image of him as a salon habitué, flatterer, and hypocrite.[27] He was even criticized for his "legendary tips," the only possible explanation for which had to be "the pathological side of his nature, his habit of 'buying' his inferiors."[28] In France, ironically for a writer who had often attacked Sainte-Beuve for confusing the man with the work, Proust's work was completely overshadowed by its author's biography, and most particularly by his "secret," which was presented as a key to the work by Henri Massis in *Le Drame de Marcel Proust* (1937).

All of this helps to explain the overwhelming mediocrity of French Proust criticism, virtually none of which need detain us after the posthumous publication of Jacques Rivière's articles, *Quelques progrès dans l'étude du cœur humain* (1927). This lack is all the more glaring in view of the fine work on Proust that began to appear abroad: in 1925, Ernst Robert Curtius published an excellent article, which was translated into French in 1928, the year in which Leo Spitzer published a 130-page essay on Proust's style that remains authoritative today. Spitzer saw something in Proust's style other than its slow pace and digressiveness, boredom and obscurity. Samuel Beckett's *Proust,* published in London in 1931, was, along with those of Curtius and Spitzer, one of the few works to take an interest in the novel as such without being blinded by the reputation of the author. There was nothing of a similar nature in France, where the monopoly of the novel by the *proustolâtres* encouraged endless refinement of the supposed "keys" to the novel. There was much speculation about the psychology and mysticism of an author whom the university had yet to embrace. Albert Feuillerat's scholarly book, *Comment Marcel Proust a composé son roman,* based on the galleys for the second volume published by Grasset in 1914, came out in the United States in 1934, where Proust attracted the attention of important philologists such as Douglas Alden (the author of *Proust and His French*

Critics, 1940) and Philip Kolb (who became editor of the correspondence in the 1930s). In France, only women were allowed to study Proust, and not in huge *thèses d'État* but in frivolous university doctoral theses that led nowhere. They were the first to explore Proust's aesthetics, still deemed a subject of minor importance, in studies of Proust and Ruskin, Proust and music, Proust and painting. If men dared to speak of Proust in the universities, even after the war, it was as a philosopher (the eternal parallel between Proust and Bergson), metaphysician (Henri Bonnet, *Le Progrès spirituel dans l'œuvre de Marcel Proust,* 1946 and 1949), or moralist (Jacques Nathan, *La Morale de Proust,* 1953), and it did not augur well for their careers if they did.

The Proustian Empire

"Combray, seen from afar, at a distance of ten miles around, from the railway when we arrived in the last week before Easter, was nothing but a church, which stood for the city" (I, 47). In *Du côté de chez Swann* Proust described everyday life in a town in *la France profonde.* This may be one key to his postwar rehabilitation. In the teeth of his reputation for decadence and byzantinism, people now emphasized his rather nostalgic provincialism, his roots in the soil of the Beauce, his love for Françoise, the type of the big-hearted servant and personification of the French soul, and, last but not least, his affection for churches and the liturgy, churches typified by Saint-Hilaire in Combray and Saint-André-des-Champs, the quintessential *opus francigenum,* to use an expression that Proust himself borrowed from Émile Mâle, for whom it expressed the priority of French over German gothic. The church is at the root of a myth of *la France profonde* that runs through the *Recherche* from "Combray" on:

> Often, too, we took shelter indiscriminately with the saints and patriarchs of stone beneath the porch of Saint-André-des-Champs. How French that church was! Above the door, the saints, the knight-kings with lilies in their hands, the nocturnal and burial scenes, were portrayed as they might have been in the soul of Françoise (I, 149).

Saint-André-des-Champs is thereafter identified with French purity, which is found in the aristocracy, in Saint-Loup, as well as in the people, in Morel, "to France's immortal glory" (II, 702). In *Le Temps retrouvé,* during the war, Proust identified the grandeur of France with that of the church to such an extent that "the French of Saint-André-des-Champs" became an expression designating fighting France.

The Société des Amis de Marcel Proust et de Combray, founded in 1947 by Philibert-Louis Larcher, who served as its secretary general until 1972, played, as its name indicates, on this aspect of Proust, transforming Illiers, not far from Chartres, into a sacred Proustian pilgrimage site.[29] Larcher faithfully restored the home of Marcel's uncle, Jules Amiot, the modest house of a merchant who had done well for himself and which supposedly served as a model for the far more sumptuous home of Aunt Léonie in *Du côté de chez Swann.* He carefully chose the furniture to fit the descriptions given in the *Recherche.* In 1971, for Proust's centenary celebration, he persuaded the reluctant municipal council of Illiers to rename the town Illiers-Combray, and a Marcel Proust Museum containing Proustian memorabilia opened in the grocery shop adjoining the house. An amateur botanist, Larcher also reconstituted Uncle Amiot's exotic garden along the Loir, the Pré-Catelan, the model for Swann's park. Thanks to his efforts, the hawthorn promenade, inaugurated by Robert Proust in 1934 on the steep path bordering the Pré-Catelan, is a "must" for any Proustian. To turn Proust into a champion of countryside and family, a poet of "old France," was a risky enterprise but not a wholly unfounded one if one remembers Proust's Barrèsian plea in favor of abandoned churches at the time of the law separating church and state; it was also an adroit way of rescuing the writer from Sodom and Gomorrah. Still, Illiers is not fond of its great man. Strangers used to be welcomed, it seems, with shouts of "More Proustians, for heaven's sake. Pederasts, those people, and water is all they drink."

But Proust's identification with Illiers is important today not because it has made it possible to create a local shrine to the writer but because it encourages a convenient, idealized identification of reality with fiction, which always makes for easier reading. Thus, when excerpts from Proust were once again included in a sixth-grade reader, the four passages chosen—"Françoise's New Year's Gift," "The Magic Lantern," "Saturdays at Combray," and "Combray's Mysteries" (two of the four honoring Françoise)—were of course taken from "Combray" and lavishly illustrated with photographs of Illiers and Aunt Léonie's house.[30] What does it matter, then, if the number of people actually visiting the house is only a third of the number of visitors to George Sand's home in Nohant or Rabelais's in La Devinière, or if the Société des Amis de Proust, though the largest such group for any French author, has only 550 members, admittedly from thirty-three different countries? These numbers, like Proust's sales figures, give only an imperfect idea of Proust's eminence.

Furthermore, the main reason for the Proustian renaissance was not his connection with the Beauce. After people who had known Proust ceased publishing memoirs (for obvious reasons) and two sets of letters quite the opposite of frivolous at last appeared, namely, the correspondence with his mother (1953) and with Jacques Rivière (1955), the vast unseen labor that preceded and laid the groundwork for the *Recherche* finally became visible. The work was anything but the irrepressible, improvised gossip that it was accused of being, Proust's protestations to the con-

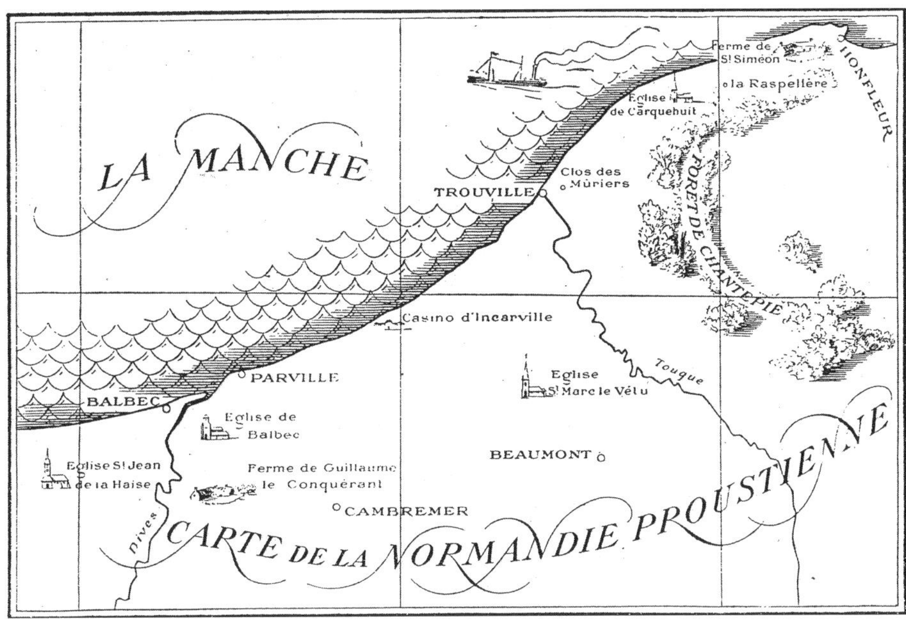

FIGURE 7.5. Map of Proust's Normandy, circa 1930.

FIGURE 7.6. Aunt Léonie's house and garden as Proust knew them.

trary notwithstanding. Indeed, it was only the tip of an iceberg. A vast submerged continent, a lifelong gestation, revolutionized the image of Proust and gave his work a memory, a historical thickness. Previously one had made do with the fable popularized by Pierre-Quint, according to which Proust's life had been tightly compartmentalized, with one part lived in society and another in sickly, studious retirement in the cork-lined room on the Boulevard Haussmann. In fact, Proust had always written, far more than his youthful work, *Les Plaisirs et les jours* (1896), and his translations of Ruskin (1903 and 1905) had led people to believe. André Maurois's book *A la recherche de Marcel Proust* (1949) was the first to deliver the writer from the ghetto of the *proustolâtres* and silence the prejudices of well-meaning readers against snobbery, dandyism, and idleness, for this excellent English-style biography was also a history of the text based on unpublished notebooks and manuscripts in the possession of Proust's family. Suzy Mante-Proust, the writer's niece, had made these available to the husband of Simone Arman de Caillavet, the daughter of Gaston de Caillavet and Jeanne Pouquet, childhood friends of Proust and models for Saint-Loup and Gilberte.

The writer's legend really began with the revelation of this gigantic cache of notebooks, with the publication by Bernard de Fallois of *Jean Santeuil* (1952), an unfinished autobiographical novel written between 1895 and 1900 and discovered by André Maurois, and then with the publication, under the title *Contre Sainte-Beuve* (1954), of excerpts from the 1908 and 1909 notebooks in which Proust, feeling his way toward the *Recherche,* still combined narrative with criticism. The failure of *Jean Santeuil* and *Contre Sainte-Beuve,* which juxtaposed philosophy with fiction, memories with criticism, without fully melding them, suddenly made the success of the *Recherche* as a total novel striking and undeniable. Far from being the spontaneous outpouring of a superior, loquacious, and extraordinarily facile writer, the book was the product of infinite labors and concealed untold suffering: one witnessed the leap from talent to genius. Claudel, who, as we have seen, still thought ill of Proust in 1947, was touched by *Contre Sainte-Beuve,* for which he thanked Suzy Mante-Proust in these terms: "It will help to dispel many of my prejudices."[31] With the publication of the Pléiade edition of the *Recherche* by Pierre Clarac and André Ferré in 1954, the effect of all these previously unpublished texts was extraordinary. Proust's drafts were now deemed worthy of publication in full. Not only did this give the work the status of a true monument by exposing its foundations, it also paved the way for its being taken up by those who would soon constitute the intellectual avant-garde.

Before long Georges Bataille published a review of *Jean Santeuil* in *Critique.*[32] Proust's involvement in the Dreyfus Affair was known, but not the naïve aggressiveness and political passion evident in *Jean Santeuil* yet well concealed behind the irony of the *Recherche.* Bataille discovered, in exploring the character of Couzon, modeled on Jaurès, that Proust had been attracted to socialism in his youth. All at once he thereby achieved legitimacy on the "left." Even more important, though in a very different way, Bataille cast a new light on all the evil in the *Recherche*—the jealousy, lies, hypocrisy, cynicism, and cruelty—which until then had been seen exclusively as immoral or amoral, neurotic or morbid, but which Bataille now characterized as "excess" and "eroticism," that is, as higher transgressions of traditional morality intended to create a more authentic morality. Thus Proust, whom Sartre had seen as the bourgeois writer par excellence, right down to his and his characters' petty perversions, presumably in contrast to the health and normality of the proletariat, was now stood on his head to become the very symbol of transgression of bourgeois morality, enlisted alongside Sade and Baudelaire, Nietzsche and Genet, and elevated to the status of hero of post-surrealist, post-Marxist modernity. Maurice Blanchot, whose review[33] of Ramon Fernandez's *Proust* in 1943 was yet another variation on the theme of Proust's mysticism—a theme that had been in vogue since the publication of *Le Temps retrouvé*—published in the *N.R.F.* in 1954 two articles inspired by *Jean Santeuil*.[34] Shifting his ground from mysticism to metaphysics, from the religion of art to the philosophy of being, these articles firmly situated Proust in a modern genealogy, as a link in the search for the essence of literature, a stage on the way to the neutralization of narrative and the ontology of art. The essential difference that Proust postulated between the social self and the deep self of the writer, confirmed by the abyss between *Jean Santeuil* and the *Recherche*, by the failure of the one and the success of the other, prefigured the future cliché of the death of the author. And so Proust found himself on the road to literature's disappearance, between Mallarmé and none other than Blanchot himself.

All the new stereotypes of the Proust myth can be found here in their nascent state. These short articles, together with a few others such as Jean Rousset's "Notes sur la structure de la *Recherche*" and Michel Butor's "Les Moments de Proust,"[35] were important because they gave Proust, for the first time in France, after surrealism and in anticipation of the existentialists' decline, *lettres de noblesse* in a camp that had never claimed him before: the intellectual avant-garde. The "right-wing" Proust was not thereby banished: the endless debate on the keys to the novel continued, as did the cries of ecstasy at the accuracy of the portrait of the Faubourg Saint-Germain. We are not yet done with attempts to prove that Proust did or did not use the Comtesse Greffulhe as a model for the Duchesse de Guermantes, the Queen of Naples as a model for the Queen of Naples, and so on. But now there is a "left-wing" Proust to stand alongside Sade and Baudelaire, Mallarmé and Blanchot, Roussel, Bataille, and Genet, or, when France looks beyond her own borders, which is not often, alongside Joyce, Musil, and Kafka. This is the Proust of the avant-gardes and the *sciences humaines*.

Yet all the works on Proust of any magnitude, whether from the camp of the *anciens* or that of the *modernes,* have come from abroad. To this day the major book on the life and the work, the keys and the models, remains George Painter's biography, published in English in 1959 and 1966 and translated into French in 1966. Painter's book was of the utmost importance for the "proustification" of Proust, that is, the perception of his life through his work. Although Proust's life was neither adventurous nor tragic nor titanic but bourgeois, stay-at-home, and all in all rather insignificant, as his correspondence shows and as Maurois faithfully represented, Painter managed to make the life exciting by interpreting it through the story of Proust's hero: "Rather than finding Proust's life in his work, we find the work in Proust's life," wrote Roland Barthes of this reversal, which abruptly transformed the life into an extension or mythic illustration of the *Recherche*: "It is not the life that informs the work but the work that irradiates the life, that explodes within it."[36] From the other camp, the work of the American professor Germaine Brée, *Du temps perdu au temps retrouvé* (1950) was the first in-depth study of the novel's structure. Hans Robert Jauss's thesis, *Zeit und Erinnerung in Marcel Proust* (1955), was the first formal analysis of Proust's temporal system. And Marcel Muller's *Les Voix narratives dans la Recherche* (1965) and Brian Rogers' *Proust's Narrative Techniques* (1965) anticipated the "narratology" that would later come to prominence in France. All these works are structuralist, in the sense that they propose formal models of the book.

The vogue for the "new novel" also had easily discernible effects on Proust's reception. New novelists such as Alain Robbe-Grillet, Nathalie Sarraute, and Michel Butor were careful readers of Proust. In fact, Robbe-Grillet believes that the new novelists were misunderstood in the 1950s because the critics of the time had not yet assimilated Proust and Joyce. The new novel demonstrated renewed interest, rare in the French tradition, in novelistic technique, and in *Figures III* (1972) Gérard Genette would bestow upon Proust the honor of offering a complete catalogue of technique for the novel in general, not just in French. Thus there were affinities. As T. S. Eliot observed, the introduction of new works into the canon can disrupt existing hierarchies, and after the new novel Proust found himself at the summit. But Sarraute, in *L'Ère du soupçon* (1956), nevertheless believed that Proust's time was nearly over:

> For most of us, the works of Joyce and Proust already loom in the distance as symbols of a bygone era. The time is not far off when people will no longer visit these historical monuments without a guide, surrounded by groups of schoolchildren, in respectful silence and rather morose admiration.[37]

She was wrong, unless of course she was using the words "historical monument" to predict the recent mad media promotion of the "Proust" trademark. In any case the new novel did not replace Proust, did not make him obsolete or turn him into a gloomy relic. Indeed, if it had an effect, it was to make people read Proust because the new novel had now arrived, like those "anticipated reminiscences" that Proust liked to discover in the works of the past.

In any event the Proustian tide has continued to rise. Although orthodox Proustians have nothing good to say about Jean-François Revel's short book, *Sur Proust* (1960), Revel usefully cleansed the work of forty years of accumulated clichés concerning time, love, and art, insisting instead on the comic, the social, and the political. Revel read Proust as a diligent realist, à la Balzac or Zola. Admittedly that is a bit much. But Proust rapidly joined the avant-garde: he was honored with ten days of seminars at Cérisy-la-Salle in July 1962. In 1963, Georges Poulet published *L'Espace proustien,* and there was also a book on Proust by Gaëtan Picon, who had evidently changed his mind since pronouncing this judgment on Proust in his 1949 *Panorama de la nouvelle littérature française*:

> If I say nothing about Proust, it is not because I am unfamiliar with him or hostile to him. It is rather that his work is remote from us not only because of its date but also because of its nature—because it is the brilliant, crowning achievement of a form of symbolism and analytic, psychological individualism that for the time being do not move us.[38]

Apparently Proust had once again begun to move.

The "Memory Portrait" of Proust that Roger Stéphane produced for French television (broadcast on January 11, 1962) marked a decisive step toward the "proustification" of Proust that Painter would consummate. Daniel Halévy, Proust's classmate at the Lycée Condorcet, who would die before the year was out, quietly told how Proust had come up to him in the school courtyard, and it was as if he still felt Marcel's hand on his shoulder. Emmanuel Berl, Paul Morand, and Jean Cocteau recounted anecdotes about his life. But above all Céleste Albaret, his housekeeper and companion in his final years, who took notes on additions to the novel right up to the last night of Proust's life and whose beautiful memoir *Monsieur Proust* would appear in 1973, put the finishing touch on the Proust myth. On the screen she played the role of Françoise, she embodied Françoise, she was Françoise, just as the Duc de Gramont, with the odd elocution of an old aristocrat, and the Marquis de Lauris, with the inimitable accent of the Jockey Club, played characters from the novel, the Duc de Guermantes and the Marquis de Bréauté. It was as if one were witnessing the "Bal de têtes" from *Le Temps retrouvé.*

From the "left-wing" Proustian camp, Gilles Deleuze's slim but celebrated *Marcel Proust et les signes* (1964) proposed a simple, systematic new model that proved persuasive to the structuralist generation. The *Recherche,* for Deleuze, was an apprenticeship in signs arrayed in circular patterns: high society, love, impressions, and finally art, which pulls everything together. The signs of art are immaterial; they reveal essences as ultimate and absolute differences. Deleuze's Proust was a Leibnizian. And thus the writer was saved, once and for all, from idealism. He had fully replaced Flaubert in the role of the great writer, the *malade des lettres,* mad for literature, that Sartre had made famous.

The year 1965 marked Proust's apotheosis for the general public. Between 1965 and 1968 a Livre de Poche edition appeared, with attractive covers designed by Pierre Faucheux and featuring a collage of photographs, manuscripts, and souvenirs. This was how I discovered the *Recherche,* as each new volume appeared. Then, like everyone else of my generation, I read Deleuze's little book, for me the equivalent of Bergotte's on Racine, and after that I devoured Painter's biography. Then 1965 brought forth a veritable feast of Proustian images: the *Album Proust* in the Pléiade, the show at the Bibliothèque Nationale with its invaluable catalogue, as well as an album in the Génies et Réalités series published by Hachette. The age of myth had begun. Sales figures confirm this, showing a regular increase in sales of the first volume of the Pléiade from the mid-1950s, when annual sales were 3,000, to 1965, by which time they had climbed to more than 12,000, settling at about 7,500 after the publication of the paperback, with another peak of more than 10,000 in 1971, Proust's centennial year.

Many years after the foreign academic works, the first French *thèses d'État* began to appear. As befits the tradition of the Sorbonne, Émilien Carassus's *Le Snobisme dans les lettres françaises de Paul Bourget à Marcel Proust, 1884–1914* (1966) and Michel Raimond's *La Crise du roman des lendemains du naturalisme aux années vingt* (1967), both excellent, situated Proust in literary history from the two recently established points of view, the worldly and the novelistic, which continued to define the way of understanding Proust. Only then could the writer become the subject of monographs such as Jean Milly's *Les Pastiches de Proust* (1970), on style, and Jean-Yves Tadié's *Proust et le Roman* (1971), on technique. Why had it taken so long? Does the fault lie, as some people have whispered to me, with a certain professor who for years dominated the study of modern French literature in France? Or was it the general skittishness of French academics before, broadly speaking, 1968? After that date the trail becomes much harder to follow.

The hundredth anniversary of Proust's birth in 1971 and the fiftieth anniversary of his death in 1972 were marked by a veritable explosion of Proustian fireworks, with an endless series of celebrations and more than 600 publications in two years. All the reviews published homages to the writer: *Europe, L'Esprit créateur, Les Nouvelles littéraires, Paragone, L'Arc, La Nouvelle Revue française, La Revue d'histoire littéraire de la France,* and so on. On the "left," the works of Gérard Genette (*Figures III* [1972]), Jean-Pierre Richard (*Proust et le monde sensible* [1974]), Serge

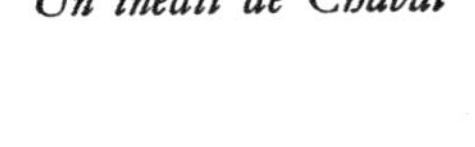

À Combray, pour la première fois, le petit Marcel goûte un peu de madeleine trempée dans du thé.

Les années passent, Combray s'éloigne...

Les années continuent à passer. Le petit Marcel grandit.

Le petit Marcel est devenu Marcel Proust.

Marcel Proust écrit...

Pour la deuxième fois Marcel Proust goûte une madeleine trempée dans du thé...

Marcel a réussi à se souvenir : c'était à Combray, chez sa tante Léonie.

Proust ne peut arriver à définir en lui la sensation gustative provoquée par la madeleine...

FIGURE 7.7. A literary comic strip by Chaval, published in *Le Nouvel Observateur* (1969).

Doubrovsky (*La Place de la madeleine* [1974]), and many others made it clear that the "new criticism" had taken hold of Proust and had no intention of letting him go. A few books began exploring the prodigious volume of manuscripts that the Bibliothèque Nationale had acquired in 1962 as an American university was negotiating to buy them from Suzy Mante-Proust. Several of these are important, including Henri Bonnet's *Marcel Proust de 1907 à 1914* (1971), a biography limited to the crucial years for the genesis of the novel, and above all Maurice Bardèche's *Marcel Proust romancier* (1971), a comprehensive study of the composition of the *Recherche* based on the notebooks. The same year saw the founding of the *Études proustiennes,* primarily devoted to the publication of the unpublished notebooks, which took their place in the new series of *Cahiers Marcel Proust.* Since then, Proust has become the main focus of "genetic criticism," which has tended to dominate the field: the Centre National de Recherche Scientifique even established several permanent positions. The Proust archives are an incomparable source: four *carnets,* sixty-two notebooks of drafts, increased to seventy-five in 1983–84, when the Bibliothèque Nationale acquired those in the collection of Jacques Guérin, and manuscripts, including twenty notebooks numbered I to XX containing the manuscript of the end of the *Recherche* written during the war, from *Sodome et Gomorrhe* to *Le Temps retrouvé,* typescripts, abundant proofs, and the famous *paperoles,* sheets to which Proust glued other sheets folded in accordion fashion, some measuring more than a yard long.

Add to this Percy Adlon's film *Céleste* (1981) and Volker Schlöndorff's *Un amour de Swann* (1984); the burst of activity that followed the expiration of the copyright on Proust's work in 1987, with new editions from the Pléiade, Garnier-Flammarion, Bouquins, Folio, and Livre de Poche; the "Quid de Marcel Proust," whose unfortunate inclusion in the front of the Bouquins edition spread the "Painter effect" to new generations; the continuation of Kolb's edition of the *Correspondance* (of which the twenty-first and final volume was published in 1993, one year after Kolb's death); the publication of Proust's correspondence with Gaston Gallimard (1989); a handful of Proust biographies on the shelves or in press; the restoration, at the Musée Carnavalet in 1989, of the room in which Proust died; and the astronomical prices that the least slip of paper with Proust's handwriting on it can claim at public auction—all this confirms that Proust is firmly established at the zenith of French letters. With the exhaustion of surrealism, *la littérature engagée,* the new novel, and other avatars of the avant-garde and the quieting of the polemics between literary historians and new critics, the return to Proust has taken on gargantuan and universal proportions.

The Novel of Two Centuries

How in the world did a Jewish homosexual and snob become the uncontested paradigm of the great French writer? If Proust was long dismissed for his neglect of the "social question," because his predilection for high society and his sexuality were seen as limitations of experience leading to despicable hypocrisy, the Proust myth really took off after the "social question" ceased to be paramount, when people stopped insisting that literature represent the classes of society and became interested in various forms of marginality. The coincidence between Proust's consecration and the inception of consumer society is also worthy of note. It became fashionable to read Proust on the train. But why did people now identify so enthusiastically with a novel so closely associated with a bygone era and a vanished society?

There is in fact a fairly high degree of compatibility between the beginning of the *Recherche*, the "Combray" episode that opens *Du côté de chez Swann*, and the new individualism that took hold with the vogue for the *sciences humaines* and psychoanalysis. "A sleeping man holds in a circle around him the thread of hours, the order of years and worlds" (I, 5). To the person who naïvely opens the book, involuntary memory can be understood first of all as a resurrection of the lost paradise of childhood, a technique that had only recently acquired a new legitimacy. The *Recherche* is the novel of childhood and of dream, of introspection and self-analysis, which were rehabilitated in the 1960s after a long period of being taboo. There was nothing new in the association of Proust with Freud; as for the association with Bergson and Einstein, it had been attempted even before the writer's death and was one of Rivière's *idées fixes*. As early as 1925, Curtius was speaking of a Proustian reconquest of the individual. Yet at that time and after, it was surrealism rather than Proust that most people identified with Freudianism, owing to a misinterpretation: the surrealists were interested in the products of the unconscious, which they fetishized, whereas psychoanalysis, like the long Proustian sentence, is concerned with interpreting the meandering course of desire. Proust and Freud acquired mass audiences at the same time: the *Three Essays on Sexuality* and *Du côté de chez Swann* could be read line against line, for both spoke ingenuously of the child's relations with the mother, of the oedipal complex, of infantile sexuality, and of adolescent masturbation. The page where the hero's father surrenders his wife for the night—"Go with the boy" (I, 36)—still stuns readers. Proust was lucky enough to belong to the last generation of writers for whom psychoanalysis did not play the role of a superego, or censorious judge, so that psychoanalytic interpreters have been able to have a field day with his work.

Yet many other more serious and substantial explanations also come to mind, in particular the prodigious ambiguity or even duplicity of Proust's work, which allows for two contradictory readings. The *Recherche* is at once a novel of the world and a novel of the novel, or again, a novel of the nineteenth century and a novel of the twentieth century, an encyclopedic book and a metabook, a "total" book in the two senses of extension and comprehension. Proust is our book of books because he can be read at once as Balzac and Blanchot, because he gives the reader the impression of being stupid and intelligent at the same time—and in that he is unique. He thus wins across the board, appealing to both the classic and the modern, the realist and the experimentalist in the readership generally as well as in each individual reader.

An encyclopedic book, the *Recherche* enchants us in particular as a literary summa. All French literature appears to be contained in this single vast work. It was Rivière, once again, who linked Proust to the "great classical tradition" in a 1920 article published amid the furor aroused by the Prix Goncourt.[39] The connection between Proust's work and the work of the French moralists became a cliché of traditional criticism, which delighted in drawing dictums and maxims from the *Recherche*. And since the notion of "intertextuality" has more recently allowed Proust's relation to previous literature to pass for modern, everyone is happy, modernists as well as traditionalists. The number of allusions and references in the *Recherche* is dazzling, and, beyond literature, allusions to all the arts—theater, painting, music, architecture, and history—as well as to contemporary knowledge—of medicine, genealogy, diplomacy, toponymy, strategy, and manners—make the *Recherche* a world, a veritable treasure trove, or repository, of French culture, or at any rate of a certain kind of French culture. Clearly, history has no monopoly on memory. Recent critical editions of the *Recherche*, following on the heels of Proust dictionaries and thematic indexes, have revealed the novelist's extraordinary appetite, prodigious enough, it sometimes seems, to have swallowed the whole of France's cultural memory.

This idea is correct but misleading. No doubt that is why it has spread with the tenacity of myth. It is correct because Proust's culture is truly colossal, yet it is false because that culture is also anarchic, fragmentary, and rather superficial. From literature, the Middle Ages, the Renaissance, and the eighteenth century are totally absent; Proust is at home only with the seventeenth and the nineteenth centuries. It is sometimes said that he was thoroughly familiar with Mme de Sévigné, Saint-Simon, and the Grand Siècle of Louis XIV in general. Yet the allusions to the *Letters* and the *Memoirs* are limited to a few pages, many of them close together, and there is nothing to suggest that Proust's erudition went much beyond the passages he quotes. The same is true for Racine and La Fontaine. As for Baudelaire, whose affinities with Proust are often pointed out, the novelist apparently knew the poet better from Fauré's settings of the poems than from direct reading of the *Fleurs du mal*, and he doesn't seem to make much of a difference between the settings of Sully Prudhomme's verses and the best of Baudelaire. Almost all his citations, from memory, are inaccurate, most of his references are approximate, and there was nothing systematic about his culture, which is precisely why it is memory rather than history, culture rather than learning. Proust's culture was that of the liberal Parisian *grande bourgeoisie* of the late nineteenth century: it drew on *La Revue des deux mondes*, the Comédie-Française, and fashionable concerts rather than on education and direct knowledge of works, and in the final years of Proust's life it yielded some of the best articles on Flaubert and Baudelaire. For a lover of music and painting, even an ailing lover, Proust spent little time in concert halls and museums. The most learned references, which came to him we know not how, coexist with citations of the social register, and everything is on the same plane. Proust drew on some of the most mediocre works of his time in ways that have yet to be fully explored. Anne Henry, in her *Marcel Proust: Théories pour une esthétique* (1981), shows how much the *Recherche* owed to the philosophy of Lachelier, the diplomacy of Hanotaux, and the sociology of Tarde. She does so in order to diminish the writer and accuse him of plagiarism, but one really ought to praise his receptiveness and his ability to transform this disparate material into a novel.

All the ingredients of the myth of the cultural memory book are there, and yet one doesn't need to be very erudite to read Proust. A few fin-de-siècle commonplaces are all one requires: Botticelli and Vermeer, Wagner, Émile Mâle's Middle Ages, and of course the seventeenth and nineteenth centuries. Proust put culture on stage, he dramatized it more than any other novelist, and he was also the last to do so. Today's readers are more attuned to this vast historical and cultural theater than to the symbolist dream of a synthesis of all the arts that animated Proust, so that we no longer understand his criticism of Balzac's *Comédie humaine* and other great nineteenth-century cycles as suffering from insufficient planning and composition. We read the *Recherche* as the culmination of French literature, as well as of the English and Russian novel—Eliot and Hardy, Dostoevsky and Tolstoy figure centrally in the discussion with Albertine in *La Prisonnière*—an extraordinary, monstrous pastiche of all our culture, to the point where, through a paradoxical, perverse effect, we can no longer read the books that Proust kept at his bedside without referring to him. We read the Sévigné of Proust, the Saint-Simon of Proust, and they are now forever identified with the clichés he attached to them, for instance the marquise's ambivalent feelings about her daughter, whom according to Proust she loved more because she lived far away and could write to her. All the books about Sévigné since Proust have stressed this point, seeing the marquise's love of her daughter as a Proustian love: Proust is not the only one to be affected by "proustification."

More than as an encyclopedic work, however, the *Recherche* has since the 1950s been reclaimed by the avant-garde as a metabook, a mirror book, a book *mise en abyme*, that is, a novel about the novel, containing its own criticism and incorporating a philosophy. *Le Temps retrouvé* has been compared with *Comment j'ai écrit certains de mes livres*, and Proust with Raymond Roussel. Symptomatic in this regard is the evolution of Roland Barthes, whose few allusions to Proust in *Le Degré zéro de l'écriture* (1953) show that he still did not know the writer well. But soon Barthes would discover the notion of "metalanguage" and apply it to the twentieth century's substitution of literature about literature for literature *tout court*. Proust, Barthes wrote in 1959, stands for "the hope of avoiding literary tautology by, as it were, postponing literature until tomorrow, by declaring indefinitely that one *is about* to write, and by turning that declaration into literature itself."[40] Formalism as applied to Proust—unfolding the first person, distinguishing between the hero, the narrator, and the author, complicating the system of voices and times—is based on this sort of observation.

Barthes returned frequently to this idea, which was not new: *Le Roman d'une vocation* was the title of a book published in 1925, even before *Le Temps retrouvé,* by Auguste Laget, who saw that art gave the *Recherche* not only its subject but also its form. The only difference was that Laget still believed that one could become a writer, whereas Barthes did not: since Mallarmé, "not only have writers become their own critics, but their work often states the conditions of its inception (Proust) or absence (Blanchot)."[41] Always ambiguous, however, Proust offered the agreeable advantage of being a writer easier and more fun to read than Mallarmé or Blanchot. "The story of a desire to write," said Barthes, hence still a story, and after insisting on Proust's modernity, Barthes apparently became increasingly aware of the pleasure he took in reading the *Recherche,* whose *problématique* was modern but which could be read like a good old novel: "The *Recherche du temps perdu* is one of the great cosmogonies of which the nineteenth century in particular was so prolific (Balzac, Wagner, Dickens, Zola), cosmogonies whose formal and historical nature was precisely that of being *endlessly explorable* spaces (galaxies)."[42] We can always reread Proust, and when we do we never skip the same pages. He gives us a world which, once we have entered it, we never leave, a breviary, a bedside companion, as the letters of Mme de Sévigné were first for the grandmother and then for the mother in the *Recherche*: "I understand that Proust's work is, at least for me, *the* reference work, the *mathesis universalis,* the mandala of all literary cosmogony."[43]

Anyone could say much the same thing. Book of books as well as metabook, memory as well as mirror, the *Recherche* is our bible. Telescoping literature and philosophy, exploring all genres—including the novel of initiation, the social novel, the analytic novel, the adventure novel, and the poetic narrative—this total, self-contained book is unique in all literature. Whence the incredible diversity of orthodox and heretical readings to which it has given rise. When it comes to talking about the *Recherche,* or to talking about oneself through the *Recherche,* all methods are good because everything is already in the book. It can serve as a pretext for any critical view, as a focal point for any desire: it is a galaxy in which the most singular idiosyncrasies can coexist. Barthes ultimately produced an expressly identificatory reading of the *Recherche,*[44] as if it were possible, once Proust had been firmly established as a modern writer on the path from Mallarmé to Blanchot, to begin reading his work once again, with a clear conscience, as a novel of high society. Proust having been recruited to the avant-garde, there was no longer any reluctance to indulge in the pleasures of kitsch or camp readings, à la Montesquiou after Mallarmé, juggling between a narratological *distinguo* and a genealogical subtlety and enjoying both.

But if contemporary Proustians are still divided into two camps, a "right" and a "left," admirers of the novel of the world and admirers of the novel of the novel—to say nothing of those sly readers who, having paid their respects to the novel of the novel, have been only too glad to rediscover the novel of the world, as the socialists have been to rediscover the notion of profit—the fact remains that the object of fascination is the same for all: the improbable contrast between Proust's long and painful impotence and the dazzling success of the *Recherche,* and this contrast is further heightened by the fact that the writer's impotence seems to be represented in the novel itself by the hero's endless "procrastination" between the precocious discovery of his vocation in *Swann* and the belated revelation of his instrument, metaphor, in *Le Temps retrouvé.* So goes the legend: in 1896, Proust published *Les Plaisirs et les jours,* his promising debut in the literature of the salon; but then he strayed with *Jean Santeuil* and amused himself with translating Ruskin. He did not reemerge until 1908–1909, mysteriously, with a novel in 1908, a series of pastiches, and *Contre Sainte-Beuve,* before at last conceiving the great novel and setting to work on it in 1909. Rare is the critic who has not dreamt of discovering the key to this miraculous transformation—the equivalent in the author's life (from a biographical standpoint) or in the structure of the work (from a formalist standpoint) of the madeleine in *Swann* or, rather, of the flood of reminiscences that overwhelms the narrator one afternoon at the Princesse de Guermantes's in *Le Temps retrouvé.* There have been any number of hypotheses. Each commentator has his own and pleases himself with believing that he has found the true origin of the work, its philosopher's stone, the pregnant moment (logical or chronological) in which the book jelled, after which Proust continued writing without letup until the day of his death.

At bottom, then, the *Recherche* exerts the same charm on critics of every stripe, including the most illustrious, and on "well-intentioned readers." Is it not quite simply the subject of the work that subjugates them, because it brings them face to face with every Frenchman's secret desire: to write, to become a writer? It is difficult, I said earlier, for young people of the current fin-de-siècle to see themselves in the novel's narrow, old-fashioned themes. Yet as French society has become more and more democratic, growing numbers of people have been able to identify with one of the book's themes, by no means the least important: the desire to write, the central subject of the *Recherche.* This was Proust's stroke of genius. For ordinary readers, Proust's biography corroborates the universality of the myth; for scholars, the slow genesis of the work attested by the manuscripts plays the same role. Every reading of the *Recherche* in some sense casts the work as a "story of the desire to

FIGURE 7.8. Allée Marcel-Proust in the Tuileries.

write." Because every Frenchman, from the president of the Republic on down, dreams of becoming a writer, everyone reads his or her own story in Proust, and his work therefore has a chance of remaining the polestar that guides us, or the will-o'-the-wisp that leads us astray, as long as there are people who want to write.

A Vast Cemetery

"People will read me, yes, the whole world will read me, and you'll see, Céleste. Remember this: it took a hundred years for Stendhal to become known. It will not take Marcel Proust as many as fifty." This appeal to posterity, so unlike Proust, which he allegedly confided to his housekeeper, was answered more quickly than even he anticipated. Proust did not have a historical understanding of art, and a merely historical understanding, counting on progress to win acceptance for works of the avant-garde, cannot explain why he is today, for us, literature incarnate: "The work . . . must create its own posterity," he believed (I, 522). The new writer and the original painter are not immediately recognized. They are disconcerting because they propose a new vision of the world. A new writer appears just as people are becoming accustomed to the style of Bergotte. What is an original artist? How does one become a classic? What is the role of time? Proust wrote:

> People of taste tell us nowadays that Renoir is a great eighteenth-century painter. But in saying this they forget Time, and the fact that it took a great deal of it, even in the middle of the nineteenth century, for Renoir to be hailed as a great artist. If they are thus to win recognition, the original painter, the original artist, must proceed as oculists do. The treatment afforded by their painting or prose is not always agreeable. When it is over, the practitioner says, "Now look." And then the world (which was created not once but as many times as there have been original artists) strikes us as entirely different from the old world yet perfectly clear. Women pass by in the street, and they are different from the women of the past because they are Renoirs, the very Renoirs we previously refused to see as women. The automobiles are also Renoirs, and the water, and the sky. . . . Such is the new and perishable universe that has just been created. It will endure until the next geological catastrophe unleashed by a new and original painter or writer. (II, 623)

Proust has durably imposed his view of the world. It took time, but not a lot of it, less than fifty years. It took a change in the vocation of literature, which ceased to be the representation of classes, and it took a change in attitudes toward snobbery and homosexuality, which no longer offend. The world that Proust created is still our world. Not that there have not been original writers since Proust. But we still wear the lenses that the *Recherche* gave us, and we judge all literature by its standard.

In *Le Temps retrouvé*, however, Proust proposed limiting the role of the writer to that of an optician offering the reader an instrument for looking not at the world but into himself: "Every reader is, in reading, a reader of himself. The writer's work is merely a kind of optical instrument, which he offers the reader so that the latter may make out things in himself that he might otherwise not have seen" (IV, 489–490). According to Proust, reading is one of the most subjective of activities, and authors, rather than impose themselves, should "allow the reader the greatest possible freedom by saying, 'See for yourself whether you see better with this lens or that one or some other"' (IV, 490). But things did not work out that way, and paradoxically, Proust's success has made it impossible for us to do without him and caused us to reject all other lenses. It is still with the Proustian lens that we see best, and it is in reading Proust that we read best in ourselves, for we learned to read and to see the world through Proust's eyes, so that every party we attend is a "Bal de têtes" and every love we experience is "Un amour de Swann." We cannot get outside Proust, whose optical instrument has become our mental organ.

Proust and Lucien Daudet amused themselves by associating people they knew with certain paintings, a habit that Swann picks up in the *Recherche*, where he compares M. de Palancy to a Ghirlandaio, Dr. du Boulbon to a Tintoretto, and of course Odette to a Botticelli. It was a fin-de-siècle fashion to confound art with life, a malady, one that afflicted John Ruskin and Oscar Wilde and that Proust dubbed "idolatry." We are all *proustolâtres,* who see Mme Verdurin, Cottard, and Brichot in people we know. Proust himself for want of a better word described as "a Charlus" a man whose "taste, as Saint-Simon said, was not for women" (III, 720). We indulge in a similar antonomasia, using Proustian proper names to designate species and types. Is there any better proof of Proust's power over us?

Proust's work has so shaped our expectations that, since gaining acceptance, he has inevitably been imitated: memories of childhood, analytic narratives, novels of sexual or aesthetic initiation—these Proustian models, now that they are firmly established, have destroyed French literature. Because the *Recherche* contains all novels and all genres, it is the paradigmatic novel, and the best we can do is imitate it. Even though Proust was never really "in" with the *Nouvelle Revue Française,* he killed it, and every publisher receives truckloads of manuscripts in the Proustian manner. A summa of literature, the *Recherche* was also in a way the end, which only further accentuates its supremacy.

For us the *Recherche* is a magical *lieu de mémoire,* not only because it can be seen as something like our literary guide, a compendium of our culture; not only because it is a book that contains its own world and ends with its own beginning, because it is circular, like a monad; but because ultimately the work itself is based on a richly suggestive elaboration of the notion of a *lieu de mémoire.* Proust did not conceive of the mnemonic site in terms of classical architecture or a Palladian theater, as rhetorical memory was conceived in antiquity or the Renaissance, nor did he think of it in the form of an *encyclopédie raisonnée* or a positivist library, the models, respectively, of the eighteenth and nineteenth centuries. Or, rather, he conceived of memories in all these ways, but without a key, a scheme of classification, for consulting what was stored in an orderly, linear, chronological fashion. Recall his comparison of his book to a cathedral, never complete yet always finished, in which each new object of worship finds its place, but by chance. Proust thought of the architecture of memory as a work of time, a mansion with wings in many different styles:

> If our souvenirs are truly ours, they are so in the manner of one of those properties with hidden gates of whose existence we are often unaware and which a neighbor opens for us, so that by some route we have never taken before we find ourselves back home. (IV, 76)

Proustian memory includes and presupposes forgetfulness. It comes after things have been forgotten, plucking them from oblivion. It does not preserve but resurrects. The entire novel is summed up in this image: "A book is a vast cemetery in which the names on most of the tombstones can no longer be read" (IV, 482). Such is the Proustian *lieu de mémoire,* a cemetery, a monument to the dead:

C'est une pyramide, un immense caveau,
Qui contient plus de morts que la fosse commune.
[It is a pyramid, an immense vault,
That contains more dead than the potter's field.]

But in yet another paradox stemming from the consecration of the *Recherche*, some of the people on whom Proust drew in composing his characters, such as Charles Haas, Mme Straus, and even Montesquiou, have not seen their names obliterated but have remained vivid in our memories because of Swann, the Duchesse de Guermantes, and Charlus, who have made us curious about their models. Who would really be interested in Montesquiou if it weren't for Proust? We must not complain. Thanks to Proust, the Mémoire des Lieux association had the idea of marking the Pré-Catelan in Illiers with a plaque, and as a result at least one late-nineteenth-century decorative garden will be saved: Jules Amiot deserved as much. In one of the strangest passages in the *Recherche,* anticipating the death of Swann, Proust is no longer clear whether he is talking about Swann, the fictional character, or Haas, the real model. Speaking to Swann in the grave, he says: "Already it's because a person whom you must have looked upon as a little imbecile made you the hero of one of his novels that people are starting to talk about you again, and you may survive" (III, 705). Swann will survive in the book that the narrator is in the process of writing: we are in the fiction. But the next sentence leaps without warning into history, where it is a question not of Swann and the narrator but of Haas and Proust himself. The author of the book we are reading now addresses Haas: "If, in Tissot's painting of the balcony of the Cercle de la Rue Royale, where you are with Galliffet, Edmond de Polignac, and Saint-Maurice, people so often speak of you"—that is, of Haas, who posed for this actual portrait of twelve members of the Cercle—"it is because they see traits of yours in the character Swann." Indeed, Haas has survived in Swann to such an extent that, in yet another proof of Proust's "proustification," he has recently been treated to a biography that in fact shares many of the characteristics of fiction.[45]

Proust had no liking for the documentary, positivist kind of memory that served up, like a series of photographs of Venice, only snapshots, that is, artificial images, ludicrous surfaces without depth. What comes back to Marcel when he trips on the paving stone in the courtyard of the Prince de Guermantes's hôtel is all Venice, Venice as it really is. In the book, thanks to art, as in the reminiscences, what is recovered or redeemed is not lost time or things past but the truth of the past, "a little bit of time in the pure state" (IV, 451). Only the ephemeral can save the ephemeral: time is always time. Every single instant, every detail, every *intermittence* encompasses the whole of eternity. Because the tissue of detail in the episodic novel far outweighs the global unity, the book is truly the manifestation of the reality that eludes history's grasp: "All these people, who had revealed truths to me and who were no more, struck me as having lived lives that benefitted me alone, as if they had died for me" (IV, 481).

If we now turn to the *Recherche* in search of our own memory, it is because we do not find that memory in the same form in works of history. Meditating on the profound changes in society caused by the war, Proust expresses doubt that these are any more important to us than apparently insignificant incidents with infinite repercussions:

> The song of a bird in the Parc de Montboissier or the fragrance of mignonette in a breeze are obviously of less consequence than the great events of the Revolution and Empire. Yet they inspired Chateaubriand to write passages of infinitely greater value in the *Mémoires d'outre-tombe* (IV, 306).

The froth of time need not be lost forever. The "philosophy of the *feuilletoniste*, according to which everything is destined to oblivion," is no more true, according to Proust, than the "opposite philosophy, which would predict the preservation of all things" (I, 469). The anecdotes, humorous stories, and gossip about which we say, "Who will remember any of that in ten years?" sometimes wait to be rediscovered. Proust mentions his delighted astonishment the day he discovered in a book by Gaston Maspero "that they knew the exact names of the hunters that Assurbanipal invited to his hunting parties ten centuries before Jesus Christ" (I, 469), when so many presumably more significant events are for us completely nonexistent.

Proust's narrative is neither chronological nor centered on events. He objected to thinking of the novel as a "cinematographic procession of events" (IV, 461) and mentions certain crucial events, such as the death of Swann or Bergotte, only in passing, after the fact or in anticipation. He recounts isolated moments without telling us anything about the intervals. The *Recherche* is full of holes, a tissue of omissions, yet it presents itself as a web of *lieux de mémoire*—a tune as in Chateaubriand, a mildewed odor, a flavor, a color—so as "to awaken consciousness of unconscious phenomena, which, completely forgotten, sometimes lie in the very remote past."[46] And that past can even be historical, as in the splendid passages of *La Prisonnière* in which Proust discovers the persistence of twelfth-century French in early-twentieth-century Parisian street cries.

Proust is always attentive to etymology and genealogy, which are the memories embodied in words and flesh. He has his ears peeled for those private words which are mysteriously transmitted in each family to refer, he says, "above all to annoying things": "This type of expression is generally the balance that remains from a previous state of the family accounts" (III, 829). A word unexpectedly restores a distant past, a syllable of Hebrew or patois reveals a Jewish or provincial background. Proust also observes bodies in search of ancestors, for example, Charlus, whose laugh, a sort of chuckle, reveals his hidden nature, which has come down to him through history:

> He had a little laugh that was all his own—a laugh that probably came to him from some Bavarian or Lorrainian grandmother, who herself took after some ancestor in just the same way, so that this same laugh could have been heard unchanged for quite a few centuries in the small courts of old Europe, where its precious quality was savored as one savors certain old instruments that have become extremely rare (III, 332–333).

This alertness to linguistic and physical atavisms intersects with the issue of heredity and race, which obsessed the fin-de-siècle and about which Proust tells us more than any treatise when he describes it as a perception of the world itself as a kind of *lieu de mémoire*.

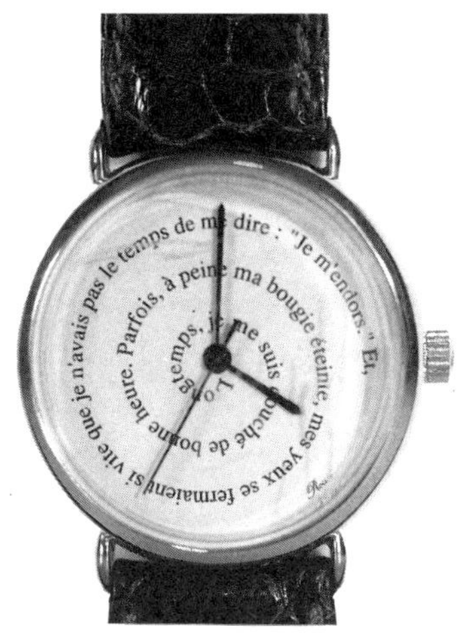

FIGURE 7.9. Wristwatch featuring the first sentence of Proust's novel. The spiral evokes the structure of the novel, the flight of time, and the traditional watch-spring.

In "Combray," as a prelude to the episode of the madeleine, Proust proposes his own theory of *lieux de mémoire*, a theory inspired by contemporary doctrine yet highly personal. He suggests that the past is never dead in us but survives, potentially, in the most insignificant things:

> I find quite reasonable the Celtic belief that the souls of the departed are captive in some lower form of being, an animal, a plant, an inanimate object, lost for us until the day, which for many never comes, when we happen to pass the tree or come into possession of the object in which they are imprisoned. Then they flutter, they call out to us, and the moment we recognize them the spell is broken. Delivered by us, they have conquered death and come back to live with us (I, 43–44).

The source of the belief to which Proust alludes is not clear: Michelet, Renan, Anatole France—it could be any of them, because the idea was in the air. Yet none of these writers spoke of inferior beings or inanimate objects as repositories of dead souls. That was the Proustian version of the cult of the dead that Fustel de Coulanges lauded and in which the Third Republic placed its faith. It turned the world, as in the *Mémoires d'outre-tombe*, into a vast echo chamber of history. In 1815, when the remains of Marie-Antoinette and Louis XVI were exhumed, Chateaubriand recognized "in the midst of the bones . . . the head of the queen by the smile that that head had directed [toward him] at Versailles" when he was introduced to the court in 1787, the only time he ever saw her. Resurrection is a matter of chance, the product of an accidental encounter. No determinism can lay claim to the rediscovery of the past. This idea figures centrally in *Le Temps retrouvé:*

> Minds that like mystery want to believe that objects preserve something of the eyes that looked at them, that monuments and paintings reveal themselves to us only through the palpable veil that love and the contemplation of so many admirers have woven for them over the centuries. (IV, 463)

History lives in *lieux de mémoire*. In the Prince de Guermantes's library, the narrator discovers *François le Champi*, which, however mediocre the book, brings back the forgotten night when his mother read it to him in Combray. *Du côté de chez Swann* serves for us the same function that George Sand's book served for the narrator of the *Recherche*. Alongside the documents of history *lieux de mémoire* lie in slumber. We turn certain books, like the *Mémoires d'outre-tombe* and *A la recherche du temps perdu* into very special *lieux de mémoire*, and they become essential to us because they help, because literature helps, us to think of memory in terms other than historical.

PART III

SINGULARITIES

FIGURE 8.0. A meeting of the Académie at the Louvre, after 1672. The portrayal is certainly not exact: everything has been embellished and ennobled for the glory of the monarchy. At the far end of the hall the engraver has placed an empty throne, like the one that awaited the sovereign at the Parlement of Paris in case he decided to hold a *lit de justice.* The two vignettes above the imaginary arch of triumph depict a reception of academicians by Louis XIV and Queen Marie-Thérèse at a court ceremony.

CHAPTER VIII

La Coupole

Marc Fumaroli

> As luck would have it, I, having camped on a hill among Iroquois and in a tent among Arabs, having donned the buckskin of the savage and the caftan of the Mameluke, found myself at table with kings and then plunged once again into indigence. I took part in peace and war, I signed treaties and protocols, I witnessed sieges and conclaves and the reconstruction and demolition of thrones. I made history, and I could write it. My silent and solitary life proceeded amid sound and fury with the daughters of my imagination—Atala, Amélie, Blanca, and Velléda—to say nothing of what I might call the realities of my time had they been anything but alluring illusions. I fear that my soul was of the kind that an ancient philosopher once termed a sacred malady.
>
> *Chateaubriand, Mémoires d'outre-tombe, ed. Levaillant (Paris: Flammarion, 1949), 5: 602.*

1. In this peroration to the *Mémoires d'outre-tombe*, Chateaubriand summed up that entire work by reciting the *curriculum vitae* that he hoped to see engraved forever in the marble of France's ideal pantheon. The composition of this epitaph observes precise rules of precedence, which are respected with all the punctiliousness of a courtier of the Ancien Régime. First comes the career of the public man, who was in turn a political exile, an advisor to the prince, a statesman, and a diplomat. Next, and less prominently, come the various phases in the career of a man of letters. This second career, moreover, is carefully indicated to have been entirely subsidiary to the first, thus warranting the author's work against any imputation of vulgar or venal sophistry. As an actor in the history of France, he is therefore also entitled to be its bard, adding narrative to deeds and thus contributing his full measure to the French epic. As a historian as well as an actor in history, he has, in addition, practiced a sub-genre of historiography based, like historiography itself, on firsthand experience: the travel narrative, a variant of historical narrative, to which the great witness devoted himself in exile. At this noble level, then, he has excelled in the supreme genres: the *Iliad*-History and the *Odyssey*-History. Descending a few notches, Chateaubriand now cites his work as a lyric poet and author of prose idylls: *Atala*, *Les Martyrs*. Eloquence, his-

tory, poetry: Homer, Bossuet, Fénelon. Next we hear the music of elegy, first in the allusion to fleeing Daphne, who in any number of beloved guises always manages to escape, and then in the avowal of that melancholic temperament that Aristotle reserved for heroes and geniuses. We understand that the *Mémoires d'outre-tombe* are the *Aeneid* of an Aeneas who was evidently his own Vergil. In a few lines Chateaubriand has sketched himself at the center of the allegorical scene from the *Inspiration of the Poet* by his beloved Nicolas Poussin. At the same time he has summed up the whole academic ideal of the Ancien Régime and, by stating it in the first person, has translated it for the romantic French nineteenth century. This modern translation would not have been possible without the "I" of Rousseau's *Confessions*. But what transformations that "I" has undergone! Formerly unfathomable and untamable, it has become the mainspring of a threefold public career, which it has shrouded in its mystery: a career in the State, a career in Letters, and a career that one dares not call private because its legend had been public for so long before finding its "ultimate" expression in the *Mémoires*—what Chateaubriand called "the realities of my time," which bestowed upon his idyllic and elegiac work the authentic warrant of autobiography. Here was Rousseau revised and corrected by Fénelon's *Lettre à l'Académie*. In a prodigious interplay of mirrors, the longest, most splendid academic eulogy in all of French literature was delivered by the very man who was also its subject.

To pull off or even hazard a tour de force of this kind, however, one has to be fully and serenely certain that it will be understood and even avidly savored. Neither Chateaubriand's life nor his earlier work were enough to create that expectation by themselves. He had to know that he was sustained by a generally recognized hierarchy of values and canonical forms, mastery of which guaranteed their "Enchanter" an infallible recognition: the grand style, the great genres, the major forebears—Homer and Vergil, Tasso and Fénelon, Poussin—all orchestrated by a man who wed undisputed official rank to the allure of Letters, an allure that by itself might have seemed suspect. No single writer or œuvre could have created all these implicit conditions of success: Chateaubriand knew that he was sustained by a majestic national tradition revered by his audience. Much older than the writer himself, that tradition would survive him. It was not fundamentally different from the tradition that sustained Ingres in the *Apotheosis of Homer*. For French men of letters, that tradition was associated with the Académie Française, with its social and aesthetic norms, and with the cultural order that it authorized as the *commonplace* of national grandeur and glory. Standing at the center and summit of the French nineteenth century, Chateaubriand took that tradition, which the Revolution and Empire had not eradicated but revived, and reinterpreted its basic assumptions, just as Ingres did for the traditions of which the Académie des Beaux-Arts was the repository. There is no better evidence of his vitality than the virtuosity with which he took Rousseau's singular, disjunct self and turned it, for his own glory and that of French letters, into a classic case of inspired melancholy, whose natural vocation since Aristotle had been for *great* tragic roles, in drama that Rousseau reviled but that, in the *Mémoires d'outre-tombe,* became none other than the *tragic stage* of Antiquity and the Renaissance, at the center of the city or court: a theater in which admiration takes precedence over terror and pity and whose relatively few and recurrent uses respected the rules of classical dramaturgy, formulated when the Académie was founded: unity of place (Paris, to which all roads lead), time (a "century"), and action (a career as statesman and man of letters). Chateaubriand also took love—but love according to Petrarch, the essential ingredient that our classical tragedy added to its Greco-Latin models—and added it in turn to the norms of Ancien Régime literary biography: after him, the French-style "great writer"—the official or unofficial *académicien*—was entitled to a Muse publicly incarnated in "the realities of his time": Hugo and Juliette, of course, but before Hugo, Lamartine and Elvire, and after Lamartine, Barrès and the Comtesse de Noailles, Lemaître and the Comtesse de Loynes, France and Mme Arman de Caillavet, and, even more recently, Malraux and Louise de Vilmorin, Aragon and Elsa, Sartre and Simone de Beauvoir. In France the "great writer" with his official mistresses is still a public man even in private life, just like kings, whose private lives were stylized as legend in accordance with time-honored models.

2. Though Rousseau's posterity—fascinated, to be sure, by the heroic career of Napoleon—proclaimed itself alien to the world and its philistine ways, it took the mechanisms of public recognition and ennoblement that the Ancien Régime had, in moderation, made available to men of letters and caused or allowed them to operate with unprecedented intensity. Racine, Boileau, and La Fontaine had merely joined other "illustrious men" of various professions in Perrault's ideal academy of "Moderns." The "geniuses" of romanticism sought grandeur of a quite different kind, a spiritual magisterium that Malraux later translated into technocratic terms by having himself named minister of cultural affairs and thumbing his nose at the Académie. Probably the first appearance of a magisterium of this type in France dates from the court of the Valois. The "palace academy" whose patron was Henri III himself and whose first "perpetual secretaries" *avant la lettre* were Guy du Faur Pibrac and Jacques Davy Du Perron had already played a role in recognizing Ronsard as the kingdom's official orator-poet. It had served Du Perron himself well in his brilliant literary and later ecclesiastical career. And the first *discours de réception* in French history was surely Du Perron's funeral oration for Ronsard, which was delivered at the Collège de Boncourt in 1585.[1] But obviously it was Richelieu's founding of the Académie Française that permanently associated the rites of passage of the literary vocation with the acknowledgment of public utility and the

entry into a sort of national pantheon. Based on the theater of the court and in accordance with an etiquette that would be elaborated little by little, a Parnassus was created in which men of letters had their place and which gave them, along with the honors of the court, the right to share in the immortality and authority of the monarchy. This was not yet the magisterium of genius, but it was at least for literary reputation, in itself evanescent and suspect, a legitimate status, which established its rank alongside the offices and charges dispensed by the state. It was rescued from the whims of patrons, the shifting favors of the public, and the prejudice against professionals of the pen, a prejudice scarcely less humiliating than the anathema on tumblers. At its inception this legitimation was quite modest. Membership in the Académie Française under the Ancien Régime preserved a man of letters from the common condition because there, and there alone, he could mingle as a colleague with the ministers of state, great lords, and high dignitaries who gave the Company its true brilliance. Still, it was a royal company, and men of letters derived from those of their number who belonged to it a luster sufficient to bestow upon their social group the authority it would later enjoy under Louis XV and Louis XVI, rivaling that of such traditional authorities as the magistracy, the clergy, the nobility, and the court. What is more, this "royalty" of men of letters during the Enlightenment laid the groundwork for what Paul Bénichou has called the "sacralization"[2] of the romantic writer: this was a "Napoleonic" sacralization, in which the writer, acclaimed by the *vox populi,* crowned himself rather than accept his crown from any established authority. Yet Napoleon's coronation took place in Notre-Dame, in the presence of the Roman pontiff. Chateaubriand himself, always so eager to hold important diplomatic and political posts, considered it natural to take his seat in the academy, which translated his literary glory into the language of officialdom. Indeed, as the postrevolutionary Académie reemerged by degrees after its abolition in 1793, it was more than ever an institution of state, a *grand corps* at once attesting and ensuring that in France literature was a matter of public utility. All the great romantics from Lamartine to Musset eventually became members, and Baudelaire himself considered it natural to become a candidate. This, as we shall see, is not to say that there was not growing tension between literary notability of the academic type and the centrifugal subjectivism of romantic and post-romantic poetics. In Paris, however, not even literary subjectivism and gnosticism could resist the temptation to create a public persona and exercise a form of magistracy. The link established by the Académie Française between the mastery of eloquence and participation on a footing of equality in public life became a natural assumption of even the rebellious writer. Thus, when the Académie was itself rejected, denigrated, and combatted, its adversaries internalized its principle and took it into their own camp. The cliques that form around a journal, a publishing house, a manifesto, or a great man are apt to reproduce within their midst something very like academic rituals. More than that, they aspire to occupy a legitimate, universal, and central place in the life of the mind and ultimately in public life as well. Even though what is now called literary life, with its seasonal prizes and juries, has shrunk considerably in comparison with the past, it is invariably a copy, faithful but ephemeral, of the formal model impressed on French national memory in 1671, when the Académie Française awarded its first prize for eloquence.[3] The king and his court, whose prestige the Académie reflected and refracted onto men of letters, have disappeared, yet the state and fashionable Parisian society still turn to the Académie and its numerous satellites in search of the mediators and exchangers through whom the art of good writing brings access to notoriety, visibility, and perhaps even authority.

3. In the fragmentary texts published under the title *Contre Sainte-Beuve*,[4] Proust picks apart what Chateaubriand, in our introductory quote, apprehended as a synthetic whole: namely, "genius" and the various hierarchically ordered careers that had projected that genius onto the stage of history. According to Proust, all that should matter to us is the literary work of genius, the work alone. The work contains its own secret, and the social man, public and private, that Chateaubriand took such care to present as the warrant for his work is of no use in deciphering that secret. Literary genius pertains only to the work that manifests it, art pertains only to art. What about the historical and social worlds? These were but obstacles for genius to overcome, stereotypes and illusions to be dispelled. Accordingly, Proust rejected Sainte-Beuve's entire critical method, which in so many ways expressed the academic spirit of the nineteenth century: that method proceeded systematically from the social man, the public man, to the work, which doomed it to miss the genius revealed only by the work itself. Inevitably it dwelt on a host of mediocrities who enjoyed a rank and place in society but for whom literature was merely an ornament, albeit perhaps the most precious ornament, of their "distinction." In Sainte-Beuve's *Lundis*, Vicq d'Azyr receives as much attention as Victor Hugo, Daru as Stendhal, Molé as Baudelaire, Mérimée as Balzac—and much more sympathy. The *Lundis* were for Proust what the Académie was for Arsène Houssaye: the "forty-first chair" was always vacant.[5] Yet Houssaye's son, Henry, became one of the Forty. And in *Mémorables*, Maurice Martin du Gard tells a story he heard from Maurice Barrès, in which Proust pays a midnight call on the author of *Colette Baudoche* to sound him out about the possibility of becoming a candidate for the Académie.[6] The election to the Académie of one of Baudelaire's most fervent admirers would have been revenge for the poet's own failure, which elicited from "Uncle Beuve" this savage report: "When one reads [in the Académie minutes] the last sentence of your acknowledgment, conceived in such modest and polite terms, one says out loud: Very good. So you've left a good impression of yourself. Isn't that something?"[7]

Proust was not wrong to see Sainte-Beuve as the chief enemy of the gnosis of art elaborated throughout the nineteenth century in protest against academic conventions. But in refusing to confine himself within literature in the gnostic sense, did Sainte-Beuve betray letters? Working tirelessly against the current that swept along his century and his friends, he pointed out that literature was not a sect, even of occasional geniuses, but a national Port-Royal open to all sorts of talent, provided they demonstrated, in proper order, a love of language and "classical" wisdom, which together constituted for him the common ground of French men of letters. Thus, to Proust's dismay, the *Lundis* were a vast extension of the nineteenth-century Académie Française, welcoming consecrated "geniuses" but reluctant to accept contemporary and controversial ones, and welcoming even more those who played supporting roles, whose honest talents strengthened institutions and enabled them to endure. Proust refused to see that for Sainte-Beuve French literature was a national institution and that his column in the *Constitutionnel* was a vigilant contribution to the well-being of that institution.[8] Among other things the institution had to be protected against the captiousness and irresponsible improvisations of exceptional "geniuses." And if France, for Sainte-Beuve, was the literary nation par excellence—as it was, in the realm of painting, for Diderot or Delescluze—it would remain so not so much by the brilliance of a few exceptions as by an abundance of regular talents, by their variety and authentic solidity, and by the appetite for high literary standards that this very abundance would foster outside the ranks of professional writers. Proust's doctrine—found also in embryo in Flaubert and the Goncourts—was in short the despair of the unanointed. To the extent that the Académie was the head and exemplar of the literary nation, moreover, it was only natural that it should be a company, in the sense that the Comédie-Française was a company, that is, not a collection of stars but a gathering of people of various skills, including supporting actors. The Société des Gens de Lettres was quite capable of defending the corporate interests and publishing rights of professional clerics. That was something else entirely. Sainte-Beuve had a "nobler," less pure conception than Proust of both his critical authority and that of the Académie Française: the impurity as well as the nobility preserved the character of the national literary common ground, where abilities of various kinds, and not just writers who were only writers, could seek public recognition and consecration.

Art historians, freeing themselves from the prejudices of modernism, have studied the central role of the Académie Royale de Peinture with its Prix de Rome and its Salon in the extraordinary development of the art of painting in France from the seventeenth to the nineteenth century.[9] Even the privilege that this academy long bestowed on "history painting," and the institutional and theoretical structures that derived from that privilege, provoked, in reaction, a long series of felicitous heresies that made French painting what it is. It was the same in Rome in the seventeenth century, where the canonized, monumental models of the High Renaissance spurred reaction as often as emulation. It is less obvious that the Académie Française played a similar role in literary history. Once the question is raised, however, it becomes fairly clear that the Académie continuously occupied a central position in the symbolic economy that governed the fate of letters in France, both in the national imagination and in the ranks and motifs of French society. The anecdotes, capsule biographies, and chronological narratives that fill all too many histories of the Académie veil what Paul Valéry called the "mystery" of the institution. That "mystery," which others might call its esprit de corps, has nothing to do with literary "genius" or "creativity." It is a collegial sense of attending to what Valéry still called the Académie's "function," which is to epitomize the inscription of letters in the fabric of the French state and society. That inscription is so profound and so traditional that only those members of its body in possession of its secret are aware of its existence. France is the first—and indeed the only—country endowed with an official "literary corps," election to which is the supreme honor that can be bestowed on people from all walks of life and not just those who pursue literary careers: academicians have come from the army, the church, the government bureaucracy, the bench, the diplomatic corps, the legal profession, and the university, as well as from science, "society," and, more recently, from the world of cinema and television. Having bestowed prestigious "grandeurs of establishment" on men of letters, the Académie also gave them an ideal of literary glory. No serious analysis of the relationship between literature and the nation-state in various periods can afford to overlook the "mystery" and "function" of the Académie Française.

4. Academic literary history, fluctuating between positivist methodology and the romantic ideals, has failed to show much interest in institutions. Though much concerned with establishing the lives of writers, it has paid only intermittent attention to any possible academic ambition or to the position of the writer with regard to academic norms. It has left the history of the Académie Française to a subspecialty, the "history of the Institut." And that subspecialty, with the exception of an interesting essay by Paul Mesnard (1857!),[10] some "insider" remarks by Sainte-Beuve,[11] and an admirable pre-Lansonian thesis by Lucien Brunel,[12] has been too limited in scope even to glimpse the role that the Académie may have played in establishing a nexus among literature, state, and society, in establishing the various forms of the writer's public *persona*, or in the history of literary genres. Do the introductory remarks above suffice to suggest the potential benefits to historians of adopting the central and panoramic view that the Académie Française affords? Far from limiting perception to the academic microsociety and its immediate fringes, which in themselves deserve greater attention than they have received, this approach shows how the negation of the academic literary paradigm has shaped the idea of literature that currently prevails in France. In Simone de Beauvoir's *Les Mandarins*, where the

very terms *Académie* and *academician* are insults,[13] the coterie of "committed" journalists and novelists that forms the subject of the novel is sustained by a French idea of literature, which is implicit for them and obvious to their public. And that idea, from which they derive their strength, is essentially to live without admitting it on the income from the capital of prestige of which the Académie is the Banque de France. Instinctively and without resistance on the part of their audience, they behave as if their writerly gifts bestowed national authority on them, a universal moral and political authority that immediately grants them as much of a right to be heard as political leaders and public officials. What has happened here is the same thing that historians of art have found among painters who shaped their work and their careers in opposition to the closed system largely controlled by the Académie des Beaux-Arts: they instinctively occupied the niche of "great painter" that the Académie had patiently imposed on the national imagination from the day it was founded. They inexorably hoisted their works up to the level of the "great genres" whose supremacy the Académie had established over the centuries: Picasso, with *Guernica*, by far his most famous painting, created a great "history painting," which in another age would have entitled him to submit his candidacy for the Académie de Peinture, much as Watteau did after the *Embarkation for Cythera* or Greuze after *Severus and Caracalla*. Even the genre of academic encomium, the keystone of the entire edifice, is reflected in the deforming mirror held up by the cenacles refractory to established literary authority: the academic idea is a perennial everywhere in France, and perhaps especially where one seeks to supplant its official incarnation. For the regular visitors to Mallarmé's cenacle on the Rue de Rome,[14] the poet's "eulogies" (subsequently models for the properly academic eloquence of Valéry and Claudel) resurrected the rites of the cathedral on the Quai Conti within the confines of a literary chapel. And in the surrealist and later the existentialist coteries, the eulogy (often a privilege reserved for the leader of the group) was instinctively linked to the group's ancestor worship and adoption ritual. The *discours de réception* by the surrealists' *secrétaire perpétuel* André Breton were as celebrated as his anathemas on the excluded candidates. And in the work of Sartre, who became the *secrétaire perpétuel* of the Academy of *Les Temps Modernes*, the enormous eulogies dedicated to the ambiguous ancestor, Flaubert, and the adopted outcast, Genet, can be seen as rather monstrous but still official excrescences of a national genre, the panegyric of the *séance solennelle* or *séance de réception!*

This is because the panegyric—a genre widely decried by the semi-cunning—is not content simply to return repeatedly to the source of literature's power to act as a social bond, to create a symbolic suture between the living and the dead, between people of varying ages and functions in the "tribe." A magical mirror of all the major oral genres—hymn, epic, and funeral oration—the panegyric stands at the center of any celebration that renders a society present to itself and gathers it around a shared, sacred *patria* and patrimony. Now, the panegyric is the institutional genre of the Académie Française, where its public role is not occasional but fundamental. For three centuries it has established the rhythm of the academic year. There it serves not simply as the "monstrance" of the national language, which has been placed in the Académie's charge and whose proper use it monitors. It also reaffirms the preeminence of the grand style and the major genres of eloquence, history, and poetry, whose exemplary place in French Letters the Académie has upheld for three centuries, because its ambition is to succeed at once as eloquence, as history, and as epic-lyric-elegiac poetry. The effect of this central genre on our literature, if only by ironic or outraged reaction, has been immense. We glimpsed this in the introductory quote from the *Mémoires d'outre-tombe*. We might equally well have glimpsed its remote and satirical refraction in the speech at the agricultural fair in *Madame Bovary*, in Jarry's "pataphysical" parodies, and in Jules Romains's send-ups.

5. Thus in two respects, sociopolitical and literary, consideration of the Académie Française ought to be a prolegomenon to any history of modern and contemporary French literary culture. Here, however, I can do no more than stake out the territory and offer a few suggestions for analysis. But even within these necessarily quite modest limits, how can I avoid reflecting on the foundation of the Académie, which coincided with the first flourishing of both the modern French state and modern French literature?

Richelieu, a cardinal of the Holy Roman Church, must have deemed it appropriate to his station to establish a private academy with himself as patron. Along with building palaces and castles and libraries and collections, founding an academy was a natural part of the exercise of one of the virtues inherent in a prince who was also a clergyman: magnificence.[15] Other Roman and French cardinals, including one who was in many ways Richelieu's model, Cardinal Du Perron, had preceded him down this path. Accordingly, in 1624, Richelieu formed a group of men of letters to serve as his "academy in the fields," and so it would remain, despite the disgrace of some old members and the adoption of some new ones, until the cardinal's death. The purpose of this academy was that of all private academies: to please and instruct. This, of course, required the knack of praising the master and if necessary engaging in polemics on his behalf. But the fact that a substantial contingent from this private academy (Sirmond, Silhon, Boisrobert, Hay du Chastelet, Desmarets, La Mothe le Vayer, Chapelain) entered the Académie Française during Richelieu's lifetime cannot hide one essential fact: the Académie, established in 1635 by letters-patent signed by Louis XIII, was a royal foundation, instituting a *corps de l'État*, whose status was radically different from that of a private academy. The members of a private academy are isolated individuals who serve their master in a personal capacity and who may be dismissed at any time. The members of the Académie belong to a "corps," and even if their election depended on approval by the cardinal and very likely on his prior suggestion, once elected they benefitted, like the members of similar bodies, from the permanence of the monarchy and were no longer subject to the ephemeral will of a minister, even when that minister was named Richelieu. Boisrobert, in disgrace, was expelled from the cardinal's "academy in the fields" in 1641 yet remained a member of the Académie Française until his death in 1661. The Académie's chosen motto, "To Immortality," referred not only to literary glory but to the corporate transcendence of the life of any individual, a transcendence that medieval jurists conceptualized on the model of that mystical body the Church.[16] Despite Richelieu's statism, derived from that of Jean Bodin, and despite his cavalier treatment of the Académie, the cardinal respected, as much as it was in him to respect, the autonomy of the corps he had created. One can place this construction on the care he took never to appear at academic sessions, thereby marking the difference between a royal establishment and his own private academy.

But why run the long-term risk of granting men of letters an autonomous Company, thereby according to French literature the status of an institution and the independence, modeled on that institution, of a veritable "mystical body"? Those specifically French phenomena, the philosophy of the Enlightenment and the romantic coronation of writers, are inconceivable anywhere other than in a country where, *on principle,* in Montesquieu's sense, literature was provided with a transcendent and immortal "body." There are two ways of responding to the question. In order to associate men of letters with the state, the only legal instrument available to Richelieu was the old concept of corporation, which Jean Bodin had tried to limit but had been unable to replace.[17] Before it could be replaced, the very concept of monarchy had to be demolished. And then, even if, as we may suspect, Richelieu perceived the difficulty, the men of letters he had before him may well have aroused his suspicion, yet they caused him no immediate anxiety. Indeed, they were men of letters who practiced in the vulgar tongue, whose prestige and influence were still uncertain and whose gratitude he was able to win by taking a step that granted them a publicly useful status. In terms of contemporary European culture, that step was not fundamentally dissimilar from the ordinance of 1641 granting respectable civil status to actors, who previously had lived on the fringes of society, sometimes celebrated, at other times treated as vulgar mountebanks.[18] The craving for respectability on the part of men of letters working in the vulgar tongue, disdained by humanist magistrates and often dependent on the whims of a great lord, was too powerful at the time for their nascent esprit de corps not to work in favor of the Académie's founder.

What is more, the *lettrés* writing in the vulgar tongue whom Richelieu deemed it wise to associate with the state by founding for their benefit a respectable and permanent institution shared with the *lettrés* in his own entourage a commitment to the doctrine of Malherbe.[19] And that doctrine, which Richelieu knew at first hand, from Malherbe himself, with whom he had been a frequent visitor at Cardinal Du Perron's, had what was needed to reassure the statesman. "Malherbe's doctrine" does not enjoy a good reputation today. A great deal of scorn has been poured on the narrowness of Malherbe's purism and even more on Boileau's "Enfin Malherbe vint." In fact, there was no French writer after 1630 who did not accept Malherbe's doctrine, which in any case lent itself to a variety of interpretations. Everyone acknowledged the strategic correctness of the poet's views: if writers were successfully to "defend and give luster" to the vulgar tongue, they needed to put less emphasis on *inventing*, in the manner of the Pléiade writers, and more on stabilizing the *elocution* of the language by bringing it into line with universally accepted conventions. The Pléiade method had not succeeded; indeed it had failed to dislodge the humanists' Latin from its pride of place as the language of learning and immortality. Malherbe's more modest method, that of a grammarian, metrician, and gourmet of words, succeeded in putting literary French on the road that would transform it into a living Latin. This success did not come without sacrifice: by concentrating his efforts on the language, the Malherbian writer was forced to content himself with commonplaces, those most apt to bring out the elegance of his style. This was all the more true in that the living referent of "correct usage" in accordance with which the writer sought to *fix* his language, was the conversation of the court and of the "*grand monde*," whose oral "naturalness" could not easily accommodate learned *invention* or bold individuality. On both of these points, a statesman like Richelieu could not help sympathizing with the new method of "adding luster" to the national language. That method, and the properly literary asceticism it required, tended to make men of letters wary of inventive and troubling enthusiasm, which often went hand-in-hand with heresy and political nonconformity. The requirement that literary language align itself with the living speech of the court guaranteed that the court would enjoy unquestioned priority over men of letters.

Finally, the example of Malherbe himself proved that his method lent itself admirably to the genre of official encomium, precisely because encomium aspired, more than any other literary genre, to that royal "immortality" and "eternity" that Malherbian language claimed to have achieved. The poet who could write "Ce que Malherbe écrit dure éternellement" was a man whose primary vocation was to celebrate kings and ministers and who did not wish their glory to be ephemeral. Richelieu himself had been the subject of three panegyric poems by Malherbe between 1624 and 1628.[20] And even before the founding of the Académie,

Malherbian poets had not stinted on lyrical odes to the cardinal.[21] Furthermore, Malherbian prose had proved its worth in polemics and apologetics by writers in the cardinal's service such as Silhon, Sirmond, and Faret.[22] The founding of the Académie honored and gave official status not only to a specific type of man of letters but also to a quite specifically located historical idea of literature, both apparently offering various guarantees of loyalty to the state.

In the proposal submitted to the cardinal on March 22, 1634, and intended to make the Académie the official repository of Malherbe's doctrine, for example, one could read that the "lectures" of the future Company would ensure the supremacy of French over Latin, a goal to be achieved by taking "greater care than heretofore with elocution, which was not in truth all of eloquence but which constituted a very substantial and considerable part of it."[23] Now we can see why the Académie, which briefly hesitated over the name Académie d'Éloquence, preferred the title Académie Française: like the poet according to Malherbe, the best French stylist, the Company too specialized in that part of eloquence that was concerned with words *(élocution)* and bestowed on them the weight of things.

6. Why did Richelieu not entrust the task of verifying French words to a body of specialists, grammarians or experts in prose and poetry? In the Académie's first years its members included, evidently with the cardinal's approval, a mathematician, Claude Bachet de Méziriac; a physician, Marin Cureau de la Chambre; diplomats, Bautru and Servien; and a statesman-magistrate, Séguier. Prelates, great lords, and military leaders would take their place during the reign of Louis XIV, by which time no one was surprised by such things. The coexistence, within a single body, of men of letters and dignitaries of the state, church, army, and university has remained the most persistent and striking feature of the Académie: the Académie honored Letters, and in the long run Letters could avail themselves of that honor to look down on the court from on high. This refusal to specialize from the outset might seem to contradict the apparently quite specialized purposes for which Richelieu had created his Académie. In reality, that specialty was a specialty only in relation to the humanist ideal of *Eloquentia,* according to which "things," understood in an encyclopedic sense, took priority over "words," over the art of awakening interest in "things." The wholly tactical distinction that Malherbe proposed between "things" (left in suspense, in brackets, as it were) and the "words" of French, which were, above all else, to be made as stable, clear, and elegant as the words of Latin, had a properly *universal* meaning, but now in relation to the *royaume des lys* and its unity, centered on the royal court. The language, reformed in accordance with the "doctrine of Malherbe" and, later, the principles of Vaugelas, was proposed as the kingdom's *common denominator,* its Place Royale, where the various orders, professions, corps, provinces, and intellectual disciplines could enter into

dialogue and work toward a common understanding, conscious that they shared a common fatherland. They could do this thanks to the place, the commonplace of a linguistic convention accepted by all. And these "words," this *elocution,* whose standard of reference was the language as spoken in the king's entourage and the "sounder part" of the court, made it indispensable for the Académie to include *speakers* from the court, living examples of the *correct usage* of the royal tongue, alongside professional men of letters. Their presence ensured that the men of letters would remain, even in the practice of their art, dependent on the court, which in the final analysis was the repository of the kingdom's linguistic orthodoxy. Vaugelas, a grammarian and amateur linguist, was above all an attentive and docile interpreter of "correct usage" as defined by the court.[24] By contrast, a professional linguist like Ménage and a lexicologist of all too vast knowledge such as Furetière would later have bones to pick with the Académie. The language of the Académie did not prevent scholars, philosophers, and theologians from adjusting their "things" to its "words." But they first had to adapt their specialized knowledge to the requirements of a style that the *honnête homme* of the court could understand without effort, and only then one suited to all the specialists. From the outset the Académie was seen as an intermediary body between men of letters and the court, its mission being to establish a linguistic middle ground acceptable to the entire kingdom, now that the court, since the Valois, had become the epitome and crossroads of the entire realm.

The purpose of the dialogue, within this intermediary body, between men of the court and men of letters was not solely to honor the latter. It institutionalized one of the essential features of Malherbe's doctrine, which was to mask the discrepancy between *written* literary language and the language spoken in the "best society" at court. This presupposed the exclusion of all technical words from the lexicon. More than that, it forbade men of letters from forming, as sixteenth-century poets had done, a learned caste whose works ultimately could be understood and savored only by their peers, those who possessed the arcana of Greek and Latin and were virtuosos of rhetorical and poetic *tours de force.* The men of the court were in the Academy to make sure that the men of letters did not give too free rein to their professional penchants and that their art remained within the bounds of clarity and elegance by virtue of which their thought and expression would be immediately accessible to all *honnestes gens.* Classical French, it has been said, was the language of an elite. It was much less so than the language of Scève or even Ronsard, whose French derived from scholarly written language. And it was not the language of an elite at all if we agree that the *honnestes gens* who were its touchstone were regarded as representatives of the "common sense" that Descartes believed was the thing in the world most widely shared. Malherbe made a similar point when he said that he wanted to be understood by the "porters of the Port-au-Foin." The language that

FIGURE 8.1. An allegorical composition in which academicians and their patrons are represented as ornaments on the king's crown of laurels along with other symbols of the sovereign's immortality: his motto, the trumpets of renown, and the fleurs de lis decorating the globe.

the Académie was charged with preserving and correcting was intended to be a royal language, common to the entire kingdom: its principal superiority over the various sociolects—popular or noble, provincial or professional—lay precisely in the intention that it be used to create a social bond linking the various groups that made up the kingdom and that could no longer pull in separate directions. Here was a remedy for Babel: a literary language that sought to be only literary would itself be one of the technolects of Babel. What Latin had been for the various peoples of Europe (each with its own vernacular)—a tie to Christendom and later a means of diplomacy and learned communication—French, reformed in accordance with Malherbe's method, was to become for the mosaic of orders, provinces, and specialized corporations that composed the kingdom. This *logos* had nothing in common with what emanated from the Pantocrator in Byzantine apses and cathedral portals. It was a "gentle," "clear," "elegant" tongue, filtered by courtly taste and verified by the Académie so as to become a standard for all communication and social interaction. It would convey, it was hoped with grace and wit, the system of commonplaces acceptable to the entire court and hence to the entire kingdom. But the *doxa* that the "Ancients" of the Académie would later wish to bring into conformity with the *philosophia perennis* established once and for all by Erasmus's *Adages*, Alciati's *Emblems*, and Montaigne's *Essais* was now set free from learned tradition: the opinion of the "Moderns" would introduce a leaven of fashion and novelty that the worldliness of the court, imitated by that of the city and then imitating the city's in turn, would ardently set to work at the end of Louis XIV's reign.

Malherbian French, attuned to a worldly culture, dismissed the poetic heritage of the Pléiade as archaic. More than that, the ideal that the Académie Française had set for itself directly undermined the more senior authority of another monarchical institution: the *parlements*, and especially the foremost among them, the Parlement of Paris.[25] Since the Renaissance, this prestigious corps, which thought of itself as guaranteeing the continuity of the monarchy, had forcefully asserted its authority over French scholarly culture and the national language. Guillaume Du Vair, the first theorist of "old-style" French eloquence, had legislated with the Parisian "Senate" in mind. For a long time to come, anthologies of magistrates' remonstrances and attorneys' pleas would rival those of academic speeches. The leading French humanist scholars came from the ranks of the *noblesse de robe* (that is, the *parlements*), including philologists and antiquarians of the caliber of J.-A. de Thou, the Dupuy brothers, and Peiresc, all dismissed as Latinizing "pedants" by courtly and academic *honnêteté*. Indeed, all the great French philologists came from the world of the Palais: men like Étienne Pasquier and Claude Fauchet, the direct forebears of men like Gilles Ménage and Furetière. Enmeshed in erudite neo-Latin culture, the Parlement was also associated with a civic conception of eloquence and a concept of the vulgar tongue inherited from Varro and Pliny the Elder, curious about archaisms, professional jargons, and piquant turns of phrase. This whole world of learned bourgeois jurists, more solid than they were brilliant, was held up to ridicule and indeed identified with professional pedantry by the elegant world of the court, with its "imperturbable *honnêteté*," and its language made official by the Académie Française. Surely Richelieu was not displeased that he had played such a cruel trick on the *parlements* and *robins*, who, along with *les Grands*, were the heart and soul of the resistance to *la raison d'état*. But the wide-ranging consequences of placing the royal seal of approval on "court usage" of the French tongue exceeded even his predictive capacities.

7. What is true for language and style was also true for genres. The statutes of the Académie prescribed its task as the establishment not only of a grammar and a dictionary but also of a rhetoric and a poetics. Yet the institution wisely avoided a pedantic attitude remote in spirit from both Malherbe, despite his abrupt manner, and still more, Vaugelas (a friend of St. Francis de Sales). By looking at who was accepted and who was rejected one can make out a guiding principle in the Académie's attitude toward literary genres. It came into being even as the "classical doctrine" was taking hold, the doctrine that Boileau would sum up in his *Art poétique* (1674) before taking his seat among the Immortals. The Académie quite clearly adopted the tripartite division of literature accepted by the rhetoricians of antiquity and the humanists of the Renaissance: Eloquence, History, Poetry. Present in the Académie from the first generation were the three genres of profane eloquence (political, represented by the polemicists serving Richelieu; judicial, represented by lawyers like Olivier Patru; and epideictic or panegyric, represented by all academicians). These were soon joined by sacred eloquence, represented by Bossuet and Fénelon. History had its own distinctive place, with royal historiographers becoming members almost automatically, starting with Eudes de Mézeray, soon followed by Racine and Boileau.

But this eloquence and this history were reoriented to suit the needs of the court, which replaced the Parlement as the standard of the best French style. Poetry also found its place in the Académie, but in accordance with the tradition of courtly encomium inaugurated by Malherbe. Epic poetry, with Chapelain, lyrical genres with Saint-Amant and Malleville, and tragedy and comedy with Desmarets and Boisrobert, soon followed by Corneille, bore the hallmark of courtly order and *doxa*. The lighter genres, associated with courtly amusements, were by no means ostracized from the nascent Académie, which had a horror of "stuffiness" and "pedantry" and refused to limit itself to the solemnity of the *grand style*. Voiture and Benserade were the first talents of the *genre galant*, or witty and lively poetry that appealed to women, to be received among the Forty. If La Fontaine became a member, it was probably not, as we see him, as the talented author of the *Fables*, but rather as a virtuoso of the *style galant et plaisant*, and in the implicit "section" of the Académie that has tacitly been reserved for this genre ever since. From Collin d'Harleville to Labiche, the Académie, even at the height of Victorian stiffness, has always welcomed laughter and entertainment, humor being the social bond par excellence and as such particularly prized in the best society in all ages.

By contrast, the novel, despite its popularity as early as the seventeenth century, and despite its efforts to emulate epic and history, found no place in the Académie from the time of Richelieu onward. Some academicians may have written prose fiction, as would again be the case in the nineteenth century, but it was not their prose fiction that earned them their place in the Académie. Gomberville was a prolific novelist but above all a moralist and a historian.[26] Desmarets, the author of an *Ariane* that sold well, was above all Richelieu's collaborator in the theater.[27] Tristan L'Hermite, the author of the *Page disgracié*, owed his respectability to his plays and lyrical poetry. And Georges de Scudéry, who published under his name serial novels written either by his sister or in collaboration with her, entered the Académie as a playwright.[28] Later he wrote an epic, *Alaric*.[29] The novel's fate in the Académie was sealed in the seventeenth century, and so it would remain until the end of the nineteenth century. By contrast, the moralists, the Prévost-Paradols of classicism, were at home in the Académie from the outset: men like Nicolas Faret and Jacques Esprit were the first of a long line. And translators, whose status has since fallen so low, were then honored in the person of Jean Baudoin and Nicolas Perrot d'Ablancourt.[30] Of course they translated Latin and Greek masterpieces and thus played a prominent role in the task of the Académie, which was to "perfect" the French language by placing it on a footing of equality with the classical tongues, as well as to bridge the gap between men of letters and men of the world.

Ambiguous and unformulated, the Académie's attitude toward the various genres nevertheless left a definite mark on the national perception of literature until the end of the nineteenth century and the insolent triumph of the novel over the *alexandrin*. Basically, it favored genres of general interest for the formation of "good taste," a solid average culture, and a sound moral complexion. It made room for the one trait of the French "national character" most widely acknowledged in pre-Revolutionary Europe: gaiety. This was the yeast that, mixed in the right proportions with an excellent flour, yielded the fine bread of traditional literary France. Paul Valéry, in the acceptance speech he gave on joining the Académie, poked fun at the "highly composite fragrance" of the work of Anatole France, work that was the product of a civilization "of extreme old age," of that "perpetuated culture" whose tenacious vehicle the Académie had been for three centuries. "Our great writers," he added, "are not grand, isolated figures such as one sometimes sees in other countries. But there exists in France a sort of atmosphere for Letters that is found nowhere else and that was quite beneficial to your colleague."[31] Mallarmé's disciple, having been accepted by the Académie, retrospectively avenged his master. Yet with eyes of irony he saw things right.

8. The archetypal reign of Louis XIV completed the task of acclimatizing France to that "atmosphere for Letters" of which Mallarmé spoke, so that the French forever after looked upon Mount Parnassus as a prominence of "gentle slopes." The Académie proved its corporate solidity by negotiating without mishap both the regency of Anne of Austria and the Fronde. It may have suffered from the triumph of Surintendant Foucquet, whose patronage was ill adapted to academic regularity. It benefitted fully from the sympathy of Colbert.[32] In 1672 the minister persuaded the king to proclaim himself in person the protector of the Académie. The French Parnassus had found its Apollo, who offered the permanent hospitality of the Louvre. In exchange for a munificent tribute of praise, the Académie acquired considerable additional authority. Its meetings became public, and the ritual of the *discours de réception*, or acceptance speech, was established. It began awarding an annual prize for eloquence and, from 1701 on, a prize for poetry, whose "normative" character, though never as definitive as that of the Prix de Rome, would exert substantial influence on the classical seventeenth century and the neoclassical eighteenth century. Colbert himself had done the Académie the honor of joining its ranks in 1667. Henceforth, it became the rule for tutors of the children of France and royal historiographers to be elected members (Voltaire would benefit from this tacit law). Some very great lords and titled prelates aspired to membership. Academic pomp matched the majesty of the institution's protector. *Séances de réception* (sessions to welcome new members), masses in the chapel of the Louvre on the anniversary of the death of Saint Louis, and funeral masses for academicians became noteworthy events in the life of the court. All the great writers of the reign—except Molière, an actor, and Saint-Évremond, a political exile—were members of the Académie, which implies a consonance, to us surprising, between "personal merit" and the academic norm. A common fund of ancient models, a poetics and rhetoric implicit but unanimously accepted (all the more so because they lent themselves to exegesis and jurisprudence), and a general agreement as to language and style as "reformed" by Malherbe explain this "providential" convergence of a reign, genius, and official taste.

Corneille and Racine, Bossuet and Fénelon, La Fontaine and Boileau, La Bruyère and Fontenelle sat alongside high dignitaries of the nobility and state as well as fashionable society writers such as Quinault and Benserade and *abbés galants* such as Cassagne and Cotin. The partition of the old humanist encyclopedia, still rudimentary under Louis XIII, was officially consecrated under Louis XIV: the Académie des Sciences was founded by Colbert in 1666, and the Petite Académie, which in 1701 would become the Académie des Inscriptions, made its appearance in

1663. The latter was initially an assemblage of members of the Académie Française versed in Greek and Latin and prepared to put their knowledge at the service of the monarch's glory. This specialization of the traditional *Litterae* in an academy of their own, at first devoted to the task of recording the king's great exploits in a language of eternity, resulted in a legal conflict with the Académie Française. This was an institutional version of the Renaissance drama in which the languages of the scholars and the vernacular tongues were cast as rivals. The conflict came to a head under Louis XIV in the so-called *Querelle des inscriptions*, and its resolution demonstrated the central, and no longer merely ideal, role of the Académie Française in the literary economy of the Ancien Régime.

The first clash in this dispute took place on the fringes of the Académie. It involved the neo-Latin poet Charles Du Périer and the magistrate Louis Le Laboureur.[33] The latter, replying to an ode of Du Périer's to the Dauphin recommending that the future king's education begin in Latin, dedicated his 1667 treatise *Avantages de la langue française* to Habert de Montmor, a member of both literary academies. Wedding arguments taken from Vaugelas to others borrowed from the Cartesian Cordemoy, Le Laboureur put together the first of a long series of apologia for the French language and its universality, extending all the way to Rivarol.[34] His enthusiasm for the Malherbian tongue was based above all on his belief that it was a language suitable for use by children and women as well as adults and men of learning, and by human beings as well as angels. It was a *living* bond, a *vital* common ground, as opposed to Latin, which was the preserve of specialists and frozen in funereal stasis. The good fortune of having, in French, a "royal place" in which all the king's subjects could come together was surely connected with the sense of security and civil peace to which the new kingdom had given rise.

From 1667 to 1676, the *querelle* roiled the ranks of the academies, pitting Abbé de Bourzeis against François Charpentier, both members of the Académie Française as well as the Petite Académie.[35] Charpentier waited until after Bourzeis had died in 1672 to write and publish, in 1676, a *Défense de la langue française pour l'inscription de l'arc de triomphe, dédié au roi*.[36] He expanded this into a vast, two-volume work, *De l'excellence de la langue française*, published in 1683, shortly before Perrault's "modern" offensive.[37] Also in 1676, Abbé Tallemant publicly replied during a meeting of the Académie to a speech that the Jesuit Lucas had delivered in Latin during a celebration at the Collège de Clermont attended by the king, the court, and a delegation from the Académie. Father Lucas's thesis was that "public monuments should bear Latin inscriptions." This was entirely consonant with the views of the king and even more of Colbert, who, though himself a member of the Académie Française, had created the Petite Académie to compose, among other things, just such Latin inscriptions. Furthermore, Father Lucas was entirely in agreement on this point with the late Abbé de Bourzeis, a highly learned man, who had been one of the first members of the Académie Française to be invited by Colbert to join the Petite Académie. Abbé Tallemant wrote:

> What makes one language more universal and common than another? The fact that it was at one time the language of the most flourishing empire. Why do we hold that language in higher esteem and find more grace in it than in others? Because victory, plenty, and peace have brought more civility into a kingdom and given the Arts the means to grow. And why, finally, does a language remain at a certain degree of beauty, seemingly having attained its ultimate perfection? Because great geniuses have consecrated it through immortal works, which remain models from which one cannot depart with impunity; and though it may subsequently not cease to change, that change is called corruption; and one holds that it was perfect in the time when it flourished most. . . . It is not difficult, Gentlemen, to draw from what I have just said an infallible consequence for the beauty and duration of our tongue.[38]

The point is that François Charpentier and Abbé Tallemant, who had held the posts of director and perpetual secretary, felt bound to defend, with all the tenacity characteristic of the corps of the Ancien Régime, the interests of the Company they represented, at the expense of those of the more recent Petite Académie of which Charpentier was merely one member among many. Here we see evidence of the esprit de corps of the Académie Française even at the height of absolutism. The tactic—a shrewd one—was already one that Charles Perrault would take up in impressive fashion later on: to broaden the debate about language to a debate about civilization. A thesis officially supported by the king was vigorously combatted, but the attack was veiled in clouds of incense to the same monarch. The king could not take offense, because the idea under attack coexisted in official thinking with its opposite: Colbert, in creating the Petite Académie, implicitly recognized the vocation of Latin to express immortality; but in making the king the protector of the Académie Française, he also recognized the excellence of French and its vocation to celebrate the king's glory. Indeed, the king could only feel flattered by the zeal of the Académie Française, which held that only the language that it was charged with defending was suitable for singing his praises. The whole dispute might seem to be little more than a rivalry among men of letters over a fundamentally unimportant issue. But beneath this innocuous or even pointless appearance, a far more serious issue lay hidden. In relegating Latin (and the Petite Académie) to the second rank, in identifying the honor of the king with that of the French language alone and therefore of the Académie Française, the spokesmen for that institution worked to discredit antiquity. And with antiquity the whole theological political order that was founded on the idea that the revelations—of Christian faith and of classical wisdom—had come at the very beginning and were transmitted primarily through the language of learning, Latin. Thus the Académie's esprit de corps, manifest in the ardent apologia for the privileges of French and hence for its own institutional privileges, compromised the prestige of parlementary humanism and indeed of traditional theology. It winked at the new masters of opinion: worldly society, whose culture was wholly French and modern, women, *honnestes gens.* The authority of the Académie derived from the mission with which it had been entrusted with regard to the nation's language: in the course of this quarrel over language, the Académie discovered that the logic of its mission naturally associated it with a public for which "well-spoken French" was one *raison d'être* and whose "common sense" was now sovereign in all intellectual debate. Out of this was born a quintessentially French alliance that for three centuries would dismiss as worthless pedantry the ancient authority of the clerical and the learned.

9. By 1687, when Charles Perrault scandalized Boileau by reading to the Académie his poem *Le Siècle de Louis le Grand*, which initiated the Quarrel of the Ancients and Moderns, the case had already been made, because it was intimately associated with the Académie's esprit de corps.

Perrault limited himself to drawing the ultimate logical conclusions from the apologia for the French language and French eloquence first proposed by Le Laboureur and developed by Tallemant and Charpentier. Scholars have shown quite easily that from the Renaissance on, the superiority of the Moderns over the Ancients recurred regularly *in utramque partem* as a theme of dispute among humanists. If Perrault, in reviving this old controversy, elicited so great a response, it was not for his intellectual audacity. For the first time, the polemical and scholastic thesis of the Moderns emerged from the schools and libraries into the public arena, taking for its stage an academy protected by "the greatest king in the world" and for its heroic and monumental setting the most populous and powerful monarchy of the modern era. Formulated in the royal tongue and to the glory of the living king, this thesis came to signify true redemption for a modern and worldly public previously intimidated by a sense of its own "ignorance" and by respect for the learned, who alone were initiated into the secrets of Antiquity. Perrault anticipated a feeling that, though already widely shared, needed to find eloquent formulation from an official rostrum before it could accede to the status of a tranquil certitude. The Académie Française itself, despite the remarkably discreet objections of men like Boileau and Huet, saw Perrault's thesis as the most profound justification of its own existence in the face of an older and traditionally more authoritative corps such as the Parlement of Paris, which since the Renaissance had associated its own eloquence with humanist erudition, with the evocation of ancient precedents. The Sorbonne remained aloof from this dispute, which seemed to be circumscribed within the order of the profane. In the long run it too would suffer from the prerogative accorded to the present against antiquity. The works in which Perrault developed his thesis (*Parallèles des Anciens et des Modernes* and *Hommes illustres qui ont paru en France pendant ce siècle*[39]) were extensions of the academic genre par excellence, the panegyric, specifically, panegyrics of illustrious contemporaries of the inception and development of that recent, modern Company, the Académie Française. Only the Académie could have produced a voice that dared to characterize as "modern," hence "unprecedented," the historical success of the Most Christian Kingdom, which had yet to situate itself consciously "at the center of Time." Only the Académie had an interest, for its own prestige, in pursuing to such lengths the hyperbolic praise of its protector and his entire reign, and of the people who were fortunate enough to be his subjects and contemporaries, to speak his language, and to share in his glory. The gallery of illustrious men whose portraits Perrault collected marked a decisive step toward the pantheon of "great men" that the Age of Enlightenment would openly substitute for Plutarch's *Lives* and the *Lives* of the saints and doctors of the faith. It was now possible for a living language to transform its own present into glorious immortality without the mediation of a dead language and its literary models. French, and before long European, "consciousness" no longer needed to embark on a lengthy journey through time: truth and grandeur could reveal themselves in the very present. And that self-coincidence, which seemed at first to benefit only the royal Sun, in fact simultaneously exalted the Académie Française, worldly society, and the men of letters whose wholly French eloquence was capable of bestowing upon the Present the epiphanic dimension formerly restricted to the Past.[40]

The price to be paid for this, in the long run, was the dissipation of the sacral shadows that once shrouded the mysteries of faith and wisdom, mysteries that only the learned, those initiated into the scholarly tradition, could penetrate. In the short run, during the devout reign of the Great King himself, the price was the devaluation of profane humanism, of literature that relied on erudite memory, and of those *lettrés* in the Parlement and the University who sought their methods and models of truth in the teachings of the Ancients.

10. Yet another dispute, known as the Quarrel of the Dictionaries, would publicly mark the break between the purely French literary order, of which the Académie was the keystone, and an older order, erudite and European. This dispute, which erupted in 1684 and claimed Furetière, an academician since 1662, as its victim, sheds remarkable light on the way in which, under the Ancien Régime, the academic institution *revealed*, dramatized, and resolved disputes that without this allegorical French Parnassus would have remained shadowy.

Furetière was one of the great scholars of Louis XIV's reign, the heir of Étienne Pasquier and Claude Fauchet and the ancestor of Littré. He had been elected to the

Académie, however, not because of his scholarship but because of his minor work as a poet and society critic. In 1684 he had gained a dispensation to publish his life's work, the *Dictionnaire contenant tous les mots français tant vieux que modernes et les termes de toutes les sciences et de tous les arts.* This was a monumental masterpiece, combining the best lexicographic, linguistic, and scholarly work of the time. It was also a dangerous rival for the *Dictionnaire de l'Académie,* which, as Furetière, who had collaborated on this still unfinished project, knew better than anyone, was conceived for a different purpose in accordance with different principles. Indeed, he believed that the radical difference between the two works would justify his request to publish his own. Unfortunately for him, the Académie's perpetual secretary, Régnier-Desmarais, did not see it that way, and, invoking the exclusive privilege the Académie had obtained for its dictionary in 1674 (thanks to the then powerful Perrault), had Furetière's work banned. It was eventually published in The Hague, but not until 1690, two years after the author's death, to the unanimous acclaim of scholars throughout Europe. More than that, Régnier-Desmarais persuaded his colleagues to expel Furetière, who from then until his death defended his cause in a series of briefs and pamphlets. With the bitter candor of one who has nothing more to lose, the great philologist, pugnacious to the end, disclosed a number of truths that but for this incident would have remained hidden. Throwing off the gaudy finery of French "authorship" that he had hitherto worn out of respect for the Académie, he now spoke as a citizen of the Republic of Letters. He stressed the immeasurable distance between his *Dictionnaire,* a veritable summa of French language and culture, and the Académie's, which, when finished, would confine itself to recording the limited and quite modern "correct usage" of the language by *honnestes gens,* in other words, French as it was spoken by *beaux esprits* and in the *grand monde,* the polished French of the best local society. That is, an idiolect, indeed a "snapshot" of that idiolect, rather than an exhaustive portrait of the language throughout its history and in all its richness, technical, scholarly, and popular. In this respect the Quarrel of the Dictionaries overlapped the Quarrel of the Ancients and Moderns. Furetière pointed out that the Académie, since the end of the Fronde, had admitted a great many superficial and modern *beaux esprits* because fashionable and ignorant society liked to have them at its feet: Abbé Cotin, Claude Boyer, Michel Le Clerc, Abbé Cassagne, François and Paul Tallemant, Ballesdens, Quinault, Benserade, Charpentier, Barbier d'Aucour, and, last but not least, the perpetual secretary, Régnier-Desmarais. For Furetière, men like Corneille, Bossuet, Racine, and Boileau (he left out La Fontaine, whom he regarded as a traitor) were ill at ease in a Company dominated by *les petits marquis des belles-lettres*:

> Finally, I make so bold as to say that the craftsmen engaged on this incomparable Dictionary know how to write sonnets, rondeaux, rhymed couplets,

FIGURE 8.2. Allegorical composition in honor of Voltaire's apotheosis in 1778 at both the Comédie-Française and the Académie.

> madrigals, and coquettish verse, but they have no tincture of science, and rather than delve deeply into things, they only skim the surface. They call themselves men of Belles Lettres when they have read a few French poets and by chance a few Latin ones. They think they know everything when they know the words of their own language necessary for daily living and everyday conversation. They are enemies of all erudition and hunt down any word or phrase that gives the slightest appearance of such a thing.[41]

The tyranny exercised by "second-rate minds" backed by a "society" unfamiliar with the arcana of true knowledge was detrimental not only to scholars but also to "first-rate minds" whose inventive genius lay in their erudite manner, arousing the jealousy of their apparent peers in the Académie. "What pains me most, Monseigneur," Furetière wrote to Chancellor d'Aligre, "is that I have been unable to make you understand that my opposition is directed not against the entire Académie but only against a small cabal of its members, who are envious of the quality of my book and ashamed of the defects of their own."[42] Indeed, he praised the "profound erudition" of his former colleague Pierre-Daniel Huet, one of the last "encyclopedists" of the Renaissance, as well as "M. Racine," who, in contrast to his unworthy rivals Boyer and Leclerc, "has honored so many heroes by the character he has given them," and of course Bossuet and Boileau. True learning is the brother of true talent. Both measured themselves, in different ways incomprehensible to the vulgar herd, not by modish success but in comparison with the masters of Antiquity. Obviously there was nothing national or "modern" about such a criterion. Furetière expressed regret, moreover, that such "sublime spirits" were joined in the Académie by fops rather than men like "Du Cange, Ménage, Président Cousin, Thévenot, Varillas, Baillet, and Amelot de la Houssaye," that is, the Varros and Plinys whose value the ignorant were incapable of comprehending. The name of Ménage, included here as a candidate for the "forty-first chair," is particularly pertinent in this context. The author of *Origines de la langue française* (1650), *Observations sur la langue française* (1675), and many other masterpieces that made him at once the Brunot and the Warburg of the seventeenth century, he seemed destined to occupy a place in a Company whose mission was to keep watch over language. What is more, he had managed to make his vast knowledge as a Romanist acceptable and desirable if not comprehensible to the most select society: he was a close friend of Mme de La Fayette, Mme de Sévigné, and Mlle de Scudéry. Apparently his satire, entitled *La Requête des dictionnaires à messieurs de l'Académie pour la réformation de la langue française* (circulated against his wishes in 1649), had made his truly learned irony suspect in the eyes of the same "small cabal" that later undermined Furetière. He had dared to point out that the fine literature of French was but a pale shadow of the ancient literature to which scholars of his caliber held the only keys:

Ils sont les Docteurs des docteurs,
Les Précepteurs des précepteurs,
Les Maîtres des maîtres de classe
Et tels, qu'on a cru savantasses
A la faveur de leurs bons mots,
Sans eux n'étaient que des sots.
. . .
Mais sans parler ici des autres,
Vous savez que parmi les vôtres,
Les plus renommés traducteurs,
Et les plus célèbres auteurs,
Qui s'en font maintenant accroire,
Nous sont obligés de leur gloire.
Et cependant, ô temps, ô mœurs!
Ce sont eux qui, par leurs clameurs,
Aujourd'hui dans l'Académie,
Nous traitent avec infamie.
Il est pourtant véritable
Que ce qu'ils savent de la Fable
Ils l'ont appris des versions
Qu'à l'aide de nos dictions
Il fut autrefois nécessaire
De leur faire en langue vulgaire.

[They are the doctors' Doctors,
The preceptors' Preceptors,
The schoolmasters' Schoolmasters,
And some who were thought learned
Because of their witty remarks
Were without them mere fools.
. . .
But to say nothing here of others,
You know that among your number,
The most renowned translators
And the most celebrated authors
Who are now puffing themselves up
Are obliged to us for their glory.
And yet, O the times, O the customs!
It is they who, with their clamor,
Today treat us so vilely in the Académie.
Yet it is undeniable

That what they know of Myth
They learned from the translations
Into the vulgar tongue
That with help from our dictionaries
Used to have to be made for them.][43]

Yet even if Ménage had shown greater self-control, there was no place for him in an institution that was in a sense created to *combat* the learned Republic of Letters and to defend only the literature of the court of France. The evolution of the Petite Académie into the Académie des Inscriptions et Belles-Lettres would open up the latter to men of his quality and learning in the eighteenth century, too late for the great scholar. Under Louis XIV only the title of bishop could excuse the superior erudition of Bossuet, Fénelon, and Huet. In the eighteenth century "philosophical" prelates would seek to have their episcopal titles overlooked for the sake of their prestige within the Académie. And it must be said that only the genres accessible to all *honnestes gens*, in which they excelled, excused men like Racine, Boileau, La Fontaine, and La Bruyère for all that they owed to their meditation on the ancient and European literary traditions, their education and even erudition.

Furetière's protests changed nothing—and would change nothing even after the Académie des Inscriptions had achieved its final form: henceforth the Académie Française held the keys, unjustly perhaps, to the national literature. Its choices were based on criteria defined by a *doxa* at once official and social and no longer consonant with the specialized knowledge of a small minority of scholars in France or in Europe. This convention was perhaps never adhered to as scrupulously or consistently as by the "small cabal" that had its home in the Académie under Louis XIV and that used it to fuel the overabundant production of panegyrics to the glory of the monarch. In his *Essai sur les éloges* (1773), a key work about which I shall have more to say later on, the academician Antoine-Léonard Thomas wrote this about the "century of Louis le Grand":

> One might with equal truth call it the century of encomia. Never was praise so plentiful: it was, as it were, the nation's malady. . . . Louis XIV was praised more during his reign than all the kings of the previous twelve centuries. . . . It was forty years of intoxication. Style everywhere acquired I know not what tone of panegyric [and Thomas showed that satire, tragedy, epic, ballet comedies, and even fable itself were all linked in one way or another to the central genre]. Last but not least, one can add the spate of compliments and panegyrics pronounced before the Académie Française, which for sixty years was a kind of temple consecrated to this cult.[44]

In this extraordinary chorus of encomia to the protector of the Company, whose harmonious scores today repose in thick anthologies of academic speeches, even "scholars" and "sublime spirits" had their part, leaving Furetière's pamphlets aside. Their commonplaces reflected the nature of the language as it was conceived, after Vaugelas, in the *Dictionnaire de l'Académie*. For Louis XIV's subjects, the old formulas became a common denominator. They translated the ancient conventions of princely panegyric into the French of *honnestes gens* and adapted them to the contemporary glory of the king of France. Smoothed out and patined by time but revivified by the language of the Moderns, the old formulas in their setting of academic eloquence acquired something akin to the tranquil pomp of Handel's concerti grossi. Perrault's *Siècle de Louis le Grand* was but a more *vivace* version of this perpetual *largo maestoso*. These encomia established a durable national consensus around the king and a set of notions summed up in the idea of divine right. The Académie sang the king's praises but at the same time recognized itself in him. In 1671 the Jesuit Bouhours could write this of Louis XIV: "Finally, to sum up in one word, he speaks so well that his style can give a veritable idea of the perfection of our tongue."[45] The epiphany of the royal voice had by now become a commonplace of academic panegyric. In 1673, Abbé Tallemant said this to his colleagues:

> Since this Company's principal task is to apply itself to the purity of the language, Louis's natural eloquence, the felicitous ease with which he explains himself, the choice and purity of the words he uses, and the inexplicable charm with which he infuses everything he says, have justly made him Protector of the Académie.[46]

Beneath the indisputable generality of the statement we glimpse the esprit de corps: the foremost *honneste homme* in France, the archetype of the academician, the king is also seen here as the most eminent representative of the public of which the Académie claims to be the head, the "central" public of the kingdom, the "society" of *honnestes gens*, relegating raucous "pedants" to the periphery.

The masterpieces of Molière, Racine, Boileau, and La Fontaine might seem, as is only fitting, to avoid the monotonous generality of academic eloquence and link up with a more essential, more universal truth. In another sense, however, they participated in the same quest for what was acceptable to all *honnestes gens*, for what united respectable people of good society. And even the aptly named Port-Royal, though adhering to still other principles, was guided by the same concern. No one put it better than Pascal, in a text in which he rejects the external bombast and superficial unanimity of academic encomium:

> Nothing is more common than good things: it is simply a question of identifying them, and surely they are natural and within our grasp and even well known to everyone. But we do not know how to distinguish them. This is uni-

> versal. Excellence in any genre is not to be found in what is extraordinary and bizarre. We look high to find it, and we go astray; usually we must look low. The best books are the ones that those who read them think they could have written. Nature alone is good, and it is quite familiar and common. . . . The mind should not be strained: stiff and painful manners fill it with foolish presumption through a strange elevation and a pointless and ridiculous inflation, instead of solid, vigorous nourishment. And one of the principal reasons why so many who partake of such knowledge depart from the true path they ought to follow is the fancy they conceive that good things are inaccessible because they give them names like great, noble, and sublime. This misses the point. I prefer to call them low, common, and familiar, names that are more apt. I hate those inflated words.[47]

Sainte-Beuve would make this Port-Royal philosophy one of the principles of his academic criticism, one of the cornerstones of his idea of literature: a path open to everyone but hidden from the seekers of the extraordinary and the bizarre, a path leading to moral truth shared by all in an agreeable form and for that reason universally recognized. Through the clouds of incense generated by the classical Académie, we must learn to respect this invincible taste for common sense, which Louis XIV in his supreme position himself possessed to the utmost degree.

11. Common sense is not what metaphysicians call reason. It originates in, and puts to the test, a society's generally accepted opinions about things, opinions that are the product in part of traditions and in part of circumstances, the conjunction of minds. The function of the court, of courtly society in the seventeenth century, was to regulate the kingdom's common sense and the shared notions from which that common sense derived. The Académie, a repository for the common sense of the language of the kingdom and an arbiter of courtly usage, also became one of those "commonplaces" that created unanimity throughout the realm. The Quarrel of the Ancients and Moderns would reveal this tacit function. Owing to this quarrel, for which the Académie served as the stage, common opinion would adopt both the enthusiasm of the Moderns and their irony with respect to the authority of the Ancients. The victory of the Moderns created the conditions for a ready acceptance of the philosophy of the Enlightenment. Indeed, that philosophy assumed that everything began not in Antiquity, much less in the Renaissance, but in the century of Louis le Grand. Voltaire could become "king" after Perrault and Fontenelle had made Louis XIV and his "century" the fountainhead of Arts and Letters. This shift in generally accepted beliefs accelerated and broadened over the course of the eighteenth century. Once again it was left to the Académie Française to mark the change, stabilize it, and give it that canonical and respectable character that it alone could

confer upon novelty. In their campaign against the old certainties transmitted by the Church, the Sorbonne, and the *collèges*, the encyclopedists were well aware of the legitimating function of the Académie, and in the second half of the eighteenth century they would use it as the official translator of their own ideas into generally accepted commonplaces. High society, whose center of gravity shifted from the court to the city, willingly went along with this displacement of common sense; it would celebrate an Académie transformed into the Sacred College of the *Encyclopédie*.

This eighteenth-century displacement of common sense was gradual and irresistible, all the more so because it came about in a remarkably unanimous and tranquil aesthetic context. From J. B. Rousseau to Delille, from Fontenelle to Chamfort, the profane aesthetic canon established by Boileau under Louis XIV remained, with little-noticed variations, the eighteenth century's literary norm. Precisely because that norm was *taken for granted*, the Académie, which was its supreme champion and prudent enough never to formulate it explicitly, felt no need to reaffirm it. Some were outraged by its idleness and futility. In fact—but it was an important fact—it confined itself to reigning over what was never challenged: the primacy of classical belles-lettres over all specialized forms of knowledge. The struggle between *philosophes* and *dévots* prevented the latter from availing themselves of any forms other than those recognized by the Académie: what little theology the *dévots* could muster was obliged to borrow its literary expression, and Montesquieu could write about the spirit of the laws *(De l'esprit des lois)* only by writing about the law in an amusing way *(de l'esprit sur les lois)*. The force of the *philosophes*, and the relative ease with which they won academic authority to their side, was due in large part to their sincere belief (Diderot and Rousseau excepted) in a national grammar, poetics, and rhetoric over which the Académie enjoyed tacit authority. That authority, entirely profane, did not trouble them. Indeed, it told against the scholarly faith of the Church, in keeping with a principle set forth by Boileau, who failed to anticipate all its consequences:

> De la foi du chrétien les mystères terribles
> D'ornements égayés ne sont pas susceptibles
> [The terrifying mysteries of the Christian faith
> Cannot be embellished by jolly ornament.]

The rules of the game were thus accepted by all though favorable to men of letters and unfavorable to the Sorbonne, indeed to the Church in general, whose finest minds turned to belles-lettres and "modern" worldliness. The prize was French opinion. The court acted as arbiter, and it wavered. The Académie was a central pawn in the game: it possessed royal legitimacy in the area of belles-lettres, it was in a position to consecrate a *doxa*, and it constituted a body which, though closely tied by origin and tradition to the court, enjoyed real independence from the corps of the Ancien Régime. Between the court and the city, the Académie eventually threw in its lot once and for all with the city and joined in a rebellion against the court.

Geography favored this evolution. The Académie, installed in the Louvre by Colbert in 1672, had opened its formal sessions to the public. It did not follow the court to Versailles, either in 1682, when Louis XIV set up in residence there, or at the end of the Regency, when Louis XV returned there from Paris. It had had the time to become one of the city's "scenes" and sights. The salons and cenacles of Paris in which literary reputations were made and unmade exerted growing influence on elections to the Académie. They had no other way to consecrate their "stars," since men of letters could not be ennobled: this was a major error on the part of the court. Mme de Lambert, Mme de Tencin, Mme du Deffand, Mme Geoffrin, Mme Necker, and Mlle de Lespinasse—all efficient "literary agents"—were naturally *grandes électrices.* They played a shrewd game with the court, where they had their allies, and generally the court, after giving vent to its humor, bowed to their wishes. The very success of the osmosis between court and city that Richelieu and Louis XIV had promoted in matters of custom, manners, and taste, an osmosis of which the Académie was one conduit, was so complete that the city dictated its will to the court and transformed itself into the interpreter of a rebellious public opinion that the Parisian Académie had to take into account.

12. This took time. Until the election of Voltaire and even more of Duclos in the following year, 1747, the Académie remained essentially a court organ: prelates, great nobles, and important state officials jostled one another to the deteriment of men of letters. Cardinal Fleury kept a wary eye on religious orthodoxy, and Abbé Olivet[48] interpreted the Académie's esprit de corps to mean a strict fidelity to Bossuet's pious classicism. The cult of Louis XIV, celebrated every year on the occasion of the mass for Saint Louis and at the reading honoring the Clermont-Tonnerre Prize in poetry, established in 1701, bore the pious stamp of the end of Louis's reign. Not even the Regent himself could challenge the expulsion of Saint-Pierre, guilty in his *Polysynodie* of the crime of lèse-majesté against the Sun King.[49] Accordingly, Montesquieu (*Lettres persanes,* 1721) and Voltaire (*Lettres philosophiques,* 1734) poked fun at an institution that they deemed set in its ways, but whose latent authority derived from the fact that it perpetuated the monarchical and Catholic doctrine of the reign of Louis le Grand. Montesquieu's election in 1727, which was the handiwork of Mme de Lambert, and Marivaux's in 1742, which was that of Mme de Tencin, scarcely affected the behavior of the institution. And in order to be elected in 1746 after two failures in 1731 and 1743, Voltaire had to feign piety in various sermons, which cost him virtually nothing and fooled no one but

FIGURE 8.3. Of the three candidates, only Victor Hugo would be elected to the Académie. The novelists Alexandre Dumas and Honoré de Balzac were never admitted (1839).

without which the support of Mme de Pompadour and the Marquis d'Argenson would have remained without effect. By now, however, the seventeenth-century Académie was nearing its end. When Duclos became perpetual secretary in 1755, the accelerating modernization of the institution was confirmed. The court reacted, but too late. Now the Académie's esprit de corps began to work against the Church. On March 10, 1760, Le Franc de Pompignan delivered his *discours de réception*. He launched into a vehement attack on the philosophical spirit and, in barely veiled words, on Voltaire. He summoned the Académie to return to respect for the throne and the altar. Immediately, a series of poisonous pamphlets, emanating not only from Ferney but also from Abbé Morellet, the "theologian of the *Encyclopédie*," poured ridicule and scorn on the agent of Versailles. Pompignan thought he could count on the *succès de scandale* scored by Palissot's comedy, *Les Philosophes*, which was opportunely performed in May at the Théâtre-Français. Morellet circumvented the danger by publishing his pamphlet *La Vision de Palissot*, which earned him a stay in the Bastille but put the laughter of the city, and hence that of the court, on the side of the *Encyclopédie*. In late May, Pompignan published a *Mémoire justificatif* addressed to the king, urging the monarch to purge the Académie. In June, Voltaire leapt into the fray. He issued three satires, *Le Pauvre Diable*, *Le Russe à Paris*, and *La Vanité*, which crushed Pompignan and forced him to retire to southwestern France, from which he never dared to return to his seat in the Académie. The contest had been brutal, but the victory was complete. Duclos, whose influence in the Académie had been great even before 1755, would contribute, with the aid of various salons, to the election of a majority of encyclopedists.

Henceforth, the Académie, pleased as a body to feel itself supported by public opinion and rejuvenated by an influx of incontestable talent, enjoyed what it called its "freedom." Thus after 1760, the new doctrine symbolized and embodied in the *Encyclopédie* became, thanks to the legitimation it received from the "philosophical" majority in the Académie, the very focus of French common sense. Anyone who departed from its norm exposed himself to the same withering laughter that Molière had unleashed against anyone who departed from the doctrine generally accepted by the *honnestes gens* of the court of Louis XIV. And conversely, by putting itself, as Sainte-Beuve said, "on a level with outside literary opinion," the Académie had gained a vitality and brilliance comparable to what it had enjoyed in the most luminous moments of the *grand règne*.

13. That vitality was such that the academic genres themselves were rejuvenated by it. They regained, or received for the first time, the enthusiastic ear of the public. Irritated by this independence, which Richelieu had failed to foresee, Maupeou under Louis XV and Maurepas under Louis XVI considered abolishing the Académie or merging it with the Académie des Inscriptions. The grip on the Parisian audience, for which the Académie was criticized, protected it, as did the prudence and respect that the Ancien Régime always maintained toward its recalcitrant corps. As a focal point of intrigue in Paris salons seeking rewards for their literary stars, the Académie discovered a vocation for the eloquence of the forum, which the monarchy had banished as contrary to its principles. Having burned incense to the court and served as a royal chapel until 1755, the academicians now took up civic eloquence with a rebellious tinge, turning their formal meetings into political and social events. The *discours de réception*, enlivened by philosophical enthusiasm, in turn stirred the enthusiasm of the public. When pronounced by academic abbés who supported the new thinking, the annual encomia for the mass of Saint Louis elicited complicitous smiles and applause from the public. The prize for eloquence, which Guez de Balzac had founded in a spirit of pious contrition, and the Clermont-Tonnerre Prize for Poetry, founded to celebrate the Most Christian King Louis XIV, were recast by Duclos in 1759: henceforth the competition was to feature profane and civic eloquence in praise of "the nation's celebrated men."[50]

Antoine-Léonard Thomas, the first to win the new prize, established the rules and style of the new genre, which might be characterized as philosophical homily. He was hailed as the laureate for several years running, leading ultimately to his own election to the Académie in 1767. The novelty of Thomas's declamatory style, which delighted Voltaire and the whole philosophical party, was limited. In fact, it reflected the long-standing nostalgia of French humanism for a "republican" style of eloquence, one that would resurrect Demosthenes and Cicero for the Moderns. It was related to exercises in prosopopoeia practiced in eighteenth-century *collèges* and should not be seen as a move toward a deliberative and therefore openly political genre. Thomas's *Éloges,* for all their "patriotic" pathos, remain *within* the genre of academic panegyric: they represent its secularized version. In his *Essai sur les éloges*[51] Thomas became the historian and theorist of the genre that he had so illustriously practiced, and the very title of the work shows that if, at Duclos's behest, he had moved beyond the homiletic and para-ecclesiastical version of the genre, he never ventured outside the epideictic, of which he continued to offer a civic variant. This was nevertheless a step toward the political eloquence of the revolutionary assemblies and clubs, but it was a step taken without premeditation and in the belief that it was merely reviving the ancient republican art of panegyric, Plutarch exalted by the virtuous vehemence of Cicero. Still, Thomas's declamatory civism served the purpose of state reform and thus illustrated in its own way the *doxa* of the *Encyclopédie.* "If there were a country," Thomas proclaimed in his *Éloge de Sully,* "where disorders and misfortunes were one and the same, where abuses were transformed into laws, customs degraded to the point of corruption, and the mainsprings of the State gone soft, I would write for that country."[52]

In the decades preceding the Revolution, both perpetual secretaries wrote essays that touched on the status of *gens de lettres* in French society—an issue with which the Académie was involved by definition. Duclos's tone was moderate, d'Alembert's spitefully haughty. In his *Considérations sur les mœurs de ce siècle* (1751), Duclos remarked on the decline of "studious men" and the broadening "taste for Letters, the Sciences, and the Arts." He noted the welcome softening of manners that resulted from the osmosis between "those who cultivate Letters" and the "World" that found pleasure and profit in their acquaintance. If the "World" deliberately ignored the scholars, who were too narrowly specialized and too withdrawn, if it readily acknowledged the works of men of talent but shunned its authors as too individual for its taste, it celebrated *gens d'esprit,* adopted them for itself, and even forgot the distinctions of rank for their benefit. In the tradition of the seventeenth-century moralists, Duclos attempted to define the undefinable: true superiority of mind *(esprit)* in a worldly society that had become accustomed to recognizing intelligence *(esprit)* as a principle of social distinction but easily confused it with *le bel esprit,* or wit. This lesson in tact addressed to men of the world was complemented by a lesson in moderation addressed to men of letters, who among themselves all too easily fell prey to envy and rancor: "Carefully wrought works and reasonable, severe, but just and honest criticism, which notes beauties even as it points out defects so as to open up new perspectives: that," wrote Duclos, "is what one is entitled to expect from men of letters."[53]

14. It is not surprising that the Académie enjoyed one of its proudest moments under the leadership of a perpetual secretary as firm about the interests of his corps as he was aware of the more robust tendencies of his time and country. His successor, d'Alembert, was by nature a less happy man who took a less serene view of his functions. This could have been anticipated simply by reading his *Essai sur la Société des gens de lettres et les Grands* (1751), where the affectation of Stoic brevity à la Tacitus exudes the rancor of resentment and partisanship. D'Alembert ambitiously presents himself as a "writer without wiles, without intrigue, without support, and therefore without hope, but also without worries or desires." This figure of excessive modesty is already alarming. The embittered commonplaces that this paragon of rectitude reels off one after another confirm this baleful impression. Claiming that Richelieu's goal in founding the Académie was to establish a model of *equality,* the academician calls for party solidarity among "men of letters": "Fortunate at least are men of letters if they recognize at last that the surest way of winning respect is to live united and almost apart, among themselves. Through unity they will easily succeed in setting the law for the rest of the nation in matters of taste and philosophy."[54] In 1753, a year before his election to the Académie, he wrote to Mme du Deffand, at that time his fervent patron: "That is how those people must be treated. We are not of the Académie; we are Quakers, and we keep our hats on when we pass the Academy and those who get people into it."[55] He was elected nevertheless and, despite principled resistance from the court, even succeeded Duclos as perpetual secretary in 1771.

With such views, it is not surprising that d'Alembert strove to turn the brilliant and respected Académie he had inherited from Duclos into the foremost of those "societies of thought" whose role in laying the groundwork for the French Revolution was denounced by Augustin Cochin. Whereas Duclos had restored the Académie to its role as central mediator, d'Alembert closed out all but the encyclopedist spirit, which itself had shriveled to the spirit of a sect. Sénac de Meilhan, in his essay *Du gouvernement des mœurs et des conditions en France avant la Révolution* (1814), could write without exaggeration that after Voltaire's death d'Alembert held "the scepter of literature" in France and became the "dictator of Letters" precisely because he "controlled all the seats in the Académie." Setting the tone for public sessions, he used his voice to transform them into a forum for a new Juvenal. Even Voltaire, before his demise, worried about the aggressive turn taken by a triumph that he would have preferred to see accomplished in a more tranquil and magnanimous spirit. Yet no one had done more than the author of the *Dictionnaire philosophique* to ensure the definitive triumph in the Académie of the *philosophes*, and no one had worked harder to present the Académie uniformly as the antithesis of the Sorbonne, the spearhead of the battle against *l'Infâme*. Among other signs of this vigilance, consider this letter that Voltaire sent to Palissot from Ferney on February 13, 1767:

> What a pity, I said, that a man who thinks and writes so well should have made implacable enemies of extremely meritorious people who think and write as he does. Had you turned your talents in another direction, I would have had the pleasure of having you before my death as a colleague in the Académie Française.[56]

Shortly thereafter Palissot replied:

> I shall not be a member of the Académie Française, I think, but if I deserve to be, then so much the worse for it. And the polite regrets that you have been kind enough to express to me in connection with this minor disgrace are more than sufficient consolation.[57]

Hence it was only fitting that on the very day of Voltaire's apotheosis at the Comédie-Française, the Académie honored him with a reception befitting a pontiff. But then Voltaire conducted himself as a pontiff rather than a party leader. The legitimate heir of Boileau and Racine—and d'Alembert, who delivered the welcoming speech and described him as superior to those two past masters—he revealed himself, in a final and admirable burst of vitality, as what he had fundamentally always been: the incarnation of the French academic spirit in its most spiritual, most enticing, most radiant form. Though dying, he wanted to press ahead with his old plan of recasting the *Dictionnaire de l'Académie*, exhorting his colleagues, circulating letters, and not hesitating to assume responsibility himself for the letter A! He died on May 30, and his project was buried with him. In any case Voltaire's plan had run counter to the tradition of Vaugelas: Voltaire had set writers up as the arbiters of language, whereas for Vaugelas the golden rule was the usage of high society, corroborated by an Académie in which "authors" had only a consultative voice. Still, in this ultimate and almost testamentary expression of love for language, Voltaire demonstrated his vocation for that which unites: he had always opposed the catholicity of the Church with the catholicity of the Enlightenment, and it was to this, around this, enlightened conclave that he called the Académie in a supreme *Sursum corda*. It was a beautiful utopia. The golden age of the *Encyclopédie* died with him. D'Alembert took it upon himself to complete the transformation of *mystique* into *politique*. His iron discipline quelled any remaining enthusiasm, and only the musical dispute between the partisans of Gluck and the champions of Piccinni seemed to amuse the Académie in the years preceding the Revolution.

15. The Enlightenment had set its philosophical church against the Church of Darkness, and the Académie Française, as the sun in a solar system of academies that had grown up throughout France and Europe, ultimately became the Sacred College of Reason on the March.[58] The fact that the Ancien Régime could have allowed one of its court institutions to become the authority sanctioning the transformation of "men of letters" into militants working for its own reform reveals the extent not so much of its blindness as of its moderation. In retrospect, the decree of August 8, 1793, by which the Convention with one stroke abolished the whole constellation of Ancien Régime academies, clarifies the nature of that moderation. Richelieu's intention had been to use the vanity of men of letters to bind them to the state. In order to honor them, he had been obliged to avail himself of France's venerable corporate model, which Jean Bodin's critiques, dating back as far as the sixteenth century, had not been enough to render obsolete. After its founder's death, this "literary corporation" developed its own esprit de corps, which, thanks to the collegial spirit and life tenure of its members, proved immune to attacks from the court. Won over to the eloquence of the Enlightenment, the Académie thus became just another component in the fragile and complex "balance of power" that limited and even hamstrung the exercise of public authority in the old monarchy. The Revolution then lost no time in attacking precisely those intermediate corps that the royal government had so meticulously respected. The Constituent Assembly abolished all the *grands corps* that had exercised a modicum of political power: the *parlements*, the provincial estates, the assemblies of the clergy. The Convention abolished the rest: the ecclesiastical congregations, the universities and colleges, and the guilds. The academies suffered the same fate. The logic of this action was that of the Enlightenment's faith in a natural law which, recognizing only individuals "free and equal in rights" and a general will that was the only place in which they came together in common purpose, rendered illegitimate any mediation between the subjectivity of individuals and the objectivity of the general will. The academies in fact fell within the purview of a different law—medieval, customary, Catholic law—which saw the monarchy, in the image of the Church, as composed of separate corps whose collegial identity, privileges, and purpose had been revealed gradually over time, and saw each person as the sum of memberships of various corps, orders, colleges, congregations, and corporations that defined that person's form and "estate" within the state. In militating for reforms and setting itself up as a Counter-Church, the philosophy of the Enlightenment had nevertheless been caught up in this mold, and in conquering the Académie it had even accepted the rules of the

FIGURE 8.4. Montalembert, dressed as an abbé and armed with one of his historical works, knocks at the door of the Académie, which had in fact just elected him (1850). Daumier is here reflecting the views of the rebels who, under the Second Empire, set themselves up as a secessionist movement of artists, novelists, and poets who rejected the official order of letters upheld by the Académie.

game. The "philosophical" man of letters of the eighteenth century, starting with Voltaire, derived from the Académie the certitude of having an "estate" in the real society, if only that of reflecting on and reforming that society. No one challenged this belief. Thus by using the Académie as its Sacred College, the Church of the Enlightenment remained in a sense "catholic." It was rooted in a terrestrial city, which bore the mark of the dark centuries' sin, and it endeavored to transfigure that city into the City of Reason. But in that interregnum, untormented by apocalyptic urgency, its clerics had a regenerative function that was universal in the strict sense, and this gave them a powerful sense of belonging, indeed of belonging felicitously.

Rousseau introduced heresy into this Counter-Church, which in so many respects was a child of the Counter-Reformation: for him, a Pietist, any mediation between the heart and its God, any expectant or diplomatic compromise with whatever stood in the way of the purity of natural law, any limit on the infinite expansion of the inner self, the sole witness to the original state of grace, was by nature Evil. Only a utopian General Will had the right to obedience and respect *perinde ac cadaver*, and that General Will was the product of a contract between minds which, like his own, had been revealed unto themselves. All the literary subjectivism of the nineteenth-century artist, from René to Ménalque, stems from the Rousseauist heresy, which the heirs of the Enlightenment would often combat with more conviction than the heirs of the *Génie du christianisme*. A dividing line separated those who chose to emigrate from reality from those who, whether reactionary or progressive, sought first to honor what history had given them, namely, a society with a distinctive and present reality of its own, a society that might, by emulating either ancient models or supposedly superior modern ones, be made more perfect, but in which, in the meantime, it was possible to achieve form, figure, and estate. The romantic heresy and its innumerable sects would strive to make literature—and the arts—a *bateau ivre* on which the pure, the exiled, and the damned could embark, cutting themselves loose from established society. In this new context the Académie Française would discover a more exposed, more dramatic symbolic function than under the Ancien Régime: for now it was the very principle that literature has a natural place in society that was violently challenged in the name of a purer literature, a literature freed from its carnal envelope and set up as the foundation of a new kingdom. Reinstituted de facto by the Consulate and Empire and restored to its preeminence and former title by the Restoration, the *corps littéraire* that the Convention had abolished became for some the temple in which France celebrated the high mass of its last national religion, for others the ghostly site where literature, enslaved by its executioner, sacrificed to the impious cult of honors, vanity, and sham—and so it has remained to this day. The dark pathos with which the Goncourt brothers treat the Vatican and Saint Peter's in their novel *Madame Gervaisais* is of exactly the same order as that with which they treat the Académie Française and its literary pope, Sainte-Beuve, in their *Journal*. Paralleling the political drama of the nineteenth century and determining it at some deep level, the literary drama of the century cannot be understand without that obscurely obsessive Arlésienne, the Académie Française. Barbey d'Aurevilly was speaking for the whole romantic rebellion when he wrote in 1863 that "it is good that young people become disgusted with Academies and their spirit when they see how that spirit shrivels the talent of talented men."[59] He was thinking not only of the Académie Française but also of the Académie des Beaux-Arts, which, as art historians know, played a central role both in maintaining a high tradition of craftsmanship and in spurring the *refusés* to invent a new form of artistic legitimacy. The role of the Académie Française, though less visible and less easy to grasp, was no less important in the literary sociopsychology of nineteenth-century France.

16. The abolition of the academies on August 8, 1793, in the wake of a report submitted by Abbé Grégoire, was preceded by a polemic in which the principal target was the Académie Française, the oldest of all the academies and, because of its composition, the most exposed to the sophisms of the *esprit de géométrie* and the vehemence of *ressentiment*. As early as 1791, Chamfort, despite having been first a laureate and then a member of the Académie, published a diatribe in which he concluded that it was useless and ought to be abolished. Abbé Morellet, himself an adept of the Enlightenment and quite devoted to the Company that had elected him, answered his colleague but in an almost clandestine pamphlet, which was circulated to a few trustworthy friends and sold secretively. After saving the Académie's archives from revolutionary vandalism, the same Abbé Morellet joined with Suard to become, after the Convention was dissolved, the tireless artisan of the institution's slow and difficult reemergence.[60]

Of all the academies, the Académie Française was, owing to its association with the court, the high nobility, and the high Church, the most *ci-devant*, or prerevolutionary, in spirit. But the constellation of academies that the Ancien Régime had slowly accreted seemed intolerable to encyclopedic reason when, encouraged by the first revolutionary events, it discovered haste. Talleyrand and Condorcet came up with fine programs for a system of "public instruction," an imposing edifice to be topped off by an Institut National in which all research would be coordinated and progress in concert.[61] This new institution, twice approved in principle by the Convention, was finally established by decree of the Directory on October 25, 1795.[62] Of the three classes of the Institute (Physical and Mathematical Sciences, Moral and Political Sciences, Literature and Fine Arts), only the first corresponded to one of the old academies, the Académie des Sciences. The prerevolutionary "men of letters" who had owed their luster under the Ancien Régime to the Académie Française and who had done so much to lay the intellectual groundwork for the Reign of Reason, found themselves reduced to a very meager place in the new institution: only two sections of the "third class," or twelve members in all of the hundred and forty members of the Institute, were in a position to claim, under the heads of "grammar" and "poetry," what was left of belles-lettres. And this was even less than it might appear, since the proposed mode of recruitment was election by general assembly, that is by all "classes" and "sections" combined. Instead of an illustrious corps in which men of letters mingled as colleagues with dukes, marshals, and cardinals, they now found themselves lost in a huge contingent and treated just like any other employee of the state, entitled to a stipend "appropriate to both the modesty of the true scholar and the severe economy of republican government." So much for the court privileges that the Académie Française had enjoyed. Relegated to the ranks, men of letters would henceforth be obliged to advance, in Daunou's phrase, toward the "common center" to which, "by a natural and necessary inclination" must lead "everything great, fruitful, and beautiful that springs each year from the fertile soil of France."[63] This encyclopedia on the march was nevertheless profoundly restructured by the Consulate in 1803. The class of Moral and Political Sciences, which included those whom Bonaparte called Idéologues, was abolished. Two new classes, French Language and Literature and Ancient History and Literature, reconstituted (without explicit acknowledgment) the Académie Française and the Académie des Inscriptions. The institution of the perpetual secretaries was reinstated. Henceforth elections were to be by class rather than by head. These successive and authoritarian restructurings might have augured a future of incessant "reforms" at the whim of each new political regime, but the Napoleonic reform limited the danger in advance by creating the conditions for a new esprit de corps, capable in the long run of resisting administrative and political caprice. In addition, scholarly belles-lettres and advanced studies, which had known a golden age under the Ancien Régime and which were intimately associated with the politeness of its customs, once again found a place that the Directory had denied them. Yet one source of recruitment had dried up for good: ecclesiastics, who were henceforth deprived of the training they had received from the old university and of the benefices of various kinds that, under the Ancien Régime, had guaranteed them the leisure and material independence indispensable for works of the mind.

In 1801, the First Consul, quite proud of belonging to the first class of the Institute, gave orders that his colleagues be issued an official uniform designed by David, the famous "green coat" embellished with embroidered olive leaf, which, but for minor modifications, has remained the academic uniform ever since. After becoming emperor, Napoleon I, in a decree issued on March 20, 1805, ordered that the Institute, cramped in a "Grand Louvre" now packed with art treasures streaming in from all quarters of the Empire, be moved to the building that had formerly housed the Collège des Quatre-Nations. The Institute established itself there in August 1806.

17. This was much more, in appearance at any rate, than the Ancien Régime had done for its academies. When Louis XIV installed the old academies in the Louvre, he put them in close proximity with the artists and craftsmen who worked for the Court and who had been lodged there since the reign of Henri IV. In moving the Institute to the other side of the Seine, to a building that would eventually become its own, Napoleon had aimed to elevate it to a new sublimity. His choice could not have been more appropriate: the college and chapel of the Quatre-Nations, closed down by the Revolution, had been conceived by Colbert (Mazarin's executor) as an edifice worthy to stand opposite the New Louvre.[64] The architect Le Vau had designed a building that, whether in homage to Mazarin and his Roman roots or as a challenge to the Holy See, could pass for a scaled-down, elegant variation on the theme of Saint Peter's of Rome. The half-moon facade was reminiscent of Bernini's colonnade, but in a minor key. And the cupola, erected on an elliptical drum above the chapel crossing, soared above the facade, as Michelangelo's would have done had not the addition of a Latin nave and the massive Maderno portico not pushed it far to the rear. The French state thus established its Sacred College of Reason in a setting and beneath a vault that rivaled those of the basilica of the Roman pontiffs. Corresponding to the inscription *Tu es Petrus* in gold capitals on the interior face of the drum of Michelangelo's cupola was this quotation from Ezekiel (31:17) beneath Le Vau's cupola: *Sedebit sub umbraculo ejus in medio nationum.*

To be sure, the cupola of the Quatre-Nations was masked, during the Consulate, by another, in trompe-l'oeil, designed by Vaudoyer. But the prophetic inscription, long hidden, once again shone forth in all its luster above the amphitheater after renovations carried out while André Malraux served as minister of culture. Instead of the modest prerevolutionary Parnassus in the Louvre, the postrevolutionary state thus created an empyrean in the form of a cupola that secularized sacred Neoplatonic and Christian symbols. Through the crossings in Vaudoyer's false cupola or the high windows and skylight in Le Vau's restored design, the light of the French Logos beamed down on academic assemblies, now the sole custodians of that light since the death of the king-pontiff and the disappearance of Parlement and the old Sorbonne.

This architectural assumption was not without its price. The state, which had created the Institute out of nothing and bestowed upon it something of its official majesty and even, with the sword, its military pomp, intended to make sure that the Académie was utterly and entirely devoted to its service. And so it was—under the Directory, the Consulate, and even more, if possible, under the Empire, when the Institute was required "to report" each year to Napoleon I. On February 27, 1808, a deputation led by Marie-Joseph Chénier, president of the second class of the Institute (French Language and Literature), presented to His Majesty the Emperor and King, in his Council of State, a *Rapport historique sur l'état et les progrès de la lit-*

térature. Here we see the revenge of Arnauld and Nicole's *Logique* on Vaugelas's *Remarques*, the triumph of the "school of Port-Royal, that source as inexhaustible as it is pure, to which all sound doctrine and classical literature can be traced," over the tradition of the old Académie Française.[65] Despite Napoleon's suspicion of the Idéologues, the report of the second class awarded Condillac and his heirs, Destutt de Tracy and Cabanis, the honor of continuing the tradition of Port-Royal and symbolizing the brilliance of French literature. Imperial neoclassicism saw itself as inheriting the intellectual mantle of the Gallican Counter-Reformation in its most radical form, that of the "gentlemen" of Port-Royal, and hailed them, not without historical justice, as the unwitting fathers of French Enlightenment philosophy. When Sainte-Beuve produced his monumental *Port-Royal*, dedicated to the learning and piety of the Jansenist *solitaires*, he demonstrated his devotion to the original inspiration of the Institute, that creature of the Revolution, and showed that he was also its most profound interpreter.[66]

By 1808, however, the *Génie du christianisme* had already been out for six years. It was not mentioned in the report, and it received no prize from the Institute. Chateaubriand was elected a member in 1809, but only on orders from Napoleon, and he would not be welcomed until the Restoration: his speech contained an encomium on liberty that he refused to omit. Like Rousseau, Chateaubriand, the greatest writer of the century, owed his literary glory to his genius alone, and like Napoleon he owed his crowning as hero solely to his own will. This was a bad sign for the future of the relationship between the Académie and literature.

Although the Restoration restored the old names of the academies and reinstated the old prerogatives of the Académie Française, the purge that it decided to order in 1816 once again revealed the Institute's lack of independence vis-à-vis the government. But the utopia of an encyclopedic corps, all of whose organs worked steadily in concert like the "gentlemen" of Port-Royal or the collaborators of Diderot, had already vanished under the Empire. And the danger of having a corps of functionaries obedient to each new ministry soon evaporated as well. In 1825, Stendhal could write that

> in fact, in a country where there is an opposition, there can no longer be an Académie Française. The Ministry will never allow it to admit the great talents of the opposition, and the public will always persist in being unjust toward noble writers paid by ministers, for whom the Académie will become an Invalides.[67]

On April 19, 1827, the Académie Française elected Royer-Collard, the opposition's most spellbinding orator. Its esprit de corps triumphed over the bureaucratic temptation. Thereafter the Académie remained liberal, which set it in tune with the July Monarchy, put it in opposition under the Second Empire, and kept it in a sort of senatorial *juste milieu* under the Third Republic. For successive governments its loyalty was not a political issue serious enough to get worked up about. More important, the Académie, thanks to the reform of the Institute under the Consulate, was able to fill its ranks with the kind of "notables" who made nineteenth-century French society relatively stable and harmonious.[68] Regardless of their birth, noble or common, and regardless of their profession, the members of the new aristocracy from which the Académie drew its membership, and which included or came to include journalists, political orators, playwrights, poets, historians, and university critics, inherited something of the authority of the Ancien Régime institution: stability, gravity, a dynastic sense, a taste for landed property, and an idea of literature associated with a large library. This notability of letters was something that the "great romantics" like Lamartine, Hugo, and Vigny could all the more easily assume because it was but one facet—an important one, to be sure—of their public persona, and in any case they knew how to embellish their academic uniform with garb that appealed more directly to the imagination. But the common denominator between a Hugo and a Guizot, a Lamartine and a Mignet, a Vigny and a Montalembert, assumed that the poets shared a social *habitus* not within reach of writers who were not so well-born, writers who were merely writers. The gap between the notables and senators of nineteenth-century literature and the nervous sons of the bourgeoisie with literary vocations grew wider as the century progressed: the model of the notable, a noble variant of the bourgeois type, provoked an allergic reaction among the minor romantics and their heirs, an allergy that swelled the ranks of literary heresy. Indeed, that allergy, which had as much to do with a lifestyle as with aesthetic and political ideas, was reciprocal: the Notables of Letters despised the multifarious "bohemia" that proliferated outside the Institute and ostentatiously affected to ignore its very existence. University professors conformed to the academic mold more easily than "artists." Many professors would join the Académie during the Third Republic, but their place had been marked out for them by Victor Cousin as early as the July Monarchy. Gaston Boissier (1876), Ernest Renan (1878), Hippolyte Taine (1878), Ernest Lavisse (1892), Fernand Brunetière (1893), and Émile Faguet (1899) added their austere but eloquent learning and their "Victorian" idea of the French academician to a portrait whose essential features had been sketched in by the peers in the upper chamber under Louis-Philippe.

18. "A haven of gloomy old herons," to borrow a phrase from Barbey,[69] the nest of burgraves in which the same Barbey was outraged to find Hugo and Musset ("in academic garb, a pack on Ariel's back") was indeed notable for the high average age of its members, who "entered" later than was usually allowed in the eighteenth century. The relative aging of the "academic body"[70] in the nineteenth century (dating

back to the time of the Directory) would have done it no harm in a traditional society, in which old age was respected for its experience and wisdom, but it took on a new meaning in a society in which generational conflict was acute, and youth, along with the future, was in the process of becoming a supreme value. Furthermore, the rites of passage from adolescence to adulthood, especially in privileged and educated milieus, worked less effectively in the nineteenth century than they had under the Ancien Régime. School-age youth, studying rhetoric in preparation for various professions, easily succumbed to the spell of a literature that ever since Rousseau had invoked enthusiasm, dream, and desire against scholastic and academic pedantry. But Villemain and Saint-Marc Girardin linked the Académie with the university, Barbey called Sainte-Beuve "professor," and under the Third Republic, numerous members of the faculty of the École Normale Supérieure entered the Académie Française.

The Académie was not content to be a senate of old men, an assembly of notables, and the seat of a literary orthodoxy odious in principle to the rebellious younger generation. The Prix Montyon and any number of other prizes for virtue and achievement, academic awards reflecting the charitable spirit of the nineteenth century—a spirit to which Hugo's *Les Misérables* stands as a durable monument—only irritated "artists" and the youth of the Latin Quarter all the more. Baudelaire's ironic "Let's bludgeon the poor," a motto that Manet or Degas might have taken for his own, stood romantic and Victorian sentimentalism on its head. Bohemia, in all its more or less impoverished variations, had one thing in common: the alliance of writers and painters in furtherance of their rebellion against their respective academies. Bohemian habits, which smacked more of the studio than of the salon, encouraged promiscuity with the demimonde and a taste for the open air in a countryside that had nothing to do with respectable castles. The novels of Champfleury as well as of the Goncourt brothers, especially *Charles Demailly*, revealed the gap between the bohemian lifestyle (broadly understood) and that of the official notables.

Those novels were written in the Second Empire, but since the days of "Jeune France" any number of Parisian groups and cenacles had arisen to challenge official taste and search for new thrills utterly foreign to officialdom.

In France, this polarization in the life of arts and letters—misleadingly confused with the "vanguard" of progress in the sciences and politics—took on an almost archetypal character and is today the golden legend of official culture. This is because the existence of prestigious academic institutions in France has given the debate there a particularly clear outline and raised it to a neurotic pitch. Do the academies play the role of a terrifying father or a castrating mother? Be that as it may, they did in any case introduce into the "family romance" that nineteenth-century arts and letters became an oedipal figure so powerful that the band of brothers

FIGURE 8.5. Sainte-Beuve dressed in the uniform of the academician. He was the most profound and intelligent nineteenth-century interpreter of the academic norm.

was obliged to squander fortunes of talent, imagination, seduction, and irony to defy it and even perhaps to internalize it.

As early as the Restoration the quarrel between "classics" and "romantics" defined certain recurring features of the nineteenth-century French literary drama, casting the Académie from the outset in the difficult but central role of "noble father." In many respects Stendhal established the outline of the plot in the two successive versions of his pamphlet *Racine and Shakespeare.*

He even anticipated the violent tone that the conflict would take under the Second Empire. This was because his own literary position was eccentric, and in the long run this made him the precursor of every form of discomfort and insolence. Stendhal, the heir of the Enlightenment and admirer of Bonaparte, was an ironist unmoved by Chateaubriand's pathos, but he was also a reader of Rousseau, an admirer of Italian painting and music, and a man bored by La Harpe's neoclassicism. The first version of *Racine et Shakespeare* (1823) pitted an academician against a romantic: the mere fact of belonging to the Académie was enough to designate a champion of dreary, conventional taste, a mechanical emulator of the Ancien Régime. In April 1824, Auger, then director of the Académie Française, answered Stendhal indirectly with an attack on romanticism in a speech delivered to a plenary session of the Institute. The debate dealt mainly with dramatic art. Warming to the contest, Stendhal responded with a second version of *Racine et Shakespeare,* whose irony was now aimed directly at the Académie. In two facing columns, H. B. (Henri Beyle, that is, Stendhal) listed the nonentities (as he judged them) who sat in the Académie after its "reform" by the Restoration on one side and, on the other, the talents of the day who were not represented. The vigor of the reply found no immediate imitators, particularly since the leading lights of romanticism, starting with Lamartine in 1829, ignored the pioneer who led the way and threw themselves into the academic game, thus obviating Stendhal's most vehement complaint. But under Napoleon III the theme would be developed by Arsène Houssaye, and after Baudelaire failed to gain admission a whole generation of writers, slowly rediscovering Stendhal, came to share his contempt for the sterile conformism of which the Académie in their eyes was a symbol.

19. The misunderstanding that separated the nineteenth-century Académie from what has become, for us, according to an absurdly restrictive definition, literature, grew much worse during the Second Empire. Filled with historians, political orators, eloquent poets, and critics, the Académie as a body greeted the novel as a genre with Olympian contempt. Novels sold well, and novelists were the only writers who could live by their pens. The novel was the popular genre par excellence, and serialization made fiction available to a hungry public.[71] The novel was also a genre in which women, its most inveterate readers, excelled as authors. Mme de Staël, Mme

de Krüdener, Mme de Duras, and above all George Sand had stood or stood even now at the head of the pack. Prose fiction thus earned the scorn of the notables. The Académie had accepted the lyrical genres of romanticism and even romantic theater, but in its novelistic form—a dragon with a thousand heads—it inspired contempt. That contempt, which was concentrated and publicly and officially expressed in the form of academic exclusion, was not without consequences on the evolution of the French novel. Balzac's struggle to achieve academic respectability for himself and for the novel was one of the driving forces behind his life and his literary strategy.

La Comédie humaine, with its references to Dante and Molière, was an obvious bid to escape the curse on the novel by any possible means. Indeed, Balzac carefully avoided the very word "novel," characterizing the various segments of his social epic as "studies" and "scenes" and spicing his narratives with digressions intended to give him the stature of a historian, economist, philosopher, and theorist of the moral and political sciences. This passionate desire for official recognition was in no way at odds with the generous impulse that caused him to publish, in 1834 in the *Revue de Paris,* a "letter to nineteenth-century writers" calling for the creation of a Society of Men of Letters, which was in fact legally constituted in 1838 to monitor the material and moral situation of writers.[72] Balzac recognized that the collection of authors' royalties, to which the Convention had granted legal status, could become an instrument for the economic emancipation of men of letters, providing resources for mutual assistance. Of course this was profoundly alien to the academic tradition, which consistently ignored the corporate concerns of writers, and ignored their economic concerns even more. Bear in mind that the Company was not and never had been just a club for writers. Its honor as a body even impelled it to exclude from its ranks, which included so many notables, writers whose social and financial position was not fully attested and secure. It could not run the risk of seeing one of its members hounded or imprisoned for debt. Indeed, it was to just such certain and enduring respectability that Balzac aspired both for itself and as a necessary if not sufficient prerequisite for academic consecration.

In the admirable chapter of *Choses vues* in which the academician Victor Hugo recounts his visit on August 18, 1850, to the dying Balzac on Avenue Fortunée, we read the report of a disaster. After two unsuccessful attempts to enter the Académie, Balzac had recently enhanced his status by marrying Mme Hanska and moving into a luxurious dwelling furnished with the taste of an antique dealer. He died too soon to discover whether this final effort would have been enough to overcome the resistance of the Academy. At his funeral, in which Hugo and Alexandre Dumas served as pallbearers, the poet heard the minister Baroche offer this belated judgment: "He was a distinguished man." Twelve years later, the Académie elected Octave Feuillet, the successful author of the *Roman d'un jeune homme pauvre:* it was not so much the novelist, who in his acceptance speech begged pardon for writing novels, that the Académie chose to honor as it was George Sand's rival, the man who had championed Victorian morality in the very arena where Sand had preached for bohemia.

In 1844, Prosper Mérimée was elected to the Académie, but not for *Clara Gazul* or for his novellas. A member of the Académie des Inscriptions since 1843, he had all the credentials of an erudite historian, and in any case would subsequently sacrifice his gift for writing fiction to his admirable work as an inspector of historical monuments and his career as a politician and courtier under the Second Empire. The next novelist to be admitted to the Académie was Paul Bourget, who was not elected until 1894. This academic bravado, which Sainte-Beuve noted with satisfaction in an 1862 article,[73] did not diminish. Meanwhile, novelists responded to the challenge by seeking another form of ennoblement in aesthetic irony: Flaubert slaved like a dog to embellish apparently "vulgar" and "scandalous" subjects with a sumptuous style as dense as anything found in the highest poetry. And Edmond de Goncourt was convinced that his brother Jules died from his exertions in perfecting the style of *Madame Gervaisais,* a novel that Sainte-Beuve, himself dying but still merciless, lived long enough to skewer cruelly. Indeed, the literary rehabilitation of the novel by Flaubert and the Goncourts and later the "naturalists" relied on the art of description rather than the philosophical digression favored by Balzac. In a roundabout way this tightened the old alliance between writers and painters, an alliance ratified under the July Monarchy by the voluntary exile of bohemia, the sworn enemy of both the Académie Française and the Académie des Beaux-Arts. The "rejected" novelists could readily believe in an increasingly refined art, just like the "rejected" painters, who also bestowed the brilliance of the noble genres on subjects disdained by the Prix de Rome. It did not matter that both painters and writers moved in excellent bourgeois circles: Flaubert and the Goncourts were regular visitors at Princess Mathilde's and in the best society. For the Notables of Letters, *lettres* meant the traditional trilogy: eloquence, history, and poetry. By rehabilitating the great poetic genres—epic, lyric, and idyll—Lamartine, Hugo, Vigny, and Musset had earned the right to sit beneath the Cupola. The eloquence of the liberals, historiography, and even journalism, which was seen as a genre of eloquence, all had their place in the Académie. But the novel posed an intolerable threat to the equilibrium of the genres. Indeed, its appetite clearly demonstrated its ambition to occupy a central, invasive, and ultimately exclusive place in literature, and ultimately that ambition was fulfilled. Sainte-Beuve saw the danger quite clearly. His reasoning about poetry was the same, moreover. When he characterized *Les Fleurs du mal* as "Kamchatka" and "madness," he was thinking of poetry in terms of geography or of a garden with a center, a privileged point of view; and the value of that *commonplace,* the standard of reference for all, was too great to run the risk of sacrificing or weakening it for the sake of qualities that were too singular or too peripheral. He thus proved himself to be the nineteenth-century academic sage par excellence, the custodian of a tradition without which there is no Church. It is worth noting that Paul Valéry, who was almost without peer in his understanding of the "function" and "mystery" of the Académie Française, shared the Institute's longstanding aversion for the novel, against which he unleashed, in the presence of a delighted André Breton, the famous epigram: *La marquise sortit à cinq heures* ("The marquise went out at five o'clock"). The novel has since taken its revenge, but—the victim of its own overwhelming victory, the sole survivor in the arena of genres—it slowly disintegrates with each new round of literary prizes into a thousand *sonnets d'Oronte.*

20. The revenge of the novel was predictable by the end of the nineteenth century. What the novel had going for it was its large print runs, number of readers, and even the patent of nobility acquired by those martyrs of hard labor, Balzac and Flaubert, and later by the nonchalant Stendhal, who was opportunely rediscovered in the 1880s as the great ancestor of the family.[74] Manifestos and literary debates, which in the age of romanticism had revolved around drama, now focused increasingly on the novel. In 1888, Alphonse Daudet summed up the complaints of three generations of novelists disdained by the Notables of Letters: he published *L'Immortel.* The plot of this pamphlet-fiction turns on the antithesis between a prototypical academician, Laurent Astier-Réhu, and an artist, Védrine. Skillfully, Daudet refrained from introducing a novelist into this allegory: he chose instead to give the positive role to an artist, a rebel from the other academy, which was in any case more picturesque. A lover of the outdoors, enthusiastic, generous, humorous, and gifted with a protean genius, Védrine is as great a painter as he is a sculptor and architect. Yet despite all this he is modest and happy. As for the sinister and pitiful Astier-Réhu, he is a caricature of a long line of historians who, from Guizot to Taine, from Mignet to Sainte-Beuve, from Thiers to Montalembert, fearlessly defended the eloquence of facts against the invasion of fiction, beloved of bohemia. His undoing and suicide, inspired by an actual incident, come as just punishment for his naïve, fanatical confidence in the archival document: it turns out that his work was based on forged signatures sold for a small fortune, just as his life was based on his ambition to receive counterfeit honors. Daudet's melodramatic pathos seems pale today. Yet the novel reveals something more than social resentment pure and simple: a genuine debate, begun early in the century with the vogue for Walter Scott, here found its vengeful conclusion. At stake was the cognitive value of fiction, which was challenged by academic eloquence and its devotion to the True, the Beautiful, and the Good.

It did Émile Zola no good to wrap himself in the scientific method of Claude Bernard and Tarde's theories of heredity or to cast his *Rougon-Macquart* (on the model of *La Comédie humaine*) as a "social history of the Second Empire": his credentials as a historian and scholar did not impress the Académie, to which he sought admission twenty-four times, in vain. It was not until Paul Bourget made his *Essais de psychologie contemporaine* and his novels the vehicles for his Catholic, aristocratic, and emotional views of the modern world that a novelist was able to enter the Académie *qua* novelist. Into the breach thus opened rushed André Theuriet and Anatole France (1896), René Bazin (1903), and above all Maurice Barrès (1906). At last, it was said, the novel had proved its ability to grapple with the high moral, political, and spiritual concerns that formed the substance of the Académie's magisterium.

In contrast, drama, and especially boulevard comedy, was warmly welcomed by the nineteenth-century Académie, which saw such social comedy as one of the classic "commonplaces" of French society, perfectly at home in the canon of literary genres. Scribe (1834), Émile Augier (1857), Alexandre Dumas *fils* (1874), and Eugène Labiche (1880) all sat beneath the Cupola. Hence it was only fitting that the playwrights of the *gaiété parisienne* should cleanse the stain left by *L'Immortel:* in 1912, Robert de Flers and Georges de Caillavet's *L'Habit vert*, masquerading as a witty send-up, used laughter to dispel the last remaining clouds of naturalist wrath. Caillavet was to the manner born: his mother was the celebrated Mme Arman, the principal of one of the most influential academic salons and the Egeria and impresario of Anatole France. But it was Robert, Marquis de Flers, who outlived his collaborator and was elected to the Académie in 1920. The institution may have been grateful to him: *L'Habit vert* had in fact heralded one of the most brilliant and successful periods in the history of the Académie Française. Between 1918 and 1939, military glory, literary glory, and the relative youth of the Académie's new members lent its public sessions a luster comparable to that which it had known at the end of the reign of Louis XV. King Valéry seemed able to exert an influence comparable to that of King Voltaire. And Gide, excluded on moral grounds, could be seen as a reincarnation, with variations, of Rousseau the Enchanter.

In those happy years, the disciples of the Mallarmé cenacle, the disciples of Barrès, and even the converts from Rimbaud infused the literary image of the institution with fresh blood and life, while the Church and the victorious army contributed figures of undeniable prestige. The Académie could calmly hold its own against the numerous heretical chapels that claimed to be exploring new and remote literary "Kamchatkas."

The Académie Goncourt and its annual prize, established by the will of Edmond de Goncourt, came on the scene in 1903. The members designated by Edmond de Goncourt were all novelists: Daudet, Huysmans, Hennique, Mirbeau, Rosny (elder and younger), Geffroy, and Margueritte. This was clearly an attempt to promote the naturalist tradition of the novel. The success of the Prix Goncourt led the Académie to establish its own Grand Prix du Roman in 1914, for the purpose of recognizing a "work of inspired imagination." The quarrel was over, but it had ended with the victory of the long-ostracized genre. The Nobel Prize for Literature, first awarded in Stockholm in 1901, was something like a Prix Montyon (a prize awarded by the Académie for "virtue") for internationally known writers. It presented a long-term challenge by implicitly opposing an international common sense, defined in Sweden, to the national common sense represented in Paris by the Académie Française. But the French academy had been accustomed to seeing itself as universal for too long to worry much about an upstart that in any case proved in practice to suffer from provincial philistinism.

21. By contrast, the literary cenacles and magazines that had emerged in the nineteenth century as rivals of the venerable salon formula for launching and sustaining literary careers, or simply for providing writers with a vital milieu, ultimately gave rise to a veritable institution, whose influence was without precedent in French literary history, not even in the *Encyclopédie* of d'Alembert and Diderot.

Geneva versus Rome: at bottom it was a reformed "Academy," intended initially to be above compromise with honors, society, and respectability, that formed in 1904 around André Gide, Jean Schlumberger, and Jacques Copeau and attracted a first generation of writers to *La Nouvelle Revue Française (N.R.F.)*: Jean Giraudoux, Valery Larbaud, Jacques Rivière, Alain-Fournier, and Alexis Léger.

Others have analyzed or will analyze the development of this exclusively literary Geneva, which Claudel and Maritain, a latter-day Francis de Sales, would attempt to convert (with occasional success). Students of the subject will rightly attempt to distinguish between the initial group and what the *N.R.F.*, with its distinctive white dust jacket, became after the war at the behest of the powerful publishing house Gallimard, namely, more ecumenical but already in possession of the keys to an earthly kingdom. Here it will suffice to note what distinguished the *N.R.F.*'s Geneva from the Académie's Rome. Literature, for the Académie, was the commonplace of all of French society, represented not only by professional writers but by prominent people from society, Church, and state. The "*N.R.F.* movement" was precisely the opposite: originally and in theory literature was here, as in the Académie Goncourt, the privilege of men of letters, indeed of novelists, yet it did not renounce its right to exercise moral and even political authority over the entire realm of the spirit, an authority above that of the traditional notables. In the *N.R.F.*, the type of writer forged in the anti-academic struggles of the nineteenth century would merge with the type of "intellectual" that had emerged in the Dreyfus Affair. The novel, which the Académie had excluded for so long and which the Goncourts had wished to promote, in its naturalist form, to the status of a major genre, was also the pivotal genre for the *N.R.F.* But there it was seen as a public spiritual exercise addressed to the moral conscience. Gide, with *Les Cahiers d'André Walter*, *L'Immoraliste,* and *Si le grain ne meurt*, established a canon that Roger Martin du Gard, Jacques Rivière, Marcel Jouhandeau, Albert Camus, Jean Genet, and Jean-Paul Sartre would respect, each in his own way. Moving beyond these fiction-meditations, the writer-intellectuals of the *N.R.F.* set out to conquer the theater, art criticism, philosophy, and politics, yet never lost sight of the house genre. From Gide to Sartre, the growing authority of the "white cover" was based on the alternation between the essay and the novel, between ideas and fiction, in both cases with a marked penchant for autobiographical orison with Rousseauist overtones. The ecumenical spirit of Gaston Gallimard's editorial "patronage" did less than one might perhaps think to obscure the initial logic of the *N.R.F.*

As different as the accounts of Jean Delay *(La Jeunessse d'André Gide)*, Auguste Anglès (*André Gide et le premier groupe de la* N.R.F.), and Simone de Beauvoir *(Les Mandarins)* are, a type emerges: the literary intellectual, privately anxious yet ready to lay before the public the fruits of reflection on his private suffering. In the 1920s and after World War II a touch of bohemia was added to the rather austere style that the founders took from their bourgeois and puritanical backgrounds. Surrealists liberated from the leadership of André Breton and, later, defrocked *normaliens* liberated from the university turned the café—the Dôme and the Coupole in Montparnasse, the Deux-Magots and the Flore in Saint-Germain-des-Prés—into a substitute for the library and the salon, and the cast-iron table with its marble top, café-crème, and ashtray became the writer's desk. In interpreting the nonconformist ways that the existentialists made legendary, one must not neglect the example of the American novelists in Paris, who lived on memories of the romantics' bohemia: Hemingway, as he recounted his own story in *A Movable Feast*, was already a legend for Sartre, Beauvoir, and their friends. All, incidentally, were published by Gallimard.

The *N.R.F.*, magnified by Gallimard, thus set itself up as a triumphant Counter-Academy with universal ambitions. Its moral ambitions led it into politics in the 1930s, both on the extreme left with a certain Gide, Aragon, and Malraux and on the extreme right with Drieu la Rochelle and, after 1945, Céline. But this "reformed" literature continued to interrogate itself and to seek to recapture its pure essence. Fashionable society was not too much of a threat, but moral and political preaching was a constant temptation. Thus there were reforms within the Reform.

With Maurice Blanchot the *N.R.F.* returned to Gide's Mallarméan sources, which soon became clouded: looking back to André Walter's biblical meditations and beyond, Blanchot's "literary space" imprisoned the writer in a sublime but melancholy dungeon; writing was set up as an absolute. By contrast, ironists like Jean Paulhan[75] and Raymond Queneau pointed out how much the subjective "originality" of the writer depended for its expression, despite protestations to the coun-

FIGURE 8.6. The Académie in person; photograph by Henri Cartier-Bresson, 1953.

try, on preestablished commonplaces and topics, which the old rhetoric had refused to hide. Meanwhile, the "white dust jacket" saw no dereliction of duty in lending its authority to the novel, theater, and ideological essays that offered a tumultuous mix of philosophy and pathos. If the Académie Française was indeed the paradigm in terms of which nineteenth-century cenacles defined themselves in order to legitimate their literary manifestos, then perhaps the striking success of the *N.R.F.* gave rise to analogous projects or imitators. In conjunction with the journal *Esprit*, the Éditions du Seuil have also relied since the Liberation on the Gidian formula of alternating between novels and doctrinal essays. The same publisher has also welcomed the "human sciences," which have extended the existing literary genres with a series of hybrids combining elements of intellectual autobiography, the bravura essay, and the philosophical treatise. Yet another house that has imitated Gallimard and Seuil on a smaller scale is the Éditions de Minuit, an academy serving both the *nouveau roman* and the "hard human sciences."

22. In a world of specialists where literature itself has become a specialty, one competence among many others that are far more important, or at any rate think that they are, what role lies in store for the Académie Française? In a world eroded by utilitarian language and by a transnational subculture, in an age when every group, fleeing this gimcrack universality, is seeking a reality, perhaps wholly imaginary, in its own distinctive roots, what future lies in store for the French idea, which is too difficult to translate into the universal argot and too universal to become one patois among many? These questions must remain unanswered. But the mere fact that they can be asked sheds light on the past function of the Académie Française in a national tradition that has always seen itself as *both* exemplary and universal. It was the Académie's apparent futility, its insignificant "corporate" yield, its monumental and relative immobility that ultimately preserved its central and vital function in the most visible as well as the most buried corners of the national consciousness.

The Académie, though not the inventor of the founding myth of modern France, was nevertheless instrumental in spreading that myth: the myth of Louis le Grand, who, but for the Quarrel of the Ancients and Moderns and the academician Voltaire of the *Siècle de Louis XIV*, could never have subsumed Saint Louis, François I, Henri IV, Richelieu, and Colbert in a single symbol—the Sun—and thus would never have occupied the invincible place that he holds in French imagination and thought. The Académie is also associated with another national myth, a myth that is all too often confounded with that of the Revolution, namely, the *Encyclopédie*. Without the official consecration that the Académie conferred on the encyclopedic synthesis, without the institutional majesty that the Company bestowed on all its contributors, the magnificent effort of Ancien Régime France to remain in the vanguard of modern nations would never have enjoyed the worldwide influence that it achieved and that was then distorted into an intellectual alibi for the Revolution. Finally, the Académie is linked with the French myth of beautiful language, of belles-lettres, indeed of literature in the sense of moral and spiritual authority with which romanticism invested the term and which it retains to this day. And if the Académie Française by its mere presence was able to fulfill this truly and continuously royal function in spite of changes in the political, social, and cultural regime, indeed in spite of the growing protests that its apparent changelessness has provoked, it was not because of the base passions of which Daudet portrayed it as the focal point. An implicit idea embodied itself in this corps so deeply that it never needed to be formulated explicitly, but only with reverent discretion. That idea was Ciceronian and Roman, and it is easy to understand why it met with increasing resistance as technological modernity triumphed. It consists in the belief that the truth of the scholar, the doctor, the politician, or any other specialist cannot become truth for everyone if it is content to express itself in technical terms. In order to reach the place where it can be perceived by all, truth must learn to forgo the pride of its specialty and become *eloquence*. This assumes a choice of words attested and tempered by universally recognized usage, a felicitous elegance and clarity that make truth appealing and transparent to all, and a pathos and imaginative power capable of driving that truth home to every heart.

This is the price that must be paid if truth is to become politically *religious*, and in that sense truly royal. The history of the Académie Française, seen from its noble side, which is the only one that matters to the sage, is a never-ending meditation, adapting itself to the winding course of history, upon the *tao* of language, which the Académie, properly understood, has made a national secret but which aspires to universality. The highest justification of literature lies in its ability to facilitate exchange, to enable all specialties to accede to eloquence, to rise above their laboratories to the forum of the mind. But that justification, which the Académie has always conferred on literature, implies limits that cannot be transgressed without peril. When one studies the esprit de corps of the Académie Française over the long term, nothing is more striking than that institution's instinctive repugnance for any temptation on the part of literature to turn inward, to set itself up as a specialty, an ideology, a gnosis. If this perdurable French insistence on language made literature the royal and central point in which minds converge, it was not only to prevent the fragmentation of the social and the political and of knowledge but also to prevent literature itself from giving in to its penchant for following Narcissus, from losing itself in private contemplation of its own beauty, its own seductiveness, its own power to make itself loved. The academic norm, like the rhetorical, is not content to link truth to the beauty and vitality of discourse; it is careful also to link it to the common notions and common sense that specialists disdain and that the purely literary lose sight of. The mission of eloquence—and in this sense the poetry of the great French romantics is eloquence—is none other than to serve as a mediator between truth and common notions, to bring them together in the universally acknowledged light of beauty and enthusiasm, or *wit (l'esprit)*. The masters of the French *tao* seem to have been too severe or too stubbornly silent and cruelly narrow, as the Oriental spiritual masters that Jean Paulhan admired could also be, to the point of apparent injustice. On the whole and as a body they have never wavered from the task of indicating the proper measure: neither art without truth nor truth without art. Louis XIV's panegyrists, the encyclopedists, and the notables who opposed naturalism and symbolism acknowledged changing times and ideals yet always held the national literature to a steady course, focused on its universal vocation: to serve as an eloquent forum of the mind.

FIGURE 9.0. Civic honors are a lesson in morality. That is why the participation of children is important.

CHAPTER IX

Monuments to the Dead

Antoine Prost

The idea of treating monuments to the dead as important sites of republican commemoration may seem paradoxical. In ceremonies at war memorials, men festooned with decorations parade, and the tricolor flaps in the breeze above the strains of "La Marseillaise": symbols such as these might seem more appropriate to a meeting of right-wing nationalists than to a republican memorial.

The ambiguity is long-standing. On November 11, 1923, in Choisy-le-Roi, a contingent of veterans marching to the cemetery behind their banners encountered a group of protesters marching to *L'Internationale* and shouting "Down with war!" The local veterans' organization objected that there had been a "distressing misunderstanding": "The purpose of these parades is to eliminate war by remembering its victims, whom the marchers wish to mourn and honor."[1] In Grenoble, on November 11, 1932, the socialist mayor ordered veterans' groups to join with the rest of the crowd at the inauguration of a war memorial and asked them to leave their banners home, on the grounds that these were "militaristic warrior symbols." The outrage of the former *poilus* (infantrymen) forced the mayor to back down.[2]

Thus there are two ways of interpreting the cult of which the monuments to the dead serve as altars, and in order to decide between them we shall first look at their origin and then study the associated ceremonies and speeches with an anthropologist's eyes and ears.[3]

The Building of Monuments to the Dead

The idea of raising monuments to the dead did not originate with World War I, but no other war spawned so many. Hardly a commune (township) in France is without a monument to the dead of that conflict.[4]

To be sure, the Great War was the "greatest" of all French wars. The entire nation was mobilized. Eight million men—one fifth of the population—served in the military; 1,450,000 died, and virtually every family suffered at least one death. The proliferation of monuments reflected the depth of the nation's trauma, and it is doubtful that so many villages would have erected monuments if they had not been obliged to mourn several of their sons. After the Franco-Prussian War, by contrast, only some cantons and départements erected monuments.[5] Perhaps the outcome of the war was also a factor. Conceivably, the defeat of 1871 did not lend itself to commemoration as easily as the victory of 1918. Should the monuments therefore be interpreted as nationalist symbols? Were they monuments to the dead or monuments to victory?

We can begin to answer these questions by looking into who decided that these 38,000 monuments should be built, and when. The monuments to the dead of the Franco-Prussian War were the result of belated private initiatives. They were not built in the throes of national mourning but twenty or thirty years later, after the Boulangist episode and at the beginning of the twentieth century, when the Republic seemed to avert its eyes from the blue line of the Vosges. They were built by committees that raised the necessary funds from public subscriptions and by an association, Le Souvenir français, which was founded especially to preserve the memory of those who had died in the Franco-Prussian War by dedicating monuments to them in cemeteries and on the battlefield. The monuments thus expressed the views of that segment of the public that nursed wishes of revenge. They did not involve the nation as a whole or its official representatives at either the local or the national level.

The World War I monuments were quite different. Their construction involved citizens and local as well as national authorities in close cooperation. A law of October 25, 1919, on "the commemoration and glorification of those who died for France in the Great War" established subsidies for local governments "proportionate to the efforts and sacrifices they are willing to make to honor heroes who died for their country." Thus there was no legal obligation to build a monument, only an official recognition coupled with a relatively modest financial incentive.[6] But the existence of the subsidy obliged local governments to take an active role in filing applications with the prefecture: the initiative could not be purely private.

In fact, many municipalities enlisted the support of the population in building their monuments. Some municipal councils handled the matter on their own, but most created a committee for the purpose. In some cases government simply offered its backing to privately organized committees. In others, officials may have sought additional financing or a broader consensus by appealing to persons outside the council such as a parish priest. Some private committees clashed with local authorities, who of course had the last word.[7] What one had, then, was not a purely private initiative or a purely governmental enterprise but a convergence of municipal actions. The decision to honor the war dead was taken not by a citizens' group or by the national government but by individual communes, that is, by citizens in their most fundamental civic cell. Evidence of this can be seen in the inscription most commonly engraved on the monuments: "The commune of . . ., to its children, dead for France." This established a precise relationship among three terms: the commune, which asserted its collective initiative; the dead citizens, recipients of the people's homage; and France, which received and justified the sacrifice of its soldiers.

The building of monuments proceeded rapidly, as if in response to a contagious necessity, which everyone took for granted. The law providing subsidies was passed before the election of the "sky-blue Chamber" (so called because there were so many veterans among the deputies), and communes had initiated their efforts even before the law was passed. Most village monuments were inaugurated before 1922, as each township vied with its neighbors. By contrast, there was less of a consensus in the cities, where opinion was more divided, monuments were more complex, their meanings were contradictory, and construction took longer: inaugurations were still being held in the early 1930s. But the fact that the cult of the dead that spawned the monuments preceded their actual construction is of the utmost importance for comprehending their meaning. Even before the armistice the dead had already become the object of such a cult, with demonstrations in their honor by maimed and incapacitated comrades. These took place in cemeteries on November 1 or 2, the traditional day of the dead. They continued until monuments were built and sometimes longer.[8] Could a cult born when it was still possible that the war might end in defeat have been a cult of victory?

Clearly, then, to interpret these monuments as nationalist when they were built not as a result of a cold official decision or partisan effort but in response to a broad and deep popular movement that preceded the victorious outcome of the war, one would have to assume that all of France was nationalist, except for a handful of militant socialists.[9] Does the visible reality of the monuments bear this out?

Typology and Semiology of the Monuments to the Dead

It is difficult to combat prejudices. One of the most tenacious of prejudices on the left, even among historians, is that the monuments to the dead are an expression of jingoistic nationalism. To see this, we are told, one has only to look at the statues of heroic *poilus* (infantrymen) that crown many of these sculptural ensembles.

But is there any truth to this? Just how many monuments feature triumphant *poilus*? Research has conclusively demonstrated that the claim is false: *poilus* occupy only a small minority of France's village squares.[10] What is more, no simple catalog of monuments can do justice to the complexity of the matter. War memorials

embody an intricate system of signs, and to concentrate on the statuary alone is tantamount to deciphering a long sentence by focusing on a single word: misreadings are inevitable.

The significance of the monuments stems first of all from the fact that the space in which they stand is charged with meaning. The choice to build in a schoolyard, in the square in front of a town hall or a church, in a cemetery, or at a busy intersection was not an innocent one. To be sure, village space was not always clearly marked (here, I leave aside cities, where monuments were much more complex and often polysemic). Often the church and the town hall were located on the same square, which might also be the busiest place in town. Thus the significance of the location cannot always be clearly defined. In some cases, moreover, one has to allow

FIGURE 9.1–9.3. Victory monuments: La Bourboule, Angerville,and La Roche-en-Forez.

for changes brought about by an evolving road system. Usually, however, location was significant. Other signs complemented this fundamental choice.

The nature of the monument, and above all the presence or absence of statues, constituted a second set of signs. Monuments with statuary are clearly in the minority, whether because they inevitably cost more than monuments without statuary or for ideological reasons. Although the most common statue was indeed the *poilu*, it was by no means the only possible choice. Eliminating the composite monuments from our sample, we find 91 *poilus* all told compared with 224 bare steles, 19 steles topped by a funerary urn or torch, and 30 steles topped by a *croix de guerre* (soldier's cross). When the statue was that of a *poilu*, its meaning depended on whether the sculpture was realistic or idealistic, on any allegories with which it might have been associated, and so on. Elsewhere, statues of widows and orphans or elderly parents expressed the grief of survivors more explicitly than did statues of weeping or proud women that might equally well stand for wives, mothers, France, or the Republic.

Finally, inscriptions on the monuments constitute a third group of signs. Little is to be gleaned from the lists of names, arranged sometimes in alphabetical order, sometimes in chronological order of death; in only about four percent of the monuments in the sample were the names arranged hierarchically by rank. But the frontal inscription and accompanying commentary was often explicit or easy to decipher, from the laconic "To our dead" to heroic epigraphs such as "Glory to our heroes," to say nothing of the many pregnant quotations, ranging from the high-toned to the grief-stricken and moralistic.

By combining these three sets of signs, one can establish a typology of memorials that points to a range of local sensibilities. The most common type of monument—the "canonical" form, in a sense, accounting for 60 percent of the cases in the sample—was the naked stele, erected in a space symbolically dominated by the town hall, listing the names of the dead together with a time-honored inscription: "The commune of . . . [or simply the name of the town] to its children, dead for France." There was also a closely related variant: "dead for the Fatherland *(la Patrie)*." Indeed, this was the "official formula" inscribed on death certificates for soldiers killed in the war and thus had a recognized legal significance. To use it was to speak the official language of the Republic, not the language of local tradition and sentiment. Indeed, that was why one leading veterans' group asked that any other formula be prohibited.[11]

Monuments of this type were typically quite bare. The stele featured no allegorical emblem except perhaps the *croix de guerre*, the decoration awarded to soldiers who died for France. The ultimate simplicity was achieved in certain Protestant villages in the Cévennes, where a plain plaque was affixed to a wall of the town hall.[12] Emphasizing the source of the homage, namely, the commune, that is, living citizens in their local organization, as well as the recipients, namely, the dead, in their concrete individuality, attested by their names and in some cases movingly reinforced by photographs placed in glazed medallions—that went straight to the heart of the matter.[13] Both civic duty and the duty to remember were affirmed, and each individual was then free to do as he or she wished with grief or patriotic pride. The monument did not prejudge the opinions of the town's citizens: in that respect it was republican and secular. Religious symbols were indeed avoided.[14] These were *civic* monuments, defined as such by a double refusal, and they took on their full meaning in contrast with monuments of other types. In fact, it took very little to inflect a monument's meaning from civic to patriotic or funerary.

Like the civic monument, the *patriotic* monument was erected on a public square, at a crossroads where it would be in plain view. Its iconography and inscriptions set it apart, however. The formula *morts pour la Patrie* already indicated a timid tilt from the civic toward the patriotic. The shift could be accentuated by adding phrases from the semantic realm of honor, glory, and heroism: "Glory to the children of . . .," "To our heroes . . .," "To the children of . . . gloriously [or *heroically*] fallen on the field of honor." Sometimes there was insistent repetition: "Glory to our heroes." Or a patriotic inflection could result from inscriptions engraved on the sides of monuments, including perhaps excerpts from celebrated poems:

> Ceux qui pieusement sont morts pour la Patrie
> Ont droit qu'à leur cercueil la foule vienne et prie.
> Entre les plus beaux noms, leur nom est le plus beau,
> Toute gloire près d'eux passe et tombe, éphémère
>   Et comme ferait une mère
> La voix d'un peuple entier les berce en leur tombeau.
>   Gloire à notre France éternelle!
>   Gloire à ceux qui sont morts pour elle!
>   Aux martyrs! Aux vaillants! Aux forts!
> [Those who have died piously for the Fatherland
> Are entitled to have crowds come pray beside their coffins.
> Theirs is the most beautiful of all beautiful names.
> Compared with them all glory is ephemeral,
>   And the voice of an entire people
> Is like a mother's lullaby to them in their graves.
>   Glory to eternal France!
>   Glory to those who have died for her!
>   To the martyrs! To the valiant! To the strong!]

These lines do not take us outside the republican tradition, however. Indeed, we are at its heart. Their author is Victor Hugo, one of the fathers of the Republic, which laid him to rest in a national funeral.[15] The poem was taught in all public schools and even sung to music by Hérold, another great republican. Above all, the poem glorifies not victory over the enemy but the defeat of monarchs. These lines were written for the first anniversary of the Revolution of 1830. The dead celebrated in the poem fell not at the border defending French soil but on the barricades for love of liberty.

Further signs were therefore necessary to mark the difference between republican patriotism and out-and-out nationalism. The most common of these were allegorical in nature: the Gallic cock, for example, which we find atop 6 percent of the steles in our sample. Or the triumphant *poilu,* brandishing a crown of laurels as in Eugène Benet's widely copied statue, or waving a banner in the wind in imitation of Delacroix's allegory of the Republic.[16] Some statues depicted a soldier trampling on a spiked helmet or an imperial eagle. Others went still further, portraying a Victory with wings outspread and holding a crown. Such signs could be combined with others to create a whole spectrum of superlatives. In Brissac (Maine-et-Loire), for example, a monument features a *poilu* surmounted by a cock, brandishing a flag and kicking a spiked helmet. It was not uncommon, moreover, for a winged Victory to crown a *poilu.*

Nevertheless, the language of allegory was less explicit than the language of inscriptions, and ambiguity was possible. The crown and even the palm could indicate mourning rather than victory. Female images were particularly polysemic. Victory was identifiable by her wings and perhaps helmet, but a woman without wings could represent France or the Republic.[17]

The same was true of statues of the *poilu:* not all were patriotic. Some appeared in purely civic monuments, like the sentinel who appears to be standing guard, his rifle at parade rest beside him, in front of the wall on which the town of Maisons-Alfort engraved the names of its dead in the town hall square. These were descriptive, realistic statues. Patriotism came with idealization. A step in that direction was taken by C. Pourquet, for example, in his statue of a *poilu* that bears the title *Resistance.*[18] At first glance it seems to be an accurate likeness. All the details are correct: the haversack, the cartridge pouches, the open collar, the pulled-up overcoat. Nothing is missing except the canteens. But the attitude seems posed: the jaw juts out too forcefully, the look is too proud, and the stance, at parade rest blocking the path of an imaginary enemy, is hardly the pose of a combat soldier. This is not a realistic image of the *poilu* but an illustration of the celebrated formula "They shall not pass." The monument is on the borderline between republican patriotism and nationalist exaltation. A brandished crown or unfurled flag is all it would take to push it over the line.

Among the many variations of the *poilu* with flag, care should be taken not to

FIGURE 9.4–9.6. Civic monuments
FIGURE 9.4. (Above, left) Magny-le-Freule.
FIGURE 9.5. (Below, left) Brissac.
FIGURE 9.6. (Above, right) Sermaises.

confuse two distinct families. Besides the triumphant *poilus,* there are also the "aggrieved," as one might have said in the sixteenth century: mortally wounded, they fall clutching the flag in their final agony or even using it as a winding sheet.[19] These are undeniably patriotic monuments: they proclaim the legitimacy of the sacrifice called for by the nation, which is sometimes represented as a woman bending over the dying man to gather in his last breath. But these monuments also signify that the dead are indeed dead: they are not only patriotic but also funerary.

There are enough such monuments to treat them as a distinct type. Other iconographic features also distinguish funerary from republican patriotic memorials. The former are often located in cemeteries or close to churches, outside the civic space dominated by the town hall. Crosses appear on many of them. Indeed, they glorify not the victorious Fatherland, the grandeur of France, or the triumph of the *poilu* but the sacrifice of the dead. Their lesson is that of the conservative tradition: man is great and can realize himself fully only in total, unconditional obedience to transcendent realities. Hence it is not enough simply to do one's duty; love of country and devotion to duty are also essential. Like religion, patriotism is a school of self-denial and sacrifice, through which man fulfills his destiny and is saved. In this conservative tradition, the Fatherland, like God, becomes a transcendent reality, which justifies the sacrifice that becomes martyrdom, witness, and act of faith. This is a long way from the

FIGURE 9.7. Civic-funerary memorial: Percy-en-Auge.

republican spirit, for which the individual is the ultimate end of society and which proclaims a message of individual and collective emancipation.

These *funerary-patriotic* or *conservative-patriotic* monuments are found mainly in Christian regions, and the "dying *poilu*" is not the only form they take. The most basic version is the flag laid on a tomb or draped over the arms of a tombstone cross. One also finds busts of *poilus* kissing a flag, a variant suitable for poorer communes. Elsewhere, religion is emphasized: the monument features a large cross, a soldier, and a flag. An extreme form of this alliance of patriotism and religion is the statue of Joan of Arc, combining martyrdom for both faiths, the very symbol of "Catholic and French forever."

Eliminate the reference to *la Patrie* and the funerary monuments take on a different meaning. To fail to signal explicitly the legitimacy of sacrifice was to admit the possibility that it might not be entirely legitimate. This was a step toward pacifism. One finds evidence of this in monuments that realistically depict dying or dead soldiers, as at Fay-de-Bretagne at the foot of a calvary in a cemetery: here, faith in God is the only recourse. The resources of classical funerary statuary could be mobilized, with recumbent figures and weeping women, but these representations were a little too conventional to express the pain of survivors. The dead had to be mourned by real people. In rare cases this might be a comrade-in-arms overwhelmed by the horrors of war. More commonly, it was a woman plunged into grief, a wife or mother (or both at once), reminiscent in some instances of the *Mater dolorosa* of the Catholic *pietà*. In Brittany and the Basque region it was not uncommon for this woman to be dressed in a regional costume as a way of emphasizing local roots and bestowing concreteness on a universal figure. Elsewhere it might be a widow flanked by one or two children or an elderly father and mother or a grandfather and grandson meditating over a grave. In the Saint-Étienne region the local sculptor Joanny Durand did several statues that expressed the grief of survivors in concrete and moving fashion.[20]

Funerary monuments did not necessarily feature statues. They could derive their meaning simply from their location in a cemetery, reinforced perhaps by a frontal inscription omitting any reference to France or the Fatherland. One frequently finds epigraphs such as: "The commune of . . . to its dead children" or "to its dead" or even "To the soldiers killed in the war" or, more laconically, "To our dead," as on the remarkably sober stele in the center of the cemetery in the tiny village of Oison in Beauce.

In rare cases the pacifism was made explicit, more through inscriptions than iconography. The monument in Levallois-Perret is a case apart. It became an object of polemic when someone claimed that it featured a soldier shot for mutiny in 1917. The mutinous soldier was scarcely identifiable, but the monument does indeed portray a worker breaking a sword, an allegory for the proletariat putting an end to war. The best-known pacifist monuments are those of Saint-Martin-d'Estreaux (Loire), whose rear face bears a long and interesting moralistic inscription,[21] Gy-l'Évêque (Yonne: "War on war"), and Gentioux (Creuse), in which a child raises his fist before an inscription that reads "A curse on war."

Pacifist monuments are too rare to count as a distinct type. They represent an extreme form of the purely funerary monument without patriotic justification. We thus have four main types of memorial: civic monuments, the most common and the most secular, and fully republican; patriotic-republican monuments, which often celebrate victory as well as sacrifice in a more or less overt fashion; funerary-patriotic monuments, which glorify sacrifice; and purely funerary monuments, which emphasize the depth of grief without offering any justification for it and thus tend toward pacifism.

This diversity, which corresponds fairly closely to the range of local political climates at the time the monuments were built, obviously rules out treating the triumphant *poilu* as the typical form of war memorial. The reality is more complex, more fruitful, and more profoundly republican. Apart from patriotism, most monuments gave voice to republican civism with its rather cold, bare, and dryly secular spirit. Not even the most patriotic monuments honored the army, moreover—there were no officers here—and they remained faithful to their essential function, which was to preserve forever the name of each of the town's dead. In this respect for individuals (not found in the cantonal monuments to the dead of the Franco-Prussian War), we see a fundamental feature of the republican spirit, which held that citizens are equal before death as before the law and hence equal as well in the memory of future generations.

The significance of the monuments to the dead does not lie solely in their material reality, however. It also resides in what history has made of them. As we see them, they reflect the intentions of the municipalities that built them at the time when they were built (if we ignore later modifications: changes of inscription, additional inscriptions for the dead of World War II and the colonial wars, changes of location, etc.). But citizens have subsequently used the memorials in a variety of ways, thereby bestowing new meanings on them, just as "La Marseillaise" is no longer a revolutionary song. The ceremonies that have unfolded around the monuments have invested them with a significance they did not originally possess.

Ceremonies and War Memorials

Investigating the history of ceremonies at war memorials is a particularly tricky business. For one thing, what we can observe of ceremonies today does not tell us all we need to know about the ceremonies that took place between World Wars I and II. For another, the ceremonies were probably no less diverse than the monuments themselves, and there were not insignificant differences between villages and large cities.

This double uncertainty pertains in particular to the role of the army in these ceremonies. Not only did the army have no role outside garrison cities, but even in such cities it was not as large as it is today. As survivors of World War I died off and grief subsided, Armistice Day, November 11, became less of a popular holiday, and the crowds at memorial ceremonies thinned. To some extent the government stepped in as popular emotion waned, and this had an effect on the role of the military.

In order to get a better idea of the original significance of these memorial ceremonies, we must look to the interwar period, for which certain interesting sources are available. The early Armistice Day celebrations led some veterans to reflect on how they were organized, and the veterans' press contains articles that set forth their expectations and desires and justify their views. In addition, certain local veterans' papers reported on Armistice Day ceremonies, especially in the period 1930–1934. Finally, every local or national veterans' convention included a memorial ceremony of some sort: some of these ceremonies were described, and these descriptions are particularly interesting because they establish a standard of reference.

The first point to make is that these memorial ceremonies were not originally official government occasions. They were organized not by the government but by veterans' groups.[22] Indeed, Armistice Day almost failed to become a national holiday. In 1919, of course, the first anniversary of the armistice was celebrated. And in 1920, November 11 was the day that Gambetta's heart was laid to rest in the

Pantheon, after which the same procession moved on to deposit the remains of the unknown soldier beneath the Arc de Triomphe. Hence the date was once again a holiday. But in 1921, the "sky-blue Chamber," worried more about work than about the fatherland, postponed the commemoration of the armistice until Sunday the 13th. This provoked an outcry among veterans, who boycotted the official ceremonies and eventually secured passage of the Law of 24 October 1922 declaring Armistice Day a national holiday. The commentaries at the time were explicit: the veterans had forced the legislature to make *their* holiday a *national* holiday. And it was their holiday in two senses: because it was they and not the government that had won the war, and because they had gotten out of it alive. This was the point of a poster hung by the Mutilés des Hautes-Pyrénées in advance of Armistice Day 1921: "OUR HOLIDAY, Armistice Day, is none other than November 11! Our dignity obliges us to pay homage to our cherished dead on the *anniversary* of the day the vile slaughter ended!" In another poster the following year the same group declared: "If the morning of November 11, 1918, was our only day of happiness . . ." They had won, and they were alive: what deliverance—but at what price![23]

A second feature of these ceremonies was that they were not military. On this point the veterans' groups were unanimous. The Union Fédérale, radical-socialist in its leanings, issued a categorical demand at its 1922 convention: "The national holiday on November 11 shall not be observed by any military ceremony,"[24] and the same demand was echoed by a doctor of a more rightist stripe, soon to be elected to the Chamber, Marcel Héraud. On the right, the Union Nationale des Combattants was of the same opinion even though it was headed at the time by a general: in an article offering the group's views on how the 1922 Armistice Day celebration should be organized, one official suggested that the army have no place in the event except possibly at the head of the procession, where there might be "a delegation of generals, officers, noncommisioned officers, and ordinary soldiers who took part in the war."[25] A "delegation" rather than a "detachment" of any sort: this was to nullify the army as an organized force. Deliberately and not by oversight: at the end of the ceremonies, the president of the Republic was to review not troops but a group of war victims. Not only was the army not honored, it was not even recognized. If further corroboration that this was a unanimous attitude is needed, it can be found in an article by the editor of the *Journal des mutilés*, the most important of the veterans' papers and the only one sold at newsstands: "What matters ultimately is that the celebration of November 11 be free of any military pomp. No armed salutes, no reviews, no parades. We are celebrating a festival of peace, not a festival of war."[26]

Thus the ceremonies were neither official nor military but funerary in nature. The monuments were graves, and the ceremonies were funeral services. This was especially clear in regions of robust Catholic tradition such as the Loire and Vendée, where the clergy played a central role in the ceremonies. After the Armistice Day mass, the priest remained in his robes, and a parade, or rather procession, formed up to proceed to the monument, led by choir boys in surplices bearing the processional cross and carrying lighted candles. If the procession was lengthy, canticles were sung. At the monument the chorus might sing another canticle or the *De profundis*. In some cases, the priest even absolved the monument while the *Libera* was sung: the monument thus occupied the place of the empty catafalque in the service for the anniversary of a death, and the priest walked around it and sprinkled it with holy water. To be sure, such ceremonies took place in only a few regions. They nevertheless reveal a broader climate of emotion.[27]

Other details confirm the funerary character of these ceremonies. One frequently attested practice was the reading of the names of the dead: before or after a minute of silence (the secularized form of prayer), it was customary to read all the names, perhaps as many as a hundred. After each name, a schoolchild or veteran would respond: "Dead for France" or "Dead on the field of honor."[28] This reading, also taken from the Catholic liturgy, gave the ceremony its meaning: to commemorate the anniversary of the death of those killed in the war.[29]

The laying of wreaths or flowers had a similar significance. Wreaths were more common, and the mortuary connotations are interesting. Since Armistice Day came shortly after All Saints' Day, when families visited the graves of their dead and laid flowers on them, the meaning of the gesture was plain: if people placed flowers or wreaths on war memorials, it was because they regarded them as tombs. In some towns, moreover, the procession stopped first at the cemetery, where flowers were laid on the grave of each individual soldier buried there. The decoration of monuments was a way for the community to emulate the individual acts of piety of its members.

But what about the singing of "La Marseillaise"? Care is in order here, for it is easy to jump to the conclusion that the singing of the national anthem at war memorials was inevitable. It was not. To be sure, singing often began at the end of the ceremony, but this was not a strict rule or a general practice. Indeed, uncertainty about what it was appropriate to sing and play on these occasions persisted for some time, and often the decision depended on what local resources were available. Not every town had a drum and bugle corps or a choral society. If someone had to sing, the job usually fell to the church choir, to "kind ladies,"[30] or frequently to schoolchildren. It may be that "La Marseillaise" was sung but not mentioned in our reports, but we have accounts detailed enough to be certain that in some villages, at least, it was not sung, perhaps because it was feared that too few of the participants would be able to sing along, perhaps because schoolteachers had been reluctant to teach it to their pupils for the occasion, or perhaps because it would have seemed too aggressive and triumphal. In its absence we find the psalms and canticles mentioned earlier, funeral marches played by a brass band, the "Hymn to the Dead" of Frédéric Bataille or

FIGURE 9.8. Funerary-patriotic memorial: Pouldrezic.

Victor Hugo, Maurice Bouchor's "For Those We Mourn," and various hymns to peace.[31]

Given this diversity, it is striking that there was eventually almost universal agreement about the playing of a bugle call "To the Dead" (analogous to taps) during the minute of silence that was the high point of the ceremony. Indeed, this particular bugle call was unknown in the French army. In the 1920s the minute of silence was preceded and followed by two bugle calls, "To the Field" or "Attention" at the beginning and "To the Flag" at the end. "To the Dead," as we know it today, was composed by the music director of the Republican Guard and was officially adopted in 1932. It slowly but surely gained in popularity until by the eve of World War II it had become the standard bugle call for war memorial ceremonies, never played on any other occasion but always played on that one. Here, then, is still further proof that what we are dealing with is a funerary ritual.[32]

But that ritual contains only part of the meaning of the memorial ceremonies. These were complex affairs involving several protagonists in a structured, oriented space. The meaning of the ritual depended on the placement and gestures of the participants.

After mass, everyone marched in procession to the monument, sometimes by way of the cemetery. The schoolchildren marched in rows, shepherded by their teachers. In many villages, when the children reached the monument, each would place a flower or small bouquet on its pedestal. Then they would take up a position to one side, ready to sing like the choir in a church. Other villagers, content merely to watch the ceremony, would also take up places alongside the monument, leaving a substantial area open in front. With the stage now set, the ceremony could begin.

On the morning of Armistice Day, veterans would gather at the town hall and prepare to march to mass with their banners. They marched at the tail end of the procession—the place of honor in religious processions, in which the officiant always came last.[33] Just as the clergy always entered the choir last to begin the service, the veterans would then march around the monument and array themselves in a semicircle behind it. If there were too many, some of them, bearing their flags, would stand there to represent them. Opposite them, and some distance away, thus creating an empty space in front of the monument, stood the authorities, the mayor and the municipal council.

What was particularly significant about the location of the veterans was that they remained in place throughout the ceremony, while others (the authorities always and the children if they had not already placed flowers upon arriving) left their places to place flowers on the monument. The veterans thus occupied the place next to the monument, just as the family in a funeral ceremony sat at the graveside and received the condolences of other mourners. Their position in the ceremonial space silently affirmed the solidarity of the living and the dead. In presiding over the cer-

FIGURE 9.9. Funerary-patriotic memorial: Marguy-en-Matz.

emony honoring the dead, the veterans received the indirect homage of the entire community in its concrete manifestation. Hence the presence of many members of the community along with its official representatives was essential; it would have been unthinkable for the authorities not to pay their respects.

The Armistice Day ceremonies were perhaps the only successful republican cult in France, and they enjoyed widespread popular support. Republican ceremonies have always had a problem with the difficulty of personifying the Republic. Crowds simply do not respond to the goddess Reason or even Marianne: everyone knows that these are just symbols. The Bastille Day celebration has become fairly popular, but it took a great deal of work before it caught on, as well as the fortuitous timing of the summer vacation.[34] It is a national holiday but an impersonal one.

The fundamental innovation of Armistice Day, which set it apart from all other republican ceremonies, was that it celebrated not abstract principles but concrete citizens. The monuments, as we have seen, respected the individuality of each soldier and bore the name and sometimes the picture of each of the dead. Each man's name was read during the ceremony. Thus the event honored citizens who had done their duty, and the survivors, who had also done their duty, took up their place alongside the dead.

What was celebrated at the war memorials was thus not the army or the fatherland. Instead, the fatherland paid its respects to its citizens, as the function of the flags suggests. It is a serious mistake to ignore the importance of these flags. When the flag was raised on the parade ground of a military base, at a scout camp, or at an elementary school under Vichy, it was a patriotic act not because the flag was there but because it was to be honored, saluted. There was only one flag because there was only one France. In military parades with regimental flags, the troops first formed up in ranks, and then, when the colors were brought in, the troops presented arms. Finally, the troops marched past the colors, paying their respects to the unique symbol of the fatherland. Once again, the flag was honored.

The Armistice Day ceremony was very different. Often there was more than one flag, representing not only the nation but various groups as well. No one marched before the flags. Instead, the flags marched to the monument. During the minute of silence the flags were dipped as a sign of respect for the dead, just as flags were dipped in church before the consecrated bread and wine at the elevation. To argue that the presence of the flags made the memorial ceremony a homage to the nation rather than to the dead would be as absurd as arguing that the presence of flags at mass meant that the purpose of the mass was not to honor God. At the war memorial as in church, the flags were instruments of the ceremony, not its objects.

Thus the Armistice Day ceremonies were originally republican, not patriotic. Of course all the participants agreed that the sacrifice of the dead was legitimate and that citizens have the duty to die for their country if the country demands it in a just

cause. But the occasion was not to honor the fatherland; it was not held out as a supreme value or a self-subsistent divinity. On the contrary, it was the fatherland that honored its citizens, and it was this that made the occasion republican, for the Republic held precisely that its citizens were the supreme value and ultimate end of society.

The Armistice Day celebrations were also republican in that they were educational. The Republic did not stand for unconditional obedience and submission to natural authorities such as the family, the army, or the monarchy. Through universal suffrage its citizens chose certain of their number to lead it. In order for the Republic to function well, it therefore needed enlightened and virtuous citizens who internalized the constraints of the social contract. Without instruction and education the Republic was therefore inconceivable. Hence it needed to ensure that each citizen acquired the

FIGURE 9.10–9.11. Funerary memorials: Ganges and Suippes.

knowledge necessary to fulfill his role as a citizen of a democracy. And it needed to make sure that every citizen shared its norms and values. As a liberal regime, based on elections and the rule of law, the Republic required citizens who accepted the need for collective discipline and respect for others. This resolved the classic problem of liberty: if republican education succeeded, liberty would have no enemies. Thus when the Republic paid its respects to those citizens who died in the line of duty, having "freely consented," it was said with slight exaggeration, to a necessary discipline, it hoped to make better citizens by touching and moving those who survived. The civic cult was also a lesson in ethics.

That is why the participation of schoolchildren was so important. Being young, they were open to influence. They had yet to comprehend what the Republic was. It was essential that they subscribe to its principles: respect for all citizens, respect for the law, civic duty. That is why they were asked to attend the ceremonies, to deposit flowers, to sing, and to answer for the dead before a grave and emotional audience. The ceremony was supposed to impress them and thereby influence them. In some places they were rewarded for their participation with a brioche while their elders drank the ceremonial wine. The Republic was a regime that obtained social conformity by inducing its citizens to subscribe individually to its fundamental values. For this it needed a civic cult and a method of moral education, which it found ultimately in the memorial ceremonies for the dead of World War I.

Ceremonial Speeches

The civics lesson did not come entirely from the orchestration and staging of the Armistice Day ceremonies. It was also delivered explicitly in the form of speeches, for people spoke at these monuments, and it mattered who spoke and what they said.

Two groups of people had a claim on the right to speak in these ceremonies: elected officials, because they embodied the entire community, and veterans, because only those who had fought in the war were entitled to draw its lessons. In fact, the two groups often overlapped, and compromises were always possible: perhaps the mayor had fought in the war, or perhaps there could be two speeches instead of one. For the veterans, however, the very idea of delivering a personal speech was shocking. Whoever spoke on Armistice Day must not speak in his own name but in the name of all veterans, living and dead. In 1921 the Mutilés du Loiret drafted an appeal that they sent to all their sections to be read at their respective monuments. In 1935 the Union Fédérale, the largest of the national veterans' groups, adopted this practice nationwide, and ultimately it became universal.[35] Indeed, the republican Armistice Day cult did not need to single out individuals. The Republic was a regime whose citizens were supposed to learn how to serve in a disinterested and impersonal manner.

The very form of the Armistice Day speech was the first significant thing about it. The medium reinforced the message. Neither the victorious army nor its leaders were mentioned. Not a word was said about Foch or Joffre or Pétain. The spirit of the occasion was hostile to militarism or any cult of personality. Revanchist demands and Alsace-Lorraine were rarely mentioned. Defeated Germany never figured as a nation or people: it was always imperial or militarist Germany, and France, fighting for right and freedom, stood ever ready to respond to militaristic and imperialist aggression.

Most Armistice Day speeches were constructed in two parts. Part one: the past, the war, the dead. Part two: today, peace, the living. The first part invariably consisted of a panorama, which could be more or less lengthy and detailed, of the horrors of war: victory was never mentioned without a reminder of what it had cost. For the veterans present, this would have been a grave omission, for it would have meant overlooking both the death of their comrades and their own suffering. It was repeatedly stated, therefore, that war kills, that war is carnage, slaughter, massacre, and butchery.

The fact that these dark portraits drew some protest only confirms their importance and frequency. Listen, for example, to Sergeant Tapin, the secretary general of the Office des Mutilés de la Meuse:

> Read the programs for the Armistice Day celebrations. . . . What will you find eight times out of ten? Nothing but visits to the cemetery, parades in front of memorial monuments, and the laying of palms on graves. . . .
>
> No, gentlemen, no! That is not what Armistice Day is all about! . . .
>
> On November 11 I would like to see "La Marseillaise" sung loudly at every crossroads. I would like to see all our kids jumping, shouting, and cheering for Foch and Pétain. I would like to see our gymnastics, soccer, and rugby clubs in work clothes showing their biceps, and I would like to see our theaters and concert halls bursting with shouts in honor of the *Poilu*. . . .
>
> You heat up a race, gentlemen, you don't give it chrysanthemums to sniff for two weeks. That is dangerous, and it is too much.[36]

Here, the writer has allowed himself to be carried away, but elsewhere he himself went in for terrifying tableaus, because he felt the need to root out any remaining vestiges of foolish prewar patriotism, which wished for nothing better than an invigorating, joyous war. The dark vehemence of certain Armistice Day speeches was a way of settling scores with the pro-war jingoists of 1911 and with those who preached war during the fighting from safely behind the lines. These dark passages also served to heighten the optimism of the speeches' conclusions.

Armistice Day speeches, as has been said, were often in two parts. The first part stressed the need to keep the memory of the war alive. The second part was introduced by a transitional passage, which could take two forms: the speaker might ask his listeners to behave today in such a way that yesterday's sacrifices would not have been in vain, or, in a related strain, he might exhort the living to show themselves worthy of the dead. The first transition placed the accent on the meaning that the combatants themselves gave to their sacrifice: they were fighting the war to end all wars, and this justified a pacifist conclusion. Organizing the peace was the citizen's duty for two reasons: it would help preserve society from the scourge of war, and it was also the right thing for a "citizen of humanity" to do, for just as villages were organized into provinces and provinces into states, states themselves, it was argued, must seek a superior form of union. Republican patriotism thus found purity and fulfillment in subscribing to a League of Nations that would work toward a "universal republic."

The second transition placed greater emphasis on the virtues of the dead, whose example justified every moralistic appeal. The lesson to be drawn from their sacrifice varied from orator to orator and moment to moment, but it was also civic in nature. For some it was the need for absolute devotion to public affairs, for giving precedence to the general interest over any special interest, for loving and obeying the law and the duties to the community that were created by the rights the law guaranteed for every citizen. For others it was the concrete equality that citizen-soldiers experienced in their miserable living conditions and in their equality before blind death that revealed the true meaning of the formal equality of citizens before the law. From this came a concept of discipline freely accepted and of leaders recognized because they were the most meritorious of their fellow citizens. Not authoritarian and distant leaders like the frequently reviled officers of the regular army but familiar and humane leaders, basically identical to the men they commanded, who like themselves were mobilized citizens, leaders who exercised authority only briefly and who confronted suffering and death along with their men. Last but not least, there was the fraternity of the trenches, no doubt somewhat polished up for the occasion but at times felt with sufficient conviction to kindle memory. Keeping faith with that memory implied tolerance and respect for one's fellow citizens, which meant an end to sterile conflicts like the religious disputes of the turn of the century and to politics insofar as it created artificial divisions. Shaken by the death of so many citizens once mutually hostile to one another, the Republic now signified reconciliation.

"Thus there is a purely civil profession of faith, the terms of which are to be set by the sovereign, not like the dogmas of religion precisely but like sentiments of sociability without which it is impossible to be either a good citizen or a loyal subject." In the last chapter of the *Social Contract* Jean-Jacques Rousseau argued the need for a civil religion. "It is important to the State that each citizen have a religion that causes

FIGURE 9.12–9.13. Pacifist memorials: Auxy and Pouilly-lès-Feurs.

him to love his duties. But the dogmas of that religion are of interest to the State and its members only insofar as those dogmas relate to morality and to the duties that he who professes it is required to fulfill toward others."

The republican cult of the war dead, as constituted and practiced between the two world wars, is perhaps the only example in history of a civil religion in Rousseau's sense, and it emerged at a specific point in time. With the separation of church and state, the state could no longer call upon organized religion to foster love of its laws. The war, moreover, had been a terrible calamity, and the sacrifices it required went beyond what could be expected from mere civic obedience. The need for citizens with a love of duty was widely felt. Finally, death had come indiscriminately to republicans and conservatives, freethinkers and clericals alike. The Republic ceased to be a party: it became France itself, and that reconciliation needed to find expression for the purpose of consolidation.

The monuments to the dead thus became the centerpiece not of a memory of the Republic (that was the role of republican sculpture) but of a republican cult, a civil religion, whose distinctive features we shall review by way of conclusion. It was first of all an open cult. Its ceremonies took place not indoors, in enclosed spaces, but in public places, places with a center, a pole, but belonging to no one in particular because they were the property of all.

Second, it was a secular cult, without gods or priests. Or, rather, gods, priests, and believers were all one. In truth, this was a religion in which citizens celebrated themselves. It was a cult in which citizens paid heartfelt homage to those of their fellow citizens who had done their civic duty. In preserving their memory, the monument became a civic site. The purpose of the memorial was not to deify the army or the fatherland. Recording the names of citizens killed in the war and reading them out one by one was a way of indicating that the Republic was nothing but its citizens. The dead were honored by citizens like themselves: the living were exactly the same as the dead, one might say, only luckier. They were the ones who had escaped the slaughter and who could speak of it in the language of soldiers, as well as those who had not been called upon to serve: women, old men, and children. The initiative for the monument as well as the holiday came not from the government or social authorities: it came from municipalities, committees, and veterans' groups. If, moreover, those groups played a major role in Armistice Day ceremonies, it was not because of their character as groups but because of the duty that their members had individually fulfilled. We have seen how they tended to merge into a single collective actor speaking an impersonal rhetoric: since all citizens are equal before the law and have the same civic duties, one cannot step forward from the ranks to speak in the name of all unless one has been mandated to do so, and even then one's words must have been scripted by the group.

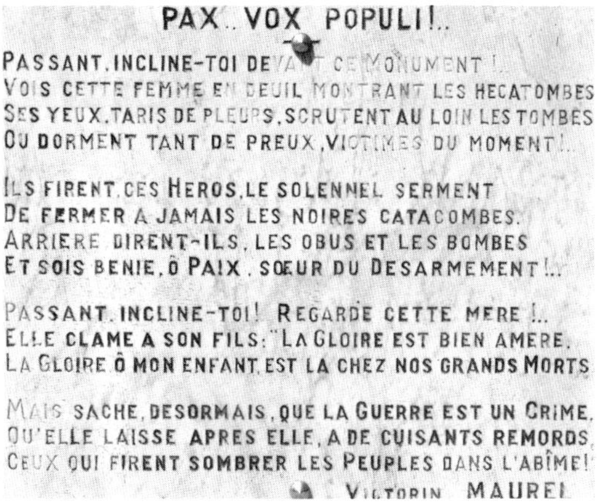

To celebrate those citizens who had done their duty was to exhort others to do theirs. In one form or another, the memorial speeches repeated what the memorial ceremony had already said through its minute of silence and dipped flags and what the monument itself affirmed throughout the year by its mere presence: because it was profoundly good to do one's civic duty, those who paid the supreme price in doing theirs must never be forgotten; and conversely, to honor those citizens who died for the Republic was to uphold the importance of civic duty.

FIGURE 9.14–9.15. Antimilitarist pacifist memorial: Château-Arnoux.

This commemoration was therefore at the same time a form of civic proselytism and pedagogy. Armistice Day was a time for citizens to celebrate themselves. It strengthened their civic spirit and passed it on to the younger generation. Where a cold official initiative might have failed, this anonymous collective enterprise succeeded. It depended on broad popular support and on the sincere conviction of its participants, a conviction that was itself the fruit of the republican elementary schools, for that was where republican dogmas were taught. To those dogmas the cult of the dead added the power of shared collective emotion. To that end it mobilized religious customs borrowed from a Catholicism that was still familiar to most Frenchmen, creating a distinctive ritual that orchestrated movement and immobility, silence and song, symbols, gestures, and words.

In itself the republican ideal was abstract and legalistic. In the grave and contemplative atmosphere of Armistice Day, it shed its austerity and dryness and became a vital bond among human beings. The republican cult can of course be looked at skeptically, and it is no more immune to irony than other religions. Its goal was not simply to improve the standard of living or make people happier: it embodied values and offered a kind of salvation. It therefore required a cult in which its ideals could be celebrated, that is, recognized and shared. Without the republican cult, there is no longer a republican faith or republican virtue. What reigns in their stead is a disenchanted regime, in which the social contract is overshadowed by functional necessities.

A Republic that does not teach itself and does not celebrate itself is a dead Republic, that is, a Republic for which people are no longer willing to die. This was apparent in May 1958, and even earlier in 1940. But if the Republic is not already alive in the hearts of its citizens, then teaching is sterile and celebration artificial. Under those conditions one can sustain the memory of the past, but it no longer has any impact on the present or meaning for the future. This has happened to the monuments to the dead and the Armistice Day ceremonies. Today abandoned by the popular fervor that created them, they are merely war memorials, and it is easy to forget that barely half a century ago the confident French Republic invited all its citizens to gather around them as celebrants and objects of their own republican cult.

FIGURE 10.0 AND 10.1. Soldier and peasant.

CHAPTER X

The Good Soldier Chauvin

Gérard de Puymège

> J'suis français, j'suis Chauvin,
> J'tapp' sur le bédouin!
>
> *La Cocarde tricolore, 1831*

"The man is a chauvinist!" "We're all a little bit chauvinistic." The word is commonplace. The epithet even gave rise to a noun, "chauvinism," which first appeared in 1840.[1] If the fortunes of any word are worth paying attention to, this has to be one of them. A relatively colloquial neologism, *chauvin* has remained current in French, and, because it expressed a new attitude, it was taken up by all the principal Western languages: one finds *Chauvinismus* in German, *chauvinism* in English, *chauvinismo* in Spanish, *sciovinismo* in Italian, *shovinizm* in Russian, *szowinism* in Polish, and *šovinismus* in Czech. Lenin used the word to condemn exaggerated and ridiculous attitudes of which he disapproved, while the phrase "male chauvinist pig," coined by American feminists, has conquered the planet.[2]

If we look up the etymology of *chauvinism* in the dictionary, we find that the word, which means "exaggerated, aggressive patriotism, fanatic nationalism," derives from the name of a French soldier who served in the armies of the Revolution and the Empire, a man from Rochefort by the name of Nicolas Chauvin. A grizzled hero, he is supposed to have distinguished himself by his passion for Napoleon and his patriotic frenzy, only to be held up to ridicule later on by various playwrights and caricaturists.

No book or in-depth article has yet been written about this picturesque character, despite his obvious interest for historians of political thought, popular attitudes, and international relations. The major works on the armies of the Republic and Empire make no mention of him. Countless works on nationalism in French and other languages, though much given to the word *chauvinism,* tell us nothing more about the man than the dictionaries do. Yet a new word that enters the language at a specific point in time and meets with such stunning success obviously points to a distinctive phenomenon, the key to which must lie in the biography of the man who gave it a name.

Neither Nicolas Chauvin's patriotism nor his passion for the Emperor can possibly account for his having been singled out to such a degree from his comrades in arms, for these were qualities shared by the army in general. What extraordinary yet forgotten escapade, what memorable propaganda campaign, gave this man such unrivaled notoriety, only to plunge him later into obscurity as he was overshadowed by the very word to which his name had given rise, in much the same way as other men whose names have passed into the language such as Boycott and Poubelle (the Paris prefect whose regulation of refuse disposal containers earned him the distinction of making his name a synonym for dustbin)?

Clues

Nicolas Chauvin appears to have been forgotten even in his own time. When the explorer and vaudevillist Jacques Arago wrote an article on chauvinism in the *Dictionnaire de la conversation* in 1845—an article that marked the first appearance of the word in any dictionary—he informed his readers of the true identity of the grizzled veteran as if he were offering a remarkable revelation:

> As I was putting the finishing touches on this brief study, specific information reached me from the archives of the War Department. Nicolas Chauvin, the very man who gave the French language the word that stands at the head of this article, was born in Rochefort. A soldier at age eighteen, he participated in all the army's campaigns. He received seventeen wounds, all from the front, had three fingers amputated, suffered a shoulder fracture and a horribly disfiguring facial wound, and was honored with a saber, a red ribbon, and a pension of two hundred francs—such is the grizzled old veteran *[vieux grognard]* who lies in the sun in his native soil still awaiting a wooden cross to mark his grave. . . . *Chauvinism* could hardly have a nobler patron.[3]

Copying Arago, Pierre Larousse completed the portrait in 1867: "This grizzled old veteran *[vieux grognard]* attracted so much attention in the camps for his naïveté and exaggerated sentiments that his comrades eventually held him up to ridicule. From the army, Chauvin's reputation spread to the civilian population, and soon the word 'chauvinism' came to denote Napoleonic idolatry and, in general, exaggeration of any kind, primarily in politics."[4] Debidour in turn borrowed from Larousse for an article for the *Grande Encyclopédie*, not on the adjective this time but on

Nicolas Chauvin himself: "Chauvin (Nicolas), French soldier born in Rochefort, wounded seventeen times during the wars of the Revolution and the Empire. The naïve intensity of his patriotism and his admiration for the emperor, no less than his valor, had made him famous throughout the army."

In an article entitled "Le Chauvinisme," published in *Le Siècle* on October 12, 1854, Louis Jourdan complained that "the Académie, which trundles along slowly behind the language, has not yet accepted into its dictionary this pleasant word, which will endure because by itself it sums up a whole period of our contemporary history." Indeed, it was not until the seventh edition of the *Dictionnaire de l'Académie* was published in 1879 that one found "*Chauvinisme:* masculine noun, a very colloquial term that has been used to ridicule an excessively high estimation of French military glory." About Nicolas Chauvin himself, the Académie, which examined the word between January 5 and 12, 1871, said nothing.

In an article published in *Le Temps* on January 3, 1913, in praise of Nicolas Chauvin, Jules Claretie, after quoting Arago without crediting him, offered this additional biographical information:

> The retired Chauvin returned to Rochefort, where he served as a guard in the *préfecture maritime*. During Napoleon I's brief stay in Rochefort before embarking for Saint Helena, Chauvin refused to leave the door of the bedroom in which his master lay sleeping. The Emperor's departure and the return of the white flag left him beside himself. He took an old tricolor banner home with him and had a pair of sheets made from it. More grizzled than ever, Chauvin murmured, "I will die in those sheets." He kept his word.

More recently, the historian Jean Lestocquoy offered this emotional tribute to Chauvin in the introduction to his *Histoire du patriotisme en France*: "I sometimes think of that sadly forgotten soldier who fought in the wars of the Revolution and Empire, Nicolas Chauvin, a native of Rochefort." This was followed by a repetition of the same details provided by Arago.[5] In 1983, a history of Rochefort devoted a chapter to "Rochefort, cradle of chauvinism": "In those days a soldier of the Revolution and Empire by the name of Nicolas Chauvin lived in Rochefort. He became famous for the intensity of his patriotic feeling," etc.[6]

Finally, the American historian Gordon Wright mentioned Chauvin's role in demonstrating for a revision of the treaties of 1815 under the Restoration: "The campaign took on a chauvinistic tinge (and the language gained a word) through the demonstrations of Napoleonic veterans such as Nicolas Chauvin."[7] Concerning the nature of this agitation Wright unfortunately provides no details, and we are still without any distinctive, symptomatic exploit that might serve as the basis of Chauvin's renown. Indeed, that is the crucial question facing anyone who seeks to understand the origin not of the word but of the thing itself, the original meaning of *chauvinism*. We must therefore turn to the archives for traces of Nicolas Chauvin. But when we do so, oddly enough, we find ourselves in a no-man's-land between the absence of history and the loss of memory, where everything seems to have been arranged deliberately to lead us astray.

Looking for Chauvin

The name Chauvin, one of the most common in France, is encountered primarily in the western part of the country. It occurs frequently in Rochefort and the Charente-Maritime. But the first name Nicolas, which is common in northern France, is quite rare in the west. There is no trace in the archives of the Charente-Maritime of a Nicolas Chauvin born in this period in the Rochefort region, and of the various Chauvins one does find, none appears to have been the exemplary soldier singled out by Arago.

There is, however, a Nicolas Chauvin file in the archives of the Ministry of War. It contains two letters from Americans asking for information about the heroic soldier, together with the ministry's response: a photocopy of the article from the Larousse encyclopedia. What became of the information provided to Arago? In the army's personnel records one finds a dozen Chauvins, but no Nicolas. The only one whose record was in any way out of the ordinary was one Henri-Guillaume Chauvin, born in Falaise on June 9, 1744, a soldier from 1761 on, captain in Year IV, who stood out when he prevented his men from joining street disturbances in Paris. Later, Napoleon awarded him a saber. Old and sick, he begged the Emperor to allow him into the Invalides, but without success. According to a file in the police archives, he committed suicide, bequeathing his saber to the emperor, but neither the press nor anyone else showed any interest in his fate.

Among the members of the Legion of Honor in 1814 there were ten Chauvins, none of whom was named Nicolas. Only one stands out: Charles François Régis Chauvin, born in Cruas (Ardèche), a copy of whose oath of allegiance was deemed to be a curiosity worthy of display in the Legion's museum: "M. Chauvin, retired grenadier of the Imperial Guard, having stated that he does not know how to write, has made a cross instead of his signature." The war archives contain additional information about this Régis Chauvin.[8] If we compare this information with Arago's portrait of Nicolas, some disturbing similarities emerge:

The most suspicious item is obviously the number seventeen: seventeen campaigns for Régis as against seventeen wounds for Nicolas, who clearly resembles Régis too closely for it to be a mere coincidence. Arago, blind at the time he wrote his article, did not do his own research: "Specific information *reached me* from the

TABLE 10.1

Régis	Nicolas
Born in Cruas (Ardèche)	Born in Rochefort (Charente-Maritime)
Enlisted at age eighteen	Enlisted at age eighteen
Seventeen campaigns	Seventeen wounds
Corporal on June 2, 1792	Corporal on occasion
Disabled veteran	Disabled veteran
Pensioner	Pensioner
Honorary saber	
Legion of Honor	Legion of Honor

archives of the War Department," he wrote (italics added). Might it be that Arago entrusted the job of research to a facetious student of legitimist leanings, who decided to play a trick on the notoriously jingoistic author by concocting, from the records of Régis, Henri-Guillaume with his saber, and other sources, an ideal Chauvin, a rustic hero who had returned to his family farm after the fall of the emperor? Perhaps. If so, dubbing this invented character Nicolas, a name that was frequently ascribed to village worthies in popular literature and that was pinned on Napoleon himself by *ultra* propaganda under the Restoration, after the deposed emperor's departure from Rochefort for Saint Helena, was an inspired choice.

In any case, we are compelled to forgo any hope of identifying Nicolas Chauvin from archival sources. We turn next to prints and the theater, the media that preserved the hero's memory.

The Identification and Execution of Chauvin

The dictionaries cite two vaudevilles in which Nicolas Chauvin was supposedly caricatured, along with two prints by Charlet. The most commonly cited vaudeville, *Le Soldat-laboureur*, falsely attributed to Scribe, was in fact the work of playwrights Francis, Brazier, and Dumersan and enjoyed a successful run in 1821. None of its characters is named Chauvin, and far from mocking the "soldier-peasant" of the title, whose name is Francœur, the play unabashedly glorifies him. The second piece, *La Cocarde tricolore* by the Coigniard brothers, was the only play of the 1831 season to treat the capture of Algiers, an event that had been overshadowed by the July Revolution. It, too, was quite popular, and among its characters there was indeed a Chauvin—Jean Chauvin, not Nicolas. Jean is a peasant, a native of Falaise, and a farmer and soldier (thus the erroneous reference to *Le Soldat-laboureur* was not altogether unjustified), but he is not a veteran of the Grand Army. He is rather a young recruit in the armies of the Restoration, who, following various heroic and amorous adventures, takes the dey of Algiers prisoner after slapping him around a bit to the cry of:

J'suis français, j'suis Chauvin,
J'tapp' sur le bédouin
[I'm French, I'm Chauvin,
I bop the head of the
Bedouin].

He also seizes the dey's harem, thus avenging the slap administered to the French consul, Duval. In return, he is promoted to corporal, which fills him with pride: "Corporal! What an honor! It takes my breath away. . . . Oh, Sophie! You will be proud of your lover." An admirer of the French military exploits that he hears about from the veteran La Cocarde, Chauvin is above all proud of his rural background. When he is poisoned by camel meat, he weeps and says, "I'll never see my hamlet again": "Oh, my Falaise, my papa, my mama!" he moans. Thus the play's hero is no proud warrior but a young and craven recruit fresh from the farm. Terrified at the first shots, he musters up his courage by the second volley:

C'est vrai que j'eus peur au premier coup de feu
Mais quoiqu'jadis j'n'ai manié que la bêche,
J' fus bientôt r'mis, et de Chauvin, corbleu!
On n' rira plus; car j'étais sur la brèche
Au second coup de feu.
[True, I was afraid when the first shots rang out,
Yet I got over it soon enough even though
The only weapon I was used to wielding was the spade.
Damned if anybody laughs at Chauvin again,
Because when the second volley came,
I was back on the attack.][9]

What about the portrait of Chauvin by Charlet? None of Charlet's engravings, which are well catalogued, bears Chauvin's name.[10] Furthermore, while Charlet did draw hundreds of fictitious veterans and recruits, he did few portraits. Nevertheless, in an *Alphabet philosophique à l'usage des petits et des grands enfants* from 1836, we find, under the letters *R* and *S* ("Regrets" and "Souvenirs"), a "Chauvin, soldier in the 61st." He is a young peasant who longs for his farm while in the service but who, after returning home, remembers the good old days in the army. He, too, served in the armies of the Restoration and not under the Revolution or Empire. Note, moreover, that he displays no patriotism, and while he does experience nostalgia when he sees soldiers marching past his cottage, it is not because he dreams of rushing off to the front lines but because his years in the service "were my good times. . . . All I had to think about were my chores, inspections, reviews, stints on guard, and drills. . . . I was free and happy." We recognize the same soldier in other engravings by Charlet. Some of these were inspired by *La Cocarde tricol-*

ore, such as "None of That's Worth My Sweet Falaise," (1834), in which Chauvin, a French soldier in Algiers, laments that "there's not a single apple tree anywhere in this wretched country." Others predated the play, which in turn borrowed some of its themes from the artist only to set them against the exotic backdrop of Algeria ("The First Volley" and "The Second Volley," for example, were Charlet engravings from 1824). The same subject was treated by Martinet and others: it symbolized the way in which heroism supplanted fear in the young recruit, who overcompensates for his initial hesitation. Finally, "I Wasn't Careful Enough About the Girl," shows Chauvin being treated for a venereal disease in a military hospital (1824). This lithograph was inspired by a song attributed to Chauvin himself by a facetious writer not mentioned in any dictionary of pseudonyms and who must remain anonymous (the Chauvin of *La Cocarde* alludes to this song when he whimpers, "I wasn't careful enough about the meat in Africa").[11] In various songs originally published as sheet music, examples of which have survived, Chauvin has the same characteristics as the peasant-soldier in *La Cocarde.*[12] The tone is similar: broadly humorous in praise of wine, women, and war. The hero describes himself this way:

Moi, je m'appelle Chauvin
Mon nom rime avec du vin
[Me, I call myself Chauvin,
My name rhymes with wine][13]

and sings in martial tones of his female conquests:

Moi, j'ai toujours été vainqueur
En amour comme en guerre.
[I've always been victorious
In love as in war.]

Chauvin's bluff manner, that of the village worthy still present in the character portrayed in *La Cocarde tricolore,* expresses a primary sexuality: "fit for military service," Chauvin is also "fit for the ladies." For him, sexual arousal and patriotic sublimation are closely intertwined, even when the consequences are unfortunate:

Je suis criblé des souvenirs
De l'amour et de la victoire.
[I am riddled with souvenirs
Of love and victory.][14]

Still, this spoiled child of ribaldry and military glory has no regrets:

Je suis borgne . . . mais j'suis sergent
Un œil c'est assez suffisant.

[I'm half blind . . . but I'm a
sergeant,
One eye is plenty good enough.][15]

Indeed, his good conduct is rewarded not so much by his modest rank as by the bonus of sensual pleasure to which he is entitled. In *La Cocarde tricolore* Sophie will be "proud of her lover" who has been promoted to corporal, and in the verse just quoted the "amorous sergeant," one-eyed, one-armed, and one-legged but happy, comes to claim his due:

Ous qu'est celle qu'elle a mon cœur
Qué jé lui fasse son bonheur?
[Where is the woman who has my heart,
So I can make her happy?][16]

The ulterior motive behind a more noble pretext, sex thus turns out to be the ultimate driving force behind Chauvin's actions. He is not so much a fanatical patriot as a "male chauvinist pig," an expression that, unbeknownst to those who coined it, thus proves remarkably apt.

The anonymous author also insists on his character's youth in the notice at the beginning of the 1833 anthology: "A Chauvin [the wording suggests that we are dealing with a type] is still just a conscript. . . . He still has much of his peasant accent. . . . [He] has big feet and talks stupidly."

And yet in the same volume Chauvin sometimes expresses himself as an old trooper. In the song "Chauvin's Loves Continued," he reminisces with his son Jean-Jean and proclaims himself "a widower and an old man."[17] From the outset, then, there was something ambiguous about our hero's age. Though basically a young recruit, Chauvin, an amalgam of rural society and the army, easily mutated into an old soldier. Over time, this increasingly common transformation would become one of the features distinguishing Chauvin from contemporary and later comic troopers whose age remained fixed (such as Dumanet, Pacot, and later Ronchonot and Camember).

A metamorphosis in the opposite direction can be found in a vaudeville of 1840, *Les Guêpes,* in which the neologism "chauvinism" occurs for the first time. In the play, Chauvin meets Alphonse Karr's "wasps," whose stings punish society for its foolishness. He first appears on stage as a grizzled veteran of the Grand Army, singing "French soldier, born to obscure peasants. . . ." He is greeted with insults: "Old fossil! . . . Chauvinism is out of date."[18] A well-known song from *Le Soldat-laboureur* is parodied (and once again, the connection to the other play is worth noting):

Je reconnais ce militaire
Je n' l'ai pas vu sur l'champ d'honneur.

FIGURE 10.2. Revelation of the mystery: sacred and inviolable, the soil of France is compounded of the bodies of its heroes.

[I recognize this soldier;
I never saw him on the battlefield.][19]

But the old duffer quickly regains the advantage: "You laugh at Chauvin. . . . But come danger . . . I hope you can find 300,000 rabbits like me."[20] A roar of cannon is heard. Napoleon's ashes are being returned, but everybody thinks the enemy is attacking. Those who had been laughing panic, but Chauvin is transformed into a dashing young recruit: "The story is always the same! Always Chauvin. . . . In France, Chauvin never dies!" he exclaims. "When the time comes to charge [the enemy], Chauvin will be there to protect you!" The eternal, immutable shield of a country given to neglecting its defense, Chauvin now commands the allegiance and respect of all. The most virulent of the wasps loses its stinger and changes into a canteen girl in love with the hero. Thanks to Chauvin, France recovers her martial virtues and stands unified and reconciled against the foreign invader.

Chauvin's regained youth is fleeting, however: he appears as a senile trooper in the songs of the Second Empire, those of Nadaud, who admired him, and of Avenel, who was the first to be outright hostile. Nadaud's Chauvin is an alcoholic old veteran who is beaten by his wife. Back on the farm, he instills patriotism in the local youth by telling stories of the Grand Army on the terrace of the local café:

Lorsque Chauvin se met à boire
Il raconte ses hauts faits
Et quand il parle de gloire
De boire il ne cesse jamais.
[When Chauvin gets to drinking,
He recounts his exploits,
And when he talks of glory
He never stops drinking.][21]

His audience of young peasants communes with him in his bouts of patriotic drunkenness. They drink themselves under the table, all caught up in the same patriotic fervor symbolized by the earth on which they roll about, the warm protective mother of all: "Chauvin, let's stay stretched out on the ground, holding hands and all united."

A fierce opponent of "Badinguet" (Napoleon III), Paul Avenel looked upon the old duffer as an accomplice of the hated regime. Chauvin distracts hungry people with stories of far-off wars that France has no stake in:

Contre son bât le peuple en vain réclame
Mais les âniers restent sourds à la voix;
Pour l'occuper Chauvin l'emmène en Chine

En lui mettant sa culotte de peau,
Et Populus bêtement s'imagine
Qu'on vit de gloire à l'ombre du drapeau.
[In vain do the people cry out against their burden,
But the mule-drivers remain deaf to their cries.
To divert them, Chauvin takes them to China,
Donning his old uniform for the purpose,
And Populus foolishly imagines
That you live on glory in the shadow of the flag.]

The Second Empire could find no better publicist. Sincere in his stupidity, deceived as well as deceiving, Chauvin was also the ideal Frenchman, above suspicion, totally disinterested in his love of army and country. He was *Saint Chauvin*, that ineffable paragon of beatitude: "Saint Chauvin believes that the Second Empire is a real paradise for the French."[22] But the regime's spokesman is also its first victim:

Pauvre vieux, tu n'es qu'une brute
Dans une culotte de peau . . .
Tu t'admires dans ta misère.
La belles chose que la guerre!
Sonnez, clairons, battez tambours! . . .
Hélas le chauvinisme en France
Tient lieu de toutes les vertus.
[Poor old man, you're nothing but a brute
In uniform. . . .
You preen in your misery.
How beautiful war is!
Sound, trumpets! Beat, drums! . . .
Alas! Chauvinism in France
Takes the place of every virtue.][23]

We have seen Chauvin grow old. Alphonse Daudet would dramatize his death. In the aftermath of the defeat of 1870, a condemnation like Avenel's was no longer tolerable. To be sure, Chauvin was an imbecile, but once again he overcame his own ridiculousness and compelled respect. What we see now is no longer an old man or a young recruit but a middle-aged man. Although Daudet does not portray him directly as a peasant, at several points he makes it clear that the man rolls his *r*'s, a trait suggestive of peasant roots.

Originally a figure of ridicule, as in *Les Guêpes*, Daudet's Chauvin gradually gains in stature as France suffers a series of misfortunes, only to die an accidental and wrenching death in a brawl during the Commune.

FIGURE 10.3–10.4. The Revolution and the restoration of order (1795–1847).

When he first appears in Daudet, Chauvin is treated even more harshly than by Avenel, who still felt some pity for him: he is an "irritating and stupid character," "always angry," with a "low, narrow, obstinate forehead," insisting on "war at any price," an "unbearable thought." But by the time August brought the first French defeats, "already Chauvin no longer seemed quite so ridiculous." When the siege of Paris begins, Chauvin, still foolish and a figure of fun, takes on a more noble dimension: "This heroic simpleton's soul took possession of all of us. . . . Any Parisian will tell you: without Chauvin, Paris would not have held out for a week." After the surrender, the return of peace brought with it social divisions and tensions. Chauvin immediately called for revenge, "but nobody would listen to him any more." Then came the Commune: "Paris in the hands of stooges," Napoleon's statue taken down as the Prussians snicker, "Ah! Ah! Ah! Mossié Chaufin." And after that, the army's entry into the capital and the "bloody week" of May 22–28. Placing himself between the troops and a barricade while shouting *Vive la France!*, Chauvin falls, a "victim of civil war." And Daudet concludes: "He was the last Frenchman."[24]

Thus the laughter that Chauvin provokes is of a very special kind, a benevolent, shamefaced derision. We laugh, but he is right and we are wrong. If Chauvin is ridiculous, Arago wrote, it is because "society, as we have made it, seems to make a point of spoiling whatever it grazes with its finger or lips. . . . Chauvinism thus became ridiculous only by the fault of those who failed to understand devotion."[25] This is because of "the very French disposition to grasp rapidly and to jeer at the commonplace side of things," according to Jourdan, writing in *Le Siècle*, the newspaper of which he was editor and which he proudly proclaimed to have been chauvinistic when chauvinism was appropriate: "Yes, *Le Siècle* was chauvinistic, and it will be chauvinistic again. . . . There is no reason to fear chauvinism. . . . Modern chauvinism is simply an ardent desire that the triumph of common decency and justice should teach absolutism a harsh and incontrovertible lesson."[26] And Pierre Larousse added that Chauvin "with his slightly stupid, slightly idiotic air" honored the country "under the noses of the Prussians and the Austrians in a heroic if Pontoise French . . . with his silly antics and his cannon." What Chauvin proclaimed was in fact "the dogma of the patriotic faith," Larousse concluded, so "let us not make fun of him: brought up with wooden sabers and tin rifles, conscious since childhood of the sound of the drum, we all rediscover, on those solemn occasions when the *brutal* intrudes in our affairs, an old reserve of chauvinism at whose expense we enjoy a good laugh with the powerful minds who dream of world peace but which we would never seriously consider toning down."[27] This was all the more true because Chauvin was not a creation of "the powerful minds who dream of world peace" or of the "cosmpolitans" whom Louis Jourdan castigated, but essentially of Charlet and hawkish, militaristic, jingoistic vaudevillists. Indeed, Daudet first ridiculed the "last Frenchman" the better to glorify him in the end. "Chauvinism," wrote Lorédan Larchey, "has its ridiculous side, but it also has its grandeur. Much fun was made of it, and the reaction has been a thousand times worse, but locating the middle ground is not a French quality."[28]

The search for a real Chauvin fits within this desire for legitimation: make fun if you wish, but Chauvin exists, or once existed: an old man, an obscure hero in an epic adventure, whose flesh bears the marks of his heroic battles. Hats off to him!

From 1820 to 1840 Chauvin was almost always a young peasant recruit. Later, in *Les Guêpes* (1840), Arago (1845), and Nadaud (1860), he was increasingly a grizzled old veteran of the Grand Army. He thus grew older not because some actual veteran had grown older but by dint of the very process by which his conduct was legitimized. As an ideal Frenchman of the age of state nationalism, he was ageless, because in France "an old soldier never dies," or rather, he can take on whatever age one wants him to have.

As we have seen, when Chauvin first appeared in songs, prints, and plays, he was not an old hero steeped in memories and history but a callow youth about to embark on a series of interesting adventures. Hence biographical research is clearly pointless. The very question of whether or not Chauvin really existed becomes almost meaningless. In some respects, of course, this "fellow adopted by the people as a symbol of the soldier"[29] was modeled on a real person or persons, but that model was copied hundreds of thousands of times by young recruits plucked from their farms to be initiated and trained at various army bases and all too often sent into battle. The name Chauvin, which is almost as common in France as Martin or Dupont, may have been chosen at random or may have been intended to poke fun at a friend (or enemy) of Charlet or the author of *La Guirlande*. But if Chauvin had an actual, living model, it could only have been a young peasant recruit known to one of those authors and remarkable for his naïveté and awkwardness. His personal life, noteworthy only for its banality, is of no interest to us.

A French Soldier, Born to Obscure Peasants

Two things deeply buried in the French collective memory and apparently repressed do interest us, however: namely, what Chauvin *recounts* and what he *embodies*. What Chauvin recounts is the peasant's discovery of patriotism and warfare. What he embodies is an old myth, dating back to biblical and Roman times and refurbished by the progressive spirit of the Enlightenment, namely, the myth of the soldier-peasant, of which the Chauvin story is the ultimate modern and popular version, as well as the most "French" with its Rabelaisian *gauloiserie*.

Neglected until now by historians despite his ubiquity, the soldier-peasant is the first great collective plebeian hero of "modernity." As such, he is in a sense the ancestor of the proletarian (with a line of descent passing through the songs of Debraux, Béranger, and Pierre Dupont, for example, and above all through the *peuple* of Michelet), as well as of the political soldier of the Nazi and fascist totalitarian regimes. Before the notion of "popular masses" became attached to the working class, it first emerged and evolved in France around the peasantry.

The soldier-peasant was the founder of the paradigmatic community in that happy time when, as Vertot wrote in 1719, "the first Romans were all farmers, and farmers were all soldiers."[30] This was the golden age of civic republicanism, with which revolutionary France deeply identified, and the soldier-peasant was the humble vehicle of some very profound symbols. In particular, he symbolized the cyclical transformation of military hardware (swords) into farm implements (plowshares) and vice versa, traces of which can be found in Vergil's *Georgics*[31] and even earlier in the Bible.[32] Totally forgotten in the Middle Ages and right up to the end of the Ancien Régime, he belatedly reappeared, in the writings of the *philosophes*, as the Vergilian antithesis of the corruption of court and city and of monarchical despotism. He covered himself with glory in the wars of the Revolution and attained maturity in the *grognard,* the veteran of the Grand Army, and even the emperor himself was depicted with spade in hand or behind the plow by Las Cases and Dr. Antommarchi and subsequently by any number of lithographers.[33] Finally, after various theatrical and literary adaptations (by Francœur, La France, La Valeur, and Pierre Giberne, to name a few), he took the definitive form of Chauvin, a "French soldier born to obscure peasants," as he would describe himself in *Les Guêpes*.

A hardworking, productive, patriotic small landowner, he was poles apart from the shepherd of prerevolutionary pastoral idylls, the medieval serf, or the hired farmhand. *Classical* yet progressive and resolutely modern, he was free from the nostalgic medieval overtones that we associate with the romantic hero or the ethnic hero of Celtic and Germanic folktales. As such, he was wholly original, and it was precisely this mixture of progressivism with classical Latinity that made him purely French. The soldier-peasant, whether personified by Chauvin or not, was a plebeian hero, the basic cog of disciplined and virtuous democracy in arms. The historical, literary, and moral sources that underlay this symbol were developed by the agronomic and physiocratic movement and brought up to date by the philosophy of Rousseau, for whom "the veritable education of the soldier was to be a farmer."[34] The first theorists of the soldier-peasant date from the late eighteenth century. Guibert's *Essai général de tactique* was published in 1772, and Servan's *Le Soldat-citoyen* appeared in 1789. These works of military doctrine not only enjoyed a wide audience (Voltaire characterized Guibert's *Essai* as a "work of genius," and Servan became minister of war in 1792) but soon inspired several attempts at implementation. Plans were made to settle soldiers of the Convention in conquered lands, and to a limited extent and without much success these plans were carried out by Napoleon in Piedmont and the Rhineland in 1803.[35] These efforts were the forerunners of Bugeaud's settlement projects in Algeria.

The symbol of the soldier-peasant was taken up by legitimist propaganda in the 1820s; this built a striking consensus, ranging from the Jacobins on the extreme left to the ultramonarchists on the right and encompassing the Bonapartist Caesarian left and the utopian socialists. The soldier-peasant came to embody the profoundly rural and martial essence of France, which was henceforth rejected only by marginal provocateurs and social outcasts such as Baudelaire.

Under the Restoration and July Monarchy, the soldier-peasant theme found expression beyond print, song, and stage. The myth was *lived* in military and agrarian rituals, typified by the *comices agricoles,* which were inaugurated in the 1820s and gradually spread throughout France. The term *comices,* from the Latin *comitia,* or assembly place, indicates the civic, patriotic, and national character of these events.

FIGURE 10.5. The rustic ideal.

Something like the American county fair, the *comices agricoles* were of course immortalized by Flaubert in *Madame Bovary*. They were part practical instruction, part civics lecture, and part orgy. Bugeaud was one of their main promoters, and though the fairs were agricultural, it was as much warrior France as peasant France that was exalted, and the goal was as much to train enlightened soldiers as enlightened farmers. Plowing contests and awards of medals to worthy husbandmen and farmhands took place to the sound of military bands against a backdrop of uniforms and banners. Prominent citizens delivered chauvinistic speeches. Listen, for example, to the liberal deputy Dupin, *président de la Chambre*, speaking at the *comice agricole* of Seine-et-Oise on June 7, 1835, and offering this pastiche of Rousseau for the edification of the rural masses:

> He who best cultivates the soil is also best at defending it. *Good farmers also make the best soldiers.* . . . He who from earliest childhood has lain on hard ground while tending his flocks is not afraid of bivouac. In repulsing the enemy, he thinks of his village, of the field that he has planted. And having done his time, he returns home to water with his sweat the earth for which he has shed his blood. Honor to the soldier-peasant!"[36]

At the other extreme of the political spectrum, the powerful voice of Michelet echoed that of this conservative *grand bourgeois*. Joining Toussenel to condemn cosmopolitan, Jewish, Anglo-Saxon "financial feudalism," the national historian praised France as a "great agricultural and military nation of twenty-five million people" and extolled its "vast and deep legion of peasant-landowner soldiers, the strongest base that any nation has had since the Roman Empire," this being the group that for him constituted *le peuple*. In considering the Algerian trooper's return to the farm—Chauvin's return—Michelet raised the agrarian question in the same terms as Dupin: "Do you wish to form a judgment of our peasants? Look at them when they return home from military service! . . . Barely back from Africa . . . you find them uncomplaining and nonviolent, looking for the most honorable ways to accomplish the holy work that is the source of France's strength: I mean the marriage of man and soil."[37]

Given this dominant discourse, it is not surprising that we find the theme of the soldier-peasant implicit in the vast majority of projects to create agricultural colonies not only of veterans but also of orphans, proletarians, and delinquents. Such projects were the mainstay of social thinking in this period. We also find them in the thinking of utopian socialists such as Cabet, Considérant, and Enfantin, and Fourierists such as Toussenel. In his pamphlet *Les Juifs, rois de l'époque*, Toussenel, like his later admirer Drumont, contrasted such alleged social "parasites" as the Jew, the industrialist, and the merchant with "the useful worker, the worker of the soil in possession of a surety whose value is known." He dreamed of "productive armies" subjected to the discipline of the barracks as a virtuous base for the world of the future.[38]

Whether fantasies or actualities, these colonies were generally organized in a military manner, modeled on the most prestigious of all, that of Mettray.[39] The colonization of Algeria, which offered a possible dumping ground for France's subversive poor, opened new prospects for colonial planners who, from the most conservative to the most revolutionary, all aimed at achieving the same ideal. This movement provided the framework for the attempt to establish villages of soldier-peasants launched by Bugeaud, the governor general of Algeria, whose efforts earned the backing of the Fourierists and Considérant. What is more, the marshal saw himself as the living incarnation of the myth. "I am merely a soldier-peasant," he proclaimed to the Chamber on April 21, 1832. When he became duc d'Isly, he chose a sword and a plowshare for his coat of arms and *Ense et aratro* [By the sword and the plow] as his motto.

All these plans and military-agrarian colonies had one professed goal: the elimination of pauperism and criminality and the establishment of social peace. Progressives saw this as the realization on earth of an ideal harmony, a utopia.

France's eminently agricultural character also formed the basis of the most celebrated project of philanthropic colonization, that of Louis Napoléon Bonaparte. In his essays *L'Extinction du paupérisme*, *La Question des sucres*, and *Les Idées napoléoniennes*,[40] the future emperor pointed out that for Napoleon, agriculture was "the soul, the bedrock of the Empire," and he suggested ways in which the proletariat could be given roots in the soil.[41] By means of a system of agricultural colonies organized in military fashion, the nation, regimented, virtuous, and prepared for the mass warfare typical of modernity, would also present a united front against the "feudalism of money"[42] that Napoleon condemned along with Toussenel and Michelet.

In 1848, the soldier-peasant enjoyed the approbation of the extreme left. Felix Pyat, a socialist deputy from the Cher, offered a toast to peasants that was reprinted numerous times and published in *Le Républicain des campagnes*, Eugène Sue's campaign newspaper in the Loiret. Pyat extolled the "men of the small plot," "true sons of the soil," who had "the religion of the fatherland and of freedom" in their blood and who combined "hatred of kings" with "love of country." Pyat glorified the very word "peasant," giving a definition of it that gave rise to a litany which would be passed on to Pétainism and repeated *ad nauseam*: "Peasant is the word for patriot par excellence. 'Peasant' means a man of the country, cultivator of the country, defender of the country." Pyat ended exactly as his adversary Dupin did, linking the farmer to the soldier: "Honor to the soldier! Honor to the farmer! Honor to the peasant twice over!"[43] At the same time, Pierre Joigneaux, a working-class deputy from the Côte-d'Or in 1848 and 1849 and the founder of *La Feuille du village*

(1849–1851), addressed his "rural brethren" in preaching the advent of a "republic of peasants, democratic and social,"[44] a theme that would reappear in 1870 in the speeches of Gambetta. At about the same time Pierre Dupont composed the *Chants des paysans* and *Chants des soldats* that made him famous; Déroulède would later borrow these titles for his two principal anthologies. Peasants and soldiers were conflated in a republican regeneration leading to the triumph of the soldier-peasant in the spirit of 1793:

> Soldats, citadins, faites place
> Aux paysans sous vos drapeaux,
> Nous allons nous lever en masse
> Avec les fourches et les faulx.
> [Soldiers, city dwellers, make room
> For peasants in your ranks.
> We shall rise en masse
> With our pitchforks and our scythes.][45]

Although many leading republicans of 1848 were sent into exile after the coup of December 2, 1851, not to return until 1870, Pierre Dupont, spared this fate, published an *Almanach de Jean Guestré, rustique et guerrier*, devoted entirely to the glory of the soldier-peasant, in which the "Peasant of France" appears as in Pétainist rhetoric as a "good husband and good father," "inexorable in his judgments, pure and simple in his habits, and as hardworking as an ox." Supreme among Frenchmen, born of the soil itself, a "child of the earth, he pays his taxes, defends the fatherland, and feeds everyone."[46]

The agrarian enthusiasm of a revolutionary discourse that harked back to the ancient symbol of Roman virtue soon drew a conservative response that sought not to condemn the peasant but to co-opt him, as conservatives had done under the Restoration. The soldier-peasant, having shouted *Vive la République! Vive l'Empereur!* and *Vive le Roi!* now, in the writings of Abbé Devoille, became a soldier of Christ. As a successful author of popular novels, Devoille reserved an important place in his work for the peasant warrior. During the Second Empire he published a series of works described as the memoirs of the soldier-peasant Mathieu Charrue: *Mémoires d'un vieux paysan* (1851), *Lettres d'un vieux paysan aux laboureurs ses frères* (1852), and *Le Paysan-soldat* (1853). In addition, he was the author of one of the first novels of the rural exodus to condemn industrial civilization, *La Charrue et le comptoir, ou la ville et la campagne* (1854), which preceded René Bazin's *La Terre qui meurt* by several decades.

Devoille borrowed all the soldier-peasant themes of the socialists of 1848 and added a new one: religion. It is because his soldier-peasant is a Christian that he is able to develop the moral and martial virtues that he derives from the soil. It is because "the agricultural class" is pious and respects the village curé that it "will save France," this being the leitmotif of the *Lettres d'un vieux paysan*. Mathieu Charrue warns his fellow farmers: Beware of the socialists who deceived you in February. Their goal was the abolition of property. Follow your priests instead! He goes on to urge rural people to mobilize against the internal enemy: "You constitute, as it were, an impenetrable mass, like those square formations of soldiers against which enemy battalions strike to no avail. . . . Farmers! Farmers! Attention!"[47] The martial virtues of the Catholic peasant also work wonders against foreign enemies. "There is nothing more beautiful than a Christian soldier," Devoille wrote of his hero, who, in *Le Paysan-soldat*, undergoes an initiation analogous to that of Chauvin: he panics at the first volley of shots, displays heroism at the second, and is promoted to corporal, only to rediscover his "life's ambition, a quiet existence as a farmer."[48]

During the Second Empire the soldier-peasant also had an important place in poetry. Although Joseph Autran, who became a member of the Académie Française in 1868, is forgotten today, his works sold impressively well in his own time. In 1869, according to the critic Pontmartin, "not one poet of the past fifteen years, with the exception of Victor Hugo, has sold as many copies." His most celebrated anthology, *Laboureurs et soldats*, "was sold out in a week."[49] It was followed by *La Vie rurale* (sold out in two weeks, according to Pontmartin) and *Les Épîtres rustiques*.

Autran can be seen as a kind of conservative counterpart to Pierre Dupont. His tone is nobler, less that of the popular song, yet he remains, in the words of Roman d'Amat, the "poet of the humble . . . a populist poet *avant la lettre*," who ordered that his tomb be inscribed with the epitaph *Exaltavit humiles*. His poems apotheosized the soldier-peasant in a violent repudiation of urban and industrial corruption similar to that of Devoille, whose faith he shared, though less militantly. His poetry was eminently chauvinistic, portraying the peasant as a soldier above all and celebrating the Crimean War and the patriotic cohesion of a regimented nation:

Aimez la France! aimez cette terre où nous sommes,
Pays toujours si riche en sève, en fière ardeur,
Que l'univers admire à jamais sa grandeur.
Heureux qui maniant l'épée ou la charrue,
Sent sa gloire agrandie ou sa fortune accrue!
J'eus, Dieu merci, l'honneur de ce double mandat
Moi, laboureur du sol où j'ai marché soldat!
[Love France! Love this land of ours,
A country always so full of sap, of ardent pride,
That the world is forever admiring of its grandeur.
Happy are those who, with sword or plow,

Gain glory or fortune!
Thank God, I was honored with this dual mission,
I who worked the soil on which I marched as a soldier.][50]

After the disaster of 1870, when the "Republic of peasants" theme resurfaced, the soldier-peasant continued his career. *L'Histoire d'un paysan,* Erckmann-Chatrian's fictional biography of a republican farmer-soldier, first published in serialized form in 1868, was reprinted. Then Déroulède, like Pierre Dupont in 1848, associated *Chants du paysan* with *Chants du soldat,* the message being identical in both cases. The ideal peasant and warrior

O race bonne aux combats
De corps vaillant, d'âme sublime
[O Race fit for combat,
Strong of body and sublime of soul]

once again experiences the chauvinistic emotion of the baptism by fire:

C'est au hasard qu'il fait feu
A la première escarmouche
A la seconde, morbleu!
Il guette, il ajuste, il touche.
[In the first skirmish
He fires at random.
In the second, by God!
He waits, he aims, he hits the target.]

Finally, as a pure patriot, heroic soldier, and purveyor of food to his fellow citizens, the peasant in arms is also the most apt to reconcile classes and parties:

Dans la France que tout divise,
Quel Français a pris pour devise
Chacun pour tous, tous pour l'État,
Le soldat.
[In a France that so much divides,
What Frenchman has chosen for his motto
"One for all, all for the State"?
The soldier.][51]

This homogenizing reconciliation can also be found in Barrès's notion of the union of the French as a "race of hunters, farmers, and vine-growers" created by the determinism of *la Terre et les Morts,* the Land and the Dead, to be achieved not only through revanchist war but also, once again, through an internal "struggle of the land and the race against the barons of finance."[52]

On the eve of World War I, Jules Méline, the former minister of agriculture under Jules Ferry and father of the protectionist tariff that bears his name as well as the founder, in 1885, of the Order of Agricultural Merit, modeled on the military organization of the Legion of Honor, published *Retour à la Terre.* A disciple of Rousseau and Michelet, Méline, like Devoille and Autran, expressed his revulsion in the face of France's urban, commercial, and industrial corruption. The only salvation from the moral and physical degeneracy of society and the race lay in a return to the soil. There was, Méline wrote, an urgent need to create "an army of small landowners that could provide France with an inexhaustible reserve force and an incomparable guarantee of social and political equilibrium."[53]

When, shortly thereafter, in the trenches, Méline's ideal France of soldier-peasants gave a foretaste of the miracles it could accomplish, the former minister saw this as proof of the excellence of his system. If the rural, autarkic, yet powerful nation he dreamed of was to be achieved, it was more important than ever for more and more people to return to the soil. Such a return became the object of a veritable crusade, which Méline launched with a book published in 1919, *Le Salut par la terre.* In it, he detailed his plans for raising an "agricultural army" through "mobilization" of "farmer-soldiers," a "sacred phalanx" of "rural *poilus*" (infantrymen) for a "new battle" that these "army corps" would soon be obliged to wage and that would naturally lead them to "victory."[54] Méline was not alone in this crusade. He was accompanied by a host of agrarian and patriotic writers,[55] emulators of René Bazin, whose novel *La Terre qui meurt* (1899) Méline saw as redeeming a literature made rotten by pornography. In 1916, Bazin published two more books extolling the soldier-peasant: *Aujourd'hui et demain* and *La Campagne française et la guerre,* vibrant appeals for a return to the soil.

The same spirit presided over the burial of the unknown soldier on November 11, 1920, a ceremony that was coupled with celebrations of the fiftieth anniversary of the Third Republic and the translation of Gambetta's heart to the Pantheon. In the week prior to the celebration, the republican historian Gabriel Hanotaux published in *L'Illustration* a text entitled "1870–1920" in praise of the *union sacrée* (government of national unity) that represented the culmination of fifty years of republican rule. If France, which had lost the war in 1870, had won in 1918, Hanotaux wrote, it was because she finally fought "not just as an army but as a nation." If unity had proved fruitful, moreover, it was because "the Republic was supported by the deepest strata of the country." As its founders Thiers and Gambetta had foreseen, "this broad-based democratic Republic was above all a republic of peasants." The peasantry stood for "physical vigor, endurance, calloused hands, the salt of the earth." These robust men of the fields were warriors in the depths of their souls. "At the first sound of the drum," therefore, "the old martial *peuple* had awakened." The result was that felicitous synthesis, the soldier-peasant, which was just what the situation required, "for this war was an affair of *land-people;* it hid itself in trenches; it was on land, with men of the land, that France defended herself." Hanotaux then echoed Méline's call for a return to the earth, for salvation through the soil: for "this peasant, this Frenchman of the war overnight became the typical Frenchman, the grassroots Frenchman of the peace. . . . This France, strong, moderate, and earnest, is the France that won the war. After the victory it returned to its furrows."

The great torchlight parade that Dilly conceived to accompany the unknown soldier to his final resting place on the night of November 11 was nothing less than an enactment of the soldier-peasant myth. Preceded by horsemen, cyclists, and Gallieni's taxis and followed by a float representing the colonies, France was represented by a series of agrarian symbols surrounding the float for Alsace: laurels, oak leaves, and hollyhock were followed by a tank converted into a farm tractor (a beating of swords into plowshares adapted to the industrial age), the Gallic cock and flowers, and symbols of the harvest and grape-picking. Roses, wheat, wine, and laurels along with swords converted into plowshares: all the symbolism of chauvinism, just as it had appeared in the songs, vaudevilles, and prints of the Restoration, was now compressed into a parade whose connotations need no commentary.[56]

The trinity of "Work, Family, Country," the cult of military discipline and of the leader, the chauvinistic exaltation of the soldier-peasant by Méline and his epigones—all this leads directly to Pétainism. In fact, the marshal's program, in yet another time of national disaster, was essentially an attempt to implement Méline's program and construct, by means of a "National Revolution," the true France, that of the soldier-peasant. The best formulation of that program can be found in the text of a speech that Pétain delivered on November 17, 1935, at the inauguration of a "monument to the peasant dead" of Capoulet-Juniac in the Ariège. All of Pétain's later declarations about the glory of the soil were inspired by this speech, from which entire paragraphs were lifted word for word. The marshal, as we have seen, was merely carrying on a long national tradition that transcended party boundaries: the virtues of the peasant (visceral love of the soil, patience, tenacity in battle, persistence in toil) "are also the virtues that make the true soldier." He is solid and "does his military duty with the same quiet assurance with which he carries out his agricultural duties." Forever being called to action, "whatever happens he faces up to it, he stands his ground." He is France. It was the soldier-peasant "who made France through his heroic patience, who ensured the country's economic and spiritual equilibrium." He is "the source of moral strength" because "he derives [that strength] from the very soil of the fatherland."[57] With these principles in mind, Pétain in 1940 could pronounce: "The land does not lie. It remains your refuge. It is the fatherland itself."[58]

Along with Sully and Olivier de Serres, whose *Théâtre d'agriculture* was reprinted in 1941 with an excerpt from the Capoulet-Juniac speech as an introduc-

FIGURE 10.6. Beating swords into plowshares: agricultural and military France accompanies the unknown solder to his final resting place.

tion, Pétainist literature celebrated Bugeaud, the farmer-soldier par excellence, the marshal who joined the sword to the plow. The glorification of this stereotype of Bugeaud provided an ideal opportunity to develop another side of Pétain's image, *un autre maréchal.* An old soldier proud of his rural origins, Pétain, the "peasant marshal," was yet another embodiment of the soldier-peasant—indeed, the last of the line, which ended with his disgrace. The founding myth, now covered in shame,

LE SOLDAT LABOUREUR

SOLDATS de l'Armée d'Alsace, nous servons en combattant, mais chacun de nous demeure ce qu'il était hier encore : artisan ou laboureur et, quand le combat s'apaise, nous reprenons la charrue et nous retrouvons l'outil. Derrière les avant-postes, dans les terres désertées, artilleurs ou fantassins, nous traçons notre sillon là même où l'aurait tracé le paysan alsacien. Paysans des Pyrénées, du Cantal ou de Savoie, nous labourons cette terre comme celle de chez nous. Nous préparons les semailles, nous préparons les moissons. Nous en ferons la récolte, avec les filles d'Alsace, aux Fêtes de la Victoire.

FIGURE 10.7. On the front lines of the grain war: national unity through joint effort.

was repressed by the national consciousness. Forgotten, ignored, all but hidden, the soldier-peasant, banished from memory as well as from museum collections, disappeared along with all the portraits of the marshal that had once adorned the walls of the humblest cottages in France.

Chauvin's Testament

In characterizing the soldier-peasant typified by Chauvin as a "founding myth," I am using the concept in the strong sense, namely—to paraphrase the well-known definitions of Denis de Rougemont, Mircea Eliade, and Lévi-Strauss—a didactic narrative of unknown origin conveying images that serve as comprehensive justifications for everyday behavior. These images, charged with very powerful emo-

FIGURE 10.8. Work, Family, Fatherland: a France of peasant-soldiers.

tional content, reveal sacred mysteries. Hence the myth also fulfills a function: it dictates behaviors and attitudes that ensure the cohesiveness of a group.

The repetitive, interchangeable adventures of Chauvin, whether stories of old men or experiences of young troopers, make it possible, by their very silliness, to escape from the vicissitudes of daily life and hark back to the Glorious Times when everything was still new. For republicans and Bonapartists, those days were all the more exalting because they were still recent: the revolutionary rupture of 1789, wreathed in the glory of the wars of the Revolution and Empire. That glory, episodically revived in Spain, Greece, Algeria, and the Crimea, was messianically cherished as far back as 1815 and right up to World War I in the idea of *revanche*. For reactionaries, a similar role was assigned to the reign of Henri IV, the conquering peacemaker and reconciler and champion of agrarian France through his intermediary Sully, who was brandished by Restoration propagandists against the crushing image of Napoleon.

In order to effect a link with the Glorious Times of old, one has to abide by certain rules and perhaps even invoke a magic formula or two. The myth of the soldier-peasant thus dictated certain attitudes, and Chauvin, who embodied that myth, far from being a caricature, should be placed in the category defined by Miklós Molnár: he was a *cultural model.* A cultural model is an artistic and literary production, not so much a reflection of reality as an ideal representation of what the government or a party or, in a more confused way, the public itself would like reality to be.[59] By conforming to society's rules, real or ideal, spoken or unspoken, the cultural model enjoys a "successful" career and is rewarded accordingly. This was the case with Chauvin, who, rather than a hero or a fanatical patriot, turns out to have been the perfect conformist. Ideally adapted to the hierarchical structures of the army (for him, happiness and freedom simply mean obeying orders), he was also perfectly adapted to the sacrificial requirements of mass warfare.

Though he fit the very definition of "cannon fodder" (an expression that first appeared during the Empire, as Chateaubriand and Charlet tell us[60]), once back at his plow he adapted with remarkable ease to the demands of productivity that bourgeois society made its dogma. His modest talents were meagerly rewarded by his notoriety and his corporal's or sergeant's stripes, which made him happy and even became a source of pride. A plebeian model within the reach of all, even the stupidest of cretins, since he was himself an imbecile, Chauvin under the Restoration and July Monarchy infiltrated traditional moral rhetoric through pictures, songs, and eventually textbooks. Moralistic tales such as Jussieu's *Simon de Nantua* (1818) and *Pierre Giberne* (1825), read by schoolchildren and soldiers, added a missing military-agrarian note to the maxims of Benjamin Franklin, thus adapting Franklin's message to French society.

What, finally, was the ultimate, profound *function* of this chauvinistic rhetoric? Through prints, poetry, and songs echoing the themes of a number of famous paintings, including one by Horace Vernet,[61] the history of the soldier-peasant almost inadvertently made people aware of an ineffable mystery, revealed in the veiled, allegorical manner of myth. The mystery was that of the sacred character of the national soil, its loam compounded of the flesh of heroes whose bones were sometimes unearthed by the blade of the plow. Inspired by Vergil's *Georgics*,[62] this scene, captured in song, painting, engraving, and sculpture, became, in its new context, the first and most powerful image of the carnal, sacrosanct, inviolable, "taboo" nature of the native soil. The soldier-peasant, and he alone, enjoyed a privileged relationship to this august and sanctified ground, made fertile by his own flesh and blood. Pesquidoux, in his acceptance speech at the Académie Française on May 27, 1937, said that the soil of France was "*incarnated* in its peasantry": it is the farmer's very flesh, and vice versa. Such images, at once primordial and very powerful, first emerged around 1820 but harked back to ancient sources whose prestige allowed them to immortalize a still recent history: the traumatic events of Waterloo and the battle of France. In memory, moreover, that history established links through the ancient sources to the structures of myth. What we see is the formation of a folklore that was no longer local but national yet still retained a crude, tribal character, the "degree zero" or raw material that a later, more coherent and elaborate discourse, that of Barrès and Maurras, would rationalize and transform into a nationalist *ideology* linked by a mystical and biological solidarity to the Land and the Dead.

Finally, the function of myth is also to ensure the cohesion of a group after giving voice to its origins and profound nature. It lays the foundations of society and establishes rules and rites through which unity is ensured. The soldier-peasant Chauvin was the vehicle of a dream of national reconciliation over and above class and party antagonisms, to be achieved through exaltation of the soil, military values, and hatred of the foreigner. This, too, is contained in the story of Chauvin, expressed to perfection in the Charlet engraving in which a lieutenant separates two young soldiers about to fight a duel. "We are all French, Chauvin, things can be worked out," the old veteran tells one of the men. The phrase, repeated on the stage, became famous even as its origin was forgotten. It would be repeated throughout the century, often with fervor but at times with mordant irony. Thus Louis Reybaud puts these words in the mouth of his ridiculous *bonnetier* Jérôme Paturot in a confused paean to protectionism and "Frr-rrrench wools."[63]

A memory of the essence of the fatherland as well as a model of behavior and attitudes revealing of national stereotypes *in the process of formation*, Chauvin embodied a myth that far transcended his person. A vehicle of cultural and moral regression, of latent sexist, racist, and xenophobic violence, sullied by the Pétainist episode, which no amount of mockery has managed to efface, that myth has been eliminated from the selective national memory of the French of which it was the product, at once ridiculous and glorious. But it has not vanished without a trace. Every now and then an attitude, an apparently absurd political reaction or slogan, a strange return of the repressed, unwittingly confronts us with an inescapable echo of the soldier-peasant, an obscure voice that is also, at times, the voice of France.

CHAPTER XI

Street Names

Daniel Milo

Street names are undeniably a rich subject. The sequence of names sometimes holds an irresistible charm. Some provoke mirth: the medieval Rue de Poil-au-Cue (Hair-in-the-Ass Street) became the Rue Purgée (Purged Street) in 1792, then the Rue de la Barrière-des-Sergeants in 1800, and finally the Rue du Pélican in 1806. Or again, the thirteenth-century Rue Brenneuse (the name means "soiled with fecal matter") became Rue Merderet (*merde,* of course, meaning "shit"), then Rue Verderet and Rue Verdelet (meaning "greenish" or "hale and hearty") before ending as the Rue Étienne-Marcel (1880). And the Rue Tire-Vit (Pull-Cock Street) became Tire-Boudin (Pull-Sausage) and much later Marie-Stuart (1809).[1]

Who can deny the ingenuity of the revolutionaries of Reims, who renamed their Rue Tire-Vit the Rue de Foi-Conjugale (Street of Marital Fidelity)?[2] Or that of the municipal council of Saint-Étienne, which rebaptized the Rue Saint-Honoré as the Rue Honoré-de-Balzac in 1905 and then just Rue Balzac in 1907?[3] The Parisian revolutionaries particularly excelled in this exercise: Rue Mont-Martre became Rue Mont-Marat, and Rue Madame became the Rue des Citoyennes in 1793, to mention just two examples from a long list. Sometimes the changes were almost absurd: for instance, Rue Marie-Louise and Rue Marie-Antoinette, named, respectively, for the daughters and wife of two Paris landlords, were renamed in 1879 Marie-et-Louise and Marie-et-Antoinette. *République oblige.*

Everyone who has written about street names has succumbed to such anecdotal charms, collecting "interesting" cases without giving too much thought to their significance or representativeness. But once the charm has dwindled, there is good reason to ask if the author of a report to the Council of Paris dated 17 Nivôse, Year II, was not right to affirm that "in general [the street names of Paris] are insignificant, and taken together they are of no interest."[4]

In order to escape from the anecdotal, authors have generally resorted to *classification*, which they took to be its opposite. Here, the focus has been primarily on medieval names. Historians have taken indefatigable pleasure in classifying and reclassifying medieval names into five (Quentin), six (Grégoire, Vallet, and Hillairet), eight (Cousin and Lacombe), or nine (Heid) categories.[5] Among these various categories, based on religious edifices, public buildings, trades, geographical references, social and ethnic groups, signs, and so on, there were repetitions and overlaps. The authors in question accumulated examples without analyzing their historical elements. One might suppose that this approach was due to the absence of documentation for the medieval period in the form of archives, municipal protocols, or reports. But modern street names were dealt with in similar fashion, simply substituting new categories such as statesmen, military leaders, and writers for buildings and signs.[6]

The same spirit prevails in the properly historical parts of the works in question. Instead of compiling and classifying names, our authors collect and order key dates: 1600 (Sully), 1728 (street signs), 1779 (Place de l'Odéon), Revolution, Empire, 1815, 1830, 1848, 1853, 1860 (the great Haussmannian annexation), and 1871. To be sure, there is nothing wrong with this series of dates. But apart from the fact that it is largely tautological, we shall see that it conceals a far more complex historical reality, which at times purely and simply contradicts what the sequence is supposed to imply. In this respect, the first date mentioned is perhaps the most significant. It is true that Sully was the first to think of institutionalizing the naming of streets and honoring the great men of the kingdom by inscribing their names on the map of Paris. But as Jules Cousin pertinently remarks, it was not until the construction of the Place de l'Odéon in 1779 that "we witness the inauguration of a new system" that is truly different from the old medieval nomenclature.[7] Thus a century and a half separated the idea from its application, and what matters to us is the moment when innovation was accepted.

While it is always wise to refine or even to recast existing works from top to bottom, other questions must be answered first: Why study street names? Why are they important? Are they a good subject as well as a rich one for the historian?

The utter absence of documents and references proves that medieval authors ignored the topic, which was of little interest to them. The Ancien Régime touched on it only rarely. It fascinated the revolutionaries of Year II and interested Napoleon, but since then, this public domain has been the private preserve of municipal councillors—along with a few scholars in the second half of the nineteenth century and of course local history buffs.

Such intermittent curiosity makes it quite clear that street names are of limited interest in themselves. It makes sense to study them only if we look beyond them to the societies that produced and used them or else ignored them. For anyone interested in the constitution of *lieux de mémoire*, street names might perhaps serve as clues, in two respects: as manifestations of a community's collective memory and as external signs of notoriety. And that notoriety was in turn perpetuated by the fact that street names guaranteed it.[8]

The idea that street names reflect and preserve collective memory is dear to the champions of medieval names: "This was the original system of nomenclature, the only true and logical and significant one, because it derived from the very nature of things and quite simply represented the affirmation of a fact, so that later, when the fact itself had disappeared, the memory thus preserved retained its importance and interest," as J. Cousin remarks.[9]

But what was the value of a memory that could only be reconstituted, if at all, with the aid of scholarship (and more often than not the original meaning was lost forever)? A more numerous group of scholars holds, therefore, that street names are *supposed* to represent collective memory, now understood in a national rather than a local sense. For them, street names are not a treasure of folklore that must be safeguarded but an official honors list that must be promoted. This short excerpt from Louis-Sébastien Mercier's *Tableau de Paris* about the inauguration of the Rue Marivaux (1784) is indicative of this tendency:

> Crispin is quite right to say that there are good-for-nothing street names not intended to *furnish memory*. In all the multitude of streets that emerge daily from the bowels of the earth, you see hardly any that remind you of a name dear to the nation. You would search in vain for the names of Duguesclin [the Rue Du Guesclin dates from 1816], Turenne [1811], Amboise, or Sully [1807]. Wouldn't the names of La Fontaine [1865], Massillon [1804], Fénelon [1804], and so many others conjure up far more pleasing ideas and establish themselves in the memory in quite a different way from the name Croulebarbe [a family of thirteenth-century millers]?[10]

Yet the optimism displayed by those who would make street names conservators of memory or promoters of renown has no obvious justification, quite the contrary. To see this, one has only to question oneself or one's neighbors. Among inhabitants of the Latin Quarter, the fact that Royer-Collard, Le Goff, Paillet, and Malebranche have all had streets named after them has not done much for their public reputation, even locally. Such skepticism is not new. It can already be detected in Raoul Morand's anxious remarks at the beginning of the twentieth century: "It is all very well to honor these geniuses and accomplishments. But we must also find ways to make that honor persist in human memory, which is all too often thankless and fleeting." It seems clear that a street name is not sufficient, or necessary for that matter, to renown. But just how important are street names in the perpetuation of memory? The title of Morand's pamphlet (*On the Instruction of the Masses through Things of the Greatest Utility: Street Signs,* 1906) suggests that he considered their role to be quite important indeed, provided that the signs in question offered information about "who this man was and when he lived." And Morand was not alone. Speaking of Rouen in 1864, Léon de Duranville wrote that "a few marble or bronze plaques at our street corners would constitute a kind of biographical dictionary for the child, the passing workman, or the foreigner."[11] Countless similar reports were presented to the municipal council of Paris.[12]

Between unwarranted optimism and radical doubt, there is, however, room for a prudent middle way. Even if what street names teach about collective memory and renown remains ambiguous, they do tell us about the *establishment*'s representations of the national memory and the nation's great men as well as about the means of promoting those representations.

Let me mention one final pitfall, the most dangerous of all, in the study of street names. I am thinking of the case study of a single city, that city invariably being Paris. I confess that I myself followed the same (false) trail. Paris is an exception. In order to generalize from findings in the case of Paris, one would have to begin by investigating the status of Paris in relation to other French cities. It is striking that none of our authors seems to have noticed the problematic nature of studies focused exclusively on the capital.[13] Paris is obviously prime territory for anyone interested in the government's attitude toward naming. But that is precisely why the example of Paris is the least representative for the historian interested in reconstituting not official but collective memory. Nor is Paris ideal for tracing the rise and fall of reputations over time, in part because of the influence exerted by institutions on urban nomenclature and in part because of the sheer number of streets (more than 5,000 in 1950). Renown is above all the result of a selection, but in Paris one finds anything and everything. Still, the capital is the richest case of all, and the most spectacular. Hence in spite of everything it will be the subject of much discussion in what follows.

From Popular Initiative to State Monopoly

The study of street names reveals an extended Middle Ages during which the initiative in naming streets was left to the "users," that is, to the inhabitants. It was this direct relation between the community and street names that led admirers of the medieval system to regard it as "natural," the perfect conservatory of popular memory. Today, medieval nomenclature strikes us as coming from another planet:

who can now imagine living on the Rue de l'Enfant-qui-Pisse (Pissing-Child Street existed in Lyons until the early nineteenth century) or on Rue Merderet? In order to decipher this strange semiology, one has to situate it in its historical context and relate it to other contemporary naming systems, such as place names,[14] medieval nicknames, and even family names.

The problem in understanding this nomenclature is not only its strangeness but its inherent logic. Is it not surprising that among the many categories so frequently invoked, one is utterly absent, namely, *history*? Indeed, one would search the medieval nomenclature in vain for the two basic elements of modern collective memory: events and heroes. Was medieval collective memory as reflected in street names therefore ahistorical (in the modern sense of the term)? Let me leave this question in abeyance and move on to the institutional era, which is the true focus of my research.

"It was only at the beginning of the seventeenth century, under the reign of Henri IV, that Sully, in his capacity as Grand-Voyer de France [Master of the Highways], conceived, in concert with the provosts of the guilds and the aldermen, the idea of adopting names that had no direct relation to the place to which they were attached."[15] All the authorities accept the date 1600 as separating two distinct periods. Before that date, private initiative; afterward, public monopoly. The problem is then to explain this transformation. But on that point the authorities are silent.

The change, however, was no accident, nor was it a simple stroke of genius on Sully's part. The nationalization of the right to name was part of a much larger evolution described by Norbert Elias in *The Civilizing Process*.[16] Elias showed that the history of France was one of monopolization by the state and the monarch of certain strategic powers, in particular, of the right to use violence and to tax. According to Elias, the reign of Henri IV marked the definitive triumph of that monpolization, which ended in absolutism. At the same time the royal government established a monopoly on naming. Elias's main thesis is that the monopolization of violence gave rise to court society, and with it civility: the corollary of this new creation was the refinement of manners and language. Hence a long process of purging the nomenclature of Paris began in 1600. Medieval oddities and, even more, obscenities were replaced by more respectable names: Pute-Y-Muse became Petit-Musse and later Petit-Musc; Pied-de-Biche became Fossoyeurs (1620) and ultimately Servandoni (1806); Pet-au-Diable gave way to Tourniquet and then Washington (1810); and so on.

The naming monopoly did indeed coincide with the military and fiscal monopolies. But whereas the impact of the latter was swift and dramatic, the former had relatively little effect for nearly two centuries. By 1760 Paris boasted some 800 public streets, but of that number, impressive for its time, only three paid homage to the great men of the nation: Richelieu, Mazarin, and Colbert (all three streets were named between 1640 and 1680). If we count the royal family and great noble houses, the figures are obviously higher, yet still not imposing: a dozen in 1636 (out of a total of 550),[17] and around sixty by 1760. Cousin is right to remark that if "kings and princes cannot be regarded as having had absolutely nothing to do with the streets they ordered to be built, the names registered at the corners were intended more as an acknowledgment of paternity than as straightforward homage, and strictly speaking these names should be classed in the original series of the old nomenclature."[18] Indeed, this was the case with three celebrities mentioned above: the Rue Richelieu bordered the Palais-Cardinal; the Rue Colbert was put in almost directly opposite the Hôtel Colbert; and the Rue Mazarine owed its name to the Collège des Quatre-Nations, which the cardinal founded.

Everything changed in 1765, when

> the circular street around the new Halle de Blé [central grain market] was named Viarmes in honor of the provost of the guilds, M. Camus de Pontcarré, seigneur de Viarmes, and the radial streets were named for Sartine, the lieutenant of police, Babille, Devarenne, and Mercier, aldermen, Vannes, the royal prosecutor for Paris, and Oblin, the building contractor. . . . Before long this privilege was accepted in principle, [and] under Louis XVI it became the rule.[19]

A cohort of functionaries invaded the city over a twenty-year period, establishing what can only be called a local honorific system that had a bright future ahead of it. What distinguished this practice from the system that Louis-Sébastien Mercier advocated was that the individuals honored were always living: they commemorated themselves, without awaiting the verdict of posterity. Mercier could hardly find words strong enough to condemn the practice: "Good God! What possessed the people who named these streets? Might it be the same spirit that gave us the *Rues du Pet-au-Diable, des Rats, du Foin, des Marmouzets*, or *Pierre-au-Lard* and *Jean-Pain-Mollet*?"[20]

Mercier was wrong: it was a new spirit that gave rise to these names, the spirit of the eighteenth century. This was the same spirit that glorified that rather strange genre, the eulogy, which Jean-Claude Bonnet has studied.[21] Street names reflected an obsession with individual honor and glory, signs of a reconfirmation of individuality. There is general agreement about the importance of 1779, the year the Odéon was built: for the first time names honored not contemporaries but the nation's "true" glories. Mercier took pride in this in an oft-cited passage:

> On the square in front of the new theater of the Comédie-Française, one can see the Rues de Corneille, de Racine, de Molière, de Voltaire, de Crébillon,

and de Regnard, which will at first scandalize the Aldermen (as is only to be expected) as a usurpation of the glorious and ancient prerogative of bestowing only their own illustrious names on streets. Little by little, however, they will grow accustomed to this innovation and come to look upon Corneille, Molière, and Voltaire as their companions in glory. Ultimately, Rue Racine will appear alongside Rue Babille without undue surprise on the part of the *quarteniers*, *dizeniers*, and other officers of the Hôtel de Ville.[22]

The birth of the modern honorific system must therefore be situated in 1779. The Ancien Régime discovered it quite late and made very little use of it. There were five occasions in all: the Place de l'Odéon, the construction of the Comédie-Italienne (enclosed in 1784 by Rues Marivaux, Grétry, and Favart), Place Vauban and the Avenue de Saxe (which date from 1780), and the Avenue de Matignon (1787). The importance of these innovations should not be overestimated, however. After the experiment with Corneille, Racine, and Molière, almost all the honors went to near contemporaries: Marivaux died in 1763, the Maréchal de Saxe in 1770, Favart and Grétry were still alive in 1784, and only Vauban and Matignon, who died in 1707 and 1729 respectively, were truly ancient glories. But these exceptions confirm the rule. Clearly, the discovery of the national honorific system did not by any means disrupt the Parisian landscape. The tool existed; it was the awareness of how to use it that was lacking.

The Counterexample: The Provinces Before 1789

There was no fundamental difference between pre-1600 Paris and contemporary provincial cities. One finds the same types of names, referring to religious edifices (at least a third of the total), trades, shop signs, and so on. This tends to corroborate the idea that the medieval system was "natural" or at any rate "spontaneous." Urban nomenclature in London and Brussels reflected the same principles, moreover.[23]

Before 1600, France, and for that matter Europe, offered the traveler a highly homogeneous urban landscape. With Sully, however, that harmony was disrupted, as a comparative study of provincial town maps from the late Ancien Régime reveals.[24] The conclusion is unambiguous: the national honorific system was totally unknown in the provinces, as the following table indicates:

In Marseilles (maps of 1787 and 1790), the system was more advanced. Of the nine quays in the city, five bore "modern" names: Dauphin, Monsieur, Marquisat, Calonne, and Breteuil. And among seventeen squares we find Dauphine and Noailles. All told, the modern names accounted for only three percent of the city's public ways. But the important thing was the direction of change, and that change

TABLE 1 STREET NAMES ASSOCIATED WITH THE NATIONAL HONORIFIC SYSTEM IN PROVINCIAL CITIES BETWEEN 1770 AND 1790

City	Date of Map	"Honorific" Names	Remarks
Toulouse	1770	Rues Royale and des Nobles	Dozens of streets with religious names
Lille	1784	Rues Royale, Dauphine, d'Anjou	Of a Princesse, total of 200 streets
Metz	1784	Pont Royal	Streets bearing names of 14 churches, 32 convents, and 4 Benedictine institutions
Rennes	1787	Place and Rue Royale, Rue Dauphine	
Rouen	1789	Cours Dauphine	*Extra muros . . .*
Reims	1790	Place and Rue Royale	
Lyons	1789	Places Louis-XV and Louis le-Grand, Place and Rue Dauphine	59 of 230 names were religious
Bordeaux	1791	Places Louis-XVI, Royale, Dauphine, Berry,[1] Rues de la Porte-de-Richelieu, de Berry	

1. F.-G. Pariset, Bordeaux au XVIIIe siècle, vol. 5 of Histoire de Bordeaux, ed. by C. Higounet (Bordeaux, 1968), p. 565, claims that the Porte and Rue du Berry were named for the dauphin's son. Note, however, that this 1754 project was never implemented and that Tourny, who was its originator, was fond of using province names for his new constructions (I am indebted to Christian Jouhaud for this information).

came, of course, from Paris, as evidenced by the Place de la Comédie, surrounded by the Rues de Molière, Corneille, and Rameau.

It was in Nantes, however, that the new spirit had made the most headway. The city had been the site of enormous public works projects since 1760 and especially after 1780: "On the eve of the Revolution, Nantes was a vast construction site. Men were at work everywhere."[25] New names were naturally under discussion. The debate revolved primarily around the Graslin district, one of the most prestigious and original urban reconstruction projects in Europe at the time. L.-F. de Graslin, a famous economist and *receveur des fermes* (a tax collector of sorts) in Nantes since 1758, and M. Crucy, a disciple of Boullée and *architecte voyer* (road planner) of Nantes since 1758, chose to model their new creation on the Place de l'Odéon in Paris. The Theater and the Place Graslin were surrounded by Rues Crébillon, Corneille, Molière, Racine, Voltaire, Jean-Jacques-Rousseau, Gresset, Piron, and Regnard. The project had to overcome numerous obstacles, but by 1788 it was a reality, as the famous English traveler Arthur Young noted: "The quarter of the *Comédie* is magnificent, all the streets at right angles, and of white stone." What is more, the new theater left Young dazzled.[26]

The fact that Nantes, France's fourth largest city and second leading port, grew dramatically in the eighteenth century is well known, but why was its "naming system" so far in advance of that of other provincial cities? The specialists are silent on the question. Was the city more "modern" or enlightened than other cities? There is no evidence to support this assumption. Perhaps the innovative naming was the work of men open to the influence of the Enlightenment, such as Graslin. This idea offers a hint: the theater.[27] The Théâtre-Français and Opéra-Comique in Paris, the Comédie in Marseilles, and the Graslin theater all inspired "national" names, as if the national glory and consensus must inevitably involve the Republic of Letters and its most popular organ, the theater. This hypothesis finds support in the construction of the Grands-Hommes district in Bordeaux, where the Théâtre-Français was surrounded by Rues Montesquieu, Montaigne, Jean-Jacques-Rousseau, Voltaire, Buffon, Mably, and Condillac. But construction there was undertaken during the Empire (in 1806), whereas the Grand Théâtre of Bordeaux, inaugurated in 1780, did not inspire "modern" names. The case of Nantes remains unexplained.

The Revolutionary Upheaval

"When one reconstructs a government from nothing, no abuse should be allowed to escape the reforming scythe. Everything must be republicanized. . . . Patriotism demands a change of names," Abbé Grégoire affirmed in his report to the Convention in Year II.[28] Yet even as he was voicing his opinion, the "reforming scythe" had already cut its swathe.[29] As early as June 22, 1790, in fact, the Constituent Assembly had considered the question of names for the forty-eight sections of Paris: "The committee was at first tempted to name each of the forty-eight sections for the famous men whose ashes reposed within their limits," but ultimately it opted for the medieval system. "It decreed names taken from places, fountains, or major streets."[30] Not for long, however. The need for a new approach was quickly felt. On the day of Mirabeau's funeral, April 4, 1791, the Marquis de Villette sent the following letter to the Jacobins:

> *Brothers and Friends,*
>
> *I have taken the liberty of removing the inscription "Quai des Théatins" from the corner of my house and substituting "Quai de Voltaire." . . . We will always have a Voltaire, and we shall never again have Theatines [a religious order]. I invite the good patriots of the Rue Plâtrière to put the name Jean-Jacques-Rousseau on the*

> *corners of their houses. It is important that sensitive hearts and ardent souls should think, in crossing this street, that Rousseau lived here on the fourth floor, while it is of little importance to know that people used to make plaster on this street.*[31]

These initiatives were approved by the Conseil Général of Paris, which demonstrated its good will by substituting the name of Mirabeau for Chaussée-d'Antin, the location of "the house where [Mirabeau] died."[32]

A third important stage in the Revolution's nominative efforts came in October 1792, when P.-A. Grouvelle asked that the Rue Sainte-Anne be renamed for Helvetius and proposed eliminating all saints' names from the nomenclature on the grounds that "saints have done as much harm as princes."[33] This proposal anticipated the great wave of debaptizings of 1792–1794, when names reminiscent of the monarchy and Church were wiped off the map and replaced by revolutionary names. The Place Louis-XV became the Place de la Révolution, Quai Conti became the Quai de l'Unité, the Pont Notre-Dame became the Pont de la Raison, and the Place de la Sorbonne became Place Chalier. The movement led to some absurd changes as well, such as the change from Rue Honoré-Chevalier, named for a late-sixteenth-century baker, to Rue Honoré-Égalité in 1793. Many other examples could be cited, but there are better ways to use the space.

The Revolution surely authored the most spectacular pages in the history of street names. At no time were people more acutely aware of the ideological and, even more, the pedagogical role of naming. The widespread indifference of the past, punctuated by occasional timid experiments, suddenly gave way to an aggressively militant approach. For the revolutionaries, street names were a means of propaganda, an instrument of revenge, and an arm of punishment.

But how widespread was the phenomenon? Heid maintains that of the 900 or so *streets* in the capital in 1794, only fifty-three, or six percent, were debaptized: "This was far from from the 'general upheaval' that Jules Cousin has described."[34] But Heid minimized the phenomenon: even according to the (far from complete) list of Franklin,[35] the number of debaptized streets was seventy-three. But Franklin chose for unspecified reasons to ignore the central arteries of the capital. It turns out that the Revolution debaptized sixteen squares out of twenty-six, nine quays out of thirty, five bridges out of twelve, two crossroads, and one boulevard, or forty-seven percent all told. In addition, in 1793 it republicanized thirty-two of the forty-eight section names (thus reversing its "medieval" decision of 1790).

Hence Cousin was right to speak of a "general upheaval." But he was wrong to speak of a "mania" (as Heid also did, while Franklin used the phrase "wind of madness"). Despite its occasional "excesses" and "absurdities," the Revolution demonstrated a perfectly consistent approach to naming. One has only to identify its intrinsic logic. That logic lay in the amplitude and above all the orientation of the phenomenon. Our authorities were sensitive only to the accelerated pace: "We come now to 1792," Lacombe writes. "People were beginning to push the mania for debaptizing and general upheaval to its limit."[36] This observation, though correct, hides a more profound truth: the revolutionary evolution was more qualitative than quantitative. The change can be summed up as follows: *the Revolution moved from the honorific era into the ideological era.* In the first phase, 1791–1792, one honored men like Mirabeau, Voltaire, Rousseau, Cassini, Buffon, Franklin, Cerutti, Helvetius, Catinat, Mably, and Lafayette. In the second phase, one honored the Rights of Man, Union, Law, Reason, and the Sansculottes. Between the end of 1792 and 1794 only two proper names were honored: Marat and Chalier, martyrs of the Revolution. What is more, Rue Mirabeau became the Rue du Mont-Blanc and Rue de La-Fayette became the Rue du Contrat-Social (December 1792). This orientation was reinforced in early 1793 by an order of the Paris Commune abolishing "street inscriptions bearing the names of proscribed individuals, saints, [and] living men."[37] This measure would remain unique of its kind in the history of naming up to the twentieth century.[38] In short, the Revolution said no to names, yes to ideals.

In 1790, *Le Moniteur universel* could still write: "Bestowing the names of great men on the streets of Paris would create monuments to glory and models for other citizens to emulate."[39] This was a period of reform undertaken in a spirit of continuity. But with the radicalization of the Revolution, everything that belonged to the past became suspect: even great men and revolutionary precursors inevitably bore the stamp of the Ancien Régime. The ideal was the tabula rasa, "the representation of the Revolution as the origin of history."[40] The only memory that mattered was that of the Future, of the objectives and missions to be accomplished. This might explain why the Revolution did not even commemorate its own great exploits such as Valmy and Jemmapes. It was the "revolution"—the nostalgic revolution—of 1830 that would see to that chore. Thus a walk around Paris in 1793 or 1794 would have resembled not a history course but a civics lesson.

Such an enterprise could not be limited to Paris without contradicting its own purpose: in fact, the Revolution affected naming in nearly all French cities. In the provinces the extent of renaming was even more impressive than in Paris. Marseilles debaptized a third of its streets (200 out of 600, along with 27 of 46 squares and 2 of 4 quays).[41] Rouen "in the early days of 1794 gave ridiculous revolutionary names to the majority of its streets and squares," Peraux wrote in 1819.[42] In Reims, "the Revolution of 1789 led to a wholesale revision of the names on the city's map."[43] The municipal council of Toulon debaptized seventy streets in one session on 2 Vendémiaire, Year II.[44] Bordeaux renamed at least ninety streets.[45] On December 29, 1793, the names of most of the streets and squares in Saint-Étienne were changed.[46] And the map of Nantes in 1795 reflected a completely "purged" city.[47] In this connection, there is no more eloquent testimony to the change than the contrast between two titles: that of the Ancien Régime's only treatise on naming,

Abbé Teisserence's *Géographie parisienne en forme de dictionnaire contenant l'explication de Paris mis en carte géographique du royame de France* (1754), and that of Abbé Grégoire's 1794 *Système de dénominations topographiques pour les places, rues, quais . . . de toutes les communes de la République.*[48]

"No abuse should be allowed to escape the reforming scythe" was surely a sentiment that Abbé Grégoire shared with the 3,200 French communes that republicanized their names according to R. de Figuères's *Noms révolutionnaires des communes de France.* One hundred twenty of these communes included *Mountain* in their new names; sixty included *Union* or *Unity;* twenty, *Equality;* and twenty-one, *Marat* (these figures are grossly understated[49]), compared with one *Voltaire* and one *Rousseau.* Thus Port-Louis became Port-Liberté, Condé became Nord-Libre, Saint-Laurent became Main-Libre, Neuvy-le-Roi became Neuvy-la-Loi, and Saint-Amard became Libre-Val. Street names also paid homage to revolutionary heroes: for example, Mont-de-Marsan became Mont-de-Marat.

One would like to be able to situate this enormous wave of popular sentiment more precisely in the chronological and ideological context of the Revolution. Figuères's inventory unfortunately does not allow this, because he does not give either the dates of debaptizing or the dates of eventual restoration of the old names. Three observations suggest, however, that the wave should be associated with the "ideological" period 1793–1794. First, the names adopted by the communes were of the ideological rather than heroic type, except for *Marat.* Second, we do know the precise dates of eighty communal debaptizings, thanks to the work of James Legendre on the history of the post office.[50] Of the eighty seals cited in his book, three date from 1792 and all the rest from 1793–1794. Finally, the "Jacobin hypothesis" is corroborated by the dates of debaptizings of streets in provincial cities: there was in fact no wave of debaptizing in the provinces before 1793. As for the new names, among the twenty-two mentioned in Reims, only one honored a personality: Jean-Jacques Rousseau. In Marseilles we find some fifteen proper names out of two hundred; in Saint-Étienne, six out of eighteen. Only in Nantes did great men dominate the new urban landscape: ten painters, twenty writers, seven scholars, one musician, and ten ancient heroes (which made Nantes in 1795 more "modern," which is to say closer to our current system, than any city in France or, for that matter, the world).

Indeed, the French Revolution deserves credit for one of the great discoveries of modern times: that semantics is inevitably political. Our linguistic environment has incalculable ideological effects, and, what is more, that environment can be manipulated. Thus the Revolution laid the groundwork for modern forms of mass communication and propaganda. In fact, on August 18, 1792, the Ministry of the Interior inaugurated a propaganda section, known as the Bureau d'Esprit.[51]

Names of streets and places were but one aspect of reeducation through language. Franklin was wrong to make fun of "men named Leroi, Leduc, and Lecomte who adopted names such as Citizen August-Tenth, Citizen Equality, or Citizen Mountain" and of "restaurant menus on which *bon-chrétiens* pears were renamed *bon-républicains*."[52] Lacombe[53] was just as wrong when he mocked "the Prussian Jean-Baptiste Cloots, [who] thought he was a sage because he adopted the name *Anacharsis*;[54] François-Noël Babeuf, [who] thought he was a great politician because he named himself *Caius Gracchus;* the unspeakable Chaumette, for adopting the nickname *Anaxagoras;* [and the] scholar Millin, [who] added nothing to his learning or philosophy when he traded his given names for *Éleuthérophile.*" In effect, all these authors were imposing a Third-Republic point of view, that of a "quiet revolution," on a very different reality: "It is a mistake to read revolutionary symbolism as a mere setting, as innocent as it is transparent, for a Revolution not directly related to it. The invention and diffusion of the revolutionary symbolic repertory and the implantation of these new symbols, as well as the war waged on the old ones, were important revolutionary *acts*."[55]

From Indifference to Nationalist Counter-Revolution (1794–1815)

Michelet concluded his *Histoire de la Révolution française* with Thermidor. He certainly hit the nail on the head as far as the "naming revolution" was concerned. After Year III there were no further initiatives in naming and, more important, there was no longer any global vision of ideological symbolism. Chance, the product of indifference, reasserted its dominion. Yet the revolutionary legacy persisted, and it would take three successive "reactions"—Thermidorian indifference, the Napoleonic counterrevolution, and the formalism of the Restoration—to obliterate it completely.

The Revolution has fascinated students of street names, for good reason. By contrast, they have been completely indifferent to the Directory—and for no good reason.[56] The ideological system has disappeared: only rarely, and in contexts having nothing to do with the Revolution, does one encounter streets with names like Égalité, Contrat-Social, Raison, or Haine-des-Tyrans (Hatred of Tyrants; Bordeaux, 1793) in French cities today. As a result, in 1985, the very word *Revolution* was honored by a street name in only six of France's ninety-five prefectures, whereas President Kennedy was so honored in forty-nine. The Revolution made only one lasting contribution to French street-naming practice: the technique of political debaptizing, invented in 1791 and generalized in 1793–1794. In other respects, the contemporary era began not with the Revolution but after it, that is, with Thermidor.

After the storm came calm, and apathy. In Paris there were very few initiatives in naming: *Concorde* replaced *Revolution* in 1795 (in the same decree that abolished the death penalty).[57] The names *Quiberon* and *Hoche* appeared in 1796, along with a few others. When the press of the period talked about "streets," it was concerned not with names but with matters such as traffic, safety, and hygiene.[58]

This Parisian calm was deceptive, however, because it hid a development that would prove crucial for the future: the collapse of the national system. France, which had rediscovered homogeneity in naming thanks to the Jacobins, lost it again under the Thermidorians, as each commune regained the freedom to go its own way. In Rouen, "during the course of the year 1795, the old names of streets and squares were restored with few exceptions."[59] In Marseilles the municipal council on 26 Floréal, Year III (May 1795), approved "measures to restore the former names of streets." These measures must have been incomplete, because ten years later it was decided to "appoint a commission to eliminate inscriptions of street names and monuments made during the Revolution."[60] In Toulon revolutionary names disappeared between 1795 and 1797.[61] In Bordeaux, on the other hand, an 1804 map shows the city with its revolutionary names (though Bernadau claims that they were eliminated as early as 1801).[62] Finally, Paris kept nearly all its revolutionary names throughout the Directory. Furthermore, this anarchy did not spare the communes: some reestablished their old names in 1796–1797; others would do so later, as we shall see. The lack of consistent naming characteristic of the Ancien Régime was back, for a long time to come.

Historians are quick to sum up the following period: "The Empire celebrated its victories with the Rues d'Austerlitz, d'Iéna, and d'Ulm."[63] It "sought to substitute the names of victories and dead officers" for political names.[64] And indeed, the most visible aspect of the period was the invasion of Paris by the names of officers and battles. But that was not the whole story of Napoleon's naming policy, far from it.

As early as 1798 one detects signs of renewed interest in the naming of streets. For example, a decision of the Département de la Seine dated 9 Nivôse, Year VII (December 29, 1798) decreed that "Rue Chatenreine, where the home of the conqueror of Italy is located, shall henceforth be known as Rue de la Victoire . . . so that henceforth Bonaparte's address will be Rue de la Victoire."[65] One finds this conquering republican spirit in other new streets of that year: Mantoue, Cysalpine, Batave, Alpes, and Hoche. But that was not all. *La Clef du Cabinet* of 12 Pluviôse, Year VII (January 31, 1799) saw a "need to change the names of a large number of Paris streets." And the Bureau Central in June 1799 proposed to the département, "as a measure useful to the public, to change the names of streets that have the same denomination and substitute names recalling our victories and the great men who have lent their luster to the Republic."[66]

Debaptizings were back. Yet their motivation—"love of the public good," which is to say, administrative efficiency, to strengthen the Republic rather than obliterate the Ancien Régime—clearly distinguished this round of renamings from their revolutionary "ancestors."

The two main ideas of Bonaparte's policy in its first phase were to present himself as the administrator and above all the continuator of the Revolution. The ambiguity of his relation to the revolutionary heritage forced him to be extremely cautious in his advance. He therefore accepted certain constraints but without relinquishing his own ideas. His tactic was simple: to revitalize revolutionary policy but in one of its dimensions only, namely, nationalism. In so doing, he seemed to be carrying on the enterprise of his predecessors, who had done so much to glorify the People, the Nation, Unity, and Patriotism—in a word, France. In reality, his course was almost the opposite. This was true, first of all, because for the men of 1793–1794 the national was inseparable from the social. More than that, revolutionary nationalism was ahistorical, because any glorification of the nation's great men and great dates ran the risk of calling attention to the context that had made or at least witnessed them, which might have been the Ancien Régime. Thus the nationalism of the revolutionaries was *almost abstract.*

For Napoleon such nationalism was inconceivable, because the nation and its history were inseparable. He fully grasped the idea that the glorification of the present, in this instance his present, inevitably involved commemoration of the past. The past provided the necessary pedigree of national legitimacy. To be sure, he put his own men and exploits in the foreground, but in order to give them historical significance he set them against the past as backdrop. It is therefore a mistake to see the naming policy of the consul and later the emperor as solely one of exalting his own generals and triumphs.

Let us begin, however, with the military sphere and battles. Paris before Bonaparte had only the Place de Fontenoy (1770) to commemorate France's military glories. The Consulate and Empire generously filled this gap with some twenty squares, quays, and streets commemorating, among other things, Fleurus, Helder, Lodi, Mondovi, and Marengo (all between 1798 and 1800). But there was also a Rue de Port-Mahon celebrating the Duc de Richelieu's victory over the English in 1756. This juxtaposition of the present and the past was even more obvious in the case of military men. To the five honored by Paris before 1798—Suffren, Vauban, Matignon, La Motte-Picquet, and Hoche—Napoleon added some thirty more: two-thirds were his comrades-in-arms, but a third came from the Ancien Régime, including Chevet, Lowendal, Tourville, Villars, and Assas.

Thus, the idea of a national honorific system, initiated in 1779 but never really pursued, then adopted briefly in 1791, was finally established on a firm footing by Napoleon. But his perception of the history of France was still selective. Witness the six writers whose names he bestowed on Paris streets: Descartes, Montesquieu, and above all the four great preachers, Bossuet, Fénelon, Massillon, and Bourdaloue (circa 1805).

Thus, surprising as it may seem, Bonaparte's naming practice was governed by the same logic as that of the Revolution. But the revolutionaries simultaneously destroyed the old and constructed the new, whereas Bonaparte was forced to establish his own system, which he presented as a "continuation" of the revolutionary tradition, before embarking on an effort of destruction. He therefore waited four years—years filled with nationalist and militarist namings—before taking his first openly reactionary step: restoring the epithets *saint* or *sainte* to old names after the signing of the Concordat in July 1801. This restoration was conducted quietly, however, with Bonaparte attacking one of the revolutionary innovations that the French had been most reluctant to accept, and doing so ostensibly for practical reasons: "It was alleged that coachmen, not familiar with the book on *Esprit* and misled by the Latin word ending, commonly referred to Rue Saint-Helvetius [formerly Rue Sainte-Anne]."[67] *La Gazette de France* for 24 Germinal, Year X (April 14, 1802), was even more ironic:

> One presumes that the streets of Paris whose names were preceded by the word *saint* are going to revert to their old names. This calls to mind an excellent anecdote. During the period when the saints were in exile, a resident of the Rue *Saint-Denis* was stopped by a patrol and asked where he lived. He answered, "I live on Rue Saint . . ." "No *Saint*!" the officer cut him off. "I live on Rue De . . ." "No *De*!" "All right, then, I live on Rue *Nis*." One more remark and Rue Saint-Denis would have disappeared.[68]

In provincial cities, the elimination of *saint* from names provoked similar reactions, which explains why Saint-Étienne avoided the practice[69] and why Rouen and Toulon restored their *saints* as early as 1795. Thus Bonaparte's initiative could be presented not as an ideological challenge but rather as a useful administrative measure.

Napoleon waited four more years before striking the decisive blow. Indeed, it was a coup de grâce. The revolutionary system had become almost an anachronism in a city dominated by the names of generals and battles. The year 1806 saw the disappearance of both the revolutionary calendar and all the revolutionary slogans. Frimaire, Germinal, Liberté, Égalité, Droits-de-l'Homme, Sans-Culottes, and Bonnet-Rouge gave way to Mars, Avril, Béthune (in memory of Sully, who certainly deserved it), Reine-de-Hongrie, Roi-de-Sicile, Guisarde, and Croix-Rouge. Only acceptable historical names such as Voltaire, Rousseau, and Catinat were spared in this great purge (followed shortly thereafter by the restoration of the prerevolutionary names of the Paris sections).[70]

Kings, princes, and nobles were the first to benefit from this new revision. But the benefits were not equally distributed. Napoleon's choices could not have been more transparent. He selected "historical" names, that is, names from the period prior to Louis XIII: Clovis, Clotilde, Clotaire (adjacent to the new Lycée Napoléon), Chilpéric, Reine-de-Hongrie, Roi-de-Sicile, Marie-Stuart, Anjou, Condé, Orléans, Monsieur-le-Prince (Condé), Dauphine (the future Louis XIII), and Sully. More "political" names, such as Louis-le-Grand, Louis-XV, Louis-XVI, Bourbon, Enghien, Roi, Royale, Monsieur, and Dauphin, would have to wait until 1815.[71]

Thus nothing was left to chance—except in the provinces. Maps of Reims (1810), Lyons (1810), and Bordeaux (1804, 1808) reveal no trace of imperial policy. In Reims and Lyons "religious" names were restored. In Bordeaux revolutionary names were allowed to stand. And in Toulon, in 1798, streets were named 13-Vendémiaire, Arcole (after Napoleon's victory at Arcola in Italy), and Victoire.[72] Why did Napoleon's project end with Paris? How can we account for the difference between the Revolution's national policy and the Empire's exclusively Parisian one? There are two answers, one practical, the other symbolic.

Unlike the men of the Revolution, Napoleon was not a great proponent of debaptizing. Instead of an aggressive approach, he preferred to restore old names—or to build new streets. In restoring old names, the only exceptions he made were those that risked awakening memories of a still too recent monarchy. Such "dangerous" names were practically nonexistent in provincial cities, where the Ancien Régime was represented by religious names, which, as we have seen, did not bother the emperor. He was therefore content to rename the Place Royale or Rue Royale the Place or Rue Impériale, to substitute *Napoleon* for *Louis*, and to leave everything else up to local citizens, who did nothing. The same logic governed the restoration of commune names. Most of the religious names were restored in 1798 and afterward, as were "noble" but inoffensive names.[73] Nevertheless, Mont-Dauphin remained Mont-Lyon and Dun-le-Roi continued to be known as Dun-Saint-Aurun from 1793 to 1815, and Nogent-le-Roi remained Nogent-Roulebois from 1794 to 1815.[74]

Napoleon's forte was not debaptizing but the construction of streets, squares, quays, and boulevards that glorified his name and commemorated his men and exploits. A map of Marseilles from 1810 features a new quarter including the Rues d'Arcole, d'Iéna, de Marengo, and de Friedland. And the legend of an 1810 map of Lyons indicates that among new projects under way were the Rues d'Iéna, d'Eylau, d'Austerlitz, de Lodi, de Marengo, and de Königsberg, as well as a Cours Impérial.

This explanation is only half-valid, however, because the Empire's urban renovations were of course limited to Paris. For Napoleon, as for the Bourbons as well as for that other great urbanist, Napoleon's nephew, who would rule sixty years later, Paris was a metaphor for power. The city was the symbolic as well as the geographic center of absolutism. In matters of administration, Napoleon was certainly a great innovator on a national scale, but in matters of ideological symbolism Paris preoccupied him more than anything else.

With the Restoration: From Surgery to Cosmetics

One of the constants of the history of street names is the practice of lightning debaptizings on a large scale. Street names were republicanized in Rouen, Saint-Étienne, and Lille in one session in December 1793, and another session in October 1794 took care of Toulon. Similarly, the "return of the saints" in 1802 and the elimination of revolutionary slogans in 1806 were each effected by a single decree. This continued right through the Liberation, when all vestiges of Vichy were abolished at a single stroke. The crisis was invariably brief. What varied was the length of time leading up to it, as well as its magnitude.

No sooner had Louis XVIII taken the throne than he ordered the restoration of the prerevolutionary names of forty-nine Paris streets, quays, squares, and bridges.[75] The date was July 1815, less than a month after Waterloo, and already the new note had been struck.

When we examine the king's order closely, we find that it was aimed exclusively at the Napoleonic layer of urban nomenclature for the simple reason that the revolutionary layer had already disappeared in 1806: the Empire did a more thorough job obliterating the Revolution than the Revolution had done obliterating the Ancien Régime. The king's order struck at names that evoked the imperial *family*. Curiously, of the twenty-five battles and twenty officers for whom Napoleon had named Paris streets, the royal order eliminated only twelve and two, respectively. How can we account for this contradiction?

There is no need to invoke the generosity of the Bourbons. The actual reason is far simpler: Louis XVIII was not obliterating Napoleon, he was restoring the Ancien Régime. Unfortunately for him, the arm he chose was bureaucratic formalism. He all but ignored the fact that Napoleon, the great urbanist, had built some two hundred streets, which remained and continued to glorify his name and his work. Parisians would thus continue to move in a highly "Napoleonized" city: Rivoli, Ulm, Les Pyramides, Kléber, Desaix, and Montebello are still there to recall the glory of the Empire.

If royal revenge was far too formalist to be effective, the eclecticism of the Restoration only compounded matters. Three "specialties" emerge from the hundred or so new names chosen in this period: the Benedictine historians of Paris (seven of whom were commemorated in 1817), European cities (twenty in 1826), and functionaries and lawyers (at least fifteen, including the three defenders of

Louis XVI and Marie-Antoinette). The rest were distributed among innumerable categories: writers (La Bruyère, Byron, Chateaubriand, Pascal), composers (Dalayrac, Marsollier, Méhul, and Monsigny, all in 1829), four architects, seven scholars, only one statesman (Malesherbes), three living soldiers, Bayard (who died in 1504), and (finally) Du Guesclin, but not a single battle.[76] It must be said that these were odd choices indeed if their intended purpose was to capture the imagination of Parisians and eclipse the Revolution and Empire.

It is easy to be ironic about the Restoration, with its vengeful formalism and encyclopedic eclecticism, yet these have remained the two principal characteristics of naming policy to this day. The July Monarchy wiped out the (recent) Bourbons, imposed its own branch, added two writers (Beaumarchais and Gregory of Tours), four architects, a musician, and four politicians (three of whom had just died), along with its own military exploits (Rues Alger, Constantine, Mogador), and above all doctors and scientists from Newton to Fulton by way of Lavoisier and Jussieu, and then retired from the scene. The Revolution of 1848 went after names from the *last* monarchy and commemorated Lamartine, 24-Février, Réforme, and Fraternité, beginning as early as March 1848. But not more than fifty streets were affected, all told.[77] And the wheel continued to turn: 1851, 1871, 1940, and 1944–1945 all saw simple cosmetic treatments that touched only the (most recent) surface.[78]

Moreover, this cumulative process was accentuated at each stage. In a city whose nomenclature is uniform, a new regime presumably has a clear target. But when Louis-Philippe took power in Paris, it was not a homogeneous "restored" city that he encountered but a mixture without a strong ideological identity (only the revolutionary layer was missing). The decisive blow to any attempt to completely reshape the landscape of Paris names was of course the great annexation of 1860, which increased the number of public streets from 1,474 to 3,750. Many names had to be found, and found quickly, and they were sought everywhere. The encyclopedic tendency became irreversible.[79]

Paris had been clerical and royal; it became republican and revolutionary, then nationalist and military, and in the end simultaneously republican and royalist, clerical and socialist—in short, a brief scholarly compendium of French history. After 1815, governments ceased to rewrite history with Paris street signs. Each regime was content to add its humble chapter to the assembled treasury. The symbol of the new age was perhaps the inauguration of three tiny streets in a far corner of Paris in 1889: they were named Liberté, Égalité, and Fraternité.

Paris and the Provinces: The Gap

In 1830, Paris streets bore the names of fifteen writers, eleven architects and sculptors, seven composers, fourteen scientists, sixteen statesmen, fifty officers, thirty battles, twelve jurists, and a hundred or so princes, nobles, and bishops.[80] Proportionally, Nantes in 1832 was more advanced, with seventeen writers, four scholars, five painters (at the time there was not a single painter's name in Paris!), and several officers, statesmen, and so on. Nantes also deserves credit for honoring eighteen international celebrities as opposed to only four in Paris.[81]

But Nantes was an exception among provincial cities. In 1827, Le Havre honored only four "great men": Fontenelle and Corneille (both Normans from Rouen), Molière, and Richelieu.[82] In Rouen there were only six in 1819: Le Nôtre, Racine, Socrates, Buffon, Fontenelle, and Jouvenet, another Rouennais. By 1869 the number had increased to only seventeen (out of a total of four hundred streets).[83] Lille already honored fifty-six "historical personages and deeds" (according to the Bertrand classification of 1880) out of a total of four hundred streets, but few dated from before 1860.[84] In Marseilles in 1820, there were only two, Corneille and Molière, but in 1868 the city partially made up for lost time. The evolution of the urban landscape in Lyons and Bordeaux was identical: very few names of national stature prior to 1830, a few dozen toward the end of the Second Empire.[85]

The *national* honorific system was therefore extremely slow to get under way in the provinces. Furthermore, it was not the resistance of the medieval system that slowed the expansion of the Parisian model. On the contrary, all the evidence shows that local governments throughout France had enjoyed a monopoly of power over naming since the eighteenth century. As in Paris, municipal councils seized on this power to immortalize their members. But the *local* honorific system, which lasted only twenty years in Paris, from 1765 to 1785, persisted in the provinces for at least a century. The case of Saint-Étienne, studied in depth by A. Vallet, is typical in this regard. In 1870 its streets bore the names of fifteen "local political personalities" as against three "celebrities," Vaucanson, Foy, and Franklin. It was not until 1885 that national glories rivaled local glories: ninety new names were chosen between 1870 and 1918. "National" names enjoyed a slight advantage from 1918 to 1950: there were 129 of them and 120 "local" names.[86]

The de facto gap between Paris and the provinces is all the more surprising given the fact that the national government had claimed a monopoly on naming power throughout the country since 1816: "In the future, no gift, homage, or prize can be voted, offered, or awarded as a sign of public gratitude by municipal councils, national guards, or any other civilian or military body without our prior authorization."[87] Such was the principle. In reality, the central government took absolutely no interest in what went on outside Paris. Furthermore, only the municipal council of Paris rebelled against state intervention in what it considered a purely local preserve. This dispute over the authority to name gave rise to a series of reports addressed to the Paris council in the second half of the nineteenth century.[88] In other French cities, where state intervention was nonexistent, we find nothing comparable.

This indifference might explain the long survival of the local honorific system in the provinces. It surely encouraged the local chauvinism exhibited by Léon de Duranville of Rouen, who had this to say in 1869: "Racine, despite his very great merit, occupies a place that we would like to see filled by a Norman."[89] Or again, L. Maynard, who expressed his indignation in 1922 about the existence of Quai Jean-Jacques-Rousseau in his city: "The relations between Lyons and the philosopher of Geneva are slender."[90] The same local chauvinism explains why the city of Bordeaux, in a wave of debaptizings in 1842, added thirteen local personalities and removed three celebrities: Voltaire, Rousseau, and Franklin.[91]

But these were only rearguard actions. The historical logic according to which the center imposes its models on the periphery was always respected in the end. From the medieval system to the royal system and from the local system to the national one, cities ultimately followed the lead of the capital with exemplary docility. And then, in the 1860s, by which time the national system was definitively established in the provinces, the capital, as if to preserve the gap between center and periphery, adopted an *international* system: Rues Mozart and Léonard-de-Vinci, Beethoven and Rubens, and other foreign-named streets cropped up everywhere in the wake of the Haussmannian annexation, which greedily consumed names. It would be another half-century before this new system was adopted in the provinces.[92]

The Third Republic: Recovery of National Homogeneity

Between 1880 and 1900 the publisher Fayard produced a collection of 160 maps of French cities, with the aid of which we can study the immediate effects of the provinces' adoption of the national honorific system.[93] Three things emerge:

1. Medieval appellations still predominated, especially in city centers (the oldest quarters).
2. The central streets of provincial cities generally bore neutral names such as Rue or Avenue or Boulevard de l'Hôtel-de-Ville, de la Gare, de l'Hôpital, or du Lycée. Historical names were ultimately rather rare.
3. Four names appeared everywhere, indicating the advent of a new era: Thiers (whose prominence in street-naming was rather brief), Gambetta, Hugo, who had just died, and above all République, with almost three-quarters of all French cities honoring the nascent republic.

How do things stand today? In 1978, the *Index-Atlas de France* appeared, with maps and legends covering all of the country's prefectures. My analysis of these

TABLE 2

Name	Total	Major Thoroughfares[1]	Multiple Occurrences[2]
Rabelais	39	4	2
Racine	38	2	-
Montaigne	35	6	1
Corneille	35	3	-
Montesquieu	35	5	3
La Fontaine	32	2	2
Descartes	30	1	-
Fénelon	21	2	1
Bossuet	20	3	1
Claude-Monet	17	2	-
Poussin	5	-	-
Claude-Bernard	30	3	-

1. Major Thoroughfares: avenues, boulevards, quays, bridges, places.
2. Multiple occurrence: names appearing at least twice on the plan of a city.

data is summarized in Table 2.[94] A quick glance at the table reveals two major categories of names, one "professional," the other historical. As G. Quentin observed of Reims:

> *Political figures* account for a substantial share of names. The share of other individual names is limited, and the streets named for them are often modest: scholars, artists, and writers are ignored unless they are associated with a political attitude (Victor Hugo, Anatole France, Émile Zola). To be sure, we do find Jean de La Fontaine, but how is it possible that there is no street named for Racine in Reims?[95]

This politicization seems natural to us. Yet the system was introduced in 1779 with Rues Corneille, Racine, Molière, Regnard, Voltaire, and Crébillon. What has become of the great intellects and artists in our streets? Rest assured: France has not forgotten them. All, or nearly all, are there, but discreetly, almost hidden away, as table 3 (next page) indicates:

These results are largely corroborated by a recent German study by R. Posthaus, "French Authors and Street Names: Paris, Montreuil, Saint-Étienne, Perpignan."[96] Even if one includes, as Posthaus does, historians, journalists, and scientists under the head of "authors," they account for only 7.6 percent of street names in Paris, 7.9 percent in Perpignan, 8.2 percent in Saint-Étienne, and 9.9 percent in Montreuil. Generally, these are modest streets of secondary importance. It is as if French municipal councils discharge their "cultural" duty with-

TABLE 3 THE MOST FREQUENT NAMES IN THE PLANS OF 95 PREFECTURES IN 1978

Name	Total	Major Thoroughfares[1]	Multiple Occurrence[2]
Republic	Many	All	Numerous
. Victor Hugo	81	38	12
. Gambetta	78	45	8
. Jean Jaurès	78	39	11
. Pasteur	78	26	11
. General Leclerc	76	48	5
. Clemenceau	73	43	2
. Marshal Foch	72	45	2
. General de Gaulle	68	61	-
. Carnot	66	41	11
. Joan of Arc	63	15	8
. Pierre [and Marie] Curie[3]	63	10	2
. Aristide Briand	60	38	5
. Voltaire	60	13	3
. Anatole France	56	19	2
. Jules Ferry	55	14	7
. Émile Zola	55	11	5
. Molière	52	5	2
. Kennedy	49	28	-
. Michelet	49	10	1
. Saint-Exupéry	48	8	2
. Lamartine	48	5	4
. Jean-Jacques Rousseau	47	3	-
. Lavoisier	45	5	2
. Claude Debussy	45	3	2
. Balzac	43	3	2
. La Fayette	42	5	5
. Hector Berlioz	42	1	2
Miscellaneous Others, Grouped by Period			
Middle Ages and Ancien Régime			
Saint Louis	34	16	8
Henri IV	18	5	1
Louis[4]	12	-	-
Charlemagne	10	-	-
Clovis	8	-	-
Colbert	28	4	4
Sully	24	4	4
Richelieu	16	-	-
Revolution			
Mirabeau	25	3	-

TABLE 3 THE MOST FREQUENT NAMES IN THE PLANS OF 95 PREFECTURES IN 1978

Name	Total	Major Thoroughfares[1]	Multiple Occurrence[2]
Danton	24	1	-
Robespierre	12	1	1
Revolution	6	6	-
Hoche	37		
Marceau	37	16[5]	
Kléber	35		
Empire			
Bonaparte/Napoleon	10	-	-
Iéna	14[6]	-	-
Austerlitz	11[6]		
Islay	12	-	-
Thiers	39	12	2
End of the Third Republic			
Henri Barbusse	34	9	2
Léon Blum	27	10	1
Resistance	37	26	4

1. Major Thoroughfares: avenues, boulevards, quays, bridges, places.
2. Multiple occurrence: names appearing at least twice on the plan of a city.
3. Of which 36 are Pierre Curie (without Marie).
4. Three Louis XI, three Louis XIV or Louis-le-Grand, and one each Louis VI, Louis VIII, Louis XII, Louis XIII, Louis XVI, and Louis XVIII.
5. A major thoroughfare for at least one of three general ones.
6. Of eight cities that honor the two battles.

out much conviction so that they can move on to truly serious matters: the men (politicians, naturally) who made France—who had just made France, to be more precise.

This brings us to the third major criterion of selection, which is historical. Of the thirteen great men found in at least two-thirds of major cities, nine were connected with the Third Republic between 1882 (Gambetta) and 1932 (Aristide Briand).[97] These men's names are not given to remote streets in some far corner of town but to major boulevards, squares, and quays. If the Third Republic is everywhere, other periods of French history seem thinly represented: for the Middle Ages there is only Joan of Arc (tenth in our ranking); for the Enlightenment, Voltaire (thirteenth); for the age of Louis XIV, Molière (seventeenth); and for the early nineteenth century, Michelet (who in any case died in 1874).

Thanks to the pantheon of the Third Republic (and the Liberation), France seems at last to have regained its unity of naming, which it had lost in 1795–1796. Unlike revolutionary homogeneity, republican homogeneity seems destined to endure. But this assertion is too simple, for while unity has been restored in the provinces, Paris is once again an exception.

To be sure, the capital has its Avenues Foch, Jaurès, Hugo, and Zola. But these don't mean much: one finds everything in Paris, and with some 5,400 streets, it would have been difficult to avoid these names. What counts is not mere presence but visibility within the texture of the city. And one has to travel far from the center to find these republican names: Pasteur in the Eleventh and Fifteenth Arrondissements; Gambetta in the Twentieth; Carnot in the Twelfth and Seventeenth; Jean Jaurès in the Nineteenth. Thus all of these names appear in areas recently incorporated into the capital. Only Clemenceau and Foch are better positioned. For Paris is not a "Third Republican" city, it is still an "imperial" city. Everything attests to the fact, from the avenues around the Étoile to the Avenue des Invalides to the peripheral boulevards. Indeed, the Ancien Régime is more fully represented in the center of Paris than is the Third Republic.

Are the provinces for once in advance of Paris? The hypothesis has its appeal, but the real explanation lies elsewhere: it is a matter of urban realities. The number of streets in Paris increased from 1,070 in 1789 to 3,750 in 1860 to 5,218 in 1957 (even as the surface area of the city increased from 8,327 acres in 1789 to 19,279 in 1860 to 25,822 in 1959).[98] Given the scope of the renovations undertaken in the two Empires, there is every reason to maintain that Paris is today half *Napoleonic*, especially insofar as street names are concerned.

The growth of provincial cities was no less spectacular in the eighteenth century, the great century of urbanization. But in contrast to what happened in Paris, growth in the provinces accelerated even more after 1870. Although the case of Saint-Étienne, which tripled the number of its streets from 260 in 1870 to more than 700 in 1950, is somewhat extreme, it does reflect a general trend among French cities (including those of the Paris region, which profited from the relative stagnation of Paris).[99]

Circumstances thus conspired to allow the Third Republican pantheon to take over the French urban scene, as spectacular urban growth coincided with the definitive adoption of the national honorific system. Sheer longevity was also a factor: the Third Republic lasted longer than the Consulate, Empire, Restoration, July Monarchy, Second Republic, and Second Empire combined.

Call this combination of circumstances a *conjoncture*. But is not a *conjoncture* that lasts for seventy years almost a *structure*, especially in this age of the "acceleration of history"? A survey, "Heroes of French History," published in the journal *L'Histoire* in April 1981 gives some interesting answers (see table 4).[100]

TABLE 4

Uncontroversial Figures	Mildly Controversial Figures	Highly Controversial Figures	Bad Reputations
Vercingetorix	De Gaulle	Napoleon	Louis XI
Saint Louis	Henri IV	Louis XIV	Catherine de Médicis
Joan of Arc	Charlemagne	Richelieu	Ravaillac
Hugo	Marie Curie		Louis XV
Pasteur			Louis XVI
Jaurès			Danton, Marat, Robespierre
Clemenceau			Talleyrand
Blum			Napoleon III
			Thiers

The table reveals a very marked contrast between two groups of historical figures: uncontroversial figures from the remote past, up to the time of Henri IV, and from the Third Republic to de Gaulle; and controversial or hated figures from Ravaillac to Thiers (Catherine de Médicis and Louis XI being exceptions that are easily explained).[101] Thus, the two and a half centuries of classicism, Enlightenment, Revolution, and Empire are still a problem for the French. Curiously, this division is reminiscent of Napoleon's selection criteria: historical personages prior to Louis XIII were acceptable, "politicians" from Richelieu to Robespierre were excluded. Was not Napoleon himself later a victim of his own criteria?

The urban circumstances *(conjoncture urbaine)* that we have been describing might thus coincide with a certain set of attitudes *(conjoncture des mentalités)*, each consolidating the effects of the other. Thus street names might prove to be a "good subject" after all.

The survey we have just concluded has led us from the spontaneous, organic system of the Middle Ages to a semi–state-oriented system emphasizing history and the nation. We have thus moved, in the terms of a set of issues made familiar by the larger work in which this essay appears, from an era of "natural" memory to an era of official historical memory. But how many of the thousands of names "immortalized" by the streets of France still belong to living memory?

Finally, let us take a brief look at the "new cities" built in recent years. In the 1960s nine cities were born of the fusion of several towns and villages, so that their urban existence started from square one. What names did they choose for their streets? Without inflicting any further statistics on the reader, let me simply state the lapidary conclusion: they chose *neutral* names.[102] In Villeneuve-d'Ascq we find quarters of "impressionists," "musicians," and "classics" along with Rues Kléber, Champollion, and Jean-Jaurès. Other cities were even more prudent, drawing their inspiration mainly from nature. Consider the following two lists of street names in alphabetical order: Acacias, Barrois, Cambraisis, Dauphiné, Échoppes (Plessis-le-Roi and Plessis-la-Forêt), Falaises, Garance, Kiosque, Lacs (Le Vaudreuil), Maïs, Nénuphars, Orée-de-Nandy, Palombes, Renardière, Sablons (Nandy), Terrasses, Vieux-Village; Abreuvoir, Belle-Herbe, Canal (Bondoufle-Évry), Dames, Églantier, Féculerie, Gaboulets (Cergy), Hôtel-de-Ville, Lac, Malacombe, Oiseaux, Pépinière (Saint-Quentin-Fallavier). Perhaps what these new names allow us to glimpse is the advent of a post-history and an anti-memory.

FIGURE 12.0. Bossuet delivering the funeral oration for the Prince de Condé, March 10, 1687, at Notre-Dame.

CHAPTER XII

The Pulpit, the Rostrum, and the Bar

Jean Starobinski[1]

The realm of eloquence in the history of France extended from religion to politics, from litigation to solemn celebrations, from academic orations to everyday life. On several occasions in his famous work on legal philosophy, *De l'esprit des lois* (1748), Montesquieu refers to despotism as a form of government in which speech is not a prerequisite for the exercise of political power. The "Oriental" tyrannies, in his opinion, are regimes based on arbitrary violence in which the ruler is obeyed in almost total silence. Terror and speechlessness are closely intertwined.

We can agree to a certain extent with Montesquieu's views. In the Western political tradition there is a consensus that political power cannot impose itself by sheer force, but must result from education, agreement, and persuasion. In short, language must prevail over violence or, at least, play a significant role. Eloquence, of course, does not preclude violence, for when it uses its power of seduction, it exerts another, more subtle, less overt form of violence. A means of enforcing the law must exist, even in law-abiding regimes, which for Montesquieu could equally be monarchic, aristocratic, or republican. And once the boundary between legal and illegal behavior has been laid down, no objections should arise when the forces of law and order engage in fighting against unlawful behavior. To safeguard the well-being of its citizens, the democratic constitutional state is endowed with what the German sociologist Max Weber has called "the monopoly of violence." But each individual must also have the right to legally oppose state violence. The constitutional codes of law, starting with the constitution itself, are in principle a *matter of deliberation* between the public and its representatives in parliament. After adoption and *promulgation* by the legislators, these codes might give rise to *litigation*. Hence the need arises for special courts acting as the guardians and interpreters of the original spirit of the law. When the meaning of the law is in dispute, it is the duty of the magistrate to state the legal position and "pronounce judgment," and it is the right of the lawyers to support or contradict this or that interpretation of the law itself or a particular case in which it is deemed to apply. In a truly democratic system, the right of defense and free democratic speech should be unconstricted. Furthermore, in modern democratic regimes where church and state are separate, religious laws, usually couched in ancient texts, are *preached* to the faithful. To sum up, therefore, to eliminate violent conflicts from communal life, speech acts are expected to be performed in the making of laws *(deliberation)*, in litigation over its correct interpretation *(accusation* or *pleading)*, and in the moral and political education of individuals (*preaching* or *edifying* in the broadest sense of the word). Eloquence or its equivalents contribute toward the decision-making processes of government. Eloquence precedes and determines the tenor of the law. It shapes the convictions of the judge and the consciousness of the individual.

Moreover, the authority conferred on the legislator, the judge, or the educator must result, whether implicitly or explicitly, from some sort of general preliminary consensus about the best way of handling human affairs. From Hobbes onwards, many philosophers have taken it for granted that decisions made according to the rules must be based implicitly on the fundamental acceptance of a principle, that is, the presupposition that a set of rules is needed to regulate the relations between individuals. This fictional contract introduces an original collective speech act, from which the different forms of speech acts—legislative, judicial, and educational (or religious)—derive their legitimacy.

In classical rhetoric there were three types of eloquence: deliberative (practiced in assemblies making political decisions), judicial (used for settling legal cases), and demonstrative (mostly encomiastic, that is, laudatory, but also depreciatory on occasion). Though this classification was derived principally from the experiences of the Athenian agora, it could still be maintained in other historical circumstances. Suffice it to say that eloquence, the "art of persuasion," had been taught for centuries because it was inseparable from all forms of nonviolent collective behavior. Whether in popular assemblies or (select) courtrooms, in halls of justice, in churches or academies, eloquence was cultivated by the leaders as well as their opponents, as the art of eliciting consent. Persuasive communication has undoubtedly always pervaded all walks of life, though taking many different forms. Nowadays, commercials and advertising have unfortunately taken over some of the functions which had been ascribed to education in the past.

In these institutions, social power was both exerted and represented. Thus mastering a verbal skill was considered a first step to power within established social roles. The ancients knew it, from the age of the sophists onward. In France the classical writers repeated the lessons of the ancients. La Bruyère, among others, defines eloquence as "a gift of the soul that makes us masters of the hearts and minds of others, that enables us to inspire them or persuade them in any way we wish."[2] In the eighteenth century, agreement on this point was virtually unanimous: "The effect of eloquence," d'Alembert assures us, "is to cause the movement that animates us to pass into the souls of others."[3] Across the centuries we perceive, in regard to eloquence, an enduring dream of omnipotence. And we find this not among the hereditary possessors of political and military power but among clerics, humanists, and men of letters—people with no other weapon than language and the right to speak, in which they invested great hopes. But no sooner was the power of language acknowledged (or imagined) than its very efficacy gave rise to a suspicion: How might it be abused? What dangers lay in store for mankind if an orator, having gained power over men's minds, did not aim for the common good? When he who holds the power of language is not also a servant of virtue *(vir bonus dicendi peritus)*, he corrupts mobs, seduces princes, and sows the seeds of ruin in cities.

Such ambivalence about eloquence has always existed: language was at once a source and instrument of power, a basis of authority, yet itself in need of justification and confirmation by the moral value of the person exercising it, failing which it was open to attack as "specious eloquence," "rhetorical declamation," and "sophistry."

The pulpit, the bar, and the rostrum are places where this power of language was exercised before it was relayed by books and newspapers. These same places could also be denounced as suspect when those who used them to gain a hearing for themselves were discredited by counterpropaganda that could avail itself of the same sites as well as of instruments such as books, caricatures, and theatrical or journalistic satire.

The words survive and are still used to designate, collectively, by metonymy, preachers, lawyers, and law makers. The three nouns serve as a convenient professional classification. But the use of these words, which denote places in which discourses of a specific type are delivered, may seem rather archaic: memory burdens them with a somewhat old-fashioned formality. In modern social intercourse, obviously, the bulk of effective verbal action does not involve these three sites: religious and political orators now rely on amplifiers and loudspeakers to reach large crowds assembled in huge meeting halls. Other types of "messages" abound: posters, streamers, and wall slogans; interviews and debates controlled by "moderators"; press conferences and televised speeches. Of course it is easy to see how the resources of the old rhetoric and the old poetics still find uses, even when nothing else seems to have been learned. The art of persuasion may avail itself of new instruments, but it has renounced none of its old tricks. And the suspicion that those tricks aroused is all the more reason to remain vigilant. What is different now is that orators are no longer confined to the traditional sites; often they tend to avoid adopting the stance of an orator. The ancient figure—which one can recall with a tinge of regret—was that of an individual who, speaking in a consecrated place, made public his convictions, arguments, and feelings. From oral "delivery" to printed publication to the polymorphous and then to the seemingly anonymous "publicity" of modern times, means of persuasion have evolved from the direct to the "decentered": of the many messages in circulation, few can be traced to a speaker who has meditated and formulated his message. Public relations techniques intervene. Today's mistrust concerns not only the possible hypocrisy of the speaker but the impersonality of the "hidden persuaders": ideas that are simultaneously images and imperatives, generators of emotion, are *circulated* as pseudo-facts, doing away with the presence of a specific speaker facing a specific audience, but often only to lay the groundwork for an opportune appearance by a "leader" or "candidate." Persuasion operates through many channels. Persuasive intent is still associated with identifiable voices and faces, though engulfed in a vast sea of circulating information. Now that the technical power of those influence-amplifiers, the media, ensures an inexhaustible, endlessly renewable supply of messages, the orator on the rostrum, at the bar, or in the pulpit is an anachronistic figure, chained to a symbolic site from which the power of his speech to reach and penetrate an audience, even if magnified by currently available technologies, may seem limited. To be sure, there are still "charismatic voices." But authority and seduction avail themselves of other instruments.

These differences duly noted, it remains true that *persuasion,* which was the purpose of eloquence, is still the purpose of modern "propaganda." And it is also true that in countries where rhetorical culture goes back a long way, any out-of-the-ordinary situation triggers a revival of rhetoric, if only because a situation becomes extraordinary only when language declares it so. I am not only thinking of periods of historical crisis, during which those who would appeal to the people must find the words to make themselves understood. On ceremonial occasions, in France particularly, people seem to feel a need for elevated language, for "sublime" diction, sources for which remain ready to hand: an oration on the Acropolis, a Nobel Prize speech, or perhaps an acceptance speech from the Académie Française. More often, whenever political debate heats up, whenever voters have to be wooed or a party platform defended or an indicted official saved, rhetorical art—moving, sententious, aggressive, or malicious as the case may be—is pressed into service, and no effort is made to conceal the fact that there is not only utility in speaking effectively but also pleasure in speaking well (and gaining a hearing for one's views). One senses an almost spontaneous rhetoric in the "innuendoes" of politicians, which often suggest a kind of linguistic gratification. No doubt this was what eighteenth-century theorists had in mind when they attributed a "spontaneous eloquence" to the better minds of all classes and all peoples. Now, in France the art of speaking well is sustained by a series of glorious images that are never openly invoked, a long "gallery of great orators" coupled with a vast repertory of famous phrases, celebrated repartees, and *ultima verba* which punctuate the "collective memory" of the nation like statues along an avenue.

The system of belles-lettres, as it was generally conceived during the eighteenth and much of the nineteenth century, was divided into three main genres: poetry, eloquence, and history. But rhetoric, as it had been codified in the sixteenth and seventeenth centuries, included poetics.[4] It had the right to judge all invention and all diction. The oratorical forms per se were simply instances. Hence the speeches attributed to heroes by epic poets, playwrights, and historians fell by right under the head of eloquence. Between the time when eloquence reigned over all linguistic production (including the art of conversation) and the emergence of the modern notion of literature, a decisive change took place, the history of which has been recounted by Marc Fumaroli[5] and Paul Bénichou.[6] To us, eloquence seems to belong to a bygone world, and the works in which it most fully manifested itself seem to us, with few exceptions, to lie outside the domain of literature proper. And while the church, the courts, and the legislature are still symbolic sites whose social function remains intact, the same cannot be said of the prestige attaching within each of these institutions to the preestablished sites—pulpit, bar, and rostrum—dedicated to the exercise of linguistic prowess, as if language itself, owing to its place of origin, were doomed to remain captive to obsolete forms, owing its value solely to the importance of the decisions it influenced. This by no means rules out nostalgia for an age when public speeches received a more passionate hearing. Today's orator may succumb to such nostalgia, and depending on how well or badly he fares, he may be rewarded by seeing his audience moved or punished by seeing it smile.

The Gallic Hercules

This nostalgia is nothing new. Throughout the Christian centuries all preaching that followed in the wake of the Prophets, the Apostles, and the Fathers of the Church was suffused with a sense of having been preceded by an unsurpassable past, which set the example, providing the strong "text" on which the sermon could comment or elaborate. All discourse was merely exegesis of the prior Word.

During the Renaissance, when French *lettrés* set out to produce great works in the vulgar tongue, they called for emulation of the Latins and Italians but above all they invoked the ancient and courageous eloquence of the Gauls. Du Bellay, in his *Défense et illustration de la langue française*, gave free rein to the new spirit without losing sight of the inspiring Greco-Latin precedent. His exhortation to future poets and orators appealed to national pride. The Gauls had been conquered by the Romans; now it was time for revenge. In appropriating the spoils of the Greeks and

Romans, the new French writers would relegate them to the past. According to the myth shared by Du Bellay and his militant humanist friends, the French were the descendants of the Trojans:[7]

> We escaped from the Greek midst thanks to the Roman squadrons that penetrated to the heart of much-coveted France. And so, men of France, march courageously toward that superb Roman city, and with her spoils *embellish* your temples and your altars (as you have done more than once). . . . *Remember* your ancient city of Marseilles, a second Athens, and your Gallic Hercules, dragging peoples after him by their ears, with a chain attached to his tongue.[8]

The new language would *resurrect* Herakles Ogmios (of whom Lucian had spoken), who possessed the gift of binding peoples by the power of the word alone. The Gallic Hercules, chaining nations to his tongue, would obliterate the humiliating image of the vanquished Gauls led away in defeat behind the triumphant Romans.

Initially, the desire for a new language took the form of wanting to invent a French *poetry* and *eloquence,* "because the poet and the orator are the two pillars upon which the edifice of every language rests."[9] Of course the images of the poet and the orator are themselves ancient, passed down through the ages, so that one may say, perhaps, that in the heart of the new desire the future of the yet-to-be-born language drew on and emulated an exemplary past in which language exercised sovereign power. It is tempting to generalize by arguing that any strong linguistic project depends on a myth of the past in which language possessed a superior power which must now be reconquered: an original poetry, an original eloquence suffered oblivion and corruption from which the new language just being invented must be saved. The earlier model is necessary only because of the deficit, the lack, the enfeeblement, that stand between past and present. The energy of renewal draws on this source. It hopes to free itself, to escape from servitude.

One of the most important prerequisites of effective eloquence, moreover, is the refusal—through laughter or scorn—of gossip, jargon, and sophistry, that is, of aberrant or fallacious forms of discourse, confused words, words without relation to truth. The sixteenth century gives us, in the work of Rabelais, a perfect example: after being educated by the "mateologians," all Gargantua can do is mumble. By contrast, the young page Eudemon, raised by the humanists "of today," can deliver a perfectly articulated encomium of Gargantua that is nevertheless unduly flattering because it assumes virtues that Gargantua has not demonstrated.

> Then Eudemon . . . cap in hand, with open face, crimson mouth, assured eyes, and his gaze fixed on Gargantua with youthful modesty, stood up and began to praise and magnify him. . . . It was all proffered with such correct gestures, such distinct pronunciation, such an eloquent voice, and in such ornate and

> correct Latin that he resembled a Gracchus, a Cicero, or an Emilius of old more than a youth of this age.[10]

For "young men of today," obviously, perfection was to resemble the great Roman orators "of old." No sooner was that memory awakened than one wished to rival the illustrious figures who lived in the mind. Gargantua is humiliated when he can find no words to respond to the great models brought to life by Eudemon and can make only animal noises in response:

> But all Gargantua could do was cry like a cow and hide his face in his cap, and it was no more possible to pry a word out of it him than to wrest a fart from a dead ass.[11]

Such obvious inferiority leads to the dismissal of Gargantua's inadequate teachers and the beginning of a new education, which will turn him into a literate, well-spoken, alert, pious young nobleman. He will learn to listen to worthwhile readings (of the Gospel above all), to comment on texts, to discuss them, to memorize them, and to recite "clearly and eloquently several morals from reading the lesson." In bad weather, instead of exercising outdoors, Gargantua familiarizes himself with all the activities of the capital. After visiting artisans he enjoys other useful sights: "They went to hear public lectures, formal ceremonies, readings, speeches, the pleas of noble advocates, and the harangues *[concions]* of evangelical preachers."[12]

Gargantua, who is learning the princely craft, does not indulge in oratorical practice (circumstances will soon enough conspire to oblige him to speak like a prince). He does, however, mingle with the audience and listen to eloquence of all types and to speakers of many different kinds. We thus discover that a public of amateurs could, out of taste and curiosity, join those who listened professionally in order to learn or dispense justice. We divine that religious eloquence was not associated with formal services and was addressed to all comers, at least until the Affaire des Placards (1534). Although Gargantua does not vie with the orators he listens to, he does "try out different strokes" with the masters of fencing: the transition in the text from listening to Gospel preaching to participating in martial exercises is noteworthy. From there he moves on to the "druggists, herbalists, and apothecaries," where he learns how to mix drugs: linguistic competence, agility in combat, and knowledge of the medicinal properties of natural products constitute a unified body of knowledge, in which appreciation of the effective use of language, knowledge of infallible thrusts and parries, and understanding of authentic remedies and counterfeits are presumably varied applications of the same faculty of judgment. The final spectacle is one of playacting and comic parody, in which the serious activities just enumerated reappear as caricatures: he "went to see jugglers, conjurers, and snake-oil salesmen, and considered their gestures, ruses, leaps, and fine talk."[13] Leaving the serious register of "pleas" and "harangues," here we are back at the other extreme, in which words, gestures, and blandishments are intended to provoke mirth: eloquence is thus closely accompanied by its "carnivalization."

However much Rabelais's language oscillates between the serious and the clownish, the very hyperbole of these chapters of *Gargantua* gives us a perfectly clear-cut image of the highest eloquence *in action,* as a "magnifying" humanist reverie might have imagined it. When the "Picrocholine War" breaks out, the virtues of eloquence are deployed in fine Ciceronian periods in the letter from Grandgousier calling Gargantua to the rescue. An identical erudite solemnity animates the speech delivered by Ulrich Gallet, the *maistre des requestes* sent on an embassy to the tyrannical invader Picrochole, Grandgousier's response to the prisoner Touquedillon, and above all Gargantua's *contion* (speech) to the defeated.

Erasmus's recommendations in the *Institutio principis christiani* (Book III) were thus abundantly illustrated and amplified. We are listening to the voice of a sovereign speaker—the language is correct, magnanimous, and measured, and it brings peace—addressing the violent, who heed only their own limitless desires and who must be brought to heel by means of legitimate counter-violence, or just war. Eloquent speech is an appropriate response to the impulsive "wrath" of the ambitious traitor, who must be stopped by force if peaceful means fail.

Writing to his son, Grandgousier reveals his "deliberation," which is "not to provoke but to appease"—a decision he has taken like a monarch, without prior debate. Picrochole has inexcusably infringed a "liberty" that must be safeguarded: Picrochole "daily pursues his mad enterprise with excesses intolerable *to free persons.*" Eloquence is political wisdom's first defense against "*tyrannical* wrath." It soon becomes apparent that the liberty that needs defending is a *liberty according to the law,* a reasonable liberty. Picrochole's "tyrannical wrath" is the expression of a very different kind of liberty, a liberty of passion and excess, a liberty of the human creature dominated by his natural instincts: "I understood that eternal God had left him to the governance of his own free will and understanding, which cannot but be wicked unless continually guided by divine grace."[14] The message is communicated to Picrochole by the ambassador: "Nothing is holy or sacred to those who have emancipated themselves from God and Reason to follow their perverse affections."[15] Solemn speech attempts to erect an impediment to wicked freedom in the name of faith, law, reason, and the fear of God, which are supposed to offer incentives for preserving the bonds of an old covenant. The ambassador seeks to persuade the sinner once again to fear God. In so doing, he is fulfilling the fundamental religious function that ancient Roman custom assigned to *oratio* and the *orator.*[16] As for the king, in speaking eloquently to safeguard the highest liberty, he thus reveals his princely qualities and full authority. Along with his fine speeches he performs acts of liberality: throughout the narrative he gives generously. He replaces the five dozen *fouaces* with five *charretées;* to these he adds generous benefits for the compensation of the *grand bâtonnier Marquet;* and when he sets Touquedillon free, he not only forgoes any ransom but showers the former prisoner with gifts ("Then he gave him a handsome sword from Vienne with a gold scabbard with finely engraved vignettes and a gold necklace worth seven hundred two thousand marks"[17]). Hence Grandgousier (along with Gargantua, Brother Jean, and the exuberant troop of youths) is not only the liberator of his country but also the magnanimous prince who frees his prisoner; his material largesse is equal to the generous abundance of his discourse. In its superlative imaginary form, princely eloquence *distributes* grace, justice, and wealth. The utopia of Thélème is merely the final *fiat* of an eloquence itself quite utopian. It will be the role of the Son—the male heir—to deliver the final *contion* to the defeated enemies (ch. 50). As a good son, he sings his father's praises. What did this generous father do when he captured the king of Canarre, who had come to pillage his land? Rather than imprison him and hold him for ransom, "he treated him courteously, amiably, lodged him in his own palace, and with incredible indulgence gave him a safe-conduct and sent him on his way, laden with gifts, favors, and all the offices of friendship." This indulgent treatment elicits a similar generosity from the Cannarians in return. They respond to the gift with a counter-gift, "as an example to the world that there is as much noble generosity in us as there is generous nobility in them." Accordingly, they decide to become Grandgousier's subjects, to give themselves to him together with their lands and possessions. A huge fleet brings all the treasures of Canarre to Grandgousier. "Everyone in the crowd threw in gold, silver, rings, jewels, spices, drugs and aromatic herbs, parrots, pelicans, monkeys, civets, genets, and porcupines. Not a single honest mother's son failed to contribute something special." Grandgousier's largesse was thus a "constraining gift." It will be easy for him not to accept all that is offered, because he is being offered the servitude of an entire country (which "gave itself and its posterity as voluntary slave and serf. This was not accepted because it did not seem equitable"). Once again Grandgousier grants liberty. But the "transaction" is not to his disadvantage, and his modest words provoke yet another round of gratitude:

> The end was that my father began piteously to lament and cried copiously in view of the Cannarians' honest will and simplicity, and by exquisite words and appropriate maxims diminished the good turn they had done him. . . . What was the outcome? Instead of the ransom, taken at the highest, that we might tyrannically have demanded of twenty times a hundred thousand écus while holding his eldest hostage, they pledged themselves to pay a perpetual tribute and honor us every year with two million pieces of twenty-four-carat refined gold.

Thus Grandgousier's generosity did no harm to his interests, and the noble words that freed the enemy were amply compensated. Gargantua, who does not wish "to degenerate from his parents' kind heredity," offers a pardon of his own: "I hereby absolve you and deliver you and set you free and at liberty as before. Moreover, each of you will receive three months' pay at the gate when you leave so that you may return to your homes and families." But this freedom-granting speech is coupled with the language of judgment and discrimination *(crisis)* with respect to those responsible for the war. Gargantua, like Caesar, distinguishes between those who shall be saved and pardoned and "the authors of rebellion" who are destined to be punished. But what punishment can be imposed on the guilty after such a formal *contion*? "Gargantua did them no harm but ordered them to operate the presses in his printing house, which he had recently set up." In captivity, the violent must put their strength to the service of the written word. They shall be slaves of the book—but the books that Gargantua publishes can only be liberating books. In Rabelais's own work we can already trace the ways in which books were supplanting the spoken word. In the libraries planned for the utopian abbey of Thélème, "free men" will meet. At Thélème people do not make speeches: they converse and they gossip. When it comes to language, Rabelais playfully, as it were, expresses the highest expectations. He offers us an exemplary "discourse from the throne." This monarchical language is, as we have seen, essentially liberating and generous; it simultaneously distributes and attributes because it enunciates sovereign justice. It is against this imaginary language, exalted in the person of the prince, that we must measure all eloquent practices carried on not from the princely throne but opposite it, to alert the sovereign or his representatives: the speech of the people to the king; that of the Church and people to the king; and that of the man of law to the judge who decides in the king's name. The history of eloquence in France retains a more or less faithful memory of certain notable *statements* of sovereign discourse, but the great *texts* whose fame lives on are those that argue or protest against the usurpers who wield unjust power, those that defend the cause of public peace.

Fettered Eloquence

Of the words attributed to its former sovereigns, French national memory has retained only snatches of military eloquence, proclamations and cries from the battlefield, or else brief acknowledgments of either an excess of monarchical power ("L'État, c'est moi") or its precariousness ("J'ai trop aimé la guerre"; "Après moi, le déluge").

This is not to say that certain monarchs were not keen to gain admiration for their eloquence. As Marc Fumaroli points out, this was the case with Henri III, who "succumbed to the temptation of an eloquent monarchy," whereas "Henri IV and even more Louis XIII, who made it clear that speeches bored him, clung to an *imperatoria brevitas* consistent with monarchical authority."[18] The person who uttered the royal "We" did not need to utter it himself in public. He indicated his superiority by having his edicts and decrees *read by others.* No one could dispute the king's *bon plaisir* or *pleine puissance.*

The period of unrest and disorder that accompanied the rise of the absolute monarchy also witnessed growing dissension among humanists and religious movements. Civil peace remained elusive despite the increased importance attached to ancient models and theological authorities. These were invoked on behalf of the monarchy, which, if tolerant, could guarantee public peace. They were also plundered for powerful language with which to attack princes in the name of liberty: heroic paradigms exonerated those who called for rebellion and tyrannicide. History has preserved the memory—but not the actual words—of such "moderates" as Pibrac and above all the admirable Michel de L'Hospital, who tried to prove to their fellow citizens that discussion, and hence the recourse to persuasion, were preferable to civil war. A great scholar, Pierre Pithou, joined their cause and included a "Speech of Monsieur d'Aubray for the Third Estate" in his *Satire Ménippée.* This was a *written* speech, combined with verse, and its eloquence significantly coincided with a power vacuum during an interregnum.

Pithou, who wrote with such vehemence about the misery of the Parisian populace, did not reject ancient authorities. To justify the love affairs of Henri de Navarre, for example, he invoked Mars and Venus, Titus and Berenice. Before the Third Republic, French eloquence had seldom broken its ties with the classical past, which it interpreted, adduced, imitated, refuted, and dangerously exposed to parody. (Two pretexts for parody were erudition and solemn sublimity. The ridiculous orator, specimens of which are found in other parts of the *Satire Ménippée,* was one of the great resources of comedy: the burlesque sermons of the Middle Ages, the harangue of Janotus Bragmardo [Rabelais], the tirades of Sganarelle [Molière], and the plea of Petit-Jean [Racine, *Les Plaideurs*] were all unforgettable variants on the abuse of language that continued to amuse the public in its modern forms: it takes great art to simulate the failure of art).

Even those who, like Montaigne, were wary of political eloquence fought it with arguments borrowed from the ancients:

> It is an instrument invented to manipulate and agitate a crowd and a disorderly populace, and an instrument that is employed in sick states, like medicine. To those states where the vulgar, or the ignorant, or all men held all power—such as Athens, Rhodes, and Rome—and where all things were in perpetual turmoil, there orators flocked. . . . Eloquence flourished most at Rome when affairs were in the worst state and agitated by the storm of civil wars; as a free

> and untamed field bears the lustiest weeds. From that it seems that monarchical governments need it less than others.[19]

In fact, Montaigne, without acknowledging his obvious source, has here borrowed Maternus's argument from Tacitus' *Dialogue on Orators.*[20] Maternus knows that the peace imposed by the imperial authorities is not favorable to great political eloquence or the glory that goes with it. He has retired from public life to write tragedies, just as Montaigne had done to write his *Essais.* His *Cato,* which was "dangerously bold" and had "wounded the authorities," may have been a way for Maternus to influence the public mind indirectly, just as the teaching in the *Essais* was a substitute for the overt political action in which Montaigne, though a *parlementaire,* was unable and unwilling to engage fully. When he became a poet, Maternus claimed that he now practiced a "different eloquence, sounder and more august." Montaigne, seeking refuge "in the bosom of the learned muses," was animated by a similar conviction. But with Maternus, the conversion to poetry was not exempt from a certain note of nostalgia, even when he condemned the disorders of the republican age: "Truly great, truly striking eloquence is the daughter of that license that people foolishly call liberty. It is the companion of sedition, the goad of popular rage. Incapable of obedience and subordination, stubborn, foolhardy, and arrogant, it is unlikely to arise in any well-ordered society."[21]

The place designated in this text, which urges us to look back to the heroic age of public speaking, is the Forum of the earlier republican age, or, looking even farther back, the agora of democratic Athens. In the sixteenth century (often through references to Tacitus or even more directly to Cicero or Demosthenes and the raucous cohort of ancient orators), the Forum—that unique place, the idealized heart of the ancient city—would once again become the common ground of countless speeches delivered in any number of places in France, such as the Estates General held in various cities, the *lits de justice* in which the king pronounced judgment in the Sainte-Chapelle, sessions of the Parlement of Paris, and so on. Regardless of differences among institutions, high magistrates, who frequently aimed to achieve political eloquence, wished to be worthy of the ancient orators who spoke in the Forum or before the Senate. This ambition found opportunities to express itself in the period between the first religious struggles and the end of the Fronde (and later it would enjoy free rein in revolutionary assemblies and then, after the Napoleonic interlude, in the Chamber of Deputies). But it was a thwarted ambition. It has justly been said that Guillaume Du Vair's treatise *De l'éloquence française et des raisons pourquoi elle est demeurée si basse* (1595) formulated a program that was not destined to succeed. Du Vair's "oratorical magistracy" has remained without posterity, although he employed all the resources of persuasive invention and elocution in pleading the cause of eloquence.[22] He cited the example of Athens and Rome: "Those cities produced admirable orators, primarily in times when the popular estate ruled. Liberty nourished minds with courageous grandeur and gave them the means to extend themselves."[23] While praising the French monarchical tradition, he criticized the monarchy for not having encouraged the training of true statesmen: "Our French state has been governed since its inception by Kings, whose sovereign power has in truth delivered us from the miseries, calamities, and confusions that are common in popular states but has also deprived us of exercise for worthy minds and of the means to gain skill in dealing with affairs."

The nobility could be forgiven for neglecting the study of letters, since this failing could be converted into a virtue praised by the ancients themselves: giving priority to deeds over words, to *doing* over *saying:* "Content with the rank bestowed on them by birth or valor, they sought no honor but that of arms or, in peacetime, of administration." It would suffice, however, if noblemen, convinced of the advantages to be gained from eloquence, were to turn to "the muses." Eloquence would then become glorious once again. It would cease to be manipulated obscurely "at the bars of the Parlements or in public pulpits" by "abject persons," by the "lowest and most servile spirits." Du Vair appealed to aristocratic pride to win his readers over to the cause of public eloquence. He failed. As long as they wished to be heroic and until they could obtain the titles that were their substantial reward, nobles, while demonstrating their virtue on the battlefield, might throw their support to great royal ministers in exchange for favors, or they might turn against them. When a noble wished to become a *lettré,* it was in order to practice the art of the salon portrait or maxim, or perhaps to write a memoir in which defeat at the hands of the queen and Mazarin became the stuff of retrospective political reflection. The only resource available to men of ambition was, in Hegelian terminology, the "discourse of flattery": they could appear at court and try to please the king, his mistresses, and his high officials. In Versailles, however, the very art of conversation depended on a profound silence. The segment of the nobility that sustained the court had no choice but to perfect and abide by a complex code whose first fundamental rule was, "Never contradict the king." To please was imperative. All merit, the moralists tell us, was equated with being seen regularly at court; an individual's personal qualities had nothing to do with it.[24] When it came to signs of devotion, "manners" mattered more than speeches.

Etiquette, by bestowing significance on the insignificant, filled the space vacated by dangerous eloquence. Hobbes, the theorist of absolutism, condemned eloquence because of its destructive effects. By way of sedition and faction it rent the fabric of the state and reduced individuals to a war of all against all.

> Eloquence is nothing else than the power of winning belief of what we say. And to that end we must appeal to the emotions and concerns of the listener. . . . Seeing then eloquence and want of discretion concur to the stirring of rebellion, it may be demanded, what part each of these acteth therein? The

> daughters of Pelias, king of Thessaly, desiring to restore their old decrepit father to the vigor of his youth, by the counsel of Medea, chopped him in pieces, and set him a boiling with I know not what herbs in a cauldron, but could not revive him again. So when eloquence and want of judgment go together, want of judgment, like the daughters of Pelias, consenteth, through eloquence, which is as the witchcraft of Medea, to cut the commonwealth in pieces, upon pretense or hope of reformation, which when things are in combustion, they are not able to effect.[25]

Gianluigi Goggi pertinently reminds us that for Diderot, the dismemberment of the aged Aeson by his daughter-in-law Medea was, by contrast, emblematic of the way in which one restores "vigor to a nation" or "moral fiber to a corrupted people."[26]

The rostrum in our modern sense did not exist until the Revolution, which set up "four planks" on which orators prepared to brave peril in pursuit of glory could stand. But, *pace* Joseph Reinach,[27] the history of political eloquence in France before the Revolution is not a blank page. Sometimes that eloquence took written form and was semi-clandestine (Étienne de La Boétie's *Servitude volontaire* is the best example). It was also an eloquence of harangues, or "remonstrances." But when a *parlementaire* addressed a remonstrance to the king, he spoke with one "knee on the ground." Such a humble posture precluded the more democratic debate that the rostrum encouraged (only the chair stands higher than the rostrum). Lanson did full justice to L'Hospital and Du Vair in his *Histoire de la littérature française*. Yet he was well aware that in the final analysis their eloquence tended to confirm the absence of eloquence by conferring on the king the power necessary to restore public order. "In the midst of crisis, L'Hospital spoke to the king, Du Vair to Parlement, and both spoke forcefully, simply, and effectively. What killed eloquence was the triumph of the cause that both men served: the monarchy. Augustus had squelched Roman eloquence. . . . Henri IV, in pacifying the kingdom, shut the mouths of its orators, whom people had barely had time to listen to."[28] Indeed, it was the consistent policy of the court to reduce the function of Parlement to the registration of edicts by limiting its rights of remonstrance. Let us admire the terms in which, according to his memoirs, *premier président* Mathieu Molé addressed the queen regent Anne of Austria in June 1648:

> It can fairly be said to Your Majesty that the greatest advantage the sovereign can possess on earth consists in reigning always by love for his subjects, and that he can exercise no more baleful empire than by obtaining constant obedience through terror. . . .
>
> These faithful officeholders and luminaries established to promulgate and accredit their sovereign's will, these repositories of public law and order, and above all this Parlement of France, could well promise themselves that the

> time that heals all wounds and brings remedies to all ills would also serve for those that they had suffered to date. But owing to an extreme misfortune, new injuries occur day after day, hence these ills augment daily, and one sees, through an unfortunate encounter, that this hand, so powerful and beneficent to everyone, all too often uses its strength to weaken them, or rather to reduce them to nothing, since Your Majesty's mere name lends credence to all that they have been made to suffer.
>
> Those charged with responsibilities are not deprived of them, but they are reduced to such a point . . . that freedom of suffrage having been denied them along with knowledge of what is theirs, they remain almost without function.[29]

Omer Talon, the *avocat général,* had spoken in a similar vein during the *lit de justice* of January 15, 1648, at times adopting an even sharper tone (but at other times indulging in rather too much erudite ornament):

> You are, Sire, our sovereign lord. Your Majesty's puissance comes from on high: Your Majesty must account for your actions, after God, only to your conscience. But your glory depends on our being free men rather than slaves. The grandeur of your State and the dignity of your crown are measured by the quality of those who obey it. . . .
>
> For ten years now, Sire, the countryside has lain in ruins. Peasants, reduced to sleeping on straw, see their furniture sold to pay taxes they cannot bear. In order to maintain Paris in luxury, millions of innocent souls are obliged to live on bread, bran, and oats. . . .
>
> If you please, Madame, look into the depths of your heart and consider the misery of the people. At night, in the solitude of your chapel, consider what pain, bitterness, and consternation all the officers of your kingdom may feel at seeing their property confiscated when they have committed no crime.[30]

Here, the "very humble remonstrance" of the *parlementaire* has adopted the tone of religious exhortation. We see the possibility of a transition from a political speech to the eloquence of the pulpit. That transition was facilitated by the fact that political eloquence, reduced to silence, would abandon to the Church the entire task of denouncing misery and inequality and pointing out the "eminent dignity of the poor." Speakers would appeal to the responsibility of the powerful before God, because they could not emphasize enough how much they owed to their people. In his papers Talon added: "My speech . . . touched the Queen and displeased the ministers. In her carriage on the way back to the Louvre, the Queen spoke well of it." We have an invaluable account—from Mme de Motteville in her *Mémoires*—of the way in which the effects of this initially impressive speech were nullified in the queen's mind:

> That night, [Mazarin] made war on the Queen because Talon had ordered her to her chapel. He was seconded by the princess's personal servants, who felt that she had stayed there too long and who, interested in defending their own interests, continually reproached her for it. . . . Princes rarely encounter people who speak to them in strong terms, and such people are usually held up to ridicule by their courtiers.

Adopting a moralistic point of view, Mme de Motteville explains why remonstrances addressed to the conscience of the prince are ineffective: since "the reason" of princes "is weakened by the care that is taken to hide the truth from them, they scarcely try to distinguish between truth and falsehood. Letting their minds run to sloth and passing lightly over good and evil, they always go where it pleases their ministers to lead them."[31] Although a remonstrance might be vehement and urgent, it was open to challenge and might fail to make a lasting impression on a weak soul incapable of the effort needed to *discriminate* between good and evil and act in consequence. What Mme de Motteville shrewdly points out is true not only of the psychology of the great: eloquent language must encounter judgment and will, *critical* independence and decisiveness, on the part of a listener consequently impervious to insidious flattery.[32]

The Court, The Theater, and Preaching

The absence of deliberative eloquence in the seventeenth century does not imply an absence of oratorical art. Indeed, the opposite is true, as if the shutting off of public expression of political dissent had forced language—the desire to speak—into other channels. Marc Fumaroli quite rightly notes that "the progressive elaboration of a French rhetoric in the seventeenth century" was a "function of the realization on the part of writers and authors of rhetoric of the differences between the ancient Forum and the Court of France."[33] This new rhetoric would govern a whole "literature."

Thibaudet, placing particular stress on a favorite idea of Brunetière's, painted a picture of the seventeenth century in which religious eloquence was paramount:

> Why did the seventeenth century, alone of our four great literary centuries, sustain a powerful clerical literature, over which Bossuet presided? . . . Because of those four centuries, the seventeenth was the least bookish, the most oratorical, the one in which the spoken word predominated over the written. . . . The seventeenth century was a century of spoken genres: theater, religious eloquence, and speaking well were uniquely valued at court and in the city: it was the century of Racine, Molière, and Bossuet because it was also the century of Vaugelas. The Catholic Church was the place where orators

> spoke. A priest did not need to know how to write to his bishop. He did need to know how to speak to his flock. In a world in which the highest values were attached to speech, he had every advantage. Remember that Louis XIV never opened a book (when he could not sleep, a reader, sometimes Racine, would read to him for a while) and never read state papers, which secretaries summarized or excerpted for him. . . . Corneille, Racine, and Molière spoke to him through their actors, and the Church through its sermon writers.[34]

Although this description may seem simplistic, its aim is correct: Thibaudet portrays the king as the ultimate recipient of the words uttered on stage and of the speeches declaimed from the pulpit. Why not include within the realm of eloquence theatrical actions and dramatic situations that offered a pretext for great tirades constructed in the form of speeches? What could not be said in public life thus achieved indirect expression. Prohibitions were partially circumvented by way of fiction. On stage one could denounce the wicked counselors who, by flattering princely pleasures, led the mighty to disaster. The passions of tragedy, that unstable mix of love and ambition, must always compromise with *raison d'état*. As for comedy, when commissioned by Versailles its prologues and intermezzos had to celebrate the king's glory. But the vices and foolishness that it attacked almost always grew out of some trick of the imagination, some acceptance of illusion, from which it was not always clear that the monarch, infatuated as he was with his own glory, was exempt. Without neglecting the many ways in which this literature represented a compromise with courtly homage, one can still argue, with some justice, that it was a kind of muffled remonstrance, holding up models of true glory and generosity to the monarch while presenting him with the comic or monstrous humiliation reserved for those who forsake reason or are abandoned by grace. The theater thus performed the function reserved in discourse for the *exemplum* and oratorical narration. Furthermore, since the theater availed itself of multiple voices, it was apt to portray both a rhetoric of petition and a rhetoric of reply; it could concretely represent, in the mouths of its characters, the very different tones of sincere effusion and hypocritical insinuation. In order to speak to the king and address "the court and the city," it portrayed speakers in well-defined oratorical situations. That is why it is so common for nineteenth-century histories of eloquence to mix examples taken from the texts of orators with others taken from dramatic works.[35] When the orators of the Revolution later strove after the most dramatic effects, they did not always rely directly on the eloquence of the ancients but sometimes found models in the plays of Corneille and Voltaire.[36] There are connections between the eloquence of the classical theater and the future eloquence of the rostrum. (Conversely, theater audiences during the Revolution applauded speeches that they could apply to the current situation.)

Conflicts tend to fade with time. As we have seen, a twentieth-century critic was able to associate the names of great seventeenth-century playwrights with Bossuet as though they were fighting for the same cause (*spoken* literature) in a single lesson addressed to the king. In fact, the eloquence of the pulpit sought to reign alone, or at any rate above all others. Bossuet waged war on "comedy." He accused it of "stirring up flattering passions," and he denounced dramatic heroes for capturing our sympathy and soliciting our identification. The result was that people averted their eyes from the one model, the one spectacle that legitimately deserved their attention: "If we need spectacles, spilt blood, and love to move us, what is more beautiful or more touching than the bloody death of Jesus Christ and his martyrs?"[37] For it was only proper that the authority of Scripture, Christ, and his Church should reign supreme over all the powers of this world. The primary purpose of persuasion is to recall the voice of this authority, to revive, in the mind of the believer, the scenes of a Passion that invests all history with meaning and concerns each individual being. Through dogma and symbol the Church revealed to kings and lords the conditions under which political power and the superiorities of "rank" could be inscribed within a larger order that upheld and guaranteed them. It warned them that they were nothing, that if they were the legitimate rulers of their people it was only by virtue of a special election that made them responsible before their consciences and before God. The preacher was himself a *delegate:* he recalled an antecedent utterance which alone possessed authentic value. He interpreted, whether for demanding audiences or simple souls, a Truth and a Holy Mystery of which he himself must only be, according to Saint Augustine, the humble servant. And therein lay all the ambiguity of Christian eloquence, which was a matter of debate among the Fathers of the Church and which fueled new quarrels in the Reformation and Counter Reformation as various efforts were made to define the best way of spreading the good word. Is the "*art* of preaching" not a contradiction in terms? The first verses of the Bible (as pseudo-Longinus states) are sublime; the words of Christ and the Apostles are simplicity itself. These were the very words dictated by the Holy Spirit. Is there any need to say more or to say something else? Could the sermon, which was based on a few verses of Scripture, which it repeated step by step, be anything other than an invitation to a better understanding of the holy writ through the preacher's reasonable applications, which were shaped by the nature of the occasion and the quality of the audience? At times, preachers, inspired by their examples, might be vouchsafed an almost prophetic gift. Touched by grace, they could change the inner dispositions of their audience. But how rarely! And how much more frequently did their art—that is, their skills, their "rhetorical colors," and the portraits they painted, even if they were of the Passion—prevent them from conveying the message they they were supposed to be getting across in all its purity! Of course we know that eloquence is the art of mastering the feelings and convictions of our listeners. When it is a question of converting or opening the eyes of the ignorant or of rounding up stray souls, or of encouraging faith and good works, the sanctity of the goal justifies the recourse to the impressive resources of language: the preacher's heat or smoothness wins hearts and instructs minds, preparing them to receive a truth of which the man in the pulpit is but the "interpreter."[38]

But the time came when sermoners and preachers would be listened to and read for the pleasure they gave. What peril lay in store for the preacher who, with the purest of intentions, set out to *please* his audience! That peril lay in attaching to his own person and speech sentiments that ought to have been bestowed on more "eminent" objects. When Bossuet delineated the true powers of pulpit eloquence, he never failed to mention the perversion lying in wait for the preacher, who must seek to triumph over them.[39] Yes, "faith begins with listening." Yes, in the very Gospel, the mystery of the incarnation gives itself a "second body." Eternal Wisdom made itself perceptible in written form after "having made itself perceptible in the flesh that it took on in the womb of Mary." But God had made himself humble through his incarnation, and "the preaching of apostles must not seem brilliant." Saint Paul's true strength lay in his avowal of weakness.

> Do not expect the Apostle to come caress your ears with harmonious cadences or flatter your mind with idle curiosities. . . . His speech, far from flowing with that agreeable gentleness, that temperate evenness that we admire in orators, seems uneven and incoherent to those who have not gone into it deeply enough. And the delicate of the earth, who, they say, have sharp ears, are offended by the harshness of his irregular style.

In celebrating Father Bourgoing's merits as a preacher, Bossuet dismissed "unfaithful preachers who debase their dignity to the point of placing the ministry to teach at the service of the desire to please."[40] Bossuet, who is here speaking to ecclesiastics, warns them against the abuse of trust and distortion they become guilty of when they "do not blush to purchase acclamation with instruction, words of flattery with words of truth, and the idle fruits of frivolity with the solid and substantial nourishment that God has prepared for his children!" What do bad preachers do? Precisely what playwrights, poets, and novelists do: they move the passions for the pleasure they provide rather than for uplifting the soul; they appeal to the imagination without aspiring to overcome its spell. In a world in which the "great according to the flesh" are only too inclined to "idle ostentation," those who should dissuade them imitate them. Rather than teach and admonish, they seek to show off. La Bruyère, who agreed with Bossuet on this point, believed that amusement had taken precedence over "noble simplicity" and seriousness in religious exhortation. It is important to condemn comedy if "Christian discourse itself has become a spectacle."[41] Nothing was left but outward appearances and amusements—an aesthetic game, no more "evangelical sadness." This was

> compensated for by the advantages of expression, by inflections of voice, by regularity of gesture, by choice of words, by lengthy enumerations. No one listens seriously to the holy word any more: it is one amusement among a thousand others, a game in which there is emulation and there are chance-takers. . . . Eloquent assaults are launched at the very foot of the altar and in the presence of the mysteries. The listener sets himself up as the judge of the preacher, to condemn or to applaud, and is not converted by the speech he favors any more than by the one he opposes.[42]

It was a notorious fact, confirmed by La Bruyère, that the prize in this game was not only literary glory but also the chance of a bishopric. The pulpit from which preachers denounced the vanities of this world was a stepping stone for the ambitious. ("A man says in his heart, 'I shall preach,' and he preaches, and there he is in his pulpit with no talent or vocation other than the need for a benefice."[43])

The fact that preachers offered their audiences not the spectacle of the Passion but that of their own oratory, their artificial stagecraft, was grounds for severe moral reprobation. It was seen as a danger by people who held religious orthodoxy to be the source of all order in public and private life. If, in the ancient edifice of Christian society, the profane order was buttressed by the religious order, what was happening now was like the collapse of a principal pillar. But in a transitional period, in the eyes of the lover of belles-lettres, religious eloquence could be counted as one of the signal achievements of the age of Louis XIV. Even Bossuet's praise of Saint Paul's *unpolished* speech had an admirable rhythm, style, harmony, and color, did it not? And did he not seek to please even as he denounced preachers overly concerned with ornamentation? The system of belles-lettres included eloquence, both profane and religious, alongside poetry (epic, lyric, and dramatic) and history (sacred and profane). For defenders of the Moderns, such as Perrault, the great religious orators did more than make up for the absence of political eloquence and the relatively modest role assigned to judicial eloquence (mainly represented by the sober, lackluster, and correct Patru). In fact, the argument about the connection, the fundamental solidarity, between eloquence and liberty was raised on behalf of religious eloquence, which, it was claimed, was essential for man's inner liberty, or liberation from sin. For the Moderns, the liberating function of eloquence had not been lost but merely shifted to the spiritual plane, where it dealt with more important matters:

> Instead of stirring or quelling sedition as in the time of the ancient republics, do our preachers not use the same rhetorical figures either to exhort sinners to shake off the yoke of tyrannical passions or to quell the disturbances that

> those same passions continually provoke in the depths of their souls? Never have things been better for eloquence, for what is at stake is nothing less than salvation and eternal life.[44]

Voltaire, in the thirty-second chapter of the *Siècle de Louis XIV*, credits Bossuet with a genius that, as it flourished in the funeral oration, "resembled poetry a little" and—scandalously—generated the same interest as the theater: "The greater the woes of the deceased, the more felicitous are the subjects of these eloquent plays. In a sense it is the same *as in tragedies*, where what is most interesting is the misfortunes of the principal characters." But Voltaire, it will come as no surprise to discover, gives short shrift to the Gospel. Though an admirer of Bourdaloue, he cannot help criticizing him for clinging to "the custom of preaching on a text." In the article "Eloquence" that he wrote for the *Encyclopédie*, Voltaire mentions Massillon—the most moralistic and least theological and dogmatic of preachers, hence the one most favored by the *philosophes*—and praises him for a "painting" that has impressed the public as a great moment in the theater might. This is "what happened when M. Massillon preached his famous sermon on the *small number of the elect*":

> There came a point at which the whole audience was gripped, and nearly everyone half stood up in an involuntary motion. The murmur of acclamation and surprise grew so loud that it disturbed the speaker, and his uneasiness only increased the pathos of the passage. Here it is: "I suppose that the last hour for all of us has arrived, that the heavens are going to open upon our heads, that time is past and eternity is beginning, that Jesus Christ will appear before us to judge us according to our works, and that we are all here awaiting his decree of eternal life or eternal death."
>
> This figure, one of the boldest ever employed, is one of the finest devices of eloquence that can be read among ancient nations as well as modern ones.

Thus reclaimed for literature, the preacher's work ceased to belong to the corpus of edification and joined instead the corpus of seduction. No wonder, then, that the emergence of sensuality in the adolescent Chateaubriand found its literary culmination in Massillon, whose texts were read alongside those of Vergil, Lucretius, and Tibullus: "The volumes of Massillon containing the sermons of *The Sinful Woman* and *The Prodigal Son* never left my side. I was allowed to leaf through them, because no one suspected what I found in them."[45]

Prolegomena to the Revolution

Simplifying greatly (and leaving aside rural France, where men like Bridaine made their mark[46]), we can say that after 1715 the more or less clandestine writings of the *philosophes* supplanted preaching in shaping the public mind—or at any rate that fraction of the public mind represented by the "enlightened class." But the debate about eloquence did not end. Indeed, the *philosophes* did not fail to seek the aid of eloquence in the form of written discourse, academic encomium, "memoranda to be consulted" in conjunction with a just cause, open letters, and so on.

After Descartes, rationalism substituted *method* for rhetoric as a means of persuasion: the art of speaking was supposed to be subsumed by the art of reasoning without pointless ornament. There was no important subject not susceptible to rational demonstration.[47] This argument, developed by Malebranche, tended to disallow the artifice of appeals to the imagination and the "passions" (with an exception for poets, whose craft was to deceive agreeably). Rhetoric, dismissed as sophistry, was barred from the realm of clear and distinct ideas. This led to a dispute between Arnauld and Malebranche, in which Arnauld defended the role of the senses and the imagination in approaching the truths of faith.[48] A disciple of Malebranche, the Oratorian Bernard Lamy, began his *Entretiens sur les sciences* by condemning eloquence in the voice of Aminte: eloquence was as dangerous as poetry for individuals "of little judgment."[49] "We are wise and reasonable only when we heed the counsel of those truths that God has engraved in our hearts, that they might serve as rules for our actions and our words." Thus every person was asked to open "the eyes of the spirit" within himself or herself. But this argument was answered, in the voice of Théodose, by another pointing out the need for instruction: "Few people are capable of learning by themselves what the truth within the soul tells us. . . . Mute wisdom is useless." Instruction is necessary, and instruction requires knowledge of how to please: "Eloquence is therefore necessary, since it is through instruction that those who have reasonable thoughts and feelings form similar thoughts and inspire similar feelings in their listeners." To be sure, "false brilliance," "high-flown words," and "overly elaborate cadences" were to be avoided. Correct eloquence was a beneficial magic, which enabled the listener to *see* (as inwardly evident) what eloquence caused him to *hear:* "Eloquent is the speaker who enchants his listeners so that they are not aware that they are listening to words but imagine seeing what he tells them because the image formed in their minds is so vivid. There is no greater talent than this, nor is there any of greater utility in the principal employments of the Republic."

Now, just as, according to Descartes, "common sense is the most widely shared thing in the world," eloquence is virtually universal. All we need to communicate our ideas and feelings are strong powers of persuasion, not art. Since the word of God is "engraved in our souls," the authority we ought to heed is the truth that we *read* in ourselves in order to *show* it to others by telling them about it.

Since there is no one in whom God has not "engraved" his precepts, anyone can convey eloquently a truth of which he is sufficiently convinced. So much for the embarrassing idea that great eloquence was the exclusive property of Greece and Rome and possible only under a free government. As early as 1672, Father Rapin maintained that "eloquence can reign anywhere when it is authentic and has what it takes to command a hearing."[50] Turgot, in a youthful text (1748), seems to echo this view: "Among all peoples and in all ages, passions and affairs have produced truly eloquent men. Histories are full of powerful and persuasive eloquence in the midst of barbarity."[51] The dictates of the heart or of inner reason and enthusiasm are worth more than all the masters of rhetoric. The most eloquent representatives of the Enlightenment had no use for manuals of rhetoric. Rousseau claimed that in his case "warm persuasion" had always "done duty for eloquence."[52] Voltaire appealed to the Enlightenment above all and to genius: "In an enlightened age, genius, aided by examples, knows more than all the masters say."[53]

All these were excellent reasons for "men of letters" to claim eloquence without the sanction of a public or religious function. This egalitarian attitude (allowing for the proviso of genius, of course) anticipated and laid the groundwork for political egalitarianism. Were those who were enlightened or "warmed" by natural reason supposed to remain silent? Voltaire, the scourge of *l'Infâme*, had a church built at Ferney *(Deo erexit Voltaire)*, and there he preached. He wrote prayers, in particular the one that forms the conclusion to the *Traité sur la tolérance*. Diderot, in the pieces he gave Raynal for the *Histoire des deux Indes*, steadily heightened the oratorical tone and included any number of pathetic apostrophes; this was his way of following the example of Socrates. As for Rousseau, when he wrote the *Discours sur les sciences et les arts* (for the prize offered by the Academy of Dijon in 1750), he borrowed some of his themes—the critique of luxury, spectacles, and idle curiosity—from preachers, yet his book seemed new and scandalous because he made no attempt to contrast these culpable activities with the salvation reserved for pious souls: he denounced the ills of society without proposing any substitute other than the image of great civic virtues, virtues that corrupt countries might have irremediably lost. The burden of sin was borne by society, and conversion, which preaching demanded of individual consciences, became something that could be sought (if it was not too late) at the level of political institutions and educational methods. Men of letters thus seized upon eloquence as a way of practicing a substitute "ministry." No matter that well-born men destined for positions in public service had received a comprehensive training in rhetoric: they did not know what to do with it. The writer, who was freer and less constrained by proprieties, could be eloquent in their stead and even win them over to his cause. After 1789 his eloquence would be put to the purpose of supplanting them and assuming political responsibilities for himself.

Eloquence, which for several decades had found its place in the prose of the Enlightenment, was never as vehement as when it evoked its past grandeur, deploring in books the absence of popular assemblies and denouncing the corruption of language itself. When people in the eighteenth century read the words of Maternus in Tacitus, they no longer sensed the resignation to changed historical circumstances or the readiness to use the now idled energies of language in another art; instead what they read was a veiled condemnation of despotism. Morabin, the translator and prefacer of Tacitus' *Dialogue on Orators,* argued in 1732 that the debate over the superiority of the Ancients or the Moderns in that work was of secondary importance: "Beyond the apparent design, the author had a private one . . . which was to show that if the Moderns had degenerated, it was not their fault as much as the fault of the times or, rather, the Prince who governed at that time" (pp. xiii–xiv). This, then, was the critical intention which, at the beginning of an age of resolute criticism, was perceived as the predominant idea in Tacitus' text. The commonplace notion of a connection between eloquence and democratic liberty was henceforth revived. Criticism also relied on another authority. Pseudo-Longinus' *Treatise on the Sublime,* translated into French by Boileau, was widely read. In Chapter 44 we read:

> Why is it that in our century one finds any number of orators who know how to manipulate an argument and who even possess oratorical style . . . yet so few who can rise very high in the sublime. . . . Is it not . . . as is often said, that popular government nourishes and shapes great geniuses, for until now, almost all talented orators flourished and died with it? Indeed, . . . there is nothing, perhaps, that uplifts the souls of great men more than liberty, or that excites and awakens more powerfully in us that natural sentiment which leads us to emulation and that noble ardor to see ourselves raised above others. Furthermore, the prizes that are offered in Republics stimulate, as it were, and add the final polish to the minds of Orators, impelling them to cultivate with care the talents they have received from nature. Thus one feels the liberty of their country glowing in their speeches.
>
> But we . . . who from early childhood have learned to bear the yoke of a legitimate domination, who have been as it were enveloped by monarchical customs and ways of doing things when our imaginations were still tender and capable of all sorts of impressions; in a word, we who have never tasted that vital and fecund source of eloquence, by which I mean liberty; what generally happens to us is that we become great and magnificent flatterers.

As in Tacitus, but with greater emphasis, here we see love of liberty, hope of glory, and, more materially, the expectation of "prizes" and "awards" combine their influences so long as "popular government" allows them to hold sway. A similar text (assuredly one of many) explains the fascination that the republican idea could have held not only for (often impecunious) men of letters of the Ancien Régime but also for the privileged who had received a good rhetorical education. The notion of the close link between eloquence and literature, which was already current in the time of Longinus, enjoyed renewed favor in the eighteenth century despite being hackneyed. Voltaire, before stating that "in an enlightened age" genius can achieve eloquence with no teacher other than "examples," had subscribed to the general principle. His article "Eloquence" includes these lines:

> Sublime eloquence, it is said, belongs to liberty alone, because it consists in stating bold truths and exhibiting powerful reasons and portraits. Often a master does not like truth, fears reason, and prefers a compliment to bold strokes. . . . In France great eloquence has scarcely been known at the bar because it does not lead to honors as it did in Athens or Rome or does in London today and does not have great public interests as its object.

In his *Essai sur la société des gens de lettres et des grands* (1752), d'Alembert was concerned about the corruption of language.[54] At issue here is not just eloquence, the "daughter of genius and liberty," but the spirit of the entire nation as vested in that essential institution, language. The corruption of language was both a cause and a consequence of moral corruption. Hence d'Alembert, even as he rejects the suspect "heats" of eloquence, insists on the need to preserve the purity and propriety of terms, the simplicity and clarity of expression: the stakes were ethical and political. It was a question of protecting the nation from a mortal poison as well as preserving weapons for the cause of liberty. (Note that, in a strategy similar to the one that Jean Paulhan denounced in *Les Fleurs de Tarbes*, d'Alembert proposed and practiced an austere rhetoric in the guise of a critique of rhetoricians.) D'Alembert's advice to men of letters was to "live in unity" and take a vow of "liberty, truth, poverty." If they paid the price, they might reverse the course of events; they might even "set the law for the rest of the nation in matters of taste and philosophy." By safeguarding their independence, serving a precise logic with their words, and avoiding frivolity, men of letters might control collective opinion and hence become masters of the nation. A conditional hope was affirmed here: the threat of decadence, the distressing image of the decline of Rome, was perhaps only a rhetorical ruse to make the call for unity among "men of letters" all the more imperious. That call did not go unheeded. Whether united or scattered, many of those who had attempted to live in Paris before 1789 on literary employments, writing brochures, and accepting large or small sums for journalism—commoners, provincials who took themselves for Jean-Jacques, and black sheep of the nobility—would look upon the Estates General, revolutionary broadsheets, and political clubs and assemblies as an opportunity at last to make themselves heard, achieve fame, and wipe away the humiliations of youth.[55] "To speak to the assembled people": this, according to Rousseau, was no longer possible owing to the very defects of a refined and degenerate language. In the *Contrat social* (1762), his criticism is scathing: "Your dull tongues cannot make themselves heard in the open air, you give more for your profit than for your freedom, and you fear slavery less than misery."[56]

It will come as no surprise, then, that in 1789 the challenge was taken up by members of the clergy and the bar: now that the moment had come to regenerate the nation, was not the time ripe for a rebirth, or rather a birth, of French political eloquence? And who better to represent that eloquence than men who had learned the oratorical craft—lawyers and priests—but never practiced it at the rostrum for the simple reason that the institutions that had confined them to the pulpit and bar had never offered them any *place* resembling a rostrum from which to speak? Since the early seventeenth century *remontrances d'ouverture* and other remarkable briefs had been published with some care, but their reputation endured for little more than a generation even among *gens de robe*.[57] They failed to gain a place in long-term memory, which was "literary" and above all scholarly. In 1768, the lawyer P.-L. Gin, in a book titled *De l'éloquence du barreau*, dismissed all judicial eloquence before the age of Louis XIV.[58] Rollin, in his *Traité des études* (1726), though generally careful to provide French examples, stated that "the excessive modesty of our orators" (speaking of the most recent of them, whom he also praised) forced him to "go back to the source" and seek his models "in Athens and Rome." But things were somewhat confused. Marmontel, in his article "Barreau" in the *Encyclopédie*, set matters straight: the Moderns, among whom he mentions only Le Maître, Patru, and Daguesseau, did not need the skills of the Roman orators. The cases they tried required only a discreet use of the pathetic: "The principle of the eloquence of the bar is . . . that the judge needs to be enlightened, not moved." The confusion stemmed from the fact that the Moderns, unlike the Ancients, never pleaded before the people. Marmontel (like the other *philosophes* mentioned above) held that the people were the obligatory audience of the highest eloquence, because the people, who could change the law, were the sovereign authority whose decision the orator had to influence. If the orator's speech succeeded, he became, for a day at least, the masters' master, the legislators' advisor:

> In speaking of the Ancients, the bar is often confused with the rostrum, and lawyers are often confused with orators, no doubt because the one employment led to the other and frequently the same man exercised both.
>
> In Athens there were three sorts of tribunals: the areopagus, which judged only criminal cases and from which pathetic eloquence was banished; the tribunals of private judges, before whom non-capital cases were tried; and the tribunal of the people, who sat in judgment of laws alleged to be unjust and who had the right to abolish such laws. The first two tribunals correspond to our bar, the latter to the Roman forum or tribune.

> So long as Rome was free, the forum, in which the people were judge, was the supreme tribunal. The tribunals of the praetors, censors, equestrians, and even the senate were subordinate to the tribunal of the people. But from the time of Caesar and under the emperors, all great cases were assigned to the senate. The authority of the praetors increased; that of the people was abolished, and the eloquence of the forum perished along with freedom.

A text like this is illustrative for our understanding of the "revolution of the lawyers," that is, the presence of a considerable number of young legists in the Estates General and later in the revolutionary assemblies and among the personnel of the Revolution. And, along with many other "sources," it explains why these lawyers adopted the Roman tone. There is reason to doubt whether people in the countryside preserved precise memories of the *jacqueries* (peasant uprisings) or whether the people of Paris had clear memories of the time of the Ligue or the Fronde, even if there are striking similarities between different "popular uprisings" over time. On the other hand, lawyers, being educated men, steeped in belles-lettres, readers of pamphlets and gazettes, had a better knowledge of their predecessors, with whom they might try to identify: the revolutionaries in America, the parliamentarians of England, and above all—since the time had come to go back to first principles—the orators of the ancient Forum, before imperial despotism and decadence had reduced them to silence, and lastly, the orators of the "Carolingian fields of Mars," which Mably and the "Germanists" saw as an element of France's first constitution. These orators spoke to the people because the salvation of the fatherland depended on what the people decided. Called for by the written eloquence of philosophers and publicists, a foundational political language was made conceivable by the advent of the sovereign Third Estate in the summer of 1789. If popular sovereignty was one and indivisible, that language would have to be unanimous and unequivocal, just as the general will was simple and unequivocal (Rousseau, in order to save the general will from the risk of fragmentation, had carefully distinguished it from the "will of all," which, as the counting of individual votes reveals, is always fragmented). The unique source of the new sovereignty could only be *represented* by some spectacular *mise en scène:* collective oaths, ovations or hymns chanted by an entire nation, grandiose festivals set against a backdrop of emblems.[59] Only then would the persuasive language of the orator seem to fuse with the manifestation of the popular desire in its truth. This manifestation was supposed to be free and spontaneous even when it was obvious that the fusion was an illusion and that the popular voice was solicited, that it was responding to an appeal, almost a dictation. It was the thankless role of the opposition to suggest that the hypothetical will of the people was a fiction created by the orator who declared himself to be its interpreter. In a "Discours sur l'éloquence," quite probably written before the meeting of the Estates General, an anonymous author, who wanted modern eloquence to emulate the eloquence of the "first two peoples of the world," appealed to imagination and patriotism. But even in his encomium he could not stop himself from introducing ideas and terms that would help to make revolutionary speeches suspect: "The Nation as a body is the most ardent as well as the most flexible judge: it likes to be deeply moved and prefers the dazzling clarities of the imagination to the gentle and peaceful light of reason. The liberty of the orator *flatters* that of the Nation."[60]

Thus the orator can satisfy "a multitude of citizens who . . . want to see everything laid out in the open; who passionately desire truth, who clamor for it, and who receive it all the more warmly the more luminously it is presented." This project of an *unveiling* eloquence, which reveals a "dazzling" truth to all eyes, expresses to perfection the expectation of a reign of enlightenment and already prefigures certain romantic interpretations of revolutionary eloquence. But this "flexible" people, this imagination that triumphs over reason, this liberty that *flatters* another liberty—all these were arguments that could be turned against the eloquence of the revolutionary rostrum, reduced to mere "demagogy." It would become possible to denounce the "flatterers of the people" as it had once been possible to denounce the flatterers of the prince.

The Revolutionary Rostrum

Recent historiography of the French Revolution, interested in all aspects of a vast sociopolitical restructuring, has been no less interested in the role of oratory. Parliamentarism was born in France in 1789. And no sooner was speech liberated than it was free to speak ill of speech. The first thing to notice is that the discourse of both the rostrum (in assemblies and clubs) and the press was one that the first actors themselves knew to be far from unequivocal. Speakers discussed the good of the state but were suspected of conspiring *in secret* against the Revolution. And some conspired while *openly* denouncing conspirators. Historians, at least since Tocqueville, read revolutionary speeches and try to disentangle overt motives (radical innovation, patriotism, denunciation of plots, wisdom, virtue) from unseen consequences (the completion of the centralizing action of the monarchy) and implicit motives (the elimination of rival factions, access to employment, ideological outbidding). Attention must indeed be paid to what was said and written in public, even and perhaps especially if there is no directly discernible correlation between a complex situation (famine, inflation, war, etc.) and the opinions expressed, the motions and proclamations. Revolutionary eloquence is difficult to read, for it is at once the interpretation of a given situation and the verbal creation of a new one. As François Furet quite rightly states: "The Revolution was not merely a 'jump' from one society to another; it was also the set of means whereby civil society, suddenly 'opened up' by the crisis of power, liberated all the languages pregnant within it."[61] Even the historian must on occasion become a lexicographer and linguist. He must examine how different systems of argument, appeal, or accusation function, and he must analyze not only the style of discourse but its effect on the audience (applause, protest, response, etc.). It has proved fruitful to use the methods of pragmatics to study speeches and their audiences (H. U. Gumbrecht[62]) and a day in the work of the Convention (Peter France[63]). One can also dream about the incalculable mass of words in circulation at any given moment: brochures and gazettes, street cries, discussions related in memoirs, public debates in clubs and assemblies, paying due attention to interruptions and the sudden entry of various deputations. All this discourse has a structure, which might conceivably be represented as a polyphonic composition on several staffs, and could ultimately lead to new interpretive insights. Of course the task can never be completed, for we can never be sure of what was said: speeches were transcribed in different ways and often revised by the people who published them. Memorized words are like fiction.

Still, these multiple forms of speech command our interest, whereas in the nineteenth century people were more interested in singular individuals, whom they admired or detested and whose eloquence, whether fascinating or repulsive, inspired the style of the historians. The Revolution and its oratorical myth gave rise to imitators and adversaries, themselves stimulated by the ambition to demonstrate through similar (or superior) eloquence their own parliamentary personality: Constant and Chateaubriand, who were almost participating parties until Napoleon silenced the "metaphysicians"; Lamartine, Hugo, Thiers, and Jaurès, themselves parliamentarians who, as historians or mythographers of the Revolution, trained themselves on famous speeches they hoped to echo or refute with their own words. All of these men searched the revolutionary paradigm for coals to fire their enthusiasms or formulas for their oratorical strategies. And as long as the university was itself a place of oratorical priesthood, professors who taught courses on the Revolution could legitimately favor the great voices that protested, in the name of "talent," against the privileges of birth and the misuse of wealth: Michelet, Taine, and Aulard, each in very different ways, had reason to wax eloquent about past eloquence that for them remained a source of warmth or a motive for vengeful ardor. These approaches now seem old-fashioned: they often attached exaggerated importance to the heroes of the Revolution, to the "magic of words," to the volume of the voice, to invention, to the "storm effect." But these things were only the crest of the wave, and modern historians are more curious about the underlying currents. Still, the men of the Revolution for the most part deliberately assumed the role of orator to demonstrate their talents "in a vast theater." When popular assemblies, supported by the people and opposed by nothing more than irresolute authorities, decided on new political structures, on war, and on the death of the king, there was no reason to look upon eloquence as an epiphenomenon. It determined action—until the armies assembled by oratorical enthusiasm themselves became the dominant power.

On the death of Mirabeau, Marie-Joseph Chénier wrote a rather uninspired ode evoking in turn Mirabeau's childhood in the south of France, his role in the Estates General, and his legendary response to the Marquis de Dreux-Brézé:

Par son éloquence puissante,
De notre liberté naissante,
Je vois les ennemis vaincus:
Le despotisme en vain conspire,
Le peuple ressaisit l'empire,
Aux accents d'un nouveau Gracchus.
Sur une scène encore plus belle,
Au nom du peuple et de sa loi,
Je l'entends, plein du même zèle
Répondre à l'esclave d'un Roi.
[By his powerful eloquence,
From our nascent liberty,
I see enemies vanquished:
Despotism conspires in vain,
The people have regained power
With the accents of a new Gracchus.
On an even more handsome stage,
In the name of the people and their law,
I hear him, full of the same zeal,
Answering the slave of a King.]

Two stanzas later, the poet does not hesitate to apostrophize the rostrum itself:

Couvre-toi d'un voile funèbre,
Témoin de ses brillants succès,
Tribune que rendit célèbre
Le Démosthène des Français.
[Cover yourself with a funeral veil,
Witness to his brilliant successes,
Rostrum made famous by
The Demosthenes of the French.][64]

Chénier has forgotten neither Rome nor Greece, seeing both as brought back to life by Mirabeau-Gracchus and Mirabeau-Demosthenes. Through memoirs and histories one could trace a series of images of Mirabeau as the emblematic hero of

FIGURE 12.1. Portrait of the Marquis de Mirabeau by Lonsing.

the rostrum. In the early days of the Revolution, "everyone knew by heart" his words at the royal session of the Estates (Rabaut Saint-Étienne, 1791). Barnave is said to have called him the Shakespeare of eloquence. Mirabeau was the first "great man" of the Revolution to be "pantheonized."[65] The former church of Sainte-Geneviève was refurbished to receive his remains: "For the first time in France, a man celebrated for his writing and for his eloquence received honors formerly accorded only to great noblemen or warriors."[66] Hence his depantheonization after the discovery of his ties to the court would be all the more humiliating. But famous scribes came to the rescue: "When he shook his mane and looked at the people, he stopped them in their tracks. When he raised his paw and bared his claws, the plebs whipped itself up into a frenzy. Amid the frightful disorder of one session, I saw him immobile on the rostrum, somber and ugly: he reminded me of Milton's chaos, impassive and without form at the center of its confusion."[67] Michelet, who held that *le peuple* was the only hero of the Revolution, could not stop himself from singling out Mirabeau alone in an otherwise anonymous procession of members of the Third Estate:

> He was plainly a man, the others merely shadows. . . . Indeed! No one would hail that dawn of liberty, that renewal of the soul, more ardently than he—he said as much to his friends. He would be born again, young with France, shed his stained old coat. . . . That he more than once had fallen into disgrace but always climbed back up—that gives a very imposing idea of the power of eloquence over this nation, more sensitive than any other to the genius of the spoken word.[68]

When Louis in seizing power attacked "parliamentarism" and had the Palais-Bourbon destroyed, Victor Hugo seized on the character of Mirabeau and cast him as the founding hero of free speech:

> They chose a vast hall and erected tiers of seats along the walls, and then they took planks and with those planks constructed in the middle of the hall a kind of platform. When the platform was finished, what in those days was called the nation, namely, the clergy in red and violet cassocks, the nobility all decked out in white and with swords at their sides, and the bourgeoisie clad in black, came and sat down. No sooner were they seated than they saw an extraordinary figure climb up onto the platform and strike a pose. What kind of monster is this? asked some. What kind of giant is that? asked others. It was a singular, unexpected, unknown creature suddenly emerged from the shadows, who aroused fear and fascination. A hideous malady had given him a sort of tiger's head. Every kind of ugliness seemed to have been deposited on this mask by every kind of vice. He was dressed, like the bourgeoisie, in black, that is, the color of mourning. His wild eye caused disarray in the Assembly wher-

ever it fell. He was reproach and menace incarnate. Everyone looked at him with a sort of curiosity mingled with horror. He raised his arm and silence fell on the assembly.

And then there emerged from this deformed face a sublime speech. It was the voice of the new world speaking through the mouth of the old. It was the radiance and splendor of '89 standing erect and challenging, accusing, and denouncing to God and man all the fatal dates of the monarchy. It was the past, a majestic spectacle, the battered past in chains, branded on the shoulder, an old slave, a worn-out convict, the ill-fated past, which called forth the future, the liberating futre, in stentorian tones! That is who this stranger was, that is what he was doing on that platform. On hearing his words, which at times were like thunder, prejudice, fiction, abuses, superstitions, errors, intolerance, ignorance, infamous taxes, barbarous punishments, decayed authorities, worm-eaten magistracies, decrepit codes, rotten laws—all that was to perish trembled, and began to crumble. This formidable apparition has left a name in human memory: people were to call it the Revolution, but for now they called it Mirabeau.

From the day that man set foot on that platform, the platform was transfigured. It had been merely a trestle, it became a tripod, an altar: the French rostrum was born.

The French rostrum! It would take an entire book to explain all that this word contains. For sixty years the French rostrum has been the open mouth of the human spirit. Of the human spirit telling all, mingling all, combining all, fertilizing all, good, evil, truth, falsehood, justice, injustice, grandeur, baseness, the horrible, the beautiful, the dream, the fact, passion, reason, love, hate, matter, ideal; but in sum—for that is its sublime and eternal work—creating night to bring forth the day, making chaos to bring forth life, making the Revolution to bring forth the Republic.[69]

Here, mythification has reached its zenith. Hugo's lyrical wrath invented a man-revolution and a rostrum that resembled the Pythian tripod at Delphi. His Mirabeau was already the disfigured Gwynplaine of romantic fiction, the lord-turned-mountebank defying the House of Lords in the name of the people. In Hugo's *Quatrevingt-treize*, the Convention, an "immense place," would assume the proportions of a "Himalaya" peopled with "spirits caught in the grip of the wind." Emblems of ancient eloquence were combined with images of a cosmic epic: "An entrenched camp of the human race attacked by all the forces of darkness at once, nocturnal fires of a besieged army of ideas, immense bivouac of spirits on the edge of the abyss. Nothing in history can be compared with this group, at once senate and populace, conclave and marketplace, areopagus and public square, tribunal and accused" (book 3, ch. 1, section 2). It is no longer only the human spirit that speaks.

FIGURE 12.2. Danton at the podium.

Another voice resounds in the arena: "The Convention had always bent to the wind. But this wind came from the mouth of the people and was the breath of God" (ibid.). With such backing, it should come as no surprise that under the Third Republic, after the imperial intermezzo, Joseph Reinach offered readers (especially students) an *Anthologie de l'éloquence française* in 1894 with a preface entitled "Le Conciones français" and a section on political eloquence starting with Mirabeau and ending with Jules Ferry, including a speech by Victor Hugo to the Legislative Assembly in 1850 on freedom of teaching. Such a book, an anthology of examples and training ground for future orators, shows that the Third Republic owed a great deal to its forebears, to a great tradition starting with Mirabeau. Developing this secular tradition with a selection of texts oriented toward the liberal left, it competed with the histories and anthologies that sustained the predominantly religious and monarchist oratorical training offered by the Catholic institutes.[70] Reinach's judgment of Mirabeau was reserved, however: his replies and improvisations were better than his prepared speeches, in which "the expression of his thought . . . often lacked relief" and "the ideas are difficult to separate out from the heavy verbiage." By contrast, "each of his ripostes was a triumph" (p. xv). The myth, though still alive, was no longer intact. Lanson was no less critical. And the myth was already dead for Albert Thibaudet in his *Histoire de littérature française de 1789 à nos jours*, published in 1936, at a time when parliamentary eloquence was devalued: although he states (p. 15) that Mirabeau and Robespierre "left more pages of oratory worthy of being read" than anyone else, he does not urge us to read them with any great enthusiasm. He nevertheless helped to dispel the most common criticisms of the antirevolutionary tradition:

> The eloquence of the Constituent Assembly was not a popular eloquence. With Mirabeau, the celebrated apostrophes, adjurations, pathetic passages, spewed lava, and shaken mane take up only a very small place in his speeches, and they could even . . . coincide with a lack of common sense, which, by the way, he possessed in abundance. The speeches of Mirabeau, Barnave, Cazalès, Maury, and Robespierre under the Constituent were generally speeches of ideas and affairs, in which the pathos was only on the surface, and which were sustained by the lessons and logic of experience and culture.

Vergniaud, the orator of the Legislative Assembly, spoke "not so much for the Assembly as for the tribunes," with a "generous and vain romanticism in which one already senses the lyrical effusions of his future historian, Lamartine."[71]

After the revelations stemming from the *armoire de fer* (1793), of course, Mirabeau was depantheonized. Indeed, the critique of eloquence began during the Revolution itself. The adversary of the moment was always a slave of tyranny or a demagogue. No speech was above suspicion. Laharpe, writing under the

FIGURE 12.3. Lamartine at the podium declaring that the Orléans dynasty has been overthrown.

Thermidorian regime about "fanaticism in revolutionary language," formulated arguments that antiparliamentarians would use during the Empire and Restoration.[72] Often, however, critics of "declamation," after denouncing its seditious or seductive uses, reserved an important place in the political machine for eloquence presumed to be legitimate as well as for parliamentary debate. Condorcet, in his report on public instruction (1792), clearly differentiated between the public eloquence of the ancients and debate among representatives in modern constitutional states:

> Although a moving, passionate, appealing eloquence may sometimes lead popular assemblies astray, those who are deceived are obliged to make decisions only about their own interests. Their mistakes affect only themselves. But the representatives of a people, who, seduced by an orator, yielded to a force other than their reason, would, in making decisions affecting the interests of others, fail in their duty and soon lose the confidence of the public on which any representative constitution is based. Hence the same eloquence that

is necessary in ancient constitutions would in ours be the seed of a destructive corruption.[73]

This was to renounce the mirage that made it possible to confound the ancient Forum with the hall of the Convention and its attendant illusion of tribunes addressing the people directly. The liberty of the Moderns could not resemble that of the Ancients. Benjamin Constant would take up the same argument. In his *Esprit de conquête* (1816), he incisively analyzed the terrorist perversion of language, the way in which *conventionnel* rhetoric mobilized the eloquence of "austere ancient republicanism" to conceal various interests.[74] But the program that Mme de Staël set forth in *De la littérature* (1800) made considerable room for eloquent emulation in representative assemblies. She surely had in mind the role that Benjamin Constant aspired to play in the Tribunate, and which he would actually play in the Chamber of Deputies from 1819 to 1830. A liberal monarchy could reconcile the promotion of merit with the idea of perfectibility provided that talents were called upon to prove themselves: success at the rostrum demonstrated their fitness for high state office. This conquest of power involved a stint in the opposition, where the outstanding man could better demonstrate his mettle, winning esteem despite the numerical weakness of his group. In theory, competition for position, intellectual ability, and social progress were in no way contradictory. Of course Constant and Mme de Staël took it for granted that the exercise of parliamentary speech was aimed at safeguarding individual liberties against unnecessary state intervention. Freedom of the press was therefore important as a means of shaping public opinion and electing representatives who, at the slightest threat of arbitrary government, would demand to be heard in the Chamber. Liberal constitutionalism sought to limit ministerial power by reinforcing the combined influence of the rostrum and the press.

The Chamber and Its Actors

The restored monarchy hoped to expand its base of support by reinstating the rostrum: "We have," reads the preamble to the 1814 Charter, "replaced the ancient assemblies of the *champs de mars et de mai* by the Chamber of Deputies." Benjamin Constant, who had suddenly thrown his support to the Emperor during the Hundred Days, excused himself on the grounds that Napoleon had said to him: "See what seems possible to you. Bring me your ideas. Public debate, free elections—I want all that. . . . Especially freedom of the press—to snuff it out would be absurd. I am convinced on this point. . . . I am the man of the people. If the people really want liberty, I owe it to them. I have recognized their sovereignty."[75]

When this liberal freedom and constitutional eloquence (in Constant, Foy, Manuel, and Royer-Collard) was allowed to express itself, it had its own distinctive accent even though it was necessarily on the defensive. Its sword was not blunted, even when the debate was about the allocation of funds. Once again the battlefield was divided between "right" and "left," following the division inaugurated by the Constituent Assembly. To be sure, there had been times before 1848 when the Chamber appeared to have gone to sleep. Much can be learned from the *Livre des orateurs* by Louis de Cormenin, who signed himself Timon.[76] The book was one of the nineteenth century's best-sellers, and it is evidence of public interest in oratorical talent in general (the subject of the first part) and, in particular, in the leading parliamentary speakers from Mirabeau to Lamartine, including Guizot, Thiers, and Jaubert (whose portraits occupy the second part). Contemplating "an assembly of rich men," Cormenin describes parliamentarians "as blasé about the emotions of the soul as well as the pleasures of the mind and senses":

> Most of them have served under several governments, sworn several oaths, and squandered several fortunes; they are truly wretches with none of the illusions of youth, virtue, or liberty! . . . Those who have a great deal of property and gold are tormented less by desire of winning than by fear of losing. Those who have positions want to keep them. Those who do not want to acquire them. Given this state of mind, ministers have only three things to work with: selfishness, greed, and fear. . . . In the parliamentary comedy, all the roles are assigned and distributed, and the prompter is at his post. Everyone knows in advance who will take the rostrum, what will be avoided, and even what decisions will be made.[77]

Under the July Monarchy, Cormenin saw the press gain at the expense of the rostrum and through the latter's fault. Anthologies of speeches had no readers: "Who today buys, who reads the widely acclaimed speeches of General Foy? And since the July Revolution has there been one speech by our best orators that can withstand the test of reading?"[78] Daumier, the vilifier of the "parliamentary paunch," is here the appropriate illustrator.

Yet in periods of crisis (of which there was no shortage), interest was rekindled. The Chamber attracted ambitious intellectuals, poets whose "sacred" status as writers[79] proved satisfying only if coupled with oratorical glory and political consecration. Hugo wanted to be a magus and procreator of the rostrum. He said as much during his exile in *Napoléon-le-Petit*: "Once risen to the rostrum, the man who stood there was no longer a man. He was that mysterious workman whom one saw at night, at dusk, striding boldly along the furrows and hurling into the air, with a masterly gesture, kernels, seeds, the future harvest, the riches of next summer, bread, life" (book 5, ch. 6). Lamartine and Lamennais (a refugee from the pulpit) enjoyed a brief period of brilliance during the events of 1848. Cormenin was ironical about Lamartine: "If, with your melodious phrases, you only want to make music, we would just as soon hear Rossini."[80] Balzac borrowed from Lamartine to create the character Canalis, whom he portrayed in a salon dispensing the conventional wisdom ("modern commonplaces"):

> Mademoiselle, the rostrum is today the greatest theater in the world. It has replaced the jousting ground of chivalry. It will be the meeting place of all intelligence, as the army once was of all courage.
>
> Canalis mounted his horse and spoke for ten minutes about politics: Poetry was the preface of the statesman. Today, the orator was becoming a sublime generalizer, a pastor of ideas. When the poet could show his country the way to the future, did he therefore cease to be himself?[81]

Yet Balzac was not hostile to parliamentary eloquence on principle. To be sure, François Keller, banker and "great orator of the left," is portrayed as an outrageous figure. But Albert Savarus, the novelist's fictionalized self-portrait, has the "voice of an orator" and tries to win election as a deputy, just as Balzac himself dreamed of "dominating the Chamber" in his letters to Mme Hanska of January 1842.[82] Thus we cannot look to Balzac for a literary liquidation of political eloquence. It was rather Flaubert, in *Madame Bovary* (settling scores with the "demonstrative" eloquence of the *comices*, or county fair) or in *L'Éducation sentimentale* (ferocious on the pathos of 1848), who achieved the greatest ironic distance, at the very time when the *book*, with its written style (subjected though it might be to the test of the *gueuloir*, or reading aloud), became the object on which the writer placed all his bets. As we know, epilepsy, coupled with his desire to write, providentially dispensed him from finishing his legal studies!

Lawyers

Savarus is a portrait of Balzac as a lawyer. Also a lawyer, but without a fortune, and hence ineligible for office, was Z. Marcas, who had the genius of a "great orator": "A concise orator, solemn yet movingly eloquent, he resembled Berryer for his warmth and his sympathy for the masses and M. Thiers for finesse and skill."[83] If he had been elected, Savarus would have been a powerful ally in the Chamber for Berryer, a celebrated lawyer made even more famous by his career as leader of the legitimist opposition. Balzac implies that the courts did not afford lawyers the full scope necessary to display all their talents. Only politics offered a large enough arena:

> Eloquence is not to be heard at the bar. Rarely does the attorney employ the real power of his soul there; if he did, he would perish in a few years. Eloquence today is seldom heard in the pulpit. But it is to be found in certain

FIGURE 12.4. Berryer; caricature by Daumier.

> sessions of the Chamber of Deputies, where the ambitious man plays double or nothing, and where pierced by a thousand arrows, he shines forth when the moment is right.[84]

Cormenin said jokingly that "the lawyer is the most common matrix of the parliamentary orator."[85] Although what was decided in the Chamber was often a foregone conclusion, for the "idle and educated crowd" what went on there was more interesting than what went on in the courts. "When the press was enslaved," such people went "to hear pleas and sermons." "But now that the public has the violent and positive emotions of the rostrum and the press, it has deserted the churches, the theaters, and the courts." Is this diagnosis correct? A crowd would turn up at Notre-Dame to hear Lacordaire! Yet there was still a feeling, probably fairly widespread under Louis-Philippe, that the bar ought to lead to something higher and that the true Parisian spectacle was not unfolding at the Palais de Justice. Since the Palais was only a preliminary training ground for politicians, it enjoyed a flood of aspirants ("as many lawyers as cases"[86]) even as its hitherto faithful public faded away. Cormenin deplored an epoch of stagnation and careerism:

> Today we may not find a single lawyer capable of drafting a legal opinion. . . . One climbs onto the first rung of the ladder only to reach the second, which leads to the third, and so on. . . . The lawyer, a fine speaker, sets his sights straightaway on a ministry, not justice—come now!—but the navy or foreign affairs. Such a man! He can deal only with ambassadors or princes.[87]

But, *pace* Cormenin, what lawyer would not be tempted by a parliamentary career? Who would not want to hear it said of himself what the severe Cormenin, himself a student of the law, said of Berryer, that he was "the greatest French orator since Mirabeau?"[88] And then, things were not so bad for eloquence at the bar, at least not on the criminal side. The *président des assises*, or presiding judge, had a great role to play (and knew it); he also had an audience in front of which to perform. Eloquence, charging to the rescue, became grandiloquence in the mouth of the defense attorney: "Warming to the contest," he "would not wish to be outdone in eloquence. When his turn came, he, too, would hammer the air with his words."[89] Some improvised speeches were handwritten and preserved in *La Gazette des tribunaux* for an audience not as large, to be sure, as that for the debates of the Chamber but not limited to legal professionals, just as in the previous century volumes of *Causes célèbres* were not found only in the libraries of *gens de robe*.

Under Louis-Philippe prosecutions for the crime of antigovernment publication fostered close relations between the rostrum, the press, and the bar. To choose one of a hundred similar affairs, take the case of Ledru-Rollin at the *assises* of Maine-et-Loire, the transcript of which was published in *La Gazette des tribunaux* on November 25, 1841: the *Courrier de la Sarthe* was accused of printing a virulent election speech by Ledru-Rollin. The latter, defended by Berryer, Odilon Barrot, and Marie, assisted by Arago, energetically pleaded his case. The court nevertheless ordered the seizure of the article (which had been widely circulated in pamphlet form since July). The reader of *La Gazette* was thus able to enjoy new speeches by Ledru-Rollin and Arago along with three pleadings.

In the nineteenth century the bar lost none of its old *esprit de corps*. In addition, it had acquired a new self-consciousness. Sharing the fate of the old *parlements*, the *ordre des avocats* had been abolished by the Revolution. It was revived, but lawyers remained under surveillance during the First Empire. Berryer, a legitimist, did not fail to point out "the wrath of the despot against the exemptions of the bar." The independence of the bar became a "sacred principle."[90] Government interference would not be tolerated, and the bar would stand up against the ministries. In 1860, under a second imperial regime, Berryer did not conceal his anxiety or his determination to resist. The legist considered himself, not without reason, the last defender of liberty:

> When the rostrum is silent or when its voice is heard only through muffled echoes;
>
> When thinly disguised press censorship is exercised through unofficial warnings;
>
> When newspapers are written in fear of being suspended or suppressed without judgment;
>
> When ministerial responsibility does not exist, so that criticism of the acts of government risks being easily distorted into an offense against the head of state . . .
>
> For each citizen the independence of the bar is still a rampart against the wrath and aggression of power, against the violation of rights, against unjust persecutions. Everything is to be feared if that independence is curtailed; nothing is hopeless if it is maintained and commands respect.[91]

On this occasion, the lawyer felt that a gauntlet had been thrown down, and he agreed to play a difficult role. An aura of heroism surrounded the impartial and dauntless attorney. It even surrounded certain highly placed individuals. In his preface to the *Discours et plaidoyers* of Gustave-Louis Chaix d'Est-Ange in 1862, Edmond Rousse wrote elegantly that "I am publishing these speeches at a time when the spoken word has fallen into disgrace, and these pleadings at a time when people assure me that the reign of the attorneys is finally over."[92]. Chaix d'Est-Ange had nothing to fear: he was procurator general at the imperial court of Paris, as the title page informed his readers. And his prefacer, explaining his support for Napoleon III, did not fail to draw inspiration openly from Tacitus and Longinus: "The Republic expired almost on the appointed day, in obedience to that immutable and repeatedly forgotten law that causes silence to supplant excesses of speech and the authority of one man to supplant excesses of liberty. The rostrum would soon vanish for many years to come, replaced by a harsher discipline. 'Eloquence, like everything else, was pacified under a sovereign hand.'"[93] Clearly, the bar was no exception to the rule that liberty is a necessary condition of public speech if the speaker is to display his full talent. Now, the invocation of liberty was not simply an implicit appeal to strength of character; it also awakened a historical consciousness. There was no shortage of broad views of the history of the bar in the nineteenth century. It was left to a legitimist, Berryer, under the July Monarchy, to paint, in his *Leçons et modèles d'éloquence judiciaire* (1838), a portrait of that history and present a selection of texts going all the way back to medieval pleadings and Gerson. It was common for portrait galleries of contemporary orators and attorneys (Timon-Cormenin; Oscar Pinard, 1843; Maurice Joly, 1862) to invoke the past and paint in broad strokes a historical background behind their parade of notable figures.

But the memory of judicial eloquence is on shaky ground. If you ask today's reader what he or she knows about nineteenth-century lawyers, you will probably hear about the gesticulating attorneys in Daumier's caricatures. From Pinard's collection, the modern reader is unlikely to know a single passage from any of the celebrities of the bar whose portraits are drawn, unless their names were in some way associated with political history. To choose a few at random: Bellart? Ferrère? Odilon Barrot? Teste? Barthe? Dupin aîné? Marie? Romiguière? And Pinard himself? Someone may remember that an Ernest Pinard presented the indictments against *Les Fleurs du mal* and *Madame Bovary*. But he was not the author of the book (*Le Barreau*, 1843) in which the portraits appear; that was Oscar Pinard. Perhaps the name Chaix d'Est-Ange will also call to mind the trial of *Les Fleurs*, in which the poet was represented by Gustave Chaix d'Est-Ange. But the man whom we have briefly mentioned was his father, Gustave-Louis Chaix d'Est-Ange. Apparently what we remember about the attorneys of the nineteenth century comes to us by a roundabout route, by way of the affairs stirred up by the century's most scandalous works. Gustave Chaix d'Est-Ange was right to discern an echo of the "Christian pulpit" or "homilies of some harsh and severe father of the Church" in *Les Fleurs du mal*. But what prevailed from Baudelaire on was the ironic sarcasm toward "loquacious" attorneys unable to cherish solitude: their "supreme pleasure is to speak from the height of a pulpit or rostrum."[94] The anathema struck home. Today one would search in vain in a book for an echo of the language of Berryer or Chaix d'Est-Ange. No one—other than the professional scholar—takes up the anthologies of their speeches. Rousse, the perspicacious prefacer of the *Discours* of Chaix d'Est-Ange *père*, knew this in advance and said so in rather too ornate language. He foresaw the oblivion:

As for posterity . . . lawyers and orators rarely aspire to it. . . . The writer . . . when it comes to the future, has too many obvious advantages. . . .

Eloquence knows neither meditation nor repose. It is an anxious and confused power, which, in the tumult of our transitory passions and affairs, draws fleeting and inaccurate sketches in haste. With an unfinished word, an involuntary gesture, a cry, a glance, it stirs, enlightens, and enlists minds and hearts. But its sovereign power reaches no farther than the sound of the trailing voice and lasts no longer than fleeting speech. . . . When the orator comes before posterity, he will stands there like a dethroned king, without retinue, without luster, stripped of his fragile splendor, alone with the vain rumor of his renown and a few lackluster texts, impotent witnesses to his genius.[95]

The equality that the eighteenth-century system of belles-lettres had established between poet, orator, and historian was thus dismantled. The orator gave way to the writer, "who contemplates his thought in silence, who polishes it, arranges it and composes it at will, and then finally engraves its image in a patiently discovered form."[96] Rousse wrote these lines as a reader of *La Maison du berger* (the second part of which contains a severe critique of eloquence) and a contemporary of the Parnassians and of the poet who would write: "Take eloquence and wring its neck." No, Rousse added, "orators would not be able to contend for the tranquil immortality that the genius of letters can bestow."[97]

Memory thus detached itself from the "practitioners" of the bar, whose role was not so much to make a name for themselves as to prove in action, generation after generation, that juridical institutions are inseparable from civil society, and viable. Sometimes collective memory will preserve the names of lawmakers, or rather of those who gave their approval to the work of legists (the Napoleonic Code!) or of theorists of law such as Montesquieu. Cultural memory retains a host of caricatures from Pathelin to Bridoye, Perrin Dandin, and hundreds of others. The legal institutions themselves, quite apart from the talents they foster, continue to play a fundamental social role implicit in a state of law, where enforcement of the law is subject to disciplined scrutiny. To describe those institutions one would have to examine methods of training, rules of admission and promotion, the ritual of role assignment, and courtroom procedure. Thus "the bar" cannot be treated as an abstract *lieu de mémoire*. It is a *place* only for the time it takes to hear a case, substitute disciplined speech for natural violence, and frame a decision. Like the pulpit, the bar requires a distinct form of dress as an additional sign of institutional sacrality, which can amount to little more than dramatic flourishes. But that difference is indicated only to justify intervention in the conflicts of the moment, in the time of "affairs."

Firmly established in public life by the second half of the nineteenth century, eloquence required no mastery other than that of the living moment, the "present hour" in which decisive choices must be made: "Life is its dominating influence," Rousse declared. Bear in mind that in his separate domain (destined for memory, however), the artist who "polishes his thought" excludes himself from "life" (a secession that many poets insisted on). Subject to the exclusive authority of the beautiful, the *poetic* of the written word was no longer reducible to the *rhetoric* of persuasion, to the "art of speaking" that flows through a "crowd" like a circulating coin. Mallarmé, observing this divergence, wrote: "One indisputable aspiration of my age is to separate, as if for the purpose of different attributions, the twofold state of language, raw and immediate here, essential there."[98] Yet even so, there persists in Mallarmé, as in a dream state, the image of public reading, stage ritual, "the cries of the fairground." This, however, did not prevent Breton from attributing, with all the irony one might wish to ascribe to him, the title *Discours* to what he wrote about the "lack of reality."

Speaking to the Nation on Behalf of the Nation

In June 1850, Alexis de Tocqueville, reflecting on himself and his situation after the Revolution of 1848, weighed the success of his book on America against the disappointments of his parliamentary career. Clearly he was not made for "this miserable world of parliament" in which he had always felt "constrained and oppressed":[99]

> It did not take me long to discover that I did not have what it takes to play the brilliant role there that I had dreamed of. . . . I had mistakenly believed that I would enjoy the same success on the rostrum that I had encountered with my book. The writer's craft and the orator's harm each other more than they help. Nothing is less like a good speech than a good chapter. I soon noticed and saw plainly that I was counted among the speakers who were correct, ingenious, and sometimes profound but always cold and therefore powerless. . . . Discussion on points that were of little interest to me was annoying and on those that were of great interest, painful. Truth is for me something so precious and so rare that I have no desire to subject it to the risks of debate once I have found it. It is a light that I fear extinguishing if I wave it about.[100]

So Tocqueville was a poor tactician, not very skilled "at uniting and leading many men" and uncertain "about what was best to do each day" (p. 104). Would he now devote himself to writing books? If we take him at his word, everything was pushing him in that direction: the contempt into which "the governing class" had fallen and the comical behavior of the rioters who had taken over the Chamber on January 24. "It seemed to me that they were busy acting out the French Revolution rather than continuing it. . . . They tried to rekindle our fathers' passions but failed. They imitated the gestures and poses of their forebears as they had seen them on the stage but could not imitate their enthusiasm or feel their rage. . . . It all struck me as a wretched tragedy played by provincial mountebanks." In the face of what is nowadays called a "verbal intervention" (pp. 75 ff.), Tocqueville was attentive but not really involved: "I stepped down and took my seat. Nearly all the deputies had withdrawn. The benches were occupied by men of the people. Lamartine, still on the rostrum between two flags, continued to address or rather converse with the crowd, for there seemed to be as many orators present as there were members of the audience. Confusion was at its height."

A passage like this gives some idea of the attraction exerted on the popular mind by oratorical eloquence, especially when it supplanted institutional authority and was exercised in the very place where the owners of property had sat: the so-called Censitary Assembly [in which property, as measured by a tax called the *cens,* was an eligibility requirement—TRANS.]. This passion for speaking spread like wildfire throughout the city, spawning utopias: "Everyone proposed his plan. This one wrote in the newspapers, that one on signboards that soon covered the walls. And yet another wrote in the open air, through speech. . . . The lukewarm passions of the time were made to speak the language of '93" (p. 95). In the "thousands of strange systems" that composed the socialism of the moment, Tocqueville saw only a parody of the Terror. Yet this discovery, strikingly close to that of Marx,[101] did not end Tocqueville's parliamentary career—quite the contrary. Something more important made up his mind: the "salvation of the country," the "public good." When the time came for elections to the Constituent Assembly, he campaigned, drafted and signed a petition, and found a way to improvise on the stump an "oratorical pathos" that proved rather successful. Here the memoirist found it pertinent to point out that "speeches are made to be listened to and not read, and the only good ones are those that move."[102] He felt that his oratorical difficulties would be less of an embarrassment in the new assembly, where "character" carried more weight than "the art of speaking well or of manipulating men" (p. 105). The activities that he recalls in his *Souvenirs* are legislative and ministerial: the constitutional commission, where his colleagues included Cormenin and Lamennais, and the Ministry of Foreign Affairs.

Of course it would be useful to spell out such general notions as the "salvation of the country" and "the public good." Here I shall simply note that for Tocqueville these were sufficient reasons to return "to the arena" as well as ethical criteria in the light of which all politicians must be evaluated. In this respect his judgment of Lamartine is significant. Tocqueville granted him many qualities: learning, courage, "manners." Lamartine spoke in a "brilliant manner" (p. 128) but "before an assembly more docile than any other to the deceits of eloquence" (pp. 128–129). And here is the supreme criticism: "He is, I think, the only man who has ever seemed to me prepared to turn the world upside down for his own amusement." In Kierkegaard's terms, Lamartine was always ready to give priority to what was "interesting" and aesthetic over political morality. On the verge of defeat, he could not resolve himself to "lose [power] with glory, by saving the country." Tocqueville adds: "Lamartine was certainly not a man to sacrifice himself in this or any other way. I do not know if I have ever encountered, in the world of selfish ambitions in which I lived, a mind more devoid of concern for the public good than his. . . . Nor have I ever known a man less sincere or more utterly contemptuous of truth" (p. 126). Given these oratorical qualities and moral flaws, Lamartine as Tocqueville describes him is a negative image of Tocqueville himself.

The political analysis in this passage from Tocqueville is based on moral norms. Elsewhere he appeals to laws that apparently take precedence over any positive law: he was a candidate for the Constituent Assembly because he had resolved to devote himself to "the defense, not of any particular government, but of the laws that constitute society itself" (p. 105). To be sure, these words express the spirit of conservatism, which for Tocqueville was coupled with an insistence on liberty. For us, however, their interest is that they define reasons for speaking, reasons for sitting in a deliberative body. A final cause of political speech begins to emerge. It involves some kind of "salvation," the future of society itself. We must not be critical of the excessive generality of these concepts, because it is that very generality that justifies political speech. Such concepts have a regulative function: they are supposed to lead to concrete acts but always within limits, where the goal is universality. Tocqueville, the defender of property, was persuaded (rightly or wrongly) that he was acting on behalf of the "public good" and not in the interest of the property-owning class. With respect to the problem that concerns us here, we recognize a principle that Tocqueville certainly did not invent but that he deserves credit for bringing out into the open. To corroborate this, one has only to reread a few lines from *Democracy in America*. Although the passage I have in mind was written before Tocqueville became disillusioned with his parliamentary career, and although it is preceded by some very severe remarks on "the small side of political debate," it can be regarded as an outline for a theory of the relation between political eloquence and the nation, with the French case adduced as an example. Tocqueville begins with the hypothesis that the abolition of "privileges" and "rights inherent in certain groups *[corps]*" ends the division of society into distinct "classes." Democracy thus achieves in the political order what the Church achieved in the religious order, addressing itself to all men on an equal basis as God's people:

> I see nothing more admirable or more powerful than a great orator discussing great affairs in a democratic assembly. Since in such a place there is never any class whose representatives are charged with defending its interests, the orator always addresses the entire nation in the name of the entire nation. This magnifies his thought and heightens his language.

> Since precedents have little influence here, and since privileges are no longer attached to certain forms of property or rights inherent in certain bodies or certain men, the mind is obliged to have recourse to general truths drawn from human nature in dealing with the particular case under consideration. Hence the political discussions of a democratic people, no matter how small, take on a general character that often makes them of interest to the entire human race. All men are interested in them, because they concern man, who is everywhere the same. . . .
>
> This, as much as the grandeur of the French nation and the favorable disposition of other peoples, is the reason why our political discussions sometimes produce such a great effect in the world.
>
> Our orators often speak to all men even when they address only their fellow citizens.[103]

In a more restrained manner than Hugo but in agreement with him on this point, Tocqueville assigns democratic eloquence a universal scope. Ideally, it addresses the entire nation and reaches all mankind. But who gives the "great orator" his mandate? The nation, which appears here as the origin of the "speech act." It is the nation that authorizes him to speak and grants him authority to express "general truths." It is the nation that grants the orator the legitimate right to be heard. The circularity of the argument is striking! But that circularity defines democratic discourse. Tocqueville's text says so in a simple, powerful manner: the orator "speaks *to* the entire nation" (the recipient) and at the same time "*in the name of* the entire nation" (the guarantor). The nation is both the addressed body and the legitimating body. This circularity is not invalidating as long as the orator himself adheres to the great regulatory principles and never advances his own interests. The danger lies in the temptation of demagoguery: government by the people is then reduced to "despotism exercised in the name of the people."[104]

An expression such as "to speak in the name of" descends directly from religious discourse (in the broadest sense). The "person" in whose name one speaks occupies a transcendent position and possesses a higher authority than that of the speaker. Even in profane discourse certain formulas of adjuration remain. Indeed, Tocqueville has recourse to one in the moving peroration to a speech he delivered on the eve of the February revolution: "*In the name of God*, change the spirit of the government." At the time, and in the mouth of a secular speaker, God was the ultimate if not very effective source of legitimacy. The many priests in the Constituent Assembly received no better hearing than Tocqueville, however. He tells us that they "never could learn the language of politics. They had long since forgotten it. All their speeches turned imperceptibly into homilies."

It was nevertheless inevitable that under the Ancien Régime an insistent memory of the discourse conducted in God's name should have been projected onto and recapitulated in the discourse carried on in the name of the people. Mandated by God, authorized by the Revelation vouchsafed unto it, the Church, through its sacred orators, spoke to princes in the name of a supreme source of legitimation, whose effective power it transmitted to them. It delegated to them the task of governing human affairs, but it reserved the right to recall them to their duties and remind them that they were absolute only so long as they remained obedient to the legitimating authority and considered themselves to be the repositories—and not the unconditional possessors—of the wealth and concerns of the nation. The principal effect of eloquence in the Enlightenment was to cause this system of legitimation to be seen as a fiction. And when the nation supplanted God as the source of legitimacy, it was not so much a secularization of theological authority that was involved as a persistent need to appeal to some source of legitimation. The "modern" system required a "universal subject" (the Nation, Reason, the *vox populi*, the workers, etc.) to exercise the legitimizing role that the religious theorists of absolutism had ascribed to God and His Providence.

Speech Without a Place?

Three collective bodies: clergy, deputies, men of law. Three enclosures, or temples, to accommodate them: Church, Assembly, Palais de Justice. Within these enclosures, three places reserved for those who rise to speak: pulpit, rostrum, bar. These three places, reserved for three rituals of language, were usually decorated with emblems: the Holy Spirit above the pulpit; over the rostrum, the colors of the flag, Roman fasces, a Phrygian cap, or a full-scale representation of Liberty; on the walls of the courtroom, blindfolded Justice with her scales. The emblems allegorized three authorities: God, the Nation, the Law. Three authorities that if need be could be appealed to against the men in power. Can we call them transcendent? God, certainly. But what about the Nation and the Law? We have called them sources of legitimation. Something in their supposed antecedence, in their normativity, gives them an air of transcendence.

How to speak in these three places? Rhetoric taught how to speak but made it clear that different virtues of language must be developed for each of the three types of discourse and that the orator must possess, in addition to the appropriate natural gifts, special forms of acquired knowledge. The art of persuasion depended on whether one was speaking to the faithful in the name of God; or to the representatives of the nation in the name of a superior good, the Nation itself; or invoking the Law in the presence of a judge in the name of a "party" to a dispute. The goal was to obtain one of three types of decision: conversion (or contrition) on the part of the faithful; a vote on the part of the representatives of the nation; or a judicial decision settling the interpretation of the law in the case before the court. These decisions left their stamp on the present moment and opened the way to the future.

As we have seen, the poet, whom Du Bellay and humanism had placed on an equal footing with the orator, renounced the association according to which both were subject to the same laws of rhetoric. He freed himself (or so he thought) from precepts that defined, too narrowly for his taste, the conditions of communication. The liberty claimed was no longer the liberty of the Forum. He found liberty in the depths of his soul, in feeling, refractory to all constituted authority but eager to coincide with the force that constitutes the world and is always at work throughout the universe, a force that, in the infinite series of its manifestations, borrows the poet's voice in passing. From now on speech sees itself as so innovative that the page on which it is recorded is already the place of an absence, the trace of a migration, while the force that had inhabited the word spreads elsewhere, into temporary abodes, in other transitory forms. "Nothing will have taken place but the place except perhaps a constellation" are the words written in capital letters across the pages of one of the great poetic texts of modernity, in which chance is declared to be indestructible [Stéphane Mallarmé's *Un Coup de dés*—TRANS.]. But from this vacant yet constellated place more recent poetry has returned, with a concern for the "true place" (Yves Bonnefoy)—a habitable, terrestrial place in which the simplest objects would be named in accordance with the requirements of a truth that can be shared.

God, the Nation, and the Law are the highest sources of legitimation. As we have seen, the Nation could be invoked against the power of divine right (reserving the realm of personal beliefs for God). Against antiquated laws, one could appeal to new legislators. And more generally, from the eighteenth century on, it has been suspected that other sources of legitimation might, like the law, be the work of men. This was to dispossess God. But not necessarily the nation, that ancestral heritage, product of the work and faith of generations that had inhabited the same soil. The nation could be supplemented, although not necessarily supplanted, by a "sense of history," human progress, the future god of various historiosophies. Their preachers do not occupy places recognized by the authorities. They preach in the open air, circulate clandestine newspapers, and organize in the shadows. If we believe them, the official rostrum, pulpit, and bar are places that allow a society to conceal its true nature: places of mystified consciousness, places where human relations created by labor and material transactions never achieve full expression. In these isolated places of deception, the speech monopolized by a dominant fraction is not true speech. It is rather speech that prevents authentic exchange from taking place in the life of the community. Speech must arise everywhere, in all mouths, this time in the name of exchange itself: then the absence of authority or, what comes to the same thing, the generalization of authority would constitute the only possible legitimacy.

We have seen this dream lose its way, no doubt because speech became rumor without origin or destination until a stronger voice asserted itself. Questions quickly arise. Who is speaking? To whom? About what concerns? To what ends? The once urgent question, "Where are you speaking from?" clearly indicates the importance of the place from which one speaks, even if that place stands outside any established edifice in what is supposed to be an ultimate society or universal social group. With these questions, however, rhetoric is reborn from its ashes, for rhetoric had always insisted that the orator ask himself these questions before attempting to persuade. Are these questions clearly posed today by those who wish to recover or re-create the authority that was God, the community that was the nation, the rules of nonviolent coexistence that defined the law? These are questions that philosophy has never ceased to ask in its age-old debate with rhetoric. Moral philosophy today tends to develop as an enquiry into the conditions under which communication can best be achieved among free individuals. It tends to include the fundamentals of rhetoric among its own problems. The past and present of eloquence have become one of its most relevant topics.

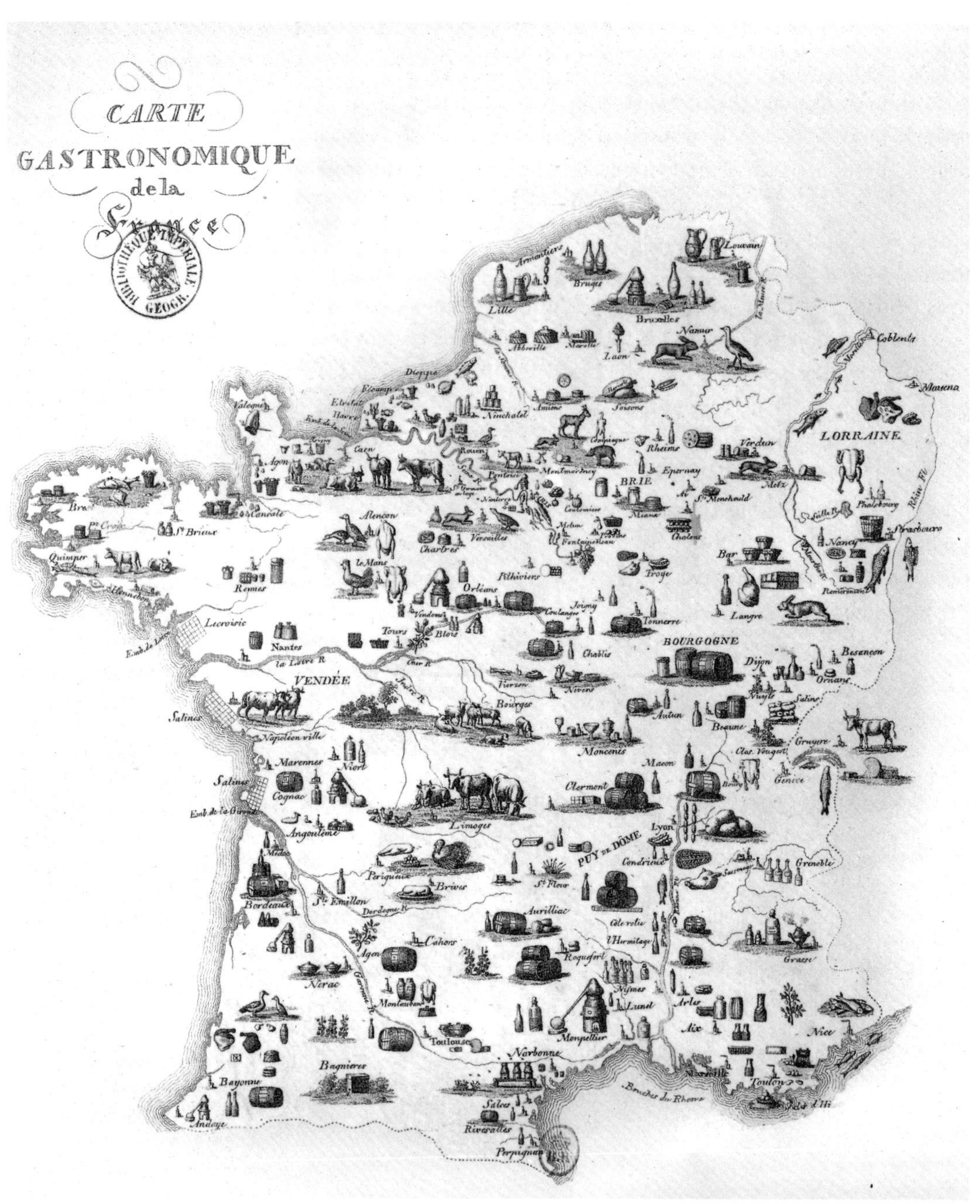

FIGURE 13.0. Gastronomic map of France circa 1800. The prototype of an iconography that has enjoyed unremitting success.

CHAPTER XIII

Gastronomy

Pascal Ory

Will French cuisine be all that remains when everything else has been forgotten? Community identity draws on many sources, but there may be only two that count, as one can see by looking at communities not at the height of their splendor but rather in the throes of demise and extinction: in acculturation, integration, assimilation. One has, on the one hand, a private history, almost a mythology, and, on the other hand, a concrete set of more or less ritual practices connoting membership, practices involving language, religion, and, of course, cooking (assuming that it is even possible to establish such clear demarcations).

The fruit of an interaction between history and environment, cooking, more than any other communal practice, is a response to a vital necessity. It invariably involves a collective ritual (the meal and its menu), a tradition (recipe and style), and critical discrimination (the product, the commentary). A cuisine is one of the most distinctive expressions of an ethnic group or, in modern times, a nation. Frequently, the last sign of an individual's attachment to his roots before total assimilation into the host community is the consumption of distinctive kinds of food, formerly at home, in the future, perhaps, owing to a breakdown of family traditions and maternal lessons, in a restaurant. Even within families we find the same kind of differentiation, where one of the few (and again dwindling) ways of asserting a difference remains the recipe, the culinary knack or "secret."

Yet when an authoritative voice, speaking on behalf of French culture, asserts that "a people's cuisine is the only accurate testimony to its civilization," one hesitates to dismiss this statement as a mere gloss on the foregoing.[1] In the minds of the speaker and many of his countrymen, the assertion is actually a metonymic syllogism: the supremacy of French cuisine, which is taken for granted, implies the superiority of French "civilization."

Facts

France is not a country with an ordinary relation to food. In the national vulgate food is one of the distinctive ingredients, if not *the* distinctive ingredient, of French identity. Writing in the shadow of 1815, the authority quoted above, a typical representative of the romantic age of French gastronomy, was not the last to seek to compensate for military and diplomatic humiliation with culinary and gastronomic triumph. Noting that "Europe sought out our restaurateurs as missionaries of civilization," he concludes that "under the Empire, the reputation of Paris restaurants rose so high that throughout Europe they did for our cuisine what the seventeenth and eighteenth centuries had done for our literature: they made it universal."[2]

Indeed, the remarkable fact is that no change in this rhetoric is discernible in the century that followed, and in particular during the lengthy period in which democratic culture took root. Indeed, the belief in the superiority of French cuisine seems to have spread beyond the milieu of chefs and men of letters, becoming henceforth the common property of all the classes of society. Auguste Escoffier, the most illustrious chef of the Belle Époque, had his own distinctive view of the matter, which he expressed in a rather clumsy metaphor: "I have 'sown' two thousand chefs all around the world. . . . Think of them as so many seeds planted in virgin soil. France is today reaping the fruits."[3] Marcel Rouff, the inventor of Dodin-Bouffant, that ideal and ultimately legendary gastronome of the *ère des notables*, was inspired by the victory of 1918 to propose a different but no less sweeping vision: "Great, noble cooking is a tradition of this country. It is an ancient and important ingredient of its charm, a reflection of its soul." From these premises he drew the following conclusion: "Simplifying an important idea of Brillat-Savarin's, we can say that everywhere else people feed themselves; only in France do they eat." He went on to establish a set of correspondences, by no means unusual in this genre of writing. Some are cultural: "There is less distance than one might think between a tragedy of Racine, for example, and a meal designed by that marvelously skilled host, Talleyrand." Others are ethnic: "If mortadella, which is surely not to be despised, comes close to Goldoni; . . . if 'Black Forest meatballs' are heavy, thick, and dense, like German thought, literature, and art; then quiche lorraine, the foie gras of Périgord, and the bouillabaisse of Marseilles . . . contain all the refined riches of France." In other words, "gastronomic taste is innate in the race."[4] It is by no means clear that the tone today, though more nuanced and cautious, is fundamentally any different, as a glance at the preface of any book by the great chefs or at certain gastronomic guides will suffice to show. Even the official report prepared by the journalist Jean Ferniot for the ministries of culture and agriculture contains sentences like this one: "Perhaps France alone . . . is still capable of training chefs, whereas other countries train cooks."[5]

Ultimately, what matters is not this smug self-satisfaction, of which French national rhetoric offers any number of other examples,[6] but the confirmation that it still elicits from abroad. Witness the current prestige of expatriate French chefs, who once served in the households of the wealthy but now tend the ovens of renowned and invariably chic restaurants, as well as the constant influx of amateur cooks from around the world but primarily from the United States and Japan, who come to France to attend cooking schools and courses in oenology and who flock to France's wine cellars and three-star restaurants. Perhaps the most decisive evidence of France's culinary supremacy is to be found in language: witness the importance of French in culinary and gastronomic terminology around the world. The fact that *Art Culinaire*, *Bon Appétit*, *Chef*, *Chocolatier*, and *Gourmet* are all titles of English-language periodicals is a telling example.[7]

The actual culinary identity of France is not really at issue: at this and other levels it could be characterized in terms of a more or less subtle relationship between the variety of *terroirs* and the centrality of the dominant classes. On the one hand an infinite variety of basic dishes, the objects of a largely ahistorical crystallization. On the other hand, a codification of noble recipes, significantly named less often for the chef than for the host, at one time the *amphitryon* (the Marquis de Bichamel, the Chevalier d'Uxelles, the Prince de Soubise, etc.), and later the client (Rossini, Melba, etc.). The question of French culinary identity is really a mirror question, a question of how the French and others see themselves and their cuisine. This raises questions about the nature and hence the origins of France's asserted (and widely recognized) superiority in this realm, the justification or lack of justification for which is of no concern in the present context.

Definitions

Let us first be clear about terminology in order to avoid the frequent confusions that arise in this area. Though long considered marginal, gastronomic literature is nowadays taken seriously in France and elsewhere. Never has more been written about the subject, and never have licensed scholars taken such an interest in it. Yet gastronomic literature has retained one significant vestige of its origins that must be eliminated if it is fully and perhaps permanently to achieve the status to which it aspires: a certain conceptual vagueness due no doubt to the conditions in which modern gastronomy was born some two centuries ago, as a *demi-genre* for a *demi-monde*, looked upon by intellectual authorities with more or less amused contempt.

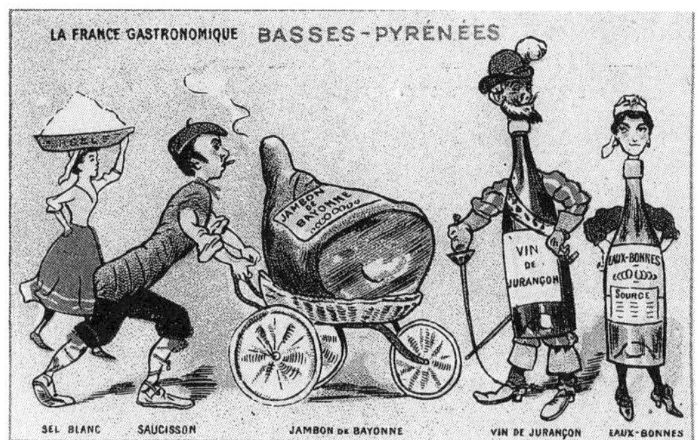

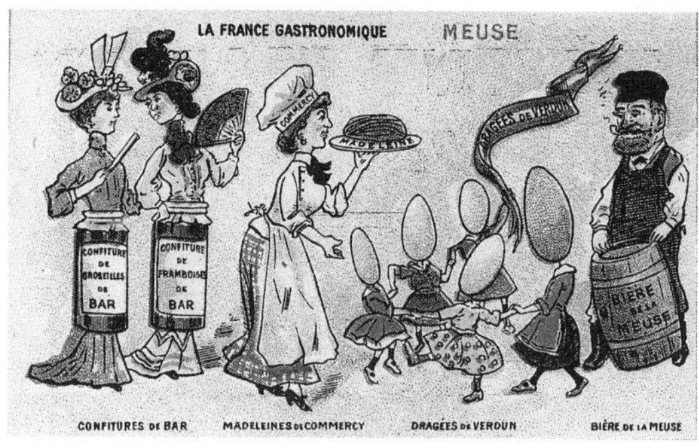

FIGURE 13.1–13.7. Gastronomic topography as conceived during the Third Republic, with its good inns and local notables; vignettes from 1910, *La France gastronomique*.

Accordingly, it is not uncommon to find even recent texts confusing such terms as *alimentation, cuisine, bonne cuisine, haute cuisine, restauration,* and *gastronomie,* none of which is a synonym for any of the others. For example, one food writer, Christian Guy, published a *Histoire de la cuisine* in 1962 and, twenty-three years later, a *Histoire de la gastronomie,* which basically dealt with the same subject—*alimentation*—in the same anecdotal manner. All that one can deduce from the change in title is that the subject matter had achieved a more noble status in the interim.

One way to find one's bearings in this morass is to follow the development of the historiography of the subject. In the late 1960s the so-called *Annales* school, bent on uncovering the history of "material civilization," inaugurated a vast project of historical anthropology which, among other things, openly called "for a history of alimentation."[8] Preceded by anthropology, and in particular by the most eminent anthropologist of the day,[9] the historians soon developed ambitions beyond the essentially positivist, if delicate, task of establishing how alimentary practices had changed or been forgotten over the centuries, the kind of work with which Fernand Braudel, being of an older generation, essentially occupied himself.[10] Emancipated from purely quantitative methods (using, for instance, statistics for the production and consumption of particular products), historians moved toward a cultural approach, looking for the systems of representation involved in the games of the table.[11] By 1974, Jean-Paul Aron's *Mangeur du XIXe siècle* had not only brought unexpected popularity to this genre but had also begun to shift the angle of attack.[12]

Aron's approach, which was not particularly rigorous and has since been questioned in several respects, in any case opened up two new avenues of research: it "modernized" the question by making it clear that the alimentary practices of the bourgeois period were no less interesting, not to say noble, than those of rural and traditional societies; and it broadened the historical perspective to include a form of culinary theater that the nineteenth century in fact invented, located primarily in a site with no true antecedent: the restaurant.

What Aron proposed, then, was a comprehensive, global, social history in which politics ultimately regained its rightful place. In opening the doors of the restaurant, he forced historians to take note of a society they had previously neglected, not to say scorned: gastronomic society. Of course gastronomic society arrived laden with the fruits of its own peculiar erudition: the abundant anecdotal history of chefs and their establishments.

Nevertheless, historians of alimentation and of the restaurant, whether or not the two were confused, shared the same objectivist concern: their first goal was to discover concrete practices. The other aspect of the question—the discourse on food—failed to engage the sustained attention of Aron or anyone else, even though its modern foundations were laid in the period he studied, which coined the term *gastronomie* in 1801. It is to this task that I now turn, following the pioneering work of Jean-Claude Bonnet.[13] I will attempt to discover the signs of a fabricated identity, of a national memory, through the various forms not of cuisine, which is endless, but of the much more restricted realm of discourse.

Brillat-Savarin's aphorism, often used and abused by gastronomes (including, as we have seen, Marcel Rouff), is well known: "Animals feed; man eats; only the intelligent man knows how to eat."[14] Beyond its immediate meaning, this statement helps to define the intellectual position of gastronomy vis-à-vis such related notions as "alimentary" and "culinary." To study alimentation is to study the whole range of practical and theoretical relations that a given society entertains with eating and drinking. To study cuisine is to focus on the elaboration of food, on implements, recipes, and menus. Finally, to study restaurants is to place the emphasis on what might be called public cuisine, which involves the interaction among chefs, publicists, and the public. By contrast, to analyze gastronomy is to choose not an object but a subject: a subject that speaks or, rather, engages in discourse—and this despite the fact that one of the greatest successes of the gastronomes is to have identified gastronomy with good eating.

Gastronomy is neither good cooking *(448 bonne cuisine)* nor fine cooking *(haute cuisine)*. It is the establishment of rules (a *nomos*) of eating and drinking, an "art of the table." In the latter expression, as one might guess, a deliberate ambiguity is maintained between the ancient and modern senses of the word *art:* here the interests of the cook and the gastronome are identical, and whereas the former is promoted to the status of artist, the latter is raised to the level of a critic of art.

Thus gastronomy is concerned with content (cuisine and its associated disciplines, oenology, the art of the menu, the decorative arts) only to the extent that it gives rise to a discourse. The gastronome in his most evolved form is not a professional cook. He is a man of letters, at least as an amateur. His real table is not the one where he eats but the one where he writes, his desk, where, having weighed and digested every item, he composes his column or treatise. No civilized person talks with his mouth full. Indeed, Saint Benedict commanded his monks not to speak at all at the dinner table, and so did certain very rigid codes of etiquette of the triumphant bourgeoisie. Afterwards, however, one could make up for lost time, in keeping with Talleyrand's dictum that after one sampled a fine wine with the eye, ear, and nose, the next step was not to drink it but to "speak of it." Ultimately, the gastronome is not the one who knows the most (the technical competence of Monselet and Curnonsky has been questioned) but the one who speaks best.

Along the way, we may, in order to explain changes in discourse, find it necessary to take account of the history of cooking implements or popular revolutions or the biographies of certain chefs or politicians. Nevertheless, the history of gastronomy is a form of literary history—the history not of a genre (because, as we shall see, it encompasses several) but of a whole literature. Perhaps there is a certain justice in this, because it is common to say of a person who speaks eloquently that we "drink in his words" or of a book that we like that we "devour" it. Gastronomy, it will emerge, can be seen as the reconciliation of two forms of orality. And here again we will discover a cultural identity, for France is a country in which things literary have long been the object of a special veneration.

Basics

The primacy of France thus has two components, gastronomy as well as cuisine: the eloquence of French gastronomes, one infers, has sustained the hegemonic image of French cuisine. Yet the question is still how to explain this double sense of superiority. There is no shortage of incompatible answers.

Nature is generally invoked as one reason. As Escoffier affirmed without hesitation, "it suffices to note that French soil enjoys the privilege of producing naturally and in abundance the best vegetables, the best fruits, and the best wines in the world," along with "the finest fowl, the tenderest meat, the most varied and delicate game, and the most beautiful fish and shellfish. Hence the French have quite naturally become both gourmands and good cooks."[15] Yet the statement itself makes it perfectly clear that "quite naturally" means first of all "quite culturally" and that the best proof of the excellence of French produce is the a posteriori proof of the excellence of French cuisine. True, other writers, not least geographers and historians, have provided more subtle glosses on the nature and above all the variety of French soil and climate. A variant of this argument takes economic geography into account. This more complex view, which has strong points that Brillat-Savarin was the first to recognize, emphasizes such factors as Bordeaux's vineyards and the density of top-rated restaurants in the region of Lyons. (But since when?)[16]

The naturalist argument rarely occurs in isolation, however. The next step is to bring in social or political factors, such as the role of the Church. Indeed, historical research, discounting pious legends and Rabelaisian anecdotes, every day turns up new evidence of the role that monasteries and cathedral chapters played for a thousand years in concocting and improving produce and recipes. Without going so far as to adapt Weber's thesis on the Protestant origins of capitalism to the history of cuisine,[17] there can be no doubt that, while modern France's choice of religion did not prevent the development of a certain anticarnal puritanism, from which Catholicism is no more exempt than any other confession, it did limit the effects of such puritanical thinking to nonrepresentative segments of French society, as any study of daily life at Versailles will show.

But this mention of the court of the Bourbons points up the weak spot in the argument. Any attempt to trace the French national obsession with "good eating" back to the country's origins or even to prehistoric times is guilty of the sin of teleology. It makes no sense to accumulate supposed gastronomic references taken out of context from Gallic or Gallo-Roman sources unless one can show by similar methods that other peoples were somehow different. In other words, there is no proof that contemporaries before at least the seventeenth century saw anything superior about French cuisine, whereas by the beginning of the nineteenth century such superiority was routinely affirmed and acknowledged. Furthermore, there is no evidence that in French culture before the seventeenth century food had the same importance it would acquire later on. Even during the final two centuries of what, after 1789, became the Ancien Régime, it is by no means certain that the subsequently undeniable signs of French hegemony were as yet an intrinsic part of the culture. When a foreign observer reported on a sumptuous French table, he was not yet describing a trait of the national character.[18] He was signalling, rather, both prosperity and, even more, a form of domination whose basis was political and cultural, the two being intimately associated in the logic of absolute monarchy, then in its heyday.

Clearly, then, it was no accident that the names of two largely mythical exemplars of ancient gastronomy, Archestratus and Apicius, were associated with the political and cultural flowerings of, respectively, fifth-century B.C. Athens and Rome from Caesar to Claudius. Even the great culinary texts of the Middle Ages and Renaissance could be linked to domination. In the seventeenth century French culture became hegemonic in Western Europe for at least two reasons: first, the political system that supported it triumphed and extended its influence throughout Europe, and second, the old relation between political power and symbolic production (that is, in modern terms, "artists," "scholars," and "ideologues") achieved its greatest intensity thanks to absolutism. If French cuisine tended to become a standard of reference, it was for the same reason, though obviously at a lower level of prestige, as the language codified by Richelieu (and not Malherbe) or the painting codified by Colbert (and not Le Brun). Just as people discriminated between good and bad French and recognized the rules and unities that were the hallmarks of good style, certain texts published at the beginning of Louis XIV's reign distinguished between good and bad in matters of culinary taste.[19] La Varenne and his immediate successors gained a European reputation that the "new cuisine" of Louis XV[20] would in no way compromise. On the contrary, a (dare I say) *palate* revolution does nothing to undermine the legitimacy of power but only alters its orientation for a time.

A comparative study of French and English diners by British historian Stephen Mennell tends to confirm this hypothesis by looking at the persistent question of

LOUIS LE GRAND L'AMOUR ET LES DELICES DE SON PEUPLE. ou les Actions de graces, les Festes et les Réjouissances pour le parfait restablissement de la Santé du Roy en 1687.

LE DINE DV ROY A L'HOTEL DE VILLE DE PARIS

CALENDRIER POUR L'ANNEE BISSEXTILE MDCLXXXVIII.

A PARIS CHEZ N. LANGLOIS RVE S.T IACQVES A LA VICTOIRE AVEC PRIVILEGE DU ROY

FIGURE 13.8. The King's Dinner at the Hôtel de Ville in Paris; anonymous engraving for the almanac of 1688.

"two cuisines" (which is also a question of "two discourses"). What emerges is that there is nothing original, much less ontological, about the French difference, which does indeed date from the period 1650–1750. As in other areas, this period saw a bifurcation of two cultures, that is, two models held out to society by the dominant classes. In France, the culinary model was that of the monarchy at Versailles: courtly, ostentatious, and sophisticated. Its ideal diner was the Sun King, reigning over a nobility dispossessed of its functions and indeed domesticated. By contrast, the English model was that of the liberal aristocracy, which held much of the country's economic and political power: it was rural, puritanical, and practical, and its ideal diner was the "gentleman," an integral part of a relatively open elite, the "gentry." It took no more than this for two culinary languages to become mutually incomprehensible.

Foundations

The origins of French gastronomy can now be interpreted in the light of the configuration of power in the Ancien Régime. The key period here, as for so many other distinctive features of French identity, corresponds to the great rupture of the Revolution.

The word *gastronomie* itself appeared in the very first year of the nineteenth century, with the publication of a didactic poem in four stanzas by an author who was both a royalist and an aesthetic "modernist," a disciple of the Abbé Delille and the immortal author of the line "Who will deliver me from the Greeks and the Romans?" namely, Joseph de Berchoux.[21] If the word was (relatively) new, its novelty was less important than its instant success.[22] This quickly led to such back-formations and derivatives as *gastronome* (1803) and *gastronomique* (1807) and above all to the extremely important publication of Alexandre Grimod de La Reynière's first work, the *Almanach des gourmands* (1803). The public snapped up the *Almanach*, which went through eight printings by 1812, leading in turn to the publication of Charles Louis Cadet de Gassicourt's *Cours gastronomique*, which already included a "gastronomic map of France."

Who was Grimod? Leaving aside certain eccentricities, he is perhaps best described as the offspring of three generations of farmers-general and the heir to one of the day's largest fortunes, half of which he lost in the Revolution. Before being forced to sell his *hôtel particulier* on the Champs-Élysées, he tried to cash in on the good taste of the defunct regime by selling it to the *nouveaux riches* of the Directory, the *parvenus* of the Consulat, and the *arrivistes* of the Empire. A man of order, he was glad to see the return of a "stable and moderate government" and sought to aristocratize the new men of the hour, who proved to be docile students. More than that, he reestablished order, hierarchy, and distinctions in the realm of good taste. He disciplined the new ebullience with a set of rules: after the *Almanach* he published a *Manuel* that he himself described as a "catechism of the art of living well." It is no exaggeration to see him, along with the Comte de Saint-Simon and Alexis de Tocqueville, as one of the founders of the modern French culture that arouse out of the defeated aristocracy, at once nostalgic for the old regime and convinced of the irreversibility of the new one.

Calling, in jest perhaps, for a chair of gastronomy to be established in all the new lycées, Grimod established the criticism of cookery at about the time that others were instituting criticism of art, literature, and drama in the salons and newspapers.[23] Very much aware of and very proud of his originality ("a mine not yet explored by any other writer"), within five years he had invented the three major forms of the genre: the guidebook, the gastronomic treatise, and the gourmet periodical. The *Almanach des gourmands* was virtually an annual "Guide Grimod." The *Manuel des amphitryons*[24] demonstrated the gastronome's power over the consumer: henceforth producers controlled only cookbooks. And finally, the *Journal des gourmands et des belles*, an epicurean newsletter, was the first gastroliterary periodical, and one would be hard put to say whether the writing exalted the food or the food the writing.[25]

Before Grimod there was of course a literature of eating and drinking, but it had no status, being linked to three quite distinct genres. The most common was the technical literature, the literature of cooks or their ghostwriters.[26] This began to appear at about the same time as other technical literatures, such as those for cabinetmakers and glassblowers, as well as works in home economics. Although these cookbooks were essentially practical, focusing on recipes, many contained prefaces or afterwords that offered opinions on the good and the beautiful, the rules of cooking and infractions thereof, and the history and philosophy of dining. The works were not read for these glosses, however, and this technical literature was not killed off by the advent of an autonomous gastronomy. The second genre was the work of physicians and would-be physicians, Ever since Hippocrates, medicine had been not just medicine but also, if not primarily, a form of hygiene, and every great era in medicine had its dietetic discourse: the Middle Ages had John of Milan and the School of Salerno, the seventeenth century had Gui Patin, and the eighteenth century had whoever wrote the prefaces to the *Dons de Comus*.[27] With their newfound prestige in the nineteenth century, the doctors became the gastronomes' valued comrades. Indeed, the two were often one and the same, and some doctors found it hard to reconcile their profession with their gourmandise. Yet until the middle of the twentieth century the basic texts of the discipline tended, in reaction against the old medicine, to avoid the concern with diet. In this area the field was open.

The third origin of gastronomic discourse, and the one that is often forgotten today because, though originally the most important of the three, it is the only one that has not survived, lies in the literature of gourmandise, a somewhat debased version of the heroicomic and the burlesque. Traditionally, revelers celebrated the hedonism of the palate along with the hedonism of the flesh, *la chère* and *la chair.* Such celebration developed its own forms of eloquence and poetry (bacchic verse, for example), which achieved their most polished form on the eve of the Revolution. Unlike the cookbooks, which were works of the uninitiated, these forms were practiced by men of letters and in general reflected the elitist sociability of bacchic societies promoting an epicurean philosophy. In a period of moral order they were a sign of nonconformism. Under Charles X, for example, a writer who began a book with the epigraph "All great thoughts come from the stomach" was indicating a muffled, "Voltairean" opposition to the established order. This gourmet literature, which flourished between 1750 and 1850, lost its prestige as it became more democratic and regional in character, with local poets writing alexandrines in praise of bouillabaisse and cassoulet.[28] Even back then, however, such writers of light verse were not necessarily considered to be full-fledged gastronomes.

Grimod thus had these three literatures at his disposal: the literature of the profession, the literature of science, and the literature of art. His personal contribution was to synthesize all three and move food writing onto a new plane. From the technical recipes he borrowed the didactic tone that justified such titles as "manual" and "almanac." From the medical treatises he borrowed observations on hygiene, which allowed him to write of, say, the artichoke as "a very healthful food, stomachic, astringent, and slightly aphrodisiac." And the eloquence of the gourmands was responsible for the lyrical flights and literary allusions, for the parallels between, for example, Raphael and pigs, since the painter used brushes made of hog's bristles. The subtitle of the *Journal des gourmands et des belles* gave as clear an indication as one could wish of what Grimod was drawing on: "Compiled by the author of the *Almanach gourmand*, several guests at the Vaudeville Dinners, and a doctor of medicine."

Origins

We can now begin to answer the question raised at the outset: Why the primacy of French cuisine? Because unlike any other country in the world, France went from the most absolutist of regimes to the most systematic destruction of absolutism, meanwhile retaining many aspects of the old regime under the new one, in particular a "modern" centralized organization. As in the age of monarchy, cooking and gastronomy continued to inspire rivalry among patrons and a concomitant emphasis on innovation. Patrons made the fortunes of particular dishes or products, some of which remained luxury items (such as *foie gras* during the reign of Louis XVI) while others soon became items of popular consumption (for example, Camembert cheese under Napoleon III). Chefs engaged in endless competition to come up with new dishes, with the consequence that changes in cooking styles spread rapidly and cooks were open to foreign ideas, though these of course had to be adapted to French tastes. The most obvious legacy of all this is the extreme centralism of French cuisine, with the center now shifted from Versailles to Paris: Grimod said that Paris offered "the best eating in the world,"[29] and Briffault said that Paris took from the provinces "the tithe and best part of what Providence thought it was distributing equally."[30] All over the world Paris had its admirers, "attentive to its tastes, whims, desires, and caprices."[31]

The most distinctive feature of the French scene, however, must be placed under the sign of rupture rather than continuity. One regime was radically undermined. A short time later a new order was established under the aegis of Napoleon, who in gastronomic matters relied on two illustrious survivors of the monarchy, Cambacérès, whose authority was disputed, and Talleyrand, who was universally acknowledged as an arbiter of good taste. "Sire," the latter addressed his new master, Louis XVIII, during the Congress of Vienna, "I need saucepans more than I need instructions" (in words that also meant: "I need spies more than prosecutions"). Of course this pragmatic loser meant his gnomic philosophy to be taken in jest, but it nevertheless marked the beginning of a new age of political gastronomy. "Meals," Brillat would observe, "have become a means of government."[32] Still, the full implications of this political rupture become apparent only when we recognize that it points up an undeniable crisis in aristocratic society, a crisis signaled as early as the reign of Louis XVI by the emergence of the restaurant, a French invention that subsequently "made the rounds of Europe."[33]

For our purposes it is unimportant to know who was the first Parisian restaurateur. Some say it was a man named Boulanger, who in 1765, as the old corporatist structures were collapsing, persuaded a judge to allow him to serve "restoratives" *(restaurants)* to clients of his establishment, thus breaking the monopoly of the household caterers. Others say the honor belongs to Champ d'Oiseau or Lamy some five to nine years later. But the most likely candidate is Antoine Beauvilliers, who in 1782 quit the service of none other than the king's brother, the Comte de Provence, to open a restaurant, which according to several observers he was the first to decorate in the manner of an imposing household: "An elegant salon, well-attired waiters, a carefully stocked cellar, and a superior kitchen."[34] There is reason to believe that the first two qualities counted as much at this stage as the last two: the establishment that Beauvilliers opened was not just another restaurant but the first "great restaurant," which immediately bestowed nobility on the whole new family. "The restaurateurs' accomplishment was a social feat," Briffault later observed. "Under the regime that they succeeded, good eating was the privilege of opulence; the restaurateurs put it within reach of everyone."[35] Never mind the overly

FIGURE 13.9. (Top) The Grand Buffet of Modern Cuisine; engraving by Hibon from an idea of Carême for the latter's Maître d'hôtel français. The stylish chef competes with the architect.

FIGURE 13.10–13.11. (Left) Frontispieces engraved by Mariage, after Duant, for Grimod de la Reynière's *Almanach des gourmands*, circa 1804. There is no better illustration of the idea that the gastronomer is an art critic whose true worktable is his writing desk.

schematic character of this assertion, the idealization of "everyone," and the neglect of the role played earlier by cabarets and inns, which are summarily dismissed as lacking in quality: the "social feat" remains. We discern the same genealogy behind '89 and '82: the conquering bourgeoisie.

Like Beauvilliers, several of the first "great chefs" had served in the kitchens of *grands seigneurs* in the waning years of the Ancien Régime. The custom of nobles' serving dinner to their friends in their own homes was beginning to fade, though just beginning, even in France, as the new desires of wealthy commoners came to the fore: namely, to dine well without maintaining a costly staff, to dine out on the town without having to depend on a complex system of selective invitations, and, last but not least, to dine out without having to endure the social promiscuity of inns and *tables d'hôte,* which had previously been the only authorized venues of public "restoration." The Revolution did not create this trend, but it did accelerate it in two ways. First, it put many domestic cooks on the street, and second, it set many *nouveaux riches* in search of good places to eat, *nouveaux riches* in search of respectability and well aware that the dinner table has always served as a place to administer qualifying examinations to the upwardly mobile.

To bring the founding age to a close, then, all that remained was for Brillat-Savarin to produce his theoretical, not to say dogmatic, summa, the *Physiologie du goût.* Brillat, born in 1755, was an almost exact contemporary of Grimod (born in 1758), and his "meditations on transcendental gastronomy" offer a complementary view of the period. Whereas Grimod, the son of a farmer-general, made a busy life out of what came naturally to one born with a silver spoon, Brillat came to prominence only after the Revolution as a *conseiller* on the Cour de Cassation. At a time when Grimod was regarded as an eccentric at best or at worst a parasite, Brillat was prospering under every regime except the Terror: he was forced to flee the country in 1793, but it would later be put down to his credit that the two countries he chose to visit in his flight were republics.[36] Whereas Grimod issued his pronouncements in the name of tradition, Brillat invoked science and reason. Grimod conceived of his work in moral terms, though his "philosophy" was amiable and unsystematic. Brillat was a disciple, ironic yet convinced, of the Ideologues, the leading intellectuals of the moderate Republic.

He had read Condillac's *Traité des sensations* and Dr. Cabanis's *Rapports du physique et du moral,* which offered praise of dietetics, and he made his debt to them explicit in the title he chose for his book and for its chapters and paragraphs: "On the Senses," "On Taste," "Theory of Frying," "Osmazome" [an old technical term for the part of meat that gives it its distinctive smell and taste.—TRANS.], "Purgative Diet." The important point is that these trappings of wit and scientific theory, both rather cumbrous, did not disqualify their author. On the contrary, his successors were encouraged to abandon their anonymity, still quite common in this

RF

EXPOSITION UNIVERSELLE

Banquet des Maires de France

Sous la Présidence de

M. ÉMILE LOUBET, Président de la RÉPUBLIQUE FRANÇAISE

MENU

HORS-D'ŒUVRE

Darnes de Saumon glacées Parisienne

Filet de Bœuf en Bellevue

Pains de canetons de Rouen

Poulardes de Bresse rôties

Ballotines de faisans Saint-Hubert

Salade Potel

Glaces Succès. — Condés

DESSERT

VINS

Preignac en carafes ✣ St-Julien en carafes

Haut-Sauternes

Beaune ✣ Margaux J. Calvet 1887

Champagne Montebello

(Potel et Chabot)

PROGRAMME

SALLE DES FÊTES

La Marseillaise

DANSES
DE JADIS ET DE NAGUÈRE

I. — Danses Barbares

II. — Danses Grecques

III. — Danses Françaises

IV. — Danses Modernes

LE CHANT DU DÉPART

Avec le Concours de

LA COMÉDIE-FRANÇAISE

et de

L'ACADÉMIE NATIONALE
DE MUSIQUE ET DE DANSE

(Orchestre de l'Opéra.)

FIGURE 13.12. The great years of the republican banquet were 1888, 1889, and 1900, when huge feasts were staged to symbolize the postprandial unity of the French nation. Here, a menu from the French mayors' banquet of 1900.

genre of writing, and set out in search of a cultural authority that was limited, to be sure, being remote from the more exalted sources of legitimation, but solid and popular. The nineteenth century thus saw the emergence of a French gastronomic school, which drew on Grimod's technique and Brillat's philosophy.

The prestige that both men enjoyed redounded to the credit of contemporary French cuisine: the third element of the founding trilogy was of course the chef-writer. At about the same time, in 1815, the illustrious Antonin Carême inaugurated the long line of loquaciously pontificating chefs that runs by way of Escoffier all the way to Paul Bocuse and beyond.[37] Significantly, Carême's career took him from Napoleon's ovens to those of the czar of Russia (after 1815, of course) and ultimately to the kitchens of Rothschild. The "chef to kings" thus bears witness to an age when glory could come to the "king of chefs," whose greatest joy was to be considered, if only briefly, not just a superior pâtissier but a master of the supreme art: architecture. The "Palladio of the kitchen," as a contemporary gastronome called him, was the author not only of *Pâtissier pittoresque* but also of a series of architectural plans for the "embellishment of Paris and Saint Petersburg."[38] A century later Escoffier liked to tell people that his first vocation, from which his parents dissuaded him, was sculpture.

FIGURE 13.13. (Left) One of the wine tents from the 1900 mayors' banquet.

FIGURE 13.14. (Above) A view of the kitchens for the 1900 mayors' banquet.

Can one dialectically transcend the chicken-and-egg question, "Does the chef make the gastronome or vice versa?" Grimod or Carême? Bocuse or Gault-Millau? It is a good bet that in substance culinary evolution is largely independent of gastronomic evolution, but in form the two are obviously closely related. Vigorous criticism encourages emulation among restaurants. If a gastronomic school does not reflect a noticeable change in culinary practice, it has to reflect a change in a society's relation to its cuisine. The cuisine that Grimod promoted owed more to the Age of Louis XV than to the Revolution, but the setting in which it was served had changed completely. Conversely, it was around 1880 that the "Russian service," in which courses are served in succession, definitively supplanted the "French service," in which dishes are served simultaneously. This marked a real culinary change, and while it did not lead immediately to a dramatic change in critical discourse, it did ultimately enrich the content of criticism by allowing for clearer discrimination between dishes.

Structures

French cuisine and gastronomy have long enjoyed a privileged status, yet both have been subject to the same forces as other aspects of culture. Like theater, philosophy, or the physical sciences, gastronomy can thus be seen as the fruit of a combination of structural factors stemming from the realms of technology (primarily agro-alimentary and culinary technologies), the economy (obviously associated with the history of the social movement), and finally, of course, the cultural domain itself, where the experimental and the human sciences, aesthetics and politics, often go hand in hand.

Take, for example, the relatively easy to decipher yet still richly significant "modern age" of gastronomy, which began in the late 1960s under the banner of a pair of writers whose place in history is already assured, Henri Gault and Christian Millau, the authors of a celebrated guidebook and coiners of the phrase *nouvelle cuisine.* Although the point is often overlooked, it is nevertheless obvious that, just as the New Wave in French cinema depended on certain technological advances such as lightweight cameras, certain of the culinary innovations introduced by the chefs honored by Gault and Millau depended on advances in kitchen appliances, food preservation techniques, especially freezing, and faster transportation, without which the fetish for "fresh ingredients" could hardly have existed. Similarly, the now commonplace "internationalization" of cuisine, which goes far beyond the traditional "naturalization" of foreign ingredients and recipes, depends on a flourishing international traffic not just in material goods but in people. Finally, both the menu and the commentary on the menu have been greatly affected by progress in oenology since the 1950s: the wine of 1980, meticulously analyzed and systematically processed, bears only a distant relationship to the wine of 1950 and probably no relationship at all to what was called wine in the Middle Ages.

Even more important, however, is the economic factor. There is no hyperbole in saying that the economic evolution of contemporary Western societies, beginning with urbanization and the growth of the service sector, has been revolutionary. For one thing, more and more women now work, so that in the not too distant future "home cooking" will be a thing of the past. As a result, diets have become more standardized, and the "pleasures of the table" have increasingly been associated exclusively with restaurants, thus giving food writers a more explicit social role—helping people decide where to eat—which is why food columns are increasingly common in newspapers and magazines. Clearly it was no accident that nouvelle cuisine came into vogue in the final years (1965–1975) of a thirty-year period of economic growth, that is, at the height of the great cycle of democratic prosperity inaugurated by the era of postwar reconstruction: the overall progress of the economy installed two new generations of "decision-makers" on either side of the kitchen door.

On the inside, by the ovens, young chefs were determined to control their own kitchens and indeed to own their own restaurants. "Kitchens to the cooks!" was the operative slogan of the eldest of the group, Paul Bocuse, in a move that was reminiscent of other transfers of power in not dissimilar realms of the economy and culture.[39] In the dining room, meanwhile, the clientele changed, with the new opinion-makers drawn from the upper reaches of the growing service sector, who expected to find reflected in their plates the same values that were paramount in their social

FIGURE 13.15–13.17. Nouvelle cuisine.

lives: transparency, dynamism, and innovation. The fans of Knoll furniture and ecotourism listened with respect to those who advocated a new simplicity in three areas: the preparation of dishes, the vocabulary of the gourmet, and the decor of restaurants. Of course they were still willing to pay high prices for all this simplicity, because though distinction may change in form, it will always come dear. The Gault-Millau line fit in with these new aspirations, with its offensive against "a replete France, slouching toward Bibendum,"[40] its crusade against long cooking times, flambés, sauces, table linen, *feuilletés* and other disguises, high game and marinades, all in the name of what Bocuse called "the cuisine of the marketplace"[41] and Michel Guérard called "cuisine minceur."[42]

This last argument suggests that the new state of affairs needs to be interpreted primarily in cultural terms. To be sure, the new cuisine reflects the current state of technology, but it is even more indicative of the current state of science, and especially the latest thinking about diet and nutrition. Whether they have read him or not, the views of the proponents of nouvelle cuisine cannot be understood without knowledge of the work of Dr. Trémolières, the founder of modern nutritional science, and a whole range of nutritionists and dietitians (who are increasingly gaining recognition of their professional status), organizations, and food suppliers, to say nothing of the ecology and consumer movements. As for the style in which the new wisdom was expressed, it is of some interest to know that it was developed by two journalists connected with a small but distinctive literary group, the so-called *hussards* [a name bestowed in the early 1950s on the novelists Roger Nimier, Jacques Laurent, Antoine Blondin, and Michel Déon—TRANS.]. Gault and Millau wrote for the daily *Paris-Presse* and the weekly *Nouveau Candide,* the two newspapers that in the early 1960s best typified the "impertinent" and "nonchalant" style that the writers of this group employed in their running battle with the academic, "committed" writers they detested—the "leftists," in a word.[43]

This polemic also had an aesthetic dimension: it was an attack on a gastronomy that was associated with an academic spirit, just as Jacques Laurent had earlier taxed "Jean-Paul" (Sartre) with being the heir of "Paul" (Bourget): "Gastronomy was invented by pedants who dreamed of being taken seriously."[44] Gault and Millau even launched a metonymic attack against the style of the traditional food writer as "dripping with cream sauce."[45]

Of course, as is often the case in such cultural battles, the very vigor of Gault and Millau's "modernist" attack on the "ancients" signaled their arrival as members of the family, their inclusion in the unbroken chain of gastronomic generations. For our purpose, which is not to reconstruct the chain but to indicate how it matches up with changing views of French identity, that is the principal lesson to be drawn from the case of the nouvelle cuisine.

Establishment

With this in mind, it is fairly easy to look back over the past two centuries and trace the evolution of gastronomical writing. Brillat-Savarin died in 1826, Carême in 1833, and Grimod de la Reynière in 1838. Drawing on all three, the gourmets of the next generation laid the groundwork for a veritable gastronomic society, with its sacred establishments, forms of sociability, rituals, and rhetoric. The first daily gastronomic column appeared,[46] as did the first periodical exclusively devoted to the subject.[47] This first gastronomical era, which corresponded roughly with the period of constitutional monarchy, from the fall of Charles X to the defeat of Mac-Mahon, gradually gave way to a new sensibility as a more democratic culture took root. The two periods can easily be confused in more than one respect, and in fact what French gastronomic memory has preserved of the century and a half between the publication of the *Physiologie du goût* and that of the *Guide Julliard de Paris* mingles, in the greatest imaginable confusion, images of the copious and the pompous both on the dinner table and in gastronomic publications. The only thing that stands out is the debonair but rather too portly figure of the "prince of gastronomes," the exact contemporary of the "prince of poets," Paul Fort—a fact that does little to enhance gastronomy's intellectual prestige.[48]

If one looks closely at gastronomic discourse, however, it is easy to distinguish two different sensibilities, with a transition from one to the other whose timing depends on whether one is dealing with a chef or a man of letters, a hotel restaurant or an inn, a Paris restaurant or a provincial establishment, etc. Auguste Escoffier owes his strategic importance precisely to his intermediate position not only in time (1846–1935) but also in the world of great international hotels. It would be surprising if this were not so, as it would be surprising if there were no noticeable difference between the gastronomy of 1830 and that of 1930, between the last flickering embers of aristocratic society and the absolute triumph of the petite bourgeoisie, which is attested in the realm of dining by the transition from French to Russian service.

The difference is evident even in writers as similar as Charles Monselet[49] and Curnonsky. Both moved in the same world, that of the Paris boulevards, though a half century apart. Both partook of that "true Parisian" spirit whose history has yet to be written but that was one of the most explicit ingredients of France's self-image throughout both periods in question. The *culture boulevardière* was marked by gaiety of tone and hedonistic values. Together these might have given rise to excesses potentially threatening to the social order, but they were kept within bounds by an overt philosophy that took the form of "cultivated" allusions to old-fashioned writers while avoiding doctrinaire criticism of any kind. But the two men addressed themselves to different audiences, as did the less well known but more substantial critics Eugène Briffault for the first period and Marcel Rouff for the second.

The audience in the later period was not only geographically and socially more diverse but, even more important, lived in a different intellectual universe. The republic, universal suffrage, and democratic associationism underwent a similar evolution, with their subtle equilibrium between a basic Jacobinism and a more explicit provincialism than is often acknowledged. At first, then, the idea was that, between bohemianism and the Parisian life, the only educated palates were to be found in Paris. But later, even though gastronomic discourse continued to be elaborated in the capital, it was tinged with regionalism or even frankly regionalist. The high point of this latter discourse was the Exposition Internationale of 1937, at which the first "class in gastronomy" was held at the Centre Régional.[50] Clearly, then, the most illustrious chefs of the Second Empire, such as Urbain Dubois and Jules Gouffé,[51] still belonged to the monarchical system, whereas those whom Curnonsky and Rouff sought to promote in their twenty-eight-volume *France gastronomique* (a title unthinkable in the Romantic era, when the typical gastronomic book was entitled *Paris à table*[52]) were identified as Alexandre Dumaine *of Saulieu* or Fernand Point *of Vienne*, as if they were feudal barons ensconced in their estates.

Grimod's nostalgia for "the Old Court" and its ability to keep alive "the sacred fires of good eating" now gave way to Curnonsky's nostalgia for "home cooking" and regional dishes. In 1926, the illustrious "Cur" launched a vogue in high society for a tart that he attributed to the Tatin sisters of Lamotte-Beuvron, and during the war and for some time thereafter he chose to live in epicurean retirement at Chez Mélanie in Riec-sur-Belon. In the late teens of the twentieth century the Burgundian Rouff painted a portrait of the ideal gastronome in his *Dodin-Bouffant*. Although the portrait was largely inspired by the Parisian Brillat-Savarin, Rouff deliberately obscured this essential aspect of the model and preferred to portray his hero as a prominent citizen of *la France profonde*.

In fact, the gastronomic society of the Third Republic was based on a less exalted network of notables, a network in which, as in parliament or the *conseils généraux*, professional men rubbed shoulders with independent entrepreneurs in the gourmet clubs that proliferated between the Franco-Prussian War and World War I. Such groups as the Club des Cent and the Club des Purs-Cent, the Académie des Gastronomes, and the increasingly common gastronomic confraternities[53] attest not so much to the survival of aristocratic institutions (for these were generally mere pastiches rather than authentic reconstitutions of aristocratic clubs) as to the tortuous fate of such fanciful notions in a republican century. Between the lascivious monk and the publican as the devil's henchman, medievalism enjoyed the favor of the gastronomes in Curnonsky's principality, obsessed as they were with the stereotypical images of the *fabliaux* and *rabelaiserie*.

Such old-fashioned pomp, also evident, even today, in the writing of many food columnists, was by no means contradictory with a real sensitivity to some of the more important structural changes in French society. Gastronomic decentralization was of course connected with the development of new means of transportation, and above all, at mid-century, with the most bourgeois of all forms of transportation, the automobile. Nothing is more significant in this connection than the role played by the Automobile-Club de France (A.C.F.), the Touring-Club de France (T.C.F.), and the Michelin guide in the gastronomic mapping of the nation.[54] Outside Paris, the most famous restaurants of the post–World War II era have been found chiefly along the major tourist routes defined by the main national highways. In the same period, doctors, disproportionately represented among gastronomes,[55] have rediscovered their old concern with hygiene, whose leading postwar spokesman has been Édouard de Pomiane.[56]

Thus gastronomic France had already considerably evolved between romanticism and realism, between the sumptuous lyricism of Alexandre Dumas's *Grand Dictionnaire de cuisine*[57] and the "coziness" of Curnonsky's *Cuisine et vins de France*,[58] or, on the more technical side, between Dubois's *La Cuisine classique*[59] and Prosper Montagné's *Larousse gastronomique*.[60] Nevertheless, there was probably still a gap between an Escoffier-style *haute cuisine* beyond the reach of the ordinary gourmet, a Curnonsky-style "naturist" discourse ("cuisine is when things taste like what they are"), and a *bonne cuisine* likely to go heavy on the sauce and more likely to be over- rather than underdone. When the prince died, this culinary aesthetic was ripe for systematic *flambage,* the height of a showy if "rustic" conception of dining, even as France was beginning to declare itself to be "resolutely modern."

Modernism

The modern age of gastronomy has been fully in harmony with the economic and cultural changes of the past forty years. Modern gastronomy was defined by the *hussards,* and its values, dietary preferences, and audience were drawn from the upper echelons of the service sector. But these facts do not explain everything. For one thing, Gault and Millau had the advantage of presiding over an authentic culinary mutation, a change whose effects were quickly felt throughout "the profession." For another, eating gained a new intellectual respectablity, which affected both gastronomic discourse and the status of restaurants. The historiographic movement mentioned earlier was only one manifestation of a change in the French intelligentsia's attitude toward these issues after 1968, the year, it is worth recalling, in which Claude Lévi-Strauss published *L'Origine des manières de table.*

Was this unpredictable change due in part to the outspoken hedonism of the 1968 generation, despite its initial hostility to *la grande bouffe* as a symbol of the antinatural disequilibrium of consumer society? Or, on the other hand, should one see it as a striking demonstration of the retreat into individualism of the decade 1975–1985? Probably it was a little of both: many "postmoderns" are aging *soixante-huitards.* Hence it was probably no accident that the success of Jean-Paul Aron's *Mangeur du XIX*^e^ *siècle* came in the mid-1970s, which marked both the beginning of the "postmodern" decade and the end of thirty years of postwar progress.[61] The most important factor, however, is one common to both periods: the exaltation of the body, freed at last of the ideological vestments in which it had been wrapped by secular as well as religious puritanism. It would have been surprising if a society that suddenly and belatedly discovered the importance of physical discipline in activities ranging from sports to dancing to yoga,[62] and that called fervently for the "liberation" of the body, had not also begun to take a less condescending attitude toward eating and drinking than had been common only a short while before, when the only "intelligent" writing on the subject had been Roland Barthes's quite ironic chapters in *Mythologies.*[63]

Until the late 1960s, writing about food was the preserve of amateurs (such as gourmet doctors) and writers without intellectual authority (journalists, local writers, and dilettantes). Within a period of ten years, however, a new type of discourse appeared. Anthropologists and sociologists from Marcel Detienne to Michel de Certeau still maintained a prophylactic distance from the object of their inquiry.[64]

FIGURE 13.18. Stamp honoring French gastronomy, 1980.

But there were also "serious" books that were nevertheless deeply implicated in the subject, such as Jean-François Revel's *Festin en paroles*, Frédéric Lange's poetic anthropology,[65] Noëlle Châtelet's psychoanalysis,[66] and Jean-Louis Flandrin's historical gourmet columns.[67] In 1975, Barthes abandoned sarcasm in his preface to a new edition of the *Physiologie du goût*,[68] and a short while later one of his disciples, Jean-Claude Bonnet, published the first modern edition of Grimod de La Reynière. In 1985, Michel Serres, another admired essayist, accorded the culinary sensibility a place of honor in his *Cinq Sens*.[69] And in a sign of the times, the orthodox Lacanian journal *L'Ane, le magazine freudien*, devoted a special issue to cooking in 1983: its title was "We Eat Signifiers."

Six years later, in 1989, two young philosophers, Michel Onfray and Michel Field, published best-selling books. Onfray's *Le Ventre des philosophes* interpreted the works of the great philosophers in terms of their relation to food.[70] And Field's *L'Homme aux pâtes* is an erudite fiction containing, among other things, a reinterpretation of history in terms of a "battle of pastas" that mobilizes all the field marshals and captains among the day's intellectuals.[71] The mode was still ironic, to be sure, but the irony was now second-degree, an exaggeration rather than a negation of reality.

An analysis of the press further corroborates the extent and nature of the new concern with food. Reprints and new editions proliferated in the late 1960s, and within twenty years all the old classics, from Taillevent's *Viandier* to Rouff's *Dodin-Bouffant*, were once again available to food lovers. The leading newspaper *Le Monde* expanded its gastronomic column, which had been written since shortly after the war by Robert Courtine. In 1989 an Étude pour la Valorisation de la Recherche en Sciences Humaines (E.V.R.S.H.) launched a prestige publication that borrowed Platine's title *L'Honnête Volupté* and added a subtitle proclaiming that "Culinary Art [is] Major Art."[72]

One of the leading food writers of the 1990s, Gilles Pudlowski, can be seen as a pure product of the '68 generation, a writer who moved imperceptibly from poetry and political militancy to the poetics of the table and culinary militancy by way of a passionate reflection on France's national identity and his own personal identity.[73] The son of Polish Jewish immigrants who had settled in Alsace, he has several times expressed how important gastronomy was in providing him with access to French culture. After such books as *Un judaïsme tranquille* and *L'Éternité à Port-Royal*, his first essay on gastronomy included chapters with titles like "Wine Also Speaks to Me in Yiddish" and "Gourmandise Is a French Quality." Indeed, for Pudlowski, that is precisely the point. "I love this country. And this book is nothing but a love song."[74] These words, written in 1984, recall the gastro-patriotic literature of the turn of the century, yet he points out that "the best wine specialists are men with names like Alexis Lichine, Steven Spurrier, John Winroth, Hugh Johnson, and

Henri Elwing. . . . And all this, I told myself, makes for excellent Frenchmen."[75] Does it also make France? Pudlowski is ready with an answer: "The France I'm talking about does not exist. At least these inns existed."[76] "In short, the only France I know is gourmet France. . . . So don't hold it against me if my *French,* my *exemplary French,* are master chefs or master vintners, cellar men, and vine growers. . . . This country, as vast, multifarious, and well-fed as it is gourmand, is indeed a gigantic, convivial, perpetual, quotidian feast" [italics in the original].[77]

"Love of Country" and "The Frenchman's Duty": these titles of two of Pudlowski's essays may well stand as a conclusion to this first attempt to interpret gastronomy as a source of French national identity. I hope to have shown that the history of gastronomy's origins and transformations does not merely reflect the history of France but sheds new light on certain of its aspects. What we find is an old country that has long been unified and centralized (it hardly needs pointing out that the two terms are not synonymous). More than that, France is a country that has been quick to intellectualize its unity and centrality, and often this has meant, to some extent at any rate, codifying them. But once we move beyond such generalities, gastronomic legitimation draws on a typically French tendency to take seriously activities elsewhere deemed trivial, a characteristic of France that is likely to provoke puzzlement or irony abroad.[78] In the twentieth century this tendency can be seen at work in the role that France has played in bestowing respectability on the "minor arts" of "popular culture." From film to comic books, from the Surrealist Revolution to "hot jazz," France has taken the fore in promoting the notion that there are no limits to conceptualization and that the intellect ennobles whatever it touches.

Everything else is a matter of circumstance. France's *grande cuisine* crystallized once and for all under the absolute monarchy, while gastronomy took shape under the "conservative Revolution." In retrospect, it is difficult to deny that these two periods were the founding epochs of modern France. There are of course many other ways for a nation to look back on its past, but many French people would argue that none is more agreeable.

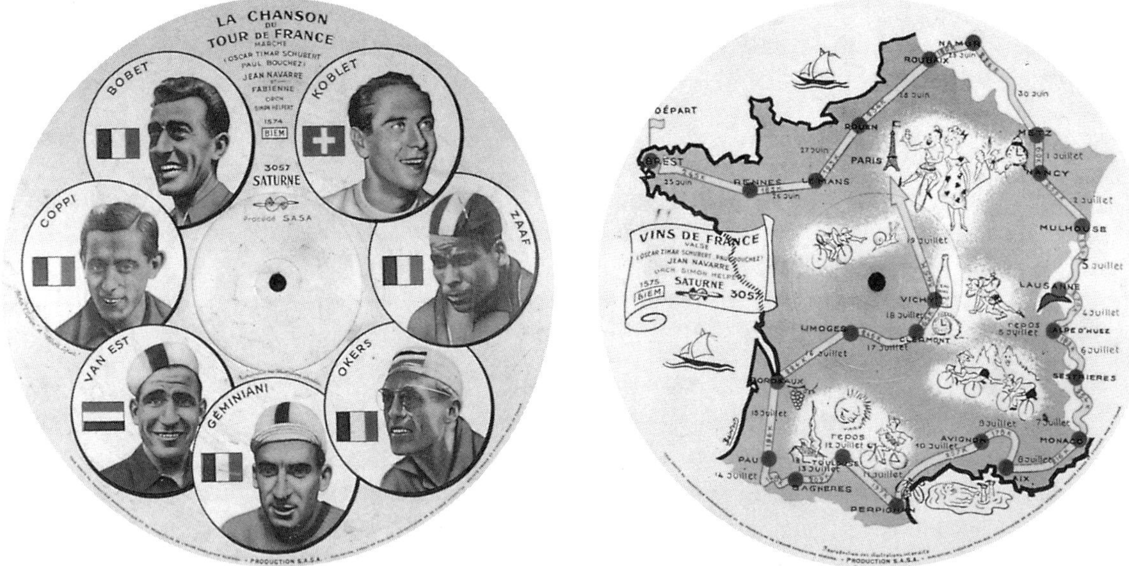

FIGURE 14.0 AND 14.1. The culture of the Tour: the endless repetition of the route, the faces of the riders, and local products sampled along the way. The race was also a focal point of recreation, song, and local culture: here, a Saturn recording of the Chanson du tour de France features the faces of champion riders on the front and the route of the Tour on the flip side.

CHAPTER XIV

The Tour de France

Georges Vigarello

When Desgrange, the managing editor of *L'Auto*, gave the starting signal for the first Tour de France one night in July 1903, he probably had no idea that he was inaugurating a lasting institution. All he wanted to do was compete with rival sports dailies by financing an important race: stories of unprecedented feats would attract new readers as well as new advertisers. But the venture quickly surpassed all predictions: the paper's circulation jumped from 20,000 to 60,000, celebrations marked the route, and wildly enthusiastic crowds turned out at every finish line. This race caught on in a way that no previous race had ever done. The annual event quickly became a tradition: its success was so visible and so familiar that the Tour came to seem a public treasure, a "national property," to borrow a phrase from Georges Rozet, a journalist who covered the race for *Le Temps* in 1908.[1] And Xavier Louy, who is in charge of organizing the Tour today, calls it "part of the national heritage."[2]

Within a few decades the Tour de France had become an established national ritual. It is by now an institution so sanctified as to seem ageless, a spectacle whose origins have been forgotten. Perhaps this is because the contest is more than just a race: it touches the collective consciousness, France's sense of community, as much as it appeals to the curiosity of sports fans. It has to do with geography, provinces, and frontiers. It presents the nation in spatial terms, using the landscape as scenery in an elaborate staging. The racecourse is more than a line on a map. Traveling the route calls to mind past encounters and events: the Tour evokes geographical memories. *Le Monde* remarked on this by invoking the poet Jacques Prévert: "Here a belfry, there Poulidor, and there Lip or Victor Hugo."[3] The course of the Tour is as much a symbol of the national heritage as it is the route of a bicycle race. The history of the Tour's setting is as important as the history of the race itself. The memory of the race combines two histories, one long, the other short, and together these two histories define its meaning.

1. Memory Tour

From the outset one image was crucial: Desgrange in 1903 called it "a ring completely encircling France."[4] The event has retained this symbol: the course is regular and above all circular. The Tour is one of those charged representations of the national territory, an idealized geography. It is the France that students learn about in elementary school, the France that Ferdinand Buisson described as "symmetrical, proportioned, and regular."[5] It is also the France of tradition, upon which monarchs attempted to impose Euclidean geometry through royal rounds and circuits. This idealized geography is not the geography of the scholars, of Vidal de La Blache, for example, whose *Tableau*, published in the same year as the first Tour de France, stressed the patchwork of the soil and the absence of any clearly defined natural boundaries.[6] Rather, it is the geography of the people, of a people more likely to respond to flattering images than to contour plots. The race was designed to appeal to the imagination, indeed it was compelled to do so by the need to attract an audience. Its professed goal was to "contemplate the marvels with which nature has endowed France."[7]

The Renewal of Tradition

Desgrange's racecourse followed a long tradition of tours of France. Circular itineraries had always exploited the symbolism of circumference. The monarch's tours suggested territorial possession and offered displays of sovereignty. The tour of the *compagnons* (journeymen) was a voyage of initiation, as workmen set out to acquire training from master craftsmen along the route. Pedagogical tours taught children about France through a kind of literary game. The circuit concocted by the editors of *L'Auto* partook of all of these: it was a demonstrative procession, a workingman's itinerary, and an educational device.

Desgrange's course most closely resembled the pedagogical and journeymen's tours. The original route closely followed the itinerary of the typical *compagnon:* Paris, Lyons, Marseilles, Toulouse, Nantes, Paris. It drew on the image of the self-sufficient laborer, who looked after all his own needs. In 1926 racers were still setting out, each with "three inner tubes on his back, extra spokes on the frame, and a spoke key in his jersey pocket, along with a safety toe clip."[8] In case of mishap they were required to repair their bicycles themselves. No help was allowed from the few "followers" or even from other racers, at least during the first few runs of the Tour. And so, in the 1913 Tour, one had the image of Christophe, "the old Gaul," welding his own front fork at Sainte-Marie-de-Campan in the middle of the night after a fall in the Tourmalet.[9] This was a latter-day version of what George Sand once called "the knight-errantry of the artisan,"[10] which the 1903 race organizers consciously evoked through repeated references to "past departures"[11] and "octogenarian *compagnons*"[12] nostalgic for the voyages of old. *Compagnon du Tour* was the title that Tristan Bernard gave to a book he wrote in 1934, but now the focus was on episodes occurring within the race itself.[13]

The race drew even more on memories of pedagogical tours of France, designed to reveal the glories of the country and bolster a sense of citizenship. The aim was to inform the spectator about the "most beautiful parts of France."[14] Here we detect the influence of the embryonic tourist trade, with its early photographic essays and its guidebooks such as the Guides-Joanne and Guides-Conty. But we also sense the enthusiasm aroused by the republican primary schools, which had produced the *Tour de la France par deux enfants*, a text still in widespread use in 1903.[15] Mme Fouillée's book had sold more than six million copies by the time of the first Tour de France. It was the canonical example of the trip transformed into an educational journey, the most celebrated version of the adventure story as pedagogical device. Of course none of the book's detail could be incorporated into Desgrange's project. No race could provide an exhaustive inventory of the country's riches nor "present the fatherland in the noblest possible light," as Mme Fouillée's book claimed to do.[16] Nevertheless, there was a resemblance, for *L'Auto* openly avowed its educational ambitions and at times dwelt at length on places and towns through which the racers passed. Nantua, for example, was described as a "tidy little town bathing its feet on the shore of a majestic lake."[17] The climate of the Midi was graphically depicted for the benefit of readers in Paris: "You Parisians, my friends, you have no idea what the dust of the Midi is like!"[18] The Tour, almost in spite of itself, took up the educator's dream of teaching the country about itself.

There was also a more specific educational intention: *L'Auto* proposed not simply to inform its readers about the various regions of France but to transform those regions. It was a self-consciously modern project in which sport was to become a "gigantic crusade," a herald of progress and discovery. The paper had a rather grandiose sense of mission: "The racers will carry the ideal of the new life to the most tranquil of hamlets and the most out-of-the-way cottages. They will teach people, or remind them, that the conditions of life are changing every day."[19] Champions were to become "superb sowers of ideas" and "rude awakeners of energy."[20] The whole extravaganza was to instill a new morality and spread "the good athletic word."[21] The Tour thus reproduced the discourse not only of educators but of the early-twentieth-century elite, with its insistence on athletics as a healthful activity capable of halting alcoholism, poor hygiene, and physical decrepitude in its spectators. Wouldn't the race help get people "out of the tavern?"[22]

FIGURE 14.2. Written reports of the race were soon embellished with photographs. The reporting told the story of the race that the immobile spectator could not see. This accounts for the importance of race journalism and its exploitation by advertisers. Here, the cover of *La Vie au grand air* featuring the first Tour de France, 1903.

Wouldn't it help them rediscover "the secret of all moral energy?"[23] Here is Bergson's answer to the questions put by the *Gaulois littéraire* in 1912: "What I like best about sports is the self-confidence it generates. . . . I believe in a renaissance of French morality."[24]

Thus the tradition of the tour interacted with the belief in modernism; the old journeys were exploited even as the virtues of "physical regeneration" were touted. History was superimposed on the present, as evidenced by the confrontation with technology: the racer alone on the road stood for both the *compagnon* of old and the modern worker with his machine. Man was alone but not without tools; he was bare-handed but also mechanized. He had to deal with machines: he moved on wheels rather than on foot, using devices made not by artisans but by engineers. The old journeymen's initiation rituals were revived to sing the praises of machinery: for *L'Auto*, the "fairy bicycle" was "the intelligent creature's first successful effort to free himself from the laws of gravity."[25] The bicycle embodied all the images of scientific technology, "with its chains as thin as watch chains and all but frictionless bearings that reduce the human body to an algebraic formula."[26] At the beginning of the twentieth century people were fascinated with these contraptions. The new bicycles, which had come onto the market only a few years earlier, had movable handlebars, steel bearings, and chain drives that made them incomparably easier to use than their immediate predecessors, the *draisienne* and the *grand-bi*. Not only did this type of bicycle enable people to move about quickly, it was also the first consumer product of industrialized France, with sales climbing from 50,000 in 1890 to more than a million in 1901: a "social boon," according to the contemporary bicycling press.[27] It was also a symbol of speed, as Colette observed upon witnessing the Tour in 1912: she barely caught glimpses of the racers as they passed by, faceless creatures with "hollow eyes and dusty lashes" hidden behind masks of sweat and dirt, with "black and yellow backs bearing red numbers on their arched spines. They quickly disappeared, the only silent ones amidst the tumult."[28] The Tour in a sense abolished distance, but it was also a mix of ageless labor and mechanical exploitation, of working-class identification and industrial standards, and in 1903 the bicycle was the quintessential symbol of all of these things.

The case was further complicated by the fact that the machine itself exemplified both the present and the past, the new and the old. It was linked to the age-old equestrian tradition: the rider straddled the machine, sat on a saddle, kept his head erect. The analogy proved to have a lasting appeal, which gave rise to all sorts of archaic images and anachronistic parallels. Baudry de Saunier, the first historian of the bicycle, frequently availed himself of the comparison in 1894: "The cycle rider like the equestrian has, in my view, an obligation to the public, an obligation of elegance."[29]

Even the terminology was confused: for a long time the word *cavalier* (rider) was preferred to *cycliste* (cyclist). Mallarmé referred to female cyclists as *les chevaucheuses de l'acier*, steel-horsewomen.[30] Reports of the Tour borrowed such comparisons. Rozet, describing the tougher stretches of the race and the difficulties of the riders, ticked off the movements of horse and jockey: "The animal is ill-tempered and stubborn and has to be dragged out of the mud, spurred in the flank, and reined in on downhills, and it tends to rear up on the cobblestones."[31] The "bicycle, a small machine," thus took on almost organic, animal qualities.[32] Such comparisons drew little comment and were not carried very far, yet they show that in working-class memory the Tour was still to some extent interchangeable with the noble journeys of old. Did the bicycle wreak a kind of vengeance on the horse? It was in any case a way of reappropriating space, of conquering the realm of speed, which had always belonged to "others."[33] Part of the Tour's appeal lay in this particular interaction between tradition and modernity. The machine made its mark on the very itinerary where the horse once dominated. Like the horse, it proceeded stage by stage, from post to post, following the same route as Ancien Régime travelers but moving more rapidly with the aid of modern technology.

La Vie au Grand Air

ABONNEMENTS : Paris et Départements 24 fr. Etranger 28 fr.

21 Juillet 1906 ✍ N° 409
PUBLICATIONS PIERRE LAFITTE & Cie
9 et 11, avenue de l'Opéra, PARIS ✍ Téléph. 280.52, 280.56, 254 88
Publicité : HUGUET, MINART & Cie, 11, boulev. des Italiens

PUBLICITÉ : Pages d'Annonces, la ligne 2 fr. La Page 600 fr. Encartage 750 fr.

LE TOUR DE FRANCE ✍ AUCOUTURIER RÉPARE SA ROUE BRISÉE DANS LE BALLON D'ALSACE

Aucouturier, toujours sur la brèche, fournit encore une très belle course dans le Tour de France. Mais les crampes d'estomac qui le font si souvent souffrir dans les épreuves auxquelles il prend part, de nombreux accidents de machine l'ont forcé à abandonner au désespoir de ses partisans. Notre photographie le représente en train de changer la roue d'avant de sa machine, qui vient de se briser au moment où il montait le Ballon d'Alsace. (Voir pages 510 à 512.)

FIGURE 14.3 In the early Tours the good racer was also a good worker. Here, Aucouturier repears a broken wheel in the Ballon d'Alsace; *La Vie au grand air* (July 21, 1906).

The Appropriation of the Land

The journey still marked out a territory. The land became a feature in a spectacle. Symbolism accentuated three of its qualities: immensity, beauty, and natural defenses.

The regions traversed were always infinite. To know France was to experience vastness. The racers always seemed lost in endless panoramas: "Night is falling and the mistral is still blowing on the immense plain in the midst of which a fantastic Arles looms up beneath the moon."[34] The end of the journey is never in sight. The racers obliterate local boundaries as they rush off to invisible destinations: "Through the calm of the Vendean countryside, all along the Loire, which flows slowly and silently, men are about to flee into the distance at breakneck speed."[35]

The land was not only vast, it was also beautiful. The Tour was intended to be an aesthetic experience. *L'Auto* never hesitated to pluck the strings of emotion. Crossing France magnified it: "The waters of Villefranche seen from the Corne d'Or have no rival but the sky, which joins the Mediterranean at the horizon."[36] Reports painted portraits: the images that emerged from slightly wrinkled postcards reinforced ideas acquired at school or conveyed by popular culture. The better known the sight, the more it was appreciated. The description of the "Grande Bleue" with its "sumptuous background" and "fantastic cliffs" told the reader nothing but confirmed the quasi-eternal beauty of France—confirmed rather than revealed.[37] But aesthetics was sufficiently important for it to remain a permanent feature of the Tour. When Henri Troyat was sent to cover the Tour in 1939, he chose the aesthetic vein, remarking on the "background of miraculous places" through which the racers passed.[38] *L'Équipe,* the sporting paper that succeeded *L'Auto* in 1945, also made much of the aesthetics of the Tour, though in a more touristic mode: "Shining a searchlight on the magnificence of our countryside, our sea, our mountains."[39] Nowadays, of course, the possibility of vacationing in such places tends to attach market value to aesthetic considerations: "The effect of the Tour on the national economy is virtually incalculable. Belgian and Dutch tourists would not be aware of the Causses as a place worth visiting were it not for the Tour de France."[40]

Knowledge of the countryside tended to be translated into adjectives of splendor—a device by which early providentialist descriptions of France as a country enjoying the protection of Nature could be made to seem modern. But there was also an almost physical identification with the geography. The relief and contours of the land were immediately translated into sensory, muscular terms. One discovered a France inhabited by the body, mapped out by physical effort: "A charming landscape! The riders were through it all too soon, and their backs were soon bent once again, for Nantua has its hill, a hill about two kilometers long that demands a strenuous muscular effort."[41] Every distance, every change in altitude seemed to have its energy equivalent: some places called for intense effort, others permitted a moment of relaxation, still others called for acceleration, always measured in terms of the racer's pulse: "In passing L'Isle-sur-le-Doubs the racers naturally savor the morning charm of the delightful surroundings."[42] The landscape took on palpable, individualized features. It became something not to know but to take possession of.

It was not the configuration but the character of the terrain that mattered. Strength and skill were needed to master the country in this way, and this mastery became one of the enduring features of the Tour.

In this respect mountains played a special role: they were a barrier to be overcome. In the mountains riders broke down from exhaustion, fell, or clashed with one another. The mountains made people uneasy: "The Alps loom up with roads cut into their flanks that are frighteningly steep to climb and take you through dizzying hairpins on the way down."[43] The point about the country's boundaries was reinforced: if the mountains were impressive, they were also formidable defensive ramparts. The old theme of natural borders was restated in an irrefutable form.

The first two versions of the Tour followed the old *compagnonnage* routes. The course soon expanded to the nation's borders, including the Alps (1905) and the Pyrenees (1910). Their presentation was always dramatized: they were difficult, inaccessible places. Think of Lapize's complaint to the organizers after crossing the Aubisque in 1909. Exhausted, barely able to walk, but leading the pack, he got off his bike and yelled: "You're criminals!"[44] The mountains were still a realm of frozen wastes, and accidents demonstrated what formidable barriers they were. It was precisely the riskiness and difficulty of the mountain stages, of the battle with those Molochs, the Alps and Pyrenees, those "monsters of cruelty," that demonstrated the legitimacy of France's natural borders. The mountains, seemingly impregnable, lay "in wait for the riders as if they were prey."[45] France became one: ringed by mountains and seas, it was protected and homogeneous. The age-old image of France as a country defined by nature and defended by its own soil resurfaced, and the Tour, "skirting just those seas and climbing just those mountains," confirmed it.[46] This was the same tradition of natural boundaries defended by the *Conventionnels* and the soldiers of Year II and vaunted by the nineteenth-century champions of the nation-state: "Its limits are traced by nature. We reach them in the four corners of the horizon, on the Rhine and the Atlantic, in the Pyrenees and the Alps. These are France's boundaries."[47] The Tour ensured the triumph of this popular image of a France unified by the soil, surely a stronger unity than that afforded by language or customs. Thus a very special value was ascribed to geography.

The Memory of the Earth

But there was more to the theme of grandeur than this. If the territory was to be valued, it had to be seen as ancient and durable. So the Tour not only evoked the country's size and unity but also delved into its memory. The splendid scenery was made even more splendid through allusions to history. Each new site offered yet another occasion to evoke the past: Du Guesclin at Broons in the Breton countryside, Joan of Arc at Orléans, the Poilu (infantryman) of 1914 at Metz, Nancy, and Châlons. At times the allusion was merely conventional, intended only to confirm the presence of time. Consider, for instance, the commemoration of Mme du Barry upon cross-

FIGURE 14.4. Mountains were a key feature of the Tour: they marked the nation's boundaries, protecting and unifying French territory; drawing by Pellos, 1936.

ing the Meuse: "It was not to pay their respects to Mme du Barry, Louis XV's notorious mistress, who before being decapitated on the Place de Grève was a native of Vaucoulers, that the racers picked up the pace at kilometer 160."[48] Or this even more artificial allusion to Saint Udant at Ax-les-Thermes: "It was here that Saint Udant, Attila's vanquisher, was martyred in 452 during the pontificate of Pope Leo I."[49] The commentators cited history as a guidebook might do, mentioning historical events in connection with places visited but with no particular purpose in mind other than to recall the existence of a past. Thus the final stage of the 1989 race, Versailles to Paris, evoked the Revolution: "Twenty-seven kilometers from Versailles to the Champs-Élysées, with a pass by the Tuileries the better to commemorate the bicentennial of the French Revolution."[50] Here the only point being made is that France is a land with a history.

More commonly, the nation's glories were evoked with a quite specific purpose: to demonstrate that France is also a land with many exploits to its credit. The images of the great men of the past and the riders of the present blur together to justify faith in the grandeur of France. Names are uttered in celebration: "Of course the Vendée specializes in national glories. They grow there like mushrooms: for instance,

Clemenceau and de Lattre de Tassigny, to name only the most recent. But who had any idea that on reaching the Gironde estuary, this 1972 Tour de France was going to turn up the names of eighteen staunch warriors?"[51] There were also references to battles, images of 1870 in the first Tours and of the World Wars in subsequent ones: a "charming pink sandstone chapel" stood as a "reminder of yesterday's combat" in the Vosges,[52] while reminders of "the Battle of Belgium" lay along the course through the Ardennes.[53] Some commentators were determined to bear witness to the upheaval of war, assuming a kind of moral responsibility: "We have passed through a veritable lunar landscape [Longwy, Charleville, Armentières in 1919], which the children of France must be made aware of."[54]

A frequent, perhaps even dominant, reference was to Napoleon and the Grand Army. With Desgrange this still took a rather pompous form: "The crowd will applaud as they pass, just as yesterday's crowds hailed the return of Napoleon's grizzled veterans from Spain and Austria."[55] Others took a more amused or frivolous tone, but the importance of the model is still clear: "At the starting line in Charleville, the man they used to call 'Rik Imperator' [Van Looy, the future winner] chose to celebrate the bicentennial of Napoleon's birth in his own way, beating the drums for his own French campaign on the battlefields of Bazeilles, Montmédy, and Pont-à-Mousson."[56] The aggressive strategist drew the lion's share of the attention: "Battle along Napoleon's route," ran the headline for a report on a stage near Grenoble,[57] and another, on an Alpine descent, read "Back from the Italian Wars."[58]

This was popular history, in other words, interested mainly in heroes and battles, with the national defense as its immediate background and nostalgia for a time of conquest as a more remote reference. What survived in memory was a victorious France, its past summed up in a few striking events and powerful men. It was also a nostalgic France, secretly thinking of the Napoleonic adventure as a glorious epic. The Tour reawakened memories of a triumphant country led victoriously into battle by great men, with the riders' sweat and fatigue adding a note of realism to the mix.

2. A National Institution

Surely the Tour owes much of its success to this ability to awaken memories, to reveal the country to itself from the sea to the mountains and the mountains to the sea. But the Tour project itself was not static. It had its own history and underwent its own internal transformations, influenced by the spirit of the times. And interest in the race also changed, as did its organization and staging.

The Tour naturally changed with the times. As a reflection of the ambient culture, the race can tell us a great deal about some of the important changes in popular culture over the course of the century.

FIGURE 14.5–14.6. Private enterprise chose its national symbols shrewdly, turning the Tour into a unique event, unlike any other. 14.5. The start of the 1939 Tour de France at the Arc de Triomphe. 14.6. The Finish of the 1980 tour.

The Weight of the Inaugural

A former notary's clerk and one-time racer as well as an authoritarian, ambitious managing editor, Desgrange treated the race as an investment. His goal was to use the race to sell papers and attract new readers and advertisers. And daily circulation did in fact grow quickly and steadily: from 200,000 in July 1914 to 500,00 in July

1924.[59] The crucial link between sports and industry was clearly explained by the managing editor himself: "The Tour de France has created a significant new market, so that the bicycle manufacturers were quick to recognize it as an indispensable race."[60] In other words, *L'Auto* was selling a show. It did so on behalf of a triumphant new machine, the bicycle, which had caught on with the public: the number of bicycles in use grew from one million at the turn of the century to seven million twenty-five years later.[61] The paper sold bicycles by singing the praises of mechanical progress and celebrating science and technology. From this came the enthusiasm, so evident in early commentators on the Tour, for the modern economy and economic growth: "*L'Auto* will daily sing the praises of the athletes and of industry."[62] In the early days it was the bicycle itself that was the sign of progress, pointing the way to the future, "the future of the bicycle, which the present can only dimly perceive."[63] Of course the bicycle did not remain a technological marvel for long, and the triumph of other forms of locomotion would not be without effects on the tour.

"Wounded" France

Another characteristic of the early Tours was the emphasis on "physical regeneration," for which the race became a symbol.[64] This, too, was a product of the times. The talk of a physical renaissance of course reflected the insults that France had suffered in 1870 and was suffused with nostalgia for her lost provinces. At the beginning of the twentieth century, sport, the athletic spectacle, was frequently thought of as a militant tool, a remedy for "disasters that ought to serve as lessons."[65] Of course the spectacle was still minuscule by current standards, and many people already looked upon it as strictly a holiday rather than a moral lesson. Local festivities associated with the race included such traditional activities as dances and torchlight parades. But *L'Auto*'s strong suit was pedagogical language. It invoked the notion of collective salvation. It excelled at borrowing arguments from the enlightened elite: "In recent years a new and perhaps incomparable thirst for physical exercise has given rise to an ideal of physical health which every day takes a clearer shape in our minds. We have learned our lesson: this way salvation lies."[66] Whence the staging of the race, which could seem controlled rather than spontaneous, laid on rather than responding to what people wanted. Along with it went a certain interpretation of the athletic mission: "I want people to come [to the race] more as if to a pilgrimage than to a show."[67]

The routing through the German-annexed territories takes on its full meaning in this context. The 1906 race was the first to gain the permission of German authorities to enter Alsace-Lorraine, and the same route was followed until 1911, when the Germans reneged. Each incursion into German territory became an occasion for symbolic reappropriation. The race was a kind of homecoming. The route was marked out in French with yellow signs in the colors of *L'Auto*, and a few bold souls sang "La Marseillaise": "It was perhaps the first time since the war of 1870 that exclusively French signs could be seen in Alsace-Lorraine."[68] And there were also the spectators, who came as if to a family reunion in which one could sense the approval of the local populace and the pride of the visitors.

Territorial symbolism thus received very special treatment. At times the Tour insisted so heavily on the borders that their reality became inescapable. Then the nation's wounds, which figured so prominently in the symbolism of the early races, took on a tragic dimension.

The National Ritual

The event also adopted certain national symbols. The Arc de Triomphe, for example, figured in the early Tours. Although the race really started at the gates of Paris, the riders passed through the arch as if they were warriors on parade. *L'Auto* vividly described their passing at night "between rows of curious spectators" along the Champs-Élysées and the Avenue de la Grande-Armée on their way to the starting line.[69] After 1920 the ritual was expanded to include an earlier procession along the grand boulevards: even larger crowds gathered in front of such historic monuments as the Opera, the Madeleine, the Obelisk, and the Arc de Triomphe. This *parcours des honneurs* was repeated year after year until World War II, and in 1975 it was revived in a different but no less significant form, no longer at the start of the race but at the finish, with an urban lap including the Champs-Élysées. Another tradition passed down through the decades was the red lanyard worn by the *garde républicaine* escorting the racers. The search for a suitable triumphal procession has thus been a durable feature of the Tour.

Last but not least, the participation of the authorities lent the event a quasi-official status: mayors and subprefects greeted the racers in cities along the course, as did generals and other officers at frontier fortifications. In Toulouse in 1909, for example, the official reviewers included the ten municipal councillors, the mayor, the subprefect, and a military band.[70] The race was a national event.

The Making of Heroes

There was also the physical struggle itself, and here the newspaper played a crucial role. Its job was to recount the race. It gave meaning and unity to the fleeting glimpse of the racers that the roadside spectator was likely to catch. Newspaper accounts gave the event duration. So the reporting mattered. The articles published in *L'Auto* re-created the tension of the race; they brought out the drama, creating it if need be out of whole cloth. The first segment of the 1904 race, Paris-Lyons, unfolded without notable incident, but the report in *L'Auto* created incidents anyway, noting every acceleration and every obstacle. Garin, the first winner in 1903 and the favorite in 1904, had to avoid the traps that other riders set for him: "At night a veritable pack is constantly at his heels, testing him, looking for weaknesses."[71] Bicycling, a sport of stamina and tense comebacks, lent itself to such dramatization.

Journalists spiced the drama by leaving out the boring parts. They fabricated the story of the race. More than that, they focused admiration. They singled out certain exploits for special attention. On the road to Lyons, Garin became superhuman: "I felt the same admiration for Maurice Garin that I had felt as a child for the heroes of legend," Desgrange admitted.[72] The "Italian chimney sweep," a naturalized citizen of France and winner of the 1903 Tour, was described as a "superb fighting animal," a "Hercules of the highways," a "giant." "Heroes are necessary," the organizer of the Tour pointed out.[73] Here we see the other purpose of the race: the creation of a mythical space, the description of exemplary men. The early Tours witnessed the emergence not only of Garin but of "sport's sacred battalion": Aucouturier, with lungs like "the bellows of a forge,"[74] Christophe "the old Gaul," Faber, the "giant from Colombes," and Pottier, who won in the Ballon d'Alsace in 1906 and was immortalized by a monument that Desgrange commissioned at the summit two years later. There was nothing surprising about any of this: it is the job of the press to magnify. Enthusiasm became its normal tone. It did not seek to persuade its readers but to impose its point of view. The marketing logic was impeccable: *L'Auto* organized a race that only a newspaper could report. No effort was spared, as Jean Calvet points out in his fine book, *Le Mythe des géants de la route*, to make the race "a popular epic and create a myth."[75]

The mythological creation succeeded. Its heroes acquired a solidity, a density that did not depend on what the journalists wrote. Witness the crowds that turned out to greet them: in 1914 the Vélodrome of Marseilles filled two hours before the cyclists arrived, and the gates had to be closed. Songs and novels were written about the racers: in 1924, for example, Darcaux and Decoin published *Le Roi de la pédale*, which was quickly made into a film.[76] The Tour created a gallery of heroes, men who, according to *L'Auto*, were made of "a different flesh and blood from the rest of us."[77]

Did this mean that traditional cultures and religious beliefs disappeared? Not necessarily. But just after the turn of the century athletics did give rise to a totally new system of representations, a repertory of actions and symbols with which people identified. The new heroes were at once proximate and remote, familiar and elusive. Therein lay the novelty: the Tour bestowed legendary status on men who triumphed over the mountains, but "these feats were performed by ordinary men."[78] The adventure, as Desgrange pointed out, remained "human, athletic, egalitarian."[79] When the exhausted Aubisque shouted "you are criminals" at the organizers in 1910, he was demonstrating that even heroes are human. The champion was "beyond" mere mortals, but what set him apart was his talent and energy, and these were accessible traits. Winners were human and yet more than human, like other men yet still incomparable. Suddenly a vast social dream became possible. The Tour, like all sports, gave people a way to think about the contradiction inherent in any democratic society: the conflict between an equality of principle and an inequal-

ity of fact, between a contract of right and an accommodation of force, of real disparities. Through sports "anybody could become somebody" without disrupting the social hierarchy.[80] In any case, the race was inextricably intertwined with the business of creating heroes. The mechanism was crucial, and it would remain a constant feature of the Tour.

This national sporting institution did change in other respects, however, especially in regard to staging and context. We turn next to these.

"Free Time" Festivity

A significant change in the organization of the race came about in 1930. National teams replaced the manufacturers' teams, so that the competition was no longer between

FIGURE 14.7–14.8. Over the years, advertising spread to the racers' hats, uniforms, and support vehicles and also appeared on buildings in towns along the route. But publicity was a part of the Tour from the beginning, as ads in the early issues of *L'Auto* indicate. 14.7. Finish of the first Tour de France, with Garin, 1903. 14.8. The victory of Eddie Merckx, 1969.

brand names but between countries. This meant an end to the domination of the race by certain firms, which were suspected of favoring selected riders and rigging the spectacle. The reasons given for the decision would thus appear to have been technical: to limit the power of the bicycle manufacturers (who had been hurt by the economic crisis) and end their meddling in the competition. The consequences, however, were far-reaching, affecting the inner workings and staging of the race itself.

International Alliances and Battles

The focus on national teams after 1930 changed the way in which the battle was reported if nothing else. The drama was simplified to focus on the clash of national monoliths: "the day of the Belgians," "the health of the Germans," "the hotel of the French."[81] And the number of countries competing increased. Desgrange canvassed all Europe for racers. Besides the usual Germans, Belgians, and Italians, he signed up teams from Romania, Yugoslavia, Austria, and Luxembourg. His paper piqued the interest and curiosity of its readers: "What tactics will the Belgians use?" "The Romanian team has left Bucharest." "The Yugoslavian team has arrived in Paris."[82] Other changes soon followed. Political allusions, for example, began to crop up in race reports. The battles of the Tour echoed the important international debates of the interwar period: the question of grand alliances, the negotiations of the 1930s, and, after Hitler's accession to power in 1933, the signing of secret as well as public defensive pacts. The phraseology of post-1930 Tour reporting reflected these diplomatic concerns, re-creating a world of pacts, mutual assistance agreements, and national conflict, but in its own simplified, pictorial manner. German riders often wore "mournful masks," the Italians had "conspiratorial looks," and the French, like Leducq, the winner of the 1930 and 1932 Tours, were "more jovial."[83] In this almost involuntary transposition, the Tour was reassuring. It reduced tensions, putting a tolerable face on the intolerable, transforming anxiety into hope: nations clashed throughout the 1930s in these summertime races along their borders; they fought hard, sometimes aggressively, but always within the framework of a sport that people liked to think of as reconciling differences. A symbol of this was the photo of the start of the race on the Champs-Élysées, with the Arc de Triomphe in the background, that *L'Auto* published in 1930: "Friend and sister nations climbing toward the triumphal arch," read the caption.[84] Another symbol was the new emphasis on Strasbourg, a stop on the way to Geneva: "The racers in the capital of the League of Nations."[85] Within each team, moreover, riders now helped each other out, reflecting the newfound solidarity of the working class.

Prolific Procession

Other changes were even more important. The disappearance of the manufacturers' teams along with (some of) their paid advertising led to the introduction of new

FIGURE 14.9. Selling drinks and cycling newspapers was always a goal of the Tour. Here, spectators await the arrival of racers in the 1935 Tour; photograph by Robert Capa.

publicity techniques: companies paid the organizers of the race for the privilege of joining the caravan of vehicles bearing various signs and messages. The racecourse itself was now exploited, and its spectators were addressed directly and not just through the pages of the newspaper. This transformed the spectacle. In 1930, for example, the race caravan was headed by a truck from Meunier Chocolate, which distributed five thousand paper hats bearing the firm's name. The company's agents distributed tons of chocolate bars. At every mountaintop, Meunier representatives offered cups of hot chocolate to spectators and riders alike.[86] More than twenty companies having nothing to do with bicycling participated in the 1930 event, sometimes handing out free samples to the public. The Lion Noir wax firm sent a truck with a giant can of wax. Various alcoholic beverage manufacturers sent cars to which colossal cardboard replicas of brandy bottles had been attached, standing up, lying down, or set at an angle to the roof and so huge that they dwarfed the vehicles on which they were mounted.[87] The caravan naturally made the Tour an even more festive affair.

Indeed, the colorful procession itself became the symbol of progress, replacing the bicycle. It was a palpable, noisy sign of modernity, at a time when the bicycle

FIGURE 14.10. The parade of advertisers has been an integral part of the Tour since 1930. The photograph is from 1990.

manufacturers could no longer afford to maintain their dominance of the race (by 1929, the number of bicycles in use stood at around seven million, but the rate of increase had slowed to a few tens of thousands annually).[88] The procession, with its ads and slogans, its loudspeakers and trucks, was now the harbinger of things to come: "Industrial plenty on the march toward the future."[89]

At a deeper level, the caravan changed the explicit meaning of the celebration. Its purpose became recreation rather than morality, pleasure rather than education. It widened the gap between the organizers' vague intentions (the "celebration of energy") and the public's immediate pleasure, the exciting presence of things to buy or to dream of buying. What was the Tour if not a raucous celebration of industrial abundance?

The Tour, with its summer caravansaries and spendthrift, prodigal crowds packing sun-drenched highways, was also a harbinger of the workingman's vacation. Photographs signal the change: vacation spots suddenly appeared in the pages of *L'Auto* and the *Miroir des sports* around 1930. Although beach resorts were still extremely rare, they already connoted sensuality: "At La Garonnette, in front of a large crowd of pretty bathing beauties wearing even less than last year though more than they will be wearing next year and the year after that, Fréchaut, Vierni, and Cosson decided to leave their nearly seventy comrades in the dust."[90] Other photos tell the same story: the number of spectators on the mountaintops suddenly increased in the 1930s. This of course reflected the success of the race, but it was also a sign of the greater mobility of the spectators themselves, of their willingness and desire to travel. Compare the scant, all-male crowd at the peak of La Faucille in 1928 with the several rows of spectators pictured on the same peak ten years later, with far more women among them.[91] Although it is impossible to estimate just how many people turned out to see the Tour each year, such photographs are suggestive. A new kind of celebration was invented in the 1930s, with sports and advertising combining in unprecedented ways. In this we see a glimmer of the future of leisure consumption and the dream of recreation.

And there was also a new way of being present at the race: the radio, which first began broadcasting news in 1927, began providing regular reports on the Tour in 1929.[92] Roadside commentators such as Georges Briquet gave new meaning to the excitement of the event: incidents were immediately flashed to the audience, along with results and interviews. As a result the Tour became noisier and more frenetic than ever. The race was important enough for news of it to be broadcast hourly, and the excitement was palpable enough to fill the airways. A sport thus became a sporting *event,* reinforcing the logic of the new modes of communication, which also allowed the captive audience to see hitherto inaccessible aspects of the event. As always, the race existed because it was talked and written about.

Mediatization

Since 1947, when *L'Équipe,* the successor to *L'Auto,* began organizing the Tour, the festival aspect has become more important than ever. The caravan is still a central feature of the event, and the distribution of free gifts makes it seem as though a "hot-weather Santa Claus" has come to town.[93] Banania has replaced Meunier, distributing 21,000 packets of chocolate daily and more than nine tons at the end of the race in 1985. Coca Cola gives away more than sixty tons of beverages.[94]

Nevertheless, there have been changes since the Tour resumed after the war, as the consumer aspect of the event was accentuated while its role as an educator of the nation has been played down.

A Model of Consumption

When the organizers discuss the race today, they do so without invoking any moral ambitions or edifying intention—there is no transcendence, or at any rate very little. The goal is to create pleasure, to go after it and exploit it. Jacques Goddet, the race director who presided over the fiftieth anniversary of the Tour in 1963, was silent on the subjects of physical regeneration and the importance of will: "This is a holiday in the absolute sense of the word, that is, an opportunity to cast aside your habits and forget your worries and go to a place where a spectacle will be brought to you, a show that, happy or sad, is always beautiful and colorful and full of interesting new ideas, a fantastic display of commercial intelligence thanks to the advertising caravan, which makes people glad they stuck it out through the long waits to see the temporary displays set up in the cities along the route."[95] The Tour became more than ever a form of recreation. Realism replaced lyricism. The eschatological and philosophical interpretations were a thing of the past. From now on the organizer's job was simply to lay out the route. No more militant speeches. One sees many similar shifts in contemporary culture: the virtual disappearance of public discourse and public models, the investment in the present rather than in some visionary future, and the demise of moralistic rhetoric. As democratic societies develop, one finds less of a search for federation, less of an impulse toward unification.

Last but not least, television has only added to the exploitation of the race by advertisers. Television has been recording finishes since 1948 and transmitting live images of mountain segments since 1958. Since 1962 it has been able to broadcast the last thirty kilometers of the event using miniaturized wireless cameras mounted on motorcycles.[96] Television has unified the event, while its images have given the spectacle a new lease on life. Not only is the televised event more realistic than the newspaper or radio account, it has transformed the technique of advertising. To publicize a brand name, for instance, care is taken to make sure that it appears on the screen during live segments, indeed that it appears everywhere. As a result, advertising has become part of the very backdrop of the race: it appears on the riders' jerseys, on moving signs, on speakers' podiums. National teams were eliminated in 1962 under pressure from advertisers wanting to sponsor teams of their own. The benefits were immediately tangible and significant. Peugeot multiplied its television exposure tenfold when it sponsored a team in 1978 instead of spending the same amount to finance a standard publicity campaign. The monthly magazine *Vélo* calculated that it cost 192,000 francs per month to maintain a racer in 1978, compared with 110,000 francs for a thirty-second publicity spot on the main television network, TF1 (at 8 P.M. on a weekday).[97] Thus it cost a company far less to get its name on television by sponsoring a team than by running ads.

Finally, television has vastly increased the number of spectators. So much so that in 1987 Jean Leuliot described the Tour as "the most popular sporting event on the tube."[98]

Anachronisms?

Increasingly, however, the race has had to cope with geographic constraints: traffic, urbanization, and huge summer crowds blocking the caravan's path. Hence there has been a tendency to avoid certain places (like the Côte d'Azur), and since 1960 the race has ceased to follow the outline of France's borders. But these changes merely reflect changing circumstances.

Far more significant are the regular excursions abroad. It is nowadays common for parts of the Tour to take place in other countries. Segments of the race are staged in foreign capitals and countries. This was rare before 1940 (apart from occasional

FIGURE 14.11–14.12. The number of spectators in the mountain stages increased steadily. The Tour encouraged tourism.

14.11. (Top) A mountain pass in 1920.

14.12. (Left) A mountain pass in 1986.

visits to the German-annexed provinces, isolated incursions, and a more or less regular stop in Geneva) but has become common since the resumption of the race in 1947. In 1949 there were visits to Belgium, Switzerland, and Italy. In 1965 an entire segment of the race was run in Belgium, along with a start in Germany and a long excursion into Spain. Almost every Tour since 1947 has crossed the border at some point. There have been repeated proclamations that "the Tour is a link between nations."[99] It is a sign, one indication among others, of a decreased national "concentration." Yet there are reasons to be cautious: every attempt to create an international bicycle tour has failed or at best met with limited success. For example, the Tour of Europe in 1954 crossed twelve borders without arousing the slightest interest, and the experiment was not repeated.[100] The Tour de France remains rooted in French soil. It lives in France. Its foreign excursions are merely a sideshow.

There is also a financial reason why the Tour no longer cleaves to France's borders. Cities now pay for the privilege of being visited, from which they directly profit: "It is easy to understand the Tour's appeal to tourist and real-estate interests in view of the fact that Orcières-Merlette [a winter sports resort in the Alps] became famous overnight when Ocaña beat Merckx in that segment of the race in 1971, and this instant notoriety brought an immediate influx of French and foreign tourists."[101] Cities therefore engage in subtle competition to have the Tour routed their way. That is why the twisting course passes some cities by: a closed circuit is no longer as important as the commercial interests at stake. Most people nowadays are willing to accept breaks in the route as the riders travel to international sites by train or airplane. But there has been some criticism of the abandonment of old landmarks, coupled with fears that nothing but fragments of the old Tour will remain: "If a region is no longer susceptible to the Tour's appeal, the racers will make several laps of the host city, then hop a plane and fly off to a place where the welcome is likely to be warmer."[102] The 1982 Tour, for example, consisted of a dozen separate segments, some of them separated by hundreds of miles.[103] France as a geographical entity is no longer the centerpiece of the circuit.

In the long run there are signs that the future of the race may not be secure even in France. For one thing, popular culture has changed: today it is less intimately bound up with local customs and as a result, perhaps, less interested in an event that traverses different regions. As local disparities diminish, the Tour can no longer aspire, as Desgrange hoped, to bring out "differences in customs and speech."[104] The danger is that the whole idea of the Tour may come to seem quaint, a bit of folklore from the past. This is compounded by the fact that other multi-stage races have taken adventure to new venues: the Paris-Dakar automobile race, for example, offers new images of immensity, powerful machines, and a dangerous confrontation with nature.[105] Audience surveys show that the television audience for the Tour is aging.[106] Will it eventually come to seem a relic of the past?

FIGURE 14.13. The Tour de France has come to include excursions beyond the country's borders, an acknowledgment of the growing permeability of frontiers and increased international tourism: Puigcerdá, 1965.

There is no way to be sure whether or not the Tour is today perceived as an anachronism. Indeed, the race has polished up its image considerably. It has modernized itself. It has transformed its televised appearance, overhauled its advertising techniques, and increased foreign participation (the presence of American, Canadian, and Australian riders in Tours of France during the 1980s sharply increased interest in those countries and spurred the bicycle market in places where it had previously been quite limited).[107] Above all, the Tour has constructed its own history, indeed its own legend. The race looks at itself, judges itself, evaluates itself in the light of this knowledge of the past. It combines its own distinctive memory with its present-day incarnation. The Tour has a culture of its own. This memory surely adds to the appeal of today's spectacle, so that it is hard to call the Tour anachronistic.

3. The Memory of the Tour

The Tour thus has its own temporal existence—not just the list of past winners but a veritable history of important events. Spectators remember these events and turn them over in their minds to create a distinctive set of representations. Memory links the race to various sites along its route, a veritable historical atlas: "A new map of France has taken shape inside the old one, a map in which the provinces bear the colors of the champions who made their names there while at the same time making the names of the provinces."[108] And then, too, the race has its own mythology, with its rituals and sacred sites, which also tell us a great deal about popular culture and representations.

The Commemorative Will

The desire to create a specific memory was present from the earliest races. In introducing each new race, *L'Auto* would remind readers of incidents from previous runnings. It would quote old reports stage by stage, constructing an anthology. This recapitulation had its rules: the events selected had to enhance the image of the race. There was little or nothing said about the dark side of the competition or the occasional outbreaks of violence. The attacks on certain racers in the second Tour during the Col de la République segment were carefully expunged from subsequent retellings. Yet these were serious incidents: Gerbi lost a finger, and César, a modest rider from Nîmes, was left in a coma after being beaten up by thugs hired by rival racers.[109] Also expunged from the record were the poisonings of certain favorites, to say nothing of the repeated bargains struck between riders or teams to fix the race. And for years nothing was said about accidents due to drugs and stimulants: for example, Simpson's death on Mont Ventoux on July 13, 1967, was officially blamed on heat and exhaustion even though the autopsy report mentioned "dangerous substances" in the athlete's body.[110] The history of the race has its darker side, which has been purged from memory. The business of making heroes makes no room for disturbing realities.

Monuments, on the other hand, exemplify the kind of memory that enhances the image of the athletes: the stele on the Ballon d'Alsace erected in 1907 in honor of Pottier was the first of its kind, and other riders in the early part of the century saluted it in passing "as soldiers might salute a flag captured by their elders."[111] Similar monuments have been erected at various places along the route: in 1948, for example, a high stone tower was built on the summit of Le Galibier to honor Desgrange, who had died a few years earlier; a plaque was dedicated in Sainte-Marie-de-Campan as a reminder of Christophe's accident in 1913 and his single-handed repair of his bicycle; and another plaque serves as a memorial to Simpson, the rider who died on Mont Ventoux. Even the creation of the Tour is commemorated in marble at the Café de Madrid on the Boulevard des Italiens, where

Desgrange is supposed to have announced the plans for the first race. Another symbolic gesture is the commemorative ceremony at the start or finish of a segment: in 1988, for example, the mayor of La Haye–Fouassière dedicated the Place Jacques-Anquetil at the start of one short segment.[112] In other words, the creation of the Tour's memory has its own rituals. It also has its own texts, its golden books, its "tales and legends," which regularly recount past races or introduce new ones. The unity of the national contest is affirmed over time. But certain Tours stand out above all others, and certain events have engraved themselves particularly deep in memory.

The Grand Tours

Some races have left more indelible traces than others, and some versions of the race have been more successful, especially those in which unexpected incidents and reversals seemed to magnify the riders' exploits. Take, for example, the 1930 Tour, the first race run with national teams. From the outset the dominant rider was André Leducq, a popular racer with a brilliant record whom *L'Auto* dubbed the "French ragamuffin" (*gavroche national*, after the character in Victor Hugo's *Les Misérables*). He still held a clear lead after the first Alpine segments, despite the strong performance of Benoît Faure, "a climber of astonishing talents."[113] But he took a hard fall after Grenoble during the descent of Le Galibier and lost nearly a quarter of an hour to the racers closest to him in the overall ranking. The champion, his knees bloodied, could barely stand. The race was lost: that, at any rate, was the firm opinion of the radio reporters on the scene, present for only the second year on the Tour. But the impossible happened: with help from other racers on the French team, Leducq made up the time he had lost. He even managed to outdo his rivals and win the Évian segment—a "stunning victory" according to the reporters.[114] Leducq was crowned the winner in Paris.

Immediately the episode was heralded as a sign of energy and team spirit. Was this not the first French team? Leducq's return concretely demonstrated what a team effort could accomplish: a rider could be protected from the wind by his teammates, reducing the effort required to maintain the pace. But the exploit took on even greater importance in the weeks and months that followed with the publication of photos of Leducq's fall, including one that inspired sculptor Arno Breker's *Wounded Warrior*.[115] Certain facts were forgotten as well. And the participants themselves offered explanations. Some of them continued to attend races and became a kind of living memory. For example, Marcel Bidot, a teammate of Leducq's who served as manager of the French team in 1950, had this to say about the exploit twenty years after the fact: "All the ingredients needed to turn the event into legend were present, including the role of fate and providence."[116] The reporting turned Leducq's feat into an indelible act.

FIGURE 14.14. Team strategies tended to promote rivalries between team leaders. The 1964 Tour, in which the top two riders were separated by only fourteen seconds, has become legendary and immortalized the names of Anquetil and Poulidor.

Equally strong images emerged from the 1964, in which Anquetil, the favorite, fell far behind in the Alps. "Flagging," read the headline in *L'Équipe*.[117] But when he made up for lost time in the Hyères-Toulon segment, the headline read "Incredible Ride."[118] The champion clung to his small lead through the Pyrenees. Then came the Puy de Dôme and the duel with Poulidor. The contest was intense. Anquetil's overall lead was reduced to fourteen seconds by the time the riders reached the summit, but he held that lead in Paris: "The Final Battle of an Unforgettable Tour."[119]

The great Tours were always being compared to plays and films. In 1923, *L'Auto* went so far as to compare Henri Pélissier's victory in the Nice-Briançon segment to the theater of Racine. Pélissier slowly gained on the leader before scoring a defini-

FIGURE 14.15. Pottier with his bicycle in 1905. The early machines were heavy and simple and had no gears, and so allowed no finessing of the difficulties of the route.

tive victory, putting other favorites out of the running: "All day long, Henri Pélissier put on a show that can rival any work of art. His victory was as beautifully orchestrated as Racine's plays."[120] If the race was in fact more situation comedy than Racinian tragedy, the fact that the action extended over several days allowed reporters to keep readers in suspense, as if watching a cliffhanger. The great Tours were those in which a dominant hero had to contend with some sort of surprise. Accidents, of course, did introduce a genuinely tragic note, as in the 1960 Tour, when Rivière fell into a ravine in Le Perjuret. Though favored to win the race, he was seriously injured and had to drop out. Or again, in 1919, Christophe broke his front fork a second time in the penultimate segment, when he was leading the pack. The "old Gaul" lost the race: "Huge, dirty gray clouds filled the sky. Nature seemed to be in mourning," according to *L'Auto*.[121] The tragedy was seen as an even greater injustice than in 1913: a collection was taken up to alleviate "poor Christophe's despair," and the amount collected was considerably greater than the winner's purse.[122]

The Tour turned cycling into a serialized drama, a transformation facilitated by the tactics of the sport: riders raced ahead of the pack or overtook it or fell behind it or were overtaken by it, they helped one another, and they created surprises. It was easy to weave a narrative around such events. The device of dressing the current leader in a yellow jersey, the famous *maillot jaune,* was adopted in 1919. By marking out the position of the leader and making him visible despite the vicissitudes of the course, this practice heightened the daily drama of the race. In this respect the Tour was a model of its kind. It was also a model in creating memory. More than other kinds of sporting events, the Tour was sustained by its history. It required a past, and it needed the recounting of that past. The Tour was better appreciated as a story than as an event glimpsed from the side of the road. Narration brought it to life. And the narrative particularly favored comebacks, which the artful narrator could then compare to other comebacks. It was common to weave together narratives of different races, to compare one with another. This gave rise to a kind of culture of the Tour. The memory of the Tour became part of the race itself. It was only logical for Anquetil to compare his weakness in the mountains in 1964 to Coppi's in 1952.[123] And it is only logical for *Le Miroir du cyclisme* today to devote a regular column to "Tales and Legends of the Tour de France."[124] This realm of legend can tell us a great deal about popular imagery and its evolution.

The Legendary Imagination

Not only did certain races stand out from the rest, but so did certain men. In 1988 the magazine *Vélo* ran an article entitled "The Soloists of Le Galibier" about the great climbers of the past: Bartali, "imperial" in 1937, and Coppi, "knocked out" in 1952.[125] Exploits were projected into a timeless realm where heroes mingled. Thus Kubler, photographed in the timed segment of the 1949 Tour "on the verge of becoming a legend,"[126] belonged to the same world as Buysse, who crossed Le Tourmalet in a storm in "a legendary segment" in 1926.[127] The time of myth directly infiltrated the present: Anquetil condemned the refusal of other riders to run the Tarbes-Valence-Agen segment in 1978 on the grounds that "the legend requires it."[128] It bears repeating: the Tour was for creating heroes.

The Generational Issue

Legend, which Chateaubriand called the "mirage of history,"[129] had a specific function in the world of the Tour. The rider who became a hero drove home the truth of the imaginary France that the race evoked. He served as a kind of mediator between the memory of the soil and the national geography suggested by the Tour. He breathed life into a France that was at once discovered and rediscovered, enhancing it with heroic feats performed in what Roland Barthes has called a "Homeric geography" fraught with accidents and natural challenges.[130]

The heroic rider of course took his place among the other figures of sports mythology. As we saw earlier, such heroes serve as social mediators. They are familiar yet inaccessible, "giants" who help bridge the gap between the legal equal-

FIGURE 14.16. Le Mond with his bicycle in 1990. Paradoxically, the bicycle, though easily outrun by swifter, more modern vehicles, seems capable of endless technological improvement.

ity and de facto inequality of democratic society. Riders often receive nicknames as tokens of this deceptive proximity: Alavoine was "Boy Jean," Gauthier was "Nanar," Lauredi was "Nello," Marinelli the "Parakeet," and Hinault the "Badger." These names were revered yet familiar: "In the diminutives attached to bicycle racers there is a mixture of servility, admiration, and privilege that makes the people voyeurs of their gods."[131]

This athletic Olympus creates the agonizing rivalry that has become characteristic of the Tour. The very nature of the race tends to create rivals: riders can run side by side for long periods, they can enter into alliances or break them off, and they can clash in duels. Rivalry takes all the classic forms. Sometimes the hero is so dominant that he brooks no competition: Bartali in 1938 was so far ahead of his adversaries that the commentators spent all their time just describing him: "His thin arms and prominent veins remind you of ivy climbing the trunk of an oak tree."[132] At other times the hero is threatened by a close rival: Anquetil's battling it out with Poulidor on the Puy de Dôme in 1964 was described as a fratricidal struggle: "It was Cain cutting Abel's throat, and this ultimately established a kind of fraternity between the two men."[133] More profound as well as more common was the theme of rivalry between a younger man and an older one, combining generational conflict with athletic competition: for example, Vietto, "King René," a twenty-year-old climber,

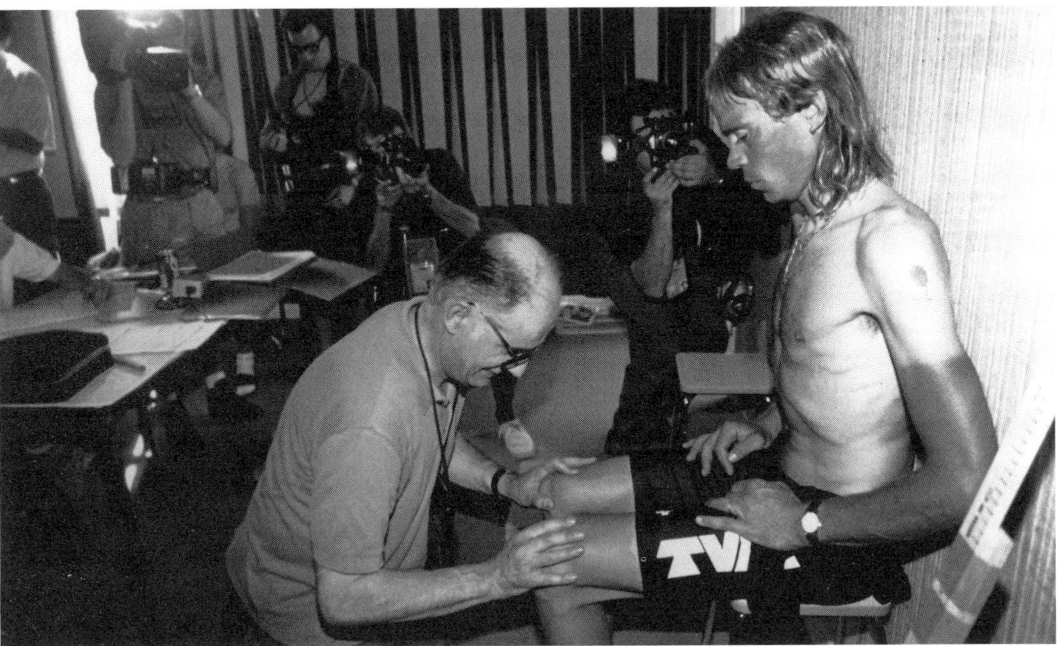

FIGURE 14.17–14.18. The bicycle racer is like everyone else and yet very different, which only intensifies the tendency of spectators to identify with riders.

14.17. A break during the 1920 Tour.

14.18. A break during the 1991 Tour.

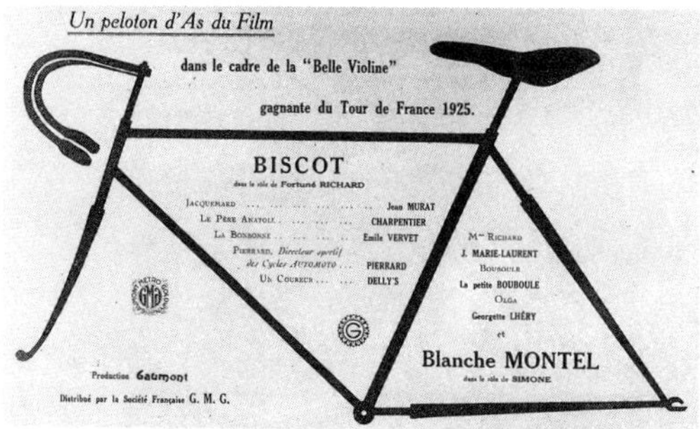

FIGURE 14.19. The Tour also gives rise to a culture of its own, a culture of popular fiction and drama: film poster for *La Belle Violine,* winner of the 1925 Tour de France.

sacrificed his chances in the 1934 Tour to backtrack during a descent in the Pyrenees and give his wheel to Antonin Magne, the acknowledged leader. Or, conversely, in 1952, Bartali, the aging champion, gave his wheel to Coppi for a major descent. The generational theme is surely the most persistent: Christophe and Lambot in 1919, Bottechia and Pélissier in 1923, Vietto and Magne in 1934, Robic and Vietto in 1947 ("King René" was now the mentor), Gaul and Bobet in 1944, Merckx and Ocaña in 1971, Hinault and Le Mond in 1986. Although such clashes could take a variety of forms, the focus was generally on youthful energy. For Desgrange the contest was between "young wolves" and "old veterans."[134] In this respect Vietto's gesture in 1934 created a canonical image: the martyr sacrificed to the older leader, even though *L'Auto* believed that the young man from Cannes was "exactly what the Tour needs, a brave and bold young hero, determined but careful, fierce yet sensible, a wingèd young climber whom the crowd adores."[135] Vietto's sacrifice was seen as weakness. In this there was no doubt an oedipal component but also a more historical element. Athletics confirmed the growing importance of a new social value: precociousness as a prize, youth as a form of success. It was a new world in which adolescents could perform great feats. Sports, and especially the Tour with its duels between rivals, symbolized the conflict between generations. Here, the content of the legend clearly revealed a new aspect of contemporary culture.

From the "Bulldog" to the "Computer Technician"

The timeless heroes of the Tour had psychological profiles, social identities, and images that changed from decade to decade. Time inevitably affects myth, even if certain dominant polarities remain.

For example, the qualities attributed to champions changed dramatically over the years. In particular, the description of the ideal racer's body was refined. Garin in 1904 was a "bulldog," a "wild boar," a "fighting animal" who knew how "to charge with his head down."[136] These traits were deemed "remarkable" by sportswriters at the turn of the century. And Faber, the "colossus of Colombes," won in Metz in 1909 because he could "charge like a brute."[137] The racer's silhouette was massive. His body was dense, even heavy. Power belonged to those whose strength was visible, whose bodies were compact, robust, and rugged.

By 1920 things had changed considerably: the bulldog was out, the jackrabbit—in the form of Henri Pélissier, the winner of the 1923 Tour—was in. There was a new attention to the shape of the body: "powerful without being heavy or fat, with a slim waist: he has the speed of a rabbit."[138] Strength shed pounds, so that calculation and subtle strategy became essential. The "beasts of burden" had had their day, *L'Auto* proclaimed in 1923.[139] This refinement of body type continued over the next few decades: in 1955 Agostinho was not only svelte but showed off the "harmonious curves of his muscles and impeccable jerseys."[140] Anquetil's tall, thin profile was accentuated by the "purity of his style" and the "finesse" of his movements.[141] Appearances and styles had gradually changed over the course of the race's history until they were now the opposite of what they had been.

More broadly, the Tour participated in a major twentieth-century transformation of the culture of the body: strength was increasingly understated, and the ideal body grew slimmer and suppler. Greater attention was paid to physical qualities and appearance. This may have been related to the growing "psychologization" of behavior and perhaps, at a deeper level, to associated consumer values.[142]

The "workingman" racer of the past was a far cry from the "businessman" racer of today. Once again, the Pélissier brothers typify the change. They substituted a more complex, perhaps more carefully honed image for the worthy journeyman and soldier of the early Tours. When they quit the race in protest in 1924, refusing to be "highway slaves," they marked a shift in sensibility: riders were now better prepared and more careful, wary of old rules of thumb and obscure assignments.[143] They were no longer merely workers but technicians, in conformity with the new standards of industrial competence, the standards of the manager and engineer. They also expressed themselves differently: "My name is Pélissier, not Azor."[144] Labor's aristocracy aspired to greater knowledge, greater freedom, and the possibility of advancement. This trend has continued with the recent appearance of manager heroes and businessman heroes. "The victory of management," trumpeted an advertisement exploiting Hinault's success in 1985: the champion had ostensibly managed a team of "computer technicians, trainers, and doctors." The old image had been stood on its head. The winner was no longer a mere technician but the head of a firm. He symbolized the race's financial success, the profits to be made. Above all, he pointed up the degree to which sports and the economy were intertwined: the manager-champion had a role to play in a larger firm, helping to meld his athletic team with the firm's overall goal. The success of one helped the success of the other: it was "a real love match between two winning teams."[145] Such convergence offered a somewhat surrealistic version of the dream of social mobility symbolized by the hero.

The Tour de France exploited and promoted French geography, the nation's roots in the soil. It bestowed value on memories and exploits of the past, if need be magnifying the setting and enhancing the splendor of the scenery. In this sense, the

Tour was a staging of French geography, of a national heritage rooted in space and time. It also offered an appealing, protective, homogeneous vision of that heritage. At the same time it updated a long tradition of "tours" of France, by kings, journeymen, and teachers. It transformed the past even as it recaptured it. It even claimed to be ushering in the future with its emphasis on machinery, signs, and consumable objects. Whence the interest in its own history. The Tour de France, as it evolved over the decades, illustrates the transition from a France of *terroirs* to a France of tourism and from voluntarist pedagogy to consumptionist pedagogy, until ultimately the sense of the nation itself was transformed and, it must be said, relieved of its anxiety. The sport was as much a product as it was a faithful mirror of society.

NOTES

1. BIBLIOGRAPHY FOR CHAPTER 1.

Agache, Roger. *La Somme préromaine et romaine d'après les prospections aériennes à basse altitude,* Mémoires de la Société des antiquaires de Picardie, no. 24 (Amiens: Société des Antiquaires de Picardie, 1978).

"Avec nos sabots," *Autrement,* no. 14 (June 1978).

Blanc, Jean-François. *Paysages et paysans de l'Ardèche* (Annonay: by the author, Imprimerie du Vivarais, 1984).

Bloch, Marc. *Les Caractères originaux de l'histoire rurale française* (Oslo: H. Aschehough, 1931; new ed., Paris: Armand Colin, 1952).

Bozon, Pierre. *L'Ardèche, la terre et less hommes du Vivarais* (Lyons: L'Hermès, 1978).

——. *La Vie rurale en vivarais: Étude géographique,* 2d ed. (Valence: Imprimeries Réunies, 1963).

Brunet, Pierre, and Marie-Claude Dionnet. *Présentation d'un essai de carte des paysages ruraux de la France au 1/1 000 000* (Atlas de la DATAR, 1962).

CNRS. *La Préhistoire en France,* esp. vol. 2, *Les Civilisations néolithiques et protohistoriques de la France* (Paris, 1976).

Dion, Roger. *Essai sur la formation du paysage rural de la France* (Tours: Arrault, 1934; new ed., Paris: Flammarion, 1991).

Duby, Georges, and Armand Wallon, ed., *Histoire de la France rural,* 4 vols (Paris: Éditions du Seuil, 1977).

Frémont, Armand. *L'Élevage en Normandie,* 2 vols. (Caen: University of Caen, 1968).

——. *Paysans de Normandie* (Paris: Flammarion, 1981).

George, Pierre, ed. *Études de géographie rurale,* supplement to the *Bulletin* of the École Normale Supérieure de Saint-Cloud, 1959.

Guilaine, Jean. *La France d'avant la France, du néolithique à l'âge de fer* (Paris: Hachette, 1980).

Hélias, Pierre Jakez. *Le Cheval d'orgueil* (Paris: Plon, 1978).

INSEE. *Tableaux de l'économie française* (Paris, 1987).

——. *Statistiques et indicateurs des régions françaises* (Paris, 1988).

Juillard, Étienne, et al. *Structures agraires et paysages ruraux* (Nancy: Faculté des Lettres de l'Université, 1957).

Léger, Danièle, and Bertrand Hervieu. *Le Retour à la nature, ˇAEau fond de la forêt à l'État ˇAF* (Paris: Éditions du Seuil, 1979).

Le Roy Ladurie, Emmanuel. *Montaillou, village occitan, de 1294 à 1324* (Paris: Gallimard, 1975).

Mendras, Henri. *La Fin des paysans* (Paris: SEDES, 1967; 2d ed., Paris: Armand Colin 1970).

——. *Voyage au pays de l'utopie rustique* (Arles: Actes Sud, 1979).

Merle, Louis. *La Métairie et l'évolution agraire de la gâtine poitevine de la fin du Moyen Âge à la Révolution* (Paris: SEVPEN, 1958).

Meynier, André. *Les Paysages agraires* (Paris: Armand Colin, 1967).

Papy, Louis, ed. *Atlas et géographie de la France moderne*, 15 vols. (Paris: Flammarion, 1976–1983).

Renard, Jean. *Les Évolutions contemporaines de la vie rurale dans la région nantaise* (Les Sables d'Olonne: Le Cercle d'Or, 1976).

Riou, Michel. *Guide de l'Ardèche* (Lyons: La Manufacture, 1987).

Roupnel, Gaston. *Histoire de la campagne française* (Paris: Plon, 1932; repr., 1981).

Tavernier, Bertrand. *Une semaine de vacances*. Film, 1980.

2. THE CATHEDRAL

1. On the administrative status of French cathedrals, see Philippe Geffre, "La Loi et la cathédrale," *Monuments historiques*, no. 153 (1987): 11–15.
2. Jacques Dubois, "La Carte des diocèses de France avant la Révolution," *Annales E.S.C.*, vol. 20 (1965; repr. Paris: Gallimard, 1976).
3. As Georges Duby has shown in *Le Temps des cathédrales: L'art et la société, 980–1420* (Paris: Gallimard, 1976).
4. A good summary of the question for the early Christian centuries can be found in Paul-Albert Février's essay in the catalogue for the exhibition *Premiers Temps chrétiens en Gaule: Antiquité tardive et haut Moyen Âge* (Lyon, 1986), pp. 63–69, and, also by Février, "Religiosité traditionnelle et christianisation," in vol. 1 of Jacques Le Goff and René Rémond, ed., *Histoire de la France religieuse* (Paris:Éditions du Seuil, 1988), pp. 147–168.
5. Marie-Madeleine Gauthier, *Les Routes de la foi: Reliques et reliquaires de Jérusalem à Compostelle* (Fribourg: Office du Livre, 1983).
6. Louis Duchesne, *Fastes épiscopaux de l'ancienne Gaule*, 3 vols. (Paris, 1907–1915).
7. There is no comprehensive study of this topic for France. For Italy, see Jean-Charles Picard, *Le Souvenir des évêques: Sépultures, listes épiscopales et culte des évêques en Italie du Nord des origines au Xe siècle* (Rome-Paris: École Française de Rome, 1988).

8. See Pierre du Colombier, *Les Chantiers des cathédrales* (Paris: Picard, 1973).
9. See André Vauchez, "Le Christianisme roman et gothique," in Le Goff and Rémond, *Histoire de la France religieuse*, esp. pp. 328–338.
10. See the excellent study by Jean-Louis Biget, "Recherches sur le financement des cathédrales du Midi au XIIIe siècle," in *La Naissance et l'essor du gothique méridional au XIIIe siècle*, Cahiers de Fanjeaux, no. 9 (Toulouse: Privat, 1974), pp. 127–164.
11. Hans Reinhardt, *La Cathédrale de Strasbourg* (Paris: Arthaud, 1972), pp. 79–92.
12. Jacques Le Goff, "Saint Marcel de Paris et le dragon," in *Pour un autre Moyen Âge* (Paris: Gallimard, 1977), pp. 236–279.
13. Jean Gimpel, *Les Bâtisseur des cathédrales* (Paris: Éditions du Seuil, 1958), p. 42.
14. Pierre Desportes, "Villes et paroisses dans la France du Nord au Moyen Âge," *Histoire, économie et société* (1985): 163–178, and "Réflexions sur la paroisse urbaine en France du Nord au bas Moyen Âge," in Jean de Viguerie, ed. *Histoire de la paroisse* (Angers: Centre Culturel de l'Ouest, 1988), pp. 45–58.
15. See Jean Hubert, "La Vie commune des clercs et l'archéologie," in *La vita commune del clero nei secoli XI et XII* (Milan: Vita e Pensiero, 1962), 1: 106–111.
16. Colette Beaune, *Naissance de la nation France* (Paris: Gallimard, 1985).
17. Bernard Guenée, *Les Entrées royales françaises de 1328 à 1515* (Paris: Centre National de Recherche Scientifique, 1968).
18. See Bernard Mahieu in the catalogue for the exhibition *Notre-Dame de Paris, 1163–1183* (1963), pp. 4–6.
19. See Jules Leflon, "Notre-Dame de Paris pendant la Révolution," *Revue d'histoire de l'Église de France*, vol. 50 (1964): 109–124, and Hans Reinhardt, *La Cathédrale de Reims* (Paris: Artaud, 1963).
20. Texts quoted in Pierre Léon, *La Vie des monuments français: Destruction, restauration* (Paris, 1951), pp. 256 ff.
21. René Limouzin-Lamothe, "La Dévastation de Notre-Dame et de l'archevêché en février 1831," *Revue d'histoire de l'Église de France*, vol. 50 (1964): 125–134.
22. Texts quoted by Charles Morice in his introduction to Auguste Rodin, *Les Cathédrales de France*, 2d ed. (Paris: Denoël-Gonthier, 1983).
23. Jacques Mallion, *Victor Hugo et l'art architectural* (Grenoble: Arthaud, 1962).
24. Émile Mâle, *L'Art religieux du XIIIe siècle en France* (Paris, 1910), p. 458.
25. Louis Vitet, *Études sur l'histoire de l'art* (Paris, 1864), pp. 128–129.
26. Ibid., pp. 131–132.
27. On the origins and spread of this myth, see Gimpel, *Les Bâtisseurs*, pp. 139–140.
28. Eugène Viollet-le-Duc, article "Cathédrale," in *Dictionnaire raisonné de l'architecture française du XIe au XVIe siècle* (Paris, 1866), 4: 281.
29. Ibid., pp. 391–392.
30. On Montalembert's defense of the cathedrals, see Jean-Michel Leniaud, *J.-B. Lassus (1807–1857) ou le temps retrouvé des cathédrales*, Bibliothèque de la Société française d'archéologie, 12 (Paris: Arts et métiers graphiques, 1980), pp. 35 ff., and Léon, *La Vie des monuments*, pp. 116 ff.
31. Mâle, *L'Art religieux*, p. 353.

32. See the remarkable study by Eugène Ollivier, "La Cathédrale de la Révolution à nos jours," *Monuments historiques,* no. 153 (1987), pp. 17–23.
33. Thierry Soulard, "L'Achèvement de la cathédrale de Limoges au XIXe siècle," ibid., pp. 37–41. A colloquium, Achèvement et transformations des cathédrales au XIXe siècle, was held in Limoges in November 1988.
34. Rodin, *Les Cathédrales,* p. 20.
35. Paul Verlaine, *Sagesse,* X, ed. J. Borel (Paris: Gallimard, 1962), p. 249.
36. John Ruskin, *La Bible d'Amiens,* trans. and with preface by Marcel Proust (1903; repr. Paris: Union Générale de Éducation, 1986), p. 33.
37. Joris Karl Huysmans, *La Cathédrale* (Paris: Plon, 1986), p. 278.
38. Simone Fraisse, *Péguy et le Moyen Âge* (Paris: Honoré Champion, 1978).
39. Marcel Proust, "La Mort des cathédrales," in *Chroniques* (Paris, 1927), p. 159.
40. Jules Michelet, *Histoire de France,* book 4, in *Œuvres complètes,* ed. Paul Vaillaneix (Paris: Flammarion, 1974), 4: 604.
41. Charles Péguy, *L'Argent,* in *Œuvres en prose* (Paris: Gallimard, 1957), p. 1050.
42. On resistance to Gothic art in France in the eighteenth century and the first half of the nineteenth century, see Jules Corblet, *L'Architecture du Moyen Âge jugée par les écrivains des deux derniers siècles* (Paris, 1859).
43. Viollet-le-Duc, *Dictionnaire raisonnée,* 1: 71.
44. Rodin, *Les Cathédrales,* p. 144.
45. Henri Focillon, *Art d'Occident,* vol. 1, *Le Moyen Âge* (Paris: Le Livre de Poche, 1965), pp. 109, 138.
46. Georges Duval, "Rouen ou la résurrection d'un chef-d'Œuvre," *Monuments historiques,* no. 153 (1987): 54–57.
47. Bernard Huet, "Meurtre près de la cathédrale," *ibid.,* 25–29.

3. THE COURT

1. François-René de Chateaubriand, *Mémoires d'outre-tombe,* ed. M. Levaillant (Paris: Flammarion, 1964), part 4, book 4.
2. Pauline M. Smith, *The Anti-Courtier Trend in Sixteenth-Century French Literature* (Geneva: Droz, 1966), with useful medieval precedents; Nicole Ferrier-Caverivière, *L'Image de Louis XIV dans la littérature française de 1660 à 1715* (Paris: Presses Universitaires de France, 1981); idem., *Le Grand Roi à l'aube des Lumières, 1715–1751* (Paris: Presses Universitaires de France, 1985).
3. Konrad-Ferdinand Werner, ed., *Hof, Kultur und Politik im 19. Jahrhundert* (Bonn: Röhrscheid, 1985).
4. Louis-Sébastien Mercier, *Tableau de Paris* (Amsterdam, 1782), 2: 470, and more generally pp. 461–472. The beginning of Chapter 346, "The Gallery of Versailles," sets the tone: "On Pentecost the Parisian takes the *galiote* as far as Sèvres and from there hastens to Versailles to see the princes, the procession of blue ribbons, the park, and the menagerie. He is admitted into the grand apartments but kept out of the small ones, which are the most sumptuous and interesting. Crowds gather at noon in the

gallery to contemplate the king on his way to mass, and the queen, and Monsieur and Madame, and his lordship the Comte d'Artois. Then they ask one another, 'Did you see the king?' 'Yes, he laughed.' 'That's true. He laughed.' 'He seems happy.' 'I'll say! He has what it takes."' Ibid., p. 461.

5. *Mémoires de Madame Campan* (1822), ed. C. de Angulo (Paris: Mercure de France, 1988). See p. 22: "Etiquette still existed in this court [that of Louis XV, to which the author came in 1768 at the age of sixteen] with all the forms it had acquired under Louis XIV. All that was lacking was dignity. As for gaiety, there was no longer anything of the kind. If you were looking for a place where French wit and grace gathered, Versailles was not the place to go."

6. True, Diderot's remarks continue by borrowing from Montesquieu's *De l'esprit des lois* (and indeed the critical anticurial tradition) to attack the court's underside and artificiality. It is significant, however, that the beginning of the article repeats the definitions of the court that can be found in most of the major dictionaries of the late seventeenth and early eighteenth centuries.

7. Mme de Sévigné, *Correspondance*, 3 vols., ed. R. Duchêne (Paris: Gallimard, 1972–1978). See especially vol. 1, p. 414 (letter of January 13, 1672, to Mme de Grignan); vol. 1, p. 617 (letter of November 13, 1673, to the same); vol. 2, p. 13 (letter of July 24, 1675, to the same); vol. 2, pp. 902, 1027 (letters of April 12 and July 28, 1680, to the same). The theme crops up in the marquise's letters with increasing frequency as her visits to the court become more and more infrequent in the 1680s. Abbé de Bellegarde, *Modèles de conversation pour les personnes polies*, 3d ed. (Amsterdam, 1699), pp. 59, 179, etc. Saint-Réal, *Œuvres* (Amsterdam, 1730), 4: 27–28 (quoted by Raymond Picard, *La Carrière de Jean Racine* [Paris: Gallimard, 1961], p. 483). A late (1759) version can be found in the work of that model of the well-adjusted courtier, the Duc de Croÿ: *Journal inédit du duc de Croÿ*, 4 vols., ed. Vicomte de Grouchy and P. Cottin (Paris, 1906), 1: 437.

8. See Jacques Revel, "Une Cour en République? Du bon usage des formes," *Le Débat*, no. 57 (November–December 1989): 186–190. On contemporary versions of ritualized forms of authority, see Marc Abelès, "Inauguration en gare de Nevers: Pèlerinage à Solutré," *Les Temps modernes*, no. 488 (March 1987): 75–97. In a rather different vein, I explored the history of rulers' journeys in Jacques Revel, ed., *L'Espace français*, vol. 1 of André Burguière and Jacques Revel, ed., *L'Histoire de la France* (Paris: Éditions du Seuil, 1989), pp. 72–81.

9. There has been a vast amount of (mostly mediocre and in any case repetitious) journalism on this subject. The assumption of power by the Socialists, the reelection of François Mitterrand in 1988, and the tenth anniversary of his first election in 1991 all provided occasions to explore the theme. See, for example, the set of articles in *Le Point* (November 21, 1988), under the title "Mitterrand: Le roi et sa cour," with the following paragraph-long subtitle: "The spirit of monarchy invades the president's second term. His institutional behavior reflects this. His daily life proves it. And his entourage is becoming a court" (p. 70). Of course the same weekly was quick to proclaim the regime's alleged drift toward "Social Monarchy" in a headline published in

its October 19, 1981, issue, only months after Mitterrand's first election. A more stylish effort to chronicle the Mitterrand court as early as May 1992 appeared under the signature of the Duc de Saint-Magloire, "Barbichets et Barbelets," *Le Débat,* no. 20 (1982): 18–27.

10. A comparative history of different court systems has yet to be written, and the absence of such comparison is probably the weak point of Norbert Elias's great work *Die höfische Gesellschaft* (Neuweid: Luchterhand, 1969; Fr. trans., *La Société de cour* [Paris: Calmann-Lévy, 1974]; rev. trans. with a preface by Roger Chartier [Paris: Flammarion, 1985]), trans. into English as *The Court Society* (New York: Pantheon, 1983). There is much useful information in Arthur G. Dickens, ed., *The Courts of Europe: Politics, Patronage and Royalty, 1400–1800* (London: Thames and Hudson, 1977), and additional bibliographic information can be found in Pierpaolo Merlin, "Il tema della corte nella storiografia italiana ed europea," *Studi Storici,* no. 27 (1986): 203–244. For the past ten years, such a comparative history has been the goal of an Italian project, Europa delle corti, the title of a series of books published by Bulzoni. Two valuable monographs call attention to the singularity of the French model: John H. Elliott, "The Court of the Spanish Habsburgs: A Peculiar Institution?" in Phyllis Mack and Margaret C. Jacob, ed., *Politics and Culture in Early Modern Europe: Essays in Honour of H. G. Koenigsberger* (Cambridge, England: Cambridge University Press, 1987); and Hubert Ch. Ehalt, *Ausdruckformen absolutischer Herrschaft: Der Wiener Hof im 17. und 18. Jahrhundert* (Munich-Vienna: R. Oldenburg, 1980).

11. For a recent, quite useful overview, see Jean-François Solnon, *La Cour de France* (Paris: Fayard, 1987), which has an excellent bibliography. Unfortunately it does not cover the courts of the thirteenth to fifteenth centuries.

12. Duc de Saint-Simon, *Mémoires,* ed. Coirault (Paris: Gallimard, 1985), 5: 531.

13. Yves Coirault, *L'Optique de Saint-Simon: Essai sur les formes de son imagination et de sa sensibilité d'après les Mémoires* (Paris: Armand Colin, 1965).

14. *Médailles sur les principaux événements du règne de Louis le Grand* (Paris, 1702).

15. Dangeau, *Journal,* 19 vols., ed. Soulié and Dussieux (Paris, 1854–1860); Sourches, *Mémoires du marquis de Sources sous le règne de Louis XIV,* 13 vols., ed. Cosnac and Pontal (Paris, 1882–1893).

16. Mercier, *Tableau de Paris,* 2: 467.

17. Dangeau, *Journal,* 1: 79–80.

18. Saint-Simon, *Mémoires,* 4: 999.

19. Mme de Sévigné, *Correspondance,* 3: 429 (letter of December 15, 1688, from Louis-Provence de Grignan to his mother). Among many other examples, including Primi Visconti, *Mémoires,* ed. Solnon (Paris: Librairie Académique Perrin, 1989), p. 12, see the similar testimony of the Duc de Croÿ, who presented his son to the court of Louis XV in 1758 (*Journal inédit,* 1: 426).

20. Mme de Sévigné's correspondence with her daughter harps incessantly on this theme: one must not stay away from court for too long, even if one is serving the king. See, for example, the letter of January 12, 1674 (*Correspondance,* 1: 668), as well as this

rather disillusioned observation from a letter of January 12, 1680: "The king has been immensely generous. Truly, one shouldn't lose hope: although one isn't his *valet de chambre,* it may happen that, in paying him court, one will happen to be under whatever he chooses to toss out. What is certain is that away from his presence, all services are for naught. It used to be the opposite" (ibid., 2: 793–794).

21. Saint-Simon, *Mémoires,* 5: 1150.
22. Elias, *The Court Society.* This work, first published in 1969, some thirty years after it was written in the 1930s, should not be isolated from Elias's great work, *Über den Prozess der Zivilisation: Soziogenetische und Psychogenetische Untersuchungen* (Basel, 1939; abridged in English as *The Civilizing Process* [New York: Urizen Books, 1978; paperback ed. Cambridge, Mass.: Blackwell, 1994]), which was also slow to gain recognition.
23. See, for example, the overview by Roger Mettam, *Power and Factions in Louis XIV's France* (Oxford: Blackwell, 1988), which orchestrates some very useful revisionist themes from English and American research. On the French side, see, for example, the work of Daniel Dessert, especially his *1661: Louis XIV prend le pouvoir— Naissance d'un mythe* (Brussels: Éditions Complexe, 1989), and Arlette Jouanna, *Le Devoir de révolte: La noblesse française et la gestion de l'État moderne* (Paris: Fayard, 1989).
24. I borrow this expression from an unpublished paper by William Beik, "A Social Interpretation of Louis XIV," presented to the colloquium L'État absolutiste, Paris, École des Hautes Études en Sciences Sociales, May 1991.
25. Saint-Simon, *Mémoires,* 5: 997.
26. The most recent commentary on this great symbolic occasion (based largely on Charles Perrault, *Courses de testes et de bagues faites par le Roi* [Paris, 1670]), is that of Jean-Marie Apostolidès in *Le Roi-machine: Spectacle et politique au temps de Louis XIV* (Paris: Éditions de Minuit, 1981), pp. 41 ff. One need not follow Apostolidès's rather venturesome general sociological hypotheses, however. Note that this *carrousel* is *Parisian*—the only one of its kind and, given the date, significantly staged on the principal scene of the Fronde—and was the first of a series in which the king actively participated through 1676. Other *carrousels* are mentioned through the late 1680s. See Dangeau, *Journal,* 1: 135–136, 170, 184, 276–277, 385; 2: 72–73, 305, 327, 363–364; Sourches, *Mémoires,* 1: 224–249, 340–342.
27. A late echo (from a time when the solar theme had lost much of its symbolic and political importance) can be seen in connection with the funeral of Condé in 1686, which Mme de Sévigné described in a letter to Bussy-Rabutin (*Correspondance,* 3: 283, March 10, 1683). Mottoes dispersed through the cortège evoked the various phases of Condé's life. When it came to his collusion with the Spanish, the emblem depicted a dark night on which the motto commented: *Laetant quae sine sole* (Things that are done far from the sun must be hidden). See *Les Honneurs funèbres rendus à la mémoire du très haut, très puissant, très illustre et très magnanime prince Monseigneur Louis de Bourbon, prince de Condé* (Paris, 1687).
28. *Relation des magnificences du grand Carrousel du roi Louis XIV* (Paris, 1662), p. 3.

29. Louis XIV, *Mémoires*, ed. J. Longon (Paris: Taillandier, 1978), p. 134.
30. Ezechiel Spanheim, *Relation de la cour de France en 1690*, ed. Schaffer (Paris, 1882); Sourches, *Mémoires*, 1: 10–22 ("small portrait of the court," September 1681).
31. Élisabeth-Charlotte de Bavière, Duchesse d'Orléans, Princesse Palatine, *Lettres de Madame la duchesse d'Orléans*, ed. O. Amiel (Paris, 1981), pp. 334 ff. This text was recently commented on by Emmanuel Le Roy Ladurie, "Auprès du roi, la cour," *Annales E.S.C.*, no. 1 (1983): 21–41.
32. See Le Roy Ladurie, "Auprès du roi," and the still useful essay by Henri Brocher, *A la cour de Louis XIV: Le rang et l'étiquette sous l'Ancien Régime* (Paris, 1934). See also Solnon, *La Cour de France*, pp. 315–372, and Jean-Pierre Labatut, *Les Ducs et pairs de France au XVII*[e] *siècle* (Paris: Presses Universitaires de France, 1972).
33. Of Dangeau, Fontenelle wrote that he "was quite learned in history, especially modern history, in the genealogies of the great houses, in the interests of princes, and indeed in all the sciences of a man of the court." Quoted in the introduction to Dangeau, *Journal*, 1: xliii–xliv. Other acknowledged court connoisseurs of genealogy included d'Hozier, of course, as well as Pomponne and Bouchet.
34. Saint-Simon was contemptuous of the privilege but noted, when he received it, that "all France came to compliment me on this 'Pour.'" *Mémoires*, 5: 357.
35. Ibid., 3: 58 ff.
36. Quoted in Corrado Fatta, *Esprit de Saint-Simon* (Paris: Correa, 1954), pp. 40–45.
37. Saint-Simon, *Mémoires*, 3: 702–708; 4: 747.
38. Le Roy Ladurie, "Auprès du roi." Ladurie explicitly takes his inspiration from Louis Dumont's work on the hierarchical societies of India. See Dumont, *Homo hierarchicus* (Paris: Gallimard, 1966).
39. Saint-Simon, *Mémoires*, 5: 1141.
40. Visconti, *Mémoires*, p. 146.
41. Elias, *La Société de cour*, p. 94, and, more generally, ch. 3 and 4.
42. *Mémoires de Madame Campan*, p. 75.
43. Visconti, *Mémoires*, p. 100.
44. Mme de Sévigné, *Correspondance*, 3: 489 (letter of January 28, 1689, from Mme de Coulanges to Mme de Grignan); 451, 497, 498, 501, 505, 506, 508–509, 519–520, 550–551 (Mme de Sévigné to Mme de Grignan, January-February 1689). See also Mme de La Fayette, *Mémoires de la cour de France pour les années 1688 et 1689*, ed. G. Sigaux (Paris: Mercure de France, 1965), pp. 150–152 ("what should have been looked upon as a convent comedy became the most serious affair of court"). On the performance of *Esther* as a social event, see Picard, *La Carrière de Jean Racine*, pp. 396–407.
45. Saint-Simon, *Mémoires*, 4: 871.
46. Visconti, *Mémoires*, pp. 18, 48–49. An example in the opposite sense is offered by the return to Versailles of the Princesse des Ursins, who was out of favor with the royal couple: "Few people apart from her old friends and members of her old cabal saw her arrive . . . and solitude reigned, for after people noticed the success of her trip to Versailles, they allowed her to wait a few days." Saint-Simon, who reports the episode, was one of her friends, but he was still cautious: "The moment I saw her

leave, I went to M. le Duc d'Orléans, whom I told of what I had just done; that it was not a visit but an encounter." *Mémoires*, 5: 190, 228–229.

47. "I felt that all our plans should be in our heads, and quite clearly worked out, and that we should all be convinced and in agreement before setting any machinery in motion." Saint-Simon, *Mémoires*, 3: 532.
48. Emmanuel Le Roy Ladurie, "Système de la Cour (Versailles vers 1709)," *L'Arc*, no. 65 (1976): 21–35. See also Coirault, *L'Optique de Saint-Simon*, pp. 360 ff.
49. Elias, *La Société de cour*, pp. 77 ff.
50. Émile Magne, "Les Marlys," *Revue de Paris*, no. 6 (1934): 119–149.
51. This is what happened when Louis XIV bought Meudon from Mme de Louvois, as we know from two letters that Mme de Coulanges wrote to Mme de Sévigné in the summer of 1695. In early July: "The king is going to Marly for two weeks. If the Duchesse du Lude accompanies him, it will be the third time in a row. Such distinctions charm when one is from that place. Happy are those who can see it as it should be seen." On August 12: "The king is to go to Meudon on Saturday for two days. At the moment the distinctions are being handed out for Meudon and not Marly." Mme de Sévigné, *Correspondance*, 3: 1112 and 1115.
52. Saint-Simon, *Mémoires*, 2: 170.
53. Ibid., p. 174.
54. Ibid., 3: 26–32.
55. Mme de Sévigné, *Correspondance*, 2: 14 (letter of July 24, 1675, to Mme de Grignan). Quotations from Bossuet are taken from Élie Longuemare, *Bossuet et la société française sous le règne de Louis XIV* (Paris, 1910), ch. 2.
56. Mme de La Fayette, *Histoire d'Henriette d'Angleterre*, ed. G. Sigaux (Paris: Mercure de France, 1965), p. 21.
57. Mme de Sévigné, *Correspondance*, 1: 724 (letter of June 5, 1675, to Mme de Grignan).
58. Visconti, *Mémoires*, pp. 121 and 138. A good example of the confusion of court and stage can be found in a famous letter of Mme de Sévigné's, in which she comments on the tragicomic episode of the thwarted love of Mademoiselle and Lauzun: "It is a fit subject for a tragedy conforming to all the rules of the theater. . . . M. de Lauzun played his part to perfection. Mademoiselle was also very good. She cried well." *Correspondance*, 1: 143–144 (letter of December 24, 1670, to Mme de Coulanges).
59. Mme de La Fayette, *Histoire d'Henriette d'Angleterre*, p. 76.
60. Here, the comparison with Spain is enlightening. In Spain the king made few appearances, mainly in connection with religious ceremonies, and remained aloof. Saint-Simon became aware of the distance between the two courts when he was sent as an ambassador to the Spanish Bourbons. See Elliott, "The Court of the Spanish Habsburgs."
61. Ralph E. Giesey, *Cérémonial et puissance souveraine, XVe–XVIIe siècles* (Paris: Armand Colin, 1987). Giesey, following many other authorities, places an emphasis on the ritual significance of solar symbolism at the court of Louis XIV that is not entirely convincing, however, and has been subjected to useful criticism: see, for example, Hélène Himelfarb, "Versailles, fonctions et légendes," in Pierre Nora, ed., *Les Lieux de mémoire*, part 2, *La Nation* (Paris: Gallimard, 1986), 2: 235–292, esp. pp 252 ff.

62. Saint-Simon, *Mémoires,* 5: 381–382.
63. Sourches, *Mémoires,* 1: 463, recounts this significant episode (which occurred at the time when the king was suffering from a fistula): "Some say that one day, when he was supposed to receive in his apartment and was in extreme pain, Mme the Dauphine, in tears, said that there should be no reception and that she could not dance when he was in such a state, to which he answered: 'Madame, I want there to be a reception and I want you to dance. We are not private individuals. We owe ourselves entirely to the public. Go and do the thing gracefully.'"
64. See Saint-Simon, *Mémoires,* 1: 36–37: "What was called the 'reception in the king's apartments' was a gathering of the entire court from seven until ten in the evening, during which the king sat at a table in the great apartment between the salons at the end of the grand gallery and the chapel rostrum. First there was music. Then there were tables in all the rooms set for various kinds of games. . . . When this reception was first established, the king went and played for a while. Although he stopped going after a while, he nevertheless wanted others to attend regularly, and everyone was eager to please him. He, however, spent his evenings in Mme de Maintenon's apartments working with various ministers."
65. Visconti, *Mémoires,* pp. 27 and 148.
66. Ibid., pp. 29 and 100. This report is confirmed by Saint-Simon, *Mémoires,* 5: 997–1005.
67. Baldassar Castiglione, *Il libro del cortegiano* (Venice, 1528). The most recent French translation is that of Alain Pons (based on the version of Gabriel Chappuis, Lyons, 1580): *Le Livre du courtisan* (Paris: Éd. G. Lebovici, 1987). Recent English translations include Charles S. Singleton, trans., *The Book of the Courtier* (Garden City, NY: Doubleday, 1959).
68. *Le Livre du courtisan,* book 1, ch. 12, p. 34.
69. The latest of the old translations was that of Abbé Jean-Baptiste Duhamel, published in 1690: *Le Parfait Courtisan et la dame de cour: Ouvrage également avantageux pour réussir dans les belles conversations, et pour former les jeunes personnes de qualité de l'un et l'autre sexe* (Paris, 1690).
70. I describe these adaptations in "Les Usages de la civilité," in Roger Chartier, ed., *De la Renaissance aux Lumières* pp. 169–209 (Paris: Éditions du Seuil, 1986), vol. 3 of Georges Duby and Philippe Ariès, ed., *Histoire de la vie privée,* Eng. trans. by Arthur Goldhammer, *The History of Private Life* (Cambridge, Mass.: Harvard University Press, 1991). On these questions the standard reference is still Maurice Magendie, *La Politesse mondaine: Les théories de l'honnêté en France, de 1600 à 1660,* 2 vols. (Paris, 1925).
71. Saint-Simon, *Mémoires,* 2: 174.
72. Mme de Sévigné, *Correspondance,* 2: 352 (letter of July 29, 1676, to Mme de Grignan); ibid., pp. 766, 854 (letters of December 8, 1679, and February 28, 1680, to the same).
73. La Bruyère, "De la Cour," in *Les Caractères,* in *Œuvres complètes,* ed. J. Benda (Paris: Gallimard, 1951), 63: 236.
74. Ibid., 2: 215.
75. Saint-Simon, *Mémoires,* 4: 803.

76. Baltasar Gracián, *L'Homme de Cour,* trans. by Amelot de La Houssaie (Paris: Grasset, 1924), maxim 13, pp. 9–10.
77. Voltaire, *Le Siècle de Louis XIV* (1751), ed. A. Adam (Paris: Garnier-Flammarion, 1966), 2: 18; 1: 320, 373.
78. Himelfarb, "Versailles, fonctions et légendes"; Jean-Pierre Néraudau, *L'Olympe du Roi-Soleil: Mythologie et idéologie royale au Grand Siècle* (Paris: Les Belles Lettres, 1986); N. Ferrier-Caverivière, *L'Image de Louis XIV.*
79. Félibien, *Relation de la fête de Versailles du 18e juillet 1668* (Paris, 1668), p. 4.
80. Molière, *Les Amants magnifiques,* foreword. See Néraudau, *L'Olympe du Roi-Soleil,* pp. 138–143; Jacques Vanuxem, "La Scénographie des fêtes de Louis XIV auxquelles Molière a participé," *Dix-septième Siècle,* nos. 98–99, pp. 83–110. On an earlier example, see the remarkable demonstration by Marc Fumaroli, "Microcosme comique et macrocosme solaire: Molière, Louis XIV et *L'Impromptu de Versailles,*" *Revue de sciences humaines,* no. 145 (1972): pp. 95–114.
81. Combes, *Explication historique de tout ce qu'il y a de remarquable dans la Maison royale de Versailles et en celle de Monsieur à Saint-Cloud* (Paris, 1681).
82. Quoted in Apostolidès, *Le Roi-machine,* p. 136.
83. See, for example, the commentary of Mme de La Fayette: "The goal was also to make the river Eure flow opposite to its natural penchant" (*Mémoires de la Cour de France,* p. 106). In discussing the gardens of Versailles, Saint-Simon mentions the king's pleasure in "tyrannizing and domesticating nature with much help from gold and silver" (quoted in Elias, *La Société de cour,* p. 256).
84. Louis XIV, *Manière de montrer les jardins de Versailles,* ed. S. Hoog (Paris: Réunion des Musées Nationaux, 1982).
85. Saint-Simon, *Mémoires,* 5: 381.
86. Of course the move to Versailles did not result in a completely sedentary court, far from it.
87. It was of course emulation that prompted Mercier's irony: "The atmosphere of the court suffuses even the servant and the watchman, who, mimicking the great lords, affect a modest demeanor only to appear proud and cool on another occasion. The valets take a tone that anywhere else would be utterly ridiculous." But Mercier no longer believed in courtly values. See *Tableau de Paris,* 3: 229.
88. Revel, "Les Usages de la civilité," pp. 192 ff.
89. Quoted in Roger Picard, *Les Salons littéraires et la société française, 1610–1789* (New York: Brentano's, 1943), p. 88.
90. Magendie, *La Politesse mondaine,* pp. 569 ff., esp. 581–582.
91. On the undefinable "Mortemart wit" that so fascinated Proust, a great reader of Saint-Simon, and caused him to write at length about the "Guermantes wit," see Dirk Van der Cruysse, *Le Portrait dans les* Mémoires *du duc de Saint-Simon* (Paris: Nizet, 1971), pp. 261 ff; and above all D. J. H. Van Elden, *Esprits fins et esprits géométriques dans les portraits de Saint-Simon: Contribution à l'étude du vocabulaire et du style* (The Hague: M. Nijhoff, 1975), pp. 44 ff.

92. Abbé de Bellegarde, *Réflexions sur le ridicule et sur les moyens de l'éviter, où sont représentés les différents caractères et les mœurs des personnes de ce siècle*, 4th ed. (Amsterdam, 1695), p. 202.
93. See the useful reminders of Jacques Thuillier, "Réflexions sur la politique artistique de Colbert," *Un Autre Colbert* (Paris: Presses Universitaires de France, 1985), pp. 275–286.
94. Picard, *La Carrière de Jean Racine*; Alain Viala, *Les Institutions de la vie littéraire au XVIIe siècle* (Lille: Atelier de Reproduction des Thèses, 1985), and *Naissance de l'écrivain: Sociologie de la littérature à l'âge classique* (Paris: Éditions de Minuit, 1985).
95. The text was carefully annotated by Boileau and Racine: see Marc Soriano, *La Brosse à reluire sous Louis XIV: L'*Epître au Roi *de Perrault annotée par Racine et Boileau* (Paris: Schiera-Nizet, 1989), pp. 40–44. On the sharing of qualities between king and artist, see Martin Warnke, *L'Artiste et la Cour: Aux origines de l'artiste moderne* (French trans., Paris: Éditions de la Maison des Sciences de l'Homme, 1989), which unfortunately treats few French cases.
96. Saint-Réal, *Œuvres* (Amsterdam, 1730), 4: 28, quoted in Picard, *La Carrière de Jean Racine*, p. 483.
97. Mme de Caylus, *Souvenirs*, ed. Lescure (Paris, 1873), p. 86; Picard, *La Carrière de Jean Racine*, p. 483.
98. Bellegarde, *Réflexions sur le ridicule*, p. 35; F. de Callières, *Du bon et du mauvais usage de s'exprimer: Des façons bourgeoises de parler et en quoy elles sont différentes de celles de la Cour* (Paris, 1691).
99. Marc Fumaroli, "Le Langage de cour en France: Problèmes et points de repère," in *Europäische Hofkultur in 16. und 17. Jahrhundert* (Munich, 1979), 2: 23–32; and of course Ferdinand Brunot, *Histoire de la langue française* (Paris: Armand Colin, 1905–1939), 4: 1.
100. Erich Auerbach, "La Cour et la ville," in *Vier Untersuchungen zur Geschichte der französischen Bildung* (Berne, 1951), pp. 12–50, available in English in Auerbach's *Scenes from the Drama of European Literature* (College Point, Md.: Meridian Books, 1959). The very conception of the work of the Académie Française and the composition of the Company illustrated this historic compromise: see Marc Fumaroli, "La Coupole," in this volume, esp. pp. ff.
101. Charles Perrault, *Parallèle des Anciens et des Modernes* (Paris, 1692), 3: 113–114.
102. Werner, *Hof, Kultur und Politik*; Anne Martin-Fugier, *La Vie élégante ou la formation du Tout-Paris, 1815–1848* (Paris: Fayard, 1990), ch. 1–3.
103. Marcel Proust, *Le Côté des Guermantes*, ed. P. Clarac and A. Ferré (Paris: Gallimard, 1956), p. 426.
104. Alexis de Tocqueville, *De la démocratie en Amérique*, ed. François Furet (Paris: Garnier-Flammarion, 1981), part 2, ch. 7, vol. 1: 355–358.
105. The last protocol revision was approved by the council of ministers in September 1989, in the midst of the bicentennial of the French Revolution. The previous one dates from 1907.
106. An example of these can be seen in the Pascalian theme of the king without amusement. If carried to an extreme, the sovereign function can easily become so grandiose that it is

always in danger of bursting like a bubble. Primi Visconti wrote of Louis XIV as the sovereign who commanded everything, even the weather: "In spite of it all, I am sure he was not happy." (*Mémoires*, p. 167.) Today, of course, the gloominess and disillusionments of power are among the favorite themes of journalists covering the president.

107. Louis Marin, *Le Portrait du roi* (Paris: Éditions de Minuit, 1981), available in English as Martha Hode, trans., *The King's Portrait* (Amsterdam: Benjamins, 1985).

4. LE TOUR DE LA FRANCE PAR DEUX ENFANTS:THE LITTLE RED BOOK OF THE REPUBLIC

1. Aimé Dupuy, "Les Livres de lecture de G. Bruno," *Revue d'histoire économique et sociale*, no. 2 (1953). We are indebted in many ways to the pioneering article of Aimé Dupuy, who not only studied the diffusion of *Le Tour de la France* but also drew our attention to the files preserved by the publisher Belin and initiated the discussion of Daniel Halévy's brilliant but misleading presentation of the book.
2. Among many studies, let us single out the excellent postscript by Jean-Pierre Bardoz to the centennial facsimile edition, which reproduces the 1877 version of the text in its entirety.
3. In the 1910 parliamentary debate on textbooks, Ferdinand Buisson made this point explicitly: "In composing the ethics textbook, the writer thought about the second reading that would someday be made of it."
4. In 1886, the municipal council of Paris acceded to the request of a teacher on the council and refused to approve funds for the purchase of Bruno's books for use in elementary schools. The reason or pretext given was their alleged religious *(confessionel)* tone, which was said to be incompatible with the schools' policy of neutrality in matters of religion.
5. In a parliamentary debate in January of 1910, the right launched a strong attack on the "secularizing" revision of the text, which right-wing critics saw as mechanical and absurd. In an article published in *Le Temps* on February 11, 1910, Fouillée summarized the convergent attacks: "I would have to go on forever if I were to tell you all the remarks, contradictory claims, and maneuvers that G. Bruno's text has occasioned on account of its extraordinary success and the jealousies that has aroused."
6. Jean-Marie Guyau, whose first philosophical work *(La Morale d'Épicure)* appeared in 1878, made his debut three years earlier, at the age of twenty-one, with a *Première Année de lecture courante* (Paris: Armand Colin, 1875).
7. The epithet is from Bardoz (see n 2), who wrote that "no schoolchild in France could possibly identify with André or Julien."
8. The revised or "secularized" edition of *Le Tour de la France* appeared in 1905.
9. We have made extensive use of the teacher's handbook (in its first edition of 1885), because it is explicit where Mme Fouillée "glides" over things and because it is always careful to associate items in the official curriculum with the corresponding pages of *Le Tour de la France*. A contract in the Belin files proves that Mme Fouillée was the sole author of the handbook. It is identical in every point to the contract for the book itself.

10. The *compagnon*'s itinerary depended on the group he belonged to and of course the city from which he started but always moved clockwise from east to south to west. André and Julien's itinerary is close to the typical one of the *compagnon*, but nevertheless bypasses the valley of the Loire. See J.-P. Bayard, *La Compagnonnage en France* (Paris, 1979).
11. It was a commonplace at the time to say that Sedan was a victory for German schoolteachers, who had taught their students geography, and that even French generals didn't know whether "the Rhine flows south to north or north to south" (see *La République française*, November 27, 1871).
12. This argument was repeated by J.-M. Guyau in *Éducation et hérédité* (Paris: Alcan, 1889). As for how to awaken the child's interest in geography, Guyau, like his mother, believed that it was always best to begin with the emotions: "I have seen a three-year-old child take an interest in America after he was told that the sun would be shining there when it was night here, so that the little children of that extraordinary country would be starting to play when he was thinking about going to sleep."
13. As Dominique Maingueneau states in an otherwise very stimulating book on G. Bruno, *Les Livres d'école de la République 1870–1914* (Paris: Le Sycomore, 1979).
14. Alfred Fouillée, *Esquisse psychologique des peuples européens* (Paris: Alcan, 1903): the idea is that in France, the community and individuals are more alike than in other countries.
15. One could be "proud of being Jurassien," for example, because the Jura had given France "the important idea of association."
16. Émile Guillaumin, *La Vie d'un simple* (Paris: Stock, 1905).
17. On this point, see Maingueneau, *Les Livres d'école:* "To travel the nation's roads was a way of learning about commerce, a typical form of generalized communication."
18. Ibid.
19. See Maurice Crubellier, "L'Histoire dans les livres de lecture courante" (paper presented at the Colloque sur les manuels d'histoire et la mémoire collective, April 1981, University of Paris VII). Crubellier counts the number of mentions and number of lines devoted to various figures of grandeur in *Le Tour de la France*: 22 mentions and 687 lines on benefactors of humanity, 16 mentions and 694 lines on military heroes, 8 mentions and 273 lines on writers and artists, 4 mentions and 133 lines on statesmen.
20. Daniel Halévy, *La République des ducs* (Paris: Grasset, 1937).
21. Mme Fouillée began her career as a writer of textbooks with another best-seller: *Francinet: Principes généraux de la morale, de l'industrie, du commerce et de l'agriculture*, which appeared in 1869, carried a shorter title in subsequent editions: *Livre de lecture courante.*
22. The quoted phrase is from Aimé Dupuy, summarizing Daniel Halévy's views.
23. See, for example, Claude Digeon, *La Crise allemande de la pensée française, 1870–1914* (Paris: Presses Universitaires de France, 1959). Digeon writes that, in *Le Tour de la France*, "the ideal of Revanche is diminished to the point that it almost totally disappears. War is always reviled, and Alsace and Lorraine seem forgotten." Roger

Thabault is more subtle. He praises Halévy for his insight but notes that "we see only one thing: two orphans driven from their conquered region by Germany, who discover France and do their best every day to better themselves and make themselves more worthy of being French." Roger Thabault, *Mon village* (Paris: Delagrave, 1944).

24. Gérard Varet and Groussau were not attacking any particular author, however. In the debate of January 14, 1910, Varet said, "I think he is dead."

25. Religious instruction was made optional after October 1882. Ethics courses continued to include certain vague negative duties toward God. The issue of a totally secular edition of *Le Tour de la France* did not arise until after the separation of church and state.

26. The right-wing critics implicitly acknowledged the work's impact. Groussau noted that "in a book now in its 331st edition, *Le Tour de la France par deux enfants*, 'My God!' had been replaced by 'Alas!' or 'Oh!' or simply eliminated."

27. In the January 1910 debate, Jaurès's remarks confirm that the work was conventionally attributed to Alfred Fouillée: "*Le Tour de la France*, signed Bruno, is by M. Alfred Fouillée."

28. Alfred Fouillée, *Revue bleue*, December 17–24, 1898: "On what basis should moral and social instruction rest in the schools of a parliamentary democracy?"

29. Despite the revised edition, the original edition, referred to by the publisher as "early," remained in print until 1967. The revised edition continued to be available for another ten years, until the publication of the centennial edition, which reverted to the original version.

30. In *La France au point de vue moral* (Paris: Alcan, 1900), Alfred Fouillée stated in no uncertain terms that Sundays were not the property of religion.

31. Fouillée justified the cuts in a letter to *Le Temps* on January 11, 1910, citing the teacher's legitimate desire for peace, "hence abstention. Abstention is not negation."

32. On this point we differ with Dupuy, who found the remark "quite curt." In fact, Julien had no need to say more, and it was quite effective simply to note that history had repeated itself.

33. Mme Fouillée's third best-seller, *Les Enfants de Marcel*, appeared in 1887. It was a book of "moral and civic instruction in action," a reader for the middle course.

34. Fouillée's words.

35. On this point see Eugen Weber, *Peasants into Frenchmen: The Modernization of Rural France, 1870–1914* (Stanford, Ca.: Stanford University Press, 1976).

36. Despite the francocentric theme of *Le Tour de la France*, not all of its imitators were French (like *Le Tour de France d'un petit Parisien*, by C. Améro, published after 1899, whose hero was also an orphan from Lorraine and whose story is filled with references to the journeys of *compagnons*). Among the foreign works inspired by the book was Selma Lagerlöf's story of the journey of Nils Holgersson.

37. Fournière objected that in contrast to the timorous writers of textbooks, "the unbelieving masses have moved beyond deism."

38. In *La France au point de vue moral*.

39. Others, like Gérard Varet and Reinach, were even less well informed than Jaurès and asserted that the author was dead.
40. These biographical details are borrowed from an article by Robert Vellerut, which appeared in the January-March 1969 issue of *Nice historique*. Vellerut had access to the unpublished correspondence between the Foncin and Fouillée families. Mme Foncin, the wife of the geographer, was a friend of Mme Fouillée's.
41. In 1885, G. Bruno told her friend Mme Foncin of her marriage by remarking that the world wrongly believed her to be a widow: "For twenty-eight years, I have been loved and adored by the noblest heart I know."
42. The scene is described in Alfred Fouillée, *La Morale, l'art et la religion*, 4th ed., expanded, with appendix, which traces Guyau's life. The passage depicts the death scene as a *pietà*: "The mother in tears, as pale as her son, makes one think, in spite of oneself, of the descent of Christ from the Cross."
43. Alfred Fouillée, *Tempérament et caractère selon les individus, les sexes et les races* (Paris: Alcan, 1895).
44. "From their twinned youth falls a ray of light / That gilds their transfigured brows in endless dawn"; Jean-Marie Guyau, *Vers d'un philosophe* (Paris: G. Baillière, 1881).
45. Francisco García Calderón, *Profesores de Idealismo* (Paris: Sociedad de Ediciones Literarias y Artísticas, 1910).
46. Fouillée, *La Morale, l'art et la religion*.
47. In 1888, when little Augustin was four years old.
48. In fact there were several houses, in Nice and Menton, prior to the construction of "the" house described by Augustin Guyau in his memoirs, which was completed in 1887.
49. As a letter to his publisher shows.
50. In his brief life—he died at thirty-three—Guyau had time to look into ancient ethics, English ethics, and contemporary aesthetics as well as to write verse and books for children. In addition, he published the two books on which his reputation rests, *L'Esquisse d'une morale sans obligation ni sanction* (Paris: Alcan, 1885), and *L'Irreligion de l'avenir* (Paris: Alcan, 1888).
51. Pierre Ulric, *Aux domaines incertains* (Paris: L. Theuveny, 1906), and *Parmi les jeunes* (Paris: Grasset, 1911), with a preface by Alfred Fouillée.
52. Alfred Fouillée, *La Science sociale contemporaine* (Paris: Hachette, 1880). Fouillée indicated his debt in the preface to the 1910 edition.
53. Jean Macé, *Histoire d'une bouchée de pain* (Paris: E. Dentu, 1861). One of the favorite themes of this other public school best-seller, and quite well done indeed, was: "Get those hands moving so you can take your morning coffee!"
54. For example, Alfred Fouillée, *La Conception morale et civique de l'enseignement* (Paris: Éditions de la *Revue bleue*, 1902), and *Enseignement au point de vue national* (Paris: Hachette, 1891).
55. Especially in *Éducation et hérédité* (Paris: Alcan, 1889).
56. Augustin Guyau entered the École Supérieure de l'Électricité in Paris in 1907. He graduated as an engineer and was working on a thesis under Paul Janet, who wrote a note included in Guyau's posthumously published works.

57. Augustin Guyau, *Œuvres posthumes: Voyages, Feuilles volantes, Journal de guerre.* Faithful to the family tradition, Augustin Guyau also wrote a book on the work of his grandfather, *La Philosophie et sociologie d'Alfred Fouillée* (Paris: Alcan, 1913), in which he included biographical details he had from his grandmother.
58. Fouillée, *La morale, l'Art, et la religion.*
59. Alfred Fouillée, preface to *Parmi les jeunes.* He credited the phrase to Pierre Ulric, that is, to his daughter-in-law.
60. Fouillée files, preserved by the publisher Belin.
61. One of her swooning heroines says: "Who knows if, after a complicated cycle, our reasoners and scholars will not some day be brought back to convictions their companions could never stifle?"
62. Fouillée, *Tempérament selon les caractères, les sexes et les races.*
63. Fouillée, "La Réforme de l'enseignement philosophique et moral en France," *Revue des Deux Mondes* (1880), 39.
64. The story of this defense, in 1872, is retold in François Maury, *Figures et aspects de Paris* (Paris, 1910).
65. The Institut, for which his candidacy in 1893 was sponsored by Ravaisson, Janet, Barthélemy, and Saint-Hilaire, rejected him on the grounds of "socialist leanings." The rumor was spread by his longtime rival, the religious traditionalist Ollé-Laprune.
66. On all these matters, see the illuminating article by Yveline Fumat, "La Socialisation politique à l'école du *Tour de France de deux enfants* aux manuels de 1977," *Revue française de pédagogie,* no. 44 (July–September 1978).
67. Guyau, *La Première Année de lecture courante* (Paris: Armand Colin, 1875).
68. On the relation between the republican idea and the quasi-contract, see Claude Nicolet, *L'Idée républicaine en France* (Paris: Gallimard, 1982).
69. He acknowledged this in the second preface to the 1910 edition of *La Science sociale contemporaine*: "We owe the original idea to Mme Fouillée, who, in writing the first of her masterly textbooks, delved deeply into economic and social issues." He was speaking of *Francinet.*
70. See Fouillée, *La Propriété sociale et la démocratie* (Paris: Hachette, 1884).
71. See the teacher's handbook: "Why do people still refer to charity as fraternity? Because it makes us aware of all men as brothers."
72. A. de Margerie, "La Philosophie d'A. Fouillée," excerpt from *Annales de philosophie chrétienne* (Paris: A. Roger and F. Chernovitz, 1897).
73. Fouillée, *La Science sociale contemporaine,* second preface, 1910 ed.
74. Significantly, after the war, Mme Fouillée bequeathed another relic to the elementary school in Menton: Jean-Marie Guyau's school desk.

5. LAVISSE, THE NATION'S TEACHER

1. L. Lemonnier, *Revue internationale de l'enseignement,* January-February 1923.
2. C.-V. Langlois, *Revue de France,* September-October 1922.
3. Jules Isaac, *Expériences de ma vie* (Paris: Calmann-Lévy, 1959), pp. 265–267.

4. René Doumic, *Écrivains d'aujourd'hui* (1894). However, this essay, which is concerned primarily with the basic history primer, gives only oblique consideration to the content of Lavisse's work on Germany and of the important collective works (to which the volume on Louis XIV was a contribution).
5. Lavisse, *Discours à des enfants* (Paris: Armand Colin, 1907); *Nouveau discours à des enfants* (Paris: Armand Colin, 1911).
6. Lavisse always maintained close contacts with Saint-Cyr, whose entrance examination he tried to reform (see "L'Examen de Saint-Cyr," *Revue de Paris,* April 1896). He was a history and literature professor at the school at the height of the Dreyfus Affair in 1899. His younger brother, who died a general, was a graduate of Saint-Cyr and became head of the Saint-Maixent School.
7. Lavisse, in *Études et étudiants* (1895).
8. I have been unable to discover how the two men met, but their friendship lasted until Duruy's death in 1894. Duruy concluded his *Notes et souvenirs* (written in 1892 and published in 1904) with a report of his satisfaction with the success of his children and of his disciple: "And my former secretary for public instruction, Ernest Lavisse, who for more than thirty years I have regarded as one of my children, has been admitted to the Académie Française" (p. 312). See also Ernest Lavisse, "Un Ministre: Victor Duruy," *Revue de Paris,* January–March 1895.
9. Lavisse himself entrusted the letters to the Bibliothèque Nationale. When large portions were published in the *Revue des deux mondes* in April 1929, Lavisse's publisher, Armand Colin, reacted vehemently. Max Leclerc, director of the house at that time, immediately asked Lavisse's heir, Mme Jeanne Quiévreux, to stop "a publication likely to injure the memory of her uncle, for these letters are truly 'too young' and wholly out of character with what we know he later became." Mme Quiévreux then turned against General Lavisse's widow, Mme Suzanne-Émile Lavisse, who had been pleased to read "these letters, which do honor" to her brother-in-law. M. Mignot, who is currently literary director of Armand Colin, was kind enough to make the house files on Lavisse available to me, for which I am extremely grateful.
10. He used whatever came his way, says Jules Isaac, who in a private conversation told me that he found in Lavisse's works whole sentences lifted from letters he himself had written him. And no one but M. Esmonin himself can tell us who contributed what to their joint work on Louis XIV.
11. By 1927 seventeen editions of the work had been published.
12. My italics. Note, however, how much of the luster of Michelet's fine phrase is lost in Lavisse's rendering.
13. The original plan dated back quite a way: "I really think it would be useful for students to learn the history of France," Lavisse wrote to Gaston Pâris on April 7, 1878. "The trouble is, their teachers don't know any. . . . How wretched our national education is, and how little we are doing to fix it!" Bibliothèque Nationale, Nouvelles Acquisitions Françaises, 24–25, fols. 278–294.
14. He was less interested in secondary education. It is significant that Lavisse was not a member of the committee on secondary education that was established in 1882.

15. See Lavisse, *Les Questions d'enseignement national* (1885) and *Études et étudiants* (1890).
16. See the speech to the École Normale Supérieure, November 20, 1904. The *normaliens* of the class of 1905 reacted vigorously. Some, including Dean Davy, from whom I heard the anecdote, recall the ruckus that greeted the new director, who with his slow step walked to the school from his home on the Rue de Médicis only to be greeted with shouts of "Save the school in spite of its director!"
17. See Barrès,"Toute licence contre l'amour" (1902).
18. Claude Digeon, "La Nouvelle Université en Allemagne" ch. 7 of *La Crise allemande de la pensée française* (Paris, 1959).
19. See Lavisse's critique of Father Didon's *Les Allemands,* in *Questions d'enseignement national,* and the article "Jeunesse allemande, jeunesse française," in *Études et étudiants.*
20. Ibid.
21. Lavisse, *Études sur l'Allemagne* (Paris, 1881), p. 98.
22. Lavisse, *La Question d'Alsace dans une âme d'Alsacien* (Paris: Armand Colin, 1891).
23. Daniel Halévy, *Péguy* (Paris: Grasset, 1941).
24. Charles Péguy, *Un Nouveau Théologien, M. Fernand Laudet* (September 1911). *L'Argent* (February 1913) and *L'Argent: suite* (April 1913).
25. "I am well aware of all the other vile things on top of this vileness and hatred and envy and filth and shame." To his friend Lotte, Péguy confided: "For eighteen months I have not been able to say 'Our Father."' Péguy, thirty-two years younger than Lavisse, was in the class of 1894.
26. In *L'Argent: suite* (p. 1146 of the Pléiade edition), from which all the quotes are taken.
27. This point was confirmed by M. Esmonin, who provided me with invaluable information.
28. Archives of Armand Colin Publishing.
29. See the section on contemporary history, which was made available at this date to purchasers of the old edition.
30. Letters of April 29 and May 5, 1880 (archives of Armand Colin Publishing).
31. The Armand Colin files contain mostly notes between author and publisher. The publisher proposed typefaces and design ideas and repeatedly advised the author to be "simple and *interesting*." Lavisse was endlessly scrupulous. For instance: "I am still counting on having someone reread the text after I do to check the chapter numbers, questions, and stories, to verify dates, and so on. I have worked hard to eliminate abstract words and difficult turns of phrase. I have read, reread, and read some more, but I am still not sure if any are left, and, if so, I would be happy to have them pointed out to me, along with any repetitions of words" (August 27, 1881).
32. The most widely used, in addition to the Mame texts, were apparently the primers by Abbés Lucien Bailleux and Victor Martin, by Alfred Baudrillard, by Abbé Vandepitte, by Abbé Godefroy, by Father Dom Ancel and Gabriel Maurel, and by Abbé P. Gagnol.
33. See Lavisse to Armand Colin (November 5, 1896): "I have seen the Mame books. What shameless imitation!"

34. It is virtually impossible to come up with exact figures on the number of copies printed. The average press run was apparently 150,000, from which it would follow that the Lavisse primers had several million readers. As a rough gauge, note than in the year of his death, 1922, Lavisse's account at Armand Colin was credited with 70,000 francs and his account at Hachette with 15,000 francs.
35. A major campaign was launched to defend republican primers. See, for example, Mme. J. Guiot, *Les Attaques contre les manuels d'histoire*; Guiot and Mame's response (1910); or Paul Lorris, *Ce qu'ils enseignent? Est-ce vrai?: Étude sur les manuels condamnés par l'épiscopat.*
36. Here, I treat the Mame and Aulard-Debidour texts as typical, respectively, of private and republican public school textbooks.
37. Even allowing for the fact that this was a primer, how impoverished this seems compared with Michelet! For Michelet, Jeanne symbolized the people, the virgin, the victim of the clergy, salvation through woman, hostility to England, the Passion, the identification of France with a woman—seven different symbols. Here, Jeanne was simply the memory of France, who was truly herself only in misfortune.
38. Lavisse, *Discours à des enfants: L'école laïque* (1904).
39. This sentence, which was included in the 1882 insert *("dévelopement de la partie contemporaine")*, was eliminated from the "new work" of 1884.
40. Lavisse, *Nouvelle Deuxième Année d'Histoire de France* (1895), p. 415.
41. Lavisse, "L'Enseignement de l'histoire à l'école primaire," taken from the *Dictionnaire de pédagogie*, revised and expanded in *Questions d'enseignement national.*
42. See the description of this patriotic elementary teaching by Georges Goyau in *L'École d'aujourd'hui* (Paris: Perrin, 1899, 1906).
43. Lavisse, "L'École d'autrefois et l'école d'aujourd'hui," in *A propos de nos écoles* (Paris: Armand Colin, 1895).
44. Lavisse, *A propos de nos écoles: Une école d'enseignement socialiste révolutionnaire* (1895).
45. V. Jeanroy-Félix, *Fauteuils contemporains de l'académie française* (1896).
46. Pierre Lasserre, *La Doctrine officielle de l'Université* (Paris, 1912).
47. Maurice Barrès, *Toute licence sauf contre l'amour* (Paris: Perrin, 1892).

6. VIDAL DE LA BLACHE'S *GEOGRAPHY OF FRANCE*

1. Born in Pézenas (Hérault) in 1845, Vidal de La Blache ranked first in the 1863 entrance examination for the École Normale. After also scoring first in the history *agrégation*, he was sent by Duruy to the École Française in Athens from 1867 to 1870. His thesis, defended in 1872, was still, in keeping with tradition, in history, but, traumatized by the defeat, he was probably affected by a report published at the time by Émile Levasseur (a geographer who in many respects anticipated Vidal) showing the disastrous consequences of the insufficient emphasis on geography in French education compared with the importance attached to the subject in Germany. After assuming, in 1873, the chair in history that Fustel de Coulanges had held in Strasbourg, now moved

to Nancy, Vidal decided to devote himself entirely to geography, which he did until 1877, when he was named to the École Normale, of which he eventually became assistant director. There, over the next twenty years, he would create the new French school of geography. In 1898, the retirement of Auguste Himly, who had doggedly kept faith with the old school of historical geography that originated in the seventeenth century, paved the way for Vidal's appointment to the Sorbonne, where he gained acceptance for his views and taught students until his retirement in 1908. From then until his death in April 1918, Vidal continued to dominate French geography. In addition to his *Tableau,* he gained prominence for his *Atlas* (1894) and his famous wall maps as well as for works such as *La France de l'Est* (1917). His many lectures and articles in the *Annales de géographie,* which together with Lucien Gallois he founded in 1891, also attracted considerable attention.

The *Tableau* is the first volume of Ernest Lavisse's *Histoire de France,* 27 vols. (Hachette, 1900–1911), but it was not the first volume published: by 1902, seven volumes had already appeared, covering the origins of France to the fifteenth century. The 395-page *Tableau* was reprinted several times without change (1905, 1908, 1913, and 1930). An edition in a different format appeared in 1908 under the title *La France: Tableau géographique.* The text is essentially the same (the only changes having to do with the fact that this volume was no longer part of a series), with the addition of a foreword (see n. 17 below).

All these editions contain a color map of France and Europe marking "the history of the occupation of the land." This map was omitted from the facsimile of the 1903 edition published in 1979 by Tallandier, with a preface and appendices by Paul Claval. Page references in the text are to this edition.

2. Numa Broc, "La Géographie française face à la science allemande, 1870–1914," *Annales de géographie,* 86 (1977). See also the article "Ratzel" in the *Encyclopaedia Britannica.*
3. Paul Claval, *Essai sur l'évolution de la géographie humaine,* Cahiers de géographie de Besançon, 12 (Paris: Les Belles Lettres, 1964).
4. The influence of Ratzelian determinism on Vidal de La Blache is a complex question, which I shall try to sort out in the remainder of this essay. I cannot agree with Mariel Jean-Brunhes Delamarre, who wrote that "Paul Vidal de La Blache and his student Jean Brunhes vigorously rejected Ratzelian determinism" (chapter "Géographie humaine et ethnologie" in Jean Poirier, ed., *L'Ethnologie générale* [Paris: Gallimard, 1968], p. 1477). One must distinguish different aspects of Ratzel's ideas. As for the texts of Ratzel's that were used (with some distortion of Ratzel's intentions) to justify calls for German *Lebensraum,* there can be no doubt that Vidal expressed his doubts, as the *Tableau* shows. But Vidal continued to refer to Ratzel and in 1898 published in the *Annales de géographie* an article entitled "La Géographie politique à propos des écrits de M. Frédéric Ratzel," which does contain a discreet warning about a "dogmatic formalism having little to do with the relativity of phenomena" (p. 99) but in which Vidal also warmly recommends the works of the great German geographer, who he says offers "a conception of political geography consistent with the present

state of the science" (p. 111). The article shows that Vidal had more refined views than Ratzel on geopolitics but nevertheless appreciated the richness of his colleague's work.

5. Jules Michelet, *Introduction à l'histoire universelle.*
6. "Débat sur le nationalisme et le patriotisme"(1905), in Émile Durkheim, *Textes* (Paris: Éditions de Minuit, 1975), 3: 180.
7. *Annales de géographie,* 5 (January 15, 1896): 138.
8. On the relation between ethics and geography, see Vincent Berdoulay, *La Formation de l'école française de géographie, 1870–1914* (Paris: Comité des Travaux Historiques et Scientifiques, Bibliothèque Nationale, 1982).
9. See Philippe Pinchemel's chapter on Vidal de La Blache in *Les Géographes français, Bulletin de la section de géographie du Comité des travaux historiques,* vol. 81 (Paris: Bibliothèque Nationale, 1975), pp. 9–23.
10. Claval, *Essai,* p. 48.
11. Jean-Yves Guiomar, "Le Désir d'un tableau," *Le Débat,* 24 (March 1983): 90–106.
12. I am quoting from the edition prefaced by Charles Morazé: Jules Michelet, *Tableau de France* (Paris: Bibliothèque de Cluny, Armand Colin, 1962), pp. 82–161.
13. Paul Vaillaneix, *La Voie royale* (Paris: Flammarion, 1971), p. 256.
14. Berdoulay, *La Formation,* ch. 4. Vidal de La Blache wrote an important article on regionalism, "Les Régions françaises," in *Revue de Paris* (December 15, 1910). For a biography of Pierre Foncin, see J.-B. Duthil in the *Revue de géographie commerciale de Bordeaux,* 1925–1926.
15. Ch. 2, of vol. 1, "Situation de la Gaule dans le monde ancien," pp. 40–56.
16. On progress in physical geography in France between 1890 and 1914, see André Meynier, *Histoire de la pensée géographique en France* (Paris, 1969), and Numa Broc, "Les Débuts de la géomorphologie en France: Le tournant des années 1890," *Revue d'histoire des sciences,* 28 (1975).
17. For the geographer, the landscape is a synthesis of physical and human characteristics. The 1908 Hachette edition was advertised in a lavish photographic spread. "A landscape is a complex ensemble of elements of varying ages and shapes." The photographs illustrate the nature of the geographer's perception of the landscape. "The pleasure of philosophizing mingles with the pleasure of seeing. An educated eye can detect what is interesting in landscapes that might seem insignificant or mediocre to a tourist or even an artist," but the photography "must be done in a geographic spirit by people who know how to ferret out nature's secrets."
18. Albert Demangeon evolved considerably after his 1905 thesis on Picardy, which was entirely in the Vidalian spirit. In ch. 15 he examines, in a sequence not without significance, "Human settlements. Houses. Villages. Towns and cities." A change was already evident in Camille Vallaux's 1906 thesis on lower Brittany: ch. 11 is entitled "Cities, Roads, Trade." But Vallaux would become a dissident.
19. See Michel Denis, "La Géographie et les origines des déséquilibres régionaux en France," *La Pensée géographique française contemporaine: Mélanges offerts à André Meynier* (Saint-Brieuc: Presses Universitaires de Bretagne, 1972), pp. 683–691.

20. Lucien Febvre, *La Terre et l'évolution humaine*, part 3 (1922; repr. Paris: Albin Michel, 1970).
21. See Paul Vidal de La Blache, "Les Conditions géographiques des faits sociaux," *Annales de géographie*, 11 (1902), and "Rapports de la sociologie avec la géographie," *Revue internationale de sociologie*, 12 (May 1904).
22. "Les Pays de France," published in *La Réforme sociale* (September 1–16, 1904).
23. *Annales de géographie*, 20 (1911), p. 297.
24. In 1908, his friend and collaborator Lucien Gallois published an important work on *Régions naturelles et noms de pays*, which Vidal reviewed in the *Journal des Savants* (September-October 1909).
25. Camille Vallaux, *La Basse Bretagne, étude de géographie humaine* appeared in 1906. Vallaux was then a professor at the École Navale.
26. Julien Gracq, *En lisant, en écrivant* (Paris: José Corti, 1981), p. 87. Gracq was of course a teacher of history and geography.
27. Fernand Braudel, *Écrits sur l'histoire* (Paris: Flammarion, 1969), p. 31.
28. Georges Duby and Guy Lardreau, *Dialogues* (Paris: Flammarion, 1980), p. 95.
29. On all these points see the extensive discussions in Berdoulay, *La Formation*, ch. 3, 4, and 5.
30. Ibid., ch. 2.
31. See Pierre Nora, "Lavisse, The Nation's Teacher," in this volume.
32. Numa Broc, "Histoire de la géographie et nationalisme en France sous la IIIe République, 1871–1914," *L'Information historique*, 32 (1970).
33. Berdoulay, *La Formation*, ch. 6.
34. All this can be related to the well-known debate between Vidalian geographers and Durkheimian sociologists at the beginning of the century. The debate concerned the foundations, methods, and subject matter of geography.
35. Paul Vidal de La Blache, "Des caractères distinctifs de la géographie," *Annales de géographie*, 23 (1913), quoted in Berdoulay, *La Formation*, p. 211.

7. MARCEL PROUST'S *REMEMBRANCE OF THINGS PAST*

1. References to *A la recherche du temps perdu* are to the Pléiade edition edited by Jean-Yves Tadié (Paris: Gallimard, 1987–1989), 4 vols.; translations by Arthur L. Goldhammer.
2. Jean-Yves Tadié, *Proust* (Paris: Belfond, 1983), p. 9.
3. Xu Jun, "Proust en chinois," *Le Monde* (October 6, 1989): 48.
4. See the article by Avner Ben-Amos, "Les Funérailles de Victor Hugo," in Pierre Nora, ed., *Les Lieux de mémoire*, part 1, *La République* (Paris: Gallimard, 1984), pp. 473–522.
5. See André Vauchez's article "The Cathedral" in the present volume.
6. Thanks to MM. Jean-Pierre Chauvière and Jean-Pierre Dauphin for providing these figures.
7. Gustave Lanson, *Hommes et livres: Études morales et littéraires* (Paris, 1895), pp. 296–297.

8. See Daniel Milo, "Les Classiques Scolaires," and Olivier Nora, "La Visite du grand écrivain," in Pierre Nora, ed., *Les Lieux de mémoire,* part 2, *La Nation,* vol. 3 (Paris: Gallimard, 1986): 517–526 and 563–589.
9. Gustave Lanson, *Méthodes de l'histoire littéraire* (Paris: Les Belles Lettres, 1925), pp. 41–42.
10. Louis-Ferdinand Céline, *Romans* (Paris: Gallimard/Pléiade, 1981), 1: 74. See Marie-Christine Bellosta, *Céline ou l'art de la contradiction: Lecture de* Voyage au bout de la nuit (Paris: Presses Universitaires de France, 1990), pp. 96–101.
11. Letter to Jacques Boulenger, [4 December] 1920, *Correspondance générale* (Paris: Plon, 1932), 3: 229–230.
12. Louis-Ferdinand Céline, *Bagatelles pour un massacre* (Paris: Denoël, 1937), p. 187.
13. Letter to Lucien Combelle, "Révolution nationale," February 20, 1943; *Cahiers Céline,* no. 7 (Paris: Gallimard, 1986), p. 180.
14. Marcel Proust and Gaston Gallimard, *Correspondance,* ed. Pascal Fouché (Paris: Gallimard, 1989), p. 371.
15. Céline, *Bagatelles,* p. 169.
16. Letter to Milton Hindus dated June 11, 1947, in Milton Hindus, *L-F. Céline tel que je l'ai vu* (Paris: Éditions de l'Herne, 1969), p. 142.
17. "L.-F. Céline vous parle" (1957), in Céline, *Romans,* 2 (1974): 932.
18. Proust and Gallimard, *Correspondance,* p. 302.
19. If "the death of Bergotte" appeared as early as 1926 in Marcel Braunschvig's anthology, *La Littérature française contemporaine étudiée dans les textes, 1850–1925* (Paris: Armand Colin), the intended audience for which is not clear and which went beyond the school curriculum, the presence of "the grandmother in the garden" excerpt from "Combray" in a 1928 reader for the sixth, seventh, and eighth grades, *Morceaux choisis des auteurs français* by G. Dulong and H. Yvon (Paris: Delalain) is more surprising, because Proust would make no further appearance in textbooks for this level until the 1960s, with the notable exception of an anthology compiled by Pierre Clarac, a future editor of the *Recherche* in the Pléiade edition, who in 1941 included two pages of Proust, "the magic of place-names" and "the idle chatter of an elderly diplomat" in a book for the eighth grade, *La Classe de français* (Paris: Belin).
20. Léon Pierre-Quint, *Marcel Proust, sa vie, son Œuvre* (Paris: Le Sagittaire, 1976), pp. 254, 265.
21. Ibid., p. 273.
22. Jean-Paul Sartre, *Situations I* (Paris: Gallimard, 1947), p. 32.
23. Jean-Paul Sartre, *Situations II* (Paris: Gallimard, 1948), p. 20.
24. Paul Claudel, *Œuvres en prose* (Paris: Gallimard, 1965), p. 650.
25. Proust and Gallimard, *Correspondance,* p. 267.
26. Ibid., p. 578.
27. Pierre-Quint, *Marcel Proust,* p. 280.
28. Ibid., p. 274.
29. Thanks to Mme Anne Borrel, the current secretary general, for information about the Society.

30. M. Domerc, G. Hyvernaud, and J. Sirinelli, *Plaisir de lire,* Collection Jean Guéhenno (Paris: Armand Colin, 1961). Proust is given less space in the 1970 edition.
31. Letter of December 23, 1954, *Œuvres en prose,* p. 650, n. 4.
32. *Critique* (July 1952; repr. in Georges Bataille, *La Littérature et le mal* [Paris: Gallimard, 1957]).
33. Reprinted under the title "L'Expérience de Proust" in Maurice Blanchot, *Faux Pas* (Paris: Gallimard, 1943).
34. Also reprinted under the title "L'Expérience de Proust" in Maurice Blanchot, *Le Livre à venir* (Paris: Gallimard, 1959).
35. *Revue des sciences humaines* (July–September 1955; also published in *Monde nouveau* [December 1955]).
36. Roland Barthes, "Les Vies parallèles," *Quinzaine littéraire* (March 15, 1966).
37. Nathalie Sarraute, *L'Ère du soupçon* (Paris: Gallimard, 1987), p. 84.
38. Quoted in Tadié, *Proust,* p. 162.
39. Jacques Rivière, "Marcel Proust et la tradition classique," *La N.R.F.* (February 1, 1920; repr. in *Nouvelles Études* [Paris: Gallimard, 1947]).
40. Roland Barthes, *Essais critiques* (Paris: Éditions du Seuil, 1973), p. 59.
41. Roland Barthes, *Critiques et vérité* (Paris: Éditions du Seuil, 1966), p. 45.
42. Roland Barthes, "Une Idée de recherche" (1971), in *Le Bruissement de la langue* (Paris: Éditions du Seuil, 1984), p. 308.
43. Roland Barthes, *Le Plaisir du texte* (Paris: Éditions du Seuil, 1973), p. 59.
44. Roland Barthes, "Longtemps je me suis couché de bonne heure" (1978), in *Le Bruissement de la langue.*
45. Henri Raczymow, *Le Cygne de Proust* (Paris: Gallimard, 1989).
46. Letter to Camille Vettard, undated, *Correspondance générale,* 3: 194.

8. *LA COUPOLE*

1. Jacques Davy Du Perron, *Oraison funèbre sur la mort de Monsieur Ronsard* (1586), critical ed. by Michel Simonin (Geneva: Droz, 1985). On academies in the France of the Valois, see Frances Yates, *French Academies in the Sixteenth Century* (London: Warburg Institute, 1960).
2. *Sacre:* from the title of his book *Le Sacre de l'écrivain* (Paris: Corti, 1973).
3. On the Prix Balzac for eloquence, first awarded in 1671, see Bernard Beugnot, *Guez de Balzac, bibliographie générale* (Montreal: Presses Universitaires de Montréal, 1969), pp. 27, 84, 118, 148, and *Supplément* (1969), p. 71.
4. Marcel Proust, *Contre Sainte-Beuve* (Paris: Gallimard, 1954).
5. Arsène Houssaye, *Histoire du quarante et unième fauteuil de l'Académie française* (Paris: Hachette, 1856). Houssaye was primarily a novelist. His son Henry, who entered the Académie, was a historian. From one generation to the next, the family had moved up in the world.
6. Maurice Martin du Gard, *Mémorables* (Paris: Flammarion, 1957), 1: 277. See also *Correspondance Marcel Proust–Jacques Rivière, 1914–1922* (Paris: Plon, 1955), pp. 105–

107 (May 1920). See also letter to Maurice Barrès (June 1921): "I will not speak to you, after such an important subject, about my petty academic ambitions. You advised me to declare my candidacy immediately at the first vacancy, before minds were made up about the seat. But I do not know how such a declaration is made, and perhaps M. Aicard's chair has not yet been declared vacant. Last but not least, I've heard vague rumors that Claudel may try for it. I do not know him and have no reason to stand aside for him. But his great fame and political connections would probably leave me with no chance." Recall that Proust won the Prix Goncourt in November 1919 and received the Legion of Honor on September 29, 1920.

7. Quoted by Proust in *Contre Sainte-Beuve*, p. 202.
8. See especially in the *Nouveaux Lundis* (Monday, January 20, 1862), "Des prochaines élections à l'Académie," concerning speculations about replacements for Scribe and Lacordaire. Sainte-Beuve casts himself as interpreter of the academic tradition, "combining" the "inspirations and influences" of the Ancien Régime, the Revolution, and the Restoration. This is the article in which he describes "Baudelaire's Madness," the possibility of his succeeding Scribe. In the end Octave Feuillet was elected.
9. See, among other things, the preface by J. Thuillier to the anthology *Les Grands Prix de Rome au XIX*[e] *siècle* (Paris, 1982), and Donald D. Egbert, *The Beaux-Arts Tradition in French Architecture, as Illustrated by the Grand Prix de Rome*, ed. David Van Zanten (Princeton: Princeton University Press, 1980).
10. Paul Mesnard, *Histoire de l'Académie française depuis sa fondation jusque 1830* (Paris: Charpentier, 1857). One can also profitably consult the Duc de Castries, *La Vieille Dame du quai Conti, une histoire de l'Académie française* (Paris: Librairie Académique Perrin, 1978).
11. See note 8 above.
12. Lucien Brunel, *Les Philosophes et l'Académie française au XVIII*[e] *siècle* (Paris: Hachette, 1884).
13. Simone de Beauvoir, *Les Mandarins* (Paris: Gallimard, 1972), 1: 190.
14. On the circle of the Rue de Rome that gathered on Tuesday evenings around Mallarmé from 1885 on, see Henri Mondor, *Vie de Mallarmé* (Paris: Gallimard, 1946), and the memoirs of Édouard Dujardin, *Mallarmé par l'un des siens* (Paris, 1936), which quotes the memories of Bernard Lazare, Albert Mockel, Henri de Régnier, and Camille Mauclair. Valéry, in *Variété* (*Œuvres* [Paris: Gallimard, 1957], 1: 619–706), also offers a version of the "academic" discussions that took place around the man whom Dujardin compares to Socrates.
15. Aristotelian and Thomist ethics legitimated patronage as a way of making wealth, even ostentatious wealth, demonstrate the grandeur of the soul to the vulgar.
16. One should distinguish between *corps*, or corporations, whose origins are lost in the mists of time, and *compagnies*, founded by the king; but it was common to think of companies in terms of corporations. See Ernst Kantorowicz, *The King's Two Bodies: A Study in Medieval Political Theology* (Princeton: Princeton University Press, 1957), which discusses the medieval theory of corporations and its debt to the theology of the Church as "mystical body."

17. See Jean Bodin, *Les Six Livres de la république*, book 3, ch. 7 ("Des corps, collèges, états et communautés"): "Thus we can say that every corporation or college is a right of legitimate community under sovereign power." Bodin, while acknowledging that corporations helped to maintain "friendship" (in Aristotle's sense) and thus a society's political well-being, and that they could not be abolished except for just and powerful reasons, nevertheless enumerated cases in which the state was entitled to suppress or abolish them if they betrayed their purpose and involved themselves in or aggravated public disputes. The jurisconsults of the Ancien Régime, elaborating Bodin's views in a manner still more favorable to state power, eventually accepted the idea that the state is free to abolish corporations for reasons of convenience rather than justice. This laid the groundwork for the revolutionary *tabula rasa*.
18. In 1641 the Palais-Cardinal theater opened its doors, and a royal ordinance equivalent to a patent of civil respectability for actors was promulgated. Nevertheless, more than a few bishops and theologians held to the "severe" doctrine according to which exercising the profession of actor meant automatic excommunication. For that reason Molière could not become a candidate for the Académie. However, in the course of the Balzac-Goulu dispute (1626–1630), it emerged that for many in the clergy and in *parlement*, writers in the vulgar tongue, especially those concerned with art, were mere sophists and potentially libertines, dangerous to sound morals.
19. See the classic works of Ferdinand Brunot, *Histoire de la langue française*, and his thesis, *La Doctrine de Malherbe d'après son commentaire de Desportes* (Paris, 1901).
20. Malherbe, *Œuvres*, ed. A. Adam (Paris: Gallimard, 1971), pp. 156–157.
21. Gombauld, Chapelain, and Godeau, three poets belonging to the Conrart circle even before its "discovery" by Boisrobert and Richelieu, began "making sacrifices" of praise to the cardinal at this time. In 1634, Boisrobert published *Le Sacrifice des Muses au grand cardinal*, an anthology of "Malherbian" poems celebrating Richelieu.
22. See Maximin Deloche, *Autour de la plume du cardinal de Richelieu* (Paris, 1920; B.N., 8° Ln[27] 81157).
23. Paul Pellisson-Fontanier, *Relation contenant l'histoire de l'Académie françoise* (Paris: P. Le Petit, 1653).
24. See Zygmunt Marzys, "Pour une édition critique des *Remarques sur la langue française* de Vaugelas," *Vox Romanica*, no. 34 (1975): 124–139.
25. On the victory of the court and failure of Parlement, see my *Âge de l'éloquence* (Geneva: Droz, 1980), part 3, passim.
26. Marin Le Roy de Gomberville, *Tableau du bonheur de la vieillesse, opposé au malheur de la jeunesse* (Paris: Lacquehoy, 1614).
27. See Desmarets de Saint-Sorlin, *Visionnaires*, critical ed. by G. Hall (Paris: S.T.F.M., 1963).
28. He was Corneille's rival in the quarrel over *Le Cid* and the author of several tragedies that Richelieu liked.
29. G. de Scudéry, *Alaric ou la Rome vaincue*, heroic poem (Leyden, 1656).
30. See R. Zuber, *Les Belles Infidèles ou la formation du goût classique* (Paris: Armand Colin, 1968).

31. Paul Valéry, "Remerciement à l'Académie française," in *Œuvres* (Paris: Gallimard, 1957), 1: 728. The whole piece is worth reading for its epitome of "Mallarméist" taste, *N.R.F.* taste, and academic taste in a soaring diplomatic tour de force.
32. On Colbert and the academies, see the catalogue of the Colbert exhibition, Hôtel de la Monnaie, 1983, pp. 355–363 and 447–480. It is clear that Colbert, in contrast with the individual, *grand seigneur* style of Foucquet, took an institutional view of royal patronage. See also J. Thuillier, "Réflexions sur la politique artistique de Colbert," in *Actes* of the colloquium Un Nouveau Colbert (Paris, SEDES, 1985), pp. 275–286.
33. Charles Du Périer (b. Aix [?], d. Paris, 1692), *Ad Delphinium* (Paris, n. d.; B. N. Yc 2770). He traded translations of fables (including those of La Fontaine) with Charles Perrault and *le père* Commire.
34. The famous *Discours* of Rivarol, a man also associated with a French-style academy, that of Berlin, has been studied by Baldensperger, *Comment le XVIII*[e] *siècle voyait l'universalité de la langue française,* in regard to its sources and immediate reception. The history of the myth celebrating the language is inseparable from that of the Academies.
35. On Amable de Bourzeis (1606–1672), see O. H. de Bourzeis, *Un Académicien oublié, l'abbé de Bourzeis* (Paris, 1879). On François Charpentier (1620–1702), see "Éloge de M. Charpentier," *Journal des Savans* (1702): 506–508, and d'Alembert, "Éloge de François Charpentier," *Histoire des membres de l'Académie française* (Paris, 1787), 2: 127–159.
36. François Charpentier, *Défense de la langue françoise pour l'inscription de l'arc de triomphe* (Paris, 1676). The tireless Charpentier was also the author of a *Discours de l'utilité et de l'excellence des exercices académiques* (1695).
37. François Charpentier, *De l'excellence de la langue française,* 2 vols. (Paris, 1683). On this dispute, see my "L'Apologétique de la langue française classique," *Rhetorica,* 2, no. 2 (1984): 139–161.
38. "Discours prononcé par M. l'abbé Tallemant le jeune le 23 décembre 1676, pour servir de réponse à celui du R. P. Lucas, jésuite," in *Recueil des harangues prononcées par Messieurs de l'Académie françoise dans leurs réceptions* (Paris: Coignard, 1698), pp. 295–307. Abbé Tallemant reflects on the history of the debates over this issue within the Petite Académie, and he reveals that, while there was agreement on excluding any "ancient disguise" for the king and his family, the language of inscriptions was a problem, and there was spirited debate between Bourzeis and Charpentier.
39. On the origins of the dispute and the decisive contribution of Charles Perrault, see, in addition to Hubert Gillot, *La Querelle des Anciens et des Modernes en France, de la* Défense et illustration de la langue française *aux* Parallèles des Anciens et des Modernes (Paris: Champion, 1914), the articles by P. Bonnefon in the *Revue d'histoire littéraire de la France* (1904, 1905, and 1906).
40. Lack of space compels me to pass over the "Quarrel of Homer," which pushed the Quarrel of the Ancients and Moderns to its ultimate consequences. There is an admirable analysis in Noémi Hepp, *Homère en France au XVII*[e] *siècle* (Paris: Klincksieck, 1968), pp. 629–754. On the seventeenth-century reversal of the relation

between time and knowledge (a reversal often reduced to the decline of the argument from authority), see the essays collected in *XVII*[e] *siècle,* no. 131 (1981). Krzysztof Pomian has recently published, from a somewhat different perspective, an essential work for anyone interested in the subject: *L'Ordre du temps* (Paris: Gallimard, 1984).

41. Antoine Furetière, *Second Factum par Messire Antoine Furetière, abbé de Furetière, abbé de Chalevoy, contre quelques-uns de l'Académie française* (Amsterdam: Henry Desbordes, 1686), pp. 26–27.
42. Antoine Furetière, *Second Placet et très humble remonstrance à Mgr Le Chancelier* (no place or date; B.N. X 2551[3–8]).
43. Ménage, *Requête* (Paris, [1649]), unpaginated.
44. Antoine-Léonard Thomas, *Essai sur les éloges* (Paris, 1773), ch. 37. See his *Œuvres complètes,* 2 vols. (Paris: Belin, 1819), 2: 207.
45. Dominique Bouhours, *Entretiens d'Ariste et d'Eugène* (Paris, 1671), quoted from the 1947 Paris ed., p. 92.
46. *Panégyrique du roi prononcé le 25 août 1673 par M. l'abbé Tallemant le jeune* (Paris: Coignard, 1693), p. 48. It is not surprising that Abbé Tallemant, a proponent of French in the quarrel over inscriptions and an enthusiastic and indefatigable panegyrist of Louis XIV, was the author of the *Panégyrique funèbre de Charles Perrault,* delivered at the Académie Française, Paris, 1704.
47. Pascal, "De l'esprit géométrique et l'art de persuader," *Pensées,* ed. Lafuma (Paris: Éditions du Seuil, 1963), pp. 358–359.
48. The Abbé d'Olivet (Pierre-Joseph Thoulier, 1682–1723) was the continuator of Pellisson in his *Histoire de l'Académie française depuis 1652 jusqu'à 1720* (Paris, 1729). See Charles-L. Livet's ed. of the two *Histoires* (Paris, 1858). In Edmond and Jules de Goncourt, *Portraits intimes du XVIII*[e] *siècle* (Paris, 1858), there is a quite succulent portrait of Abbé d'Olivet (1: 237–287).
49. On the exclusion of the Abbé de Saint-Pierre, see, in addition to the various *Histoires de l'Académie française,* the *Chroniques des élections à l'Académie française* (Paris: Firmin-Didot, 1886), pp. 66–67 (the Abbé de Saint-Pierre's election in 1695 had symbolized the victory of the Moderns); pp. 88–89 (his expulsion marked the beginning of the influence of Cardinal Fleury, elected in 1717).
50. On Duclos's reform, see Mesnard, *Histoire de l'Académie,* pp. 80–81, and Brunel, *Les Philosophes,* p. 58.
51. Published in 1773, this essay was an a posteriori justification of Duclos's reform, but it was also an excellent study of the panegyric genre.
52. Quoted in Mesnard, *Histoire de l'Académie,* p. 83.
53. Duclos, *Considérations sur les mœurs de ce siècle* (Paris: Perrault, 1751), p. 229.
54. D'Alembert, "Éloge de Richelieu," in *Mélanges de littérature, d'histoire et de philosophie* (Berlin, 1753), 2: 156; "Exhortation aux gens de lettres," ibid., p. 162.
55. Quoted in Brunel, *Les Philosophes,* p. 41.
56. Letter of February 13, 1767, from Ferney, in Besterman, ed., *Œuvres complètes,* D 13951.
57. Response from Palissot, circa February 20, ibid., D 13984.

58. On the network of academies in eighteenth-century France, readers may wish to consult the fundamental work by Daniel Roche, *Le Siècle des Lumières en province: Académies et académiciens provinciaux, 1680–1789*, 2 vols. (Paris: Mouton, 1978).
59. Barbey d'Aurevilly, "Médaillon de Sainte-Beuve," in J. Petit, ed., *Le XIX*[e] *siècle des Œuvres et des hommes* (Paris: Mercure de France, 1966), 2: 38.
60. On the Chamfort-Morellet quarrel and Morellet and Suard's role in saving the archives and resurrecting the Académie, see *Mémoires inédits de l'abbé Morellet sur le dix-huitième siècle et la Révolution*, 2 vols., ed. Lemontey (Paris: Ladvocat, 1821)
61. On the projects of reform and instruction conceived by Talleyrand and Condorcet, see *Une Éducation pour la démocratie, textes et projets de l'époque révolutionnaire*, presented by Bronislaw Baczko (Paris: Garnier, 1982).
62. On the abolition of the academies and the creation of the Institute, see Georges Perrot, "L'Institut," in *L'Institut de France* (Paris: H. Laurens, 1907), pp. 37–94.
63. See, in series Le 38 of the Bibliothèque Nationale, the texts by Daunou concerning the reform of teaching and the creation of the Institute. For example, his report to the Committee of Public Safety (1793, B.N. 8° Le 38 2371).
64. On the history of the Collège des Quatre-Nations, see Alfred Franklin, *Histoire de la bibliothèque Mazarine et du palais de l'Institut* (Paris: Welter, 1901).
65. Institut de France, Classe de Langue et de Littérature française, *Présentation à S. M. l'Empereur et Roi, en son Conseil d'Etat, du rapport historique sur l'état et les progrès de la littérature, le 27 février 1808* (Paris, 1808). The deputation consisted of MM. Chénier, president; Volney, vice-president; Suard, perpetual secretary; and the members Morellet, Boufflers, Bernardin de Saint-Pierre, Andrieux, Arnauld, Villars, Cailhava, Domergue, Lacretelle, Layon, Raynouard, and Picard.
66. See the article cited in n. 8 above, in which Sainte-Beuve fully embraces the difference between the Institute, founded by the Revolution, and the Académie Française of the Ancien Régime.
67. Stendhal, *Racine et Shakespeare*, ed. Fayolle (Paris: Garnier Flammarion, 1970), p. 82 ("Avertissement" to the second version of *Racine et Shakespeare*, published in 1825).
68. See the essential work by André Tudesq, *Les Grands Notables de France, étude historique d'une psychologie sociale* (Paris: Presses Universitaires de France, 1964), and Daniel Halévy, *La Fin des notables* (Paris, 1880).
69. Barbey d'Aurevilly, *Le XIX*[e] *siècle*, p. 35.
70. See Jacques Véron, "L'Académie française et la circulation des élites, une approche démographique," *Population*, no. 3 (May–June 1985): 454–471.
71. On the diffusion of the novel in the nineteenth century, see *L'Histoire de l'édition française*, vol. 2, *1660–1830* (Paris: Promodis, ????). On the nineteenth-century Académie's complaints against the novel, see Paul Bourget, "Le Roman à l'Académie," in *Trois siècles de l'Académie française par les Quarante* (Paris: Didot, 1935), pp. 213–221.
72. On the material situation of the writer in the nineteenth century, see Bernard Vouillot, "La Révolution et l'Empire: Une nouvelle réglementation," in *L'Histoire de l'édition française*, pp. 526–535. The Convention had dissolved the Communauté des Libraires

et Imprimeurs de Paris in 1791. It had also abolished both the author's privilege and the bookseller's privilege. By contrast, in 1793, on Lakanal's recommendation, it issued a decree (21 July) defining literary property. This would become the basis of authors' royalties in the nineteenth century as well as of Balzac's call for the creation of a Society of Men of Letters charged with defending authors' rights and interests.

73. See Sainte-Beuve, *Nouveaux Lundis,* p. 399: Octave Feuillet is mentioned for his dual success "in reading and the theater": the word "reading," which calls to mind that nineteenth-century institution, the *cabinet de lecture,* or reading room, was a euphemism to avoid pronouncing the obscene word "novel." At the end of his article, Sainte-Beuve, following the example of his admired Daunou, imagines his ideal academy consisting of the following sections: 1. Language and grammar; 2. Theater; 3. Lyric, epic, and didactic poetry; 4. History; 5. Eloquence; 6. Eloquence and art of writing. At the end of the list he adds, *cum grano salis,* a seventh section, "Novels, novellas, etc.," with the following comment: "This very modern genre, for which the Académie has thus far made little room."

74. On the "social ascension" of the novel and novelist, which slowly followed the *economic* triumph of the novel (and of novelists like Dumas, Sue, and Féval), more research is needed. Hugo clearly derived his prestige from poetry and his income from the popular novel, at which he excelled. In the novels of Paul Féval, digressions on the injustice of the critics and the pretentiousness of "worldly" novelists are frequent. Paul Bourget was the first declared novelist to live among the cream of society. The Académie demonstrated sure social and literary instincts when it elected him in 1892. Without *both* Edmond de Goncourt's *artistic* indictment of the Académie *and* the ennoblement of the novel and its academization by Bourget, there would have been no Proust. Readers may consult with profit, but not without precautions, the article by Priscilla P. Clark, "Stratégies d'auteurs au XIXe siècle," *Romantisme,* nos. 17–8 (1977): 92–103.

75. Author of *Les Fleurs de Tarbes ou la Terreur dans les lettres* (1941), in which he wittily rehabilitated rhetoric against "terror," Jean Paulhan was elected to the Académie on February 27, 1964, which cooled his relations with the Gallimards. In his acceptance speech, Paulhan prophetically contrasted the Académie's grammatical wisdom with the pretensions of ancient and modern linguistics.

9. MONUMENTS TO THE DEAD

1. *La Voix du combattant* (December 2, 1923).
2. *Le Poilu dauphinois* (December 1932) and ibid. (January 1933) for the mayor's response.
3. See my *Les Anciens Combattants et la société française, 1914–1939,* vol. 3, *Mentalités et idéologies* (Paris: Presses de la Fondation Nationale des Sciences Politiques, 1977), or the English translation of my shorter book: *In the Wake of War: "Les Anciens Combattants" and French Society* (Providence and Oxford: Berg Publishers, 1992). See also Monique Luirard, *La France et ses morts* (Le Puy-en-Velay: Imprimerie

Commerciale, 1977), and June Hargrove, "Souviens-toi," *Monuments historiques*, no. 124 (December 1982–January 1983). Further research has been done since this article was first written and published in French: see, in particular, the special issue on war memorials of the French journal *Guerres mondiales et conflits contemporains*, no. 167 (July 1992), for comments on recent work.

4. Fewer than one percent of the 38,000 French communes have no monument to the dead. In those cases there is at least a plaque in the church, and the quick initiative of the clergy made the erection of a monument seem pointless to the overwhelmingly Catholic population: see Luirard, *La France et ses morts*, p. 19. Sometimes, also, the social unit is not the commune but the parish, which includes several communes, and one finds an intercommunal monument as in Fraroz, La Latette, and Cerniébaud (Jura), where the monument is in any case next to the church.

5. In addition to the examples mentioned in Luirard, *La France et ses morts*, pp. 13–14, and in Prost, *Les Anciens Combattants*, pp. 38–39, there is also the monument to the *mobiles de l'Allier*, built by public subscription in Moulins, in the Place d'Allier.

6. The schedule of subsidies was established by the law of July 31, 1920. The main subsidy ranged from 4 to 15 percent of the total expense, depending on the number of dead relative to the size of the population. There was also an additional subsidy determined by the wealth of the commune, ranging from 11 percent for the poorest to 1 percent for the richest. Mme Luirard, who was apparently unaware of this practice, points out that there were also departmental subsidies, and in some cases she is able to cite the share of the expense raised by subscription and the share drawn from municipal funds (p. 24). For 128 monuments, she cites the total cost: 28 under 5,000 francs, 48 between 5,000 and 10,000 francs, 39 between 10,000 and 25,000, and 13 above 25,000. According to one foundry catalogue, a cast bronze statue of a *poilu* cost at least 4,800 francs, a simple bust around 2,000. See price list, May 1921, of Fonderies et Ateliers de Construction du Val d'Osne.

7. These disputes generally involved the priest's insistence on adding a religious symbol of some kind to the monument, and the council's refusal to do so. See Prost, *Les Anciens Combattants*, pp. 39–40.

8. In Lyons, at the cemetery of La Guillotière, November 1, 1916 (minutes of the *conseil d'administration* of the Union des Mutilés et Anciens Combattants du Rhône, November 5, 1916); in Nîmes, November 1, 1917 (*Après la bataille* [November 1917]); in Orléans, the same (minutes of the *conseil d'administration* of the Mutilés du Loiret, October 20, 1917).

9. This minority formed two associations: the Association Républicaine des Anciens Combattants and the Association Ouvrière des Mutilés, associated with the C.G.T., which later became the Fédération Ouvrière et Paysanne des Mutilés. The A.R.A.C. and the F.O.P. were the only organizations to refuse to join in the celebrations of Bastille Day 1919 after the government agreed that they should be preceded by a memorial vigil in honor of the war dead. But the demonstration organized at Père-Lachaise cemetery drew about a thousand people. The A.R.A.C. was a very small

association before 1940, while the F.O.P. was larger but still much smaller than the major veterans' groups. In 1927, moreover, it pulled out of the (Communist) Veterans International.

10. The sample was chosen to include all regions of the country and designed to be exhaustive in each area looked at. I personally viewed 306 monuments, and colleagues viewed 51 others. In addition, 500 questionnaires were sent to teachers in eleven regional groups of communes. I received 201 responses, so that in all the survey included 564 monuments in 35 different départements. See Prost, *Les Anciens Combattants*, p. 42.
11. This request came from the Mutilés du Loiret (minutes of the *conseil d'administration*, November 5, 1931), one of the first associations of disabled veterans, whose president, Henri Pichot, was probably the most eminent veterans' leader between the two wars and for a long time the president of the largest national veterans' group, the Union Fédérale.
12. In Ayhere, for example.
13. Saint-Martin-d'Estréaux (Loire), Brassac (Tarn), etc. Luirard, *La France et ses morts*, p. 27, mentions four communes in her département, but not Saint-Martin-d'Estréaux.
14. The law on the separation of church and state prohibited affixing religious emblems to memorial monuments but not to funerary monuments. Monuments to the dead were considered to be funerary if they were located in cemeteries. In some communes, however, monuments were planned for public squares without crosses only to have crosses added later. See Prost, *Les Anciens Combattants*, p. 40.
15. Victor Hugo, "Hymne," *Les Chants du crépuscule*, 3.
16. This statue was produced by the Durenne Foundries and is referred to as model EE in their catalogue (Établissements métallurgiques A. Durenne, *Statues et ornements pour monuments commémoratifs* [Paris: Imprimerie Puyfourcat, 1921], p. 5). Unfortunately we do not know the price. This statue is found in 2.6 percent of the monuments in our sample. If the sample is representative, there would be 900 similar statues in French village squares.
17. It would be interesting to extend this study by systematically analyzing the images of females in these monuments. Maurice Agulhon, *Marianne au combat* (Paris: Flammarion, 1979), contrasts the popular Republic, wearing a Phrygian cap, the symbol of liberty, and the moderate Republic, robed and sober, crowned with ears of wheat or laurels. I found few Republics with Phrygian cap on any war memorial. Luirard, *La France et ses morts*, reproduces a photograph of one, in La Ricamarie in the Loire. Agulhon saw one in Provence. I found mainly women in ancient garb, which I am inclined to interpret as symbols of the Republic even when wearing helmets, as in Boën-sur-Lignon and La Courneuve. Agulhon, p. 211, also notes a helmeted Republic: the bust of Clésinger in the Senate. If my impression is correct, World War I marked the triumph of the sober, moderate, conservative Republic, which then became identified with France, for it was subsequently accepted by all the French, who had been willing to die for it regardless of their political views; the

Republic was no longer a party. This was already the theme of de Marcère's speech upon the inauguration of the statue of the Republic on the Champ-de-Mars, June 30, 1878; see Agulhon, p. 218.

18. No. 854 of the catalogue of the Fonderies du Val d'Osne, this statue cost 5,300 francs in cast bronze. It was not very common (only four appear in our sample), but other sculptors treated the *poilu* in similar terms, as a sentinel or lookout.
19. The most common statue of this type appears to have been that of Gourdon, which turned up seven times in our sample, but it was apparently copied frequently.
20. See Luirard, *La France et ses morts*, for the monuments of Chazelles-sur-Lyon, La Fouillousse, Leigneux, and Sorbias.
21. The inscription is a triptych. In the center: "Results of the war: more than twelve million dead! An equal number unborn! Still more maimed, wounded, widowed, and orphaned. Billions of francs in damages. Scandalous fortunes built on human suffering. Innocent people hanged on the gallows. The guilty rewarded. The disinherited plunged into misery. A huge bill to be paid. Has war at last caused enough suffering and misery, killed enough men, that men may find the intelligence and will to kill war itself?" And the last panel on the right reads: "A curse on war and those responsible for it."
22. This was easy when there was only one veterans' group. When there was more than one, their presidents generally formed a committee.
23. *Le Combattant* (Tarbes; November 10, 1921, and November 1, 1922).
24. *Compte rendu* of the Clermont-Ferrand conference (Paris: Presses Universitaires de France, n.d.), p. 291.
25. F. Malval (Hubert-Aubert), *La Voix du combattant* (July 30, 1922).
26. A. Linville (A. L'Heureux), "La Fête du 11 novembre," *Le Journal des mutilés et réformés* (October 14, 1922).
27. For the Loire, see, for example, *Le Poilu de la Loire* (December 1934)—*De profundis* at the monument: Chuyer, Montregard, Saint-Maurice-de-Lignon, Chassigny-sur-Dun; absolution: Arthun, Saint-Victor-sur-Loire, Sevelinges, Chazelles-sur-Lavieu. For the Vendée, see *Le Combattant vendéen* (December 1930). There were similar ceremonies in the Ardennes (see *Le Combattant sanglier* [December 1933]) and in Normandy. At Henqueville (Seine-Inférieure): "After the mass the procession formed, led by the clergy, and proceeded to the monument singing the *Libera*. At the monument there were the usual prayers, a blessing, the laying of a wreath, the reading of names, and a speech by Président Levasseur [a summary is given]. Return to the church singing *Te Deum*." (*La Flamme* [November 1934].)
28. The reading of the names of the dead is explicitly mentioned in 11 of 29 communes in the Ardennes in 1931 (*Le Combattant sanglier* [December 1931]). It was common in Isère, Aveyron, etc.
29. In many parishes at this time the sermon began with a necrology: the priest read a list of names of the dead and at the end the Lord's Prayer was said for them. Then came the sermon proper. Similarly, at the monuments, the speech generally came after the reading of the names.

30. Williers (Ardennes), 1930: "Kind ladies sang a canticle for the occasion." *Le Combattant sanglier* (December 1930).
31. Prost, *Les Anciens Combattants*, p. 59.
32. C. Vilain, *Le Soldat inconnu, histoire et culte* (Paris: Maurice d'Hartoy, 1933).
33. Manent is explicit about this in *Le Combattant* (Tarbes; October 1, 1921).
34. Rosemonde Sanson, *Les 14-juillet, fête et conscience nationale* (Paris: Flammarion, 1976), explains how this ceremony was organized.
35. On the initiative of the Mutilés du Loiret, *La France mutilée* (October 29, 1922), *Le Journal des mutilés et réformés* (November 4, 1922), *Le Combattant du Pas-de-Calais* (November 9, 1922). See also the advocacy of speeches by veterans rather than elected officials in Linville, *Le Journal des mutilés et réformés* (October 14, 1922), and Bruche, *Le Combattant du Pas-de-Calais* (November 9, 1922.
36. In *Le Béquillard meusien* (November 1926).

10. THE GOOD SOLDIER CHAUVIN

1. Jean-François Bayard and Philippe Dumanoir, *Les Guêpes*, performed for the first time in Paris on the stage of the Palais-Royal, November 30, 1840 (Paris: Henriot, 1841), scene 9, p. 11.
2. The phrase "male chauvinist" seems to have been coined by Germaine Greer in 1970: "It is a male chauvinist position to suppose that any creature that bleeds from the site of its torn-off sexual organ ought by rights to be a maniac." See *The Female Eunuch* (New York: McGraw-Hill, 1971), p. 77. For the use of the term in this sense, see also Edgar Berman, *The Compleat Chauvinist: A Survival Guide for the Bedeviled Male* (New York: Macmillan, 1982). And Marcella Markham and Dominic Poelsma, *A Chauvinist is . . .: An Irreverent Book of Cartoons for Oppressors and Oppressed Alike* (Watford, Herts: Exley Publications, 1979).
3. Jacques Arago, "Chauvinisme," in the supplement, letter C, of M. W. Duckett, ed., *Dictionnaire de la conversation et de la lecture* (Paris, 1845), p. 455.
4. Pierre Larousse, "Chauvinisme," *Grand Dictionnaire universel du XIX*[e] *siècle, 1866–1879*, 34 vols. (Geneva: Slatkine Reprints, 1982), 3 (1867): 1111.
5. Jean Lestocquoy, *Histoire du patriotisme en France des origines à nos jours* (Paris: Albin Michel, 1968), pp. 13–14.
6. Centre d'Animation Lyrique et Culturel de Rochefort, *Rochefort: Trois siècles en images, de Napoléon à nos jours* (Rochefort: Maury, 1983), p. 36.
7. Gordon Wright, *France in Modern Times, 1760 to the Present* (Chicago: Rand MacNally and Co., 1962), p. 242.
8. Archives de la Guerre, Garde Impériale, first regiment of *grenadiers à pied* (20-Yc 4).
9. Théodore and Hippolyte Coigniard, *La Cocarde tricolore*, episode from the war in Algiers, vaudeville in three acts, first performed in Paris at the Théâtre des Folies-Dramatiques on March 19, 1831 (Paris: Bezou, Barba, Quoy, 1834), act 2, scene 8, p. 17, and scene 9, p. 18; act 1, scene 5, p. 5; act 2, scene 2, p. 20. Chauvin here says that he is a native of Falaise. Although there are indeed families by that name in Falaise,

none of our specimens, not even Henri-Guillaume, has left any trace there corresponding to the Chauvin we are after. By contrast, the peasant from Falaise was a fixture of popular songs from the early nineteenth century.

10. Colonel de La Combe, *Charlet, sa vie, ses lettres,* 2 vols., with a catalogue of his lithographical work (Paris: Paulin and Le Chevalier, 1861),
11. Coigniard, *La Cocarde tricolore,* act 1, scene 5, p. 5.
12. *Œuvres poétiques de Chauvin,* three military romances (Paris: Gaultier-Laguionie, 1825). *Guirlande poétique et militaire de Chauvin,* 2d ed., rev. and expanded (Paris: Firmin-Didot, 1833).
13. "Les Amours de Chauvin et de la belle Janneton," *Œuvres poétiques de Chauvin,* p. 8.
14. "Suite des amours de Chauvin," *Guirlande poétique et militaire de Chauvin,* p. 21.
15. "L'Amoureux Sergent," *Œuvres poétiques et Chauvin,* p. 11.
16. Ibid.
17. "Suite des amours de Chauvin," *Guirlande poétique et militaire de Chauvin,* p. 21.
18. Bayard and Dumanoir, *Les Guêpes,* scene 9, p. 11.
19. Ibid. This was a parody of the vaudeville by Francis (pseudonym of Maris François d'Allarde), Nicolas Brazier, and Théophile Marion Dumersan, *Les Moissonneurs de la Beauce ou le Soldat-laboureur,* a rural comedy, first performed at the Théâtre des Variétés on September 1, 1821 (Paris: Tresse, Delloye, 1840), scene 14, p. 7: "Je reconnais ce militaire / Je l'ai vu sur le Champ d'honneur."
20. Bayard and Dumanoir, *Les Guêpes,* scene 9, pp. 11 and 12.
21. Gustave Nadaud, "Chauvin," *Chansons de Gustave Nadaud,* 8th ed., rev., with 39 new songs (Paris: Henri Plon, 1870), pp. 82–84.
22. Paul Avenel, *Nouvelles Chansons politiques* (Paris: Armand Le Chevalier, 1878), pp. 25, 26.
23. Paul Avenel, "Chauvin," in Anonymous, *La Chanson française du XV*[e] *au XX*[e] *siècle,* with musical appendix (Paris: La Renaissance du Livre, 1912), pp. 278–279.
24. Alphonse Daudet, "La Mort de Chauvin," *Les Contes du lundi* (1873; repr. Geneva: Édito-service, 1968), pp. 108–112.
25. Arago, "Chauvinisme," p. 452.
26. Louis Jourdan, "Le Chauvinisme," *Le Siècle* (October 12, 1854).
27. Larousse, "Chauvinisme," *Grand Dictionnaire universel du XIX*[e] *siècle.*
28. Lorédan Larchey, "Chauvinisme," *Dictionnaire historique d'argot* (Paris: Dentui, 1888), p. 97.
29. Larousse, *Grand Dictionnaire.*
30. Abbé de Vertot, *Histoire des révolutions arrivées dans le gouvernement de la République romaine,* 2 vols. (1719; repr. Avignon, 1810), 1: 5.
31. Vergil, *Georgics,* 1.508: "curvae rigidum falces conflantur in ensem" [the crooked pruning-hooks are forged into stiff swords; Fairclough's trans.].
32. Isaiah 2:4; Joel 3:10.
33. See, for example, Frey, *Le Jardinier de Sainte-Hélène* (1829; Bibliothèque Nationale, Prints, Ef 217, Collection de Vinck, no. 9785). And the interesting commentary by

Anne-Marie Rosset,"La Restauration et les Cent-Jours," in *Inventaire de la collection de Vinck*, 5: 272.

34. Jean-Jacques Rousseau, *Projet de constitution pour la Corse*, in *Œuvres complètes* (Paris: Gallimard, 1975), p. 905.
35. On the Bonapartist soldier-peasant colonies, see Isser Woloch, *The French Veteran from the Revolution to the Restoration* (Chapel Hill: The University of North Carolina Press, 1979).
36. André Marie Jean-Jacques Dupin, speech to the *Comice Agricole* of Seine-et-Oise at Grignon on June 7, 1835, reproduced in Dupin, *Des comices agricoles et en général des institutions d'agriculture* (Paris: Videcoq fils aîné, 1849), p. 101.
37. Jules Michelet, *Le Peuple* (1846; repr. Paris: Flammarion, 1974), pp. 118, 89, 132, 90.
38. Alphonse Toussenel, *Les Juifs, rois de l'époque: Histoire de la féodalité financière* (Paris: Librairie de l'École Sociétaire, 1845), pp. 105 and 276.
39. On agricultural colonization, the most complete study is that carried out by L. F. Huerne de Pommeuse at the behest of the minister of agriculture, the Comte d'Argout: *Des colonies agricoles et de leurs avantages* (Paris: Imprimerie de Mme Huzard, 1832), followed by *Questions et réponses relatives aux moyens d'établir en France des colonies agricoles de divers genres* (Paris: Imprimerie de Mme veuve Huzard, 1836). See also the various plans for military colonies in Algeria by Bugeaud and Abbé Landmann, as well as Jules de Lamarque and Gustave Dugat, *Des colonies agricoles établies en France en faveur des jeunes détenus, enfants trouvés, pauvres, orphelins et abandonnés*, a historical and statistical précis (Paris: Imprimerie et Fonderie de Rignoux, 1850); F. Martin-Ginouvier, *Mise en valeur de notre empire colonial par le Soldat-laboureur marié faisant souche* (Paris: A. Challamel, 1898); and the law thesis of Paul Jaillet, *Essai historique et critique sur la colonisation militaire* (Paris: V. Giard, E. Brière, 1903).
40. Louis Napoléon Bonaparte, *Œuvres*, 3 vols. (Paris: Librairie Napoléonienne, 1848).
41. Bonaparte, *Les Idées napoléoniennes* (1839), ibid., 1: 240.
42. Bonaparte, *Extinction du paupérisme* (1844), ibid., 2: 266.
43. Félix Pyat, *Aux paysans de la France*, speech delivered to a banquet on February 24, 1849, anniversary of the proclamation of the Republic (Le Mans: Imprimerie de J. Tousch, V. Labbé, L. Beaudoire et Cie., 1849; and Paris: Bureau de la Propagande, 1849; repr. in Eugène Sue, Félix Pyat, Pierre Joigneaux, Victor Schoelcher, and Pierre Dupont, *Le Républicain des campagnes*, new ed. [Paris: Librairie de la Propagande démocratique et sociale, 1851], pp. 61–64).
44. Pierre Joigneaux, "A mes frères des campagnes," in Sue et al., *Le Républicain des campagnes*, p. 68.
45. Pierre Dupont, *Le Chant des paysans* (Paris: by the author, 1849). Reproduced in Sue et al., *Le Républicain des campagnes.*
46. Pierre Dupont, *Jean Guêtré, Almanach des paysans, des meuniers et des boulangers, pour 1854* (Paris: J. Bry aîné, 1853), pp. 15, 16. The 1860 issue of this almanac, *Almanach de Jean Guestré, Rustique et guerrier* (1859) has as its epigraph Bugeaud's motto, *Ense et aratro.*

47. Augustin Devoille, *Lettres d'un vieux paysan aux laboureurs ses frères* (1852), *Mémoires d'un vieux paysan suivis des lettres d'un vieux paysan aux laboureurs ses frères* (Paris: J. Vermot, 1859), pp. 212–215.
48. Mathieu Charrue, *Le Paysan-soldat: Épisode de la Révolution et du Consulat* (Besançon: Cornu, 1853), p. 382.
49. Armand de Pontmartin, *Nouveaux Samedis* (Paris: Michel Lévy frères, 1870), 7: 93.
50. Joseph Autran, *Laboureurs et soldats* (1854; 2d ed., Paris: Michel Lévy frères, 1854), p. 28.
51. Paul Déroulède, "En route," *Chants du paysan* (1894; repr., Paris: Fayard, 1908), p. 111.
52. Maurice Barrès, *Scènes et doctrines du nationalisme,* definitive ed., 2 vols. (Paris: Plon, 1925), 1: 97 and 2: 180.
53. Jules Méline, *Le Retour à la terre et la surproduction industrielle* (1905; 3d ed., Paris: Hachette, 1905), p. 218.
54. Jules Méline, *Le Salut par la terre et le programme économique de l'avenir* (Paris: Hachette, 1919), pp. 77, 218, 190, 81, 83, and 226.
55. For example, Paul Harel, *Voix de la glèbe* (Paris: A. Lemerre, 1895); Maurice Rollinat, *Paysages et paysans* (Paris: E. Fasquelle, 1899); Emmanuel Labat, *L'Âme paysanne: La terre, la race, l'école* (Paris: Delagrave, 1919); Pierre Caziot, *La Terre à la famille paysanne* (Paris: Librairie Agricole de la Maison Rustique, 1919); Joseph de Pesquidoux, *Sur la glèbe* (Paris: Plon-Nourrit, 1922); Michel Augé-Laribé, *Le Paysan français après la guerre* (Paris: Garnier, 1923).
56. Drawings reproduced in *L'Illustration,* no. 4054 (November 13, 1920): 360.
57. Marshal Philippe Pétain, speech at the inauguration of the Monument to the Peasant Dead of Capoulet-Juniac, November 17, 1935, reproduced in its entirety in José Germain, *Notre chef Pétain* (Paris: La Technique du Livre, 1942), pp. 181–182.
58. Philippe Pétain, speech of June 25, 1940, in *La Doctrine du Maréchal classée par thèmes* (Paris, 1943), p. 94.
59. Miklós Molnár, "Le Modèle culturel stalinien," in *Cahiers Vilfredo Pareto,* vol. 19 (Geneva: Droz, 1981), pp. 101–113.
60. "Contempt for men's lives and for France had reached the point where conscripts were referred to as *raw material* and *cannon fodder,*" Chateaubriand wrote of Napoleon's armies, speaking of "those unfortunate wretches plucked from their cottages before reaching the age of maturity . . . and used as *cannon fodder* in the most dangerous places to draw the enemy's fire." See "De Buonaparte et des Bourbons" (March 30, 1814), *Mélanges politiques et littéraires* (Paris: Firmin-Didot, 1857), pp. 179 and 186. In 1838 the ultramilitarist and Bonapartist Charlet, in the unfinished preface to his *Vie civile politique et militaire du caporal Valentin,* wrote this of his hero: "Men of this sort are referred to as the battlefield meat course because they feed the fire well." Quoted in La Combe, *Charlet, sa vie et ses lettres,* p. 119.
61. In 1818, Pierre Roch Vigneron painted a farmer-soldier, and in 1820 Horace Vernet also took up the theme in a painting that, though forgotten today, enjoyed, according to the critic Paul Mantz, writing in *L'Artiste* (November 22, 1857; p. 179), "greater

sucess than any painting by Gros." A host of lithographs, woodcuts, and bottle labels were inspired by this work.

62. Vergil, *Georgics*, 1.493–497, "Tilling." Abbé Delille, the most celebrated classical poet of the eighteenth century, gave the following French translation, which was often quoted in legends of lithographs depicting the soldier-peasant:

> Un jour le laboureur dans ces mêmes sillons
> Où dorment les débris de tant de bataillons,
> Heurtant avec le soc leur antique dépouille
> Trouvera sous ses pas des dards rongés de rouille;
> Entendra retentir les casques des héros,
> Et d'un œil affligé contemplera leurs os.
> [Some day, the farmer, working the same furrows
> In which so many battalions lie slumbering,
> Will strike their ancient remains with his plow,
> And find rusted blades beneath his feet;
> He will hear the ring of heroes' helmets
> And contemplate their bones with grieving eye.]

Abbé Jacques Delille, *Les Géorgiques de Virgile* (1769), in *Œuvres complètes* (Paris: Firmin-Didot, 1865), p. 320.

63. Louis Reybaud, *Mémoires de Jérôme Paturot, patenté, électeur et éligible*, 2 vols. bound as one (Brussels: Méline, Cans et Cie., 1843), 1: 234.

11. STREET NAMES

1. Information on sequences of Paris street names is for the most part taken from Jacques Hillairet, *Dictionnaire historique des rues de Paris* (Paris: Éditions de Minuit, 1963), and *Supplément* (1972).
2. Quentin, "Les Noms de rues de Reims," *Revue internationale d'onomastique*, vol. 2 (September 1950): 177–192.
3. A. Vallet, *Les Noms de rues et toponymes divers de la commune de Saint-Étienne* (Lyons, 1961).
4. "Sur quelques mesures à prendre en changeant les noms de rues," *Rapport au Conseil général de la Commune de Paris* of 17 Nivôse, Year II.
5. Abbé H. Grégoire, *Système de dénominations topographiques pour les places, rues, quais . . . de toutes les communes de la République*, Rapport de la Convention nationale de l'an II (Paris); Jules Cousin, "De la nomenclature des rues de Paris," *Mémoires de la Société de l'histoire de Paris*, vol. 26 (1899): 2–4 (the article was written in 1877); P. Lacombe, "Les Noms des rues de Paris sous la Révolution," *Revue de la Révolution*, vol. 7 (1st semester 1886): 101–102; M. Heid, "Les Noms de rues de Paris à travers l'histoire: Problèmes linguistiques et sociologiques" (thesis, Tübingen, 1972), pp. 14–151.

6. See Vallet, *Les Noms de rues*; Heid, *Les Noms de rues*; P. P. Clar, "Lire la rue: Pour sémiotique de l'espace" (manuscript, 1984).
7. Cousin, "De la nomenclature," p. 4.
8. For a more expansive statement of the issues treated here, see Daniel Milo, "Aspects de la survie culturelle" (thesis, École des Hautes Études en Sciences Sociales, Paris, 1985).
9. Cousin, "De la nomenclature," p. 4, as well as Lacombe, "Les Noms des rues," p. 102, and Quentin, "Les Noms de rues," p. 192.
10. Louis-Sébastien Mercier, "Marivaux," *Tableau de Paris* (Amsterdam, 1789), 11: 150.
11. L. de Duranville, "Quelques observations sur les noms des rues et places de Rouen," *Revue de la Normandie* (June 1869): 10.
12. See the reports by Beudant (1872), Mesurier (1885), and Fleurot (1912) in *Rapports et documents du conseil municipal de Paris* (annual publication).
13. Even authors who write about provincial street names are interested only in their own cities, as if comparative studies did not exist.
14. J. Cousin remarked on the kinship between medieval street names and geographical names but did not pursue the idea very far.
15. Lacombe, "Les Noms des rues," p. 102.
16. And, especially, "La Sociogenèse de l'état" in *La Dynamique de l'Occident* (Paris: Calmann-Lévy, 1975), translation of the second part of *Über den Prozess der Zivilisation: Soziogenetische und Psychogenetische Untersuchungen* (Basel, 1939; abridged in English as *The Civilizing Process* [New York: Urizen Books, 1978; paperback ed. Cambridge, Mass.: Blackwell, 1994]).
17. Heid, *Les Noms des rues*, p. 165.
18. Cousin, "De la nomenclature," p. 7.
19. Ibid., pp. 6–7.
20. Mercier, "Marivaux."
21. J.-C. Bonnet, "Naissance du Panthéon," *Poétique*, no. 33 (1978): 46–66, is especially interested in Thomas, the master of the genre.
22. Mercier, *Tableau de Paris*, 2: 202.
23. For London, see E. Ekwall, *Street-Names of the City of London* (Oxford, 1954), and H. A. Harben, *A Dictionary of London* (London, 1918). For Brussels I have consulted the *Plan routier de Bruxelles* (1792; Département des Cartes et Plans de la Bibliothèque Nationale, Paris). One finds fewer "religious" names than in Paris or London but far more trade names.
24. Marseilles, Lyons, Bordeaux, Nantes, Toulouse, Lille, Metz, Rennes, Rouen, and Reims constitute a satisfactory statistical sample, in my view. The choice of dates was dictated by the documents available in Paris. All the maps consulted are in the Département des Cartes et Plans de la Bibliothèque Nationale, Paris, except those in Nantes.
25. P. Lelièvre, "L'Urbanisme et l'architecture à Nantes au XVIIIe siècle" (thesis, University of Paris, Nantes, 1942), p. 61.

26. Arthur Young, *Travels in France During the Years 1787, 1788, and 1789*, ed. Constantine Maxwell (New York: Columbia University Press, 1928), p. 116 (September 22, 1788). For the theater, see the entry for the previous evening, p 115.
27. I am grateful to Bernard Lepetit for suggesting this to me.
28. Abbé Grégoire, *Système de dénominations*, p. 3.
29. On revolutionary Paris I have consulted the exemplary scholarship of P. Lacombe, "Les Noms de rues," pp. 101–111, 223–233, 280–291.
30. Ibid., p. 103.
31. Ibid., p. 104.
32. Ibid., p. 105.
33. *Le Moniteur universel* (October 8, 1792), quoted in Heid, *Les Noms des rues*, p. 198.
34. Heid, *Les Noms des rues*, p. 201; Cousin, "De la nomenclature," p. 8.
35. A. Franklin, "Les Rues," in *La Vie privée d'autrefois* (Paris, 1901), 25: 71–80.
36. Lacombe, "Les Noms de rues," p. 105.
37. Ibid., p. 229.
38. The municipal council of Paris decreed in 1904 that "no street in Paris shall be named after a person dead for less than five years," the purpose being to prevent the naming of a street after Émile Zola (Heid, *Les Noms des rues*, p. 220). But the city continued to celebrate living men such as President Wilson (1918) and Pétain (1929). This failure led to the issuing of the following order by Maurice Schuman, minister of the interior, on April 12, 1948: "The Ministry of the Interior shall rule on the naming of streets and squares when such naming constitutes a public homage to a living foreign or French personality" (ibid., p. 221).
39. *Le Moniteur universel* (June 27, 1790), quoted in P. Fleurot, "Rapport concernant la dénomination de quelques voies de Paris," *Rapports et documents du Conseil municipal de Paris*, no. 50 (1912).
40. Bronislaw Baczko, *Les Imaginaires sociaux: Mémoires et espoirs collectifs* (Paris: Payot, 1984), p. 118.
41. *Tableau des noms anciens et nouveaux des promenades . . . de la ville de Marseille* (Marseilles, 1820).
42. P. Peraux, *Dictionnaire indicateur des rues et places de Rouen* (Rouen, 1819), p. x: the date explains the tone.
43. Quentin, "Les Noms de rues," p. 184.
44. Municipal Archives of Toulon, D 10, fol. 136v.
45. M. Bernadau, *Le Viographe bordelais* (Bordeaux, 1844), pp. 42–46.
46. Vallet, *Les Noms de rues*, p. 146.
47. Coulon, "Plan de la ville de Nantes," Year III.
48. The case of Parthenay proves that it did indeed deal with "all the communes of the Republic." This small Vendean city changed the names of thirty-nine streets, squares, gates, and cantons on February 21, 1794. See P. Arches, "Noms de rues et vie politique à Parthenay, 1794–1941," *Bulletin de la société historique et archéologique "Les Amis des antiquités de Parthenay"* (1980): 26–27.

49. R. de Figuères, *Noms révolutionnaires des communes de France* (Paris, 1901). The figures are understated because they only take account of names that *begin* with *Union, Égalité,* and *Voltaire.*
50. James Legendre, *Les Noms révolutionnaires: Histoire postale des localités débaptisées sous l'influence jacobine* (Paris, 1974), the title of which is eloquent.
51. Baczko, *Les Imaginaires sociaux,* p. 54.
52. Franklin, "Les Rues," p. 65.
53. Lacombe, "Les Noms de rues," p. 291.
54. It was under his new name, moreover, that Cloots uttered these striking words: "The Republic should be assured of exclusive commerce in the raw materials of which public opinion is fabricated." Quoted in Baczko, *Les Imaginaires sociaux,* p. 54.
55. Ibid., p. 47. It is interesting to note that another cultural revolution that aimed at making a fresh start, namely, that of the Jewish people become the State of Israel, used similar methods. Tens of thousands of people hebraicized names deemed to reflect too much the influence of the diaspora, some acting spontaneously, others at the urging of the government.
56. Heid, *Les Noms des rues,* p. 205, has ten lines on the Directory.
57. Lacombe, "Les Noms de rues," p. 288.
58. According to the inventory established by Alphonse Aulard, *Paris pendant la réaction thermidorienne* (Paris, 1902).
59. Peraux, *Dictionnaire indicateur,* p. x.
60. Communal Archives of Marseilles, series 1 D, fol. 125; series 30, fol. 54–65.
61. Municipal Archives of Toulon, series D 14, fol. 213.
62. Bernadau, *Le Viographe bordelais,* p. 42.
63. Hillairet, *Dictionnaire historique,* p. 38.
64. Cousin, "De la nomenclature," p. 9.
65. Lacombe, "Les Noms de rues," p. 289.
66. Aulard, *Paris.*
67. L. de Lanzac de Laborie, *Paris sous Napoléon* (Paris, 1914), p. 108, quoted in Heid, *Les Noms des rues,* p. 202.
68. Quoted in Aulard, *Paris.* One had to be rather naïve to exclaim with *Le Patriote français* that "it is high time that our streets no longer bore the ridiculous names of a few canonized penitents" (8 Frimaire, Year VII [November 28, 1798]). The wind was blowing from a new quarter.
69. Vallet, *Les Noms de rues,* p. 147.
70. Or, more precisely, the names adopted in 1790 in accordance with Necker's proposals. *Tableau des changements à faire dans les dénominations des subdivisions de Paris* (n. d., Archives de la Seine, Vd6 8 n3). These changes took place prior to 1812, as indicated by the list in J. de La Tynna, *Dictionnaire topographique, historique et étymologique des rues de Paris* (Paris, 1812).
71. The only exception: Rue Madame, restored in 1812 for reasons that remain unclear.
72. Municipal Archives of Toulon, series D 14, fol. 213.

73. For example, Saint-Florent-le-Vieil was called Mont-Glone until 1798, Libre-Val once again became Saint-Amand in 1800, and Port-Malo became Saint-Malo. Fontenay-le-Peuple reverted to its old name, Fontenay-le-Comte, in 1802.
74. The only exception, still inexplicable: Legendre claims that Bourg-Égalité reverted to Bourg-la-Reine in 1812 by virtue of an imperial decree dispatched from Moscow.
75. On these changes, see N.-M. Maire, *Nomenclature des rues de Paris* (Paris, 1816).
76. This analysis, as well as those for 1830, 1848, and 1851, is based on the lists in L. and F. Lazare, *Dictionnaire administratif et historique des rues de Paris* (1844; repr. Paris, 1855), p. 14.
77. *Le Moniteur universel* for February 22, 1849, gives a list of thirty-five names. See also A. Mousset, "Paris raconté par ses rues," *La Revue de Paris,* vol. 4 (July-August 1937): 115–136. For a summary of these successive episodes of revenge, see Cousin, "De la nomenclature," pp. 9–11.
78. For Vichy and the Liberation, see Heid, *Les Noms des rues,* p. 224.
79. Charles Merruau, "Rapport sur la nomenclature des rues," in Conseil Municipal de Paris, *Rapports et documents* (1863), gives an idea of this unslakable thirst for names. Merruau does not discuss actual names but only categories and quantities: twenty-three victories and treaties, seventy-eight generals, forty politicians and jurists, forty-nine painters and architects, eighteen musicians, thirty-five men of letters, and a hundred scientists.
80. Figures based on the lists in Lazare and Lazare, *Dictionnaire administratif.*
81. *Tableau des rues, places . . . de la ville de Nantes* (Nantes, 1832). In Paris: Franklin, Washington, Newton, Byron; in Nantes: Copernicus, Franklin, Newton, Petrarch, Rubens; Bacon, Carracci, Columbus, Galileo, Gutenburg, Linnaeus, Milton, Pope, Raphael, Rembrandt, Tasso, Tintoretto, and Van Dyck were effaced by the Restoration.
82. *Guide du voyageur au Havre* (Le Havre, 1827).
83. Peraux, *Dictionnaire indicateur* for 1819; Duranville, "Quelques observations," for 1869.
84. A. Bertrand, *Les Rues de Lille: Leurs origines, transformations et dénominations* (Lille, 1880; repr. Marseilles, 1976).
85. Vallet, *Les Noms de rues,* pp. 132–150; see especially the summary table, p. 132.
86. Ibid.
87. Ordinance of July 10, 1816, quoted in Heid, *Les Noms des rues,* p. 209.
88. For a summary of the conflict between the national government and the city of Paris over the naming law, see the Mesureur Report, Conseil de Paris, *Rapports et documents* (1885), no. 11, pp. 3–7.
89. Duranville, "Quelques observations," p. 10.
90. L. Maynard, *Histoires, légendes et anecdotes à propos des rues de Lyon* (1922; repr. Lyons, 1980).
91. Bernadau, *Le Viographe bordelais,* p. 120.
92. In Saint-Étienne, only one foreign name (Garibaldi) was adopted between 1870 and

1918, whereas seven were adopted from 1918 to 1950. See Vallet, *Les Noms de rues,* pp. 142–143.

93. *Collection unique: Deux cent cinquante—devenus cent soixante—plans de villes françaises et étrangères* (Paris, 1880–1900). The precise dates are not known, since the maps are not dated and Éditions Fayard have destroyed their archives. Another handicap: the maps lack legends.
94. The survey was conducted without a computer.
95. Quentin, "Les Noms de rues," p. 188.
96. R. Posthaus, *Französische Autoren in Strassenverzeichnissen (Paris, Montreuil, Saint-Étienne und Perpignan)* (paper, Düsseldorf, 1975).
97. Not to forget Marie Curie, who died in 1934.
98. Hillairet, *Dictionnaire historique,* pp. 36–37.
99. Vallet, *Les Noms de rues,* p. 132.
100. "Les Héros de l'histoire de France," *L'Histoire,* no. 33 (April 1981); 102–112, and esp. "L'Amour et la haine," p. 110.
101. The great success of Murray Kendall's *Louis XI* will probably rehabilitate the king's reputation.
102. The idea is from Pierre-Yves Mauguen. The information is gleaned from the most recent maps of the cities mentioned.

12. THE PULPIT, THE ROSTRUM, AND THE BAR

1. This translation is based on a revised version of the original paper that appeared in the French edition of *Les Lieux de mémoire.* In particular, the first several pages and the conclusion do not correspond to the original.
2. La Bruyère, "Des ouvrages de l'esprit," section 55 in *Les Caractères.* The idea was formulated in almost the same terms by Abbé Fleury in 1686 in his *Traité du choix et de la méthode des études.*
3. D'Alembert, "Réflexions sur l'élocution oratoire et sur le style en général," in *Mélanges de littérature, d'histoire et de philosophie,* 5 vols. (Amsterdam, 1763), 2: 325. Only the spoken word can produce this effect: "Eloquence in books is almost like music on paper, silent, null, and lifeless. In any case it loses its greatest strength, and it needs action to unfold itself," p. 322. In speaking of action, d'Alembert is of course referring to the vocal and gestural effects of "oratorical action."
4. For example, Du Bellay, in *Défense et illustration de la langue française,* addressing the reader: "Do not be astonished if I speak of the orator as of the poet. For . . . the virtues of the one are mostly shared with the other" (book 1, ch. 12).
5. Marc Fumaroli, *L'Âge de l'éloquence: Rhétorique et* res literaria *de la Renaissance au seuil de l'âge classique* (Geneva: Droz, 1980).
6. Paul Bénichou, *Le Sacre de l'écrivain, 1750–1830: Essai sur l'avènement d'un pouvoir spirituel dans la France moderne* (Paris: José Corti, 1973).
7. For a good discussion see Charles Aubertin, *L'Éloquence politique et parlementaire en*

France avant 1789 d'après des documents manuscrits (Paris, 1882), part 1, ch. 1, pp. 9–40.

8. Du Bellay, "Conclusion de tout l'œuvre," in *Défense et illustration.*
9. Ibid., book 2, ch. 1.
10. Rabelais, *Gargantua,* ch. 15.
11. Ibid.
12. Ibid., ch. 24.
13. Ibid.
14. Ibid., ch. 29.
15. Ibid., ch. 31.
16. See Alain Michel, *Rhétorique et philosophie chez Cicéron* (Paris, 1960), pp. 6–9.
17. *Gargantua,* ch. 46.
18. Fumaroli, *L'Âge,* p. 494.
19. Montaigne, *Essais,* book I, ch. 51, "De la vanité des paroles," here quoted in Donald Frame's trans., *The Complete Essays of Montaigne* (Stanford: Stanford University Press, 1958), p. 222.
20. Tacitus, *Dialogus de oratoribus,* ed. Alain Michel (Paris, 1962), pp. 113–132. See Alain Michel, *Le* Dialogue des orateurs *de Tacite et la philosophie de Cicéron* (Paris, 1962).
21. Ibid.; Eng. trans. based on the French trans. by J.-L. Burnouf (Paris, 1858), p. 707.
22. Fumaroli, *L'Âge,* pp. 475 ff.
23. Guillaume Du Vair, *De l'éloquence française,* ed. R. Radouant (Paris, 1907), pp. 150 ff.
24. La Bruyère, "De la Cour," section 6 in *Les Caractères.*
25. Thomas Hobbes, *De Corpore Politico or the Elements of Law* (1650), vol. 4, 14 and 15, in *The English Works,* ed. Molesworth (1840; repr. Scientia Verlag Aalen, 1966), pp. 211–212.
26. Gianluigi Goggi, "Diderot et Médée dépeçant le vieil Eson," in *Denis Diderot: Colloque international,* ed. A.-M. Chouillet (Paris, 1985), pp. 173–183.
27. Joseph Reinach, *Le "Conciones" français: L'éloquence française depuis la Révolution jusqu'à nos jours* (Paris, 1894). A *Conciones français, ou Discours choisis tirés des historiens et orateurs français* by J.-A. Amar had already appeared at the beginning of the century. J.-A. Amar-Durivier is the author of *Cours complet de rhétorique,* which gained in length with each new edition.
28. Gustave Lanson, *Histoire de la littérature française,* 12th ed. (Paris, 1912), p. 313.
29. Mathieu Molé, *Mémoires,* 4 vols., ed. A. Champollion-Figeac (Paris, 1856–1857), 3: 225 ff.
30. *Œuvres d'Omer et de Denis Talon,* 2 vols., ed. D.-B. Rives (Paris, 1821), 1: 126 ff.
31. Mme de Motteville, *Mémoires,* 5 vols. (Amsterdam, 1723), 2: 15.
32. See Jean Starobinski, *Blessings in Disguise,* trans. Arthur Goldhammer (Cambridge, Mass: Harvard University Press, 1993).
33. Fumaroli, *L'Âge,* p. 5.
34. Albert Thibaudet, *Réflexions sur le roman* (Paris, 1938), pp. 224–225.
35. For example, G. L. Ferri, *De l'éloquence des orateurs anciens et modernes* (Paris, 1789).

36. In addition to readings from Cicero, Demosthenes, and Plutarch, there were also various school exercises putting history into the form of stories filled with speeches. For example, "good Rollin," whose *Histoire romaine*, according to Lanson, "is a course in republican morality." See Lanson, *Histoire*, p. 728.
37. Bossuet, *Maximes et réflexions sur la comédie* (1694) in *Œuvres complètes*, ed. E. N. Guillaume, 10 vols. (Bar-le-duc, 1877).
38. I am summarizing a debate notable for the fine *Dialogues sur l'éloquence* by Fénelon, among many other texts. One could also cite a minor author, the Rev. B. Gisbert, S.J., who wrote: "It grieves a preacher to make a generous sacrifice of all his most brilliant thoughts for the sake of his listeners' salvation. We are naturally enamoured of our thoughts, and more enamoured of our brilliant thoughts than of all the others. For our vanity, these are our most beautiful children" (*De l'éloquence chrétienne dans l'idée et dans la pratique* [Lyons, 1715]).
39. Bossuet, *Panégyrique de saint Paul*, in *Œuvres oratoires*, 7 vols., ed. Lebarq (Paris, 1891), 2: 296 ff. Cf. J. Truchet, *La Prédication de Bossuet*, 2 vols. (Paris, 1960).
40. Bossuet, *Oraisons funèbres*, ed. J. Truchet (Paris, 1961), p. 49.
41. La Bruyère, "De la chaire," section 1 of *Les Caractères*.
42. Ibid., 2.
43. Ibid., 23.
44. Charles Perrault, *Parallèle des Anciens et des Modernes*, ed. H.-R. Jauss and M. Imdahl (Munich, 1964). The argument was taken up in England by Z. Pearce in the *Spectator*, no. 633 (December 15, 1714).
45. Chateaubriand, *Mémoires d'outre-tombe*, part 1, book 2, ch. 2.
46. Jacques Bridaine (1701–1767), a missionary priest with scant literary training, enjoyed an immense success thanks to what Maury called "his rustic vigor" and "his popular and striking comparisons." See J.-S. Maury, *Essai sur l'éloquence de la chaire*, 2 vols. (Paris, 1810), 1: 135–151.
47. On these problems see Peter France, *Rhetoric and Truth in France: Descartes to Diderot* (Oxford, 1972).
48. U. Ricken, *Grammaire et philosophie au siècle des Lumières* (Lille, 1978), esp. pp. 78 ff.
49. Bernard Lamy, *Entretiens sur les sciences* (Lyons, 1694), pp. 121 ff. This was one of the books that Rousseau read at Les Charmettes.
50. René Rapin, "Réflexions sur l'usage de l'éloquence," in *Œuvres*, 2 vols. (The Hague, 1725), 2: 2–3.
51. Turgot, *Œuvres*, ed. G. Schelle (Paris: Alcan, 1913), 1: 129.
52. Jean-Jacques Rousseau, *Deuxième lettre à Malesherbes*, in *Œuvres* (Paris: Gallimard, 1959), 1: 1136.
53. Voltaire, article "Eloquence," *Encyclopédie*.
54. I am quoting from the *Mélanges de littérature, d'histoire et de philosophie*, 5 vols. (Amsterdam, 1763), 2: 325 ff.
55. See Robert Darnton, *The Literary Underground of the Old Regime* (Cambridge, Mass.: Harvard University Press, 1982).

56. Jean-Jacques Rousseau, *Du contrat social,* book 3, xv. The same accusation is found in ch. 20 of the *Essai sur l'origine des langues.*
57. Fumaroli, *L'Âge,* p. 475.
58. P.-L. Gin, *De l'éloquence du barreau* (Paris, 1768). The oldest text mentioned is the *Traité des droits de la Reine* (1663) and not an anthology of pleas.
59. Mona Ozouf, *La Fête révolutionnaire* (Paris: Gallimard, 1976).
60. [Sautreau de Marsy], *Tablettes d'un curieux,* 2 vols. (Paris-Brussels, 1789), 1: 252. The text on eloquence is attributed to "M. C."
61. François Furet, *Penser la Révolution française* (Paris: Gallimard, 1978), pp. 170–171. The various studies of Alphonse Aulard on the eloquence and orators of the Revolution are still useful: they offer mainly portraits and judgments.
62. Hans Ulrich Gumbrecht, *Funktionen der parlamentarischen Rhetorik in der französischen Revolution* (Munich, 1978). The "Réflexions sur la déclamation" by Hérault de Séchelles is indicative of the high degree of attention paid to the techniques of elocution and action. The lawyer was openly inspired by actors. See his *Œuvres littéraire,* ed. E. Dard (Paris, 1907), pp. 157–180.
63. Peter France, "Eloquence révolutionnaire et rhétorique traditionnelle: Étude d'une séance de la Convention," *Studi francesi,* vol. 24 (Rome, 1985): 143–176.
64. *Œuvres choisies de M.-J. Chénier* (Paris, 1822), 1: 71–77.
65. Mona Ozouf, "Le Panthéon," in Pierre Nora, ed., *Les Lieux de mémoire,* part 1, *La République* (Paris: Gallimard, 1984), pp. 139–166; Eng. trans. in *Realms of Memory,* vol. 3 (forthcoming).
66. Mme de Staël, *Considérations sur la Révolution française,* book 2, ch. 20.
67. Chateaubriand, *Mémoires d'outre-tombe,* part 1, book 5, ch. 12.
68. Michelet, *Histoire de la Révolution française,* book 1, ch. 2 and 3.
69. Victor Hugo, *Napoléon-le-Petit,* book 5, ch. 2–3.
70. A. Henry, *Histoire de l'éloquence,* 5 vols. (La Marche, 3d ed., 1855); Father Mestre, *Préceptes de rhétorique,* which went through twelve editions between 1883 and 1922.
71. Albert Thibaudet, *Histoire de la littérature française de 1789 à nos jours* (Paris, 1936), pp. 15–16.
72. To cite a typical work: P. S. Laurentie, *De l'éloquence politique et de son influence dans les gouvernements populaires et représentatifs* (Paris, 1819).
73. Condorcet, *Rapport et projet de décret sur l'organisation générale de l'instruction publique* (Paris, 1792), pp. 19–20. See Bronislaw Baczko, ed., *Une Éducation pour la démocratie: Textes et projets de l'époque révolutionnaire* (Paris: Garnier, 1982). The *Rapport* of Condorcet can be found on pp. 177–261. The book also contains Saint-Just's *Fragments d'institutions républicaines,* advocating a model of Spartan martial eloquence: "Lycées will award prizes for eloquence. Competition for eloquence prizes will not involve pompous speeches. The prize for eloquence will be awarded for laconism, to the person who delivers a sublime speech in a situation of danger, who through oratory saves the fatherland, recalls the people to moral standards, or rallies soldiers" (p. 386).

74. Benjamin Constant, *De l'esprit de conquête et de l'usurpation*, book 2, ch. 8, in Marcel Gauchet, ed., *De la liberté chez les modernes* (Paris: Hachette, 1980), pp. 191–195. See Jean Starobinski, "Benjamin Constant et l'éloquence," in E. Hofmann, ed., *Benjamin Constant, Madame de Staël et le groupe de Coppet* (Oxford-Lausanne, 1982), pp. 319–330.
75. Benjamin Constant, *Mémoires sur les Cent-Jours*, 2d ed. (Paris, 1829), part 2, p. 24.
76. Louis de Cormenin (1788–1868), jurist, opposition deputy under Charles X and Louis-Philippe, representative in the Constituent Assembly. See Alexis de Tocqueville, *Souvenirs*, ed. Luc Monnier (Paris, 1964), and Paul Bastid, *Un juriste pamphlétaire, Cormenin* (Paris, 1948).
77. Timon (Louis de Cormenin), *Le Livre des orateurs*, 11th ed. (Paris, 1842), p. 9. According to the catalogue of the Bibliothèque Nationale, the first edition was published in 1836, the 18th, in ten volumes, from 1869.
78. Ibid., p. 75.
79. See Bénichou, *Le Sacre de l'écrivain.*
80. Cormenin, *Le Livre des orateurs*, p. 494.
81. Honoré de Balzac, *Modeste Mignon*, in *La Comédie humaine*, 12 vols., ed. P.-G. Castex (Paris: Gallimard, 1977–1981), 1: 628.
82. Balzac, *Albert Savarus*, ibid., 1: 894. See the introduction and notes by A.-M. Meininger.
83. Balzac, *Z. Marcas*, ibid., 8: 841–842.
84. Balzac, *Albert Savarus*, p. 997.
85. Cormenin, *Le Livre des orateurs*, p. 117.
86. Balzac, *Z. Marcas*, p. 832. Balzac adds: "The lawyer had to make do with journalism, politics, and literature."
87. Cormenin, *Le Livre des orateurs*, pp. 119–120.
88. Ibid., p. 475.
89. Ibid., p. 128.
90. Antoine Berryer, *Œuvres*, 4 vols. (Paris, 1878), 4: 443 (letter to the editor, Lecoffre, about the anonymous work of Henry Moreau, *Le Ministère public et le barreau*).
91. Ibid., p. 451.
92. Edmond Rousse, preface to *Discours et plaidoyers*, by Gustave Chaix d'Est-Ange, 2 vols. (Paris: F. Didot frères, fils, 1862), p. i.
93. Ibid., p. xliii.
94. Charles Baudelaire, "La Solitude," ch. 23 of *Le Spleen de Paris.*
95. Rousse in Chaix d'Est-Ange, *Discours et plaidoyers*, p. xlvi.
96. Ibid.
97. Ibid.
98. Stéphane Mallarmé, *Œuvres complètes*, ed. Henri Mondor (Paris, 1945), p. 368. Rousse, on the contrary, toned down the contrast between orator and writer: "Between the literature and the eloquence of an era, even the eloquence of the law court, there are remarkable similarities, a great deal of mutual borrowing, many involuntary exchanges, common features, and a striking family resemblance." See Rousse in Chaix d'Est-Ange, *Discours et plaidoyers*, p. xlvii.

99. Alexis de Tocqueville, *Souvenirs,* ed. Luc Monnier (Paris: Gallimard, 1964), p. 98.
100. Ibid., pp. 102–103.
101. See François Furet, *Marx et la Révolution française: Textes de Marx présentés, réunis, traduits par Lucien Calvié* (Paris: Flammarion, 1986), pp. 244–251.
102. Tocqueville, *Souvenirs,* p. 112. Lamartine's speech on the tricolor flag—for decades an anthology piece—is a good example of Tocqueville's thesis.
103. Alexis de Tocqueville, *De la démocratie en Amérique,* 2 vols., ed. M. Laski (Paris, 1951), 2: 96 (2.1.21).
104. Tocqueville, *Souvenirs,* p. 182.

13. GASTRONOMY

1. Eugène Briffault, *Paris à table* (Paris: Hetzel, 1846).
2. Ibid., p. 149.
3. Auguste Escoffier, *Souvenirs inédits* (Marseilles: Jeanne Lafitte, 1985), p. 192.
4. Marcel Rouff, *La Vie et la passion de Dodin-Bouffant gourmet* (1924; new ed. Paris: Stock, 1984), pp. 18–19.
5. Jean Ferniot, "Rapport aux ministres sur la promotion des arts culinaires" (Ministères de la Culture et de l'Agriculture, Paris, 1985, mimeographed). Primarily a journalist but also a novelist, Jean Ferniot, the editor in chief of *Cuisine et vins de France,* is the author of such works as *C'est ça la France* (1977) and *Vous en avez vraiment assez d'être Français?* (1979).
6. Such as the rhetoric of World's Fairs, where, when it comes to gauging France's international rank, gastronomy is always featured. See Pascal Ory, "Plus dure sera la chute: Les pavillons français à l'Exposition internationale de 1939," *Relations internationales* (March 1986): pp. 26–31.
7. According to *Ulrich's (International Periodical Directory),* 29th ed. (New York: R. Bowker, 1990).
8. Jean-Jacques Hemardinguer, *Pour une histoire de l'alimentation,* Cahiers des Annales, no. 28 (Paris: Armand Colin, 1970).
9. Claude Lévi-Strauss, *L'Origine des manières de table,* vol. 3 of *Mythologiques* (Paris: Plon, 1968).
10. Fernand Braudel, *Les Structures du quotidien,* vol. 1 of *Civilisation matérielle, économie et capitalisme* (Paris: Armand Colin, 1979), pp. 81–228; Eng. trans. by Sian Reynolds, *The Structures of Everyday Life,* vol. 1 of *Civilization and Capitalism, Fifteenth to Eighteenth Century* (Berkeley: University of California Press, 1992).
11. This project was led by Jean-Louis Flandrin, a historian of collective mentalities whose work deals mainly with the early modern family.
12. Jean-Paul Aron, *Le Mangeur du XIXe siècle* (Paris: Robert Laffont, 1974).
13. Jean-Claude Bonnet, ed., *Écrits gastronomiques de Grimod de La Reynière* (Paris: GE, 1978), and "Carême, ou les derniers feux de la cuisine décorative," *Romantisme,* nos. 17–18 (1977): 23–43. See also Jean-François Revel, *Un Festin en paroles: Histoire littéraire de la sensibilité gastronomique, de l'antiquité à nos jours* (Paris: Jean-Jacques Pauvert, 1979).

14. Brillat-Savarin, *Physiologie du goût* (Paris: Flammarion, 1982), p. 19.
15. Escoffier, *Souvenirs,* p. 191.
16. See, for example, Brillat-Savarin, *Physiologie,* p. 19.
17. Challenged by Stephen Mennel in *All Manners of Food: Eating and Taste in England and France from the Middle Ages to the Present* (Oxford and New York: Blackwell, 1985; repr. Champaign: University of Illinois Press, 1995); French trans., *Français et Anglais à table du Moyen Âge à nos jours* (Paris: Flammarion, 1987), pp. 153–159.
18. See Philippe Gillet, *Par mets et par vins: Voyages et gastronomie en Europe, XVIe-XVIIe siècles* (Paris: Payot, 1986).
19. See François-Pierre de La Varenne, *Le Cuisinier françois* (1651) and Nicolas de Bonnefons, *Les Délices de la campagne* (1684).
20. Well represented by the introduction to François Marin, *Dons de Comus* (1739).
21. Joseph de Berchoux, *La Gastronomie, ou l'homme des champs à table, poème didactique en quatre chants, pour servir de suite à* L'homme des champs (Paris, 1801). The subtitle alludes to the best-known work of Abbé Delille. The work, which first appeared anonymously, went through three editions in the next four years. In 1803 the author acknowledged his book.
22. The word *gastronomie,* a translation of the title of Archestratus's heroicomic poem, first appeared in 1623, but it was not used in its "contemporary" sense until Berchoux.
23. Brillat-Savarin suggested the creation of an Academy of Gastronomes, which "the government . . . would regulate, protect, and institute." See *Physiologie,* p. 66.
24. Published in 1808. It consisted of three parts: a "Treatise on the Carving of Meat at the Dinner Table," a "Nomenclature" of typical menus, and a treatise on "gourmet manners."
25. The *Journal* soon became *L'Épicurien français,* and Grimod ceased to have a hand in it.
26. The introduction to the *Dons de Comus* is supposed to be the work of two Jesuits, Father Brunoy and Father Bouvant.
27. See notes 20 and 26 above.
28. See Robert Courtine and Jean Desmur, *Anthologie de la poésie gourmande* (Paris: Éditions de Trévise, 1970).
29. *Bonnet, Écrits gastronomiques,* p. 229.
30. Briffault, *Paris à table,* pp. 148–149.
31. Ibid., p. 8.
32. Brillat-Savarin, *Physiologie,* p. 65.
33. Ibid., p. 278.
34. Ibid., p. 283.
35. Briffault, *Paris à table,* pp. 148–149.
36. Switzerland and the United States, where he claimed to have introduced scrambled eggs with cheese. In 1792 he was close to the Girondins and served as mayor of Belley, his native city.
37. Antonin Carême, *Le Pâtissier royal parisien* (Paris: Dentu, 1815). On Carême, see Bonnet, "Carême."
38. Quoted in Bonnet, "Carême."

39. Note the "quiet revolution" that has taken place since the war: the economic interests of agriculture are now represented not by landowners but by farmers themselves through the F.N.S.E.A. In the theater, meanwhile, the power has shifted from playwrights to directors.
40. *Gault et Millau se mettent à table* (Paris: Stock, 1976), p. 20.
41. Paul Bocuse, *La Cuisine du marché* (Paris: Flammarion, 1976).
42. Michel Guérard, *La Grande Cuisine minceur* (Paris: Robert Laffont, 1976).
43. Gault and Millau met at *Paris-Presse*, where Gault had experimented with the prototype of the epicurean survey that later became the pair's hallmark and gained them their success. After World War II and until recently, many French food writers were politically on the right, if not the extreme right.
44. *Gault et Millau se mettent à table.*
45. Ibid., p. 13.
46. Ildefonse-Léon Brisse's "Propos de table."
47. Charles Monselet's *Gourmet*, launched in 1858.
48. Maurice-Edmond Saillant, known as Curnonsky, 1872–1956; Paul Fort, 1872–1960. The election of the "prince of gastronomes" was organized in 1927 by a gastronomic magazine of the interwar period, *Le Bon Gîte et la Bonne Table.* Of 3,388 votes, Curnonsky received 1,823, and the Belgian gastronome Maurice des Ombiaux 1,037. Three years later, the prince created the Académie des Gastronomes.
49. Monselet (1825–1888) is still the best-known gastronome of the third generation. Much of his fame during his lifetime rested on his *Cuisinière poétique* and *Lettres gourmandes.*
50. See the *Rapport général* of the exposition, vol. 7, pp. 199–211.
51. None other than the Jockey Club's *officier de bouche* (culinary secretary).
52. Besides Briffault, one thinks of Jacques Arago's *Comme on dîne à Paris* (1842), Victor Bouton's *La Table à Paris* (1845), and Alfred Delvau's *Cafés et cabarets de Paris* (1867).
53. Although certain Alsatian confraternities have a longer history, the prototype was established in the 1930s by the Confrérie des Chevaliers du Tastevin.
54. Published every year from 1900 on, the *Guide Michelin pour les chauffeurs et les vélocipédistes* was at first filled with ad hoc information. But a note in the first edition anticipated the guide's later development by asking readers to send reports on hotels and restaurants: "We promise to remove from our lists any hotel reported to be wanting in its dining room, bedrooms, toilet facilities, or service."
55. In the twentieth century any number of associations, periodicals, and guides have been reserved for "gourmet doctors."
56. Pomiane became famous for his prewar radio programs. Among the works of his in which hygiene is an important concern was *Bien manger pour bien vivre* (1948). He should be compared with his contemporary Dr. Alfred Gottschalk.
57. Alexandre Dumas, *Grand Dictionnaire de cuisine* (Paris: Lemerre, 1873). Written in collaboration with D. J. Vuillemot.
58. Curnonsky, *Cuisine et vins de France* (Paris: Larousse, 1953).

59. Urbain Dubois and Émile Bernard, *La Cuisine classique* (Paris: Les Auteurs, 1853). The work, subtitled *Études pratiques, raisonnées et descriptives de l'école française appliquées au service à la russe,* gives details about the timing of the transition from French to Russian service.
60. Prosper Montagné, *Larousse gastronomique* (Paris: Larousse, 1937–1938).
61. On this periodization see Pascal Ory, *L'Aventure culturelle française, 1948–1989* (Paris: Flammarion, 1989).
62. On this point see Pascal Ory, *L'Entre-Deux-Mai, histoire culturelle de la France, mai 1968–mai 1981* (Paris: Éditions du Seuil, 1983).
63. In particular the articles "Le Bifteck et les frites" and "Cuisine ornamentale."
64. Marcel Detienne and Jean-Pierre Vernant, *La Cuisine du sacrifice en pays grec* (Paris: Gallimard, 1979).
65. Frédéric Lange, *Manger, ou les jeux et les creux du plat* (Paris: Éditions du Seuil, 1975).
66. Noëlle Châtelet, *Le Corps-à-corps culinaire* (Paris: Éditions du Seuil, 1977).
67. These columns appeared regularly for several years, beginning with the first issue of the journal *L'Histoire,* published in 1978.
68. Roland Barthes, preface to "first revised and annotated edition" (Paris: Hermann, 1975).
69. Michel Serres, *Les Cinq Sens* (Paris: Grasset, 1985).
70. Michel Onfray, *Le Ventre des philosophes* (Paris: Grasset, 1989).
71. Michel Field, *L'Homme aux pâtes* (Paris: Barrault, 1989).
72. This booklet ("which can be read like a book, a book of gourmet art, to be savored"), edited jointly by a scholar from the École des Hautes Études, a graphic artist, and the editor of the *Lettre internationale,* included, along with Alain Senderens and Michel Guérard, such contributors as Marc Augé, Theodore Zeldin, Maxime Rodinson, and Bernard Frank, and texts from Francis Ponge and James Joyce.
73. Primarily in two essays on gourmet touring, *Le Devoir de français* (Paris: Flammarion, 1984), a *hussard* title unwittingly borrowed from Denis Lalanne, and *L'Amour du pays* (Paris: Flammarion, 1986).
74. Pudlowski, *Le Devoir de français.*
75. Ibid., p. 110.
76. Ibid., p. 119.
77. Pudlowski, *L'Amour du pays,* pp. 146–147.
78. Emma Rothschild, "Haute Culture, haute cuisine ou Hang-Tchéou sur Seine," *Le Débat,* no. 11 (April 1981): 125–132.

14. THE TOUR DE FRANCE

1. Georges Rozet, *Défense et illustration de la race française* (Paris, 1911), p. 28.
2. Xavier Louy, *Un Nouveau Cyclisme, avec Greg, Lucho, et Wang* (Monte-Carlo: R.M.C., 1986), p. 19.
3. "Le Tour de France," *Le Monde, Dossiers et documents* (July 1988): 1.
4. Henri Desgrange, *L'Auto* (January 20, 1903): 1. Not all articles in *L'Auto* bore titles or author's bylines. To simplify the notes, only the date and page will be indicated.

5. Ferdinand Buisson, *Dictionnaire de pédagogie et d'instruction primaire* (Paris, 1887).
6. Paul Vidal de La Blache, *Tableau de la géographie de la France* (Paris, 1903).
7. *L'Auto* (July 27, 1938): 1.
8. Marcel Bidot, *L'Épopée du Tour de France* (Paris: Orban, 1975), p. 26. On the tour de France of the *compagnons*, see Michelle Perrot, "Les Vies ouvrières," in Pierre Nora, ed., *Les Lieux de mémoire*, part 3, *Les France*, vol. 3, *De l'archive à l'emblème* (Paris: Gallimard, 1992), pp. 86–129.
9. Pierre Chany, *La Fabuleuse Histoire du Tour de France* (Paris: O.D.I.L., 1983), p. 145.
10. George Sand, *Le Compagnon du tour de France* (Paris, 1841), p. 3.
11. Rozet, *Défense*, p. 28.
12. *L'Auto* (July 7, 1932): 2.
13. Tristan Bernard, *Compagnon du Tour* (Paris, 1934).
14. *L'Auto* (July 9, 1903): 1.
15. G. Bruno (pseudonym of A. Fouillée), *Le Tour de la France par deux enfants* (Paris, 1877). See Mona Ozouf's essay on this book in this volume.
16. Bruno, *Le Tour*, preface.
17. *L'Auto* (July 12, 1909): 5.
18. Ibid., p. 3.
19. Ibid. (July 9, 1903): 1.
20. Ibid. (July 1, 1903): 1.
21. Ibid. (August 3, 1905): 1.
22. Ibid. (August 22, 1904): 1.
23. Rozet, *Défense*, p. 34.
24. Henri Bergson, interview in *Le Gaulois littéraire* (June 15, 1912).
25. *L'Auto* (July 10, 1911): 1. See also Philippe Gaboriau, *Le Vélo dans la mémoire ouvrière* (Nantes: Cahiers du L.E.R.S.C.O., 1982); Paul Gerbod, "La Petite Reine en France du second empire aux années 30," *L'Information historique*, no. 2 (1986).
26. Rozet, *Défense*, p. 95.
27. Paul Giffard, managing editor of *Vélo*, in 1902, quoted in Jacques Marchand, *Pour le Tour de France* (Paris: Gonthier, 1967), p. 31.
28. Colette, *Dans la foule* (1918), in *Œuvres complètes* (Paris: Flammarion, 1949), 4: 443.
29. Léon Baudry de Saunier, *L'Art de bien monter à bicyclette* (Paris, 1894), p. 79.
30. Stéphane Mallarmé, response to a survey by *Le Gaulois*, quoted in Claude Pasteur, *Les Femmes à bicyclette* (Paris: France-Empire, 1986), p. 57.
31. Rozet, *Défense*, p. 95.
32. *L'Auto* (July 3, 1910): 1.
33. This reappropriation of space is described, quite accurately, as a "metamorphosis of the workingman's capacities and space" in Gaboriau, *Le Vélo*, p. 4.
34. *L'Auto* (July 5, 1903): 2.
35. Ibid., p. 1.
36. Ibid. (July 10, 1933): 2.
37. Ibid. (July 24, 1939): 2.
38. Henri Troyat, *L'Auto* (July 16, 1939): 4.

39. *L'Équipe* (July 22, 1946): 2. The 1946 race was a shortened format and did not make a full circuit.
40. Marchand, *Pour le Tour de France*, p. 53.
41. *L'Auto* (July 12, 1909): 5.
42. *Le Miroir des sports*, no. 1020 (1938).
43. *L'Auto* (July 13, 1909): 4.
44. Ibid., p. 2.
45. *L'Équipe*, (July 14, 1947): 47.
46. *L'Auto* (July 19, 1923): 1.
47. Danton, speech to the Convention, January 31, 1793.
48. *Libération* (July 11, 1988): 23.
49. *L'Auto* (July 5, 1925): 4.
50. "Une Nouvelle Direction pour une Grande Boucle plus serrée," *Le Monde* (October 22, 1988): 23.
51. Antoine Blondin, *Sur le Tour de France* (Paris: Mazarine, 1979), p. 71.
52. *Libération* (July 12, 1988): 27.
53. *L'Équipe*, (July 23, 1948): 1.
54. *L'Auto* (July 23, 1919): 2.
55. Ibid. (July 15, 1903): 1.
56. Blondin, *Sur le Tour de France*, p. 74.
57. *L'Auto* (July 12, 1934): 1.
58. Ibid. (July 14, 1925): 1.
59. *L'Auto* regularly published sales figures, but they are not always reliable. See Chany, *La Fabuleuse Histoire*, p. 141.
60. Henri Desgrange, *L'Auto* (July 8, 1907): 1.
61. *Officiel de l'automobile, du cycle et de la motocyclette* (September 1937): 103.
62. *L'Auto* no. 1, quoted in Marchand, *Pour le Tour de France*, p. 27.
63. *L'Auto* (July 6, 1903): 1.
64. Ibid.
65. E. Dally, *Sur la nécessité de l'éducation physique et sur l'organisation des gymnases municipaux hydrothérapeutiques* (Paris, 1871), p. 5.
66. *L'Auto* (May 6, 1903): 1.
67. Ibid. (June 28, 1919): 1.
68. Ibid. (July 6, 1906): 1.
69. Ibid. (July 3, 1910): 1.
70. Ibid. (July 20, 1909): 1.
71. Ibid. (July 4, 1904): 1.
72. Ibid.
73. Ibid.
74. Ibid., p. 2.
75. Jean Calvet, *Le Mythe des géants de la route* (Grenoble: Presses Universitaires de Grenoble, 1981), p. 164.
76. P. Cartoux and H. Decoin, *Le Roi de la pédale* (Paris: Gallimard, 1924).

77. *L'Auto* (July 1, 1904): 1.
78. Jean Bobet, "La Légende du Tour de France," *Sport et vie,* no. 50 (1960): 53.
79. Desgrange, *L'Auto* (July 15, 1903): 1.
80. Alain Ehrenberg, "Des Stades sans dieux," *Le Débat,* no. 40 (May-September 1986): 48.
81. *L'Auto* (July 3, 1933): 2.
82. Ibid. (July 3, 1936): 1.
83. Ibid. (July 1, 1930): 1.
84. Ibid. (July 3, 1930): 1.
85. Ibid. (July 26, 1932): 1.
86. Chany, *La Fabuleuse Histoire,* p. 245.
87. Philippe Gaboriau, "L'Épopée sociale de la bicyclette" (thesis, University of Nantes, 1984), gives a good description of the caravan and analyzes the popular allusions in the Tour.
88. *Officiel de l'automobile,* p. 103.
89. Gaboriau, "L'Épopée sociale," p. 142.
90. *L'Auto* (July 20, 1938): 3.
91. *Miroir des sports,* no. 437 (July 1928) and no. 1020 (July 1938).
92. Pierre Miquel, *Histoire de la radio et de la télévision* (Paris: Éditions Richelieu, 1972), and Georges Briquet, *Soixante Ans de Tour de France* (Paris: La Table Ronde, 1962).
93. Blondin, *Sur le Tour de France,* p. 25.
94. *Libération* (July 27, 1985).
95. Jacques Goddet, quoted in Marchand, *Pour le Tour de France,* p. 51.
96. Wladimir Andreff and Jean-François Nys, *Le Sport et la télévision* (Paris: Dalloz, 1988), p. 145.
97. Calvet, *Le Mythe des géants de la route,* p. 65.
98. "Quand la petite reine veut se couronner d'or," *L'Événement du jeudi* (June 25, 1987): 55.
99. *L'Équipe* (July 14, 1948): 2.
100. Jean Durry, *La Véridique Histoire des géants de la route* (Paris: Denoël, 1974), p. 104.
101. "Le Tour de France, une épreuve capitale," *Les Dossiers du Canard* (June 1982): 40.
102. Ibid., p. 39.
103. Chany, *La Fabuleuse Histoire.*
104. Henri Desgrange, *L'Auto* (July 6, 1932): 1.
105. Philippe Gaboriau, "Les Épopées modernes, le Tour de France et le Paris-Dakar," *Esprit,* special issue, April 1987, *Le Nouvel Âge du sport.*
106. Paul Irlinger, Catherine Louveau, Michèle-Métoudi, *Les Pratiques sportives des Français* (Paris: I.N.S.E.P., 1988), 2: 529.
107. Louy, *Un Nouveau Cyclisme,* pp. 16–17.
108. Blondin, *Sur le Tour de France,* p. 24.
109. *L'Auto* mentioned these facts in 1904 in connection with an investigation it had conducted. Subsequently, however, the paper alluded to the incident only in vague terms if at all.
110. Jean-Pierre de Mondenard, *Drogues et dopages* (Paris: Quel Corps, 1987), p. 102.
111. Rozet, *Défense,* p. 31.

112. *L'Équipe* (July 5, 1988).
113. *L'Auto* (July 20, 1930).
114. Ibid. (July 22, 1930).
115. Durry, *La Véridique Histoire des géants de la route,* p. 82. See also Jean Durry, "Un Champion populaire: André Leducq, vainqueur du Tour de France cycliste," *Sport Histoire,* no. 1 (1988).
116. Blondin, *Sur le Tour de France,* p. 34.
117. *L'Équipe* (July 1, 1964).
118. Ibid. (July 2, 1964).
119. Ibid. (July 14, 1964).
120. *L'Auto* (July 13, 1923).
121. Ibid. (July 26, 1919).
122. Ibid.
123. *L'Équipe* (July 1, 1964).
124. *Le Miroir du cyclisme;* see, among others, the September 1988 issue, "Contes et légendes du Tour de France, la terrible prédiction d'Anglande" (concerning Rivière's 1960 accident).
125. *Vélo Magazine* (July 1988): 18–19.
126. Serge Lang, *Le Grand Livre du Tour de France* (Paris: Calmann-Lévy, 1980), p. 119.
127. Durry, *La Véridique Histoire,* p. 75.
128. Quoted in Noël Couédel, *Le Tour de France, la grande fête de juillet* (Paris: Calmann-Lévy, 1983), p. 22.
129. François-René de Chateaubriand, *La Vie de Rancé* (Paris, 1844), book 2.
130. Roland Barthes, "Le Tour de France comme épopée," in *Mythologies* (Paris: Éditions du Seuil, 1957), p. 128.
131. Ibid., p. 126.
132. *Le Miroir des sports,* no. 1021 (1938).
133. Blondin, *Sur le Tour de France,* p. 104.
134. Henri Desgrange, *L'Auto: Édition spéciale du Tour de France* (June 27, 1921): 1.
135. *L'Auto* (July 13, 1934): 2. See Dino Buzzati, *Sur le Giro 1949, le duel Coppi-Bartali* (Paris: Robert Laffont, 1984). See also Stefano Pivato, *Sia lodato Bartali* (Rome: Edizioni Lavoro, 1985).
136. *L'Auto* (July 4, 1904): 2.
137. Ibid. (July 8, 1909): 3.
138. Ibid. (July 15, 1923): 2.
139. Ibid. (July 18, 1923): 2.
140. *L'Équipe* (July 25, 1955): 2.
141. Ibid. (July 2, 1964): 1.
142. See the special issue of *Esprit* cited in n. 105.
143. Quoted by Albert Londres, who popularized the phrase "highway slaves" after an interview in *Le Petit Parisien* (July 2, 1924).
144. Ibid.
145. Double page of advertising in *Libération* (July 22, 1985), pp. 20–21.

NAME INDEX

NOTE: Illustrations are designated by an "i" following the page number.

Adlon, Percy, 234
Agache, Roger, 19
Agostinho (cyclist), 499
Alavoine (cyclist), 495
Albaret, Céleste, 231
Alembert, Jean le Rond d,' 282, 283–285, 393, 415
Allegrain, Christophe-Gabriel, 81i
Amat, Roman d,' 352
Amiot, Jules, 226, 243
André and Julian (fict.), 125; in 1906, 137; characterized, 126–127; journey described, 128–129; military careers, 136. See also *Tour de la France, Le* in subject index
Anquetil (cyclist), 492–493, 495, 496, 499
Apicius, 450
Arago, Jacques, 334, 336–337, 345, 432
Aragon, Louis, 223–224
Archestratus, 450
Argenson, Marquis d,' 279–280
Arnauld, Antoine, 291, 412
Aron, Jean-Paul, 447, 465
Astier-Réhu, Laurent (fict. historian), 298
Aubisque (cyclist), 481
Aubonnet, Jean, 61
Aucouturier (bicyclist), 473i, 481
Auerbach, Erich, 115
Augier, Émile, 295, 299
Aulard and Debidour, 169–171, 179, 180, 182
Autran, Joseph, 352
Avenel, Paul, 342

Balzac, Guez de, 281
Balzac, Honoré de: borrowings from Lamartine, 429; on legal eloquence, 429, 431; struggle for recognition, 280i, 296
Barbey d'Aurevilly, Jules-Amédée, 288, 292, 293
Bardèches, Maurice, 233
Baroche (govt. minister), 296
Barrès, Maurice, 160, 184, 299, 353
Bartali (cyclist), 497
Barthes, Roland, 218, 465, 495; knowledge

Index compiled by Fred Leise.

of Proust, 237–238; on Proust's life and work, 230
Bataille, Frédéric, 319
Bataille, Georges, 228–229
Baudelaire, Charles Pierre, 236, 293, 295
Baudry de Saunier, Léon, 473
Bazin, René, 299, 354
Beaune, Colette, 53
Beauvilliers, Antoine, 456
Beauvoir, Simone de, 255–256
Beckett, Samuel, 224
Bellegarde, Abbé de, 73–74, 112
Benet, Eugène, 313
Bénichou, Paul, 252, 395
Benoît, Pierre, 157–158
Benserade, Isaac de, 107
Berchoux, Joseph de, 452
Berdoulay, Vincent, 208, 209
Bergotte (fict.), 215
Bergson, Henri, 472
Bernadau, M., 376
Bernard, Tristan, 471
Berry, Duchesse de, 71, 194
Berryer, Antoine-Pierre, 429, 430i, 431, 432, 433
Bertrand, Georges, 16
Bidot, Marcel, 492
Blacas, Duke de, 71, 72
Blanc, Jean-François, 14
Blanche, Jacques-Émile (fict.), 219
Blanchot, Maurice, 229, 301
Bloch, Marc, 14, 23
Bocuse, Paul, 460
Bodin, Jean, 285
Boileau-Despréaux, Nicolas, 115, 264
Boisrobert, 258
Boissier, Gaston, 292
Bonaparte, Charles Louis Napoleon (Napoleon III), 155–156
Bonaparte, Napoleon. *See* Napoleon I
Boniface VIII (pope), 51
Bonnefoy, Yves, 440
Bonnet, Henri, 233
Bonnet, Jean-Claude, 368, 448, 466
Bossuet, Jacques Bénigne, 98, 408, 409–410
Botta, Mario, 67i
Bouchor, Maurice, 321
Bouhours, Dominique, 276
Boulanger (restaurateur), 455
Bourdaloue, Louis, 411
Bourget, Paul, 297, 299
Bourzeis, Abbé de, 267–268
Bousset, 390i
Boutemy, Eugène, 166–167
Boutroux, Émile, 176–177
Bozon, Pierre, 14
Braudel, Fernand, 206, 447
Brazier, Nicolas, 337
Bréauté, Marquis de (fict.), 231
Breé, Germaine, 230
Breker, Arno, 492
Breton, André, 224, 256, 435
Briffault, Eugène, 454, 455, 463
Brillat-Savarin, Anthelme, 447, 455, 457
Briquet, Georges, 486
Brunet, Pierre, 18, 21
Brunetière, Fernand, 292
Bruno, G. *See* Fouillée, Augustine
Bugeaud, de La Piconnerie, Thomas-Robert, 349, 350, 356–357
Buisson, Ferdinand, 166, 470
Buysse (climber), 495

Cabanis, Pierre-Jean-Georges, 291, 457
Caillavet, Gaston de, 228
Caillavet, Georges de, 299
Caillavet, Simone Arman de, 228
Calderón, García, 140
Calvet, Jean, 481
Cambacérès, Jean Jacques Régis de, 455
Campagnon, Antoine, 211
Campan, Madame, 72, 93
Canalis (fict.), 429
Capet, Hugh, 51
Capets, 53, 54, 66
Carassus, Émilien, 232

Carême, Antonin, 456i, 459
Cartier-Bresson, Henri, 302i
Castiglione, Baldassar, *Cortegiano, Il*, 102–104, 106, 111
Céline, Louis Ferdinand, 216, 219–222, 223
César (cyclist), 491
Chaix d'Est-Ange, Gustave-Louis, 432, 433
Chamfort, Sébastien-Roch-Nicolas, 288
Champ d'Oiseau (restaurateur), 455
Champfleury, Jules Husson, 293
Charles V, 54
Charles VIII, 54
Charles X, 55, 71, 453–454
Charlet (artist), 339, 360
Charléty, 151
Charlus (fict.), 244–245
Charpentier, François, 267, 268
Charrue, Mathieu (fict.), 352
Chateaubriand, François August René, Vicomte de, 244; adolescent sensuality, 411; career, 249–250; election to Académie Française, 252, 291; *Génie du christianisme*, 56; *Mémoires d'outre-tombe*, 72; opinions of legends, 495; recognition of Marie-Antoinette, 245; reinterpretation of tradition of Académie Française, 250; visit to Charles X in exile, 71–72
Chatrian, Alexandre, 144
Chauvin, Charles François Régis, 336–337
Chauvin, Henri-Guillaume, 336
Chauvin, Jean, 337–339
Chauvin, Nicolas, 332i; ambiguity of his age, 340–343, 344, 345–356; clues to his life, 333–336; comparison with Régis Chauvin, 336–337; as cultural model, 359; as founding myth, 357–360; neglect of, in history, 333–334; portrayals of, 338–343, 344–345; portrayed in songs, 339–343; portrayed in vaudevilles, 337–339; question of his existence, 346; as Saint Chauvin, 343–344; soldier-peasant, 346–358; source for term "chauvinism," 333
Chaval (writer), 233
Chénier, Marie-Joseph, 290, 420
Christian Brothers, textbooks, 170, 171
Christophe (cyclist), 470–471, 481, 494
Clarac, Pierre, 228
Claretie, Jules, 335
Claudel, Paul, 56, 61, 223, 228
Claval, Paul, 190, 196
Clovis, 52
Cochin, Augustin, 283
Coigniard brothers, 337
Colbert, Jean Baptiste, 266, 267, 268; conception of Collège des Quatre-Nations, 290; described by Lavisse, 178; street named for, 368
Colette, views on bicycles, 472
Colin, Armand, 166–167, 208
Conard, Pierre, 169, 171
Condé, Prince de, 85, 390i, 507n27
Condillac, Étienne Bonnot de, 291, 457
Condorcet, Marie Jean Antoine Nicholas de Caritat, Marquis de, 288, 426–427
Constant, Benjamin, 427
Conty, Pierre, 11
Coppi (cyclist), 497
Cormenin, Louis de, 428–429, 431
Coulanges, Madame de, 94
Courtine, Robert, 466
Cousin, Jules, 364, 365, 368, 372
Cousin, Victor, 292
Couzon (fict.), 228–229
Cur, 464
Curcy, M., 370
Curnonksy (Maurice-Edmond Saillant), 463
Curtius, Ernst Robert, 224, 235

Dagan, Luo, 214
Damas, Baron de, 72
Dangeau, Marquis de, 78–79, 88; described by Marquise de Sévigné, 105; record of courtly life, 80–81; reports of apartment assignments, 94

Danton, Georges Jacques, 178, 424
Darcaux (writer), 481
Darwin, Charles, 187
Daudet, Alphonse, 298, 343–345
Daudet, Lucien, 241
Daumier, Honoré, 286i, 430i
Debidour (lexicographer), 334
Debussy, (Achille) Claude, *Cathédrale engloutie, La*, 61
Decoin (writer), 481
De Gaulle, Charles, 64, 75, 76, 120i
Delacroix, (Ferdinand Victor) Eugène, 313
Deleuze, Gilles, 231–232
Déroulède, Paul, 351, 353
Desgrange, Henri, 469, 470; evocation of Napoleon's army, 477; expansion of participation in Tour de France, 483; opinions of Garin, 480–481; on Tour de France, 477–479, 481, 498
Desmarets de Saint-sorlin, Jean, 265
Destutt de Tracy, Antoine-Louis-Claude, Comte de, 291
Devoille, Abbé, 351–352
Diderot, Denis, 73, 413
Dion, Roger, 21
Dionnet, Marie-Claude, 21
Dodin-Bouffant (fict.), 444
Doubrovsky, Serge, 232–233
Doumic, René, 152, 157
Du Barry, Marie Jeanne Bécu, Comtesse, 475
Du Bellay, 395–396
Duby, Georges, 207
Duchesne, Cardinal, 43
Duclos, Charles Pinau, 282
Dumas, Alexandre, 280i
Dumas, Alexandre, *fils*, 299
Dumersan, Théophile Marion, 337
Dupanloup, Félix, 144
Du Périer, Charles, 267
Du Perron, Jacques Davy, 251
Dupin, 349
Dupont, Pierre, 351, 352
Dupuy, Aimé, 125, 132
Durand, Joanny, 316
Duranville, Léon de, 366, 383
Duras, Marguerite, 295–296
Durkheim, Émile, 188
Duruy, Victor, 154
Du Vair, Guillaume, 263, 402–403, 404

Elias, Norbert, 367; analysis of court life, 83–85, 93, 95, 102, 121
Eliot, T. S., 230
Enghien, Duc d,' 85
Erasmus, Desiderius, 398
Erckmann, Émile, 144
Erckmann-Chatrian (pseud.), 353
Escoffier, Auguste, 444, 449, 458, 462
Esmonin, 169
Eudemon (fict.), 396–397

Faber (cyclist), 481, 498
Faguet, Émile, 292
Fallois, Bernard de, 228
Faucheux, Pierre, 232
Faure, Benoît, 492
Faur Pibrac, Guy du, 251, 401
Fayard (publishers), 383
Febvre, Lucien, 197, 206
Félibien (historian), 107–108
Fernandez, Ramon, 229
Ferniot, Jean, 445
Ferrat, Jean, 14
Ferré, André, 228
Feuillerat, Albert, 224
Feuillet, Octave, 296
Field, Michel, 466
Figuères, R. de, 374
First Consul. *See* Napoleon I
Flaubert, Gustave, 71, 297, 349, 429
Flers, Robert de, 299
Focillon, Henri, 63–64
Fort, Paul, 462
Foucquet, Surintendant, 266
Fouillée, Alfred, 124i, 138–139; beliefs, 143,

144; monument to, 147i; private life, 140–142; views of wife, 138–140
Fouillée, Augustine (G. Bruno), 124i; allegations against, 136, 137; authorial ambitions, 127; described, 138–140; *Enfants de Marcel, Les*, 138; *Francinet*, 138; private life, 138–141; qualities, 126, 145–146; religious beliefs, 143; representation of France, 132–133. See also *Tour de la France, Le* in subject index
France, Anatole, 265, 299
France, Peter, 419
Francis, Philippe, 337
Françoise (fict.), 231
Franklin, A., 372, 375
Franklin, Benjamin, 359
Frémont, Armand, 3
Freud, Sigmund, 235
Fulin, Han, 214
Fumaroli, Marc, 249–305, 395, 400–401, 406
Furet, François, 418–419
Furetière, Antoine, 270–273
Fustel de Coulanges (historian), 245

Gallet, Ulrich (fict.), 398
Gallimard, Gaston, 222, 300, 301
Gambetta, 354
Gambetta, Léon, 317–318
Gard, Maurice Martin du, 253
Gargantua (fict.), 396–398, 400
Garin, Maurice, 480–481, 482i, 498
Gassicourt, Charles Louis Cadet de, 452
Gault, Henri, 460, 461, 462, 465
Gauthier (cyclist), 496
Genette, Gérard, 230, 232
Gérard de Puymège, 333
Gerbi (cyclist), 491
Gide, André, 301
Gilberte (fict.), 228
Gimpel, Jean, 49
Gin, P.-L., 416
Giscard d'Estaing, Valérie, 75
Goddet, Jacques, 486
Goggi, Gianluigi, 404
Gomberville, Marin Le Roy de, 265
Goncourt, Edmond Louis Antoine de, 287, 293, 297, 299
Goncourt, Jules Alfred Huot de, 287, 293, 297
Gracián, Baltasar, 106–107
Gracq, Julien, 202
Gramont, Duc de, 231
Grandgousier (fict.), 398, 399, 400
Graouilly, 49
Graslin, L.-F. de, 370
Grégoire, Abbé, 288, 371, 374
Grégoire, Père (fict.), 180
Grignan, Louis-Provence de, 83
Grignan, Madame de, 94
Grimod de La Reynière, Alexandre, 452–453, 454, 456i, 457, 466
Grouvelle, P.-A., 372
Guérard, Michel, 461
Guérin, Jacques, 234
Guermantes, Duchess of (fict.), 117
Guermantes, Duke of (fict.), 117, 231
Guermantes, Prince de, 246
Guibert, 347
Guiche, Comte de, 99
Guillaume (archbishop of Bourges), 43
Guillaumin, Émile, 130
Guiomar, Jean-Yves, "Vidal de La Blache's *Geography of France*," 187
Guise, Duc de, 85
Guitry, Sacha, 118i
Gumbrecht, H. U., 419
Guy, Christian, 447
Guyau, Augustin, 140–143
Guyau, Jean-Marie, 124i, 126; *Irreligion de l'avenir, L,'* 139, 143; monument to, 147i; private life, 141
Guyau, Mrs. (wife of Jean-Marie), 143

Haas, Charles, 243
Halévy, Daniel, 231; on *Tour de la France, Le*, 132–133, 134, 137, 143

Hanotaux, Gabriel, 354–355
Hausman, Raoul, *Our Ladies of Paris*, 361
Haussmann, George Eugène, Baron, 45, 67
Heid, M., 372
Hemingway, Ernest Miller, 301
Hendras, Henri, *La Fin des paysans*, 14
Henrietta Maria (queen consort, England), 98, 99
Henri III, 251, 400
Henri IV, 54, 359, 367, 400–401, 404
Henry, Anne, 237
Héraud, Marcel, 318
Hérold, (Louis Joseph) Ferdinand, 313
Herr, Lucien, 163
Hervieu, Bertrand, 11
Hibon (artist), 456i
Hinault (cyclist), 496, 499
Hincmar, 52
Hobbes, Thomas, 403–404
Hobsbawn, Eric, xi
Honorius III (pope), 43
Houssaye, Arsène, 253, 295
Hugo, Victor, 321; admission to Académie Française, 280i; desire for the rostrum, 428; on Mirabeau, 422–423; *Notre Dame de Paris*, 56; *Odes et ballades*, 56; poetry, 312–313; stature as writer, 212, 214; visit to Balzac, 296
Huysmans, Joris-Karl, *Cathédrale, La*, 60–61

Ingres, Jean Auguste Dominique, 250
Isaac, Jules, 152, 157–158

Jaurès, Jean, 133, 163–164
Jauss, Hans Robert, 230
Jeanroy-Félix, V., 184
Joan of Arc, 174–175, 315, 520n37
John XXII (pope), 39
Joigneaux, Pierre, 350
Jourdan, Louis, 335, 345
Julien (fict.), 137, 138
Jullian, Camille, 193

Kaiser Wilhelm. *See* William II
Kaysersberg, Geiler von, 52
Keller, François (fict.), 429
Kubler (cyclist), 495

Labishe, Eugène, 299
La Bruyère, Jean de, 105, 393, 409–410
La Fayette, Marie Madeleine, Comtesse de, 79, 99; *Princesse de Clèves, La*, 73, 98, 112
Laget, Auguste, 238
Laharpe, Jean-François de, 425–426
La Houssaie, Amelot de, 106
Laloi, Pierre (pseud.). *See* Lavisse, Ernest
Lamartine, Alphonse Marie Louis Prat de, 217, 426i, 428–429, 436–438
Lamy, 455
Langlois, C.-V., 151
Lanson, Gustave, 216, 218, 404
Lapize (cyclist), 475
Larcher, Philibert-Louis, 225–226
Larchey, Lorédan, 345
La Rochefoucauld, François, Duc de, 82, 92
La Rochefoucauld, Marie-Christine de, 210i
Larousse, Pierre, 334, 345
Lasserre, Pierre, 184
Lassus (architect), 58
Latil, Cardinal, 71, 72
Lauredi (cyclist), 496
Laurent, Jacques, 462
Lauris, Marquis de, 231
La Varenne, François Pierre de, 450
Lavisse, Ernest, xi, 150i, 151–184; assigns task to Vidal, 196; critiqued by Péguy, 161–165; described, 157–158, 164, 165; description of the Commune, 179–180; *Discours aux soldats, Pourquoi nous nous battons*, 161; election to Académie Française, 292; Empirist leanings, 155–156; *Histoire de France*, 158–160, 168i, 184; *Invasion dans le département de l'Aisne*, 160–161; "Jeunesse d'autrefois et jeunesse d'aujourd'hui," 154; *Manuel*

d'instruction civique, 176; *Manuel Lavisse*, 182–183; *Manuel Mame*, 181–182; *Mark of Brandenburg Under the Ascanian Dynasty, Essay on the Origins of the Prussian Monarchy, The*, 155; national thinking, 208; *Nouvelle Deuxième Année*, 179–180; opinions of Ancien Régime, 173–176; opinions of educational system, 153, 159; opinions of France and Germany opposed, 160–161; opinions of republicans, 156; *Petit Lavisse*, 165–176; place in Republic's institutions, 156–161; *Procédés de guerre allemands*, 161; pseudonym, 176; publications, 155; qualities, 158; Republican?, 152–165; *Souvenirs*, 152–154; summary of teachings, 181–184; *Vue générale de l'histoire de l'Europe*, 158; youth, 152–156

Le Bras, Gabriel, 59
Leclerc, Jacques-Philippe de, 64
Ledru-Rollin, 431–432
Leducq, André, 492
Legendre, James, 374
Léger, Danièle, 11
Le Laboureur, Louis, 267
Le Mond (cyclist), 496i
Lenin, Vladimir Ilich, 333
Léonie, Aunt (fict.), 226, 227i
Le Pautre (artist), 106i
Le Roy Ladurie, Emmanuel, 88, 92, 95
Lestocquoy, Jean, 335
Leuliot, Jean, 487
Le Vau, Louis, 290
Lévi-Strauss, Claude, 465
L'Hopital, Michel de, 401, 404
Lonsing (artist), 421i
Louis le Grand. *See* Louis XIV
Louis of Orleans, 54
Louis-Philippe, 381, 431–432
Louis XII, 54
Louis XIII, 112, 257, 401
Louis XIV, 70i; allegories of, 80i, 110i; aptitudes, 108, 114; arts patron, 114; courtly life under, 71–122, 93, 113i; culinary texts, 450; daily life, 80–81, 510n63–64; demonstrations of favor, 89–92, 94–95; deportment, 105i, 106i; described, 77, 107; dinner at Hôtel de Ville, 451i; effect on ranks at court, 92–93, 95–96; evaluation by Lavisse, 173–174; exhumation, 245; at Grand Carrousel of 1662, 85, 86i; "How to Show the Gardens of Versailles," 109; installation of academies in the Louvre, 290; lack of reading, 407; at Marly, 96–98; medallions of, 79i, 100i; new cuisine, 450; popular perceptions of, 75; relationship with Académie Française, 248i, 266–269, 303; relationship with Colbert, 178; relationship with Duc de Saint-Simon, 92; speech, 276; use of Cathedral of Notre-Dame, 54. *see also* Versailles *in subject index*
Louis XV, 54, 101, 173–174, 175, 505n5
Louis XVI, 145, 172, 455
Louis XVIII, 380, 455
Louy, Xavier, 469
Lucas, Father, 267

Magne, Antonin, 497
Maine, Duc du, 105
Maingueneau, Dominique, 131
Mainin, Jules, 217
Maintenon, Madame de, 114–115
Mâle, Émil, 56, 59, 63, 66
Malebranche, Nicolas, 412
Malherbe, François de, 259, 261, 263
Mallarmé, Stéphane, 256, 440, 473
Malraux, André, 224, 251
Mante-Proust, Suzy, 228
Marcas, Z. (fict.), 429
Marcel, Étienne, 174
Maréchal de Luxembourg. *See* Louis XIV
Marguerite of Provence, 53–54
Mariage (engraver), 456i
Marie-Antoinette, 101, 245
Marie-Thérèse, Queen, 248i

Marinelli (cyclist), 495
Marmontel, Jean François, 416–417
Martin, Henry, 161
Maspero, Gaston, 244
Massillon, Jean-Baptiste, 411
Massis, Henri, 224
Maternus, 402, 414
Maupeou, René de, 281
Maurepas, Jean-Frédéric Phelippeaux, Comte de, 281
Maurois, André, 228
Maurras, Charles, 165
Maynard, L., 383
Mazarin, Jules, 368
Meilhan, Sénac de, 283
Méline, Jules, 354
Ménage, Gilles, 273–275
Mendras, Henri, 7
Mennell, Stephen, 450
Mercier, Louis-Sébastien, 72, 79, 81–82, 365, 368–369
Merckx, Eddie, 482i
Mérimée, Propser, 297
Michelet, Jules, 375; on cathedral laborers, 63; *Histoire de France*, 191; historical methods, 191–192; interest in the national genius, 202; *Introduction à l'histoire universelle*, 153–154; on Mirabeau, 422; national passion, 192; on soldier-peasants, 349; *Tableau de la de France*, 191–193
Millau, Christian, 460, 461, 462, 465
Milly, Jean, 232
Milnár, Miklós, 359
Milo, Daniel, 363
Mirabeau, Honoré Gabriel Riqueti, Comte de, 420, 421i, 422, 425
Mitterrand, François, 66, 76, 120, 121i
Moisin (cartoonist), 74i, 75i
Molé, Mathieu, 404–405
Molière, 108, 116
Monet, Claude Oscar, 61
Monselet, Charles, 463
Monsieur (brother of Louis XIV). *See* Orleans, Philippe, Duc d'
Montaigne, 401–402
Montalembert, Comte de, 286i; *Lettre sur le vandalisme en France*, 59
Montesquieu, Charles Louis de Secondat, Baron de la Brède et de, 243, 279, 391
Morabin, 414
Morand, Raoul, 365–366
Morellet, Abbé, 288
Motteville, Mme. de, 405–406
Muller, Marcel, 230

Nadaud (composer), 342
Napoleon I: coronation, 55, 252; depictions of, 347; evoked by Tour de France, 477; gastronomic advisors, 455; guarded by Chauvin, 335; portrayed in *Tour de la France, Le*, 144; report from Académie Française, 290; supporters, 427; support for Institut National, 289, 290; suspicion of the Idéologues, 291; system of naming streets, 364, 377–378, 379, 387–388; views on agriculture, 350
Napoleon III, 155–156
Nicole, François, 291
Nocret, Jean, 90i-91i
Nora, Pierre, 151

Ogmios, Herakles, 396
Onfray, Michel, 466
Orléans, Gaston, Duc d,' 109
Orleans, Philippe, Duc d' (1640–1701), 85
Ory, Pascal, 443
Ouzouf, Jacques and Mona, 125

Painter, George, 230
Palatine, Princess, 88, 97
Palissot (playwright), 280–281, 284
Paris, Count of, 66
Pascal, Blaise, 276–277
Patel (artist), 82i
Paturot, Jérôme (fict.), 360

Paulhan, Jean, 415
Péguy, Charles Pierre, 46, 63, 161–165, 184; *Présentation de la Beauce à Notre-Dame de Chartres*, 61
Pélissier, Henri, 498
Pelletan, Eugène, 217
Pellos (artist), 476i
Peraux, P., 373
Perrault, Charles, 108, 114, 268, 276; Quarrel of the Ancients and Moderns, 269–270
Pesquidoux, 360
Pétain, Marshall Henri Philippe, 11, 355, 356, 357
Peuch, Denis, 147i
Philip IV (king, France, "The Fair"), 51
Philippe, Duc d'Orleans. *See* Orleans, Philippe, Duc d'
Picasso, Pablo, 256
Picon, Gaëtan, 231
Picrochole (fict.), 398
Pie, Cardinal, 59
Pierre-Quint, Léon, 222, 224
Pinard, Ernest, 433
Pinard, Oscar, 433
Pithou, Pierre, 401
Plantagenets, 53
Poincaré, Jules Henri, 163
Pomaine, Édouard de, 464
Pompadour, Marquise de, 279–280
Pompidou, Georges, 75
Pompignan, Le Franc de, 280, 281
Pomponne, Simon Arnauld, 105
Pontmartin (critic), 352
Posthaus, R., 384
Pottier (cyclist), 481, 494i
Poulet, Georges, 231
Poulidor (cyclist), 492–493, 496
Pouquet, Jeanne, 228
Pourquet, C., 313
Poussin, Nicolas, 250
Prévert, Jacques, 469
Primi Visconti, 95, 99, 101
Prost, Alain, 211
Prost, Antoine, 307
Proust, Marcel, 117, 210i, 211–246; *Albertine disparue*, 219; awarded Prix Goncourt, 217, 220, 236; bedroom, 213i; *Bible d'Amiens, La* (trans.), 60; commemorative stamp, 218i; conception of *Remembrance of Things Past*, 214; conceptions of memory, 242; correspondence, 224, 226, 234; criticism of, 219–225; cultural knowledge, 236–237; depictions of, 219, 221i, 233; on genius, 253; as great writer, 215–219, 222, 232; identification with Illiers, 226; impotence contrasted with success of *Recherche*, 239; *Jean Santeuil*, 219; lack of French criticism of, 229; as literary paradigm, 234–240, 242; models for characters in novels, 229; opinions of cathedrals, 61; opinions of Malraux, 224; opinions of Sainte-Beuve, 253–254; opinions of the novel, 244; opinions of time, 243–244; opinions of writers, 229, 241; place in French literature, 212, 214–215; political passion, 228; postwar rehabilitation, 225–234; studies of, 216, 225, 232, 233–234; varying renown, 223. *see also items beginning "Marcel Proust" in subject index*
Proust, Robert, 226
Pseudo-Longinus, 414
Pudlowski, Gilles, 466
Pyat, Felix, 350–351

Quentin, G., 384

Rabelais, 396, 398
Racine, Jean Baptiste, 94, 115
Raimond, Michel, 232
Rambaud, Alfred, 151
Ranger, Terence, xi
Rapin, Fr., 413
Ratzel, Friedrich, 187, 521n4
Régnier-Desmarais, François-Séraphin, 271

Reinach, Joseph, 425
Renan, Ernest, 292
Renoir, Jean, 241
Revel, Jacques, 70i
Revel, Jean-François, 231
Reybaud, Louis, 360
Ribbe-Grillet, Alain, 230
Richard, Jean-Pierre, 232
Richelieu, Armand Jean du Plessis, Duc de, 251,257–260, 285, 368, 377
Rik Imperator, 477
Rivière (cyclist), 494
Rivière, Jacques, 235, 236
Robespierre, Maximilien François Marie, 178–179, 425
Rodin, (François) Auguste René, 63–64
Roger, Brian, 230
Rollin, 416
Ronsard, Pierre de, 251
Rostand, Edmond, 64
Rouff, Marcel, 444, 447, 464
Roupnel, Gaston, 14
Rousse, Edmond, 432–433
Rousseau, Jean-Jacques, 250, 2867; on general will, 417; opinions of writers, 415–416; on oratorical eloquence, 413; *Social Contract*, 327–328; on soldier-farmers, 347
Rousse, 433–434, 435
Royer-Collard, Pierre-Paul, 291
Rozet, Georges, 469, 473
Ruskin, John, 60

Saillant, Maurice-Edmond (Curnonsky), 463
Saint Benedict, 448
Saint Chauvin. *See* Chauvin, Nicolas
Saint Clement (bishop of Metz), 49
Saint Donatian, 43
Sainte-Beuve, Charles Augustin: critical method rejected by Proust, 253; dressed as academician, 294i; opinion of novels, 297–298; opinions of common sense, 277; opinions on literature, 254; *Port-Royal*, 291
Saint Justus, 43
Saint Louis, 53–54
Saint-Loup (fict.), 228
Saint Marcel (bishop of Paris), 49
Saint-Marc Girardin, Marc, 293
Saint Nicasius, 41
Saint Paul, 409
Saint-Pierre, 279
Saint-Réal, César Vichard, 74, 114
Saint Remi, 52
Saint Rogatian, 43
Saint-Simon, Louis de Rouvroy, Duc de, 88; attendance at Marly, 97; on form and substance, 112–113; founder of modern culture, 453; learns benefits of dissimulation, 105–106; *Mémoires*, 92; opinions of court of Louis XIII, 112; opinions of Dangeau, 79; opinions of Louis XIV, 77, 78, 101; opinions of Rochefoucauld, 82; opinions of the court, 85, 109; opinions of Versailles, 108, 109–110; opinions on information, 116; Proust's familiarity with, 236; relationship with Louis XIV, 92; signs of distinction, 89
Saint Udant, 476
Saint Ursinus, 43
Saint Victricius, 41
Sand, George, 295–296, 297, 471
Sarraute, Nathalie, 230
Sartre, Jean Paul, 218, 223, 256
Savarus, Albert (fict.), 429
Schlöndorff, Volker, 234
Scribe, Eugene, 299
Scudéry, Georges de, 265
Scudéry, Magdeleine de, 111
Seignobos (intellectual), 163
Serres, Michel, 466
Serres, Olivier de, 13, 355–357
Servan, Joseph-Michel-Antoine, 347
Sévigné, Marie de Rabutin-Chantal, Marquise de: attends *Esther*, 95; descrip-

tion of Dangeau, 105; grandson, 83; ignored by the king, 104; opinions of the royal court, 73, 98; opinions of Versailles, 108; Proust's familiarity with, 236
Siegfried, André, 208
Silvestre, Israël, 86–87
Simon, Jules, 144
Simpson (cyclist), 491
Soufflot, Jacques Germain, 54–55
Sourches (writer), 79
Spanheim (foreign observer of the court), 89
Spitzer, Leo, 224
Staël-Holstein, Anne Louise Germaine, Baronne de, 295–296, 427
Starobinski, Jean, 391
Stendhal (Marie Henri Beyle), 291, 295, 298
Stéphane, Roger, 231
Sully, Maurice de, 52
Sully, Maximilien de Béthune, Duc de, 359, 364, 367
Sun King. *See* Louis XIV
Swann (fict.), 243

Tacitus, Cornelius, 402, 414
Tadié, Jean-Yves, 212, 232
Taine, Hippolyte, 292
Tallement, Abbé, 267, 268, 276
Talleyrand-Périgord, Charles Maurice de, 288, 455
Talon, Omer, 405
Tapin, Sergeant, 326
Taveling, Bénédicte, 210i
Tavernier, Bertrand, 27
Teisserence, Abbé, 374
Theuriet, André, 299
Thibaudet, Albert, 406–407, 425
Thierry, Augustin, 57
Thomas, Antoine-Léonard, 275, 282
Timon (pseud.). *See* Cormenin, Louis de
Tocqueville, Alexis de, 435–439, 453
Torcy, Madame de, 97
Touquedillon (fict.), 398, 399
Toussenel, 349
Trémolières, Dr. (nutritionist), 461
Trouvain, Antoine, 105i
Troyat, Henri, 474
Turgot, Anne Robert Jacques, Baron de l'Aulne, 413

Vaillaneix, Paul, 191
Valéry, Paul, 254–255, 265, 298
Vallaux, Camille, 202
Vallet, A., 382
Vandérem, Fernand, 220–221
Van Looy (bicyclist), 477
Vauchez, André, 37
Vaudoyer, Antoine-Laurent-Thomas?, 290
Vaugelas, Claude Favre, 115, 261, 291
Védrine (fict. painter), 298
Vergniaud, Pierre, 425
Verlaine, Paul, *Sagesse*, 60
Vertot, Abbé de, 346
Victrice (bishop, Rouen), 41
Vidal de La Blache, Paul, xi, 186i, 186–210, 470; analyses and descriptions of France, 189, 191, 192, 205; analyses of regions, 190–191, 193–195, 204–205; *Annales de géographie*, 189–190; attention to place names, 199–201; avoids subject of the monarchy, 203–204; biography, 520n1–520n1; desire for national position, 208; *États et nations de l'Europe*, 189; "Genres de vie dans la géographie humaine," 197–199; hostility to Catholicism, 202; influence, 206–207, 208; interest in the national genius, 202; *Marco Polo*, 197; method for defining France, 189–193, 203–205; opinions of anthropology, 207; opinions of national unity, 189–190; opinions of role of geographers, 197; opinions of the long term, 207; opinions of theory of natural borders, 189; wish to transmit his vision of France, 205–206. See also *Tableau de*

la géographie de France in subject index; Vidalian geography *in subject index*
Vietto (cyclist), 496, 498
Villemain, Abel-François, 293
Villette, Maruis de, 371–372
Vinteuil (fict.), 215
Viollet-le-Duc, Eugène Emmanuel, 57, 58, 60, 63
Vitet, Ludovic: *Monographie de l'église Notre-Dame de Noyon*, 57
Voltaire (François Marie Arouet), 266; allegorical engraving of, 272i; apotheosis, 272i, 284; concerns about Académie Française, 283–284; "Eloquence," 415; *Lettres philosophiques*, 279; opinions on genius, 413; opinions on Guibert, 347; opinions on religious eloquence, 411; satires against Pompignan, 281; *Siècle de Louis XIV*, 73, 107

Weber, Max, 391, 449
William II (of Germany and Prussia, Kaiser Wilhelm), 64
Wright, Gordo, 335

Young, Arthur, 371

Zola, Émile, 298–299

SUBJECT INDEX

NOTE: Unless otherwise noted, headings refer to things French, e.g., Revolution refers to the French Revolution. Headings to general topics are indicated by "(gen.)" Illustrations are designated by an "i" following the page number.

Abbeys, 37, 53
Academic literary history, 255. *See also* Literary history
Academic rituals, 252–253
Académie d'Éloquence, 260
Académie de Peinture, 256
Académie des Beaux-Arts, 250, 256, 288
Académie des Inscriptions, 266–267, 289
Académie des Inscriptions et Belles-Lettres, 275
Académie des Sciences, 266
Académie Française, 248i, 249–305; attitudes toward literary genres, 264–266, 295–298, 299, 300; attitudes toward novels, 265, 295–298, 299; conservatism, 254; under d'Alembert, 283–285; dialogue between courtiers and *lettrés*, 261; diversity of membership, 260–264, 266; effect of governments on, 266–269, 276, 285–288, 289, 291–292; esprit de corps, 268, 269, 304; founding of, 251, 257–260; members, 252, 262i, 292–293, 302i; modernization, 279–281; nineteenth-century paradigm, 301; possible futures, 303; postrevolutionary, 252; prizes, 162, 253, 266, 299–300; purpose, 260; relationship with literary history, 254–255; relationship with nation, x, 277, 290, 303–305; support for civic affairs, 281–283; tradition associated with, 250. *See also* Novels; Prix Goncourt
Académie Goncourt, 299
Académie Royale de Peinture, 254
Academies, 257, 288. *See also* Académie Française
Actors, 258, 527n18
Advertising: through Tour de France, 482i, 483–484, 484i, 485i
Aerial photography, 4i, 5i, 6i, 19, 19i, 20i, 21
Agricultural colonies, 349–350

Agricultural fairs, 349
Agricultural land, 3, 25, 32–33
Agricultural producers, 8–9
Agriculture: attitude of Vidal toward, 196, 197; in Brittany, 34i; modernization, 11; portrayed in *Tour de la France, Le*, 140i; productivity, 8, 20–21; Sarthe, 34i
A la recherche de Marcel Proust (Maurois), 228
A la recherche du temps perdu (Proust), 210–246; allusions and references in, 236; characterized, 235, 242–243; groundwork becomes visible, 226–228; history of the text, 228; as *lieu de mémoire*, 214, 242; literary paradigm, 234–240, 242; manuscripts of, 234; as metabook, 237, 238–239; multiple readings of, 235–236; negative reception, 220; non-chronological narrative, 244; number of readers, 215–216; publishing history, 214, 223, 228, 232; as story of the desire to write, 239–240; text used on wristwatch, 245i. *See also* Proust, Marcel *in name index*
Alaric (Scudéry), 265
Albertine disparue (Proust), 219, 223. See also *A la recherche du temps perdu*
Albi, 53i
Albigensian Crusade, 169–170
Algeria: colonization, 350; troops return from, 349
Alimentation, 448
Allée Marcel-Proust, 240i
Allegories, 80i; of Louis XIV, 80i, 110i; of members of Académie Française, 262i; in monuments to the dead, 311, 313, 316; in places of oratory, 439; of Voltaire, 272i
Almanach de Jean Guestré, rustique et guerrier (Dupont), 351
Almanach des gourmands (Grimod), 452, 453, 456i, 465
Alphabet philosophique à l'usage des petits et des grands enfants, 339
Alpine valleys, 204
Alsace-Lorraine: opinions of Lavisse, 161, 173; portrayed in *Tour de la France, Le*, 136, 137, 140i; symbolized by cathedrals, 64; Tour de France route through, 479
Amants magnifiques, Les (Molière), 108
Amiens, cathedral, 49, 54, 55, 60, 63, 66
Ammerschwir, 26i
Amour de Swann, Un (Schlöndorff), 234
Ancien Régime: academic ideal, 250; basis of oratory in, 438–439; critiqued by Lavisse, 173–176; described in *Petit Lavisse*, 166; effect on street names, 364, 369, 380; lack of references in *Tour de la France, Le*, 143–148; literary biography, 251; moderation, 285; persistence in modern life, 76; relationship with Académie Française, 252, 267, 278, 290; royal courts, 72, 117; status of cathedrals, 49–50, 55; treatise on naming, 373–374
Ancients. *See* Quarrel of the Ancients and Moderns
Ane, le magazine freudien, L', 465
Angerville, 310i
Annales de géographie (Vidal), 189–190
Annales school of history, 206, 207
Annals, 42
Anthologie de l'éloquence française (Reinach), 425
Anthropology, importance recognized by Vidal, 207
Anti-Semitism, 220, 221
Antonomasia, Proustian, 242
Apartments, as sign of royal favor, 94
Apollonian mythology, 107
Appearances, 98–107; at court, 98–107
Arc de Triomphe, 317–318, 478i, 480
Archaeology, use of soil as archive, 16. *See also* Aerial photography
Architecture, cathedrals as models, 50–51
Ardèche: agriculture, 5i, 5–7, 8; crimes, 11–12; demise of farmers, 9, 11; literature about, 13–14

Ardèche, la terre et les hommes (Bozon), 14
Ardenne, 194
Ariane (Desmarets), 265
Aristocracy, loss of power, 83
Arles, 473
Armistice Day, 317, 318–319, 321, 323, 325–330
Army, role in ceremonies at war memorials, 317
Art: confounded with life, 241–242; used to reflect cathedral history, 43
Artists, time required for recognition, 240–241
Art of the table, 448. *See also* Gastronomy
Art poétique (Boileau), 264
Arts: emergence from cathedral construction sites, 57; polarization in, 293; during reign of Louis XIV, 113–114
Athleticism: body shapes of cyclists, 498–499; creation of heroes, 481; reflected in Tour de France, 472–473, 479
Atlas of rural France, 21
Aujourd'hui et demain (Bazin), 354
Auto, L' (sports newspaper), 469, 470; descriptions of bicycles, 472; on loss by Christophe, 494; on Pélissier, 493; Tour de France, creation of memories of, 491; Tour de France, descriptions, 473, 474; Tour de France, marketing of, 471, 481, 482i; Tour de France as marketing tool for, 478–479; vacation ads, 485
Automobile-Club de France (A.C.F.), 464
Avantages de la langue française (Le Laboureur), 267
Avant-garde, intellectual, embrace Proust, 229

Back-to-the-land movement, 11–12
Bagatelles pour un massacre (Céline), 220, 221
Ball at the Petit Parc of Versailles, A (Le Pautre), 106i
Banania, 486
Bande noire, 37
Banquets, 458i, 459i
Bar (legal), 439–441; importance of independence, 432; as *lieu de mémoire*, 434; memories of, 393; prestige, 395; use of oratorical eloquence, 416–418
Barreau, Le (Pinard), 433
Basilicas, 51
Basses-Pyrènées, 446i
Bastille Day, 323
Bâtements du Roi, 54
Battle of Bouvines, 173
Battles, evoked by Tour de France, 476–477
Beauce, 62i, 200i, 207
Beauvais, 49
Belles-lettres, 278, 288; genres, 395; importance of Académie Française to, 304; oratorical eloquence as part of, 410. *See also* Académie Française
Belle Violine, La (film), 498i
Bells, 48
Besançon, 51
Bible d'Amiens, La (Ruskin, trans. Proust), 60
Bibliothèque Nationale, 210i, 232, 234
Bicycles: as consumer products, 472; popularity, 478–479; symbolism, 472–473; technology, 494i, 496i. *See also* Tour de France
Bishops, power during nineteenth century, 59
Black Gang, 56
Black Virgin, 42
Bocage (enclosed fields), 22. *See also* Rural landscapes
Body shapes, of cyclists, 498–499
Bonnieux, 27i
Books: as *lieux de mémoire*, xi, 246; portrayed in Rabelais, 400
Bordeaux, street names, 370, 371, 373, 376, 379, 382, 383
Bouches-du-Rhône, 446i
Bourges, 204
Brie (town), 19i, 200i
Brissac, 313, 314i

Brittany, 34i, 202
Bugle calls, at war memorial ceremonies, 321
Bureau Central, suggestions on street names, 376
Bureau d'Esprit, 374
Burgundy (region), 203, 205
Burlesque sermons, 401

Cabourg, 211, 213i
Cadastres (land-ownership surveys), 29–30
Cahiers d'André Walter, Les (Gide), 301
Cahiers Marcel Proust, 222, 233
Campagne française et la guerre, La (Bazin), 354
Canard enchaîné, Le (satirical weekly), 74i, 75, 75i
Canarre (fict. country), 399
Capetian monarchs, 53, 54, 66
Captive, The (Proust), 215
Cardinals (religious), patronage, 257
Carrousels (military spectacles), 85–86
Cartoons. *See* Comic strips
Cathedral (term), history, 40–41
Cathedral close, 41
Cathédrale, La (Huysmans), 60–61
Cathédrale engloutie, La (Debussy), 61
Cathedral of Albi, 53i
Cathedral of Amiens, 60; celebrations at, 66; described by Viollet-le-Duc, 63; destruction during Revolution, 55; height, 49; sculpture, 54
Cathedral of Beauvais, 49
Cathedral of Chartres. *See* Cathedral of Notre-Dame (Chartres)
Cathedral of Cologne, 56, 64
Cathedral of Coutances, 48
Cathedral of Évry (proposed), 67i, 67–68
Cathedral office, 41
Cathedral of Laon. *See* Cathedral of Notre-Dame (Laon)
Cathedral of La Rochelle, 54
Cathedral of Le Mans, 40
Cathedral of Le Puy, 42
Cathedral of Marseilles, 40
Cathedral of Meaux, 47–48
Cathedral of Metz, 64
Cathedral of Moulins, 47i
Cathedral of Notre-Dame (Chartres), 40, 62i; destruction during Revolution, 55; features, 41, 43, 44i, 46i; first national pilgrimage to, 59; height, 49; influence on writers, 60–61; support from Henri IV, 54
Cathedral of Notre-Dame (Coutances), 48
Cathedral of Notre-Dame (Laon), 42, 58
Cathedral of Notre-Dame (Paris), 45; damage to, 55; as Gallic meeting place, 51; height, 49; relics of Saint Marcel, 49; restoration, 58; sculpture, 53–54; tribute to de Gaulle, 66. See also *Notre Dame de Paris*
Cathedral of Notre-Dame (Reims), 52–53; cost of restoration, 54; damage to, 55, 64; founding, 41; height, 49
Cathedral of Notre-Dame (Strasbourg), 38, 48, 64; height, 49, 50i; symbolism, 64, 66
Cathedral of Noyon, 38, 47–48
Cathedral of Reims. *See* Cathedral of Notre-Dame (Reims)
Cathedral of Rodez, 49, 50i
Cathedral of Rouen, 38; dedication, 41; location of heart of Charles V, 54; paintings, 61; Tour de Beurre, 49
Cathedral of Sainte-Croix (Orleans), 54
Cathedral of Saint-Étienne (Meaux), 48
Cathedral of Saint-Étienne (Metz), 49
Cathedral of Saint-Étienne (Paris), 45
Cathedral of Saint-Jean (Besançon), 51
Cathedral of Senlis, 51
Cathedral of Strasbourg. *See* Cathedral of Notre-Dame (Strasbourg)
Cathedral of Tours, 47
Cathedral of Viviers, 47–48
Cathedrals, 37–68; auxiliary structures, 47;

construction sites, 57; defined, 38–39, 40; destruction during Revolution, 55; economic difficulties, 48; facades, 43–44; financing, 46; functions, 41; functions of, 40–42, 43, 50–53, 63–64; as *lieux de mémoire*, 38–39, 67; as memories, 42–45, 45–51, 64–68; modern status, 67–68; origins, 43, 57; Proust compared to, 214; size rivalry, 49; status during nineteenth century, 56–60; symbolism, 44–45, 58, 59; as temples of the royal religion, 53–60; viewed by Viollet-le-Duc, 58

Cato (Maternus), 402

Causses, 474

Céleste (Adlon), 234

Cemeteries, as *lieux de mémoire*, 242–243

Censitary Assembly, 436

Centre National de Recherche Scientifique, 233

Century of Louis XIV, The. See *Siècle de Louis XIV*

Ceremonies, royal, 54

Chamber of Deputies, 427–429, 435–436

"Chanson du tour de France," 468i

Chants des paysans (Dupont), 351, 353

Chants des soldats (Dupont), 351, 353

Chapters (ecclesiastical), 50; schools, 47

Charles Demailly (Goncourt brothers), 293

Charrue et le comptoir, ou la ville et la campagne (Devoille), 351–352

Charter of 1814, 427

Chartres. *See* Cathedral of Notre-Dame (Chartres)

Château-Arnoux, 329i

Château l'autre, D'un (Céline), 221

Château of Versailles, The (Patel), 82i

Chauvinism (term), 333, 334, 335, 342, 535n2. *See also* Chauvin, Nicolas *in name index*

"Chauvinisme, Le" (Jourdan), 335

"Chauvin's Loves Continued" (song), 342

Chefs, 455, 457–458; as architects, 456i

Chess, 105

Children, at war memorial ceremonies, 306i, 321, 325. *See also* Youth

Choisy-le-Roi, 307

Choses vues (Hugo), 296

Christian eloquence, 408. *See also* Oratorical eloquence

Churches: in *A la recherche du temps perdu*, 225; as places of oratorical eloquence, 406–410. *See also* Cathedrals

Cinq Sens (Serres), 465

Cities: centers of cultural activity, 115; emblemized by cathedrals, 45–51; factors affecting creation, 190–191; portrayed in *Tour de la France, Le*, 137

Cities of the Plain. See *Sodome et Gomorrhe*

Civic duty, 326, 329

Civic-funerary memorial, 315i

Civic monuments, 312, 314i, 316. *See also* Monuments to the dead

Civic-patriotic monuments, 314i. *See also* Monuments to the dead

Civilization, cuisine as testimony to, 443–444

Civilizing Process, The (Elias), 367

Civil religion, 327–328

Clairvaux, 37

Classicism, 63

Clef du Cabinet, La, 376

Clergy, relationship to laity reflected in church architecture, 52, 53i

Clermont-Ferrand, 55

Clermont-Tonnerre Prize, 279, 281

Coca Cola, 486

Cocarde tricolore, La (Coigniard brothers), 337, 339

Codes of law, 391–392

Collective memory, 365, 366, 434

Collège des Quatre-Nations, 289, 290, 368

Cologne, 56, 64

Colonial empire, expanded by Republicans, 176

Combray (fict. town), 225

Comédie humaine, La (Balzac), 296
Comedy: commissioned by the monarchy, 407; denunciations of, by Bossuet, 408
Comices agricoles, 349
Comic strips, on Proust, 233
Comment Marcel Proust a composé son roman (Feuillerat), 224
Commission of Arts and Monuments, 57
Common sense, 277–279, 281
Commune of Paris, 1871, 179–180, 345
Communes, 12; monuments to the dead, 308, 311–312, 532n4; restoration of names under Napoleon I, 379; street names, 374, 376
Community identity, 443
Compagnon du Tour (Bernard), 471
Compagnons (journeymen), 470
Compulsory education, presaged in *Tour de la France, Le*, 148
Concordat, 59
Confessions (Rousseau), 250
Conseil Général des Facultés, 183
Conseil Supérieur de la Langue Française, 212
Considérations sur les moeurs de ce siècle (Duclos), 282–283
Constituent Assembly, 171, 285, 371, 425
Consulate (1799–1804), 287, 289
Consumer society, effect on reading Proust, 235
Contractual organisms, 146–147
Contrat social (Rousseau), 416
Contre Sainte-Beuve (Proust), 228, 239, 253
Convention (constituent assembly), 285, 289, 423, 425
Cookbooks, 453
Cooking, 443. *See also* Gastronomy
Cormeilles, 20i
Corporation (concept), 258
Correspondance général (Proust), 224, 234
Cortegiano, Il (Castiglione), 102–104, 106, 111
Côte-d'Or, 446i
Council of Paris, 363–364
Country homes, 12–13
Coup de dés, Un (Mallarmé), 440
Coup d'État permanent, Le (Mitterrand), 76
"Coupole, La" (Fumaroli), 249–305
Courrier de la Sarthe, 431–432
Cours gastronomique (Gassicourt), 452
Court and city, 115, 279
Courtiers: behavior, 111; dependence on king, 84; importance of appearance, 103; as members of Académie Française, 261; submission to sociability, 112; in twentieth century, 119–120
Court life: analysis by Elias, 83–85; game of, 105–106; regularity, 79–81; renown as allegory of, 80i; vitality during Ancien Régime, 72. *See also* Courts (royal)
Courts (gen.), in democratic societies, 74
Courts (legal). *See* Bars (legal)
Courts (republican), 116–122
Courts (royal), 71–122; admission to, 82–85; after Louis XIV, 116–117; alliances, 95; basis of effectiveness, 75; centrality of royal persons, 83, 122; control of appearances at, 98–107; court atmosphere, 109–113, 113i; culture, 113–116; differences from salons, 112; as distinct society, 83–84; evoked in twentieth century, 117–122; in exile, 71; functions, 72, 74, 92–96, 98–99, 277; length of history, 78; as *lieux de mémoire*, 73, 74, 76, 116; logic of rank, 87–98; of Louis XIV, 72–73, 77–87; memories of, 393; models of, 103–104; opinions of Voltaire, 107; political purpose, 86–87; qualities, 73–74, 78–79; relationship to culture, 113–116; as representation of subjugation, 85–87; Spanish, 509n60; speech as standard for national language, 261. *See also* Versailles
Court systems, 506n10
Coutances, 48

Crimean War, 352–353
Crise du roman des lendemains du naturalisme aux années vingt, La (Raimond), 232
Critique de l'École des femmes (Molière), 116
Croix de guerre, 311
Cuisine, 443, 448, 454. *See also* Gastronomy
Culinary identity, 445
Cultivated land. *See* Agricultural land
Cults: of the dead, 245, 308, 328, 330; referred to in Vidal's *Tableau*, 202
Culture: contemporary, 452, 487; *A la recherche du temps perdu* as repository of, 236–237; models for, 359; relationship to royal courts, 113–116
Cupola, as synecdoche for Académie Française, 290, 297, 299
Curial contract, 104
Cyclists, body shapes, 498–499. *See also* Bicycles; Tour de France

Dead, monuments to. *See* Monuments to the dead
Décadaire religion, 55
Defense attorneys, oratorical eloquence, 431
Défense de la langue française pour l'inscription de l'arc de triomphe, dédié ou roi (Charpentier), 267
Défense et illustration de la langue française (Du Bellay), 395
De la littérature (Staël), 427
De l'éloquence du barreau (Gin), 416
De l'éloquence française et des raisons pourquoi elle est demeurées si basse (Du Vair), 402–403
De l'esprit des lois (Montesquieu), 391
De l'excellence de la langue française (Charpentier), 267
Democracies (gen.), inherent contradictions, 481–482
Democracy in America (Tocqueville), 437–438
Democratic eloquence, 437–438
Democratic systems, 391–392
Department of Historical Monuments, 57
Desire, object of psychoanalysis, 235
Determinism, in geography, 199, 206
Dialects, regional, 130
Dialogue on Orators (Tacitus), 402, 414
Dictionaries, Quarrel of the, 270–277
Dictionnaire contenant tous les mots français tant vieux que modernes et les termes de toutes les sciences et de tous les arts (Furetière), 271
Dictionnaire de l'Académie, 271, 276, 335; revision planned by Voltaire, 284
Dictionnaire de la conversation (Arago), 334
Dictionnaire raisonné de l'architecture française du XIe au XVIe siècle, 58
Dictionnaire Robert, 23–24
Directory, establishment of Institut National, 289
Disabled veterans. *See* Mutilés des Hautes-Pyrénées; Mutilés du Loiret
Discours aux soldats: Pourquoi nous nous battons (Lavisse), 161
Discours de réception, 251, 256, 266, 281
Discourse, gastronomy as, 448
Discours et plaidoyers (d'Est-Ange), 432
"Discours sur l'éloquence" (anon.), 417–418
Discours sur les sciences et les arts (Rousseau), 413
Divisions: creation imputed to Republicans, 175; treated in *Tour de la France, Le*, 130
Doctrine of Malherbe, 259–260, 261
Dodin-Bouffant (Rouff), 463
Doubs, 446i
Dramas, 299
Dramaturgy, classical, 251
Drame de Marcel Proust, Le (Massis), 224
Dreyfus Affair, 156–157, 219
Du Côte du chez Swann (Proust), 211, 239; descriptions of everyday life, 225; parallels with Freud, 235; printing history, 215, 216, 222; as recaller of memories,

246. See also *A la recherche du temps perdu*
Du gouvernement des moeurs et des conditions en France avant la Révolution (Meilhan), 283
Du temps perdu au temps retrouvé (Breé), 230

Ecclesiastical geography, 39–40
Ecclesiastical quarters, 41
École Libre des Sciences Politiques, 208
École Normale: taken over by Lavisse, 159–160; Vidal's work at, 208
École Normale Supérieure, 293
Ecology, 187
Economic evolution, effect on gastronomy, 460
Economic geography, 196–197
Editions de Minuit, 303
Éditions du Seuil, 303
Education. *See* Public education
1870–1920 (Hanotaux), 354–355
Elementary schools, 165
Éloge de Sully (Thomas), 282
Éloges (Thomas), 282
Eloquence. *See* Oratorical eloquence
"Eloquence" (Voltaire), 411, 415
Embrun, 50–51
Empire: disappearance of revolutionary calendar, 378; influence on street names, 376–380; portrayed by Fouillée, 144; relationship of Académie Française to the state, 290
Encyclopédie, ou dictionnaire raissoné de sciences, des arts et des métiers (Diderot), 73, 278, 303
Encyclopedists, 278, 281
Enfants de Marcel, Les (Fouillée), 138
England, perceptions of Vidal, 189
Enlightenment: conditions for acceptance, 277; effect of oratorical eloquence in, 439; effect on Académie Française, 285–288; personal names from, used as street names, 386
Entretiens sur les sciences (Lamy), 412
Environment, effect on countries, 188
Episcopal power, 45–46
Épîtres rustiques, Les (Autran), 352
Equestrian tradition, 472–473
Équipe, L' (sports newspaper), 474
Ere du soupçon, L' (Sarraute), 230
Espace proustien, L' (Poulet), 231
Espionage, at royal courts, 101
Esprit (journal), 301
Esprit de conquête (Constant), 427
Essai général du tactique (Guibert), 347
Essais (Montaigne), 401–402
Essais de psychologie contemporaine (Bourget), 299
Essai su le tiers état (Thierry), 57
Essai sur la société des gens de lettres et des grands (d'Alembert), 283, 415
Essai sur les éloges (Thomas), 275, 282
Estates General, 174, 175
Esther (Racine), 94
États et nations de l'Europe (Vidal), 189
Etiquette, 93, 101, 403
Étude pour la Valorisation de la Recherche en Sciences Humaines (E.V.R.S.H.), 466
Études proustiennes, 233
Eure Canal, 109
Events, conseqentialness, 244
E.V.R.S.H. (Étude pour la Valorisation de la Recherche en Sciences Humaines), 466
Évry, 67i, 67–68
Exercise. *See* Athleticism
Existentialists, 301
Experiences, lived *vs.* intellectual, 128
Exposition Internationale (1937), 463
Extinction du paupérisme, La Question des sucres, L' (Napoleon I), 350

Family life, travel as danger to, 131
Farmers, population decrease, 4
Farming. *See* Agriculture

Father Lacordaire at Notre-Dame (engraving), 52i
Favor (royal), 89–92, 94, 95, 96–98
Fay-de-Bretagne, 315
Female images, in monuments to the dead, 313
Fencing, 397
Ferney, 413
Festival of the Federation, 172–173
Fiction, cognitive value, 298
Fields, 25. *See also* Rural landscapes
Fifth Republic: political culture, 74–75; reflections of royal courts, 117–122, 120i
Figures III (Genette), 230
Films: on Proust, 234; use of rural landscapes, 28
Fin des paysans,La (Hendras), 14
First Consul. *See* Napoleon I *in name index*
First Empire, status of lawyers, 432
Flags, 323
Flanders, 2i
Fleurs de Tarbes, Les (Paulhan), 415
Fleurs du mal, Les (Baudelaire), 235, 433
Fleury, 53
FNAC (bookstore chain), 219, 221i
Fontevrault, 37, 53
Food, 129, 443. *See also* Gastronomy
Forests, 24–25. *See also* Rural landscapes
"For Those We Mourn" (Bouchor), 321
Forum (Roman), 402
Founding myths, 358
France: crossroads of the civilized peoples, 188, 206; defined by cuisine, 444–445, 448; described by Vidal, 191, 208; gastronomic legitimation, 467; gastronomic map, 442i; history of gastronomic hegemony, 449–450; history viewed by Lavisse, 158–159; models of images of, x; natural borders, 189, 475; official literary corps, 255; portrayed in *Tour de la France, Le*, 132, 137; problem of formation, 203–205, 208; as product of water's effects, 195; soil composed of bodies of heroes, 341i; symbolic representations, 355; uniqueness, 17–18. *See also* French people; *Lieux de mémoire;* Republic
France de l'Est, La (Vidal), 199
France gastronomique (Curnonsky and Rouff), 463
Franche-Comté, 2i, 51
Francinet (Fouillée), 138
François le Champi (Sand), 246
Franco-Prussian War, 136, 155, 308
Freedom of the press, 427
Freemasons, 58
Free speech, 392
"French Authors and Street Names: Paris, Montreuil, Saint-Étienne, Perpignan" (Posthaus), 384
"Frenchman's Duty, The" (Pudlowski), 466–467
French people, as descendents of Trojans, 396
French service (at meals), 458–459, 463
Freudianism, 235
Fronde, 85
Funerary memorials, 324i
Funerary monuments, 316. *See also* Monuments to the dead
Funerary-patriotic monuments, 314–315, 316, 320i, 322i. *See also* Monuments to the dead

Gallican Church, 42. *See also* Cathedrals
Gallic cock, in monuments to the dead, 313
Gallic Hercules, 395–400
Gallimard (publishing house), 222
Games, 105
Ganges, 324i
Gardens of Versailles Viewed from the North Terrace (Allegrain), 81i
Gargantua and Pantagruel (Rabelais), 397–400
Gastronomic discourse, 462–463, 465
Gastronomic writing, 462, 466
Gastronomiers, 456i

Gastronomy, 442i, 443–467; appearance of term, 452; culinary evolution, 458–459; culinary models, 450, 452; decentralization, 464; defined, 448; dual sensibilities, 462–463; facts about, 444–445; French primacy, 449–452, 454–459; gastronomic topography, 446i, 446i; historical foundations, 452–454; historiography, 447; intellectual position, 447–448; literature of, 452–454, 457–458, 460; modernism, 464–467; political, 455; stamps honoring, 466i; structural factors, 459–462; terminology, 445–448
"Gastronomy" (Ory), 443–467
Gauls, oratorical eloquence, 395–396
Gazette des tribunaux, La (legal journal), 431
Generational conflict, on Tour de France, 496, 498
Génie du christianisme (Chateaubriand), 56
Génies et Réalités publication series, 232
Genius, described by Proust, 253
Genius loci, 204, 205
"Genres de vie dans la géographie humaine" (Vidal), 197–199
Gentioux, 316
Geographical memories, 469
Géographie parisienne en forme de dictionnaire contenant l'explication de Pars mis en carte géographique du royame de France (Teisserence), 374
Geography: described in *Tour de la France, Le*, 127–129; human response to, 207; idealized by Tour de France, 470; of the land, 15–16; publishers, 208; as security, 131. *See also* German geography; Vidalian geography
Geography of France. See *Tableau de la géographie de France* (Vidal)
German geography, 187
Germany, opinions of Lavisse, 160–161
"Good Soldier Chauvin" (Puymège), 333–360
Gothic architecture, 64. *See also* Cathedrals
Gothic art, 57, 63
Gothic cathedrals. *See* Cathedrals
Gourmandise, literature of, 453–454
Gourmet clubs, 464
"Grand Buffet of Modern Cuisine" (Hibon), 456i
Grand Carrousel of 1662, 85–87, 86i, 87i. *See also* Louis XIV *in name index*
Grand Cyrus, Le (Scudéry), 111
Grand Écrivains de la France, Les, 217
Grand Écrivains Français, Les, 216–217
Grande Encyclopédie, 334–335
Grand Hotel at Cabourg, 211, 213i
Grand Siècle, Le, 114
Grands travaux, 109
Grand Trianon, 75i
Grand-Voyer de France. *See* Sully, Maximilien de Béthune *in name index*
Grenoble, 307
Guêpes, Les, 342
Guernica (Picasso), 256
Gy-l'Évêque, 316

Habit vert, L' (Flers and Caillavet), 299
Hachette publishers, 232
Haut-Jura, 201i
Heroes, created by Tour de France, 480–481, 495–496, 497i, 498, 499
"Heroes of French History," 387
Histoire de France (Aulard and Debidour), 169–171, 179
Histoire de France (Lavisse), 151, 168i, 184
Histoire de France (Michelet), 63, 191
Histoire de la campagne française (Roupnel), 14
Histoire de la cuisine (Guy), 447
Histoire de la gastronomie (Guy), 447
Histoire de la littérature française (Lanson), 404
Histoire de la Révolution française (Michelet), 375

Histoire de littérature française de 1789 à nos jours (Thibaudet), 425
Histoire d'un paysan, L' (Erckmann-Chatrian), 353
Histoire du patriotisme en France (Lestocquoy), 335
Histoire général du IVe siècle à nos jours (Lavisse), 151
Historians, 419, 473. *See also* Lavisse, Ernest *in name index*
Historical memory, 42–45
Historical studies, 151. *See also* Positivist historians
Historiography, gastronomic, 447
History: embodied in cathedrals, 45; evoked by Tour de France, 475–477; life in *lieux de mémoire*, 246; mission assigned by Lavisse, 181; in *Tour de la France, Le*, 131–132
History of France (Lavisse), xi
Holy Ampulla, 52
Holy Ampulla of Marmoutier, 54
Homme aux pâtes, L' (Field), 466
Homme de cour, L' (Gracián), 106–107
Hommes illustres qui ont paru en France pendant de siècle (Perrault), 270
Homosexuality, spread blamed on Proust, 222
Honnête Volupté, L' (E.V.R.S.H.), 466
Hôtel de Rambouillet, 111
Hôtel de Ville, 451i
Houses. *See* Rural houses
"How to Show the Gardens of Versailles" (Louis XIV), 109
Hradcany, 71
Humor, 265
Hussards, 461, 465
"Hymn to the Dead" (Bataille), 319

I (self), of Rousseau, transformed, 250–251
Idées napoléoniennes, Les (Napoleon I), 350
Identity, food as distinctive ingredient, 444
Ile-de-France, 192
Illiers, 211, 213i, 225–226, 226
Immoraliste, L' (Gide), 301
Immortel, L' (Daudet), 298
Index-Atlas de France, 383
Individuals: identity defined through memberships, 285; remembered by monuments to the dead, 316–317
Industry: portrayed in *Tour de la France, Le*, 137–138; treatment in Vidal's *Tableau*, 196–197
Infantrymen. *See Poilu*
Information, importance to rank at court, 95
Inscriptions: Latin *vs.* French, 268; on monuments to the dead, 311, 312, 314i, 316, 329i
Inspiration of the Poet (Poussin), 250
Institutio principis christiani (Erasmus), 398
Institut National, 288–289, 291. *See also* Académie Française
Intellectual avant-garde, 229
Intrigue, 72
Introduction à l'histoire universelle (Michelet), 153–154
Invasion dans le département de l'Aisne (Lavisse), 160–161
Involuntary memory, 235
Irreligion de l'avenir, L' (Guyau), 139, 143
Isle-sur-le-Doubs, L,' 474
Italy, courts, 102–104
"I Wasn't Careful Enough About the Girl" (lithograph), 339–340

Jean Santeuil (Proust), 219, 228, 239
"Jeunesse d'autrefois et jeunesse d'aujourd'hui" (Lavisse), 154
Jews, hebraicization of names, 542n55
Journal (Goncourt brothers), 287
Journal des gourmands et des belles (Grimod), 453, 454
Journal des mutilés, 318
Journey to the End of the Night (Céline), 216
Judicial eloquence, 429–435, 431, 433

Juifs, rois de l'époque, Les (Toussenel), 350
July Monarchy: Chauvin under, 359; effect on cathedrals, 55, 59; exile of bohemia, 297; portrayals of soldier-peasants, 349; relationship with Académie Française, 291; status of press *vs.* rostrum, 428; street names during, 381
Jura, 201i
Jurassic limestone, 201i

Kings: evaluation by Lavisse, 173; honor represented by French language, 268; power of, 83–84. *See also* Monarchy

Laborers, 63
La Bourboule, 310i
Laboureurs et soldats (Autran), 352
Labyrinths, 44
Lacombe, P., 37, 372–373
La Faucille, 485
La Garonnette, 485
Laity, separation from clergy, 52, 53i
Land, 2i, 3–35; appropriation, 29–35; breadbasket of Ile-de-France, 15; changes in value, 9–11, 13; domestication, 21–29; fertility, 15–21; as geographical archive, 15–16; geological history, 16–17; literature about, 13–15; ownership, 29–31; productivity, 17; urbanization, 4–5. *See also* Agricultural land; Rural landscapes
"Land, The" (Frémont), 3–35
Landscapes, 522n17
Language, gastronomic terminology, 445
Languages: apologias for, 267; arbiters of, 284; corruption of, 415; courtly, 115; importance to the nation, 260–263; monitored by Académie Française, 257; myth of past oratorical eloquences, 396; power of (*See also* Oratorical eloquence), 393; standards, 212. *See also* Académie Française
Laon, 42, 55, 57, 58
La Roche-en-Forez, 310i
La Rochelle, 54
Latin, 267–268, 268
Latin Quarter, 47
Laughs, changelessness, 245
Law, codes of, 391–392
Law of Separation (1906), 42
Lawyers: careers, 431; oratorical eloquence, 416–418, 429–435, 433; rights, 392; status during First Empire, 432
League of Nations, 326
Leçons et modèles d'éloquence judicaire (Berrye), 433
L'Éducation sentimentale (Flaubert), 429
Legal institutions, social roles, 434
Legends, function in Tour de France, 495–496
Legion of Honor, 336
Legislatures, memories of, 393
Le Havre, 382
Le Mans, 40
Le Puy, 42
Les Eyzies, 198i
Les Grands, 51
Lettrés. See Men of letters
Lettres d'un vieux paysan aux laboureurs ses frères (Devoille), 351, 352
Lettres persanes (Montesquieu), 279
Lettres philosophiques (Voltaire), 279
Lettre sur le vandalisme en France (Montalembert), 59
Levallois-Perret, 316
L'Hermite, Tristan, 265
Liberalism, 175
Liberty: reasonable *vs.* excessive, 398; relationship to oratorical eloquence, 410–411, 414–415, 433
Librarie Hachette, Grands Écrivains Français, Les, 216–217
Lieux de mémoire: A la recherche du temps perdu, 242, 244; the bar, 434; books, xi, 246; central themes, x; Lavisse, Ernest, xi; Proust's theory of, 245; street names

as clues to, 365. See also *A la recherche du temps perdu*; Ardèche; Cathedrals; Chauvin, Nicolas *in name index*; Courts (royal); Gastronomy; Land; Lavisse, Ernest *in name index*; Monuments to the dead; Oratorical eloquence; Street names; *Tableau de la géographie de France; Tour de la France pour deux enfants*; Tour de France
Lille, 370, 382
Lion Noir (wax firm), 484
Literary canon, 230, 278
Literary criticism, about Proust, 224–225
Literary culture, 257
Literary French, 259
Literary genius, 253
Literary history, 218, 254–255, 448. *See also* Academic literary history
Literary immortality, 216
Literary life, 253
Literary pantheon, Académie Française as, 251–252
Literature, 466; Académie Française's tripartite division of, 264; on courtly life, 73, 77–78; functions, 246, 254; gastronomic, 445, 452, 454, 466; justifications for, 304; polarization in, 293; relationship with oratorical eloquence, 414–415; relationship with Proust, 212, 236; royal court as inspiration for, 99; search for essence of, 229; status raised by Académie Française, 258; use of rural landscapes, 28
Livre de Poche editions, 232
Livre des orateurs (Cormenin), 428
Logique (Arnauld and Nicole), 291
Loire, 194–195, 203, 473–474
Louvre, 266, 290
Love: as social duty, 111–112; transformed by Chateaubriand, 251
"Love of Country" (Pudlowski), 466–467
Lundis (Sainte-Beuve), 253, 254
Lyons, 196, 370, 379, 382
Madame Bovary (Flaubert), 349, 429, 433
Madame Gervaisais (Goncourt brothers), 287, 297
Madeleines, 211
Magny-le-Freule, 314i
Maillot jaune (yellow jersey), 494
Maisons-Alfort, 313
Major, La (Cathedral of Marseilles), 40
Malherbian French, 263
Mandarins, Les (Beauvoir), 255–256
Mangeur du XIXe siècle (Aron), 447, 465
Manners, in royal courts, 73
Manuel (Aulard and Debidour), 182
Manuel des amphitryons (Grimod), 452, 453
Manuel d'instruction civique (Lavisse), 176
Manuel Lavisse (Lavisse), 182–183
Manuel Mame (Lavisse), 181–182
Maps: created by Tour de France, 491; gastronomic, 442i; of Proust's Normandy, 227i; reflected in *Tour de la France, Le*, 128; of Tour de France, 468i
Marcel Proust. *See* Proust, Marcel *in name index*
Marcel Proust, sa vie, son oeuvre (Pierre-Quint), 222
Marcel Proust: Théories pour une esthétique (Henry), 237
Marcel Proust de 1907 à 1971 (Bonnet), 233
Marcel Proust et les signes (Deleuze), 231–232
Marcel Proust Museum, 226
Marcel Proust romancier (Bardèches), 233
"Marcel Proust's *Remembrance of Things Past*" (Compagnon), 210–246
Marco Polo (Vidal), 197
Marges, Les, 222
Marguy-en-Matz, 322i
Mark of Brandenburg Under the Ascanian Dynasty: Essay on the Origins of the Prussian Monarchy, The (Lavisse), 155
Marly, 96–98
Marne, 446i
Marseillaise, La, 317, 319, 326

Marseilles: cathedral, 40; new construction under Napoleon I, 379; reception for Tour de France cyclists, 481; street names, 369, 373, 374, 376, 382
Masonic confraternities, 57, 58
Mayors banquets, 458i, 459i
Mazes, 44i
Meaux, 47–48, 48
Médailles sur les principaux événements du règne de Louis XIV, 79i, 100i
Medicine, dietetic discourses, 453
Mémoire des Lieux, 243
Mémoire justificatif (Pompignan), 281
Mémoires (Motteville), 405–406
Mémoires (Saint-Simon), 92
Mémoires d'outre-tombe (Chateaubriand), 72, 244, 249–250
Mémoires d'un vieux paysan (Devoille), 351
Mémorables (Gard), 253
Memorial ceremonies. *See* Monuments to the dead, Ceremonies
Memories: etymology and genealogy as, 244; in *Tour de la France, Le*, 131–132
Memory: architecture of, 242; art of, *Tour de la France, Le* as example of, 127; documentary, 243; historically aware tradition, ix; as inventor of France, xii; nonhistorical, 246; perpetuation through street names, 365–366; Proust's culture as, 236; theme of *Remembrance of Things Past*, 214; of Tour de France, 491–500. *See also* Collective memory; Historical memory; Involuntary memory; National memory
Men of letters, 258–259, 282–283, 288–289; control of collective opinion, 415; gastronomes as, 448; invocation of oratorical eloquence of Gauls, 395; oratorical eloquence of, 413
Mettray, 350
Metz, 49, 64, 370
Meunier Chocolate, 484
Meuse, 446i
Michelin guides, 464
Middle Ages: interpreted by Victor Hugo, 56; street names, 365, 366–367, 369, 386
Midi, 189, 204, 471
Militancy, portrayed in *Le Tour de la France*, 137
Military, commemorated in street names, 377
Military careers, effect of royal court on, 92
Military displays, Grand Carrousel of 1662, 85–87, 86i, 87i
Ministère des Beaux-Arts, 38
Ministry of War, 336
Miroir des sports (sports newspaper), 485
Miroir du cyclisme, Le, 495
Moderns. *See* Quarrel of the Ancients and Moderns
Monaco, 198i
Monarchs, sayings held in national memory, 400–401. *See also* Kings
Monarchy: basis of effectiveness, 75; death to oratorical eloquence, 404; demolition of concept of, 258; evaluation by Lavisse, 174–175; forms of courtly life, 72; not mentioned in Vidal's *Tableau*, 203–204; power of, 83–84; relationship to clergy, 53, 54
Monde, Le (newspaper), 466, 469
Moniteur universel, Le (newspaper), 373
Monographie de l'église Notre-Dame de Noyon (Vitet), 57
Monsieur Proust (Albaret), 231
Montreuil, 384
Monuments, to Tour de France, 491
Monuments to the dead, 306i, 307–330; canonical form, 311; centerpiece of republican cult, 328; ceremonies at, 317–319, 321, 322–325, 325–329; creation of, 307–309; female images in, 533n17; loss of impact, 330; significance, 310, 317; subsidies for construction, 532n6; typology and semiology, 309–317; victory monuments, 310i

"Monuments to the Dead" (Prost), 307–330
Moralists, in Académie Française, 265
Morality, 133, 229, 306i
Moral philosophy, 441
Moral will, 146
Moselle, 4i, 5i
Mots, Les (Sartre), 223
Moulins, 47i
Mountains, role in Tour de France, 474–475, 476i
Moveable Feast, A (Hemingway), 301
Mutilés des Hautes-Pyrénées, 318
Mutilés du Loiret, 325
Mysticism, 229
Mythe des géants de la route (Calvet), 481
Mythologies (Barthes), 465
Myths, 303–304, 360

Names. *See* Personal names; Street names
Nantes, 370–371, 373, 374, 382
Nantua, 471, 474
Napoléon-le-Petit (Hugo), 428
National Assembly, 179–180
National folklore, 360
National genius, 63, 202
National identity, 466–467
National Institute for Economic and Electoral Statistics (INSEE), 9
Nationalism, 309–310, 377
Nationality, cathedrals as symbols of, 58
National language, 259
National literature, 275
National memory, 366, 447
National rituals, 469. *See also* Rituals
National symbols, 480. *See also* Symbols
National tradition, ix
National unity, 130–131; created by Académie Française, 277; created by diversity, 189–190; fostered by common language, 262–263; given new legitimacy, 176, 184; represented by soldier peasants, 357i, 358i; of Third Republic, 354
Nationhood, origins?, 187
Naturalism, in Vidal's *Tableau*, 202
Natural landscapes, 24–25
Nature, basis for French primacy in gastronomy, 449
Nausée, La (Sartre), 223
Nazis, attempted use of Strasbourg cathedral, 66
Néo-ruraux, 11
New cities, 388. *See also* Cities
New farmers (néo-ruraux), 11
New novels, 230–231. *See also* Novels
Newspapers, food columns, 460
Nièvre, 446i
Nobel Prize for Literature, 300
Nobility, compensations from king, 84
Nobility of state, 83–84
Noms révolutionnaires des communes de France (Figuères), 374
Normandy, 195, 204, 227i
Notaries, 30–31
Notoriety, perpetuated by street names, 365
Notre-Dame: *See* Cathedral of Notre-Dame (Paris); Cathedral of Notre-Dame (Reims); Cathedral of Notre-Dame (Chartres); Cathedral of Notre-Dame (Coutances); Cathedral of Notre-Dame (Laon)
Notre Dame de Paris (Hugo), 56
Nouveau Candide (weekly newspaper), 461
Nouvelle cuisine, 459, 460, 461, 461i
Nouvelle Deuxième Année (Lavisse), 179–180
Nouvelle Revue Française, 222, 223–224, 300–303
Novels: attitude of Académie Française toward, 265, 295–298, 299, 531n73–531n73; *A la recherche du temps perdu* as metanovel, 237, 238–239; during late nineteenth century, 298; pivotal genre for *Nouvelle Revue Française*, 300–301; social ascension, 531n74. *See also* New novels

Noyon, 38, 47–48
N.R.F. See Nouvelle Revue Française
Nutritional science, 461

Oath of Koufra, 64
Observations sur la langue française (Ménage), 273
Odéon, 368, 369
Odes et ballades (Hugo), 56
Office des Mutilés de la Meuse, 326
Oison, 316
Olympus, or Louis XIV and His Family (Nocret), 90i–91i
Ombre des jeunes filles en fleurs, A l' (Proust), 211, 215, 220
On the Instruction of the Masses through Things of the Greatest Utility: Street Signs (Morand), 366
Oráculo manual y arte de prudencia, El (Gracián), 101–107
Oratorical eloquence, 390–441; in Chamber of Deputies, 427–429; criticisms of, 393–394, 425–427; defense against tyranny, 398; defined by La Bruyère, 393; ecclesiastical persuasion, 408–410; effect of rationalism on, 412–413; first prize awarded, 253; goals, 304–305, 398, 439–440; in historical texts, 400; of lawyers, 429–435; mastery linked to equality in public life, 252; places for, 439–441; prerequisites for effectiveness, 396; prologomena to the Revolution, 411–418; relationship with liberty, 410–411, 414–415, 433; relationship with literature, 395, 397–398, 414–415; remonstrances, 405–406; in service to the Revolution, 418–427; during seventeenth century, 406–411; sources of legitimacy, 438–441; ties with classical past, 401–402; types, 264, 392
Orators, 393–394, 395, 396, 433–434
Orcières-Merlette, 489
Origine des manières de table, L' (Lévi-Strauss), 465
Origines de la langue française (Ménage), 273
Orléans, 54, 203
Our Ladies of Paris (Hausman), 36i
Ouvrages magnifiques du roy Louis le Grand, Les, 110i

Pacifism, 315, 316
Pacifist monuments, 316, 328i, 329i. *See also* Monuments to the dead
Page disgracié (L'Hermite), 265
Painters, 256, 297
Painting, 254
Palace academy, 251. *See also* Académie Française
Palais de Justice, 431
Panegyrics, 256–257, 270, 275, 282
Panorama de la nouvelle littérature française (Picon), 231
Pantheon, 317–318
Parallèles des Anciens et des Modernes (Perrault), 270
Paris: boulevard culture, 463; Cathedral of Saint-Étienne, 45; center of cuisine, 454; described by Vidal, 190, 194, 196; linkage with Orléans, 203; metaphor for power, 379–380; reputation of restaurants, 444; support for Académie Française, 281–283. *See also* Cathedral of Notre-Dame (Paris); Parisian street names
Paris basin, 18, 20, 21–22, 39, 194. *See also* Rural landscapes
Paris Commune, 373
Paris-Dakar race, 489
Parisian street names, 363, 366; during 1794–1815, 375–376; changes to, 380–381; effect of Revolution on, 371–373; frequency of personal names as, 384; government monopolization of, 367–368; lack of unity in, 386–387. *See also* Paris

Paris-Presse (daily newspaper), 461
Parlement of Paris, 263–264, 404–405
Parliament, marginalized role, 120
Parliamentarians, 428
Parliamentarism, 418
Parliamentary speech, 427
Past: historical, 244; survival in the insignificant, 245; truth of, 243
Pastiches de Proust, Les (Milly), 232
Pâtissier pittoresque (Carême), 458i
Patrie, La, 176, 178
Patriotic monuments, 312–315. *See also* Monuments to the dead
Patriotic-republican monuments, 316. *See also* Monuments to the dead
Patriotism, 314; foundations of, 208; link with education, 159–160; in monuments to the dead, 316; support for war, 326; viewed by Lavisse, 172–173, 180–181. *See also* Chauvin, Nicolas *in name index*
Patronage, royal, 114
Pauvre Diable, Le (Voltaire), 281
Paysan-soldat, Le (Devoille), 351
Peace, represented by royal courts, 86
Peasants: demise, 7, 9; history in soil, 16–17; land ownership, 31–33; literature about, 14; living spaces, 26–27; traditions, 4
Peasant-soldiers. *See* Soldier-peasants
Pedagogues. *See* Lavisse, Ernest *in name index*
Percy-en-Auge, 315i
Perpignan, 384
Personal names: appearances as street names, 384, 385–386, 388; effect of Revolution on, 375
Persuasive communications, 392, 393, 394
Pétainism, 355, 357
Petite Académie, 266–267, 275
Petit Larousse, 212
Petit Lavisse (Lavisse), 151; characterizations of Ancien Régime and Revolution, 171–173; design, 177i; development of, 165–167; lack of historical judgments, 169–171; press runs, 520n34; revised version, 169; success, 167. *See also* Lavisse, Ernest *in name index*
Peugeot, 487
Phalsbourg, 136
Philologists, 263
Philosophes, 278, 411–412
Physiologie du goût (Brillat-Savarin), 457, 465
Pilgrimages, 41, 61
Place de la Concorde, 145
Place de l'Odéon, 364, 368–369, 370
Place names, 199. *See also* Street names
Places, importance in collective memory, 131–132
Plaisirs et les jours, Les (Proust), 228, 239
Plantagenet monarchs, 53
Pléiade, 259, 263
Pléiade editions, 232
Podium. *See* Rostrum
Poetry, 264–265, 312–313, 352–354
Poets, 396, 440
Poilu (infantrymen), 309, 311, 313–314, 315, 316
Poincaré Law of 1896, 159
Poitou, 194
Political gastronomy, 455. *See also* Gastronomy
Political geography, 203. *See also* Geography
Political language, 417. *See also* Language
Political parties, 120
Political power, 76, 391. *See also* Power
Political speech, relationship to nations, 437. *See also* Oratorical eloquence
Politicians, 76
Politics: devaluation, 121–122; use of persuasive communications, 394
Polysynodie (Saint-Pierre), 279
Population: farmers, 4; rural, 12–13
Port-Royal (Sainte-Beuve), 291
Port-Royal des Champs, 291

Positivist historians, 164
Possibilism, 190–191
Pouldrezic, 320i
Power: of aristocracy, 83; of bishops during nineteenth century, 59; effect of the court on, 85, 103; Episcopal, 45–46; exalted by logic of rank, 96–98; of Louis XIV, 102; of the monarchy, 83–85; political, 76, 391; represented by royal courts, 87, 122; social, 392–393; socialization of, 118; in twentieth-century France, 120, 121–122. *See also* Social power
Prague, 72
Preachers, 410
Prehistory, 24
Présentation de la Beauce à Notre-Dame de Chartres (Péguy), 61
"Présentation des *Temps modernes*" (Sartre), 223
Presidents: activity reflective of royal courts, 118–121; power, 121–122. *See also specific presidents in name index*
Présidents des assises, 431
Princesse de Clèves, La (La Fayette), 73, 98, 112
Principes de géographie humaine, 199
Prisonnière, La (Proust), 215, 244
Private academies, 257
Prix de Rome, 254, 297
Prix Goncourt, 217, 220, 236
Prix Montyon, 293
Procédés de guerre allemands (Lavisse), 161
Propoganda, 374, 394
Proust (Beckett), 224
Proust (Fernandez), 229. *See also* Proust, Marcel *in name index*
Proust archives, 233
Proust et le Roman (Tadié), 232
Proustian memory, 242
Proustification, 237, 243
Proust myth, 229, 234. *See also* Proust, Marcel *in name index*
Proustolâtres, 218–219, 222, 224
Proust's Narrative Techniques (Roger), 230
Provence, 10i
Provinces, 159, 192
Provincial cities, street names, 369–371, 378, 379, 381–383, 385–386
Prussia, 161
Psallettes, 47
Psychoanalysis, 235
Public education: described by Lavisse, 153; inducement to national unity, 130; prestige, 152; reforms, 159, 160. *See also* Lavisse, Ernest *in name index*
Public relations techniques, 394
Public works, 109
Publishers, of geography, 208
Puigcerdá, 490i
"Pulpit, the Rostrum, and the Bar, The" (Starobinski), 391–441
Pulpits, 52i, 393, 395, 408, 439–441
Puy de Dôme, 202

Quarrel of Homer, 528n40
Quarrel of the Ancients and Moderns, 269–270, 271, 277
Quarrel of the Dictionaries, 270–277
Quarrel of the Inscriptions, 267–269
Quatrevingt-traize (Hugo), 423

Racine and Shakespeare (Stendhal), 295
Radio, reports on Tour de France, 486
Rank at royal courts, 90i-91i; exaltation of power, 96–98; hierarchy, 87–88; official *vs.* de facto, 93–94; privileges, 88–89. *See also* Courts (royal)
Rapport historique sur l'état et les progrès de la littérature (Chénier), 290
Rapports du physique et du moral (Cabanis), 457
Rationalism, 412–413
Readers, 241
Reading, according to Proust, 218, 241
Real estate, price trends, 30–31

Recherche du temps perdu, A la (Proust). See *A la recherche du temps perdu* (Proust)
Recreation, at court, 105i, 106i
Refurbishing of the Grand Trianon (Moisin), 75i
Regions, analyzed by Vidal, 190–191, 193–195, 204–205
Reign of Terror, 172
Reims: cathedral, 41; street names, 363, 370, 373, 374, 379
Relics, 41, 49
Religion: basis for French primacy in gastronomy, 449; civil, 327–328; in *Tour de la France, Le*, 133–136
Religious art, 59
Religious buildings, 37. *See also* Cathedrals
Remarques sur la langue française (Vaugelas), 115, 291
Remonstrances, 407, 416
Rennes, 370
Renown, as allegory of court life, 80i
Reparative justice, 146
Republican cult, 330
Republicanism, in *Le Tour de la France*, 143–148
Republican monarchy, 75i
Republicans, 175
Republics: difficulty of personifying, 323; importance of self-celebrations, 330; signifier of reconciliation, 326
Requête des dictionnaires à messieurs de l'Académie pour la réformation de la langue française (Ménage), 273–275
Resistance (Pourquet), 313
Restaurants, 444, 447, 448, 455–456, 460
Restoration: activities of Chauvin, 335, 359; effect on of Académie Française, 287, 291; portrayals of soldier-peasants, 349; street names during, 380–381
Resurrection, 245
Retour à la Terre (Méline), 354
Revolution, 344i; acceleration of restaurant trend, 457; changes to street names, 371–375; creation of rostrum, 404; damage to cathedrals, 55; difficulty in assimilating medieval past, 56; evaluation by Lavisse, 171–172, 178–179; evoked by Tour de France, 476i; influence on power of bishops, 59; oratorical eloquence in service to, 418–427; portrayed in *Tour de la France, Le*, 145
Revolutionaries, 377. *See also* Year II
Revolutionary eloquence, 418–419. *See also* Oratorical eloquence
Revolution of 1830, 313
Revolution of 1848, 381
Revolution of the lawyers, 417
Revolutions (gen.), symbolism, 375
Rhetoric, 392, 394, 395, 441
Right and Left (political positions), divisions between, 428
Rituals: funerary, 321; military and agrarian, 349; national rituals, 469
Rivers, 194
Rodez, 49, 50i
Roi de la pédale (Darcaux and Decoin), 481
Roman d'une vocation, Le (Laget), 238
Romanticism, 56
Rood screens, 52, 53i
Rostrums, 393, 395, 423, 427–429, 439–441. *See also* Oratorical eloquence
Rouen: cathedral, 41; street names, 370, 373, 376, 378, 382
Rougon-Macquart (Zola), 298–299
Royal courts. *See* Courts (royal)
Rural France, 195–196
Rural houses, 26–27
Rural industry, 8
Rural landscapes, 21–23; in prehistory, 24; scholarly interpretations, 23–29; used in films, 27–28
Rural population, 12–13
Russe à Paris, Le (Voltaire), 281
Russian service (at meals), 458–459, 463

Sagesse (Verlaine), 60

Saint-André-des-Champs (fict. church), 225
Saint-Benoît-sur-Loire, 53
Saint-Cyr, 153, 154
Saint-Denis, 53
Sainte-Geneviève, 422
Saint-Étienne, 45, 373, 374; number of streets, 387; street names, 363, 373, 374, 378, 382, 384
Saint-Georges-en Auge, 26i
Saint-Martin-d'Estreaux, 316
Salons, during seventeenth century, 111–112
Salut par la terre, Le (Méline), 354
Sarthe, 34i
Satellite imaging, 21
Satire Ménippée (Pithou), 401
Schools, chapter schools, 47
Scrofula, 75
Second Empire: Académie Française under, 291, 295–298; collapse, 155; praised by Chauvin, 343–344; soldier-peasants under, 352; songs on Chauvin, 342–343; support for cathedral-building, 59
Second homes, 12–13
Secrecy, at court, 105
Seine (river), 194, 195
Seine, (département), 376
Sein und Werden der organischen Welt (Ratzel), 187
Semantics, 374
Senlis, 51
Sens, 46
Separation of church and state, 392
Sermaises, 314i
Sermons, ecclesiastical debates about, 408–410
Seven Years' War, 174
Sèvres, 212
Siècle, Le (newspaper), 345
Siècle de Louis le Grand (Perrault), 269, 276
Siècle de Louis XIV (Voltaire), 73, 107, 411
Si le grain ne meurt (Gide), 301
Singularities of France, x
Si Versailles m'était conté (Guitry), 118i
Sky-blue Chamber, 308, 318
Snobisme dans les lettres françaises de Paul Bourtet à Marcel Proust, 1884–1914, Le (Carassus), 232
Social advancement, 138
Social Contract (Rousseau), 327–328
Social dreams, 481
Social fictions, 103. *See also* Courts (royal)
Social hierarchy, 82
Socialists, utopian, 349–350
Social power, 392–393. *See also* Power
Société d'Économie Sociale, 197
Société des Amis de Marcel Proust et de Combray, 216, 225–226
Société des Gens de Lettres, 254
Society, place of court society, 84
Society of leisure, 219
Society of Men of Letters, 296
Sodome et Gomorrhe (Proust), 220
Soil, sacred character, 359–360
Soldat-citoyen, Le (Servan), 347
Soldat-laboureur, Le (Francis, Brazier, and Dumersan), 337, 342
Soldier-peasants, 346–358; disappearance of, 357; in poetry, 352–354; relationship to the soil, 360; as soldiers of Christ, 351–352; symbolism, 347, 348i; tradition of, 355–356. *See also* Chauvin, Nicolas *in name index*
Soldiers. See *Poilu*
Somme, 193–194
Songs, Chauvin portrayed in, 340–341, 342–343
Sorbonne, 269; Lavisse as figurehead, 184; positivist historians, 164; Proust studies, 232; relationship with Lavisse, 163, 184; Vidal's work at, 208
Southern France, rural landscape, 22–23
Souvenir français, Le, 308
Souvenirs (Lavisse), 152–154
Souvenirs (Tocqueville), 436
Space, relationship of France to, x-xi

Speech, in democratic systems, 392
Speeches, 325–329
Stamps (postage), 218i, 466i
Statues, 311
Steeples, 49. *See also* Cathedrals
Steles, 311, 314i
Strasbourg. *See* Cathedral of Notre-Dame (Strasbourg)
Street names, 45, 363–388; appearance of personal names, 384, 385–386; categorization, 364; changes to, 363, 375, 380; collapse of national system, 376; conservators of memory, 365–366; effect of Revolution on, 371–375; during eighteenth century, 368; gap between Paris and Provinces, 381–383; growing state monopoly, 366–369; honorific systems, 369, 377, 382, 383; during Middle Ages, 365, 366–367; in provinces before 1789, 369–371; during Restoration, 380–381; "saint" streets, 378; during Third Republic, 383–388; value of memories, 365
"Street Names" (Milo), 363–388
Streets, numbers of, 387
Student associations, 160
Suippes, 324i
Sun King. *See* Louis XIV *in name index*
Sur Proust (Revel), 231
Surrealist Manifesto, 224
Swann's Way (Proust). See *Du Côte de chez Swann*
Sweet Cheat Gone, The (Proust). See *Albertine disparue*
Symbolic monuments, 67
Symbols, 323; bicycles, 472–473; cathedrals, 44–45, 64, 66; of common sense, 281; of France, 355; in funeral procession of Condé, 507n27; of medieval christendom, 59; of nationality, 58; on places of oratory, 439; of revolutions, 375; soldier-peasants, 347, 348i; in Tour de France, 480, 483
Synods, 51
Système de dénominations topographiques pour les places, rues, quais . . . de toutes les communes de la République (Grégoire), 374

Tableau de la de France (Michelet), 191–193
Tableau de la géographie de France (Vidal), 186–210; allusions to pre-Christian cults, 202; ancient settlement sites, 198i; central notion, 187–188; compared with Michelet's *Tableau*, 191–193; contrasts in, 189–190, 196, 197; described, 208; development of conception of France, 202–205; farms pictured, 200i, 201i; importance of way of life, 197–202; influence, 206–207; lack of attention to cities and economy, 196–197; major accomplishment, 189; portrait of rural France, 195–196; publishing history, 520n1; relationship to Tour de France, 470
Tableau de Paris (Mercier), 365
Talmud, 220
Tapisserie de Notre-Dame (Péguy), 61
Teacher training, 159
Technology, 145–146
Television, effect on Tour de France, 487
Temps retrouvé, Le (Proust), 214, 222, 229, 239; identification of grandeur of France, 225; Proust on role of the writer, 241; publication, 223; on resurrection as act of chance, 245–246. See also *A la recherche du temps perdu*
Terre qui meurt, La (Bazin), 354
Textbooks, 165–183, 167, 524n19. See also *Tour de la France Le*
Theater: classical, 116; replacement for remonstrances, 407
Theaters, inspirations for street names, 371
Théâtre d'agriculture (Serres), 356–357
Thélème (fict. city), 399, 400
Thèses d'État, on Proust, 232

Third Estate, 417
Third Republic: based on peasantry, 355; debt to forebears, 425; gastronomic society, 458i, 459i, 463; relationship with Académie Française, 292; role of Lavisse in, 161; street names, 383–388
Three Essays on Sexuality (Freud), 235
Time: Christian concept of, 43; pure state of, 243
Time Regained. See *Temps retrouvé, Le*
"To the Dead" (bugle call), 321
Toulon, 373, 376, 378, 379
Toulouse, 370
Tour de Beurre, 49
Tour de France, x-xi, 468i, 469–500; advertising, 482i, 484i, 487; advertising caravan, 483–484, 485, 485i, 486; aesthetic experience, 474; appropriation of the land, 473–475; attacks on racers, 491; culture of, 468i, 498i; effects of changing culture, 489–490; grand Tours, 492–496; heroes, 480–481, 495–496, 497i, 498, 499; historical allusions, 475–477; marketing value, 474; meaning of, 485–486; mediazation, 486–490; memory of, 491–500; as memory tour, 470–477; model of consumption, 486–487; as national institution, 477–490, 500; national teams, 482–483, 487, 489, 492; racers as workers, 472, 473i; reflection of traditional tours, 470–473; routes, 479, 487, 489, 490i; spectators, increase in, 485, 488i; symbolism, 469, 470, 478i, 480; terminology, 473; winners, 468i; written reports of, 472i
"Tour de France, The" (Vigarello), 469–500
Tour de la France par deux enfants, Le (Fouillée), 125–148; exclusions, 132–133; France encompassed in, 128–129; lack of overt Republicanism, 144–145; as *lieu de mémoire*, 127, 132, 148; memories in, 131–132; original edition, 135i; popularity, 125–126; psychological realism, 126; publication history, 515n29; religious inspiration, 143; Republicanism in?, 143–148; revised (1906) version, 132–136; secret of authorship, 138–139; teacher's handbook, 127, 129, 130, 513n9; transformed into Tour de France, 471; treatment of regional differences, 130
Touring-Club de France (T.C.F.), 464
Tourism, 219, 470, 471. *See also* Tour de France
Tours (city), 47, 199–201
Traité des études (Rollin), 416
Traité des sensations (Condillac), 457
Translators, in Académie Française, 265
Travel, inducement to national unity, 130–131
Treatise on the Sublime (pseudo-Longinus), 414
Truth, translation into oratorical eloquence, 304
Tuileries, 85–87, 240i

Une semaine de vacances (Tavernier), 27–28
Union Fédérale, 318, 325
Union Nationale des Combattants, 318
Universities, 225, 419
Unknown soldier, 354, 355, 356i. *See also* Soldier-peasants
Urban space, 45
Utopian socialists, 349–350

Valmy, 172
Vanité, La (Voltaire), 281
Vaudevilles, Chauvin portrayed in, 337–339, 342
Vélo (magazine), 487, 495
Velvet, as sign of distinction, 89
Vendée, 171–172
Venice, in Proust, 219, 243
Ventre des philosophes, Le (Onfray), 466
Versailles, 70i, 82i; during Ancien Régime,

72; art of conversation at, 403; *Ball at the Petit Parc of Versailles, A*, 106i; caricatures of, 74i, 174; as culinary model, 450; depictions of, 78, 79i, 82i; gardens, 81i, 109; importance of Louis XIV to, 108–109; public visits to, 504n4; self-view, 78; *Si Versailles m'était conté*, 118i; systems of espionage, 101; viewed by Saint-Simon, 108, 109–110. *See also* Courts (royal); Louis XIV *in name index*

Veterans, 307, 318, 321–322, 325

Vichy, 11, 380

Victory (allegorical representation), 313

"Vidal de La Blache's *Geography of France*" (Guiomar), 187–210

Vidalian geography: determinism in, 199, 206; embodied in network of rivers, 194; neglect of French regions, 188–189, 195; origins and influences, 187; structural factors assigned to France, 188; use of principle of contingency, 208–209. *See also* Vidal de la Blache, Paul *in name index*

Vie au grand air, La (magazine), 472i

Vie rurale, La (Autran), 352

Villefranche, 474

Violence, state monopoly on, 391, 392

Vision de Palisson, La (Palissot), 280–281

Viviers, 47–48

Voix narratives dans la Recherche, Les (Muller), 230

Vosges, 141i, 196

Voyage au bout de la nuit (Céline), 216, 219–220

Vue générale de l'histoire de l'Europe (Lavisse), 158

War memorials, 307, 317–319, 321, 322–325. *See also* Monuments to the dead

War of the Austrian succession, 174

Water, as source of France, 195

Westminster, 53

White Cover. See *Nouvelle Revue Française*

Wine, portrayed by Vidal, 196

Within a Budding Grove (Proust), 211

Women: figures used in monuments to the dead, 315–316; novelists, 295–296

Working class, portrayed in *Le Tour de la France*, 137, 138

World, perceptions of, as *lieux de mémoire*, 245

World War I, monuments to the dead, 307–309

World War II: damage to cathedrals, 64; propaganda posters, 66i

Wounded Warrior (Breker), 492

Wreaths, 319

Wristwatches, Proustian, 245i

Writers: alliance with painters, 297; economic concerns, 296; effect of Revolution on, 530n72; on food, 460; functions, 212; great, 216–218, 251; social self *vs.* deep self, 229; status, 252, 292; streets named for, 378

Writing: desire for, 239–240; gastronomical, 462

Year II: armies described by Lavisse, 173; revolutionaries' interest in street names, 364

Youth, lack of relevance of cathedrals, 66

Zeit und erinnerung in Marcel Proust (Jauss), 230